GW01086969

The Ceremonies
of the Roman Rite
Described

OMNIA AUTEM HONESTE ET SECUNDUM ORDINEM FIANT.
I COR. XIV 40

QUOD MINIMUM, MINIMUM EST,
SED IN MINIMO FIDELEM ESSE,
MAGNUM EST.
ST AUGUSTINE — *DE DOCTRINA CHRISTIANA*, IV, N. 35

Adrian Fortescue, J.B. O'Connell
& Alcuin Reid OSB

The Ceremonies
of the Roman Rite
Described

Fourteenth Edition

Saint Michael's Abbey Press
MMIII

SAINT MICHAEL'S ABBEY PRESS
Saint Michael's Abbey
Farnborough
Hampshire GU14 7NQ

Telephone +44 (0) 1252 546 105
Facsimile +44 (0) 1252 372 822

www.farnboroughabbey.org
prior@farnboroughabbey.org

Cum permissu superiorum

ISBN 0 907077 41 2

First Edition	1917
Second Edition	1919
Third Revised and Augmented Edition	1930
Fourth Edition	1932
Fifth Edition	1934
Sixth Edition	1937
Seventh Revised and Enlarged Edition	1943
Eighth Edition	1948
Ninth Augmented Edition	1951
Tenth Fully Revised and Augmented Edition	1958
Eleventh Edition	1960
Twelfth Revised Edition	1962
Thirteenth Reprint Edition	1996
Fourteenth Revised Edition	2003

A catalogue record for this book is available from the British Library.

Printed and bound by Newton Printing Ltd., London.

Table of Contents

PART V—OCCASIONAL FUNCTIONS

List of Figures

List of Tables

Sources

Missale Romanum (typical edition, 1962).

Cæremoniale Episcoporum (typical edition, 1886).

Memoriale Rituum Benedicti XIII (typical edition, 1920).

Rituale Romanum (typical edition, 1952).

Instructio Clementina (1731).

Codex Iuris Canonici (published 1917).

Codex Iuris Canonici (published 1983).

Decreta Authentica Congregationis Sacrorum Rituum (1588-1926).

Acta Apostolicæ Sedis (1909-1957).

Motu Proprio "Inter Pastoralis Officii Sollicitudines" (Pius X, 22 November 1903).

Graduale Sacrosanctæ Romanæ Ecclesiæ (typical edition, 1907).

Cantorinus seu Toni Communes (typical edition, 1911).

Ordo Administrandi Sacramenta et Alia Quædam Officia Peragendi (1915).

Ritus Servandus in Solemni Expositione et Benedictione Sanctissimi Sacramenti (1963).

Ordo Hebdomadæ Sanctæ Instauratus (1956).

Ordo Hebdomadæ Sanctæ Instauratus, Ritus Simplex (1957).

Instructio de Musica Sacra et Sacra Liturgia (1958).

Rubricæ Breviarii et Missalis Romani (1960).

Excerptæ Rituali Romano pro diœcesibus Angliæ et Cambriæ edita (1961).

Enchiridion Indulgentiarum (1999).

Abbreviations

A.A.S. = Acta Apostolicæ Sedis.

C.E. = *Cæremoniale Episcoporum.*

C.I.C. = *Codex Iuris Canonici (1917 Code unless otherwise noted).*

D. = *Decretum* (of the Congregation of Sacred Rites).

D.D. = *De Defectibus in Celebratione Missæ Occurrentibus* (*Missale Romanum* typical edition, 1962).

I.C. = *Instructio Clementina* (of Clement XII regarding the Forty Hours' Prayer).

M.P. = *Motu Proprio* of Pius X (regarding the reform of Church music).

M.R. = *Memoriale Rituum.*

OHS = *Ordo Hebdomadæ Sanctæ.*

OHS (R.S.) = *Ordo Hebdomadæ Sanctæ* (Ritus Simplex).

O.M. = *Ordo Missæ* (found, normally, in the centre of the missal).

R. = *Ritus Servandus in Celebratione Missæ* (at beginning of missal).

R.G. = *Rubricæ Generales Missalis* (*Missale Romanum* typical edition, 1962).

R.G.(B) = *Rubricæ Generales Breviarii* (*Breviarium Romanum; editio prima iuxta typicam,* 1961).

R.R. = *Rituale Romanum.*

R.S. = *Ritus Servandus in Solemni Expositione et Benedictione SS. Sacramenti,* 1963.

S.R.C. = Decrees of the Congregation of Sacred Rites.

SYMBOLS USED IN THE PLANS

The Bishop, even when he wears no mitre

The celebrant wearing a chasuble

The celebrant in cope

The deacon

The subdeacon

Master of ceremonies

Assistant priest

Assistant deacons

Thurifer with incense

Thurifer without incense

Aspersory-bearer

Cross-bearer

Acolytes with candles

Acoltyes without candles

Server

Torch-bearers

Assistants in copes (pluvialistæ) at the Divine Office

Cantor

Mitre-bearer

Crosier-bearer

Book-bearer

Candle-bearer

Train-bearer

14

Preface

IT is my pleasure to present this fourteenth edition of *The Ceremonies of the Roman Rite Described*, a work originally written by the noted scholar, the Reverend Doctor Adrian Fortescue, and subsequently revised many times by Canon J.B. O'Connell. Dom Alcuin Reid OSB has continued the work of these distinguished experts on liturgical ceremonies by bringing this useful manual into line with the specific requirements of the liturgical books in use in 1962.

The permission for the reintroduction into public worship of the Roman Missal according to the typical edition of 1962 dates from the issuance of the Letter *Quattuor abhinc annos* of 3 October 1984 by the Sacred Congregation for Divine Worship. The use of this missal was further encouraged by His Holiness Pope John Paul II in his Apostolic Letter *Ecclesia Dei* of 2 July 1988. Particularly since then there has been a growing desire for the celebration of the Holy Sacrifice of the Mass in this venerable form of the Roman Rite on the part of a good number of the faithful. Likewise, a growing number of diocesan Bishops, whose responsibility it is "to control, promote and protect the entire liturgical life of the Church entrusted to him" (Second Vatican Council's Decree on the Pastoral Office of Bishops, *Christus Dominus* 15; *Code of Canon Law,* canon 838), have accepted the invitation of the Holy Father to make a "a wide and generous application of the directives already issued some time ago by the Apostolic See, for the use of the Roman Missal according to the typical edition of 1962" for the benefit of "all those who are attached to the Latin liturgical tradition" *(Ecclesia Dei* 6, c). This development has rendered Dom Alcuin's most recent revision of this manual on ceremonies a particularly felicitous one.

May the publication of this new edition of a classic work contribute to "that blended 'harmony' which the earthly Church raises up to Heaven under the impulse of the Holy Spirit" *(Ecclesia Dei* 5, a)!

Darío Cardinal Castrillón Hoyos
President
Pontifical Commission *Ecclesia Dei*
17 June 2003

Introduction

QUITE what Dr Adrian Fortescue (1874-1923)[1] would make of the longevity of this book, the task of writing the first edition of which he undertook solely *"turpis lucri gratia"*[2] in order to assist his small parish of Letchworth during the 1914-1918 war, is difficult to imagine. For Dr Fortescue was no fan of the minutiæ of ceremonial, or indeed of this book. Of the work involved in writing it, he bemoaned:

> Try to imagine for one solid year of my life...I spent all day comparing Merati & Martinucci & Le Vavasseur, to find out where the thurifer ought to stand before the Magnificat, who takes off the bishop's left glove, what sort of bow you should make at the Asperges. I had to look serious, and discuss the arguments for a *ductus duplex* or the other thing, whatever it is called, at each candlestick, when you incense the altar. Conceive a man, said to be made in the image of God, spending his time over that kind of thing. Even now that the burden is over it fills me with rage to think of those days. I could have learned a new language easily in the time. I could have gone every day to the cinema. I could have read the complete works of Maria Corelli. My cat was spending his time in sane and reasonable pursuits, chasing birds in the garden, climbing trees, or sleeping in his basket, while I was describing the conduct of the second MC at pontifical Vespers not at the throne. And they affect to believe that we lead a nobler life than the beasts...[3]

And at the prospect of continually having to revise it, he was aghast:

> ...my dreadful CEREMONIES book. Does it want more revision? I had so hoped that I had done with that filthy job for ever. However, if there are still corrections to be made in it (and I have no doubt there are), I suppose I must make them...You cannot conceive how I loathe the idea of going into all that horrid business of the minutiæ of tomfool modern ceremonies once again. I do not think there is any possible subject that seems to me more utterly devoid of interest or of any scientific attraction. It is always, of course, merely a matter of seeing what some footling Congregation of incompetent idiots at Rome has said we are to do. Not one halfpenny-worth of principle or of historic research is affected by the question whether the thurifer should stand on the left or on the right at any given

---

[1] For biographical information see: J.G. Vance & J.W. Fortescue, *Adrian Fortescue: A Memoir*, Burns, Oates & Washbourne, London 1924; M. Davies, *The Wisdom of Adrian Fortescue*, Roman Catholic Books, Fort Collins 1999.
[2] Typewritten letter dated 27 May 1918: St Edmund's College Archive 20/22-56; quoted by kind permission of the President, H.E. the Cardinal Archbishop of Westminster.
[3] Ibid.

moment. I would just as soon spend hours verifying the hours at which trains start on some railway line that I shall never use.[4]

Lest Dr Fortescue be misunderstood, it must be stated plainly that the parish of Saint Hugh, Letchworth, of which he became the founding Rector in 1907, was, under his personal direction, a centre of the full, exemplary, and sound celebration of the Sacred Liturgy. Adrian Fortescue was no liturgical anarchist or modernist. His disdain, articulated above — apart from bearing testimony to his delicious sense of humour in private correspondence, as well as his preference for different kinds of scholarly endeavour — suggests, though, that rubrical fastidiousness did not thrive in the parish of Saint Hugh.

For Canon J.B. O'Connell (†1977), however, ceremonial minutiæ were of the utmost importance, as his review of the first edition of *The Ceremonies of the Roman Rite Described* indicates.[5] His breathtakingly damning review of the second edition, which complains of "indifference" and "gross carelessness"[6] in the correction of the book, demonstrates that Dr Fortescue's aversion to the task was — to the specialist — somewhat transparent.

Providence is not, however, without a sense of irony. Following the untimely death of Dr Fortescue in 1923 it was to Canon O'Connell that the publishers turned with a request to prepare a third edition. They would do so a further nine times in the ensuing forty years.

Ceremonial and rubrics were Canon O'Connell's life's work. Yet, as an old friend, Abbot Dyfrig Rushton OSB, testified after O'Connell's death, "for all his punctiliousness over detail he was never a fanatic and could laugh at himself and others in their outrageous infringement of ceremonial law."[7]

In introducing a ceremonial manual, it is perhaps opportune to underline something of Dr Fortescue's distaste for ceremonial minutiæ and of Canon O'Connell's ability to laugh at rubrical mistakes. For we can be too serious about rubrics. Fanaticism and fastidiousness have no place in the Sacred Liturgy and, it must be said, they can and do turn away priests and others from the traditional liturgy.

Care and a concern to act correctly and in accordance with the mind of the Church, however, are essential to the celebration of the Sacred Liturgy. Rubrics are not to be ignored, for they express the mind of the Church in respect of her most sacred treasures — the mysteries celebrated in the Sacred Liturgy. They surround these central mysteries of our faith

---

[4] Typewritten letter dated 20 May 1920: Cambridge University Library, Morison Papers, I, 16-18; quoted by kind permission of the Syndics of Cambridge University Library.

[5] Cf. *The Irish Ecclesiastical Record*, fifth series, vol. XII (1918) pp. 349-352.

[6] Cf. *The Irish Ecclesiastical Record*, fifth series, vol. XIV (1919) p. 262.

[7] Cf. "A Memoir of J.B. O'Connell" in: *Pax*, vol. LXVII Spring/Summer 1978 p. 33.

with gestures and rites and prayers which both protect them and enable us creatures of flesh and blood to approach them, to begin to comprehend them, and to be sustained by them in our daily struggle to live as faithful Catholics. Rubrics also protect us from the exigencies and the frailties of our clergy by giving an objectivity to the celebration of the Sacred Liturgy which transcends the human characteristics and preferences of its ministers. The past few decades are replete with the liturgical litter of subjective liturgies in which, rubrics long since disdained, the personalities of priests and of others have all but eclipsed Him whom we worship. Rubrics are important.

Yet, in rightly dismissing the ceremonial anarchy which has blighted the Liturgy of the Latin rite for far too long, we ought not to adopt a rigidity which is not required by the liturgical books, for there are rubrics and there are rubrics, and there are customs,[8] and there are different (correct) ways of performing certain ceremonies. Before one goes to (or sends someone to) the stake over a question of ceremonial, one ought to make these necessary distinctions.

Fortescue, O'Connell and the present editor are clear that some ways of performing ceremonial actions described herein can and may be practices with which one may legitimately disagree. In such cases one ought to check the sources. Where they are silent, or where rubricians disagree on an interpretation, it would seem that sanity, sobriety and equity in the light of local conditions and of custom should prevail.

This is not to advocate libertarianism. Many rubrics are perfectly clear and universally binding. The Roman rite is a complex of ritual acts. It is also traditional — it is handed on and received with respect — and it is not substantially altered or constructed anew by any generation.

One difficulty, though, is that a good deal of time has passed since the liturgical books in use in 1962 were themselves published. Many new saints have been canonised. Canon Law has been revised.[9] There has been a reform of indulgences. Episcopal conferences have made further decisions, in accordance with their customary competence, about the timing and the obligation of the celebration of certain feasts within their territories. The regalia in possession of almost all bishops is different as are the ranks and ceremonial privileges of minor prelates. These and other developments effect the celebration of the traditional liturgy in

---

[8] One needs only to think of the various legitimate customs that persist to this day in respect of reading the Epistle and Gospel in the vernacular at Mass. In some countries they are read to the people whilst the priest quietly continues with the Latin text at the altar. In other countries they are read before the homily. In others still they are not read in the vernacular at all.

[9] Because the liturgical books in use in 1962 related to the 1917 Code of Canon Law, references in this book to the 1917 Code remain, though, where pertinent, the 1983 Code is cited.

different ways, sometimes raising questions which have, as yet, received no authoritative answer.

Priests and communities who celebrate the traditional liturgy will, at present, have to decide such matters in accordance with sound principles including fidelity to tradition and openness to sound development. The present editor has no wish to presume to provide answers or to proscribe practices where prudential judgement is what is necessary at a local level, or indeed where legitimate freedoms exist. History shall record what legitimate development of the rite occurs in response to these questions and to the circumstances in which we find ourselves. Ultimately this will necessitate new typical editions of the traditional liturgical books. Until they appear we must do as well as we are able.

In this edition errors and inconsistencies present in the twelfth edition have been corrected. The text has been brought into line with the 1962 typical edition of the *Missale Romanum*[10] which was, alas, published only after Canon O'Connell's 1962 edition of *The Ceremonies of the Roman Rite Described* appeared. Passages have been expanded, rewritten and made more explicit, and new notes have been added, in order to assist the modern reader. The diagrams have been drawn anew, corrected and expanded. Notes and the bibliography have been increased. A new chapter, "The Faithful at Mass," has brought together hitherto disparate material for the convenience of the reader.

There are further improvements that can be made to the text and it has not been possible in this edition to adopt all the meritorious suggestions made: a line has had to be drawn in the work of revision and improvement in order to get the book back into print! The editor is grateful to those who responded to his request in his foreword to the 1996 edition of this book for such suggestions—Lee Bradshaw, to whom this edition and indeed this editor owe a great deal, including the newly drawn diagrams, Arthur Crumley, Michael Daniel, Gordon Dimon, Murray Dovey and Dr Joseph Gribbon—and is pleased to reiterate the invitation for future editions.

The production of this edition has been assisted by Meigs Ghent, David Harden, Peter Harden, Rev'd Dr Peter Joseph, Christine Parkin, Andrew Rutherford and members of this monastic community, for which assistance we are indebted. It has also enjoyed the constant support and encouragement of the Very Reverend Dom Cuthbert Brogan OSB, Prior of Farnborough.

---

[10] In my foreword to the 1996 edition of this book I referred to the republication of the 1962 missal by Roman Catholic Books in the United States of America. Whilst their publication is useful, it is not, unfortunately, the 1962 *editio typica,* all printings of which bear the decree of the Sacred Congregation of Rites dated 23rd June 1962.

The singular honour paid by His Eminence, Darío Cardinal Castrillón Hoyos, President of the Pontifical Commission *Ecclesia Dei*, in providing a preface to this edition is gratefully and humbly acknowledged.

In his memoir of Canon O'Connell, Abbot Dyfrig reported that "when the present [post-conciliar] reforms came in...with characteristic humility and humour [O'Connell] accepted them all without a murmur although he realised that the work of a lifetime was now little more than a memorial of the past."[11]

Writing in 1978, Abbot Dyfrig could not have imagined that within but a few years the traditional liturgy (and the work of Fortescue and O'Connell) would no longer be simply a memory. And few who worked assiduously for the implementation of the liturgical books promulgated by Pope Paul VI could have imagined that in May 2003 the Curial Cardinal responsible for the traditional liturgy would state publicly and unequivocally that "the old Roman rite preserves its right of citizenship in the Church and cannot be considered extinct."[12]

The present editor—whose fascination with this book dates back to a copy of its first edition (with its delectable preface) to which he was directed whilst but a youth by a mentor and friend (who has himself recently published ceremonial manuals on the modern rites)—prays that this new edition will play a part in the resurgence of the traditional liturgy currently being witnessed in the Church, a resurgence which, he suspects, both Dr Fortescue and Canon O'Connell would wholeheartedly commend.

Dom Alcuin Reid OSB
Saint Michael's Abbey
Farnborough
14th September 2003

---

[11] "A Memoir of J.B. O'Connell" in: *Pax*, vol. LXVII Spring/Summer 1978 p. 33.
[12] Homily of Cardinal Darío Castrillón Hoyos, President, Pontifical Commission *Ecclesia Dei*, 24th May 2003; cf. Zenit News Report 25th May 2003.

Part I

General Principles Concerning Ceremonies

Chapter I

The Church and Its Furniture

IT is not necessary, in a book of ceremonies, to give a full account of rules for building and furnishing churches. Yet, to understand the ceremonies, one must have some idea of the dispositions of the building, and one must know the names of the vestments, vessels and ornaments used. We begin, then, with a summary account of these,[1] as far as they concern the ceremonies.

Normally a Catholic church should be consecrated by a bishop, according to the form in the pontifical; or at least it should be solemnly blessed.[2] When a church is consecrated, at least one altar (which should be the high altar, if not already consecrated[3]) must be consecrated with it. The essential condition for consecration is that the building be a permanent church, both in construction and purpose; that is, it must be solidly built and must be intended to be used always as a church. To turn a consecrated church to another use is sacrilege, unless it had previously, in accordance with the provisions of Canon Law,[4] been converted to profane use. It follows that consecration is normally not allowed till the building is substantially free of debt and mortgage.

Some churches and chapels are not consecrated, but merely blessed. Canon Law makes no provision for temporary churches. A building to be used as a church for a time only should receive the simple *Benedictio loci*.[5] A church may be blessed at first, then consecrated later.

It makes no difference to any later ceremony whether the church be consecrated or only blessed.

Plan of a Church. According to the old principle, churches were ORIENTED, that is, so placed that the celebrant at the high altar faced east. This meant, normally, that the high altar was at the east end and the main entrance at the west. In describing ceremonies we speak of the gospel and epistle sides of the church and altar. The GOSPEL SIDE is where the Gospel is read at Mass; it is usually the left side as you face the altar; the EPISTLE

---

[1] *Church Building and Furnishing*, J. O'Connell (1955), deals in detail with church appointments. Cf. also canons 1205ff. of the 1983 C.I.C.

[2] The blessing is a reserved one and is found in R.R., IX, ix, 17. A semi-public oratory *may* receive this blessing, or may be given the common blessing of a place (cf. C.I.C. 1196). There is a form of blessing (R.R., IX, vi, 2) for a private oratory.

[3] C.I.C. 1165, § 5.

[4] Cf. C.I.C. 1170, 1187.

[5] R.R., IX, vi, 3; *Excerpta*, p. 116; cf. S.R.C. 4025 § 6; C.I.C. 1196.

SIDE is the right. If the church is oriented, the gospel side will be the north, the epistle side the south.

The plan of a church varies very considerably according to its size, the architect's design, and so on. There is much latitude in planning a church. A large church will probably have a number of side chapels, each with its own altar.[6] In this case, too, the normal principle would be that each altar face the east, so that the priest looks that way when saying Mass. There may also be two or more aisles and a transept.

For the purpose of ceremonies we distinguish five parts of the church. Every church, however small, will have these, at least as theoretical divisions: the nave, baptistery, porch, choir and sanctuary. The NAVE is that part of the church where the people attend the services. Generally it is arranged in two groups of seats, one on either side, with a passage down the middle. It is not now usual in English-speaking countries to separate men from women, though this ancient arrangement was desired by Canon Law.[7]

The BAPTISTERY should be a separate chapel, or be railed off from the rest of the church.[8] It may contain an altar,[9] as well as the font.[10] The font should stand in the middle. It is covered when not in use.

Outside the main entrance to the nave is the NARTHEX, or PORCH (sometimes called *vestibulum*). This has important liturgical uses, and should never be wanting. At the church doors are holy-water stoups.

In front of the nave, generally raised by one or more steps, is the CHOIR. This is where the clergy or singers attend in cassock and surplice. It should have seats or stalls on either side, facing each other across the church. In cathedral and collegiate churches the canons have their stalls arranged in this way.

There is generally a COMMUNION RAIL between the nave and the choir. This should be of a convenient height, so that people can kneel at it to receive Holy Communion. Hanging from it, on the altar side, is the COMMUNION CLOTH of white linen, which rests on the top of the rail while communion is distributed.[11]

Beyond the choir is the SANCTUARY. Often there is no mark in the building to show the line of separation between the choir and sanctuary.

---

[6] Subsidiary altars should never be within the sanctuary, and, when feasible, each real altar should have a separate chapel.

[7] C.I.C. 1262, § 1.

[8] In the rite of Baptism the first part takes place in the narthex ("ad limen ecclesiæ," R.R., II, i, 68). Then, after the child has entered the church, an exorcism is said "antequam accedat ad baptisterium" (ibid., II, ii, 12). Similarly, churching is begun *ad limina* (R.R., VIII, vi, 1).

[9] The old liturgical books constantly suppose Mass said in the baptistery. The great baptisteries in Italy all have altars.

[10] The Roman Ritual sometimes calls the font *baptisterium*.

[11] In many places the use of the communion cloth has disappeared. The Congregation of the Sacraments in an Instruction to Ordinaries, dated 26 March 1929, directs a communion plate *also* to be used for the communion of the people.

The sanctuary is merely the end (normally the east end) of the choir near the high altar. If it is not on a higher level than the choir it is counted as beginning about where the seats or stalls of the choir end on that side.

The chief object in the sanctuary is the ALTAR[12] in the middle; this will be the high altar of the church. All others are counted as side altars.

Altars. There are two kinds of altar, the fixed *(altare fixum)* and portable altar *(altare portabile)*.

A FIXED ALTAR must be of stone with the table and base permanently united. A relic of at least one martyr is buried in it. The whole top (the *mensa*) of the altar is of stone supported by stone *(stipes, stipites)*; it is all consecrated as one thing.

In the case of the PORTABLE ALTAR the only real altar is the ALTAR STONE. This is a stone in which relics are placed and sealed up. It is comparatively small,[13] perhaps about one foot square or so, and an inch or two thick. Mass is said on this. The altar stone may be placed on a table of any material. It is not fixed to the table, so in many churches there is what looks like a large stone or wooden altar. Really this is only the framework or stand. In the middle (generally sunk into the table) is the altar stone, which alone is consecrated. In this way an altar may be built of stone, used as a portable one, having on it the consecrated altar stone, till the whole can be consecrated as a fixed altar. For ceremonial purposes there is no difference between a fixed and a portable altar.[14]

There should be some kind of canopy over the altar.[15] This may hang from the roof of the church or project from the wall (a baldachin or tester) or may stand on columns (a ciborium or civory). It should cover not only the altar, but also the footpace, or at least the priest celebrating. The high altar should not stand immediately against the wall of the church; at the consecration of an altar the rubrics require that the consecrating bishop go around it.

The high altar is raised above the floor of the sanctuary by steps. Every altar should be raised at least one step; the high altar will have three or more steps. There should be an uneven number.

The top step before the altar forms a platform on which the celebrant stands while he says Mass. This is the FOOTPACE *(suppedaneum, predella)*. It should be as long across as the width of the altar (preferably a little longer) and at least so wide in front that the celebrant may genuflect on it

---

[12] Cf. C.I.C. 1197-1202.

[13] "Quæ tam ampla sit, ut hostiam et majorem partem calicis capiat;" "It should be of such size as to hold the Host and the greater part of the Chalice;" (R.G., 525).

[14] The older principle was that, as no church may be consecrated unless a fixed altar be consecrated with it, so, on the other hand, an altar may not be consecrated except in a consecrated church. Thus consecrated church and consecrated altar always went together. But S.R.C. 3059 § 15, and C.I.C. (1165, § 5) allow an altar to be consecrated in a merely blessed church.

[15] C.E., I, xii, 13; xiv, I., S.R.C. 1966, 2912, 3525 § 2.

without having to put his foot outside it. The lower steps go round the footpace, not only in front, but at the sides, so that one can go up to it from either side as from the front. The steps of a fixed altar may be of any suitable material; but the footpace is preferably of wood as this is much easier to stand on.[16]

On one altar in the church (ordinarily, in smaller churches, on the high altar) is the TABERNACLE[17] in which the Blessed Sacrament is reserved. This is a safe or casket—permanently fixed[18] in the middle of the altar—with doors usually opening outwards, leaving enough room in front of it for the vessels and other things used at any ceremony.[19] Generally it should be an iron safe fixed solidly to the altar and so to the ground, or to the wall of the church. Inside, the tabernacle is either gold or gilt, or it is lined with white silk; and has a corporal on which the ciborium stands. Sometimes at the back of the altar, on either side of the tabernacle, there are one or more raised steps, on which the candles or vases of flowers, if used, may be placed. These are called GRADINES. Before the tabernacle in which the Blessed Sacrament is reserved, at least one lamp must always burn.[20] There ought to be—at least in greater churches—several lamps, uneven in number.

Furnishing of the Altar. The altar is covered with three cloths. Under these the pontifical requires that there be a CERE-CLOTH (*chrismale*) of waxed linen, at least for some time after the altar's consecration.[21] The cere-cloth is not counted as one of the three altar-cloths. The cloths should be duly blessed by a priest with the necessary faculty to bless them (R.R. I, lxviii). The upper cloth should be as wide as the altar, and long enough to reach to the ground on either side.

In front of the altar a FRONTAL (*pallium, antependium*) may hang, usually of the colour of the day. The tabernacle should be covered *completely* by a veil (*conopæum*) of the colour of the day or white. The tabernacle veil may never be black. At requiems it should be violet,[22] and so should the frontal. It is never lawful to dispense with the tabernacle veil where the Blessed Sacrament is reserved.

---

[16] Cf. S.R.C. 3576 § 1.

[17] C.I.C. 1268-1269; Instr. of S. Congr. of Sacraments, May 26, 1938; 1983 C.I.C. 938.

[18] But not embedded in a reredos or in gradines. It must be fully veiled by the conopæum when it contains the Blessed Sacrament.

[19] Hence the door should be split into two, so that when opened it does not project too far; unless, of course, it be a sliding door.

[20] C.I.C. 1271. The glass of the lamp should be white but coloured glass is *tolerated* (S.R.C. 3576 § 5). The Ceremonial of Bishops (I, xii, 17) requires many lamps in greater churches, three before the high altar and at least five before the Blessed Sacrament, at all events on greater days.

[21] No law orders the cere-cloth to be a permanent thing.

[22] The rubrics always use the word *violaceus*. In English the meaning of violet as a colour is not clear. As a liturgical term it means not the colour of the flower (which is blue-violet) but the colour (in varying shades) of a prelate's robes, i.e., red-violet.

On the altar stands a CROSS—with the figure of the Crucified—
sufficiently large to be seen by the celebrant and people.[23] It should stand
in the middle of the large candlesticks, its base as high as these, and the
entire cross itself higher than the candlesticks. If there is a tabernacle the
cross may not stand before it. The cross should not stand on the
tabernacle,[24] nor may it stand in the throne used for exposition of the
Blessed Sacrament, though these uses are tolerated. On every altar on
either side are at least two candlesticks with candles. The high altar of a
church will normally have six large candlesticks with candles, and in
front of these two or four smaller ones.[25] The six candles are arranged in
size to form a triangle with the cross as its apex, although custom allows
that the candles be of equal length. Other candles for Benediction,
Exposition, and so on, should be placed there for the occasion only and
taken away afterwards.

Candles. The rules about candles on the altar are these. At low Mass
(when strictly private) two candles burn all the time; according to the
rubric of the missal, a third may be lit from the consecration to the
communion.[26] At solemn Mass, solemn Vespers and all such more
solemn functions six candles are lit, three on either side of the altar cross.
At pontifical solemn Mass of the living by the Ordinary a seventh candle
is lit. At a sung Mass without ministers there may be four or six candles.
During Exposition or Benediction of the Blessed Sacrament twenty, or at
least twelve, candles must burn on the altar. For Benediction with the
ciborium, six. When the Blessed Sacrament is exposed candles at other
altars or before statues and images should be put out, at least those which
can be seen from the altar.

For other rites celebrated at the altar, such as marriage, blessings,
distribution of Holy Communion not in Mass, and for non-liturgical
prayers and devotions, two or more candles are lit on the altar.

The proportion of beeswax in church candles is regulated by law. The
Paschal candle, the two candles for low Mass, six for solemn Mass, and
the twelve necessary for Exposition and Benediction must have at least 65
per cent of real beeswax. All other candles used on an altar must have at
least 25 per cent of beeswax.[27]

---

[23] If immediately behind the altar there is a large representation of the crucifixion, this may
count as the altar cross. (S.R.C. 1270 § 2.)

[24] Cf. O'Connell, *Church Building and Furnishing,* p. 203.

[25] These smaller candlesticks, which are used for private Masses, are not part of the normal
furniture of the high altar and it is better to remove them when Mass is over.

[26] Cf. Chapter VI § 1.

[27] So the bishops of England and Wales on 4 December 1906, following S.R.C. 4147. The
bishops of Ireland, in October 1905, directed "that the Paschal candle and the two principal
candles on the altar at Mass should contain at least 65 per cent of beeswax and that all the
other candles used on the altar should contain at least 25 per cent of beeswax." A decision
of S.R.C. (13 December, 1957) allows local episcopal conferences to modify the ruling of
decree 4147.

FLOWERS on the altar are not necessary. They are not used in the great churches of Rome. But there is no law against them at certain times;[28] and in many places custom is in favour of their use on festive occasions. They should, however, be used with the greatest restraint.

When the altar is not in use the altar-cloths are covered with another cloth of some coloured material (sometimes called vesper-cloth),[29] to keep off dust. This should be removed before every service at which the altar is used.

Furniture of the Sanctuary. Near the altar, on the epistle side, stands the CREDENCE (*credentia, abacus*). During Mass this should be covered with a white linen cloth which reaches to the ground all around.[30] The vessels and books, and sometimes vestments used at Mass, are placed on the credence when they are not in use.

On the same side of the sanctuary is the SEAT (*sedilia*) for the celebrant and sacred ministers. This should be a bench with room for three persons, and, normally, covered with cloth, green or violet according to the season or occasion. The use of domestic chairs is not allowed. In cathedrals the Bishop's THRONE is on the gospel side facing the sedilia. The canopy over it and its covering and cushion are of the colour of the Mass or Office, namely, white, red, green or violet.[31] They should be of silk.[32]

Instead of the throne, a bishop who is not the Ordinary, and sometimes the Ordinary,[33] uses a FALDSTOOL (*faldistorium*). This is a stool without a back. It consists of a frame of metal or wood, shaped like the letter X, with a seat of leather or cloth stretched across its upper extremities. It can be folded flat. When used as a seat the faldstool has a covering and cushion of the liturgical colour of the Office, namely, white, red, green, violet, or black. These are of silk for a cardinal, cloth for a bishop.

The Bishop kneels, on various occasions, before the altar. According to the Ceremonial of Bishops he kneels at a KNEELER (*genuflexorium*, prie-dieu).[34] This has a covering and two cushions, one on which he kneels, the other on which he rests the arms. This covering and the cushions (silk or cloth, as before) are, for a cardinal red, or violet for mourning and times of penance; for a bishop green, or violet for occasions of mourning and times of penance.[35]

---

[28] C.E. (I, xii, 12) expressly suggests small vases of little flowers as an ornament on the altar *on greater feasts,* and Benedict XIII's *Memoriale Rituum* suggests their use "if customary" on certain days. They are mentioned for the Easter Vigil Mass.

[29] Green is the correct colour, but any colour (except black) is permissible.

[30] C.E., II, xxv, 2.

[31] Gold is reserved for cardinals. Violet is used at the throne when the vestments are black.

[32] C.E., I, xiii, 3.

[33] In the presence of a higher prelate (C.E., I, xiii, 4), at Confirmation, etc.

[34] C.E., I, xv, 5 and *passim.*

[35] For the colour worn by cardinals and bishops for penance and mourning, see Chapter II.

For this genuflexorium the faldstool may be, and often is, used. A carpet should be spread beneath; there are two cushions, one placed before the faldstool, on which the bishop kneels; the other lies on the seat, so that he rests his arms on it. The cushions are of silk for a cardinal; of cloth for a bishop. They should be of red, green or violet, according to the occasion as explained above for the kneeler.

When a bishop visits a small church which does not possess a faldstool, a chair with a low back, with a cushion, is prepared on which he will sit, and a kneeler with two cushions. They should be covered with red, green or violet, according to the rank of the bishop and the occasion as explained above.

There may be seats for the servers at Mass and other services on either side of the sanctuary; or they may sit in front of the stalls in the choir.

The LECTERN (legile) and stools for cantors in the middle of the choir, used for parts of the Divine Office, are put in their place before each such service and taken away afterwards. A lectern may be used for the Epistle and Gospel at solemn Mass. It should be covered with cloth of gold or with silk of the colour of the Office.[36]

The SACRISTY (sacristia, sacrarium) is a large room on one side of the sanctuary, or behind it, separated by a door. There should be a stoup of holy water and a bell at this door. There ought to be two sacristies, one a working sacristy which will serve also for the choir and servers, the other, the sacristy proper, reserved for the sacred ministers. In the sacristies are cupboards and presses in which are kept the vessels, instruments and vestments. In the chief sacristy there must be at least one large table on which the vestments are laid out. The celebrant and ministers vest at this table. It may form the top of presses for vestments. Over this table, or in the middle of the sacristy, a crucifix or sacred image should hang. All who enter or leave the sacristy in procession bow to this on arriving and before leaving. A card should be hung up in a conspicuous place, showing the names of the reigning Pope, the Bishop, the Titular of the church, and indicating the oratio imperata, if there be one.

The 1958 Instructio de Musica Sacra et Sacra Liturgia (no. 72) permits— but certainly does not require—the use of the MICROPHONE. In very large churches, and on pilgrimages and the like, their careful use may facilitate the people following those parts of the liturgical rites which are intended to be heard by all.[37] But vigilance must be exercised in their use lest the distinction between the different voices of the rites be lost. Nor must they be too prominent on the altar or in the sanctuary.

---

[36] C.E., II, viii, 45.

[37] A microphone on the altar (which ought not to be visible), should be switched off during the canon lest it amplify the turning of pages, etc.

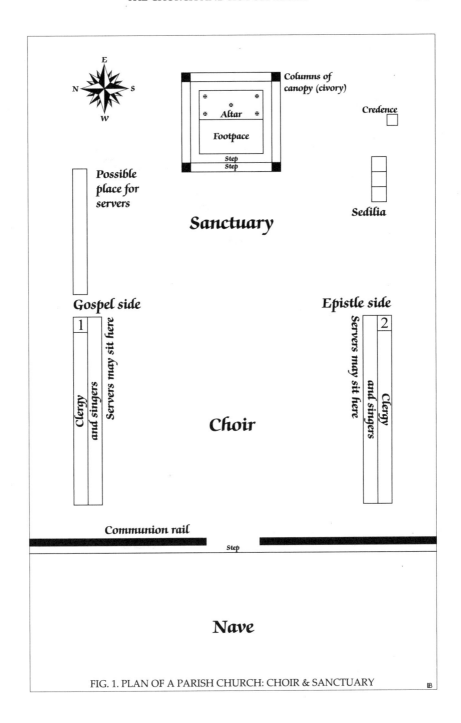

FIG. 1. PLAN OF A PARISH CHURCH: CHOIR & SANCTUARY

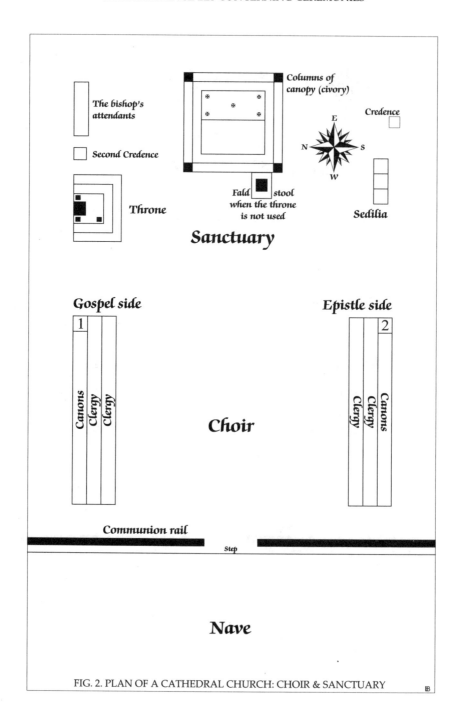

The bishop's attendants

Second Credence

Columns of canopy (civory)

Credence

E
N S
W

Throne

Fald stool when the throne is not used

Sedilia

Sanctuary

Gospel side

Epistle side

1

2

Canons
Clergy
Clergy

Canons
Clergy
Clergy

Choir

Communion rail

Step

Nave

FIG. 2. PLAN OF A CATHEDRAL CHURCH: CHOIR & SANCTUARY

Chapter II

The Vestments of the Roman Rite

THE common dress for servers and all who assist at any function in choir is a black CASSOCK *(vestis talaris)* with a white linen SURPLICE *(superpelliceum);*[1] and not the alb.[2] Certain prelates and dignitaries wear a violet cassock. Clerics have, in choir, a BIRETTA *(biretum),* a square cap of black cloth with three ridges. Some dignitaries also wear a SKULL-CAP *(pileolus, zucchetto).*[3] Canons in chapter[4] have a cape (MOZZETTA or CAPPA-PARVA) over their surplice or rochet. Prelates sometimes wear a tunic called MANTELLETTUM *(mantelletta)* having slits at the side through which the sleeves of the rochet pass.

Vestments for Mass. The celebrant at Mass, if he is a simple priest, wears over his cassock, first the AMICE *(amictus),* a rectangular piece of white linen or hemp with strings to tie it. He lays this on the head, then passes it around the neck. Then he puts on the ALB *(alba),* a long garment of white linen or hemp reaching to the feet.[5] This is tied round the waist by the GIRDLE or cincture *(cingulum),* which may be of the colour of the day, but is generally white linen, hemp or silk. On the left arm he wears the MANIPLE *(manipulus),* a band of silk of the colour of the day. The STOLE *(stola)* is a longer band of coloured silk worn round the neck — crossed in front for a simple priest and hanging straight down for anyone wearing a pectoral cross — and secured by the ends of the girdle. The CHASUBLE *(casula, planeta)* is the last garment covering all the others. It has a hole through which the head is passed and often strings on the inner side to tie around the body. Both the more ample "gothic" and the classical

---

[1] The abbreviated form is called "cotta." The ROCHET *(rocchettum)* is a garment like the surplice, but shorter, fitting the body more closely, with narrow sleeves. It is worn by cardinals, bishops, prelates, sometimes (by indult) by canons. It is generally worn under other vestments.

[2] R., II, 1. In some places servers follow the modern trend and wear an alb, contrary to the rubrics and to the tradition of reserving the alb to the sacred ministers. Where this practice persists it is imperative that the cassock (or the religious habit) be worn under the alb.

[3] The skull-cap of a cardinal is red; of a bishop (also called *biretum* in C.E.) and some abbots violet. Others may wear only a black skull-cap.

[4] Namely, normally, in their own cathedral or collegiate church (cf. Chapter V § 3).

[5] Lace is permitted on borders of the sleeves and the hem, but lace from the waist is restricted to canons and higher prelates. Coloured linings are allowed and need not relate to the rank of the wearer; S.R.C. 4048. (This ruling has long since been ignored.) When all the sacred ministers use albs with lace decoration, all three albs, but at least those worn by the deacon and subdeacon, should match.

"roman" shapes are permissible.[6] The maniple, stole and chasuble are usually silk[7] and the colour of the Mass celebrated.

A set of vestments for low Mass also includes the burse (to hold the corporal) and veil to be put on the chalice.

At Mass the deacon wears the amice, alb, girdle, maniple and stole. But he wears the stole differently from the priest. He lays it across the breast so that the middle is on the left shoulder, and the two ends under the right arm. If it is not itself joined on the side it is fixed in this position by the girdle. Then he puts on the DALMATIC *(dalmatica)*. This is a kind of tunic (often open a little up the sides from the bottom) with short sleeves, with an opening through which the head is put. It is usually silk, of the colour of the Mass.

The subdeacon at Mass wears the amice, alb, girdle, maniple, no stole, but a TUNICLE *(tunicella)* made in much the same shape as the deacon's dalmatic, but with longer and narrower sleeves and less ornate.[8]

As a rule the celebrant wears the chasuble only at Mass (and before a Nuptial Mass). Normally the maniple is not worn except at Mass.

During part of solemn Mass, namely from the offertory to the fraction, the subdeacon wears a HUMERAL VEIL *(velum humerale)* under which he holds the paten. This is a rectangle of silk, of the colour of the vestments, often with strings to tie it. It is worn like a cape over the shoulders. The object of the humeral veil is to cover the hands when something is held in them.

The Cope. During the solemn blessings in the missal (as on Candlemas, Ash Wednesday and Palm Sunday), in processions, at the Asperges ceremony before Mass, at funerals, at Benediction of the Blessed Sacrament, at Vespers and Lauds sung solemnly, at Matins from the ninth lesson, the celebrant wears a COPE *(pluviale)*. This is a large semicircular garment reaching to the feet behind, with a band[9] (having a large hook and eye) to join it in front.

Usually the cope is of the colour of the day. At Benediction of the Blessed Sacrament it is white,[10] at funerals always black. For some solemn blessings the colour is violet (e.g. the blessing of ashes). Except

---

[6] S.R.C. 20 August 1957 leaves the question to the judgement of Local Ordinaries. The shape employed for the illustrations in this book does not imply any preference.

[7] S.R.C. 2769, 3543 & 3779 forbid wool, cotton and linen. Satin, silk poplin and silk velvet are permissible. Ornamentation need not be silk.

[8] C.E., I, x, 1. The deacon and subdeacon also wear dalmatic and tunicle at the Asperges, at blessings at the altar, in processions and at Exposition and Benediction.

[9] A morse *(formale, pectorale)*, i.e., a metal clasp ornamented with jewels, etc., may be used only by the Bishop or a higher prelate (C.E., I, vii, 1; II, i, 4; cf. S.R.C. 2425 § 9) in the place of his jurisdiction.

[10] When Benediction immediately follows Mass or Vespers and the celebrant does not leave the sanctuary, the colour of the cope will be that of the Mass or Office, unless this be black (S.R.C. 1615 § 6, 2562, 3175 § 3, 3799 § 2, 3949 § 7).

for the Divine Office the celebrant wears a stole of the same colour under the cope.

At the Divine Office he wears either a surplice only, or surplice and cope. At processions and Benediction of the Blessed Sacrament he will generally wear a surplice, stole and cope. When he holds the monstrance or ciborium he has a white humeral veil. At blessings before Mass he has the amice, alb, girdle and stole. When he wears the girdle he crosses the stole before the breast. With a surplice it hangs straight down from the neck.

Other persons besides the celebrant wear the cope. The assistant priest at Mass (when there is one—cf. Chapter XIV) may do so. At Mass by a simple priest no one else may wear a cope except at a priest's first Mass when it is solemnly sung. Then the practice of having an assistant priest in cope is tolerated.[11] At the Divine Office (Vespers and Lauds) the cantors may wear copes of the colour of the Office. At certain pontifical functions and at the procession of the Blessed Sacrament at Corpus Christi some of the clergy wear copes.

When preaching the preacher, if a secular priest, wears a surplice. He may wear a stole of the colour of the day, if this is the custom. Regulars who have a habit wear no surplice as a rule. In administering sacraments and sacramentals the priest normally wears a surplice and stole. He may wear a black-lined black biretta covered in woollen material with a tuft of silk (not a pom-pom).

The Dress of a Bishop. The usual dress of a BISHOP is a cloth cassock, violet in colour, without a train.[12] The cassock is edged with and has lighter buttons, almost red. The bishop wears a violet (amaranth colour) silk belt. Over the cassock he wears a white linen rochet. Over this a bishop in his own diocese wears the mozzetta. Auxiliaries and all bishops where they have no jurisdiction wear the mantelletta instead.[13] Bishops wear a pectoral cross, which should hang from the neck by a green and gold silk cord when the bishop is wearing choir dress. At other times it hangs from a chain. They use a violet skull-cap[14] and a green-lined violet biretta.[15] On certain days of penance or mourning it is becoming, not obligatory, that the cassock, mozzetta and mantelletta be of black cloth, the cassock edged with violet. These days are all fast days (except the ember days of Pentecost), and in addition the season of Advent and from

---

[11] S.R.C. 3564 § 2.

[12] S.R.C., December 4, 1952.

[13] The mozzetta alone over the rochet is always understood to signify jurisdiction. In the presence of superiors, bishops, even in their own diocese, wear the mantelletta, and sometimes over this the mozzetta. Today, when the bishop does not possess a mantelletta, this distinction is frequently ignored and bishops wear the mozzetta even when, according to customary usage, the mantelletta ought to be worn.

[14] Conceded by Blessed Pius IX, 17 June 1867.

[15] Conceded by Leo XIII, 3 February 1888.

Septuagesima to Lent (except on great feasts).[16] Black is laudably used also at requiem functions.

The pontifical RING *(annulus)* for use when a bishop is vested must be large enough to go over the glove. Ordinarily this has a gem (though not a carved one, nor a sapphire), surrounded by brilliants. A similar but smaller ring is used on other occasions.

At functions, instead of the mozzetta, the Bishop of the diocese may wear the *cappa magna*.[17] This is a great cloak with a long train, of violet wool.[18] It has a cape and hood, which in winter is of ermine, in summer of almost red silk. When the Bishop wears the cappa magna he needs a train-bearer *(caudatarius)*. Regular bishops have the cappa, and its fur, of the colour of their order (if it has a special habit).

Blessed Pius IX instituted a kind of undress for prelates, called after him *habitus pianus*. It consists of a black cloth cassock with no train, crimson facings, a violet belt and *ferraiolone*, violet stock and stockings. This is used constantly at non-liturgical functions. Apart from those given him in the rite of consecration (ring, mitre and crosier), a bishop-elect is entitled to the use of the insignia of his office from the date of the publication of his elevation.

CARDINALS have the same dress as bishops, but always scarlet instead of violet, and violet instead of black for mourning. Round their hat bishops have a green[19] cord, archbishops green and gold,[20] cardinals red and gold.

For low Mass a bishop wears the same vestments as a priest. The only difference is that he wears the pectoral cross over the alb, under the stole. He wears the stole not crossed, but hanging straight down. He does not put on the maniple till after the prayer "Indulgentiam," except at requiem Masses.

At solemn Mass,[21] and at certain low Masses which sometimes take the place of a solemn Mass (e.g., at Ordinations or the consecration of a bishop) a bishop wears special stockings and shoes[22] of the colour of the

---

[16] C.E., I, iii, 2; S.R.C. 4355 § 1.

[17] A bishop in the place of his jurisdiction may wear his cappa magna even in the presence of his superior. In deference to the latter he does not allow the train to flow but carries it folded up. He will, however, allow it to flow if he is about to pontificate, but even then not when he walks with his superior or performs any act of deference towards him (S.R.C. 4355. II. 2). If, on an occasion where usage has the bishop wear the cappa magna, one is not available, he should wear the mozzetta.

[18] C.E., I, iii, 3.

[19] Green, not violet, is a bishop's heraldic colour.

[20] The Congregation of Ceremonial granted (3 November 1826) the use of a green *and gold* cord to the four Latin Patriarchs. This privilege was not, it would seem, extended to archbishops, but it is adopted by some of them; and its use is recognised by some authorities.

[21] But not if it is a requiem Mass.

[22] These look more like gaiters and slippers. In Latin they are "caligæ et sandalia," in English generally "buskins and sandals."

Mass. Over the rochet he wears the amice, alb, girdle, pectoral cross, stole, tunicle, dalmatic, gloves, ring, chasuble, mitre. On certain occasions a Metropolitan will wear the pallium over the chasuble. The manner of putting these on will be described later (Chapter XVI).

The tunicle and dalmatic worn by a bishop are made of very thin silk. They are of the colour of the Mass.

There are three kinds of MITRE (mitra). The precious mitre (mitra pretiosa) is generally of cloth of gold or of silver with embroidery and ornaments of gold and precious stones. Since this is supposed to be heavy and burdensome if worn all the time, its place is taken during parts of the services by the gold mitre (mitra auriphrygiata) made of cloth of gold with no additional ornament. The simple mitre (mitra simplex) is of plain white silk damask for cardinals and bishops, and of white linen for abbots (and for bishops in the presence of the Pope). It has red fringes on the ends of the lappets and is otherwise without ornament.[23] This is worn at certain functions (e.g., funerals). In his own diocese the Ordinary carries a CROSIER (baculus pastoralis). During parts of the Mass a silk veil, a GREMIAL (gremiale), of the colour of the day is laid over his knees while he sits.

On other occasions a bishop wears amice, alb, girdle, pectoral cross, stole, cope and mitre.

Certain other prelates, abbots and protonotaries, may on occasion share some of the marks of a bishop's rank (cf. Chapter V § 3).

Linens. Besides the vestments, the following cloths are used. The CORPORAL (corporale, palla corporalis) is a square piece of linen spread on the altar during Mass. The chalice and paten stand on the corporal. When it is not used the corporal lies in the BURSE (bursa), a pocket of silk, of the same colour as the vestments, strengthened with cardboard. The PURIFIER (purificatorium) is a linen cloth folded in three lengthways, used by the celebrant to wipe the chalice during Mass. The PALL (palla) is a small square of stiffened linen, used to cover the chalice at Mass. R.R. gives a blessing required for corporals and palls (I, lxix).

The HAND-TOWEL (manutergium, lavabo) is also a small linen cloth, not unlike a purifier, used to dry the fingers after washing them.

Liturgical Colours. The colours of the silk vestments and insignia (that is, of the chasuble, stole, maniple, dalmatic, tunicle, humeral veil, cope, bishop's gremial, shoes and stockings) vary according to the feast or occasion on which they are used.

The colours of the Roman rite are white, red, green, violet, black, rose-colour.

WHITE (albus) is used for all feasts of our Lord, except those of His Cross and Passion, for Trinity Sunday, for all feasts of the Blessed Virgin

---

[23] The more modern custom is to reserve the white silk damask mitre to the use of cardinals and for bishops to use the linen mitre.

Mary, of the angels, and of all saints not martyrs; as a colour *de tempore* it is used from Vespers of Christmas to 12 January, from Easter to the vigil of Pentecost.

RED *(ruber)* is used on Pentecost eve (for Mass), on Pentecost and during its octave, for the feast of the Precious Blood (1 July), the feast of Holy Cross (14 September) and for martyrs (anniversary of death, or of finding or translation of relics); and for the blessing of palms on the second Passion Sunday.

GREEN *(viridis)* is the neutral colour. It is used on Sundays and weekdays from 14 January to Septuagesima, and on Sundays (except Trinity Sunday) and weekdays (except some vigils and Ember days) in the season after Pentecost.

VIOLET *(violaceus)* is the colour of penance. It is used on Sundays and weekdays of Advent and from Septuagesima to the Wednesday of Holy Week, except (in some churches) on the third Sunday of Advent and the fourth of Lent. Violet is also used on vigils (except that of Ascension and Pentecost), when the Office is of the vigil; on Ember days, except those in Pentecost week; on the Greater and Lesser Litanies (for the Mass of Rogations); for the blessing of ashes and for many votive Masses. On Holy Saturday the lessons and collects before the Mass, with the Litanies, are said in violet vestments, the Mass itself in white.

BLACK *(niger)* is used on Good Friday (up to the communion), for Masses for the dead and at funerals.

ROSE-COLOUR *(color rosaceus)* may be used on two occasions, the third Sunday of Advent (called *Gaudete* Sunday) and the fourth of Lent (*Lætare* Sunday). If the church does not possess vestments of this colour violet ones are used instead.

The Congregation of Sacred Rites tolerates the use of *real* cloth of silver to replace white, and *real* cloth of gold in place of white, red or green (not of violet or black).[24]

The colour for processions and Benediction of the Blessed Sacrament is white. But if Benediction or a procession follows immediately after Mass or Vespers, and the celebrant does not leave the sanctuary, the colour of the day may be kept.[25] In any case, the humeral veil must be white.

---

[24] S.R.C. 3145, 3191 § 4, 3646 § 2, § 3.

[25] When Benediction immediately follows Mass or Vespers and the celebrant does not leave the sanctuary, the colour of the cope will be that of the Mass or Office, unless this be black (S.R.C. 1615 § 6, 2562, 3175 § 3, 3799 § 2, 3949 § 7).

The vestments worn by the celebrant and ministers at Mass must be blessed.[26] It is not strictly necessary to bless the cope. The burse, chalice veil, humeral veil and surplice need not be blessed but may be and often are with the other vestments.

---

[26] R., I, 2.

Chapter III

Liturgical Vessels, Instruments and Books

§ 1. Vessels

THE chief sacred vessels used in the Liturgy are the CHALICE (*calix*) and PATEN (*patena*), the forms of which are well known. The chalice, if it is not of gold, must be at least silver and gilt inside the cup; the paten must be at least silver and gilt on the concave side.[1] The chalice should have a node on the stem and a base of good size, with a cross on the base.

The CIBORIUM (*pyxis, vas*) is a vessel like a chalice with a cover, at least gilt inside, airtight, and with a small elevation inside to help gather any fragments.[2] It is used to contain the consecrated Hosts in the tabernacle. When it contains the Blessed Sacrament, or when exposed to public view[3] (e.g., on the altar before Mass awaiting consecration), it should be covered with a veil of white silk.

In the tabernacle there is also generally a PYX (*pyxis custodia*), a small box of silver or other metal, gilt inside, which contains the Host used for Benediction. This Host is usually held by a little instrument, shaped like a new moon, called the LUNETTE (*lunula*). This, too, must be at least gilt. The general principle is that the Blessed Sacrament may rest only on gold or white linen. The MONSTRANCE (*ostensorium*) is a vessel for exposing the Blessed Sacrament. It is so made—of gold, silver, or gilt metal—that the Host may be placed in it and can then be seen by the people. Often the place where the Host rests is surrounded by rays, and purely decorative or symbolic figures may adorn it, but not images of saints or angels. The Blessed Sacrament may not be touched to glass.

There is also a small pyx used when the Holy Communion is taken to the sick. This, too, must be at least gilt inside.

The chalice and paten are consecrated by a bishop or other cleric having the necessary faculty. The pyx, ciborium and lunette are blessed by a bishop or by a priest having the faculty.[4] There is no law that the monstrance be blessed but it often is.[5]

---

[1] R.S., I, 1.
[2] C.E., II, xxx, 3.
[3] So some rubricians on the principle that sacred vessels exposed to view, and not in use, are to be veiled (e.g., the chalice, the monstrance). The rubrics are not explicit, and other rubricians teach that the ciborium is veiled only when it contains the Blessed Sacrament.
[4] The form of blessing is in R.R., IX, ix, 6, 7; *Excerpta*, p. 130.
[5] Ibid.

Other vessels, not counted as sacred and *not* blessed, are:

For Mass the CRUETS *(ampullæ, hamulæ)*. These are two little jugs to hold the wine and the water. They should be of clear glass; but other material is tolerated. Sometimes their purpose is marked on them; the one having the letter V (for *vinum*, wine), the other A *(aqua*, water); or the cruet for wine has a red cross or other mark to distinguish it. Otherwise, since they should be always washed out and kept perfectly clean, it does not matter which is used each time for the wine or water. The cruets should have stoppers or lids or at least be covered, when filled, with the hand-towel, to keep out dust, insects, etc. With them is the DISH *(pelvicula)* on which they stand when not in use. This is not merely used as a stand for the cruets; when the celebrant washes his hands at Mass, the water may be poured by the server over his fingers into this dish, or, more conveniently, there is a separate bowl for this purpose. With the cruets and dish a hand-towel is laid on the credence. The celebrant dries his fingers with this after washing them.

For a bishop and certain other prelates a ewer *(urceus)* of water and a dish *(lanx, pelvis, bacile)* of silver or other metal[6] are used for washing his hands. With them is used a larger hand-towel (or several small ones).

A HAND-CANDLESTICK *(palmatoria, bugia)* is held near the book out of which prelates read. It is of gold or gilt for a cardinal; of silver or silver-plated for other prelates, and has a long handle.

§ 2. Instruments

For the sprinkling with holy water before Mass (the Asperges ceremony) and for blessing any object a portable HOLY-WATER STOOP *(vas aquæ benedictæ)* and SPRINKLER *(aspersorium,[7] aspergillum)* are used. The stoup is of metal, the sprinkler has a brush at the end, or a hollow globe with holes in it, but, preferably, a sprig of hyssop or other shrub is used.

The THURIBLE *(thuribulum)* or CENSER is a vessel, round in shape, hanging by three long chains from a disc. Held by this disc it can be swung. It has a cover which hangs by a fourth chain from a ring passing through the disc. By pulling up this ring the thurible may be opened. Generally there is another ring round all the chains to keep them together. The INCENSE-BOAT *(navicella, navicula, acerra)* is a little vessel, shaped like a boat, in which the incense is kept. It has a SPOON *(cochlear)* with which the incense is put on the burning charcoal in the thurible. In the sacristy are kept the ACOLYTES' CANDLES in tall candlesticks. The candlesticks are so made, with a node and a base, that they can stand without being held, for instance on the credence. There are also TORCHES *(funalia)* held by the torch-bearers *(cæroferarii)* at Mass and Benediction. In

---

[6] Of gold or silver-gilt for a cardinal.

[7] "Aspersory" is also used for the portable vessel.

theory these should be long torches. It is now usual to make them in the form of a separate case (practically a candlestick) into which a candle is placed. But the idea of a torch is so far preserved that they have no base, and cannot stand alone. They are kept in a rack in the sacristy.

The PROCESSIONAL CROSS is fixed to a long staff, also so made that it cannot stand alone. In Catholic churches it now always has a figure of our Lord crucified. The cross should be detachable from its staff.

For processions of the Blessed Sacrament a portable CANOPY *(baldachinum, umbraculum)* is used. It has four or more poles.[8] For short processions in the church, as when the Blessed Sacrament is carried from one altar to another, a smaller canopy *(umbella)* with one rod, like an umbrella, is used. For the Blessed Sacrament both must be white or real cloth of gold.

The SANCTUS-BELL *(parva campanula, tintinnabulum)* is a small single hand-bell (not a gong)[9] rung during Mass at the moments appointed in the rubrics of the missal. It is placed on the credence before Mass and taken away afterwards. A cushion (in silk of the colour of the Office or in leather) or a small silver or ornamented wooden stand *(legile)*[10] is needed, on which to rest the missal at Mass.

For the kiss of peace, instead of the more usual way of giving it (p. 51) sometimes a little disc is used (cf. p. 91). This is the PAX-BREDE *(pax, instrumentum pacis, tabella pacis)*. It is generally a disc of silver or gilt, with a handle to hold it. On the face it has some such symbol as the cross, the *Agnus Dei* or a pelican in her piety. If the pax-brede is used it should have a small cloth of linen to wipe it each time after it has been kissed.

Near the tabernacle where the Blessed Sacrament is reserved a little covered vessel should be kept, generally of glass, with water,[11] to purify the fingers of those, other than the celebrant who assist with the distribution of Holy Communion at Mass. It has a small purifier by it.

§ 3. Books

There are six chief liturgical books of the Roman rite.

The MISSAL *(Missale Romanum)* contains all that is needed for Mass, and for certain other functions which take place immediately before Mass, such as the blessings at Candlemas or on Ash Wednesday, and certain other blessings (of lustral water, etc.). It also has the preparation and thanksgiving of the celebrant before and after Mass.

The BREVIARY *(Breviarium Romanum)* contains all the Divine Office.

---

[8] C.E., I, xiv, 1, says it has six or eight poles and is borne by "noble laymen."

[9] The use of an Indian (hanging) gong is not permitted (S.R.C. 4000 § 3).

[10] C.E., I, xii, 15; R.G., 527.

[11] This water, and all water used for ablutions, must be put in the piscina *(sacrarium)*, a channel leading to clean earth, generally placed in the sacristy.

The MARTYROLOGY is a calendar, giving the names and a short statement about martyrs and other saints, each on his day. It is read or sung during Prime where the Divine Office is said in choir.

The RITUAL *(Rituale Romanum)* has the administration of the Sacraments, many blessings, prayers for processions and such liturgical functions, as far as they are used by a priest. There is less uniformity in the ritual than in any other liturgical book. Many countries and dioceses still have their own ritual book, based on the Roman one.

The PONTIFICAL *(Pontificale Romanum)* is the book for bishops. It contains the Sacraments and other functions performed by a bishop, such as Confirmation and Ordination, the consecration of a church, and so on.

The CEREMONIAL OF BISHOPS *(Cæremoniale Episcoporum)* is a directory of ceremonies for bishops and others who take part in pontifical functions.[12]

The PONTIFICAL CANON is a book containing the order and canon of Mass and some liturgical texts proper to prelates. It is used by them at Mass instead of altar-cards.

The ORDO HEBDOMADÆ SANCTÆ INSTAURATUS (OHS) contains the Holy Week rites (from Palm Sunday to the Easter Vigil inclusive) as does the missal.[13]

The MEMORIALE RITUUM formerly used in small parish churches was replaced for Holy Week in 1957 by *Ritus Simplex, Ordo Hebdomadæ Sanctæ Instauratus,* and by the rubrics of the missal for 2 February and Ash Wednesday.

There are other books consisting of parts of these official books printed separately for convenience. There is no reason why any special service should not be printed in a separate book, so long as it conforms to the text in the book from which it is taken, with the Ordinary's permission.

---

[12] This book (C.E.), although intended in the first place for bishops, contains very full directions for all people at many functions: so that, in spite of its title, it is really a book of ceremonies in general.

[13] One ought to be careful in using earlier editions of this book which do not include the modifications in the Holy Week Liturgy issued by the S.R.C. on 1st February 1957, or the modification ordered to the Solemn Prayers of Good Friday by the S.R.C. on 19th March 1959. The principal changes introduced are: permission to use the simple rites where there are not enough sacred ministers but only where there are sufficient well trained servers (nos 1-3); the faculty for the Ordinary to grant permission to celebrate the blessing of palms and procession in the evening on condition that this not be done in the same church in the morning, and on condition that the blessing not take place without the following procession and Mass (nos. 4-5); the faculty for the Ordinary to allow to priests in charge of two or more parishes the celebration of two Masses of the Lord's supper (no. 13), two celebrations of the Good Friday liturgy, but not in the same parish and within the stipulated times (no. 16) and two celebrations of the Easter Vigil, but not in the same parish (no. 21); the strict requirement that in churches where the transfer and reposition of the Blessed Sacrament takes place on Maundy Thursday the liturgical rites of Good Friday be celebrated (no. 14); the clarification that the Easter Vigil may be celebrated in churches where the other rites of the triduum have not, or may be omitted where they have (no. 20); tonsure, minor and major orders may not be conferred during the Easter Vigil (no. 22).

From the missal the BOOK OF LESSONS or LECTIONARY is taken. This contains the Epistles and Gospels for the year, to be used by the deacon and subdeacon at solemn Mass, and often the *Exsultet*. There may be two such books, one of Epistles and one of gospels *(Epistolarium* and *Evangeliarium)*. If the church does not possess this book, a missal may always be used in its stead. The CANTUS PASSIONIS, in three volumes, contains the chant for the singing of the passion in Holy Week. As the text in older (pre-1956) copies of these conforms to the 1962 *editio typica* of the missal, there seems to be no reason why they cannot be used with the melodies they contain. The GRADUAL *(Graduale Romanum)* contains the parts of the missal needed by the choir, with music. The Masses for the dead are often printed in a separate book *(Missæ Defunctorum)*.

There are many excerpts from the breviary. The DAY HOURS or DIURNAL *(Horæ Diurnæ)* contains all the Office except Matins. For use in the choir various extracts are made, with the music, such as the VESPERAL *(Vesperale Romanum)* and DIRECTORIUM CHORI.

In England there exists a book, RITUS SERVANDUS, approved by S.R.C. and by the hierarchy, which contains directions and the prayers for Benediction of the Blessed Sacrament, the blessing of Holy Water and the *Asperges*, prayers for the Sovereign and some non-liturgical services.[14]

The Ceremonial (I, xii, 15) says that, at pontifical functions, and at other solemn functions too, all the liturgical books used (the missal, lectionary, vesperal, pontifical canon, etc.) are covered with silk of the liturgical colour. Often a veil over the bookstand is used instead.

The ALTAR-CARDS *(tabella secretarum)* contain certain prayers from the missal, printed separately for the convenience of the celebrant. There are usually three altar-cards. The largest, containing the words of consecration and other prayers, stands in the middle of the altar, leaning against the foot of the cross or tabernacle during Mass. The altar-card which contains the prayer at the blessing of water *(Deus qui humanæ substantiæ)* and the lavabo psalm stands at the epistle end; the third, containing the last Gospel, at the gospel end. The altar-cards are used only at Mass. They should be put in their places on the altar as part of the preparation for Mass, and taken away afterwards.

A card with the prayers ordered by Pope Leo XIII to be said after 'private' Mass (and so sometimes called the Leonine prayers) is placed on the credence when these are used.

---

[14] *Ritus servandus in solemni expositione et benedictione sanctissimi Sacramenti adiectis hymnis et litaniis et orationibus quæ in ipsa expositione et in aliis quibusdam sacris ritibus adhiberi solent, editio nova,* (Burns and Oates, 1963).

Chapter IV

Common Ceremonial Actions

THERE are many actions, such as bowing, genuflecting, and so on, which occur constantly during all services. In order not to have to explain these each time, it will be convenient to say here, once for all, how they should be done.[1]

On changing from sitting to kneeling first stand, then kneel. Never slide directly on to the knees.

Genuflexions. To make a genuflexion, first stand upright facing the object or person to whom it is to be made. Unless something is held, the hands are joined palm to palm before the breast. Then, without bending the body or the head, touch the ground with the right knee at exactly the place where the right foot was. Rise again at once.

A double genuflexion is made by first genuflecting as above; then, before rising, touch the ground with the left knee where the left foot stood. Now, kneeling on both knees, bow the head and shoulders somewhat.

Everyone who passes the altar where the Blessed Sacrament is reserved, unless forming part of a procession, genuflects to It as he passes. Where It is reserved on the high altar, on entering the church genuflect before It, either as soon as you enter or before going to your place. Genuflect again before going out. In ceremonial entrances everyone except the celebrant genuflects to the altar on entering and before leaving. But the celebrant genuflects only when the Blessed Sacrament is reserved at the altar; otherwise he bows low.[2]

If the Blessed Sacrament is exposed, that is, during the rite of Exposition, on entering or leaving the church make a double genuflexion. At a ceremony everyone makes this double genuflexion on entering and before leaving the church; during the service normally they genuflect only. When the Blessed Sacrament is reserved at the Altar of Repose on Maundy Thursday and Good Friday morning It is treated as if It were exposed.

A genuflexion is made to a relic of the True Cross, if it is exposed, also to the cross when unveiled on Good Friday. A cardinal everywhere outside Rome, a bishop in his own diocese, a metropolitan in his province, a Papal Legate or a Nuncio or an Apostolic Delegate in the

---

[1] These actions are described in greater detail in O'Connell, *The Celebration of Mass*, 1964, pp. 182ff.

[2] Prelates and canons in their own cathedral or collegiate church also bow low in this case.

place of his jurisdiction, an abbot in his own church, are saluted by a genuflexion when present in vestments or in choir dress. But the genuflexion is not made to a bishop or other prelate in the presence of his superior or outside the place of his jurisdiction. Prelates, canons in their official dress, the celebrant at Mass or other services, do not genuflect to anyone. Instead they bow low.

If the head is covered it is always uncovered before genuflecting except when the priest is carrying the chalice.

If one is about to kneel immediately at the same place, as a general rule one does not first genuflect. But if one is to kneel on a step, then the genuflexion is first made on the ground. Rising, one then kneels on the step.

At the beginning and end of Mass the genuflexion is made on the ground (this is called *in plano*). During Mass it is made on the lowest step of the altar by those in sacred vestments *(parati)*.

The cross-bearer, while holding the processional cross, never genuflects.[3] When the acolytes accompany him they do not genuflect either. When an archbishop gives his blessing, then only does his cross-bearer kneel before him, holding the archiepiscopal cross turned towards him. During Holy Week the thurifer does not genuflect whilst carrying the thurible.

Bows. The rubrics prescribe several kinds of BOWS *(reverentia, inclinatio)*. Thus sometimes they say that the person is *profunde inclinatus,* sometimes that he is *aliquantulum inclinatus,* sometimes merely *inclinatus;* or they say *caput inclinat.* Formerly rubricians used to distinguish two bows of the body (deep and moderate) and two bows of the head only (deep and slight). Some even went so far—without any support from the rubrics—as to prescribe three degrees of head bow, the deepest for the name *Iesus,* the middle one for the name *Maria,* and the least one for the name of a saint or of the Pope. In the rubrics, only two kinds of bow are, generally speaking, indicated. A LOW OR PROFOUND BOW *(profunda inclinatio)* is made by bending the head and body so that the hands might touch the knees if they hung down; though, in fact, they are kept joined before the breast. The bow formerly called a medium bow of the body is now merged with a deep bow of the head. It is made by bowing the head fully and the shoulders slightly and is described in the rubrics as *inclinatus* or *caput inclinat.*[4]

The general rules for bowing are these:

In bowing always keep the hands joined before the breast, unless they hold something. The celebrant bows low to the cross at the beginning and end of services. When one does not genuflect to a prelate, then one makes a low bow. The medium bow is usually made to persons of higher rank than one's own. The medium bow is used when certain words are said: for instance, at the Holy Name; when the three Divine Persons are named *Pater et Filius et Spiritus Sanctus;* at *Oremus;* and during the *Gloria in excelsis,* and the *Credo,* at the verses so indicated in the missal. The medium bow is also made at the name *Maria* of the Blessed Virgin, at the mention of the name of the saint of the day,[5] and at that of the Pope in the canon or the *oratio imperata.* Those who are already bowing during any part of a service make no further motion on these occasions. Neither does anyone bow when he is impeded (e.g., while he is making the sign of the cross). If several names or texts, at each of which a bow should be made, follow one another immediately it is more seemly to bow once and to remain bowing till all have been said. Everyone bows, before and after being incensed, to the person who incenses him; and he bows, before and after, to the person incensed (cf. below). One does not bow before or after incensing the Blessed Sacrament.

The Hands. While standing or kneeling, when the hands are unoccupied, they should be joined before the breast; that is, they are extended and joined palm to palm, the fingers pointing upward at an angle of forty-five degrees, the thumbs crossed right over left. When sitting the hands should be extended one on each knee. In genuflecting at the altar the celebrant alone lays the hands on it while doing so; the ministers and all others keep the hands joined. When something is held in one hand the other should be extended on the breast; but the celebrant at the altar and facing it lays the other hand on it.

Walking and Turning. When walking a person must take care to maintain a straight back, keep his eyes cast down—taking care to see what is ahead where necessary—and to keep his hands joined as described above. Should the person who is walking be carrying something in one hand, the other hand (normally the left) is placed flat, with fingers extended, on the breast. One walks at a moderate pace, neither so slowly as to draw attention to one's pace, nor so quickly as to disturb recollection. It is always better not to rush. In so far as possible, care should be taken that the shoes worn do not themselves cause unnecessary noise. When turning, one always turns towards the altar cross. If in turning anyone would turn their back on the Blessed Sacrament exposed they turn by another way, or walk away slightly sideways.

Head Covering. In bowing, the head is always first uncovered. When one is taking off the biretta it is held in the right hand by the raised edge on its right side. When standing hold the biretta against the breast with

[5] The head is bowed at the name of the saint on his feast, even if only commemorated, during prayers and sermons, but not at a votive Mass in his honour and not if his name occurs in the introduction to the Gospel. The head is bowed after the consecration (if the name occur in *Nobis quoque*) as well as before. "Caput inclinat," says the rubric, R., V, 2.

both hands joined as described above, the central fin pointing to your right. When sitting rest the biretta on the right knee, while the left hand lies extended on the left knee. Those who wear a skull-cap[6] in choir take it off whenever they genuflect or bow to the altar, when they receive the sprinkling of holy water, while they say together the *Confiteor, Misereatur, Kyrie eleison, Gloria in excelsis, Credo, Sanctus, Agnus Dei* at Mass; while the Gospel is sung, while they are incensed, from the preface to the communion (inclusive), and at the Blessing. Also whenever the Blessed Sacrament is exposed; during the Gospel at Matins, at the Confession at Prime and Compline. No one wears the skull-cap when he intones the antiphons and the psalms, sings the *invitatorium,* lessons, short responsories, or Martyrology .

Sign of the Cross. In the Roman rite the sign of the cross is made thus: Place the left hand extended under the breast, hold the right hand extended also. At the word *Patris* raise it and touch the forehead; at *Filii* touch the breast at a sufficient distance down, but above the left hand; at *Spiritus Sancti* touch the left and right shoulders; at *Amen* join the hands if they are to be joined. When the sign is made with other words the same order is kept. In making the small sign of the cross, the left hand is laid flat under the breast, the right, fully extended (palm inwards), pointed towards the left, is carried to the forehead and with the left corner of the fleshy part of the thumb (separated from the fingers) a small sign of the cross with equal arms (✠) is traced on the forehead, touching the skin. This action is repeated on the closed lips in the middle of the breast.

Ceremonial Kisses. The ceremonial kiss *(osculum),* which occurs frequently, should be made by merely touching the object with the closed lips. The rule is that every time anyone hands anything to the celebrant one kisses first the object, then the celebrant's hand. On taking things from the celebrant, first his hand, then the thing is kissed. When the Blessed Sacrament is exposed, only the kisses at the Epistle, Gospel and for the chalice and paten and of the celebrant's hand when presenting them remain.[7] The thurible is then not kissed, nor the incense spoon. If the Ordinary assists at his throne, kisses of mere ceremonial politeness (e.g. when handing the thurible or biretta) to a priest-celebrant are omitted. On Good Friday and at Masses for the dead and funerals nothing is kissed (except the altar and the paten by the celebrant).

The Thurible. To handle a thurible neatly requires some knowledge. This knowledge is acquired most easily by seeing the actions done by

---

[6] When celebrating Mass only a cardinal, a bishop or a blessed abbot may — apart from Apostolic indult — wear a skull-cap (C.I.C. 811 § 2).
[7] These kisses are an intrinsic part of the solemnity of the rite of solemn Mass of the living, and are not mere acts of liturgical politeness.

someone who already knows. It is one of the many things, not really difficult or complicated, that require many words to explain.[8]

Except when the Blessed Sacrament is exposed (including the elevation at a solemn or sung Mass), incense is always blessed by the celebrant (or prelate presiding at the throne) before use. When the Blessed Sacrament is exposed and will *alone* be incensed, incense is prepared without blessing; but if both the Blessed Sacrament and, e.g., the altar are to be incensed, the incense is then blessed.

When the thurifer merely holds the thurible, while waiting for it to be used, he does so by the chains, just under the disc at top. If incense has not yet been put in ceremonially, he holds it in the left hand; when it has been put in he holds it in the right. When the thurible is not in use the lid should be raised somewhat to allow more ventilation to the burning charcoal and to keep the lid cool. To raise the lid the ring at the end of the middle chain joined to it should be pulled up.

In holding the thurible the thumb may be passed through the ring of the disc, the middle finger through the movable ring, or the thumb through this and the little finger through the disc ring. With the thumb the ring may be drawn up easily, so as to open the thurible below. Holding the thurible in this way the thurifer swings it *gently*, to keep the charcoal alight. The other hand, holding the boat,[9] should be laid on the breast. But when he is kneeling the chains are so long that, if he held the thurible this way, it would be on the ground. So, when kneeling, he holds the chains under the disc in the left hand held against the breast, takes the chains about half-way down in the right and so swings the thurible.

When the thurifer brings the incense to be blessed he hands the boat to the deacon (or MC if there is no deacon). Then he takes the chains under the disc in the left hand. With the right hand he pulls the ring up, to open the thurible sufficiently, so that the celebrant may conveniently put in the incense. He takes the chains more than half-way down in the right hand, holding them close to the top of the cover of the thurible, and so holds up the thurible in front of the celebrant at a convenient height. At the same time he lays the left hand, holding the disc, on his breast. He should not stand too near the celebrant. The celebrant needs a certain amount of room to put out his hand and put in the incense.

Meanwhile the deacon (or the MC) opens the incense-boat, takes the spoon and hands it to the celebrant, with the usual kiss of the spoon and the celebrant's hand. At the same time he says *Benedicite, Pater reverende,* The celebrant takes the spoon; with it he takes incense from the boat and

---

[8] Cf. O'Connell, *The Celebration of Mass*, 1964, pp. 412ff.

[9] In some churches it is usual to employ another server as "boat-bearer." There is no provision for such a server in any official book; nor do the authors of books on ceremonies say anything about him. Nor is he in any way useful—often the reverse. If he is employed the boat-bearer will stand or kneel at the thurifer's left, and will always hand him the boat before he approaches the celebrant and he himself will stand aside.

puts it on the live charcoal in the thurible.[10] He repeats this a second and third time. Meanwhile the deacon (or MC) holds the boat open, that he can do so conveniently. While putting on the incense the celebrant says *Ab illo benedicaris in cuius honore cremaberis. Amen.* Only on one occasion, at the offertory in Mass, is there another formula: *Per intercessionem beati Michælis archangeli,* etc., as in the missal. Then he hands the spoon back to the deacon (or MC), who receives it with the usual kisses. The celebrant, having joined his hands for a moment, makes the sign of the cross over the thurible, saying nothing, laying the left hand on his breast.

On occasions when the incense is not blessed, namely, when the Blessed Sacrament is exposed, and It *alone* is to be incensed, neither the deacon nor the celebrant says anything; nor does the celebrant make the sign of the cross.

The thurifer waits till the incense is put in and the sign of the cross made (if it is to be made). Then he lowers the thurible, and shuts the cover; if there is a ring round the chains he puts this down to hold it firm. While he is doing this the deacon gives the boat to the MC. Then he hands the thurible to the deacon (or MC) by holding the upper part of the chains under the disc in his right hand and the chains midway in his left and presents the ring at the top to the deacon. The deacon takes it and hands it to the celebrant, who proceeds to incense the altar, or whatever is to be incensed. If the deacon is performing the censing the disc is held in the MC's left hand and the chains in his right hand when passing it so that it will be taken by the deacon in the correct position for use.

Incensation. The particular directions for incensing the altar, persons or things will be given at their place in the ceremonies. Here we note only the manner of incensing any person or thing in general.

To incense anything or anyone take the top of the chains of the thurible in the left hand and place it against the breast. Take the chains close above the shut cover in the right. It is important not to hold the chains far from the cover, or the thurible will swing out too far and will perhaps get entangled in the chains. The most convenient way of holding the chains in the right hand is to pass them all together between the first and second fingers. The second, third and fourth fingers, lying together, are then under the chains. By moving the hand upwards the thurible is cast outwards towards the thing incensed.

There are two ways of incensing: with a SIMPLE swing *(ductus simplex)* and with a DOUBLE swing *(ductus duplex).*[11] The simple swing is made thus: lift the right hand to the breast only, at the same time swing the thurible out towards the person or thing to be incensed and let it fall at once towards one's self. The double swing is made by raising the thurible

---

[10] Sufficient incense should be put on *well lit* charcoal to make smoke that will last for some time. It is absurd to see a person swinging a thurible from which no fumes are issuing.
[11] A triple swing of the thurible has no basis in the rubrics.

to the level of the face, then swinging it out towards the object or person to be incensed, repeating this outward swing, and then lowering the thurible.

When incensing, the person who incenses should, as a rule, bow to the person (or object) incensed before and after. The person incensed normally bows each time in return, but stands upright with joined hands, facing the incenser, while he is incensed.

The thurible is handed back to the deacon or other person who is to receive it. He, as usual, kisses first the hand, then the disc of the thurible when it is handed back by the celebrant.

The Kiss of Peace.[12] The kiss of peace at Mass is given in this way. The two persons stand facing each other with hands joined. The one who is to receive the kiss bows. Then the one who gives it lays his hands on the shoulders of the other; the receiver clasps the arms of the other, holding them at the elbows. Each bows the head forward, so that the left cheeks of the two persons almost touch. The one who gives the kiss says *Pax tecum.* The other answers *Et cum spiritu tuo.* Then they withdraw a little and stand again with joined hands facing each other, and both bow.

---

[12] Cf. O'Connell, *The Celebration of Mass,* 1964, p. 429.

Chapter V

The Choir and Assistants at Ceremonies

§ 1. The Liturgical Choir

WE must note first that the "choir" during a service does not necessarily mean those who sing. It was so originally. In theory, no doubt, it should be so still, namely, that the singers have their places right and left of the altar and sing there. But there are often practical difficulties against this. In singing part music especially it is often difficult to produce a good artistic effect when the singers are arranged in two rows facing each other, perhaps at some distance, across the church. Often, therefore, the actual singers are placed elsewhere, in a space together at the side behind a grating, behind the altar, or in a gallery at the other end of the church. In such cases no notice is taken of them during the ceremonies.

There remains, however, the possibility that a liturgical choir may assist at the service; even if they sing only part, or none, of the chants.

Thus canons in cathedral and collegiate churches, regulars in the churches of their order, clergy of any kind, may assist in the seats or stalls on either side, before the altar. These then form the choir from the point of view of ceremonies.

They are dressed in cassock and surplice with biretta, or in their special choir dress. Dignitaries wear the dress appropriate to their rank (p. 33). Regulars generally wear the habit of their order, if this has a recognised habit; and do not wear the surplice over it in choir.

Choir Ceremonies. On entering the choir its members may come in procession (with or without a processional cross), the celebrant wearing vestments.[1] In this case the younger or inferior members walk in front of the elder or superior ones. But when they enter, not in solemn procession, that is, without either a cross or celebrant vested, the more dignified walk before the others, *seniores priores*.

They walk two and two, at equal distances from each other, with head covered till they come into the church.[2] At the entrance to the church they uncover and take holy water (unless the Asperges is to take place), the

---

[1] To wear vestments (chasuble, cope, dalmatic or tunicle) is what liturgical books mean by being *paratus*. To wear even a surplice and stole (as when, e.g., going to administer Holy Communion) is regarded as being *paratus*.

[2] Within the church and not seated, no one—whatever his rank—may wear the biretta unless he is *paratus*. A preacher may wear it in the pulpit.

one nearer the stoup giving it to his companion by dipping his own fingers and holding them towards the other, who touches them. Both then make the sign of the cross.

Before the altar each pair genuflects in turn,[3] taking care to do so exactly together. They then turn slightly and salute one another with a bow, turn back and go to their places.

In their places they either stand or kneel or sit, as will be said in the case of each function. The general rule is that when they sit they cover the head, except when the Blessed Sacrament is exposed. They never stand or kneel with covered head. Before standing they take off the biretta; they put it on again after they have sat down. Those who wear a skull-cap wear this while standing. They take it off on the occasions noted at p. 48.

While members of the choir assist at a service at the high altar they should take no notice of anything that happens in any other part of the church, for instance, private Mass said at a side altar. If, however, Mass is being celebrated at an altar in sight of the choir, and the bell be rung at the elevation (it ought not), then those in choir uncover, but do not kneel nor interrupt the Office in which they are engaged.

Entering or Leaving Choir. If anyone has to leave the choir or come to it alone, he must take care not to do so while any text is being said or sung, at which the others have to perform a ceremonial act, such as bowing. Thus, no one should leave the choir or enter while the verse *Gloria Patri* at the end of a psalm is sung, nor while those in choir are being sprinkled with holy water, nor while they say the *Confiteor, Kyrie, Gloria in excelsis, Credo, Sanctus, Agnus Dei* at Mass, nor while the collect(s), Gospel, postcommunion(s) are sung, nor while his side of the choir receives the Pax or is being incensed, nor during any short verse at which they bow or genuflect.

If a person has to enter the choir alone it is usual to kneel first in the middle, say a short prayer, then rise, genuflect (or bow if a canon or prelate and the Blessed Sacrament be not present), bow to the celebrant if he is at the sedilia, bow to either side of the choir, beginning with the side of greater dignity, and go to his place.

When anyone has to leave the choir alone he uncovers and rises; holding his biretta in his hands he goes to the middle, reverences the cross (or the Blessed Sacrament), bows first to the celebrant, if he is sitting at the sedilia, then to each side of the choir, beginning with the side of greater dignity, and goes out. As a general rule, the gospel side is considered that of greater dignity. This side will then generally be incensed before the other, will receive the kiss of peace first, and so on. The exception is that, if a person of higher rank be present, the side on

---

[3] If the Blessed Sacrament be not present, canons and prelates make a low bow to the cross of the altar.

which he sits is considered the one of greater dignity. Such a person would be a prelate, the hebdomadary,[4] and so on.

At many functions, such as, for instance, solemn Mass following Terce, the choir will already be in their places when the procession for Mass enters. In this case on the approach of the procession the clergy in choir stand and the clergy and servers in the procession bow to the choir, first to the side of greater dignity, then genuflect to the altar.

In standing and kneeling the members of the choir face each other across the church. They do not turn to the altar, except on the special occasions when the rubrics direct them to do so.

Bowing in Choir. We shall note in each case the particular rules for the choir as to standing; kneeling, bowing and so on. Here occur only certain occasions in general when the choir always bow. They are the *Gloria Patri* verse after the psalms (not the verse *Sicut erat in principio*), whenever the three Divine persons are named for honour (e.g., in the conclusion of a hymn), and whenever the Holy Name occurs. In this case they bow during the words *Iesus Christus,* not merely during the first of these. They bow the head slightly at the name *Maria* (of the Blessed Virgin), at the name of the Saint of the day, of the reigning Pope, of the Ordinary. They bow in return whenever anyone bows to them.

It is important that when there is any common action to be performed by all, such as rising, kneeling, bowing, they should do so uniformly.

Deportment in Choir. All text books of ceremonial insist on certain obvious points of deportment in choir. It goes without saying that the members of the choir should know what they have to do beforehand, so as to be ready to act at once when the time comes. Although their part of the ceremony is comparatively small, nevertheless they have a part in it. They must know this part, as the servers know theirs. They should kneel, stand and sit straight, behaving always with such reverence as to give edifying example to the people in church. They should not spend the time in choir reading irrelevant books, even pious ones. They should not, for instance, say their Office during Mass nor anticipate their own Matins during Vespers.

They should attend to the public service at which they assist, making this their prayer. When they recite or sing any text of the service they should mean what they say; *Orabo spiritu, orabo et mente: psallam spiritu, psallam et mente* (I Cor. xiv, 15). Otherwise their attendance would not be really an act of religion at all, and they would deserve the words: *Populus iste ore suo et labiis suis glorificat me, cor autem ejus longe est a me* (Is. xxix, 13).

---

[4] A choir official, i.e., the canon or religious appointed to act for a week *(hebdomada)* as the officiant at the choral recitation of the Canonical Hours and the celebration of the capitular or conventual Mass.

§ 2. Ministers and Servers

In the case of each service or function the exact number of servers required will be stated. Here a note as to the number generally needed in the average Catholic church may be useful.

Servers wear the cassock and surplice.[5] Where more than one server assists, good taste demands that the surplices used are, if not uniform, at least in harmony. Extensive lace decoration is more proper to those in major orders, or indeed to prelates.

For a simple low Mass, one server only attends. For solemn Mass, solemn Vespers, solemn Benediction, processions carried out with some pomp, and the more solemn offices generally, besides the priest who celebrates, there are the sacred ministers, that is, deacon and subdeacon.[6] At Vespers on the greater feasts there may be four or six assistants in copes. For solemn Mass, solemn Vespers and such functions the servers required are: A master of ceremonies (MC), thurifer, two acolytes. At solemn Mass two, four or six torch-bearers are needed; though there may be two only, and these, if others are not available, may be the acolytes (cf. Chapter XI § 7). At Benediction a thurifer, two, four or six torch-bearers — according to the degree of solemnity of the occasion — and at least one other server (here called MC, cf. Chapter XXIII) attend. For processions a cross-bearer is needed, except in the cases where a subdeacon carries the cross. A sung Mass *(Missa cantata)* can be celebrated with two servers only; or there may be as many as at solemn Mass (cf. Chapter XIII).

Pontifical functions require many more assistants and servers. Generally there are two masters of ceremonies of which the first is to be a priest. An assistant priest (AP) is required; and in the case of the Ordinary using his throne there are two assistant deacons there, besides the ministers of Mass. Three or four servers (called chaplains) hold the hand-candle, book, mitre and crosier (if used). If the Bishop wears the cappa he has a train-bearer. Six servers are needed to vest a bishop, though this can be managed with fewer. Altogether some twenty-three persons attend the Ordinary when he sings Mass using the throne (cf. Chapter XVI § 2). Not as many are required by a bishop who uses the faldstool (cf. Chapter XVII § 2).

At solemn processions (e.g. Corpus Christi) canopy-bearers, clergy in vestments, the choir and clergy in surplices may increase the number indefinitely.

---

[5] R., II, 1; S.R.C. 4194 § 2. The use of the alb by servers is contrary to the rubrics.

[6] In the great majority of cases the deacon and subdeacon, as a matter of fact, are also ordained priests. Cf. also Chapter XI end of § 9 "Substitute for Subdeacon." At Vespers the two, four or six assistants who wear copes, need not be in holy orders. They ought to be at least tonsured, or its equivalent — which in modern terms means having been through the rite of Admission to Candidacy for major orders or having made simple religious profession.

As a general rule, except in the case of processions and funerals (when an indefinite number of clergy, supposed to be the choir, stand around the hearse holding lighted candles), not more servers should attend than those really needed, who have some office to perform. It does not add to the dignity of a rite that a crowd of useless boys stand about the sanctuary doing nothing. Nor is it in accordance with the tradition of the Roman rite to add useless ornamental attendance. The servers needed for the ceremonies are sufficient to form the procession.

A remark by Martinucci about the behaviour of servers in church may be noted to advantage here: "They should avoid too much precision or affectation, or such a bearing as befits soldiers on parade rather than churchmen. They must certainly do all gravely and regularly; but if they behave with too punctilious a uniformity the sacred functions look theatrical."[7] Yet perhaps the danger is in the other direction, lest servers (generally young boys[8]) behave carelessly and irreverently. Considerable tact and good taste are needed in the priest or MC who trains the boys, to find the right mean between slovenliness and affectation. Servers should be trained to move *slowly* in the sanctuary, and—as far as possible—to avoid moving about during the chanting or recitation of an important part of the function (e.g., the preface or *Pater noster* of the Mass).

§ 3. Ecclesiastical Rank

Ceremonies are sometimes modified according to the rank of the person who performs them or assists at them. It is therefore important to understand such rank, as far as it affects ceremonial.

The legislation of Pope Paul VI means that prelates often do not possess the regalia formerly used by prelates of their rank, and that it is no longer usual for them to use all of the pontificalia described below at liturgical functions.[9] None of the changes made by these rules which affect the use of pontificalia should ordinarily be followed by prelates at liturgical functions celebrated according to the liturgical books in use in 1962; though in some cases it may be impossible to observe all of the customary requirements—particularly of choir dress—if the prelate concerned simply does not have access to the necessary regalia. Prelates may of course follow the provisions of these instructions in non-liturgical functions. In practice the prelate concerned will have to judge what is

---

[7] Martinucci-Menghini, II, ii, pp. 550-551, § 21.

[8] It is much to be desired that young men should, when possible, minister at the altar, instead of small boys.

[9] Cf. Paul VI, Motu Proprio on the use of pontificals, *Pontificalia insignia,* 21 June 1968; S.R.C. Instruction on the simplification of pontifical rites and insignia, *Pontificalis ritus,* 21 June 1968; Instruction of the Secretariat of State on the vesture, titles and insignia of cardinals, bishops and lesser prelates, *Ut sive sollicite,* 31 March 1969; Instruction of the Sacred Congregation for Clergy on the reform of choral vesture, *Per Instructionem,* 30 October 1970.

possible and apposite, taking into account the principles and customs outlined below.

The celebrant at Mass must be an ordained priest. For Vespers, Compline, Benediction and other liturgical functions the celebrant must be at least a deacon. The deacon and subdeacon must have received those orders. The one exception to this is that a cleric, at least tonsured, may, for a reasonable cause, perform part of the office of subdeacon at solemn Mass and other functions (cf. Chapter XI § 9). In such a case he must omit certain duties performed only by a subdeacon. No one may act as deacon (even for the singing of the Passion) unless he has received that order.

The rubrics suppose that the servers and even the members of the choir be (tonsured) clerics. The acolytes and thurifer should be ordained acolyte, the others should be in minor orders, or at least be tonsured. According to the Ceremonial of Bishops, the first Master of Ceremonies should be a priest, and the second at least in holy orders.[10] Often, however, this rule cannot be observed. It is recognised that laymen may serve at Mass or at any function, and may form the choir.

Above the rank of the simple priest are CANONS (*canonici*) in Chapter. This means, when they are present, in a body, in the church of which they are canons; or at another church at which, for some reason, the whole Chapter assists. A canon may wear his robes and special insignia throughout the diocese to which his Chapter belongs when the Chapter is present, but ordinarily not elsewhere.[11]

A PRELATE *(prælatus)* is, in the first case, a bishop. But not all bishops receive the same honours at every ceremony they may attend. There is, for instance, considerable difference between a bishop where he has jurisdiction (as the Ordinary in his own diocese), and an auxiliary or a bishop visiting a place.

The liturgical books frequently speak of GREATER PRELATES *(maiores prælati, maiores præsules)*. Under this term the following persons are understood: Cardinals[12] everywhere out of Rome, and in their titular churches at Rome, patriarchs and archbishops throughout their patriarchate or province, bishops in their own diocese, Papal Legates in the territory where they are Legates.[13]

Below these in rank come archbishops and bishops who have no jurisdiction in the place where the function occurs.

Abbots. Below bishop there are many categories of lesser prelate; the first of these is abbot. There are two chief classes of these prelates, abbots *nullius (diocesis)* and Regular ruling abbots *(abbates de regimine)*, superiors of abbeys. The former has almost all the privileges of a bishop (and

---

[10] C.E., I, v, 3.

[11] C.I.C. 409, § 2.

[12] For privileges of cardinals, see C.I.C. 239; 1983 Code canons 355-359.

[13] Under this title are included Nuncios and Apostolic Delegates (C.I.C. 267).

sometimes has episcopal orders) and does not concern us here. The latter
has certain liturgical privileges as a prelate, but to safeguard the rights of
cardinals and bishops, these abbatial privileges are regulated by a decree
of Pope Alexander VII,[14] issued in 1659, as modified by subsequent
legislation of the 1917 Code of Canon Law (canons 323, 325, 625, 811, 812
and 964), by minor changes in the rubrics of the Roman Missal (1920),
and by decisions of S.R.C. An abbot *de regimine,* who has duly received
the abbatial blessing, has, by common law,[15] the right to wear
everywhere the pectoral cross (without a gem and held by a cord of the
colour of the abbot's habit, intertwined with gold) and a ring with one
gem. An abbot wears a rochet[16] (even if it is not part of the dress of his
order) under a mozzetta within his territory (outside their territory some
abbots wear a mozzetta over a mantelletta). He does not wear the cappa
magna. He wears a black[17] skull-cap, even at Mass.[18]

  Pontifical Functions. Within his own territory, i.e., in the church of
his monastery or other places subject to his jurisdiction,[19] a ruling abbot
may: (i) use a throne (i.e., a movable armchair,[20] covered with plain silk,
and set on a platform with two steps) surmounted by a canopy (of
simpler material than that used for the canopy of the high altar); (ii) use
the pontifical insignia (mitre,[21] plain crosier, dalmatic, tunicle, buskins
and sandals, gloves, gremial, hand-candle); (iii) perform[22] functions
(solemn Vespers, Matins and Mass) with pontifical rite.[23] When coming
to the altar—in choir dress—for these functions the abbot may be
accompanied by only two monks and a master of ceremonies; he may not
bless the congregation on his way, nor the ministers or servers during the
function. At pontifical Mass the abbot has an assistant priest and two
assistant deacons, in addition to the deacon and subdeacon of the Mass,
and (at temporary benches) six monks, two in copes, two in chasubles
and two in dalmatics. He does not bless a preacher nor give an
indulgence. Should an abbot pontificate in the presence of the Ordinary
of the place using a throne on the gospel side he does so from a faldstool
placed on the epistle side of the sanctuary; he does not use the hand-
candle,[24] and the *munia* (blessings, etc.) are done by the Bishop. In his

---

[14] S.R.C. 1131.

[15] No account is taken here of any special privileges that an abbot may have by apostolic
indult or by monastic custom with the force of law.

[16] This privilege was granted to Regular *bishops* by Benedict XV in 1920.

[17] S.R.C. 1131 § 8; 31 July 1929.

[18] C.I.C. 811 § 2.

[19] S.R.C. 4098; 22 January 1948, ad 1.

[20] If the abbatial church has, by indult or canonical custom, a fixed throne, it must be draped
only at the time of pontifical functions (S.R.C., 3 February 1907).

[21] Not a precious mitre.

[22] He may not preside at a function in cope and mitre.

[23] Not, however, requiem functions.

[24] S.R.C. 4251 § 3.

territory an abbot may lay the foundation stone of a church and bless it;[25] he may give Tonsure and minor orders to his own subjects.[26] *Outside his territory* an abbot may officiate with pontifical rite only by apostolic indult and with the express permission of the Ordinary of the place.[27] He then uses a faldstool.

By common law an abbot may *not* consecrate churches or altars,[28] or bells or chalices. He may not, with pontifical rite, bless an abbess or bless and consecrate virgins. The ceremony of five absolutions of the dead may not take place at the funeral of an abbot, but he may himself be one of the absolvents at that ceremony for a deceased greater prelate.

Low Mass. At low Mass an abbot officiates like a simple priest except that he uses his pectoral cross[29] and skull-cap;[30] puts on the maniple after *Indulgentiam*[31] (except in a requiem Mass); and gives the triple blessing at the end of Mass.[32]

Lesser Prelates. By favour of the Apostolic See some ecclesiastics enjoy the honorary rank and title of prelates. There are three types: protonotaries, prelates of honour, and chaplains to His Holiness.

Protonotaries Apostolic. There are two grades of Protonotaries Apostolic. The first are the seven prelates who are Protonotaries Apostolic *de numero,* who serve as notaries at the Vatican. As prelates of the pontifical household, and, having been duly installed, when in prelatic dress they take precedence of all priests, canons or dignitaries, except a vicar general or a vicar capitular, an abbot and cathedral canons in chapter. They wear prelatic dress, i.e. (a) *choir dress:* violet cassock with red (*coloris rubini,* a violet-tinged red) trimmings, violet silk cincture with a violet silk fringe; a rochet with red lining and a violet mantelletta; violet stock and socks; a black biretta with a red pompon and a black skull-cap with red trimming; (b) *habitus pianus:* a black cassock with red trimmings, a violet silk cincture with violet silk fringe; and a plain violet silk *ferraiolo* (cloak).

The second grade is that of Protonotary Apostolic *Supernumerary.* Every Vicar General or Vicar Capitular is, during his time of office, a protonotary of this class, and is a prelate outside of Rome, but not of the Papal family. Outside Rome they may use the choir dress of a prelate as given above, but customarily this is entirely in black. When so dressed they take precedence of priests and of individual canons, but not prelates

---

[25] C.I.C. 1156.

[26] C.I.C. 964 § 1.

[27] S.R.C. 2923, 4098 § 4 and 22 January 1948.

[28] Usually the Holy See gives abbots the faculty to consecrate altars and chalices for their own churches.

[29] R., I, 4.

[30] C.I.C. 811 § 2.

[31] R., I, 4; III, 10.

[32] R., XII, 7, 8.

of the Roman curia. Other priests appointed Protonotaries Apostolic
Supernumerary enjoy prelatic dress as described above without, however,
the use of the rochet — they must use the surplice — or the mantelletta.[33]

At a sung Mass, or low Mass celebrated with solemnity, and at
Vespers and other solemn functions Protonotaries customarily use the
hand-candle, but not the pontifical canon.

Persons appointed to the various grades of the College of
Protonotaries prior to 1968 acquired certain privileges concerning the use
of pontificals in the Sacred Liturgy. Should such a person exercise those
privileges today an earlier edition of this book ought to be consulted.

Prelates of Honour (formerly Domestic Prelates). These are appointed
by papal Brief and take precedence of priests and individual canons, but
not of canons in chapter, nor of vicars general or capitular, abbots,
protonotaries or superiors-general. They use the same choir dress and
habitus pianus as a protonotary (as above), but the tuft of their biretta is
violet and they have no use of the mantelletta or of the rochet. At a sung
Mass, or low Mass celebrated with solemnity, and at Vespers and other
solemn functions, customarily, they may use the hand-candle, but not the
pontifical canon.

Chaplains of His Holiness (formerly Privy Chamberlains). This
honorary title is given to some ecclesiastics outside of Rome. They are
not prelates, but have some of the privileges of these, especially in their
dress. They wear the *habitus pianus* as described above, but the trimmings
of their black cassock are violet; their *ferraiolone* of black cloth or silk.
They use a violet stock, but black stockings. For choir dress they put a
surplice only over their *habitus pianus.*

Prelates of all categories salute the altar when the Blessed Sacrament is
not there, and the Bishop, by a bow only. During a function at which they
are present in prelatic dress they are incensed, normally with two double
swings.

---

[33] Cf. J-C. Noonan, *The Church Visible*, pp. 125-126.

Part II

The Holy Sacrifice

Chapter VI

Low Mass Said by a Priest

§ 1. Preparation

ALTHOUGH solemn Mass, historically, is the original rite, so that low Mass is really only a shortened form of that, nevertheless, in practice, the first thing a priest must learn is how to say low Mass.[1] He does so frequently, generally every day. The ceremonies of normal low Mass form, as it were, the background for all other Eucharistic rites. It is possible to describe these others more shortly, supposing that the priest is familiar with those of low Mass. Then we need note only the differences on other occasions.

Nothing is said here about the rite, as far as the prayers, etc., are concerned; that is another matter and is rather complicated.[2] Here we describe only the ceremonies.

Preparation of the Altar. Before Mass the following preparations must be made. The altar must be uncovered of the dust-cloth, leaving the three altar-cloths of white linen. It must have a cross and three, or at least two, candles, which two are lighted. They should stand at either side. The third candle, ordered by the rubrics for the consecration,[3] should stand at the epistle end of the altar, outside the others, or it may be fixed to a bracket near the altar. The frontal and tabernacle veil (if there is a tabernacle containing the Blessed Sacrament) may always be of the colour of the day for a low Mass; or — if the colour of the Mass be different from that of the day, e.g., at a votive Mass — they may conform to the colour of the Mass. When vestments are black the conopæum and frontal (if the Blessed Sacrament be present) may not be black. They must either be violet or of the colour of the day. The missal-stand or cushion is placed at the epistle side of the altar, straight, so that its front is parallel with the front of the altar. The missal lies on it, with its edges towards the cross, unless the server brings the book with him from the sacristy (which is the more correct practice). In any case, all the places should be found and marked in it before Mass begins. The altar-cards are in their place on the

---

[1] For the ceremonies of low Mass the first norm is, of course, the rubrics of the missal (*Rubricæ Generales* and *Ritus servandus in celebratione Missæ*).

[2] This aspect of the Mass is fully dealt with in O'Connell's edition of the *Rubrics of the Roman Breviary and Missal* (1960) and his *The Celebration of Mass* (1964).

[3] R.G., n. 530; R., VIII, 6. There is a widespread custom of not using this third candle, but its use is praiseworthy.

altar — the last Gospel on the gospel side, the main card at the foot of the altar cross or in front of the tabernacle, and the lavabo card on the epistle side.

On the credence[4] the cruets stand, filled with wine and water, with the dish and hand-towel, the communion plate, the bell, and the card with the prayers to be said after Mass, if this be needed. A card with the prayers at the foot of the altar may be placed on the altar step if necessary.

The Vestments. In the sacristy the vestments are laid out on the vesting table, in the order in which the priest will put them on, so that the one he takes first will be on the top. First the chasuble is laid out, conveniently so that the priest can take it at once. It is laid on the table with the front part down. On the chasuble the stole is laid, then the maniple and the girdle (customarily to form the shape IHS), then the alb and amice, in that order.

Each priest uses his own amice and purifier; so that these are kept apart for him. The other vestments are the same for any celebrant.

By the side of the vestments the chalice is prepared with the purifier, the paten, having on it the altar bread, the pall, veil and burse, with a corporal inside, as described below.

Unless the missal is already on the altar, it will be placed near the vestments, so that the priest may first find and mark the places in it. All these preparations are made by the sacristan, or partly by the server, according to the custom of the church.[5] In any case the server should look to see that all is ready in order before Mass begins.

In practice, it has become customary to celebrate Mass at almost any hour of the day. Previously the time for beginning morning Mass was not earlier than an hour before dawn nor later than 1.00p.m.[6] Evening Mass did not commence before 4.00p.m. nor after midnight.[7]

Preparation of the Celebrant. The priest who is about to celebrate must be in a state of grace and fasting from solid food and alcoholic drink. Current rules state that all must abstain for at least one hour before Holy Communion from all food and drink except water and medicine,[8] and that a priest who, on the same day, celebrates Mass a second or a third time may "consume something" (i.e., eat) before the second or third

---

[4] The more correct usage is to have the prayer-card, bell and all such things on the credence. That is what the table is for, while the altar steps are not intended — except in a passing way — for this purpose.

[5] The rubrics (R., I, 1) direct the priest to prepare the chalice himself. A cleric or sacristan may do this (S.R.C. 4191 § 1, 4198 § 15; cf. C.I.C. 1306 § 1), but the priest is recommended to do it himself (S.R.C. 4198 § 15; cf. S. Congr. Sacram. 26 March 1929).

[6] D.D. x, 1; C.I.C. 821. Any system of calculation (e.g., sun time or "summer time") could be followed. Cf. O'Connell, *The Celebration of Mass*, 1964, pp. 35-37.

[7] *Christus Dominus*, 6 January 1953, vi. Cf. O'Connell, *The Celebration of Mass*, 1964, p. 36.

[8] 1983 C.I.C. 919 § 1.

Mass even though there not be an hour's interval.[9] Previously at least three hours' fast was required, with one hour's fast from other liquids (water excepted). Piety and reverence for the Holy Sacrifice demand that he abstain from alcohol for a sufficient period before celebrating Mass.

The rubric of another rite applies very well to that of Rome too. "The priest who is about to celebrate the holy mysteries must have confessed his sins, must be reconciled to all men and have nothing against anyone. He must keep his heart from bad thoughts, be pure, and fasting till the time of sacrifice."[10]

Before Mass the priest will spend some time in saying preparatory prayers (and it is edifying if he does this in the church or sacristy) and will make the intention for which he is to offer the sacrifice. He is not bound to use the prayers given for this purpose in the missal;[11] but they certainly form the best preparation.

Vesting for Mass. Then, when he is ready, about five minutes before the time fixed for Mass to begin, he goes to the vesting table in the sacristy. It is supposed that he already wears the cassock or habit.[12] If he does not wear this habitually, he will put it on before saying the preparatory prayers.[13] The rubric directs that first he find the places in the missal.[14] Then he washes his hands at the place prepared for that purpose, saying the prayer *Da Domine virtutem*. He prepares the chalice (or sees that it has been duly prepared): the purifier laid across the mouth of the chalice, on it the paten containing a bread or breads to be consecrated, on the paten the pall, and covering all fully the chalice veil. On top of that is laid the burse containing the corporal with its opening facing towards the priest. Then he puts on the vestments. First he takes the amice, kisses the cross which is in the middle of it, places it for a moment on the head, then slips it over the shoulders, inserts the amice all round the neck, inside his collar, and ties the strings that keep it in place in front, passing them around the body. He puts on the alb (inserting his right arm into its sleeve before the left) and sees that it does not trail on the ground, but does extend to the ankles, and falls evenly all around. The alb should be evenly spread around the body and not gathered to the back. He fastens it round the body with the girdle folded double (having the part with the tassels on his right), and then lets the two ends of the girdle hang down in front. He takes the maniple, kisses the cross in the middle, puts it on the left arm and fastens it there if necessary. He takes

[9] 1983 C.I.C. 919 § 2.
[10] Rubric of the Byzantine *Euchologion* before the "Order of the Holy Liturgy."
[11] The *Præparatio ad Missam pro opportunitate Sacerdotis facienda* at the beginning of the missal.
[12] No one may wear a skull-cap while saying Mass without express permission of the Holy See. Only cardinals, bishops and blessed abbots have this right normally (C.I.C. 811 § 2). If anyone else has the privilege he must observe their rules (p. 48).
[13] C.I.C. 811, § 1.
[14] R., I, 1.

the stole, kisses the cross in its middle, puts it over the shoulders,[15] crosses it in front (the part on the right over that on the left) and fixes its ends on either side with the ends of the girdle. He puts on the chasuble, passing the head through the opening, and fixes it by tying the strings attached to it around the body. He puts on his biretta.

As he puts on each vestment he says the prayer appointed for that purpose in the missal.[16] The server should assist the priest in vesting by handing him each vestment, or by at least helping to arrange the alb, and stole.

It is fitting that the priest be ready a minute or two before the time appointed for Mass. He will then stand at the vesting table and say his prayers till that moment arrives.

From the time he has begun the prayers before Mass, he should not speak to anyone, except in case of strict necessity.

Going to the Altar. At the time for beginning Mass the priest takes the chalice in the left hand, and lays the right on the burse (its opening being towards him). Nothing but the tabernacle key — if necessary — should be on the burse. The veil should cover the chalice at least in front, so that it cannot be seen. If the veil has a cross or ornament on one side, the chalice should be held so that this be in front. Holding the chalice before his breast, he bows his head to the cross in the sacristy, [17] then follows the server into the church with eyes cast down and with his head covered.[18] At the door of the sacristy it is usual that the priest take holy water and make the sign of the cross with it, though this is not prescribed. It is also the practice in many churches that, on leaving the sacristy door, the server ring a bell there, to warn the people that Mass is about to begin. If the doors of the church mean that altar may be approached from either side, he should approach it from the gospel side and depart from the epistle side.[19]

If, on going to the altar where he will say Mass, he pass before the Blessed Sacrament, he and the server genuflect to It in passing. He bows to the high altar if he passes it, if the Blessed Sacrament is not reserved

---

[15] The position of the stole on the back is a disputed question. The best solution seems to be that the stole lie between the shoulders at the base of the neck (covered by the chasuble) neither up around the neck (C.E., II, viii, 14) nor yet down low on the back (R., I, 3).

[16] Near the beginning, after the *Præparatio.*

[17] Customarily, at low Mass the celebrant bows to the cross in the sacristy with covered head, because he already holds the chalice — but should he be comfortably able to uncover and bow, this is not proscribed. At solemn Mass the celebrant and sacred ministers bow with uncovered head.

[18] In *The Celebration of Mass,* 1964, p. 218, O'Connell states that "The rubric requiring the celebrant to wear his biretta when going to the altar is no longer of obligation." However, the basis for his opinion — R. II, 1: *convenienter caput tegit* — is questionable, as *convenienter* means agreeably, conformably, suitably, aptly; meaning that the celebrant should cover his head in the manner which conforms to his station — biretta, amice or hood. Cf. also R., XII, 6.

[19] S.R.C. 3029 § 12.

there. In neither case does he uncover to do so. If he pass before the Blessed Sacrament exposed (e.g., during the distribution of Holy Communion), he uncovers and makes a double genuflexion. This does not apply to the case of passing an altar at which Mass is being said, between the consecration and communion.[20] In this case he is to take no notice unless his attention is drawn to the part of the Mass by, e.g., the ringing of the bell. If so he is to genuflect without uncovering. But if he pass at the elevation, he kneels uncovered till it is finished.

On the way to the altar the priest does not greet anyone, except the Bishop or another priest in vestments coming from an altar. In this case he bows without uncovering.

On arriving at the altar where he will say Mass he stops before its lowest step, uncovers, and hands his biretta to the server. If the Blessed Sacrament is reserved here, he genuflects on the ground, not on the step. Otherwise he bows low to the cross.[21] If the Blessed Sacrament is exposed he makes a double genuflexion.

Then he goes up to the altar, right foot first, puts the chalice covered a little to the gospel side, takes the burse, opens it, takes out the folded corporal and puts it on the altar. He puts the burse standing upright on the gospel side, if necessary leaning it against the gradine or a candlestick. Then he spreads the corporal, placing the unfolded corporal in the middle of the altar and opening out its sides, and then the top and the bottom, ensuring that the creases face upward (so that any fragments are contained within it when it is folded again); the front edge should be about an inch from the front of the altar. He puts the chalice on the corporal, with the chalice veil covering the whole — or at least the front — of the chalice. He must take care to do this so that ample room is left in front of the chalice for him to kiss the altar. If there is a ciborium to be consecrated (which should be already on the altar — somewhat to the epistle side), it is now placed on the corporal behind the chalice on the epistle side. With joined hands he then goes to the missal at the epistle side and opens it at the introit of the Mass.[22] He comes back to the middle, bows slightly to the cross, turns by the epistle side,[23] and comes down to the ground in front of the steps in the middle. Here he turns back by the opposite side and again bows low, or, if the Blessed Sacrament be present, genuflects, this time on the lowest altar step.

---

[20] S.R.C. 4135 § 2.

[21] All such reverences as this are intended for the altar and its cross.

[22] At low Mass by a priest he must always open the book and find the places himself (S.R.C. 2572 § 5).

[23] With the exceptions to be noted, the celebrant at Mass always turns clockwise from the altar and counter clockwise back to it.

§ 2. To the Gospel

Two tones of voice are used at low Mass. All that, at solemn Mass, would be sung by the celebrant or others, at low Mass is said ALOUD, so as to be heard distinctly by all who assist.[24] The preparatory prayers are said in the same clear voice.[25] All that at solemn Mass would be said secretly is said at low Mass SOFTLY, that is, articulated in a whisper, so as not to be heard by bystanders; but the priest should hear himself.[26] While the rubrics of the missal no longer prescribe the use of the "medium" voice — low but audible to those near the celebrant — for those words in low Mass for which it was formerly prescribed, it will still be used for those parts of a solemn Mass at which the deacon and subdeacon reply to, or recite prayers with, the celebrant.[27]

Preparatory Prayers. The celebrant makes the sign of the cross, standing before the lowest altar step, laying, as always, the left hand under the breast,[28] saying at the same time: *In nomine Patris,* etc. Then he says the antiphon *Introibo ad altare Dei* and the psalm *Iudica me,* the server answering the alternate verses. He bows his head (only) to the cross at the verse *Gloria Patri* and makes the sign of the cross again at *Adiutorium nostrum.* While he says the *Confiteor* he bows deeply. He strikes his breast with the open right hand three times at the words *mea culpa, mea culpa, mea maxima culpa.* He does not turn to the server at the words *vobis fratres, vos fratres.* He remains deeply bowed while the server says the prayer *Misereatur.* Then he stands erect. He makes the sign of the cross again as he says *Indulgentiam...* He bows head and shoulders moderately during the verses *Deus, tu conversus,* to *Oremus* inclusive.

During all this time, except when he makes the sign of the cross or strikes his breast, the priest holds the hands joined before the breast.

As he says *Oremus* before the prayer *Aufer a nobis* he separates the hands a little and joins them again, but does not raise them. Having said *Oremus* he stands erect and goes up to the altar, saying *Aufer a nobis* silently. Arrived at the middle of the altar he bows moderately, laying the joined hands on the altar, so that the ends of the longer fingers rest on it. So he says the prayer *Oramus te, Domine.* At the words *quorum reliquiæ hic sunt* he bends down, separates the hands, laying each palm downwards on the altar, outside the corporal,[29] on each side of him, and kisses the

---

[24] But not so loud as to disturb other celebrants should they be near (R.G., n. 512).

[25] So are the words *Orate, fratres* and *Nobis quoque peccatoribus,* the blessing and last Gospel.

[26] R.G., 511-512.

[27] R.G., n. 513 d.

[28] This is the rule whenever he signs himself, that the other hand rest meanwhile under the breast. He should place the left hand below the lowest point of the cross he will form on himself.

[29] During Mass, except from the consecration to the communion, whenever the celebrant lays his hands on the altar, he places them, not on the corporal, but one on each side of it.

altar in the middle. To do so conveniently he should stand slightly away from it, so that, when he bends his head, he can just touch the altar with the closed lips, a little way in from its outer edge. Then, making no further reverence to the cross, he goes with joined hands to the missal at the epistle side. As he goes he continues the prayer *Oramus te, Domine.*

Sometimes the preparatory prayers are entirely omitted, then the celebrant says nothing until the introit, but kisses the altar after he has arranged the chalice.[30]

Introit.   Here he reads the introit of the Mass in a clear voice. As he begins it he makes the sign of the cross. Joining the hands again, he continues the introit. At the verse *Gloria Patri* he bows his head. In repeating the antiphon of the introit he does not again make the sign of the cross. When the introit is finished, he comes to the middle, makes no reverence to the cross[31] and here says *Kyrie, eleison* alternately with the server. If the *Gloria in excelsis* is to be said, he begins it as soon as the *Kyrie* is ended, standing at the middle of the altar. As he says the first words, he separates the hands, extends them, lifts them to about the height of the shoulders, joins them and bows his head at the word *Deo*, without, however, raising his eyes. With joined hands he continues the *Gloria in excelsis*, reading it (if necessary) from the altar-card in the middle. He bows his head at the words *adoramus te, gratias agimus tibi, Iesu Christe, suscipe deprecationem nostram.* At the last words, *cum Sancto Spiritu*, he makes the sign of the cross on himself, then lays his hands on the altar without first rejoining them, and kisses it.

If the *Gloria in excelsis* is not said, he kisses the altar, in the same way, as soon as the *Kyrie, eleison* is finished.

Prayers, Epistle, etc.   With joined hands and eyes cast down he turns, by his right, to face the people. He says *Dominus vobiscum*, at the same time extending the hands and joining them again, not lowering or raising them meanwhile. Turning back by his left he goes to the missal. While he says *Oremus* he extends the hands and joins them again, and he bows his head to the missal.[32] Then he reads the collect, holding the hands uplifted—but not exceeding the height or width of the shoulders—and extended, the fingers held close together and bowing toward the missal should the name of the saint in whose honour the Mass is celebrated occur. When he says *Per Dominum nostrum*, etc.,[33] he joins his hands. If

---

Between the consecration and the communion, when the forefingers and thumbs are joined all the time, he lays his hands on the corporal.

[30] R.G., n. 424.

[31] S.R.C. 2682 § 27.

[32] Cf. O'Connell, *The Celebration of Mass*, 1964, pp. 203, 233.

[33] The different endings of the prayers are: PER DOMINUM *nostrum Iesum Christum Filium tuum, qui tecum vivit et regnat in unitate Spiritus Sancti, Deus, per omnia sæcula sæculorum. PER EUNDEM Dominum nostrum Iesum Christum Filium tuum, qui tecum vivit et regnat in unitate Spiritus Sancti, Deus, per omnia sæcula sæculorum. QUI TECUM vivit et regnat in unitate*

the prayer ends *Qui tecum* or *Qui vivis* he joins his hands when saying *in unitate.* He bows his head again toward the missal at the Holy Name, *Iesum Christum.* If there are several collects, after the first the priest says *Oremus* and the second collect follows. If there is no other collect to be added the conclusion is made in the usual way. If there is a third collect the conclusion of the second collect is omitted and he proceeds to say the third collect, without first saying *Oremus.* The appropriate conclusion is added to the third collect.

After the last collect he either holds the book or lays his hands on it, one on each side, the palms downwards, so that his thumb or the ends of the fingers rest on the edges, while he reads the Epistle. It is usual to give a sign to the server when the Epistle is ended, that he may answer *Deo gratias.* This is best done by placing the left hand on the altar to the left of the missal, but also by raising it slightly for a moment, or by lowering the voice at the concluding words and turning slightly towards the server.

On certain days, notably the Ember days, there may be a series of lessons, each preceded by a collect, before the Gospel. In this case *Dominus vobiscum* is said only before the collect(s) preceding the last lesson. Immediately after *Kyrie, eleison* the celebrant, instead of saying *Dominus vobiscum,* goes at once to the missal. He says each collect and the following lesson in the usual way.[34] Then, at the place marked in the missal, he comes to the middle, says *Dominus vobiscum,* returns to the book and continues as above.

If *Flectamus genua* is to be said, as soon as the celebrant has said *Oremus* and *Flectamus genua* he lays his hands on the altar and kneels. With hands joined he prays for some time. Then he says *Levate,* rises and with hands extended says the prayer.[35]

After the Epistle, the priest goes on at once to read, in the same clear tone of voice, the gradual, tract, *Alleluia* or sequence, as these occur in the missal. Meanwhile he still holds his hands on the book.

In the collect, Epistle, gradual, etc., if such a word occurs as is noted above (p. 46), that is, the Holy Name, name of the Blessed Virgin, of the Saint of the day, he makes a reverence, as there described. At the Epistle or gradual, he will genuflect, laying his hands on the altar in the usual way, when the rubric directs this.

He then comes to the middle of the altar with hands joined, leaving the book open at the epistle side. In the middle he looks up to the cross,[36]

Spiritus Sancti, Deus, per omnia sæcula sæculorum. QUI VIVIS et regnas cum Deo Patre in unitate Spiritus Sancti, Deus, per omnia sæcula sæculorum. If mention of the Holy Spirit is made in the prayer, the conclusion is modified to say: *...in unitate eiusdem Spiritus Sancti...* cf. R.G. nn. 115-116.

[34] Cf. R.G., n. 468.

[35] R.G., n. 440.

[36] In looking up the celebrant always looks at the altar cross, unless it stands beneath his eyes (S.R.C. 2960 § 3). This is only a practical direction, that the action may be done

then bows low with hands joined and not touching the altar, and so says *Munda cor meum* and *Iube, Domine,*[37] *benedicere. Dominus sit in corde meo,* etc. If for any reason the server does not carry the missal across to the gospel side, the priest does so himself, bowing to the cross as he passes.[38] He lays the missal on its stand or cushion at the gospel end diagonally, so that he will turn somewhat towards the people when reading the Gospel, then comes back to the middle and says *Munda cor meum.*

§ 3. The Gospel to the Preface

When the celebrant has said the prayer *Dominus sit in corde meo,* he goes with joined hands to the book at the gospel side. He does not here turn his back to the people, but he faces half towards them looking across the gospel corner diagonally. Without separating the hands he says *Dominus vobiscum.* Then *Sequentia* (or *Initium*) *sancti Evangelii secundum N.,* adding the name of the Evangelist, in the accusative.[39] As he says these words he lays the left hand on the book. He holds the right stretched out, the fingers joined, the palm downwards and so makes the sign of the cross with the thumb on the book at the beginning of the text of the Gospel that he is about to read. Then, still holding the hand stretched out in the same way, he makes the sign of the cross with the front part of the thumb on his forehead, lips and breast, laying the left hand under the breast (below where he will sign the cross). He must be careful not to make the cross on his lips while he is speaking. If he is saying the words *Sequentia sancti Evangelii,* etc., he must pause while signing his lips. When the server has answered *Gloria tibi, Domine,* the priest reads the Gospel, with hands joined. If in the Gospel the Holy Name occurs, or any other word at which he bows, he does so towards the book. If he has to genuflect at any words, he lays his hands on the altar and does so also towards the book, unless the Blessed Sacrament be exposed. In this case he turns and genuflects towards the Blessed Sacrament.[40]

While reading the Gospel, if he has to turn a page, then, as always, he does so with the right hand, laying the left meanwhile on the altar or on the missal.

---

uniformly. In principle he looks up to heaven, as our Lord so often did in the New Testament (e.g., John xi, 41).

[37] At low Mass the celebrant says "Domine," addressing God. By a curious development the mediaeval form *domnus*, really nothing but a mispronunciation, is looked upon as the correct one when a merely human superior is addressed. So the rubrics in the R., VI, 2, and *Ordo Missæ* give the form, "Iube, domne, benedicere" when the deacon at solemn Mass addresses the celebrant; but "Iube, Domine, benedicere" when, at low Mass the celebrant prays to God.

[38] R., VI, 1; S.R.C. 3975 § 2.

[39] Matthæum, Marcum, Lucam, Ioannem.

[40] Cf. Chapter VI § 8.

When the Gospel is finished he raises the book with both hands, and kisses it at the beginning of the text, saying silently *Per evangelica dicta*, etc.[41] He stands erect and replaces the book on the stand. Then he brings the missal to the middle of the altar, raising its stand with both hands. He places it here at the middle, but on the gospel side of the corporal, turned diagonally towards the middle; it should not stand on the corporal, but as near to it as possible.

Homily. The homily, which is now of obligation on all Sundays and Holy Days of obligation,[42] may be preached from the gospel corner, the footpace, or the pulpit. The biretta is brought to the priest by the server after the Gospel if he is to wear it preaching. If the priest preaches from the footpace or the pulpit he comes to the centre of the altar, bows to the cross and descends the altar steps and reverences the altar or the Blessed Sacrament. If he goes to the pulpit, he may be escorted by the server, in which case they reverence the altar or the Blessed Sacrament upon departure and return.[43] The homily commences and concludes with "In the name of the Father, etc." during which all present uncover and sign themselves. There is no requirement to read the Epistle or Gospel in the vernacular.[44] If they are read, they are not liturgical readings and thus are not accorded any ceremony (people standing, signing oneself, etc.).

Creed. If the *Credo* is to be said, he begins it in the middle of the altar. As he says *Credo in unum Deum* he extends his hands, lifts them to the height of the shoulders, joins them as he says the words *in unum Deum* and bows his head. He says the *Credo* with joined hands, reading the text, if necessary, from the altar-card. At the Holy Name he bows his head. As he says the words *Et incarnatus est*, etc., he lays his hands on the altar outside the corporal and genuflects on one knee. He does not rise from this genuflexion till he has said *et homo factus est*. He should make the whole genuflexion slowly. He does not bow the head at these words. He bows his head at the word *adoratur* (of the Holy Ghost). As he says the last words *et vitam venturi sæculi*, he makes the sign of the cross, laying his left hand on his breast.

After the *Credo* he does not join his hands, but lays them on the altar at once and kisses it. Then he turns, by the epistle side, and says *Dominus vobiscum* in the usual manner.

If there is no *Credo* in the Mass, he kisses the altar as soon as he is at the middle, after the Gospel or homily, and turns to say *Dominus vobiscum*.

---

[41] Many rubricians suggest that the celebrant say the first half of this verse (*Per evangelica dicta*), then kiss the book, then say the rest.

[42] 1983 C.I.C., canon 767 § 2.

[43] Cf. O'Connell, *The Celebration of Mass*, 1964 pp. 483-484. The practice of removing the maniple or chasuble for the homily has no rubrical basis, but is customary in some places.

[44] Given the prevalence of peoples' missals and Mass-leaflets this seems superfluous.

Offertory. Facing the altar again, opening out, joining the hands and bowing, he says *Oremus*. In the same clear tone he then reads the offertory antiphon.

The offertory act now follows. The celebrant takes the chalice veil from the chalice with both hands, folds it and lays it on the altar at his right, just outside the corporal.[45] He lays his left hand on the altar, outside the corporal. With his right he takes the chalice by the node of its stem and stands it outside the corporal, on his right. He takes the pall from the chalice and lays it on the folded veil. If there is a ciborium[46] he unveils it and lays the veil aside. Other altar breads to be consecrated are placed on the corporal. He uncovers the ciborium and then takes the paten with his right hand, having on it the altar bread, and holds this, with both hands, over the middle of the corporal, at about the height of his breast. He should hold it with the thumb and first finger of each hand touching its edge, the other fingers joined under it. Holding it thus he looks up, and then down at the bread, and says silently the prayer *Suscipe, sancte Pater*.

When the prayer *Suscipe, sancte Pater* is finished, the celebrant lowers the paten; still holding it as before, he makes the sign of the cross with it over the corporal, tracing first a line towards himself, then one from left to right, tracing the arms of the cross about 9" (20 cm) long. He slides the altar bread on to the corporal in the middle, at the front of the fold, without touching it. Then he lays the left hand on the altar, as always in such cases, outside the corporal. He puts the paten on the altar, at his right, and slips about half of it under the corporal. The ciborium is then covered.

Putting in Wine and Water. With joined hands he goes to the epistle corner. On his way he takes the chalice at its node with the left hand, and the purifier (which lies on it) with the right. With this he wipes the inside of the chalice. Then, still holding the node of the chalice in the left hand, he puts the purifier so that it hangs over the left thumb by the side of the chalice. He takes the cruet of wine from the server in his right hand and pours as much as is needed into the chalice,[47] saying nothing, then hands the cruet back. The server holds up the water cruet. The priest makes the sign of the cross over it, as he begins to say the prayer *Deus, qui humanæ substantiæ*. He continues this prayer; as he says the words *da nobis per huius aquæ et vini mysterium* he takes the cruet in the right hand and pours a little water into the chalice, a few drops only, and hands the cruet back. In some churches a little spoon—called a "scruple spoon"—is used to measure the water. In this case he takes the spoon, dips it into the cruet,

---

[45] The rubric seems to suggest that the priest himself folds the veil. Some authors say that he may hand it to the server to fold. For more than one practical reason it is better that the priest should himself fold and put aside the veil.

[46] "Pope Benedict XIV...praised the devotion that prompts the desire of some...to receive particles consecrated at the same Mass" (Pius XII, *Mediator Dei*, Part II).

[47] Reserving some for the ablutions.

and so puts one spoonful into the chalice. Then he may wipe away any drops there may be on the sides of the chalice with the purifier wrapped around the index finger. As he says the Holy Name at the end of the prayer he bows. Having finished the prayer he puts the chalice near the corporal, with the left hand. He either lays the purifier at its place on the paten, or puts it nearby and comes to the middle with joined hands; or he may come while folding the purifier and lay it on the paten on arriving at the middle of the altar. At the middle he arranges the purifier so that, folded lengthways, it shall cover the half of the paten not already under the corporal. Meanwhile he lays his left hand on the altar. With the right he takes the chalice by its node; he holds its base with the left hand, lifts it so that the top is level with his eyes, and so holding it says the prayer *Offerimus tibi, Domine,* with his eyes raised to the cross. When this is said, he makes the sign of the cross over the middle of the altar with the chalice; as he did before with the paten. To do so he lowers the chalice; he should take care not to extend the cross over the bread. He then puts the chalice in the middle of the corporal, behind the bread. Laying the left hand on the base of the chalice, he takes the pall with the right hand and covers the chalice. He bows moderately, lays the hands, joined, on the altar in front of him, and so says the prayer *In spiritu humilitatis,* silently. He stands erect, looks up to heaven for a moment, extends and raises his hands, then lowers the eyes and joins the hands before the breast. While doing so he says the prayer *Veni, sanctificator.* At the word *benedic* he lays the left hand on the altar and with the right makes the sign of the cross over the bread and chalice together.

Washing of Fingers. With joined hands he now goes to the epistle end of the altar. Facing the server, who stands there, he holds his hands over the dish, so that the server pours water over the ends of the thumb and forefinger of each hand. Then he takes the hand-towel and, facing the altar, dries them. In doing this he should hold his hands, not over the altar, but outside it. As soon as he begins to wash his fingers he says silently the verses of the psalm *Lavabo inter innocentes* and continues while drying them. He stands at that end of the altar while saying these verses; if necessary he may read them from the altar-card. He bows his head as he says the verse *Gloria Patri* and hands back the hand-towel to the server with the left hand on the altar. Then he goes to the middle with joined hands, while saying *Sicut erat,* etc. At the middle he looks up and then lowers his eyes. Laying his hands joined on the altar before him, and bowing moderately, he says silently the prayer *Suscipe, sancta Trinitas.* Then, laying his hands palm downwards on each side, outside the corporal, he kisses the altar. Joining his hands and with downcast eyes he turns by his right to the people. Facing them he opens out his hands in a straight line and joins them again, as at the *Dominus vobiscum.* Meanwhile he says *Orate, fratres* in a clear and intelligible voice. He turns back to the altar, by his right (completing the circle), while he continues, *ut meum ac vestrum sacrificium,* etc., secretly. The server answers *Suscipiat Dominus,* etc. If the server does not say this, for any reason, the celebrant says it himself, altering the form to *de manibus meis* instead of *tuis.* At the end of this he says *Amen* aloud.

Secret(s). Then he extends his hands and holds them with palms facing one another as at the collects, without saying *Oremus.* So he silently says the secret(s), reading it/them from the missal. Only the first and last secrets have the conclusion *per Dominum nostrum,* etc., which is said with the usual joining of hands and bow of head as at the collects. At the end of the last secret (therefore of the first, if there be only one) he joins his hands as he begins silently the conclusion of the prayer if it is *Per Dominum,* but if it is *Qui tecum* or *Qui vivis* he does this at the words *in unitate.* The final words *Per omnia sæcula sæculorum* he says aloud with hands joined. Then with his left hand he finds the preface in the missal.[48] The server says *Amen,* and answers each verse of the following dialogue.

Preface. The celebrant, with his hands on the altar table, says *Dominus vobiscum.* Then he raises his hands to the height of the shoulders, holding them with the palms facing one another, as during the secrets. So he says *Sursum corda.* He joins his hands as he says *Gratias agamus;* as he says *Deo nostro* he looks up to the cross, then bows his head. As he begins the preface he holds his hands again extended on each side and remains in that position till it is ended.

At the end of the preface he joins his hands, bows over the altar moderately, not resting his hands on it, and says the *Sanctus* aloud. As he says *Benedictus qui venit* he stands erect and makes the sign of the cross. He then joins his hands again for the *Hosanna.* Then, laying his right hand on the altar, he finds with his left the beginning of the canon in the missal.[49]

§ 4. The Canon to the Communion

The celebrant looks up to the cross, extends and lifts his hands, then looks down, joins his hands, bows low, lays the tips of his joined hands on the altar and so begins *Te igitur.* When he has said *supplices rogamus ac petimus* he lays his hands on the altar, one on either side, outside the corporal, kisses the altar, then stands erect, joins his hands, lays his left

---

[48] The rubric does not determine how this is to be done. Most authors mention the way given in the text. In practice it will be found more convenient to use the right hand to seek the place in the missal, or to use both hands.

[49] When one hand is used to turn the pages of the missal, before the consecration the other hand is placed flat on the altar outside the corporal. After the consecration the pages are turned using the third and fourth fingers of the right hand using the tabs, resting the left hand on the corporal.

hand on the altar. and with his right makes the sign of the cross[50] thrice over the chalice and bread as he says *hæc✠dona, hæc✠munera, hæc✠sancta sacrificia illibata.* After the third cross he does not join his hands, but holds them extended and uplifted before the breast, palms facing each other and fingers upright, exceeding the shoulders neither in width nor height. This is the normal position of the hands throughout the canon.

At the words *una cum famulo tuo Papa nostro N.* he adds the name of the reigning Pope in the ablative case,[51] and bows his head slightly. If the Holy See is vacant at the time, he omits this clause altogether. At the words *et Antistite nostro N.* he adds the baptismal (or religious) name of the Bishop of the place where he says Mass. If the see is vacant he omits this clause.

Memento of the Living. As he says *Memento, Domine, famulorum famularumque tuarum* he raises his hands and joins them before his face or breast. He then stands a moment in this position, bowing his head, while he remembers any persons for whom he wishes here to pray. The words *N. et N.* are not expressed in practice; or rather, instead of them, he names as many persons as he likes. He may make the remembrance either verbally (in the secret voice), or entirely mentally. He may here renew the special intention for which he offers the sacrifice. He should not delay too long at the Memento.[52]

Then, standing again erect with his hands extended as before, he continues *et omnium circumstantium.* In the prayer *Communicantes,* he bows at the names *Mariæ* and *Iesu Christi.* If the name of the saint whose feast is being celebrated or commemorated that day[53] is one of those in this list he bows again as he says it. At the words *Per eundem,* etc., he joins his hands. As he begins the next prayer, *Hanc igitur oblationem,* he opens his hands and holds them spread flat, but keeping the right thumb over the left. So he stretches them over the *oblata,* so that the extremity of his fingers is over the middle of the pall. He does not touch the pall. He keeps this position while saying the prayer and joins his hands again at the conclusion *Per Christum Dominum nostrum.* So he continues the next prayer, *Quam oblationem.* He makes the sign of the cross thrice, as before—the left hand on the altar—over the *oblata,* at the words *bene✠dictam, adscri✠ptam, ra✠tam, rationabilem, acceptabilemque facere digneris.* It will be convenient to prolong this last sign of the cross a little, so that it takes as long to make as it does to say these words. Then he

---

[50] Signs of the cross should be made slowly in straight lines of equal length approximately 9″ (20 cm) long.

[51] Without the number of the Pope: "Papa nostro Joanne Paulo."

[52] Nor should he make the memory of the living (and later, of the dead) too quickly. Gavanti says: "tu memento ne Memento fiat in momento."

[53] The head is bowed at the name of the saint on his feast even if only commemorated, but not at a votive Mass in his honour. The head is bowed after the consecration (if the name occur in *Nobis quoque*) as well as before.

makes the sign of the cross over the bread only as he says *Cor✠pus* and over the chalice only as he says *San✠guis*. He raises his hands and joining them before his breast continues, bowing the head as he says *Iesu Christi*. If he is to consecrate other breads besides the one he will receive in communion he may here renew his intention of doing so. He uncovers the ciborium and lays the cover just outside the corporal, covering it again after the elevation of the Host. All bread to be consecrated must be at least partially on the corporal at this time.

He wipes the thumb and forefinger of each hand on the front corners of the corporal. In any case it is well to rub these slightly together, so as to dispel any particles of dust on them.

Consecration of the Bread. As he says *Qui pridie quam pateretur* he takes the bread between the thumb and forefinger of each hand. To do this more easily he may first lay the forefinger of the left hand on the edge of the bread; then he takes it by the lower extremity of the circle with the thumb and forefinger of the right, then in the same way with those of the left. He so lifts the bread about 9" (20 cm) above the corporal and places the other fingers of each hand, joined and extended, behind it. He does not rest the hands on the altar. Still standing erect he continues the words *accepit panem,* etc. As he says *elevatis oculis in cælum* he looks up to heaven and at once looks down. As he says *gratias agens* he bows his head slightly. At the word *bene✠dixit* he holds the bread in the left hand only, and makes the sign of the cross over it with the right. In doing this he does not keep the thumb and forefinger joined, but holds the hand straight out, in the usual way when blessing. Then, at once, he again holds the bread in both hands as before, and continues, *fregit, deditque discipulis suis dicens: Accipite et manducate ex hoc omnes.* He now bows over the altar, leaning the forearms on it. Holding the bread before him and not touching the corporal, he says, "secretly, distinctly, and attentively,"[54] the words of consecration, HOC EST ENIM CORPUS MEUM.

He should say these words in the secret voice, but so that he can hear himself.[55]

He does not touch any other breads that may be present to be consecrated. While saying the words of consecration it is usual to look at the bread he holds in his hands.

When the words have been said, without delay he stands erect, then genuflects on one knee; still holding the Host with both hands over the altar with hands on the corporal as far as the wrists. He rises at once and holds up the Blessed Sacrament, so that It may be seen by the people.[56]

---

[54] Rubric in the canon.

[55] For the form of the sacrament is part of the visible, or audible, sign.

[56] When asked if the celebrant may say in a low voice the words "My Lord and my God" at the elevation of the Sacred Host — a practice to which St Pius X attached rich indulgences for the faithful — the S.R.C. replied (6 November 1925, D 4397 § 1): "No, according to Canon 818 of the Code of Canon Law and the rubrics of the Roman Missal."

He lifts It straight up before him to such a height that It may be seen from behind, over his head. He does this slowly, taking care to hold It over the corporal all the time and keeping his eyes fixed on It. He lowers It again without pause and places it reverently on the corporal, with the right hand, at the same place as before. He leaves It there, lays his hands on the corporal and genuflects again.

From this moment till the ablutions the celebrant keeps the thumb and forefinger of each hand joined, except when he touches the consecrated Host. In turning over pages, holding the chalice, or doing any other such action, he must be careful to use the other fingers in such away as not to separate the thumb and index finger.

From now till after the ablutions every time he lays his hands on the altar he does so on the corporal.

Consecration of the Wine. Rising from the second genuflexion, he covers the ciborium. He steadies the chalice by putting his left hand on its base[57] whilst he takes the pall from the chalice with his right hand and lays it on the epistle side. Then—if necessary—he rubs the thumb and forefinger of his hands over the chalice, to let any particle there may be fall into it. He does this every time after he has touched the Host. Standing erect he says *Simili modo postquam cenatum est.* Then he takes the chalice in both hands, holding it between the node and the cup by the stem; he lifts it a little above the altar and sets it down again at once. He continues the words, still holding the chalice with both hands. As he says *gratias agens* he bows his head. As he says *bene✠dixit* he makes the sign of the cross over the chalice with the right hand (keeping the thumb and forefinger joined) and holds it, still in the same way, with the left. Then he holds the node with the right hand and the base with the left as he says *deditque discipulis suis dicens: Accipite et bibite ex eo omnes.* He bends over the altar, leaning the forearms on it. He lifts the chalice a little from the altar, putting the second, third and fourth fingers of his left hand joined under its base, the thumb and forefinger of the same hand over the base. So, in the same secret voice as before, he says the words of consecration over the chalice, "attentively, continuously and secretly," holding it a little lifted, clear of the corporal: HIC EST ENIM CALIX SANGUINIS MEI NOVI ET ÆTERNI TESTAMENTI: MYSTERIUM FIDEI: QUI PRO VOBIS ET PRO MULTIS EFFUNDETUR IN REMISSIONEM PECCATORUM. He sets the chalice in the centre of the corporal stands erect and says, HÆC QUOTIESCUMQUE FECERITIS IN MEI MEMORIAM FACIETIS.

Taking his hands from the Chalice he lays them on the altar on each side, on the corporal and genuflects. He stands, takes the Chalice with both hands, holding the node with the right hand and the base with the left partly under it as before. So he elevates it to a height where it can be seen by the people above his head, lifting it slowly and straight up, so

---

[57] This he may do every time he covers or uncovers the chalice to steady it.

that it is always over the corporal, keeping his eyes fixed on the Chalice. Without any pause he sets it down on the corporal, and puts on the pall with the right hand, the left laid meanwhile on the base of the Chalice. Then he genuflects again as before.

Standing erect and holding the hands extended on either side, but now always keeping the thumbs and forefingers joined, he continues the canon at the words, *Unde et memores*, keeping his eyes on the missal. As he says *de tuis donis ac datis* he joins his hands before his breast; then as he says *hostiam✠puram, hostiam✠sanctam, hostiam✠immaculatam* he lays the left hand on the corporal and with the right makes the sign of the cross thrice over both the Sacred Host and the Chalice. Then, as he says *Panem✠sanctum*, he makes the sign of the cross over the Host only; at *calicem✠salutis* over the Chalice only.

He extends the hands without rejoining them and says the prayer, *Supra quæ.*

Supplices. He bows profoundly, laying his joined hands on the edge of the altar before him, and so says *Supplices te rogamus* to the word *quotquot.* Here he lays his hands flat on the corporal on either side, and kisses the altar once in the middle. He stands erect, joins his hands and continues *ex hac altaris participatione,* etc. At the word *Cor✠pus* he makes the sign of the cross over the Host; at *San✠guinem* over the Chalice, as before. As he says *omni benedictione cælesti,* he signs himself with the sign of the cross, holding the left hand at the breast, but so that the thumb and forefinger do not touch the chasuble. Then he joins his hands. He extends them again slowly as he says *Memento etiam, Domine. N. et N.* may be omitted. As he says *in somno pacis* he joins his hands, raising them arc wise—not going beyond the width of his shoulders—to meet before the lower part of the face, bows his head, looks at the Blessed Sacrament before him and so prays silently for the faithful departed whom he wishes to commemorate. Then he stands erect again with hands extended and continues the prayer at the words *Ipsis, Domine, et omnibus in Christo quiescentibus.* At the conclusion, *Per Christum Dominum nostrum,* he joins his hands and bows his head.

He raises his voice just a little for the words *Nobis quoque peccatoribus.* At the same time he lays his left hand on the corporal and strikes his breast once with the right hand. He does so with the tips of the second, third and fourth fingers extended, not touching the chasuble with the thumb or forefinger. He continues *famulis tuis,* etc., erect, with hands extended. If the saint whose vigil or feast is kept or commemorated be named amongst those of this prayer, he bows his head as he pronounces the name. He joins his hands at the conclusion, *Per Christum Dominum nostrum. Amen* is not said here.

Little Elevation. With joined hands he says, *Per quem hæc omnia;* then at the words *sancti✠ficas, vivi✠ficas, bene✠dicis,* he makes the sign of the cross with his right hand three times over the Host and Chalice together, laying the left on the corporal. Steadying the base of the Chalice with his left hand, with the right he uncovers the Chalice and lays the pall at his right. Placing his hands on the corporal on each side, he genuflects and rises at once. He takes the Sacred Host with the right hand between the thumb and forefinger; with the left he holds the Chalice by its node. He makes the sign of the cross thrice with the Host over the Chalice, not extending this sign beyond the cup, as he says *Per ip✠sum, et cum ip✠so, et in ip✠so*. Still holding the Chalice in the same way with the left hand, he makes the sign of the cross twice over the corporal between himself and the Chalice, beginning at the edge of the Chalice, as he says *est tibi Deo Patri✠omnipotenti, in unitate Spiritus✠Sancti*. Then he holds the Host over the Chalice upright, holding it still with the forefinger and thumb of his right hand, by the lower edge. He may rest the lower part of his hand on the rim of the Chalice. With the left hand he continues to hold the Chalice at its node. So, with both hands, he elevates the Host and Chalice together about 4" (10 cm) above the altar, as he says *omnis honor et gloria*. Then he places the Chalice back on the corporal, and the Host in the place where it was before, in front of the Chalice, still holding the Chalice with his left hand. He rubs the first finger and thumb of each hand over the Chalice, lays the left on its base, while with the right he covers it with the pall; then genuflects, laying both hands on the corporal as usual.

Pater Noster. He stands erect, his hands still on the corporal, and says aloud *per omnia sæcula sæculorum*. When the server has answered *Amen*, the celebrant joins his hands before his breast, and bowing his head says *Oremus*. Erect, with hands joined, he says the introduction to the Lord's prayer, *Præceptis salutaribus moniti*, etc. As he begins *Pater noster* he extends his hands and looks at the Blessed Sacrament. In this position he says the prayer. When the server has answered *Sed libera nos a malo*, the celebrant answers *Amen* secretly.[58] With his left hand on the corporal he takes the paten in the right from under the corporal and purifier. He wipes it with the purifier (using the left hand to aid him if required), then lays the purifier back on the epistle side near the corporal. He holds the paten in his right hand between the fore and second fingers. He holds it outside the corporal on his right, upright, so that the concave side faces the middle, the edge resting on the altar, the left hand flat on the corporal. So he says silently the Embolism, *Libera nos, Domine*. As he says *et omnibus Sanctis*, he lays the left hand on the breast. As he says *da propitius pacem in diebus nostris,* he makes the sign of the cross on himself with the paten with his left hand under his breast. As soon as he has made this sign he kisses the paten, not in the middle, but at its upper inside edge. Then he slips the paten under the Host (laying meanwhile

---

[58] R., X, 1, has "submissa voce," however R.G., 511 would have this in the *vox secreta*, as would the rubric of the *Ordo Missæ*.

the forefinger of the left hand on the farther edge of the Host), continuing the prayer, and lays the paten against the base of the Chalice.

He uncovers the Chalice in the usual way and genuflects with his hands on the corporal. Rising, he takes the Blessed Sacrament in his right hand, holding Its lower edge between the thumb and forefinger, and assisting, if necessary, with the left. He holds It over the Chalice; then with both hands he breaks It reverently in a straight line down the middle,[59] using both hands to do this, holding each half between the forefinger and thumb of each hand. Meanwhile he continues *Per eundem Dominum nostrum,* etc. Still holding one fragment in his left hand over the Chalice he lays the other with the right on the paten. With his right hand he now breaks off a small part of the half of the Host he is holding over the Chalice in his left. Holding this Particle in his right hand over the Chalice, with the left he lays the rest of the fragment on the paten by the side of the half already there, saying *in unitate Spiritus Sancti Deus.* He grasps the node of the Chalice with his left hand, and still holding the Particle in the right over the Chalice, he says aloud *Per omnia sæcula sæculorum.* He makes the sign of the cross thrice with the Particle in his right hand over the Chalice from edge to edge of the cup, not going outside this, as he says *Pax✠Domini sit✠semper vobis✠cum.* When the server has answered *Et cum spiritu tuo,* the celebrant says silently *Hæc commixtio,* etc., and lets the Particle fall into the Chalice. He rubs his fingers over the Chalice, then at once joins the forefinger and thumb of each hand. He covers the Chalice with the pall and genuflects.

Agnus Dei. He rises and, moderately inclined towards the Blessed Sacrament, with hands joined before the breast, but not on the altar, he says aloud *Agnus Dei,* etc. He lays his left hand on the corporal; with the second, third and fourth fingers of the right he strikes his breast as he says *miserere nobis.* He does not join the hands after this, but holds them in the same position, the left on the corporal, the right resting on the breast,[60] till he says the second time *miserere nobis;* then he strikes the breast again. So, also, the third time, for *dona nobis pacem.*

Then he joins his hands and lays them on the edge of the altar, not on the corporal. Bowing moderately and with his eyes fixed on the Sacred Host he says the three prayers before communion, *Domine Iesu Christe, qui dixisti; Domine Iesu Christe, Fili Dei vivi* and *Perceptio Corporis tui.*

Then he stands upright, genuflects, and says *Panem cælestem accipiam,* etc. He now takes the Host in his left hand. The most convenient and reverent way to do this is thus: The Host lies on the paten in two halves,

---

[59] Altar-breads are generally made with a line, at the back, down the middle and another marking the division for the fragment to be put in the chalice. Some priests score the bread in the sacristy before Mass, most conveniently with the edge of the paten.

[60] Or being moved slowly away from him in preparation for the subsequent striking of the breast, or laid on the altar.

side by side, the half on the celebrant's left being without the small fragment which has been put into the Chalice. On these he lays the forefinger and thumb of his left hand, one on either fragment. So he pushes them gently forward till their upper edge projects a little beyond the upper part of the paten. He takes the two fragments here, at their upper part, between the thumb and forefinger of his right hand. The fragments are side by side, so as to form a circle, as if the Host were not broken in the middle. So he can hold them between the right thumb and forefinger together, just at the place where they are divided. Taking the two fragments thus in his right hand he places them in the left. The left hand receives them at the bottom in the same way, holding them together, just at the line of fraction, between the thumb and forefinger. Then, with his right hand, he takes the paten at the top (not separating the thumb and forefinger) and puts it under the forefinger of his left between that and the second finger. He now holds the Host in his left hand between the thumb and forefinger, and the paten under It between the forefinger and second finger. So he keeps them in front of him, not resting the forearm on the altar. Bowing moderately, he strikes his breast with the free (not joined) fingers of the right hand as he says, aloud *Domine, non sum dignus.* Then silently he continues *ut intres sub tectum meum,* etc. He does this thrice in the same way.

Communion of the Celebrant. He stands erect; with his right hand he takes the fragment of the Blessed Sacrament at his right at Its upper edge, and places It overlapping the half on the left. Then he takes the two fragments, lying one on the other, at the lower edge, with his right hand. The left hand still holds the paten as before; its thumb and forefinger are now joined over the paten. With the Blessed Sacrament he makes the sign of the cross in front of himself over the paten, not going beyond its edge, as he says silently *Corpus Domini nostri,* etc. At the Holy Name he bows his head. He leans over the altar, resting the forearms on it, and receives the Host, holding the paten under his chin. In doing so he does not extend the tongue. It is convenient to break the Sacred Species against the roof of the mouth; but he should, as far as possible, not touch them with his teeth. He then lays the paten on the corporal, rubs the fingers lightly over it, stands upright and "rests a little, meditating on the most holy Sacrament,"[61] holding his hands raised and joined before his face. It is usual here to shut the eyes. The object of this pause is that he may have time to swallow the holy Species.[62] It should not be prolonged. Then he separates the hands, and lays the left on the base of the Chalice; with the right he takes the pall, lays it aside on the epistle side and genuflects. Rising he takes the paten in his right hand, inspects it to see if he can discern any fragments of the Sacred Host, and wipes them into the

---

[61] Rubric in the Order of Mass.
[62] That is why there is no such pause after receiving the Precious Blood.

Chalice if he does. He then inspects the corporal, and collects the fragments on it, if there are any, with the paten. He may lift the edge of the corporal with the left hand while doing this. He then holds the paten over the Chalice with his left hand, and with the thumb and forefinger of the right wipes it, so that any particles fall into the Chalice. Whilst doing all this he says *Quid retribuam...mihi?* silently. Having purified the paten, he rubs his thumb and forefinger together over the Chalice to detach any fragments that may adhere to them. Saying *Calicem salutaris*, he takes the Chalice in his right hand, holding it by the node between the forefinger and the other fingers, and continues to hold the paten in his left. He makes the sign of the cross before him with the Chalice, saying *Sanguis Domini nostri*, etc., again bowing his head at the Holy Name. He holds the paten in the left hand under his chin. Raising the Chalice he drinks all the Precious Blood with the Particle in it, with one or at most two draughts, not taking the Chalice from the mouth meanwhile and not throwing back the head nor making a noise. It is usual to drink from the side of the Chalice with the cross on the base so that the ablutions may be taken on the same side.

There is no authority for making a pause to say private prayers after receiving the Precious Blood.

If no one else is to receive Holy Communion the celebrant omits all in the following section and goes on at once as directed in § 6.

§ 5. The Distribution of Holy Communion[63]

If there is anyone for Holy Communion the server will indicate this by ringing the bell (once) shortly before the communion time.

The celebrant first covers the Chalice with the pall and places it (if there be a ciborium) towards the gospel side on the corporal.

If he is to distribute Holy Communion with Hosts consecrated at the Mass, they will be on the corporal; he puts them on the paten, using the thumbs and forefingers only, and genuflecting before touching them. If they are in a ciborium he uncovers this and genuflects.

If he is to take the Blessed Sacrament from the tabernacle, as soon as he has covered the Chalice he removes the altar-card from before the tabernacle, draws aside the tabernacle veil, takes the key, opens the tabernacle, genuflects,[64] takes the ciborium from it with the right hand and places it in the middle of the corporal.[65] He shuts the tabernacle (if it

---

[63] The rules for Holy Communion are in the C.I.C. 845-869; (1983 C.I.C. 910ff.).

[64] There is only *one* genuflexion — wherever the Hosts may be — before communion and after communion.

[65] This is the moment to put into the tabernacle a (second) ciborium of Hosts that have been consecrated at the Mass or a Benediction Host that has just been consecrated in the lunette. It is also the moment to change the Benediction Host (consuming the old one) if this is to be done.

still contains the Blessed Sacrament), not locking it, unveils the ciborium, and uncovers it.[66] He takes the ciborium in the left hand at its node, or the paten at its edge between the forefinger and second finger (keeping, as all this time, the thumb and forefinger joined). With the forefinger and thumb of his right hand he takes one Host and holds It above the ciborium or paten, upright, and so turns clockwise to the people, and stands with his back to the middle of the altar.

Looking at the Blessed Sacrament he says aloud *Ecce Agnus Dei*, etc., and, three times, *Domine, non sum dignus*. When he has completed this the third time, not before, he communicates any clergy in choir (who approach as they do at solemn Mass), and the server, should he wish to communicate, and then walks to the communion rail or to the place where the communicants kneel, holding one Host above the ciborium or paten. If there are many people, he goes first to the person at the end of the epistle side. Here he says the form of administration, *Corpus Domini nostri Iesu Christi custodiat animam tuam in vitam æternam. Amen*, making the sign of the cross in front of the person with the Host he holds in his right hand. In making this cross he should not carry the Blessed Sacrament beyond the edge of the ciborium or paten. Then he lays the Host on the communicant's tongue. He repeats the sign of the cross and full form of administration to each person, however many there may be. When walking back to the epistle side of the communion rail he holds his (joined) right thumb and index finger over the ciborium or paten. He does this also when all have received Holy Communion. If there is no server, takes the communion plate from the last communicant with his right hand,[67] and goes back directly to the middle of the altar. If any Particles remain and are to be consumed, he genuflects and reverently receives them, and then purifies the paten or ciborium into the Chalice, using the index finger of his right hand carefully to gather any fragments into the Chalice. If necessary, he may present the ciborium to the server in the manner described in § 6 below for purification with wine and water.[68] If Hosts had been on the corporal he purifies this in the same manner as he did before receiving the Chalice (above).

If he has to replace the ciborium in the tabernacle, he covers it with its lid and veil, puts it back in the tabernacle, genuflects, then closes and locks the tabernacle.[69] Should there be no tabernacle and the ciborium

---

[66] The veil is placed outside the corporal, the ciborium cover on it.

[67] Ordinarily the server who holds the plate for the communicants will take it back to the altar and there hand it to the celebrant.

[68] Cf. O'Connell, *The Celebration of Mass*, 1964 pp. 289-292.

[69] In no circumstance may the celebrant consecrate one Host at Mass, reserve that and receive another for his communion. He must always break and receive the Host consecrated at the Mass he celebrates. In the case of renewing the Sacred Species in the lunette, he must consecrate two breads. The other then lies on the corporal till he, after his communion, puts It in the lunette.

must remain on the altar, the celebrant proceeds with the end of Mass as at a Mass *coram Sanctissimo* (cf. Chapter VI § 8, Chapter XII § 2).

He then removes the Chalice to the middle of the corporal again, takes the pall from it, purifies the communion plate into it, and drinks any drops that may be in it. He then holds it out with the right hand over the altar to the server, who approaches on the epistle side.

§ 6. The Ablutions to the End of Mass

If no one but the celebrant has received Holy Communion, as soon as he has drunk the Precious Blood he holds out the chalice over the altar to the server on the epistle side. Meanwhile he lays the left hand, still holding the paten, on the corporal. The server pours wine into the chalice for the ablution. Meanwhile the celebrant says the prayer *Quod ore sumpsimus,* etc. He may make a sign to the server when enough wine has been poured, by raising the chalice but slightly — the cruet should not be struck. The quantity of wine at this ablution should be about equal to the amount consecrated. The priest turns the chalice about gently, so that the wine of the ablution may gather up any drops of the Precious Blood remaining in the chalice. Then he drinks the ablution, using the same side of the chalice from which he received Holy Communion (that with the cross on the base), holding the paten with the left hand under his chin, not making the sign of the cross with the chalice and saying nothing. He lays the paten on the corporal, towards the left, and sets the chalice in the middle. He now puts the thumbs and forefingers of both hands over the cup of the chalice and grasps the cup with the other fingers. He goes to the epistle side, rests the chalice on the altar there, still holding it as before. The server pours first a little wine, then water, over the celebrant's fingers into the chalice. More water than wine should be poured. Meanwhile the celebrant says the prayer *Corpus tuum, Domine,* etc. If any other finger has touched the Blessed Sacrament, this too must be purified by having the wine and water poured over it. The celebrant sets the chalice on the altar, near, but not on, the corporal, on the epistle side; rubs the fingers a little over it, then takes the purifier and dries them. From this moment he no longer holds the thumbs and forefingers joined. He holds the purifier in his left hand under his chin, takes the chalice in his right, and drinks the ablution, saying nothing. Then replacing the chalice on the altar he grasps it by the stem in his left hand,[70] and with the right dries it with the purifier.

He places the chalice near the corporal on the gospel side, lays the purifier over it, as it was at the beginning of Mass, and the paten and pall on this. He folds the corporal beginning with the fold nearest himself and

---

[70] The most convenient way to do this is to pass the stem, just under the cup, between the first and second fingers, and to close all the fingers around the outside of the cup.

puts it back into the burse. He covers the chalice with the veil, then lays the burse on the top of all, the opening away from him. He sets the chalice in the middle of the altar, and sees that the veil covers it completely in front. If there is a cross or other ornament on the veil, this should be at the front.

Communion Antiphon. With joined hands he goes to the epistle side and reads the communion antiphon in a clear voice, his hands joined.

If, after arranging the chalice, he has to move the book himself he carries it to the epistle side, bowing his head to the cross as he passes it.

After the communion antiphon he comes to the middle, kisses the altar (with hands outside the corporal), turns and says *Dominus vobiscum* in the usual way. He goes again to the epistle side, says *Oremus*, bowing towards the missal, and says the postcommunion prayers as he said the collects, with hands extended, observing all that is said in § 2 above.[71]

If the last Gospel is the prologue of the fourth Gospel, he shuts the missal when he has fully finished the conclusion of the last postcommunion, leaving it so that the edges of the pages face the middle of the altar. If there is a proper last Gospel,[72] he leaves the book open at the place where this Gospel is printed.

He comes to the middle, kisses the altar, turns and says again *Dominus vobiscum,* as usual. Without turning back to the altar, still facing the people, he says *Ite,*[73] *missa est*, with hands joined.

But if he is to say *Benedicamus Domino*[74] he first turns back by his left to face the altar, and says this versicle in that position.

Facing the altar, bowed, and with the hands joined on the altar before him, he says the prayer *Placeat tibi, sancta Trinitas* silently. Then he lays the hands, palms downwards, on each side, kisses the altar, stands upright, looks up at the cross, extends, raises and joins his hands, and says *Benedicat vos omnipotens Deus*. As he says this last word he bows his head to the cross and with downcast eyes turns by the epistle side, lays the left hand on his breast and with the right makes the sign of the cross over the people, saying, *Pater et Filius✠et Spiritus Sanctus*. He makes this sign holding the right hand upright, with the fingers joined, the little finger towards the people. He joins his hands, turns, this time by the gospel side, completing the circle, goes straight to the altar-card at the

---

[71] During Lent in ferial Masses the *Oratio super populum* occurs. The celebrant having finished the conclusion of the last postcommunion prayer, standing before the book, extending and joining his hands as usual, and bowing towards the missal, says *Oremus, humiliate capita vestra Deo*. Then, extending his hands, he says the *Oratio*.

[72] This occurs only in Masses on Palm Sunday not preceded by the palm procession.

[73] The sense requires a slight pause after *Ite*.

[74] This occurs only when a procession is to follow the Mass immediately. When *Benedicamus Domino* is said there is no blessing (R.G., n. 508), nor last Gospel (R.G., n. 510 a), and the celebrant, having said *Placeat,* concludes Mass with the kissing of the altar.

gospel side and there says *Dominus vobiscum* partly facing the card, that is, half turned towards the people, as at the first Gospel.

Having said *Dominus vobiscum* he lays his left hand on the altar; with the right thumb he makes the sign of the cross on the altar table, then on his own forehead, lips and breast. While he signs himself he lays the left hand on his breast. Meanwhile he says in a clear voice *Initium sancti Evangelii secundum Ioannem*. As he says the words *Et Verbum caro factum est* he genuflects where he stands, laying his hands on the altar.

If the last Gospel be proper, he lays the left hand on the missal, and makes the sign of the cross with his thumb on the page, at the beginning of the text of the Gospel, before signing the crosses on himself. He does not kiss the book at the end, but, with the right hand, closes it (with the opening on the right) when he has finished.

He then may either go straight to the foot of the altar steps (or to the centre of the step immediately beneath the footpace) or he may first go to the middle, bow, and then turn by the epistle side and so go down.[75] In either case he does so with hands joined.

Leonine Prayers. According to custom, after a private Mass the celebrant with the people say the prayers prescribed by Pope Leo XIII in 1884 and 1886; which law was renewed by Pius X (1903), by Benedict XV (1915), and by Pius XI (1930, for Russia).

To say these he kneels either on the footpace or on the lowest step and says them from memory or reads them from a card provided.[76] They are generally said in the mother tongue.[77]

These Leonine prayers may be omitted after low Masses which take the place of a solemn Mass, e.g., a conventual or capitular Mass; or which are celebrated with certain solemnity, e.g., Mass for a first Holy Communion, for a general communion, for a marriage, for Confirmation, or an ordination or religious profession. They may also be omitted if any sacred function or pious exercise (e.g., Benediction, Absolution for the dead) immediately and duly follows Mass, or when a homily has been given during Mass. Also after a dialogue Mass, but on Sundays and greater feasts only.[78]

When these prayers are finished[79] he goes up to the altar, takes the chalice, holding it in his left hand by the node with the cross on the veil facing to the front of him and laying his right on it. He comes again to the foot of the steps, makes a profound inclination to the altar, or a

---

[75] S.R.C. 3637 § 8.

[76] These prayers consist of: the Hail Mary (three times); the Hail, Holy Queen; O God, our refuge and strength; the Prayer to St Michael; and the Invocation to the Sacred Heart (three times), striking the breast each time at "have mercy on us."

[77] Regarding the prayers for the Sovereign, cf. Chapter XIII § 3.

[78] S.R.C. 3697 § 7, 4177 § 2, 4271 § 2, 4305, and 9 March 1960.

[79] If any other prayers are said after Mass, with the consent of the Ordinary, those ordered by Leo XIII must be said first (S.R.C. 3682 and cf. 3805).

genuflexion if the Blessed Sacrament is there reserved, takes his biretta from the server, covers himself and so follows the server to the sacristy.

On the way he may say silently the canticle *Benedicite* or other prayers at choice. In the sacristy he first bows his head to the cross, then lays the chalice on the vesting table, takes off the biretta and unvests, in the inverse order to vesting. The server usually assists. When the priest takes off the stole and maniple he kisses the cross in the middle, as when he puts them on. Usually he puts away, in a special place, his own amice and purifier.

Having unvested, the celebrant makes a thanksgiving for a suitable time, saying the prayers given in the missal[80] or others according to his devotion. "Having adored and thanked God for everything, he goes away."[81]

§ 7. Rules when the Same Priest Celebrates More Than Once on the Same Day[82]

Every priest may say a second Mass on Easter Day if he has celebrated the Mass following the Vigil, and may say Mass three times on Christmas Day, and — according to custom — on All Souls' Day. Moreover, in case of necessity, the Ordinary may give leave to a priest to say Mass twice (or even three times) on Sundays and holy days of obligation.[83]

Each Mass must be said entirely, including the preparatory prayers at the foot of the altar. If the Masses are said without interruption (i.e., the priest does not leave the altar), in the first and second Mass, if he is to celebrate another immediately, having taken the Precious Blood the celebrant does not purify or wipe the chalice but places it on the corporal and covers it with the pall. Then, with hands joined, he says *Quod ore* and afterwards washes his fingers in a vessel[84] prepared with water and dries them. Having done this, he arranges the chalice (on the corporal) as it was at the beginning of Mass, with the purifier, paten with a new bread, pall and veil. At the offertory of the second (or third) Mass the priest, having unveiled the chalice, places it a little to the epistle side on the corporal. Having offered the bread, he does not wipe the chalice with the

---

[80] The *Gratiarum actio post Missam* after the *Præparatio ad Missam*.

[81] Rubric at the end of the Byzantine Liturgy of St John Chrysostom.

[82] R., XIV; cf. rubrics of the missal on Christmas Day and All Souls' Day and R.R., V, v S.R.C. 3068).

[83] To say Mass twice on the same day is called bination (*binatio*). It may not be done without permission, given only when otherwise, because of a shortage of priests, a notable number of people (say, twenty at least) would be unable to hear Mass on days of obligation (C.I.C. 806, § 2; 1983 Code, canon 905 § 1-2). In the case of true pastoral necessity, i.e., a requiem or nuptial Mass, such permission is customarily presumed.

[84] The water in this vessel is poured eventually into the sacrarium.

purifier, but, raising it slightly, pours in wine and water and offers it as usual.

 The 1983 Code of Canon Law mitigates the customary requirement whereby, if the Masses are said with an interruption between them, the celebrant drinks at the earlier Mass(es) the two ablutions prescribed in the rubrics, and if he is to celebrate the subsequent Mass before three hours, water only is used for the ablutions.[85]

A priest may only retain the stipend for one Mass each day with the exceptions of Christmas Day and the grounds of an extrinsic title.[86]

§ 8. Mass Before the Blessed Sacrament Exposed

Without necessity, grave cause or special indult, Mass may not be said at an altar on which the Blessed Sacrament is exposed. It is forbidden to distribute Holy Communion at the altar of Exposition.

In Masses which *by indult* are celebrated before the Blessed Sacrament exposed the prayer of the Blessed Sacrament is added, under one conclusion, to the prayer of the Mass, provided it is not a Sunday, and there is not a feast (or commemoration) of our Lord.[87]

At Mass said before the Blessed Sacrament exposed these changes must be made:

On approaching the altar the celebrant uncovers as soon as he is in sight of the Blessed Sacrament; nor does he cover himself again till he is away from the altar. Before and after Mass he makes a double genuflexion (p. 45) on the ground, not on the step. He makes no double genuflexion during Mass. When he has arranged the chalice on the altar he genuflects, laying his hands on the altar. He goes to the missal and finds the places. Coming back he again genuflects in the middle, before going down to the foot of the altar. He genuflects in this way every time he goes up to, or down from, or passes before, the middle of the altar. In coming down he must take care not to turn his back directly to the Blessed Sacrament.[88] At the foot of the altar he genuflects again on one knee on the lowest step, makes the sign of the cross, and begins Mass.

The general rule is this: every time the celebrant goes from the middle of the altar to either side, and every time he comes to the middle, he genuflects. He makes this genuflexion the last thing before leaving the centre and the first thing on arriving there. Whenever he has to turn to the people, for the *Dominus vobiscum* or other verse, he genuflects before

---

[85] Canon 919 § 2: "A priest who, on the same day, celebrates the blessed Eucharist twice or three times may consume something before the second or third celebration, even though there is not an hour's interval." Hence wine may be used at the ablutions in the earlier Masses.

[86] 1983 C.I.C., canon 951 § 1

[87] R.G., n. 355.

[88] So he comes down, not directly in the middle, but towards the gospel side.

and after turning. If he is already at the centre he makes this genuflexion last, immediately before turning (therefore after having kissed the altar or performed any other such ceremony). But when he comes to the middle in order then to turn towards the people, he observes the rule above and genuflects as soon as he arrives at the centre.

Whenever he turns, he does so, not quite in the middle, but a little towards the gospel side, and does not turn fully around facing the people, so as not to turn his back to the Blessed Sacrament. At the *Orate, fratres* and the blessing he does not turn back to the altar by the gospel side, completing the circle; but he turns by the epistle side, as at the *Dominus vobiscum.*

At the Holy Name in the Gospel he turns and bows, at the text *et Verbum caro factum est* in the last Gospel he genuflects towards the Blessed Sacrament. When he washes his hands at the *Lavabo,* he goes down from the footpace either to the step immediately below the footpace or *in plano* and turns by his left towards the people, having the altar at his right hand, so that he does not turn his back on the Blessed Sacrament.

At the ablutions at the end he need not go to the epistle side. Standing in the middle he holds the chalice towards the server; then he puts it on the altar just outside the corporal and there receives the wine and water in it over his fingers.

At *Flectamus genua* in ferial Masses he kneels facing the missal.

Having imparted the Blessing—partly turned to the people—the celebrant turns back to the altar by his left and, without any further genuflexion, goes to the gospel corner for the last Gospel.

Chapter VII

Low Mass for the Dead

AT requiem Masses the following points are to be observed: The vestments are always black. If the Blessed Sacrament be present the colour of the conopæum will be white or violet; that of the frontal violet. Should the Blessed Sacrament not be present, the frontal may be black. In the preparatory prayers the psalm *Iudica* is omitted. The antiphon, *Introibo ad altare Dei*, is said as usual, then at once the verse *Adiutorium nostrum in nomine Domini* and all that follows.

At the introit the celebrant does not make the sign of the cross on himself. He lays his left hand on the altar and with the right makes the sign of the cross over the missal, 'as if blessing someone.' *Gloria Patri* is not said; instead *Requiem æternam* is repeated.

Neither *Gloria in excelsis* nor the *Credo* is said. Normally, in Masses for the dead there is only one collect.[1]

After the prayer *Munda cor meum*, before the Gospel, the form of blessing, *Iube, Domine, benedicere* and *Dominus sit in corde meo* are omitted.

After the Gospel the celebrant neither kisses the book nor says *Per evangelica dicta*, etc. There is no *Credo*.

While pouring the water into the chalice the prayer, *Deus qui humanæ substantiæ*, is said as usual; but the priest does not make the sign of the cross over the water.

He omits the verses *Gloria Patri* and *Sicut erat in principio* at the end of the *Lavabo* psalm.

The text of *Agnus Dei* is changed. For the first two times he last clause is *dona eis requiem*; then, the third time, *dona eis requiem sempiternam*. While saying this the priest does not strike the breast. He holds the hands joined before him, not placed on the altar.

He omits the prayer *Domine Iesu Christe, qui dixisti Apostolis tuis* before Holy Communion.

At the end, instead of the verse *Ite, missa est*, he says *Requiescant in pace*. This is always in the plural, even when the Mass is offered for one person. He turns towards the altar after the *Dominus vobiscum* before this verse, and says it at the middle, facing the altar, with hands joined in front of the breast. No blessing is given at the end of Mass. The celebrant says the prayer *Placeat tibi* as usual, kisses the altar, then goes at once to the gospel corner and begins the last Gospel unless the Absolution for the dead follows immediately.

---

[1] R.G. 398.

Chapter VIII

Mass by a Priest in the Presence of a Prelate

IF a priest says Mass in the presence of a Greater Prelate,[1] the following rules are observed: A faldstool or kneeler is prepared before the altar,[2] and is adorned as described at p. 29.

If used, the pax-brede[3] is prepared, covered with a veil of the colour of the day, and a purifier at the credence. If possible, the celebrant should arrive at the altar before the prelate. Here he arranges the chalice and missal, then goes down to the ground on the gospel side and stands there, facing the epistle side across the sanctuary.

When the prelate arrives at his place, where the faldstool or kneeling-desk is prepared, the celebrant bows low to him. The prelate gives a sign that Mass may begin; the celebrant bows again to him, then makes the usual reverence to the altar, a profound bow, or he genuflects on the step if the Blessed Sacrament is reserved there. The server kneels at the left of the celebrant. The priest begins Mass as usual, but standing at the gospel side. In the *Confiteor,* instead of *vobis, fratres* and *vos, fratres,* he says *tibi Pater* and *te Pater,* turning and bowing towards the prelate.

Before going up to the altar he bows again to the prelate.

Mass proceeds as usual, with these differences. After the Gospel the celebrant neither kisses the missal nor says the verse *Per evangelica dicta,* etc. Instead, the server takes the book to the prelate open at the start of the Gospel. He kisses it and says that verse. The server makes no reverence to the prelate when he brings him the book. When the prelate has kissed the book, the server closes the book and genuflects to him (unless the prelate be outside the place of his jurisdiction, when the server bows only). The celebrant should wait to continue Mass till the server has brought back the book and has replaced it on its stand. The celebrant, not the prelate, blesses the water at the offertory.[4]

After *Agnus Dei* the celebrant says the first of the three prayers before his communion. Meanwhile, if the *pax* is to be given to the prelate,[5] the server brings the pax-brede from the credence with the veil and purifier. He kneels at the right of the celebrant and holds the pax-brede towards

---

[1] See p. 57. It is supposed that the prelate is present officially in choir dress. (See p. 35.)

[2] It may be at the epistle side, or in another part of the sanctuary, if this be more convenient (C.E., I, xxx, 1). In this case the celebrant says the preparatory prayers in front of the altar, as usual, so long as he does not turn his back directly on the prelate.

[3] Cf. p. 42.

[4] C.E., I, xxx. 3.

[5] Cf. Stehle-Rettger, *Manual of Episcopal Ceremonies,* (1961 ed.) vol. I p. 176 n. 5.

him. The celebrant kisses the altar in the middle, then with joined hands kisses the pax-brede saying: *Pax tecum;* the server answers *Et cum spiritu tuo.* The celebrant goes on with the Mass at once. The server rises and takes the pax-brede to the prelate, having wiped it with the purifier and covered it with the veil. He offers it to the prelate, uncovered, saying: *Pax tecum.* The prelate kisses the pax-brede, saying: *Et cum spiritu tuo.* The server genuflects to him wipes and covers the pax-brede and takes it back to the credence. At the blessing, when the celebrant has said *Benedicat vos omnipotens Deus,* he turns and bows to the prelate.[6] Then he gives the blessing to the people, in the direction in which the prelate is not.

At the end of Mass, when the last Gospel is finished, the celebrant does not go to the middle of the altar. He turns and kneels at the gospel end, either on the footpace or on the lowest step, facing across the sanctuary. Here he says the prayers after Mass. Then he stands there, bows to the prelate and waits till he goes. If the prelate remains before the altar the celebrant takes the chalice at the middle, as usual, comes down to the front of the altar, makes the usual reverence to it, bows low to the prelate, takes his biretta, covers himself and goes away.

If a bishop not in his own diocese is present, he receives the pax as above, but does not kiss the missal. The celebrant bows to him at the beginning and end of Mass. Otherwise Mass is said as if he were not present.

At requiem Masses the ceremonies of kissing the book and the pax are omitted. Should the Blessed Sacrament be exposed all special marks of honour to a greater prelate are omitted.

A prelate may be present at Mass unofficially, in his private dress (*habitus pianus*). In this case Mass is said as if he were not there, except that the celebrant should bow to him before and after. Even these are omitted if, for some reason, the prelate is seated outside of the sanctuary.

---

[6] "Capite inclinato, quasi licentiam benedicendi petens" (R., XIII, 3).

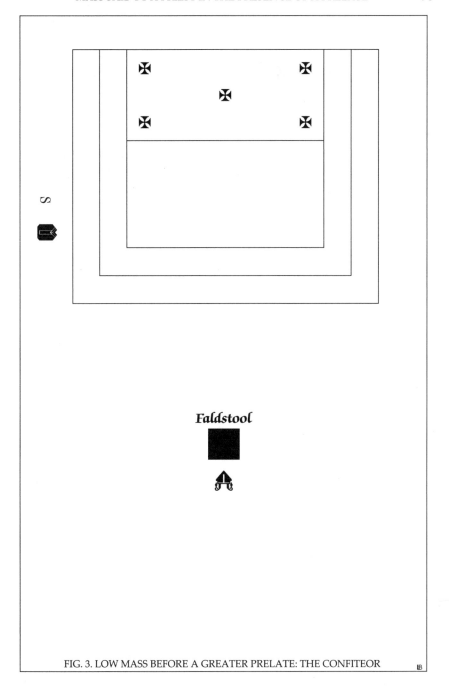

FIG. 3. LOW MASS BEFORE A GREATER PRELATE: THE CONFITEOR

Chapter IX

Low Mass Said by a Bishop

WHEN a bishop celebrates low Mass with greater solemnity, in addition to two or three servers, there should be two assistants (*capellani*),[1] one of whom should be in major orders.[2] They wear a cassock and surplice only, not a stole. The altar-cards are not put on the altar. The vestments (except the maniple) should be laid out on the altar.[3] On the credence are the chalice prepared as usual, the maniple, the larger vessel for water and the dish (*bacile*) used by a bishop, one or more hand-towels, a silver salver for the skull-cap. A faldstool or kneeler is prepared before the altar; the pontifical canon on it and the hand-candle nearby.

If the celebrant is in his diocese, he arrives in choir cassock, belt, rochet, mozzetta and biretta. In the case of a bishop not in his diocese he wears the mantelletta instead of the mozzetta. On greater feasts four candles should be lighted on the altar, otherwise two are sufficient.

The bishop makes his preparation for Mass at the faldstool. While he reads the prayers the pontifical canon lies on the kneeler; one chaplain or a server holds the hand-candle, lighted, at his side.

Vesting. When the time comes for Mass to begin the bishop takes off the pectoral cross and mozzetta or mantelletta. He puts on his biretta and washes his hands. Every time he washes his hands the water should be poured and the dish held, not by the chaplains, but by a servant or server; a chaplain holds the hand-towel.[4] The bishop takes off the biretta and hands it to a chaplain,[5] then goes to the altar and vests, assisted by the chaplains. He uses the same vestments as a priest, except that he puts on the pectoral cross over the alb, immediately before taking the stole (the ends of which he wears hanging straight down). He also wears the skull-cap and his ring. When the bishop has vested, a chaplain puts the pontifical canon open at *Oramus te, Domine* on the altar, where the central altar-card would stand.

The bishop (except at requiem Masses) does not take the maniple before Mass, but puts it on after he has said *Indulgentiam*[6] at the foot of

---

[1] C.E., I, xxix, 2.

[2] C.E., I, xxix. It is presumed in this chapter that the bishop celebrates Mass with greater solemnity, and not in the way he would celebrate in his private oratory.

[3] If the Blessed Sacrament is exposed, the bishop vests in the sacristy.

[4] C.E., I, xxix, 10.

[5] A bishop does not normally wear the biretta with vestments.

[6] C.E., II, viii, 32. The prayer (which has a special form for a bishop) he says when vesting beforehand, after the prayer for the ring.

the altar. The maniple, therefore, is held by the chaplain who kneels at the gospel side while the preparatory prayers are said, as far as the *Indulgentiam*. Then the chaplain rises, kisses the maniple at its side, not at the cross, and holds it for the bishop to kiss the cross; the chaplain puts it on the bishop's left arm and then kisses the bishop's hand.

The Chaplains. The two chaplains answer the prayers at Mass and one of them transfers the missal. At the offertory the chief chaplain brings the chalice[7] to the altar and ministers the cruets. Having poured in the wine he holds the water cruet up to the bishop saying *Benedicite, Pater reverendissime*. He hands the chalice to the bishop with the usual kisses, but does not recite *Offerimus* nor hold up the chalice; and also hands him the paten at the Embolism, kissing it and the bishop's hand, as usual. After the ablutions one of the chaplains[8] dries and veils the chalice and takes it to the credence, as the subdeacon does at solemn Mass.

During Mass the chaplains stand one on either side of the bishop, at least when he is at the middle of the altar. When he is at the side they may either stand in the same way or, according to some authors, they should then stand together at his farther side, so that the bishop is nearer the middle of the altar. Whenever the bishop reads, the hand-candle is held near the book by one of the chaplains or by a server. When the bishop is at the epistle corner it is held, normally, on his right; when he is at the centre or at the gospel corner it is held at his left.[9] Throughout Mass the chaplain nearest the book turns over its pages.

The chaplains kneel at the beginning of Mass till the bishop goes up to the altar. They genuflect each time with the bishop. They kneel during the elevation, the bishop's reception of Holy Communion, and the blessing at the end of Mass. If they are canons, they wear a surplice over the rochet and they do not kneel, but bow, at the blessing.

Preface. All bishops wear the skull-cap while saying Mass, except from the preface to the communion, both included.[10] The second chaplain removes it from the bishop's head at the beginning of the preface and puts it on again after the communion. While the bishop does not wear the skull-cap, it is put on the silver salver on the credence.

At the end of the secret(s) the missal is shut, taken from its stand and placed aside on the credence. The pontifical canon is taken from the

---

[7] Unless at least one of the chaplains is a cleric the chalice must be placed ready on the altar before Mass begins.

[8] Provided he is in major orders.

[9] The chaplain (or server) who holds the candle never kneels nor genuflects while doing so. At the prayer *Qui pridie* he puts the candle on the altar and goes to kneel on the edge of the footpace in front by the side of the other (if a server, he kneels on a step at the gospel side). As soon as the elevation is ended he goes back to the bishop's side, by the book, genuflects, and again holds the candle.

[10] Cf. C.I.C. 811, § 2. The bishop must also remove the skull-cap whenever the Blessed Sacrament is exposed.

centre of the altar and put on the missal-stand. After the ablutions the pontifical canon and missal are put back in their places as before.

When a bishop distributes Holy Communion the communicant kisses his ring before opening the mouth to receive the Blessed Sacrament[11] if the bishop thinks it fit to present his ring to be kissed.[12] After the ablutions the bishop again washes his hands.

Blessing. At the end of Mass the bishop gives his blessing in the episcopal form. Facing the altar he says the versicles, ℣. *Sit nomen Domini benedictum* (signing his breast). ℟. *Ex hoc nunc et usque in sæculum.* ℣. *Adiutorium nostrum in nomine Domini.* ℟. *Qui fecit cælum et terram.* Then he says: *Benedicat vos omnipotens Deus,* bows to the cross, and turning around makes the sign of the cross over the people thrice. ℟. *Amen.*

At low Mass the bishop never uses mitre or crosier, except at ordinations; nor does an archbishop use an archbishop's cross.

When Mass is finished, the bishop unvests before the altar at the foot of the steps; the vestments are taken by the chaplains to the altar and laid there. He puts on the mozzetta or mantelletta, the pectoral cross and receives his biretta. Then, at the desk or faldstool he says the prayers after Mass, the pontifical canon on the kneeler; a chaplain or server holds the hand-candle on the bishop's right.

If there are several servers, two of them hold candles or torches, kneeling before the altar, during the elevation, that is, from after the *Sanctus* to after the communion. If servers are not available, servants of the bishop[13] may hold these candles; or two large candles in candlesticks standing on the ground before the altar may be lit at this time and should be extinguished after the communion.

At a requiem Mass the bishop puts on the maniple with the other vestments. Nothing is kissed by the assistants (except the vestments).

Prelate Present. If a cardinal, sovereign prince, or prelate of higher rank than the celebrant be present, another faldstool or desk is prepared for him before the altar. At a bishop's Mass no one else kisses the book from which he has read the Gospel. After the Gospel another book is taken to a cardinal, or a prince or a greater prelate present; he kisses it, and the server who brings it to him observes what is said on p. 91. The pax-brede is taken to a prelate or prince assisting, as described on p. 91.

---

[11] This kissing of the bishop's ring is a remnant of the old kiss of peace before communion, as the ministers at pontifical solemn Mass kiss his cheek before receiving.
[12] S.R.C. 4395.
[13] C.E., I, xxix, 7.

Chapter X

Serving Low Mass

§ 1. General Directions

WHEN the server[1] is doing nothing with his hands he keeps them joined before his breast, unless he hold a book. Whenever he hands anything to the celebrant, he may kiss first the thing, then the celebrant's hand. In taking anything he kisses first the hand, then the thing. These are the so-called *solita oscula*.[2] They are omitted in Masses for the dead and when the Blessed Sacrament is exposed. While serving one Mass the server must take no notice of anything that may be done at another Mass, such as the elevation at a neighbouring altar. If he serves Mass at a side altar while solemn Mass or a sung Mass is celebrated at the high altar, he does not ring the bell at all. Nor does he do so at Mass at a side altar when the Blessed Sacrament is exposed in the church.

The normal place for the server is, kneeling, on the lowest altar step at the side opposite to that where the missal is.[3]

Whenever in the course of Mass the celebrant while speaking aloud bows, genuflects, or makes the sign of the cross, the server, as far as possible, does the same.

At the beginning and end of Mass, and when passing before the middle of the altar, he genuflects, whether the Blessed Sacrament be reserved there or not.[4] If It be exposed he genuflects on both knees and bows on arriving at the altar and before departing from it.

§ 2. Preparation

Before Mass the server vests in cassock and surplice,[5] and (if this is needed) goes to prepare everything at the altar.[6]

---

[1] The server is, by tradition, male.

[2] By custom these *oscula* are often omitted by laymen.

[3] At the last Gospel, the altar-card replaces the missal.

[4] S.R.C. 4193 § 1.

[5] The rubrics of the missal (R., II, 1) and the S.R.C. (4194 § 2) both require that the server who wears a cassock, whether a tonsured clerk or not, wear a surplice at Mass. Yet in many countries it is a common custom that he serve in lay dress and this usage is recognised (cf. S.R.C. 4271 § 1). Nevertheless it seems more fitting that the server be attired in liturgical vesture whenever possible. In case of necessity a woman may kneel outside the sanctuary and answer (C.I.C. 813, § 2). The priest himself moves the book, and performs the other

He takes the communion plate, the two cruets, one containing wine, the other water and the dish and hand-towel for the washing of hands, to the credence. He sees that the altar cards are in their place and that the stand for the missal is at the epistle side. If he does not bring the missal with him at the beginning of Mass,[7] he will see that it is already on the stand, closed.[8] He lights the two smaller candles used at low Mass, beginning with the one on the epistle side.

In the sacristy he then assists the celebrant to vest. He takes the missal, closed, bows with the celebrant (standing behind him) to the cross in the sacristy, and leads him (through the door on the gospel side) to the altar at which Mass will be said. In many churches it is usual that the server ring a bell near the sacristy door as he passes, to warn the people that Mass is about to begin. He may take holy water at the sacristy door and offer it to the priest. If they pass an altar at which the Blessed Sacrament is reserved, the server genuflects with the celebrant. He bows to the high altar of the church, if they pass it, unless the Blessed Sacrament be there. At the altar at which the Mass will be said the server goes to the epistle side, takes the celebrant's biretta, and genuflects as the celebrant either does so or bows. He places the missal — its opening towards the middle of the altar — on the stand or cushion (parallel to the front edge of the altar) at the epistle side, going round *in plano* (on the sanctuary floor, around the altar steps) to do so, not ascending the front steps. He puts the biretta on the credence or at another convenient place. He comes back and kneels[9] in front of the altar at the gospel side, on the ground, not on the step.

§ 3. From the Beginning of Mass to the Preface

Kneeling here a little behind the priest he answers the preparatory prayers. He does not bow nor strike his breast while the celebrant says the *Confiteor*. He bows slightly towards the celebrant while he himself says the prayer *Misereatur tui omnipotens Deus*. He bows moderately towards the altar while he says the *Confiteor,* and remains so while the celebrant says *Misereatur vestri*. At the words *tibi, pater* and *te, pater* in the *Confiteor* he partly turns towards the priest. He strikes his breast three times at *mea culpa, mea culpa, mea maxima culpa*. He bows again slightly at the versicles, *Deus, tu conversus,* and remains bowing till the celebrant has said *Oremus*.

---

actions of a server.

[6] All or part of this preparation may be made by the sacristan.

[7] The rubrics of the missal suppose that the server brings the missal with him when the priest comes out to begin Mass (R., II, 1).

[8] At low Mass the server may never open the missal, nor turn over its pages. This is done by the celebrant himself (S.R.C. 3448 § 14).

[9] He may wait for the priest to come down from the altar and bow or genuflect to do this.

As soon as the celebrant goes up to the altar the server rises too. Then he kneels again without genuflecting, this time on the bottom step of the altar. In future he always kneels on this bottom step.

At the introit he makes the sign of the cross with the priest. He answers *Kyrie, eleison, Et cum spiritu tuo*, and says *Amen* after the first and last collect, which have the conclusion. At the end of the Epistle he says *Deo gratias*,[10] and then goes at once to the epistle corner of the altar. He goes round *in plano*, genuflecting in the middle, and stands at the foot of the steps.

On certain days, for example on Ember days, there may be several collects and lessons.[11] The celebrant will not say *Dominus vobiscum* until these extra prayers and lessons are finished. The server remains kneeling at his place for these, answering *Amen* at the end of each collect, and *Deo gratias* at the end of each lesson, except the fifth. After the celebrant has said *Dominus vobiscum* the Mass continues as on ordinary days.

Gospel. The server waits at the epistle corner during the gradual or tract. When the celebrant goes to the middle the server takes the missal across to the gospel side (carrying it down and up by the middle of the steps), genuflecting in the middle, and puts it here at the corner of the altar diagonally, so that its pages face half-way towards the middle of the altar. He stands by the book on the top step (not the predella). The priest comes to read the Gospel. The server answers the versicles at the beginning, and makes the sign of the cross with the thumb on forehead, lips and breast with the priest. If the Holy Name occurs in the opening words of the Gospel the server bows his head; if not he waits for two or so lines of the Gospel to be read. Then he goes to the epistle side *in plano* and stands at that corner facing the priest, while the Gospel is read. If the priest genuflects during the Gospel, the server does so too. At the end he answers *Laus tibi, Christe*. If the *Credo* is said, the server kneels during it[12] and bows at the verse *Et incarnatus est*, etc.

Offertory. When the priest has said *Dominus vobiscum* and *Oremus* at the offertory, the server goes to the credence, takes the dish with the cruets which stand on it and the hand-towel. He spreads the hand-towel on the altar at the epistle corner, puts the dish and cruets as they are, on the hand-towel, then takes the wine cruet in his right hand, the water cruet in the left, stands at that end of the altar and there waits till the celebrant comes. He bows and hands the wine cruet to the priest and takes the water cruet in his right hand. He takes back the wine cruet with his left hand and holds up the water cruet for it to be blessed. He may

---

[10] The priest usually gives a sign at the end of the Epistle, turning towards the server or lifting his left hand, or putting in on the altar to the left of the missal-stand.

[11] Regarding the omission of some of them, see R.G., n. 468.

[12] When the congregation is taking an active part in Mass the server should – when possible – lead them in the correct postures for a dialogue Mass (p. 89), and so he will stand during the *Credo*.

kiss both (on the base or on the handle) before handing them to the celebrant, and on receiving them back, but, this time, not the celebrant's hand. Then he sets down the wine cruet either on the altar or on the credence (if he goes there to get the special bowl for the washing of the fingers), lays the hand-towel on the altar or on his left arm, takes the dish or bowl in his left hand and the water cruet in the right. The priest comes to wash his hands. The server holds the dish under the celebrant's hands and pours a little water over his fingers from the cruet. He must be careful to hold the dish under the priest's hands, so that the water poured over the fingers may go into it. Before and after washing the priest's fingers he bows to him.

He puts all back on the credence, takes the bell and goes to his place at the lowest step on the epistle side and kneels there without genuflecting.

When the priest says *Orate, fratres* the server should wait till he has again turned to the altar; then he says the answer, *Suscipiat Dominus,* etc. He answers the versicles before the preface. As the celebrant says the *Sanctus* the server rings the bell gently three times. He then goes to the epistle side and lights the third candle there if customary. This remains alight till after the communion. He comes back to his place.

§ 4. From the Canon to the End of Mass

When the celebrant spreads his hands over the bread and chalice at *Hanc igitur,* the server rings once the warning bell. He then goes to kneel on the top step, or on the footpace, at the epistle side, but near the middle. He takes the Sanctus bell with him. At each elevation he holds up slightly for a moment the end[13] of the chasuble in his left hand,[14] and rings the bell with his right, either continuously or three times. He may arrange this so that he ring once when the celebrant genuflects, once when he elevates, once again when he genuflects. Since there are two elevations the bell will be rung altogether six times. After the elevation of the Chalice and the priest's genuflexion following, the server goes back, without genuflecting, to the place where he was before, at the end of the lowest step on the epistle side, and kneels there. The server does not strike his breast at the *Nobis quoque.*[15] He strikes his breast when the priest does so at *Agnus Dei.* After *Agnus Dei* he rings the bell, once, as a sign to the people that the time of communion is at hand.

Communion. He bows while the priest makes his communion. If anyone now come to the communion rail, or if the server himself intend to receive Holy Communion, he rings the bell and rises as the priest

---

[13] Where an ample chasuble is worn, where necessary and practicable, the server may hold back the side over the right arm.

[14] Only as the priest elevates, not as he genuflects.

[15] S.R.C. 3535 § 3.

gathers the fragments from the corporal with the paten and kneels on the lowest step at the epistle side, sideways, facing the gospel side across the sanctuary. The server, by kneeling thus, indicates to the priest that there is someone for Holy Communion; but if he stands there carrying the cruets it is an indication that there is no one for Holy Communion.

If the server himself receive Holy Communion, ordinarily he does so before anyone else. If he is a cleric he will receive after clerics of a higher order than himself; if a layman, all clerics will receive before him. The server may receive Holy Communion kneeling either on the footpace at the epistle side facing the gospel side, or kneeling on the edge of the footpace in front of the altar, rather to the epistle side. He will bring with him from the credence the communion plate and hold it under his chin.

When the priest goes to give Holy Communion to the people the server will take the communion plate and hand it to the first person to receive on the epistle side.[16] After communion the priest will take the plate back to the altar and there purify it. When it has been purified the server will replace it on the credence.

Should for whatever reason the tabernacle be opened, the server always kneels till it is closed. After communion he will take the cruets to the altar for the ablutions.

Ablutions. If no one but the celebrant receive Holy Communion, the server will fetch the cruets at once, when the priest has made his communion in the form of bread and begins to cleanse the corporal with the paten. He takes the cruets on their tray from the credence. He genuflects at the foot of the altar steps (if the priest has not already consumed the Precious Blood), stands on the highest step outside the footpace at the epistle corner, and places the water cruet on the altar. When the celebrant holds the chalice towards him the server draws near him and bows. He pours some of the wine into the chalice, until the priest makes a sign. Then he bows again and goes back to where he was before. The priest, when he has drunk the wine, comes to the server.[17] The server bows and pours into the chalice a little wine, then (with his right hand) water, both over the priest's fingers. The priest will make a sign when enough has been poured. The server then bows again to the priest, puts the cruets back on the credence and extinguishes the third candle lit after the *Sanctus*. At the ablutions the server does not kiss the cruets nor the celebrant's hand.

The server then goes to the gospel side, genuflecting, as always, in the middle as he passes, takes the missal and brings it to the epistle end of the altar, again genuflecting as he passes the middle. He places the missal

[16] It is also permitted to have the plate held for the communicants by the server. He then takes it back at the end of the communion, and leaves it on the altar near the priest.

[17] The priest will rest the chalice on the table of the altar unless the server is too small to reach it.

straight on the altar, facing the people, as it was at the introit. Then he goes to kneel at the lowest step on the gospel side. He answers the postcommunions, *Dominus vobiscum, Ite, missa est,* or other versicle in its stead. During the Easter octave the priest adds *Alleluia* twice to the *Ite, missa est;* the server does so, too, after the response, *Deo gratias.* He makes the sign of the cross at the blessing, then stands.

Last Gospel. In Masses on Palm Sunday not preceded by the palm procession there is a proper last Gospel, and so the celebrant leaves the missal open after the postcommunions. This is the sign for the server. In this case, as soon as he has answered *Ite, missa est,* he brings the book again to the gospel side. He may arrange so that his genuflexion in passing the middle with the book coincide with that for the blessing. In this case he will kneel on both knees at the middle. Or he may bring the book to its place, then kneel for the blessing at the gospel side.

Standing at the gospel side on the top step of the altar and facing south, he makes the responses at the beginning of the last Gospel. Then he goes over to the epistle side, genuflecting as usual, and stands in front of the bottom step, turned towards the priest. He genuflects with him at the verse *Et Verbum caro factum est,* and answers *Deo gratias* at the end.

He waits for the celebrant at the epistle side. If necessary he hands him the card from which the prayers after Mass are said. During these he kneels on the lowest step at the epistle side and answers the prayers.

When the celebrant ascends the altar to get the chalice, the server fetches the missal from the altar and the biretta. He hands the biretta to the celebrant with his right hand; genuflects when the celebrant genuflects or bows, and then goes in front of him to the sacristy.

In the sacristy he bows, with the priest, to the cross, lays down the missal, assists the celebrant to unvest, and bows to him.[18]

Then, if he is to do so, he goes back to the altar, extinguishes the candles beginning with the one on the gospel side, and brings the cruets to the sacristy.

Lastly, he takes off his surplice and cassock.

§ 5. Requiem Mass

At Masses for the dead the server omits all *solita oscula.* The *Iudica* psalm is not said. If the sequence *Dies iræ* is said, the server does not rise to move the missal till the concluding verses. At the end of Mass, instead of *Ite, missa est,* the celebrant says *Requiescant in pace.* To this the answer is *Amen.* There is no blessing.

---

[18] In some places it is customary for the celebrant to give the server his blessing after Mass.

§ 6. Two Servers at Low Mass

On great feasts there may be two servers at Masses which are public. In this case one of the two is the first server; he does nearly all as above. The other may answer with him; he must take care to bow and genuflect with the first. The second server (who is on the gospel side) moves the missal for the Gospel and after the communion.

At the offertory the two servers genuflect at the centre and go to the epistle side. The first serves the cruets. At the lavabo the first server takes the hand-towel on the right, the second the cruet and dish. While the first goes to carry anything from one place to another the second stands. They both go up and hold the end of the chasuble, momentarily, at each elevation. The first server will hand the communion plate to the first person who is to receive. They may hold the cloth extended between them at the communion of the clergy or people, if these come to the altar.

At the ablutions the first server alone goes to the credence and serves the celebrant; the other stands at his place, until he goes to transfer the book.

Chapter XI

Solemn Mass

IN the case of solemn Mass sung by a priest it will be convenient to describe the functions of each assistant separately. Figures 6-13 show the position of each person at various moments of solemn Mass.

§ 1. The Choir at Solemn Mass

If the liturgical choir is performing its traditional function of singing the chant, it always stands when singing. If, however, there is another choir performing this function, the liturgical choir observes the following rules. For general directions for the surpliced choir at all liturgical functions see Chapter V.

The choir may enter with the celebrant and his ministers, or they may already be in their places before the altar, as when one of the canonical Hours (generally Terce) is sung immediately before Mass.

If the choir enters with the celebrant, they do not take holy water if the Asperges is to occur. They genuflect to the altar—even in the Blessed Sacrament is not reserved there, unless they be prelates or canons, in which case they bow—and, having bowed to each other, go to their places, in pairs, as described at p. 53.

If they are already in their places when the celebrant enters with the ministers and servers, they stand during that entrance and, when the celebrant bows to them, bow in return.

Standing and Sitting. They do not genuflect when the servers and ministers do so before the altar. They stand during the entire Asperges ceremony (even whilst the celebrant and sacred ministers kneel), bow and make the sign of the cross as they are sprinkled with holy water. All (except prelates) kneel during the preparatory prayers, said by the celebrant at the altar steps. While he and the ministers say the *Confiteor*, etc., the members of the choir also say them to each other, in pairs, or those in choir answer the celebrant. They should say the *Kyrie, eleison* in the same way, in pairs, while the celebrant says it. If the celebrant sits during the sung *Kyrie, eleison*, the choir sits too. They stand while he says the *Gloria in excelsis*, then sit when the celebrant has done so. They rise as he rises at the end of the *Gloria*; stand during *Dominus vobiscum* and the collect(s); sit during the Epistle—standing and then genuflecting when this is required—and the chants (gradual, tract, sequence or Alleluia verse) that follow. They stand for the sung Gospel just before *Dominus* *vobiscum* is sung, genuflect if the deacon does so, and stand while the celebrant says the *Credo.* At the verse, *Et incarnatus est,* etc., they genuflect with the celebrant, as he says it. They then sit as soon as the celebrant does so; they do not kneel, but uncover and bow, while *Et incarnatus est* is sung.[1] When the celebrant rises, at the end of the sung *Credo,* the choir stand. They sit again when he has sung *Oremus* at the offertory. After the celebrant has been incensed, they stand, and remain standing till those of their rank have been incensed. They bow before and after being incensed. When the incensation is finished they sit till the celebrant has finished the secret. They stand when he sings *Per omnia sæcula sæculorum* at the conclusion of the secret. They say the *Sanctus* with the celebrant. They kneel for the consecration[2] (when the deacon and subdeacon kneel) till after the elevation of the Chalice, then stand till the end of the celebrant's communion. They say the *Agnus Dei* with the celebrant. After the communion they kneel unless Holy Communion is not distributed, sitting when the tabernacle is closed. They stand again when the celebrant sings *Dominus vobiscum* before the postcommunion, till the blessing. They kneel for the blessing at the end of Mass, except prelates and canons in chapter, who stand bowed. All make the sign of the cross at the blessing and then stand immediately for the last Gospel (genuflecting at the words *Et verbum*), and so till the end of Mass. They stand as the procession of ministers and servers goes out, if they are not part of it. Otherwise the line up in front of the altar to genuflect with the ministers and servers.

At ferial Masses *celebrated in violet vestments* (except Christmas Eve and the Septuagesima Season) and at Masses for the dead the members of the choir kneel during the collects, postcommunions and *Oratio super populum,* also from the *Sanctus* to *Pater noster* exclusively.

Bows, Genuflections and Signs of the Cross. The members of the choir bow on all the occasions noted on p. 54. Further they bow, at solemn Mass, towards the cross during the *Gloria in excelsis* at the words *adoramus te, gratias agimus tibi, Iesu Christe, suscipe deprecationem nostram.* During the sung *Credo* they bow at the Holy Name and at the words *Et incarnatus est...homo factus est, simul adoratur.* Before the preface they bow at *Gratias agamus Domino Deo nostro.* For rules for removing the skull-cap, in the case of those who wear it, see p. 48. For the manner of giving and receiving the kiss of peace, see p. 51.

On Christmas Day and on the Annunciation at all Masses, the choir kneels at the *Credo* during the verse *Et incarnatus...homo factus est.* They kneel at the words *Flectamus genua* on fast days, rising when *Levate* has been sung. They kneel at the sung verse, *Adiuva nos, Deus salutaris noster,*

---

[1] Cf. C.E., II, viii, 53; S.R.C. 1421 § 3, 1476 § 2, § 3, 1594 § 2, 2960 § 2. If they should then be *standing* they kneel.
[2] R.G., 521.

in the Lenten tract,[3] at the verse, *Veni, Sancte Spiritus,* in the gradual of Whitsunday and its octave; during the Gospel of the Epiphany at the words *Et procidentes adoraverunt eum;* at the Epistle of the feast of the Holy Name, during the words *In nomine Iesu...infernorum;* and on all other occasions when the rubric of the missal says *Hic genuflectitur.* They do not genuflect when the celebrant says these words (except at *Et incarnatus,* etc.), only when they are sung.

The members of the choir make the sign of the cross when sprinkled with holy water at the Asperges, and together with the sacred ministers during the final words of the *Gloria in excelsis, Credo* and *Sanctus.*

For the order of receiving Holy Communion by members of the choir see § 12 below.

§ 2. Preparation for Solemn Mass

On the high altar six[4] candles are lit (four on lesser feasts). There may be reliquaries or images of saints[5] between the candlesticks, and, for great feasts, flowers — in strict moderation — may be placed on the altar (not on the *mensa,* if possible). The altar may be clothed with a frontal of the colour of the Mass; the tabernacle (if the Blessed Sacrament be present) with its conopæum of the same colour or white (but never black). The altar cards are in their places; the missal (open at the proper place) on a stand, covered with a veil of the colour of the Mass (unless the missal itself is covered with a silk cover).

At the epistle side of the sanctuary, close to the altar, is the sedilia, covered in green or in the colour of the Mass; or violet if the Mass be black or violet. A bench or stools may be prepared in some convenient place in the sanctuary for the altar servers, but not at the ends of the sedilia.

On the Credence: covered with a white cloth, extending to the floor, is placed the chalice prepared for Mass (covered with its veil) etc; the book for the lessons (marked for the Epistle and Gospel of the Mass); the cruets, finger bowl and hand-towel; the bell. If there is to be Holy Communion: a ciborium, veiled;[6] the communion cloth (if used for communion of the clergy or servers) and plate. If the Asperges precedes Mass: the aspersorium, with its sprinkler, and a book or card with the prayers. All these are covered over with a humeral veil of the colour of

---

[3] The tract *Domine non secundum peccata,* in which these words occur, is sung at ferial Masses on Mondays, Wednesdays and Fridays in Lent.

[4] At least four of which must be wax candles (S.R.C. 18 August 1949).

[5] C.E. I, xii, 12,

[6] Distributing Hosts consecrated at the same Mass is praiseworthy and has been called for by Pope Benedict XIV (*Ceriores effecti,* 1742), and Pope Pius XII (*Mediator Dei,* 1947).

the Mass;[7] and room is left at the back of the credence for the acolytes' candlesticks.

In the Sacristy: the vestments for the sacred ministers: amices, albs, cinctures and maniples for all three; stoles for the celebrant and deacon; the chasuble (centre), dalmatic (right), and tunicle (left). Surplices for the MC and servers. Also the thurible and incense boat (with a good supply of charcoal at hand, matches, etc.); the acolytes' candles; and torches— two, four, or six—for the torch bearers. Should the Asperges take place, the celebrant's chasuble is made ready at the sedilia and with it the maniples of all three sacred ministers; while a cope of the colour of the Mass is prepared in the sacristy for the celebrant. Surplices should be available for clergy assisting in choir.

§ 3. Procession to the Altar

The order of the procession to the altar will be thus, if there are torch bearers and members of the choir (or clergy) who enter with it:

(MC2)
(Verger or Mace-bearer).
Thurifer.[8]
Second Acolyte. First Acolyte.
Torch-bearers in pairs (without torches).
Choir in pairs.
Master of Ceremonies (1).
Subdeacon.
Deacon.
Celebrant.

But if the celebrant wear the cope, then the ministers walk on either side of him, the deacon at his right, the subdeacon at his left, holding the cope.[9] The sacred ministers are covered; those in choir carry their biretta when inside the church.

The MC may walk at the side of the ministers, instead of in front of them, or he may go in front of the procession, if it be necessary.

---

[7] The burse (containing the corporal) is placed on this veil, over the chalice underneath unless the *Credo* is not sung, in which case it is placed under it.

[8] Putting into the thurible and blessing incense to be carried at the head of the procession, and the use of a processional cross, are features of a pontifical Mass celebrated at the throne (C.E., II, viii, 23, 24).

[9] It is a good thing to turn in the orphreys so that the lining does not show unduly.

§ 4. The Asperges Ceremony

By universal Church law, in all cathedral and collegiate churches the ceremony of sprinkling the clergy and people with lustral water should take place before the chief Mass on Sundays. In England the bishops ordered this in all parish churches before the principal Mass, even if this be a low Mass only.

The ceremony is in no sense part of Mass. Therefore the celebrant[10] wears for it the cope,[11] not the chasuble, and does not wear the maniple. The sacred ministers wear the Mass vestments, except the maniple.

The lustral water is usually blessed by the celebrant, the water and salt having been prepared on a small table in the sacristy, but it may be done by another priest, before Mass in the church or in the sacristy. The celebrant blesses the water according to the form in the missal or ritual, before he puts on the cope.[12]

Procession to the Altar. On going to the altar the thurifer walks first, carrying the vessel of holy water and the sprinkler. The ministers walk on either side of the celebrant holding the ends of the cope. In this case no one takes holy water at the sacristy door. When entering the sanctuary the ministers remove their birettas and hand them to the MC. On arriving before the altar the thurifer goes to the right of where the deacon will be, the acolytes to each corner of the altar-steps, the sacred ministers stand between the thurifer and the second acolyte.[13] All genuflect, except the celebrant who bows low, unless the Blessed Sacrament be reserved there, in which case he, too, genuflects. All (except the acolytes who carry their candles to the credence and then kneel before it, and clergy in choir, who remain standing) kneel, even in Paschal time. The deacon takes the sprinkler from the thurifer, dips it into the holy water and hands it, with the usual kisses, to the celebrant. The celebrant takes the sprinkler and intones the antiphon, *Asperges me, Domine.* The choir continues this, the first verse of the psalm *Miserere,* the verses *Gloria Patri* and *Sicut erat* and repeats the antiphon. In Passiontide *Gloria Patri* and *Sicut erat* are omitted. In Paschal time, instead of *Asperges me,* the celebrant begins *Vidi aquam.* This is continued, according to the text in the missal and gradual.

Sprinkling the Altar. As the celebrant intones the first words from a copy of the *Ritus Servandus* or a card held by the deacon and subdeacon,

---

[10] The celebrant of the Mass that is to follow, and not another priest, performs the Asperges.

[11] If a cope be not available, he will perform the ceremony in alb and (crossed) stole, in which case the deacon and subdeacon leave off the dalmatic and tunicle also, assuming them when the celebrant vests in the chasuble.

[12] To bless the water the celebrant wears (crossed) the stole of the Mass, another priest a violet stole. Cf. O'Connell, *The Celebration of Mass*, 1964, pp. 389-390.

[13] If there is a liturgical choir, all bow to it, to the side of greater dignity first, on arriving at the entrance to the choir.

he sprinkles the altar[14] three times, first in the middle, then on the gospel side, then on the epistle side. He signs himself with the holy water on the forehead,[15] then rises, sprinkles first the deacon, then the subdeacon, who sign themselves. The Ministers and servers then rise. The celebrant hands the sprinkler back to the deacon, who receives it, as always, with the *solita oscula*. He gives it to the thurifer.

The celebrant bows (genuflects, on the lowest step, if the Blessed Sacrament be present), the ministers (on the lowest step) and thurifer *(in plano)* genuflect and go to face the choir on the side of greater dignity (normally, the gospel side).[16] The deacon again takes the sprinkler from the thurifer and hands it to the celebrant, as before. They bow to the choir, who bow in return; the celebrant sprinkles them. If there are but few persons in choir, he may sprinkle each one. If there are many, he should rather sprinkle all together three times, once in the middle, once to his left, lastly to his right. He and the ministers bow again, go to the other side of the choir (making due reverence to the altar as they cross the centre) and do as before.

If canons are present in chapter, each is sprinkled separately with one sprinkling, and the celebrant and ministers bow to each before and after and are saluted in return.

After the choir, the celebrant sprinkles the servers, who stand by the credence or altar (with a triple aspersion for all together) or he may do this after sprinkling the people. During all of this the sacred ministers recite the *Asperges me* or the *Vidi aquam*.

Sprinkling the People. Then he goes to sprinkle the people. To do this he goes, with the ministers, to the entrance to the sanctuary, and facing the people, bows, sprinkles them in the middle, to his left, and to his right and bows again. Alternatively—and indeed, entirely appropriately—he may sprinkle the entire congregation. If he goes down the church and returns by the central aisle, it is better to sprinkle the people on both sides alternately on his way down, and not at all on his return—it is not becoming to sprinkle the backs of some of the congregation and unseen by them. But if, in a large church, he goes down one side aisle and returns by the other, he will go down on the epistle side (turning to his left outside the sanctuary) and return by the gospel side,[17] sprinkling the people all the while.

During the singing of the *Gloria Patri*, the sacred ministers stand and bow towards the altar. When the sprinkling is finished the celebrant

---

[14] If the Blessed Sacrament be exposed the altar is not sprinkled.
[15] He may sign his forehead with the sprinkler, or may touch his right thumb with it and, transferring the aspergil to his left hand, make the sign of the cross with the thumb.
[16] See p. 53.
[17] Cf. S.R.C. 3114 § 2.

returns the sprinkler to the deacon with the usual kisses, who gives it to the thurifer.

The Prayer. When they have returned to the altar they make the proper reverence to it, and stand there. The MC hands the book containing the versicles and prayer, and the ministers hold this before the celebrant. When the choir has finished the repetition of the antiphon, the celebrant, with hands joined, sings the versicles (in Paschal time *Alleluia* is added to the first one), and the prayer to the second ferial tone (inflexion d'l). The choir answers.

When *Amen* after the prayer has been sung, the deacon hands the book to the MC, who puts it on the credence. The celebrant and ministers make the usual reverences to the altar and the choir (those in vestments who genuflect do so on the lowest step), and go to the sedilia. Those in choir may sit, but the servers remain standing. The thurifer should now go to the sacristy to see that the charcoal is ready in the thurible for the beginning of Mass.

At the sedilia the celebrant takes off the cope and puts on maniple and chasuble, assisted by the MC or a server. The ministers put on maniples.

All stand as the celebrant and ministers come to the altar. There they again make the usual reverence, and so begin Mass.

At a sung Mass all is done as above, except, naturally, that the deacon and subdeacon are absent. Either the MC walks at the left of the priest and holds the holy-water stoup, handing him the sprinkler and doing all the deacon does at solemn Mass, or the thurifer does so, while the MC holds the cope on the right. If there is no choir to sing the celebrant says the antiphon and the rest in an audible voice; the servers answer.

§ 5. The Thurifer at Solemn Mass

The thurifer[18] should come to the sacristy in good time before Mass begins and vest in cassock and surplice. Usually he will then prepare the thurible with a proper quantity of *well-lit* charcoal, and (if necessary) assist the celebrant to vest. During Mass (except from the consecration to the communion inclusive) each time that the he leaves or returns to the choir he bows to the clergy, normally to those on the gospel side first.

No rubric supposes the presence of a boat-bearer. The Ceremonial of Bishops always supposes that the thurifer carries the incense-boat himself.[19] If, however, there is a boat-bearer he has merely to accompany the thurifer at his left side, holding the boat, and hand it to the thurifer

---

[18] The thurifer is really one (the first) of the acolytes. He is called so constantly in C.E. (e.g., I, xxiii, 2, "ipse vero acolythus thuribulum deferens").

[19] E.g., C.E., I, xxiii, 1. Merati allows for a boat-bearer; cf. Gavanti-Merati, Pars II, tit. ii, § 21 (*ed. cit.*, vol. i, p. 107). In keeping with the principle that "no more servers should attend than those really needed," it is better that the thurifer should manage the boat himself.

when it is wanted. He genuflects and bows with the thurifer, and stands aside at all ceremonies involving the thurible.

Asperges. If the Asperges ceremony is performed before Mass, the thurifer processes as indicated in § 3 above, carrying the holy-water vessel with the sprinkler in it. He stands at the right of the deacon before the altar, genuflects *in plano* each time with the others, hands the sprinkler to the deacon and accompanies him, on his right (or in front of him), down the church, as described above (p. 109). As soon as the holy-water vessel is put back on the credence, and the celebrant and ministers go to the sedilia to put on the chasuble and maniples, the thurifer should go to the sacristy, genuflecting as usual before the altar if he passes it, to get the thurible. He brings the thurible, carrying it in his *left* hand, with the incense-boat in the right, to the church. He should arrive in the sanctuary before the end of the *Confiteor*. Genuflecting if he passes the altar, he goes to stand in the sanctuary on the epistle side.

If there is no Asperges the thurifer—usually carrying the thurible (open) in his left hand and the boat in his right—leads the procession to the church, and stands on the epistle side of the sanctuary during the preparatory prayers.[20]

For the manner of handling the thurible and of holding it while incense is blessed, see p. 48ff.

Incensation of Altar. He goes up to the altar, on the footpace, at the epistle side, as soon as the celebrant goes up to it. Here he hands the boat to the deacon, holds the thurible before the celebrant while incense is put in and blessed, hands the thurible to the deacon (taking the boat from the MC) and goes down from the footpace to the floor. He may have to remove the missal while the altar is incensed if the MC does not do so, picking up the missal and its stand and taking them both down the steps to stand well back facing north on the floor at the epistle side. He replaces the missal and stand immediately the incensation of the epistle side is completed. When the deacon incenses the celebrant the thurifer stands near him, a little behind, on his right or left, and bows with him (see fig. 6). He takes the thurible from the deacon in his right hand and carries it back to the sacristy, where he adds fresh charcoal. Then he comes to his place, between the acolytes before the credence. He stands here, waiting, till the end of the collects or Epistle when he goes to fetch the thurible from the sacristy.

When the celebrant has finished reading the gradual, etc., the thurifer takes the boat from the credence and goes to the celebrant on the footpace. The celebrant puts in incense and blesses it in the usual way. The thurifer takes the thurible (open) in the right hand and the boat in the left. He goes down on the epistle side, leaves the boat on the credence as he passes and leads the acolytes to the middle of the sanctuary before the

[20] Or he may not come out until towards the end of the *Confiteor*.

altar steps, stands some distance from the steps in front of the first acolyte or between the two acolytes or behind them and waits there (cf. fig. 11).

Gospel. The deacon and subdeacon come and stand in front of the thurifer and acolytes. When the MC gives the sign, the thurifer genuflects with the others, and bows, with them, to the choir, first to the *epistle side* and then to the gospel side. He then, with the MC, leads the procession to the place where the Gospel is sung. He stands here at the deacon's left, allowing the acolytes to pass before him (cf. fig. 11).

When the deacon has announced the title of the Gospel, the thurifer shuts down the thurible and hands it to the MC, who gives it to the deacon to incense the book, bowing with the deacon before and after. The MC hands it back to the thurifer. He raises the lid a little and stands in the same place as before. He should not swing the thurible while the Gospel is sung. When the Gospel is finished the subdeacon goes directly to the celebrant while the thurifer (with the MC) leads the deacon and acolytes to the foot of the altar (or before the sedilia). There he genuflects when the deacon does so, and handing him the thurible stands at his left, and, with him, bows to the celebrant before and after the incensation (cf. fig.12a). He takes the thurible back, genuflects with the MC and acolytes and goes to the sacristy and renews the charcoal, returning discreetly as soon as possible. If there is neither homily nor *Credo* he does not leave the sanctuary but stands between the acolytes before the credence.

Offertory. Rising with the sacred ministers at *Et exspecto*, he goes to fetch the thurible from the sacristy. He brings it out and waits at the epistle side of the sanctuary. As soon as the subdeacon has moved the missal the thurifer goes up to the altar, first taking the boat from the credence, and assists, as usual, while incense is put in and blessed. When he receives the boat back from the deacon, he takes it to the credence. He stands there, at the epistle side, with joined hands, while the celebrant incenses the altar, unless he has to move the missal. If he does this he goes around the front of the altar steps, genuflecting when passing the centre, to the foot of the steps on the gospel side. These he ascends and, taking the missal and its stand, he stands at the foot of the steps on the gospel side whilst the gospel side of the altar is incensed. When this is completed he replaces the missal and stand, returning by the same way to the epistle side. When the deacon takes the thurible from the celebrant and comes down to incense him, the thurifer goes to his side at the left, but a little behind, bowing with him before and after. He accompanies the deacon in this way while the celebrant, choir and subdeacon are incensed, bowing and genuflecting together each time.

After he has incensed the subdeacon, the deacon returns the thurible to the thurifer. He then incenses the deacon, when he has gone to his place behind the celebrant and turned round, with two double swings; then, without moving from where he stands, he incenses the MC, the acolytes and other servers, with one double swing for each, facing each where he stands, and bowing before and after.[21] He ignores—and certainly does not wait for—the MC or any server should they be occupied at the time. He genuflects in the middle of the choir, goes to its entrance, turns to the people, bows, and incenses them with three single swings, one down the middle, the next towards the epistle side (i.e., to his own left), lastly towards the gospel side. Then he bows, turns, genuflects again, and takes the thurible to the sacristy (or, if fresh charcoal is not needed, goes to the credence). Usually, the torch-bearers follow him out (p. 118). If so, they should form up in two lines behind him before the altar, all genuflect together, bow to the choir (first to the side of greater dignity)[22] and follow him to the sacristy. If, whilst crossing, the celebrant should sing *Gratias agamus Domino Deo nostro,* all stop, face the altar and bow.

Sanctus. The thurifer in the sacristy renews the charcoal in the thurible. He comes back to the sanctuary, during the recitation of the *Sanctus* by the sacred ministers, leading the torch-bearers, if possible by a longer route entering through the sanctuary gates. They all genuflect together in the middle, and then bow to the choir on the gospel side, normally, and then on the epistle side. Then the thurifer goes to the epistle side and stands there, facing across the sanctuary. Just before the consecration the MC, or an acolyte, puts incense into the thurible. The thurifer[23] incenses the Blessed Sacrament, kneeling on the lowest step at the epistle side. He makes three double swings of the thurible at each elevation (in practice, one each time the bell is rung), bowing before and after.

After the incensing of the Sacred Host at the elevation, the thurifer makes a simple genuflexion in the centre and takes the thurible to the sacristy and puts it back in its place. If the torch-bearers leave,[24] he genuflects with them and leads them out. The thurible is not used again and so the thurifer's office ends at this point. Usually he returns to choir[25] and takes his place with the other assistants for the rest of Mass. When the Mass is ended the thurifer may lead the procession, walking before the acolytes, with joined hands.

If the thurifer replaces an acolyte: Sometimes, however, the thurifer may have to replace an acolyte, e.g., if the acolytes take the place of torch-bearers, on those days when the torch-bearers remain till after the communion. In this case, then, the thurifer takes the humeral veil from

---

[21] Making only one common bow—a slight one—before and after, to each group of servers. If he incenses them collectively it will be with three simple swings (centre, to his left, to his right, p. 50).

[22] Cf. p. 53.

[23] R., VIII, 8.

[24] Cf. § 7 below.

[25] If the thurifer remains at the credence he receives the kiss of peace from the MC and gives it to the first acolyte.

the subdeacon at the words *dimitte nobis* in the Lord's Prayer, folds it and carries it to the credence. Also, when he has received the pax from the MC, or the person standing next to him, he takes the chalice veil round to the gospel side of the altar; then he brings the cruets to the altar for the ablutions, takes them back afterwards to the credence and goes back to his place before the credence.

Communion. If the clergy go to communion (cf. § 12 below) the thurifer, when he has laid the humeral veil aside, takes the communion cloth (if used), goes over to the gospel side and there kneels on the ground. Before *Ecce Agnus Dei* he comes to meet the MC in the middle. They genuflect together, each takes one end of the communion cloth, they separate and go one to either end of the altar (the thurifer back to the gospel side), stretching the cloth between them. They kneel, facing one another, on the two ends of the footpace, and hold the cloth across between them. The clergy come to this cloth and receive communion over it. Then the MC and thurifer come again to the middle, fold the cloth there; the thurifer takes it to the credence, then brings the cruets to the altar for the ablutions.

§ 6. The Acolytes

The two acolytes should be, as far as possible, of similar height. In due time before Mass they come to the sacristy, and vest in cassock and surplice. Unless someone else does this, the acolytes light the candles on the altar, each lighting those on one side. They begin lighting the candle nearest the altar cross. If one acolyte lights all the candles he begins on the epistle side. They then see that their candles in the sacristy are lit. The first acolyte assists the deacon to vest, the second acolyte the subdeacon. When the celebrant is vested they hand the maniples to the deacon and subdeacon to kiss, then put them on the left arm of each. If the Asperges comes before Mass, the maniples are not put on in the sacristy.

The normal place for the acolytes, when they are not occupied, is in front of the credence with their backs to it. At solemn Mass, when the celebrant and ministers sit, the acolytes, thurifer and other servers may sit too. They may sit on the steps of the altar;[26] often special places are appointed for them, a bench or seats in front of the choir. When they are not occupied they join the hands before the breast. When sitting they lay their hands flat on their knees. Whenever they pass before the altar they genuflect together in the middle.

Procession. The acolytes go at the head of the procession, following the thurifer, having bowed to the sacristy cross with the sacred ministers. The first walks to the right of the second. He carries his candlestick, holding it under its node, in the right hand and puts his left under its

---

[26] S.R.C. 2515 § 5. On the middle step. They may never sit at the sedilia.

base. The second holds the left hand under the node of his candlestick and puts the right under its base. It is important that they hold their candles straight and at the same height. The acolytes can verify this, without looking up, by seeing that the feet of the candlesticks are level.

When they arrive in front of the altar, they do not at first genuflect, but go at once to either side, at the corners of the altar steps. There they turn to face one another, if the clergy are in the procession, and so now go to their places in choir.[27] When the celebrant and sacred ministers arrive at the foot of the altar, the acolytes turn and face the altar, genuflect with them and then carry their candles to the credence — acolyte 1 turns right and waits for acolyte 2 to join him. They put them down there, one at each corner at the back, then kneel side by side in front of the credence.

During a function (unless attending the cross-bearer) they always genuflect when passing the centre of the altar, whether the Blessed Sacrament be reserved there or not.

Asperges. If the Asperges ceremony takes place before Mass, the acolytes stand when the deacon and subdeacon rise. They bow and make the sign of the cross when they are sprinkled and bow at *Gloria Patri*. They remain standing before the credence till the celebrant and ministers go to the sedilia. Then they go to assist them; The first acolyte hands the maniple to the deacon, the second to the subdeacon, while the MC assists the celebrant. If it is not taken by a sacristan or draped over a lectern or a stand it may be necessary for one of the acolytes to carry the cope to the sacristy. They then go back to their place before the credence. They kneel there as the sacred ministers genuflect for the preparatory prayers, making the responses, bowing and signing themselves as the deacon and subdeacon do, and they stand when the celebrant goes up to the altar.

Gloria in Excelsis. Whenever the celebrant and sacred ministers go to sit down, as at the *Gloria* or *Credo* (or perhaps during the singing of the *Kyrie, eleison* or sequence) the acolytes go to assist them at the sedilia. They go to the sedilia, the first acolyte to the corner nearer the altar, where the deacon will sit, the second acolyte to the subdeacon's place. When the celebrant has sat down the first acolyte hands to the deacon his biretta,[28] while the second acolyte hands the biretta to the subdeacon. The acolytes may arrange the dalmatic and tunicle, if feasible, over the back of the sedilia. If they pass before the celebrant they bow to him. The acolytes may themselves then sit, at some bench prepared for them or on the altar steps.

---

[27] If the clergy be already in choir the acolytes will arrive there immediately in front of the sacred ministers. On arriving at the entrance to the choir they separate, stand in a line with the sacred ministers and bow to the choir, first on the Gospel then on the epistle side. They then proceed with the sacred ministers to the foot of the altar.
[28] If there is no MC he first hands the celebrant's biretta to the deacon.

Epistle. The celebrant goes with the deacon to the sedilia and sits to listen to the chanting of the Epistle. There the first acolyte hands the celebrant's biretta to the deacon and afterwards the latter's own biretta as at *Gloria in excelsis*. After the singing of the Epistle, the celebrant returns to the epistle corner of the altar to read the gradual, etc.

Gospel. Before the sung Gospel, while the celebrant puts incense in the thurible, the acolytes take their candles from the credence and wait at the epistle corner facing west, about a yard from the bottom step. The thurifer comes down on the epistle side, and as he comes around on his way to the centre he is joined by the acolytes coming from the credence. They follow him to the centre near the foot of the altar; and stand there on either side of him or behind him and the MC (fig. 11). Then, some time after the deacon and subdeacon have come to stand in front of them, the MC gives a sign; all genuflect together to the altar and bow to the choir right[29] and left. They then go to the place where the Gospel is sung. The MC and thurifer go first, then the two acolytes side by side, then the deacon and subdeacon. The acolytes swing round, the second keeping his place to the left of the first, and stand facing the deacon, on either side of the subdeacon, slightly behind him, the first acolyte on his right (fig. 12). They stand while the Gospel is sung and do not genuflect or bow if the deacon does so, nor make the sign of the cross since they are attending the Gospel book.

When the Gospel is ended they lead the deacon to the foot of the altar, after the subdeacon has gone, and genuflect behind the deacon when he does so. After the incensation of the celebrant (cf. fig. 12a), at a signal from the MC, they genuflect again, with the thurifer, and take their candles back to the credence. They stand here, at their usual place, while the celebrant says the *Credo*; they genuflect with him at *Et incarnatus*. They go to the seats to make ready for the sacred ministers, as at the *Gloria*. But this time they stay there till the deacon comes back from having spread the corporal on the altar. They kneel while the choir sings the words *Et incarnatus est,* etc., unless they are then sitting, when they bow only. The first acolyte assists the deacon when he sits; they then go back to their place, bowing to the celebrant, if they pass before him.

Offertory. When the subdeacon comes for the chalice at the credence the first acolyte assists him to put on the humeral veil; the second acolyte folds up the chalice veil if handed to him and puts it on the credence. The first takes the hand-towel, dish and cruets, and follows the subdeacon to the altar. Here he spreads the hand-towel at the epistle end, and stands the dish and cruets on it. He hands the cruets to the subdeacon;[30] when the wine and water have been poured into the chalice he takes the hand-towel, dish and cruets back to the credence.

---

[29] First to the epistle side this time, as the procession is to go towards the gospel side.
[30] He does not kiss the cruets, since he does not hand them directly to the celebrant.

While the deacon incenses the celebrant the first acolyte takes the hand-towel, the second takes the cruet with water in his right hand, and the bowl in his left. As soon as the celebrant has been incensed they go to him at the epistle end, the first at the right of the second, and bow. The second acolyte pours water over the celebrant's fingers into the bowl, the first hands him the hand-towel. When he gives back the hand-towel they bow again, take everything back to the credence and stand before it in their usual place. They are incensed after the MC and bow to the thurifer before and after.

Consecration. The acolytes stay by the credence during the canon[31] and attend, if necessary, to the ringing of the bell—three times at the *Sanctus*, once at the *Hanc igitur*, three times at each elevation, and three times at the *Domine non sum dignus*—and to putting in incense for the thurifer before the elevation (fig. 13). Like the choir, they kneel for the consecration (with the deacon and subdeacon) till after the elevation of the Chalice, then stand. But on the days when the choir kneels till the end of the canon (cf. p. 105), the acolytes do so too.

When the celebrant sings the words *Et dimitte nobis debita nostra* in the *Pater Noster*, the first acolyte goes to the subdeacon near the footpace, takes the humeral veil from him and puts it on the credence, having genuflected with the subdeacon before and after the removal of the veil. The first acolyte receives the kiss of peace from the MC (or from the thurifer, if he be at the credence) and gives it to the second acolyte.

Communion. The acolytes bow at the celebrant's communion under both species. For the communion of the clergy (if the acolytes do not bear torches), they hold the communion cloth (where it is used) as described in § 12 below. If the acolytes receive Holy Communion, they do so after the deacon, subdeacon, and any clergy who may communicate. They genuflect on one knee before and after their communion. During the distribution of Holy Communion they kneel before the credence table.

When the celebrant gathers up fragments of the Sacred Host, the first acolyte takes the cruets to the altar and hands them to the subdeacon. On the way he genuflects to the Blessed Sacrament at the foot of the steps on the epistle side. The second acolyte meanwhile takes the chalice veil to the gospel side, genuflecting as he passes the altar in the middle at the same time as the deacon and subdeacon when changing places. He comes back to his place, again genuflecting at the middle.

The acolytes kneel at their place for the blessing at the end of Mass, stand for the last Gospel, and make the signs of the cross with the celebrant at its beginning.

Last Gospel. During the last Gospel the acolytes take their candles, come to the middle behind the thurifer—arriving just before the words *Et verbum caro*, when the Gospel is that of St John—genuflect and go to the

---

[31] If the acolytes have to act as torch-bearers, cf. § 7 below.

entrance to the choir. They genuflect again when the sacred ministers reverence the altar, and lead the procession back to the sacristy, following the thurifer. If there is no procession of clergy, the acolytes go during the last Gospel to their places at the corners of the foot of the altar; genuflect with the sacred ministers at *Et verbum* and to the altar, reverence the clergy in choir with them to left and right and lead them to the sacristy.

In the sacristy they bow to the cross, extinguish their candles and put them away, and take the maniples from the deacon and subdeacon. When the celebrant has taken off his vestments they help the ministers to unvest. Lastly they go back to put out the candles on the altar. They do this in the inverse order to lighting them (see p. 114).

§ 7. Torch-bearers

There may be two, four or six torch-bearers according to the solemnity of the Mass, of which two may be the acolytes. Clergy in choir may also fulfil this function. At least two torch-bearers are required.[32] They come to the church in the procession, after the acolytes, with joined hands. They go, after the common genuflexion, to the place prepared for them in the sanctuary, generally a seat in front of the choir. Here they attend Mass, having no special office, behaving as the members of the choir, till just before the preface.

Then they come to the middle of the sanctuary, genuflect together, bow to the clergy (normally to those on the gospel side first) and go to the sacristy in pairs with joined hands. It is usual to combine this with the moment when the thurifer goes to the sacristy after the incensing at the offertory (p. 113). In this case the torch-bearers stand in two lines behind him, genuflect and bow to the choir, and follow him out.

In the sacristy they take the lighted torches. At the *Sanctus* they follow the thurifer back to the sanctuary in pairs — each holding his torch in the outside hand, the other being laid flat on the breast — genuflect with the thurifer, bow to the choir on either side then to one another, separate and kneel in line either facing the altar (fig. 13), or at the sides facing one another.

Should Holy Communion not be distributed at the Mass, they go out again as soon as the elevation of the Chalice is ended. They rise, come together, genuflect together with the thurifer, who leads them out (p. 113), but do not now bow to the choir. So they go out two and two, put the torches back in the sacristy, come back, genuflect and, without bowing to the choir, go to their places, as before. They have no further function. At the end of Mass the torch-bearers come to the middle with joined hands, genuflect with the others, and take their place in the procession back to the sacristy.

---

[32] R., VIII, 8.

But ordinarily the torches remain till after the communion. These are fast days when a ferial Mass is said in violet vestments except Christmas eve, when a requiem Mass is celebrated, or when (as will usually be the case), other persons besides the celebrant will receive Holy Communion.

On the days when the torches remain, the torch-bearers stay on their knees in the sanctuary till after the communion; then they rise, genuflect, bow to the choir and go out two and two.

If the torch-bearers receive Holy Communion they must meanwhile hand the torches to someone else to hold while they do so.[33]

In the other case, when the acolytes of the Mass are the torch-bearers, they must go out with the thurifer at the preface, perform this function as described, then come back and go to their place at the credence.

If the acolytes hold torches, and if it is a day on which the torches remain till the communion, it follows that they cannot perform their usual service between the consecration and communion. In this case their place is supplied by others, normally by the MC and thurifer.

§ 8. The Master of Ceremonies

The Master of Ceremonies (MC) or ceremoniar[34] should know not only what he has to do himself, but also the function of everyone else. It is his business to see that the ceremony is carried out correctly by all who take part in it. What is set out in this whole section is simply a general guide to an MC. Because he is MC it is supposed that he has accurate knowledge of the entire function, and in the discharge of his duties he has no fixed place nor act. Much will depend on circumstances. He must be considered quite free in his movements in order that he may secure the most perfect possible conduct of the ceremonies, but this is no licence for gyrovagy; his movements should be purposeful and kept to a minimum. In general, of course, the (first) MC is to be regarded as chiefly concerned with the celebrant at any function and his normal place is at the celebrant's side. He must, if necessary, guide the servers by some sign, as little noticeable as possible. If a mistake is unimportant it is wiser to let it pass at the time and to point it out afterwards. Even should a major mistake occur, he must exhibit no sign of distress, but calmly attend to the necessary correction in such a way that his correction itself appears to be part of the ritual.

He comes to the sacristy in good time before Mass begins and vests in cassock and surplice. He prepares the chalice and paten, also a ciborium,

---

[33] In some places the custom of the celebrant (and ministers) coming to the torchbearers to give Holy Communion has arisen. Where there is no-one else to hold the torches, this would seem tolerable; however the freedom of the torchbearer to choose whether or not to communicate must in no way be infringed.

[34] "Magister cæremoniarum," "cæremoniarius." C.E., I, v, 1, states the requisite qualities. The Bishop should have two masters of ceremonies, the first a priest.

if it will be wanted, and puts these on the credence. He finds the places in the missal—which should be on the missal-stand open at the Mass which is to be sung—and marks them. On the credence he prepares the book of lessons, marked at the Epistle and Gospel. He ensures good order and an atmosphere of silence and recollection in the sacristy. With the acolytes he sees that the cruets, communion plate, hand-towel and bowl for the lavabo and the bell are on the credence; that the thurible, torches and everything else that will be needed are ready. He tells the celebrant and ministers when the time has come for them to vest and sees that this is done properly. The ministers should not put on the maniple till the celebrant is fully vested.

If water is to be blessed, before the celebrant puts on his cope or chasuble the MC leads the him to the place of blessing and assists.

Procession. The MC at the proper time gives the signal for the procession to go to the sanctuary. He sees to it that each person walks in his proper place. He himself goes with the sacred ministers, immediately in front of the subdeacon or to their right (p. 107). Should the celebrant have to walk *up* any steps, the MC assists him by slightly raising the front of his alb. When entering the church he may give them holy water. During the whole service he remains uncovered. When the celebrant and ministers take off their birettas the MC will take them from the deacon and subdeacon,[35] not kissing them; he genuflects and puts the birettas on the sedilia.

Asperges. The MC passes the book or card to the deacon and subdeacon at the appropriate times and leads the sacred ministers through the church as the people are sprinkled. He supervises the vesting at the sedilia and assists the celebrant. When all are ready he indicates that the sacred ministers should go to the altar.

Prayers at the Foot of the Altar. Then he kneels at the deacon's right, behind him, facing the altar, or at the epistle side facing north. He answers the celebrant during the prayers at the altar steps, in a low voice, and he makes the usual signs of the cross and inclinations.

The MC oversees the putting in of incense, ready to assist if necessary. He then takes the missal and its stand down with him and stands *in plano* with them, facing towards the gospel side; he puts them back as soon as that end of the altar has been incensed.[36] In neither case does he genuflect. While the deacon incenses the celebrant the MC stands at the epistle corner (fig. 6). He then goes up to the missal to indicate the place of the introit, standing at the celebrant's right on the step below the footpace. He points out the introit with the open palm of the right hand.

---

[35] This will occur at the entrance to the choir if the clergy are already in choir.

[36] In some churches, both at this moment and at the incensing at the offertory, the thurifer removes the missal. Liturgical authorities hold different views as to whether he or the MC should do so. The question is not decided by the rubrics and so remains an open one.

Whenever he is at the celebrant's side, and the deacon is not there, while the celebrant reads or sings, he will attend to the missal, indicating the place and turning the pages.

Kyrie and Gloria. If the choir take a long time to sing the *Kyrie,* so that the celebrant and ministers sit while they finish it, then, as soon as the celebrant has said the *Kyrie,* the MC will conduct the sacred ministers to the sedilia *per breviorem.*

Whenever the celebrant and ministers sit, the MC first hands the celebrant's biretta to the deacon and then stands, at the right hand of the deacon, facing down the church, with joined hands (fig. 8). When the choir sings the last invocation of the *Kyrie, eleison,* the MC bows to the celebrant, as a sign that he should go back to the altar. He leads the sacred ministers to the foot of the altar (seeing that they salute the choir on the epistle side and then on the gospel side), genuflects when they reverence to the altar, and goes to the epistle corner .

If the celebrant and ministers do not go to sit during the *Kyrie,* then, shortly before the last invocation is sung, the MC gives the sign to the deacon and subdeacon that they should stand in line behind the celebrant. When the choir begins the last *Kyrie* the MC bows to the sacred ministers as an indication to proceed to the middle of the altar. When the celebrant has intoned the first verse of *Gloria in excelsis,* the MC signs to the ministers to go up on either side and to say the *Gloria* with him. When they have finished reciting it, the MC leads them (after a due reverence to the altar) by the shorter way, to the sedilia. He must take care that they do not move while any of the verses are being sung at which an inclination is to be made (p. 105). If necessary, they must wait till such a verse is ended; but, if they have started, they go on. He stands by their side while they sit, as already explained, and bows to the celebrant as the sign when he is to uncover at the verses. Then the MC will himself bow towards the altar while the verse is sung.

Towards the end of the sung *Gloria in excelsis* the MC bows to the celebrant as a sign that he should go to the altar. He leads the sacred ministers back, as described above. He then goes to the missal at the epistle side, points out the collects, and turns the page (fig. 9). He goes to the credence for the book of lessons during the last collect.

Epistle. He takes the book of lessons in both hands, the openings of the pages being on his right; so he hands it to the subdeacon, bowing once before he gives him the book. He then stands a little behind the subdeacon, at his left. As the last collect is ending (having bowed to the missal at the words *Iesum Christum,* if they occur), he accompanies the subdeacon to the middle, genuflects with him, reverences to the clergy left and right, and goes with him to the place where the Epistle is sung *at a distance from the altar.* He stands at the subdeacon's left while the Epistle is chanted and gives a sign to the choir (by bowing to them) if there is any place at which they should bow or genuflect. He bows or genuflects with the subdeacon at such places. He does not say *Deo gratias* at the end of the singing of the Epistle, nor does he help to hold the book.

As soon as the subdeacon has sung the Epistle the MC (if necessary, signing to the celebrant and deacon to return to the altar, and having allowed them sufficient time to do so), goes with him to the middle; together they genuflect towards the altar and bow to the choir; they go to the epistle corner, where the subdeacon is blessed by the celebrant. The MC then takes the book of lessons from the subdeacon. The celebrant reads the gradual, etc. When the celebrant has begun the reading the MC bows to the deacon and hands him the book of the Gospels at the foot of the altar on the epistle side. He assists as before while incense is put in and blessed.

On certain weekdays of Lent (at ferial Masses on Mondays, Wednesdays and Fridays), the celebrant and ministers kneel on the edge of the footpace while the choir sings the entire verse, *Adiuva nos, Deus...nomen tuum.* In this case the incense is blessed after that verse is sung. Then the deacon says *Munda cor meum.*[37]

Gospel. While the deacon says *Munda cor meum* the MC will lead the thurifer and acolytes to the middle and wait there with them. He stands either to the left of the subdeacon or behind the subdeacon to the left of the thurifer, so that he may be in a convenient position to lead the procession to the place of the singing of the Gospel (fig. 11).

At the last *Alleluia* or at the end of the tract all genuflect together, bow to the choir *right* and left and then turning back to the right, and go in procession to the place where the Gospel is to be sung. They go in this order: first, the MC and the thurifer, then the acolytes together and lastly the subdeacon and deacon. The positions for the singing of the Gospel are according to fig. 12.

The MC makes the sign of the cross on forehead, lips and breast, with the thumb, as the deacon signs *Sequentia* (or *Initium*) *S. Evangelii*, etc.

Then he takes the thurible from the thurifer and hands it to the deacon; when the book has been incensed he passes it back to the thurifer and then indicates the start of the Gospel to be sung. During the Gospel he stands at the deacon's right a little behind him and turns the pages. If the deacon genuflects at any verse, the MC does so too. In this case, and when the deacon makes the sign of the cross at the beginning, or bows at the Holy Name, it is better that the MC should bow slightly towards the celebrant at the altar, so as to give him the sign to do so also. At the end of the singing of the Gospel he does not say *Laus tibi, Christe.*

---

[37] It may well be more fitting to prepare and bless incense and for the deacon to say the *Munda cor meum* before the *Adiuva nos* is sung, since this is the last verse of the tract — in which case the procession is formed when all rise at the end of the tract.

As soon as the Gospel is ended, the M
leads the acolytes, thurifer and deacon to the
all genuflect on a signal from the MC when t
the incensation of the celebrant (fig. 12a), the
Gospels from the subdeacon, bowing to hin
with the thurifer and acolytes and leads then
puts down the book.

If a homily follows here, the MC, having led
sedilia, may accompany the preacher to the pu
in a place prepared for him. If there is no hom
finished and he has led the preacher back to
epistle side and stands there, facing across the s

Creed. During the recitation of the *Credo* he
of the cross with the celebrant, and genuflects
incarnatus est, etc. When the celebrant has finish
MC gives a sign to him and the ministers, tha
sedilia. He arranges everything needed as they si
them, as during the *Gloria.* When the choir is sing
MC bows to the celebrant (as a sign that he shoul
facing across the sanctuary, and bows.

At the three Christmas Masses, on the feast of tl
Masses *coram Sanctissimo,* the celebrant and ministe.
incarnatus on the lowest altar step, in front or at tl
music is short the ministers may remain at the alt
edge of the footpace for the *Et incarnatus.* A cushi
prelate. The MC will give the sign and arrange everyth
kneel behind them.

As soon as *Et incarnatus est* has been sung, the MC t
and gives it to the deacon. The MC signs in the usu.
uncovering at *simul adoratur.* While *Et vitam venturi sæculi.*
the MC signs to the ministers to go to the altar. They go
way, bow to the choir and genuflect at the altar steps. The M
genuflects with them and goes to his place at the epistle c
altar.

Offertory. When the celebrant has sung *Oremus* at the offe
MC gives a sign to the subdeacon, who will then genuflect,
credence to put on the humeral veil and bring the chalice to the al

The MC may assist at the uncovering of the chalice. He assists w
blessing of the incense in the usual way. While the altar is incens
MC first waits at the epistle side; but when the celebrant, incer
comes to that side, the MC goes over to the gospel side, removes
missal and holds it, standing *in plano,* until the gospel corner of the a.
has been incensed — or the thurifer may do this while the M
accompanies the celebrant on his left during the incensation of the alta

replaces the missal close to the corporal and stands by it,
elebrant. He stays by the missal while the celebrant washes
fter the deacon has been incensed he turns round for the
cense him, and bows before and after. When the celebrant is
gin the preface the MC may give a sign to the organist, by
bowing, that the organ be silent. He bows with the celebrant
ng. The MC signs to the deacon and subdeacon to join the
or the *Sanctus* and goes to the epistle side and stands at the
. 13) — the deacon takes the MC's place at the missal.
. At the words *Hanc igitur* he, or an acolyte, puts incense into
le. Then he kneels with the thurifer at that side,[38] or he may
the gospel side, or on the footpace at the left of the deacon
the chasuble with him).
ell is to be rung at the *Sanctus*, before the consecration and at the
n,[39] as well as at the *Domine non sum dignus*. It may be rung by the
more correctly, by one of the acolytes.
r the elevation the MC rises and stands at the epistle side until the
Per quem hæc omnia.[40] Then he goes round to the missal, passing
d the subdeacon, and genuflecting in the middle. He now stands
by the missal at the celebrant's left, and turns the pages of the book.
enuflects each time with the celebrant while supporting his elbow.
re the *Pater noster*, when the celebrant sings the words *audemus dicere*,
MC gives a sign to the deacon to stand behind the celebrant. Towards
end of the *Pater* (at the words *et dimitte nobis*) he again signs to the
isters that they both genuflect and go to the right of the celebrant. He
es the sign later that the subdeacon genuflect and go to the left of the
lebrant for the *Agnus Dei*. He then steps back to make room for the
bdeacon. While the deacon receives the pax the MC goes down to the
oor of the sanctuary via the gospel side, and stands at the right of or
ehind the subdeacon. When the deacon has given the pax to the
subdeacon, the MC accompanies the subdeacon at his left as the
subdeacon gives the pax to the choir. When this is done, he comes back to
the middle, before the altar steps, with the subdeacon, genuflects there
with him (on his right), receives the pax from him, genuflects with him
again and goes to the credence to give the pax to the thurifer (or to the
first acolyte if the thurifer be not there). He then goes to the epistle side
and waits there, bowing while the celebrant communicates. He assists
with the distribution of Holy Communion to the choir and to the faithful
as described in § 12 below. He may assist at the ablutions.

[38] The MC may incense the Sacred Host and Chalice (C.E., II, viii, 70), but this is better done by the thurifer as R., VIII, 8, directs.
[39] S.R.C. 4377.
[40] If he had been on the footpace or at the gospel side for the elevation, he remains at the foot on the latter side until he replaces the deacon at the missal.

Communion Antiphon. At the reading of the communion antiphon and the postcommunions the MC turns the pages of the missal and indicates the places. If there is a last Gospel proper to the day[41] he leaves the missal open, finds the place of this Gospel and signs to the subdeacon to transfer the missal, when the *Ite, missa est* has been sung. Otherwise he closes the missal after the last postcommunion, leaving its opening facing towards the cross. During the blessing he kneels at the epistle side on the lowest step. Towards the end of the last Gospel he arranges the procession that will go out. He gives the sign to the acolytes to take their candles and to go to the middle before the altar steps. He takes the birettas from the sedilia, gives the celebrant's biretta to the deacon and stands to his right. He indicates to all when to genuflect,[42] turns and walks to his place in the procession giving the deacon and subdeacon their birettas as he passes them.

§ 9. The Subdeacon

In due time before the Mass begins the subdeacon will come to the sacristy, look over the Epistle, see that the chalice is correctly prepared (unless the MC does this), wash his hands, and vest, assisted by the second acolyte. He does not put on the maniple if the Asperges takes place and otherwise not until the celebrant is vested. He assists the celebrant to vest. He puts on his biretta after the celebrant has done so. When the MC gives the sign, he uncovers, bows to the cross, then to the celebrant, and so takes his place in the procession, immediately before the deacon. If the Asperges precede the Mass, or for any other reason the celebrant wear a cope, he walks on his left, holding the edge of the cope with the orphrey turned in. If, on entering the church, the MC or sacristan gives him holy water,[43] he uncovers to make the sign of the cross. If on entering the choir they are to bow to the clergy, the ministers stand right and left of the celebrant and bow with him (first to the side of greater dignity). In this case they uncover on entering the choir and hand their birettas to the MC. Otherwise they keep in their rank, with head covered, till they stand before the altar. On arriving at the altar the subdeacon uncovers, hands the biretta to the MC, and goes to the left of the celebrant. He genuflects[44] with the deacon.

For the Asperges ceremony, see § 4 (p. 108ff.).

---

[41] On Palm Sunday at Masses not preceded by the palm procession.

[42] Clapping or clicking the fingers is repugnant: it is better to say "genuflect" softly but sufficiently loudly to be heard by those in the sanctuary.

[43] This is not done if the Asperges takes place.

[44] The first genuflexion on arriving in the sanctuary, and the last before leaving it at the end of Mass, are made *in plano* – all other genuflexions are made on the step because the subdeacon is *paratus*, i.e., in sacred vestments.

Whenever the subdeacon stands holding nothing, he joins his hands before his breast. When he sits he rests them on his knees, palms downwards. When he holds anything in his right hand the left is laid under his breast.

Beginning of Mass. Standing before the lowest altar step the subdeacon joins the deacon in answering the prayers. He makes the sign of the cross with the celebrant. He bows with the celebrant, but does not bow while the celebrant says the *Confiteor*. He turns slightly to the celebrant, with a moderate inclination, when he says the *Misereatur*. While he says the *Confiteor* he bows low to the altar, and partly turns to the celebrant at the words *tibi, Pater* and *te, Pater*. He stands upright and signs himself when the celebrant begins the *Indulgentiam* prayer, and bows moderately during the versicles, *Deus, tu conversus,* etc.

As the celebrant goes up to the altar the sacred ministers accompany him, assisting him by slightly raising the front of his alb. They do not genuflect when the celebrant kisses the altar at the beginning of Mass.

While the celebrant blesses the incense the subdeacon remains in his place at the celebrant's left, partly facing him.

While the celebrant incenses the altar, the subdeacon accompanies him on his left, supporting him a little by putting his right hand under the celebrant's left arm.[45] With the deacon he genuflects each time they pass the middle of the altar.

When the celebrant gives the thurible to the deacon, the subdeacon goes straight to the deacon's left side. Here, he bows to the celebrant, with the deacon, before and after the celebrant is incensed (fig. 6). Then he goes with the deacon to the epistle side, behind the celebrant. He stands on the altar step below that of the deacon, or on the ground to the deacon's right (see fig. 7).[46]

Introit. With the celebrant and deacon he makes the sign of the cross at the beginning of the introit; he answers the invocations of the *Kyrie* with the deacon. If the celebrant and ministers sit while the choir sings the *Kyrie, eleison,* at the sign of the MC they go straight to the seats. When they are at the side of the altar they do not first go to the middle before going to the sedilia, nor do they make any reverence to the altar. They turn so that, in going to the sedilia, the subdeacon will be on the right of the celebrant, the deacon on his left. Then turning again on arrival they find themselves in the normal order. At the sedilia the subdeacon first holds the celebrant's chasuble over the back of the seat while he sits down. When the deacon has given the celebrant his biretta, both ministers take theirs from the acolytes (or, in the deacon's case, from the

---

[45] C.E., I, ix, 1, 5; x, 2.

[46] Most authors say that they form a kind of semicircle. The rubric of the missal says only: "diacono a dextris eius (sc. celebrantis), subdiacono a dextris diaconi stantibus in cornu Epistolæ" (R., iv, 7).

MC), they bow, not to the celebrant, but slightly to each other, sit and put on their birettas. While sitting they rest their hands on the knees. This is the rule each time they sit at the sedilia (fig. 8). They rise and go to the altar by the longer way, at the sign of the MC. First they uncover and hand their birettas to the acolytes, then they rise before the celebrant, wait till he has risen, then accompany him to the altar. They form in line to bow to the choir, first on the epistle side,[47] then, having gone some steps further, on the gospel side. The ministers genuflect on the lowest altar step. This is observed every time the celebrant and ministers sit.

Gloria. If they have not gone to the sedilia, when the choir approaches the last *Kyrie, eleison,* the ministers form a straight line behind the celebrant, when directed by the MC to do so, and then go with him to the middle. The subdeacon keeps his place on the ground or on the step below the deacon. He stands thus at the middle while the celebrant intones *Gloria in excelsis Deo;* he bows at the word *Deo,* then goes to the left of the celebrant, not genuflecting, and joins the celebrant and deacon in saying the *Gloria,* bowing with them and making the sign of the cross at the end. When they have finished the *Gloria,* the celebrant and ministers (having genuflected when the celebrant reverences) go to the sedilia and sit there, observing everything noted above. The subdeacon bows with the celebrant and deacon at a sign from the MC at the verses so marked.[48] In bowing he will always first uncover, lay the biretta in the right hand on the knee, and the left hand extended on the left knee. Towards the end of the singing of the *Gloria* the celebrant and ministers return to the altar in the way described above. The subdeacon stands behind the others, so as to be in line behind the deacon. Thus they stand while the celebrant sings *Dominus vobiscum.*[49] Keeping this rank they go to the epistle side for the collects. Here they stand in line (fig. 9). They bow to the missal each time with the celebrant.

On certain days (e.g., on Ember Saturday) a number of prayers and lessons occur before the Epistle. The lessons are sung by a reader (lector) in surplice.[50] For each prayer the deacon and subdeacon stand behind the celebrant.

If the verse *Flectamus genua* is sung by the deacon, the subdeacon kneels for the time of silent prayer and rises when the deacon sings *Levate.*

Epistle. At the beginning of the last collect the MC brings the Epistolarium to the subdeacon at his place. The subdeacon bows to the MC and takes it. He holds the book with both hands, at the bottom, shut,

---

[47] In going towards the altar, in front, they approach the epistle side of the choir first.
[48] See p. 105.
[49] If the *Gloria in excelsis* is not sung, the *Dominus vobiscum,* as above, follows at once after *Kyrie, eleison,* when the celebrant and ministers come to the middle of the altar.
[50] He does not kiss the celebrant's hand, as the subdeacon does, or get a blessing.

against the breast, having the opening of the pages towards his left. So he
waits till the celebrant has sung *Iesum Christum* in the conclusion of the
last collect. Then he bows, if and when the words *Iesum Christum* occur,
goes to the middle of the sanctuary allowing the MC to pass to his left,
genuflects, bows to the choir on either side (beginning on the gospel
side), goes and stands on the right-hand side of the choir, quite some
distance from the altar steps,[51] facing the people or the altar,[52] opens the
book and — once the choir is seated — sings the Epistle.[53] If a verse occur at
which the rubric tells us to kneel, as he sings that he genuflects. When he
has finished the Epistle he shuts the book (*Deo gratias* is not said), goes
again to the middle of the choir (not to the foot of the altar steps),
genuflects and bows to the choir, as before; he goes round to the epistle
corner of the altar, kneels there on the edge of the footpace, holding the
closed book upright. The celebrant lays his right hand on the top of the
book; the subdeacon kisses his hand and is blessed. He returns the
Epistolarium to the MC or an acolyte, and transfers the missal to the left
of the centre of the altar placing it at an angle of about forty-five degrees,
genuflecting on a step lower than the footpace as he crosses the altar. He
assists putting incense in for the Gospel, descends to the foot of the altar
and waits before the lowest step, a little towards the left, in preparation
for the Gospel.

Gospel. The deacon comes with the evangeliarium and joins him there
(fig. 11). The subdeacon genuflects and bows to the choir with the
deacon, this time beginning on the epistle side. He goes at the deacon's
left,[54] to the place where the Gospel is sung.[55] Here he turns to face the
deacon, standing between the acolytes (fig. 12). The deacon hands him
the evangeliarium. He holds it open before his breast[56] at a convenient
height, so that the deacon may sing from it. While the deacon sings the
Gospel the subdeacon neither bows, nor genuflects, nor makes any other
sign.

If a lectern is used (it should be covered in cloth of gold or of the
colour of the day), it is put in place first and taken away afterwards. The
subdeacon stands behind it, resting his hands on the upper edge of the

[51] Cf. O'Connell, *The Celebration of Mass*, 1964, p. 473 n. 29.
[52] S.R.C. 24 July 1961 states that the subdeacon *may* face the people, but not *required* so to do.
[53] If it is the custom of the church that the Epistle be sung from a lectern (C.E., II, viii, 40, 45),
the lectern will be put on the right hand side of the sanctuary before the Epistle (by one of
the acolytes). The subdeacon lays the book, open, on it; while singing the Epistle he rests the
hands on the edge of the pages. The lectern is moved away afterwards.
[54] R. says (VI, 5) "a sinistris," while C.E., II, viii, 44, directs the subdeacon to precede the
deacon. Hence the former arrangement should be followed in a non-pontifical Mass; the
latter in a pontifical one.
[55] For a detailed discussion of the correct place for the singing of the Gospel cf. O'Connell,
The Celebration of Mass, 1964, pp. 479-480.
[56] C.E., I, x, 3; II, viii, 44. Another practice — approved by many authors — is to lean the top of
the book against the forehead, thus entirely covering the subdeacon's face.

book. If the Gospel is sung at an ambo, the subdeacon stands at the
deacon's right, hands him the thurible and turns the pages. At the end of
the Gospel he receives the book from the deacon.[57]

As soon as the Gospel is ended the subdeacon waits for the deacon to
indicate the place of the start of the Gospel text and then takes the book
to the celebrant. Holding it open, he walks by himself straight to the
celebrant at the epistle side of the altar, making no genuflexion on the
way, even if the Blessed Sacrament be exposed. Arriving in front of the
celebrant he holds the book before him, pointing with the open palm to
the place where the Gospel begins. When the celebrant has kissed the
book the subdeacon stands aside to the right, shuts the book, bows to the
celebrant, genuflects towards the cross when the deacon and others
genuflect at the foot of the altar, goes down the altar steps on the epistle
side and stands there, bowing with the deacon, during the incensation of
the celebrant. He then goes to his place at the foot of the altar, or to the
left of the celebrant, and on his way he returns the evangeliarium to the
MC, bowing as he does so.

Homily and Creed. If there is to be a homily[58] at this point the
subdeacon goes to the left of the celebrant at the middle of the altar,
genuflects there with the deacon, who has come up to the celebrant's
right; so the celebrant and ministers go to the sedilia. Otherwise the
subdeacon goes to his place behind the deacon for the *Credo*. He bows at
the word *Deum*, then goes to the left of the celebrant, making no
genuflexion, and with him says the *Credo* making the usual reverences
with him. The celebrant and ministers go to sit at the sedilia, when they
have said the *Credo*, exactly as at the *Gloria in excelsis*. They uncover and
bow at the words *Et incarnatus est*.[59] They also bow at the other verses
noted at p. 105. When the deacon, during the *Credo*, rises to put the
corporal on the altar, the subdeacon rises too, first uncovering and then
holding the biretta on his breast with both hands. He will either stand the
whole time till the deacon comes back to the sedilia, or sit as soon as the
deacon has gone, then rise again when he comes back.[60] When the deacon
comes back he bows to him and sits as before.

Towards the end of the *Credo* he goes with the celebrant and deacon
back to the altar, in the way already indicated (p. 127). If there is no *Credo*
the ministers stand in line behind the celebrant as soon as he has been
incensed after the Gospel.

Offertory. The subdeacon stands behind the deacon while the
celebrant sings *Dominus vobiscum* and *Oremus* at the offertory. He bows at
the word *Oremus*, then genuflects on the lowest step and goes to the

[57] C.E., II, viii, 45. Both cases are here provided for.
[58] It would seem incongruous for a priest acting as subdeacon to preach wearing a tunicle.
[59] On certain days they kneel for this verse (see p. 123).
[60] C.E., II, viii, 54 stipulates that he should remain standing.

credence. Here he stands with his back to the people and receives the humeral veil on his shoulders from an acolyte. He takes the chalice veil from the chalice and gives it to an acolyte, then he holds the chalice at its node in the left hand bare (not through the humeral veil). On the chalice are the purifier, paten, bread and pall. He lays the right end of the humeral veil over the pall, lays his right hand on the chalice so covered, and takes it to the altar direct by the shortest way, making no genuflexion.[61] He puts the chalice on the altar a little to the right of the deacon; the deacon removes the pall and paten. Any ciboria should be moved near to the deacon. The subdeacon, still wearing the humeral veil, wipes the inside of the chalice with the purifier, then gives it to the deacon. He takes the cruets from the acolyte and hands the cruet of wine to the deacon. When the deacon has poured wine into the chalice, the subdeacon holds the cruet of water up, bows to the celebrant and says to him, *Benedicite, Pater reverende.* When the celebrant has blessed the water, the subdeacon pours a few drops into the chalice and hands the cruet back to the acolyte. The deacon gives the subdeacon the paten. He receives this in his right hand, bare, covers it with the right end of the humeral veil, and so rests it against the breast. He goes straight to his place in the middle, in front of the lowest altar step, genuflects[62] on the step and stands there, now holding the paten aloft (before his face[63] or before his breast), supporting his right elbow with the left hand, and letting the veil fall over it in front. Except for the recitation of the *Sanctus,* this is now his place till towards the end of the *Pater noster.*

At the *Orate, fratres,* if the deacon is not yet back at his place behind the celebrant, the subdeacon should answer. When the deacon comes to incense him (after the choir) he turns to face the deacon on his right, bows before and after being incensed, then turns to face the altar again. He does not genuflect.

Sanctus. At the *Sanctus,* when the deacon goes to the right of the celebrant, the subdeacon, without first genuflecting, goes up to the left.[64] Bowing, they say the *Sanctus* with the celebrant. The subdeacon does not sign himself at the *Benedictus* as he is holding the paten.[65] He returns to his place at the foot of the altar without any genuflexion or bow. When the deacon kneels for the consecration, the subdeacon also kneels, in his place (fig. 13). He rises and stands again after the elevation of the Chalice.

---

[61] If there is no *Credo* the subdeacon brings up the burse also and the deacon spreads the corporal, while the subdeacon is wiping the chalice.

[62] R., VII, 9. This genuflexion is anomalous.

[63] If it is held face high, he lowers it to his breast if he replies to *Orate, fratres,* when he is incensed, if he says the *Sanctus* and when he kneels for the consecration.

[64] R., VII, 11. In some places the subdeacon does not go up at the *Sanctus.* S.R.C. (2682 § 30) allows this custom.

[65] S.R.C. 4057 § 5.

Pater Noster. When the celebrant sings the verse *Et dimitte nobis debita nostra* in the *Pater Noster*, the subdeacon genuflects with the deacon and goes to the altar, on the epistle side, to the right of the deacon. He hands the paten to the deacon; then an acolyte, or the thurifer, takes the humeral veil from him. He genuflects and goes back to his place at the middle, in front of the steps. Here, without again genuflecting, he stands with joined hands. When the celebrant sings *Pax Domini*, etc., he genuflects, and goes to the left of the celebrant. After the *commixtio* he genuflects with the celebrant and deacon. Bowing towards the altar he joins them in saying *Agnus Dei,* etc. He strikes the breast at the words *miserere nobis* and *dona nobis pacem.* Then he genuflects and goes back to his former place, not genuflecting on arrival there.

Pax. At this place the deacon comes to give him the pax. He turns towards him, on the epistle side, bows before and after, and receives the pax in the usual manner. Accompanied by the MC he then goes to give the pax to the members of the choir, first genuflecting with the deacon on the lowest step. He gives the pax first to the person of greater dignity. If there be no such person present, he will begin with the one nearest the altar, in the farthest row, on the gospel side. Then he goes to the corresponding person on the epistle side. He comes across to him who stands nearest the altar in the second row on the gospel side; then to the corresponding person on the epistle side; and so on for each row, however many there may be.[66] Each time he passes the altar he genuflects in the middle. In giving the pax, first he stands in front of him who will receive it, while this one bows to him. The subdeacon does not bow in return. Then, leaning forward he puts his hands on the shoulders of the other and almost touches the other's left cheek with his own while he says *Pax tecum.* The other answers *Et cum spiritu tuo.* Both then join the hands and bow to each other. But if he has to give the pax to a "greater prelate" (p. 57) it is a common practice to put his arms under those of the person who receives it. When he has given the pax to the head of each order in the choir he comes back to the foot of the altar with the MC. Here he genuflects, gives the pax to the MC, genuflects, goes up to the right hand of the celebrant, and stands there. If the celebrant has already commenced the *Domine, non sum dignus,* or if he is consuming the Sacred Host or the Precious Blood, he turns toward the altar and bows, waiting until the celebrant is finished. At *Domine, non sum dignus* he bows to the Sacred Host, not striking his breast.

Communion. During the celebrant's communion in each form the sub-deacon bows low towards the Sacred Host. Before the celebrant receives the Precious Blood he uncovers the Chalice. The usual sign for him to do this is that the celebrant touches the base of the Chalice. He genuflects each time with the celebrant. If Holy Communion is distributed the

---

[66] It suffices to give the pax to the first person *of each order* of clergy on each side (R., X, 8).

Chalice he covers the chalice again. If the subdeacon receives Holy Communion he kneels at the front of the top step (to the left if the deacon also communicates) without making any genuflection. He assists with the distribution of Holy Communion to the choir and to the faithful as described in § 12 below. After the communion the subdeacon uncovers the chalice and pours the wine into the chalice for the ablution, then he pours wine and water over the celebrant's fingers and hands him the purifier. He gives the cruets back to the acolyte; then he changes places with the deacon. The deacon carrying the missal now comes to the epistle side, the subdeacon to the gospel side. They genuflect, once only, in the middle together, the subdeacon behind the deacon. At the gospel side the subdeacon dries any ciboria and then the chalice with the purifier and then arranges this across the chalice, puts on it the paten and pall, folds the corporal and puts it in the burse, veils the chalice and lays the burse on it as at the beginning of Mass. He takes the chalice in his left hand, laying the right on the burse, and carries it to the credence without bowing, genuflecting as he passes the middle.

Postcommunion. He comes back from the credence and takes his place behind the celebrant and deacon, on the ground, in front of the lowest altar step. If the celebrant is at the centre of the altar the subdeacon genuflects on arriving at his place in the middle; otherwise he does not genuflect. He stands with joined hands behind the deacon, goes with him and the celebrant to the middle, and back to the epistle side. He then goes again to the middle and stands facing the altar while the deacon sings *Ite, missa est*, or other versicle. Then, while the celebrant says the prayer *Placeat tibi*, he goes up to the gospel side, to the same level as the deacon and to his left. He kneels on the edge of the footpace[67] with the deacon for the blessing, signing himself. Then he rises, goes to the end of the altar at the gospel side and assists the celebrant at the last Gospel, holding the altar-card or turning the pages of the missal.

Last Gospel. If the last Gospel is proper to the day,[68] after the *Ite, missa est* the subdeacon goes to the epistle side, takes the missal from the altar and carries it to the gospel side, genuflecting as he passes the middle. Then he comes back to the middle and kneels at the deacon's left on the footpace for the blessing. During the last Gospel he stands on the celebrant's left and makes the responses. If he is holding the altar-card he neither makes the sign of the cross at the beginning nor genuflects. When the last Gospel is finished, he answers *Deo gratias*, puts back the altar-card or shuts the book, comes down to the floor of the sanctuary with the celebrant and deacon, genuflects on the ground with the deacon, receives and puts on his biretta and goes to the sacristy in front of the deacon. He

[67] It is better that the deacon and subdeacon kneel apart, so as not to cut off the celebrant from the people as he blesses them.
[68] On Palm Sunday at Masses not preceded by the palm procession.

will bow to the choir, if this is to be done, with the celebrant and deacon, as he did on coming in, beginning with the side of greater dignity (p. 53).

In the sacristy he stands at the celebrant's left, bows with him to the cross and clergy and then salutes the celebrant. He first takes off his maniple and then assists the celebrant to unvest, if this is the custom.

If after Mass prayers for the sovereign, or other prayers, are to be said before the altar, the subdeacon stands there with the others and assists the celebrant, holding the book with the deacon.

Substitute for Subdeacon. For a reasonable cause the place of the subdeacon may be taken by a cleric in minor orders, or by one who is at least tonsured.[69] In this case he does not wear the maniple; he may not wipe the chalice nor pour water into it at the offertory, but leaves this to the deacon; after he has brought the chalice to the altar at the offertory he does not touch it, nor does he cover or uncover it. He does not clean the chalice or any ciboria after the ablutions; this is done by the celebrant. The cleric does, however, arrange the chalice, veil it and carry it back to the credence. Otherwise he fulfils all the office of a subdeacon.

§ 10. The Deacon

The deacon comes to the sacristy in due time before Mass begins, looks over the Gospel and the *Ite* (or *Benedicamus*), washes his hands, and puts on his vestments. He does not put on the maniple at all if the Asperges is to take place, and otherwise not until the celebrant has vested. He stands at the right of the celebrant and assists him to vest. At the sign from the MC he bows with uncovered head to the cross, then to the celebrant. He walks in the procession to the sanctuary, wearing the biretta, behind the subdeacon. But if the celebrant wears the cope, the deacon goes on his right, holding the edge of the cope with the orphrey turned in. If he receives holy water from the MC or subdeacon, he first uncovers, receives the water, presents it to the celebrant, and then signs himself and puts on his biretta. If on entering the choir they are to bow to the clergy, the deacon uncovers first, waits for the celebrant, takes his biretta—kissing the celebrant's hand and the biretta—and hands them to the MC. With the celebrant he then bows to the clergy on each side (first to the side of greater dignity). Otherwise he goes to the right of the celebrant before the altar and here takes his biretta with the *solita oscula*. Before the lowest altar step he genuflects[70] when the celebrant genuflects or bows,

---

[69] S.R.C. 4181. The Pontifical Commission *Ecclesia Dei* has confirmed that the practice of an instituted acolyte acting as subdeacon may be tolerated (7 June 1993, Prot. 24/92). It is essential that the substitute be adequately prepared. A layman acting thus does not wear the biretta.

[70] The first (and the last) genuflexion is made *in plano*. All others are made on the step.

then stands to begin the Mass. If before Mass there is the Asperges ceremony, see p. 108ff.

Throughout the service, when the deacon stands he joins his hands before his breast, unless he has to hold anything. When he holds something in his right hand he lays the left extended on his breast. When he sits he lays his hands extended on his knees. When he is by the side of the celebrant he genuflects with him whenever he genuflects. Whenever he hands anything to the celebrant he first kisses the thing, then the celebrant's hand. When he takes anything from him, he first kisses the hand, then the thing. These are the *solita oscula*.

Beginning of Mass. When Mass begins the deacon joins in the prayers at the altar steps, answering the celebrant with the subdeacon. He makes the sign of the cross each time with the celebrant. While the celebrant says the *Confiteor* the ministers do not bow. They bow to the celebrant while they say the prayer *Misereatur*. They bow low towards the altar while they say the *Confiteor*, and partly turn towards the celebrant at the words *tibi, Pater* and *te, Pater*. They remain bowed while the celebrant says *Misereatur*; they stand upright at the prayer *Indulgentiam*. They bow again moderately at the versicles *Deus, tu conversus*, etc.

Incensation. The deacon goes up to the altar with the celebrant, assisting him by slightly raising his alb at the front. At the altar he takes the incense-boat from the thurifer, and hands the spoon to the celebrant, saying *Benedicite, Pater reverende*, bowing slightly to him. Only if the celebrant is a bishop does he say *Pater reverendissime*. The deacon takes back the spoon from the celebrant. When the incense has been blessed he takes the thurible, holding the chains low down in the left hand; high up, just under the rings at the top, in the right. He hands it to the celebrant, kissing it at the disc on top to which are fixed the chains, and then the celebrant's hand.

While the celebrant incenses the altar the deacon accompanies him at his right, supporting him by putting his left hand under the celebrant's right arm,[71] and genuflecting whenever he genuflects or bows. Then he takes the thurible from the celebrant, first taking in his right hand the lower part near the cover, and then the top of the chains in his left. He comes down on the epistle side, and there (see fig. 6) incenses the celebrant with three double swings, bowing before and after. He hands the thurible to the thurifer and goes to the right of the celebrant on the highest step below the footpace. Here he will stand by the celebrant during the introit joining him in making the sign of the cross and bowing. The MC points to the place and turns the pages (fig. 7). The deacon

---

[71] C.E., I, ix, 1, 5. Should the celebrant be wearing a chasuble of ample proportions the deacon may hold it back to free the celebrant's right arm. "Raising the chasuble…is not only meaningless but unsightly and unbecoming as well;" O'Connell, *The Celebration of Mass*, 1964, p. 468 n. 37.

answers the *Kyrie.* If the celebrant and ministers are to sit while the choir finishes the *Kyrie,* at a sign from the MC the deacon turns to his right so as to be now at the celebrant's left, and goes with him and the subdeacon (without any reverence to the altar) to the sedilia. Here he takes the celebrant's biretta from the MC and gives it to the celebrant. Then he takes his own, waits till the celebrant sits, bows slightly to the subdeacon, sits and puts on his biretta. When they rise, the deacon first uncovers, stands, places his biretta on the sedilia, takes the celebrant's biretta, hands it to the MC and goes back to the altar by the longer way at the celebrant's right, bowing to the choir on either side (beginning on the epistle side) and genuflecting with him in the middle before they go up the steps.

Gloria in Excelsis. If they do not sit during the *Kyrie,* towards the end of the singing of this, on a signal from the MC, the deacon stands behind the celebrant, on the top step, and at another signal, goes with him to the centre, where the *Gloria* is intoned. He bows at the word *Deo,* then goes up to the celebrant's right, not genuflecting. Here he says the *Gloria* with the celebrant, bowing and making the sign of the cross with him. When they have said the *Gloria* the ministers genuflect where they stand, go with the celebrant to the sedilia and sit there, observing all that has been noted above (p. 127). With the others, the deacon uncovers and bows at the verses so marked (p. 105). Towards the end of the *Gloria* they go back to the altar as above at the sign from the MC. The deacon stands behind the celebrant on the highest step while *Dominus vobiscum* is sung and then goes to the epistle side behind the celebrant. He stands there during the collects (fig. 9), bowing to the missal when the celebrant does so.

After the collect(s) the celebrant goes to the sedilia and sits there to listen to the Epistle. The deacon accompanies him and ministers to him as at the *Gloria.* They return to the epistle corner of the altar after the chanting of the Epistle.

Extra Lessons. On certain days (e.g. on an Ember Saturday) a number of prayers and lessons may occur before the Epistle. The lessons are sung by a reader (lector). For each prayer the deacon and subdeacon stand behind the celebrant. If the admonition *Flectamus genua* is to be sung, the deacon sings it and kneels. After a moment's prayer he sings *Levate* and rises.

Preparation for the Gospel. When the subdeacon has been blessed, and the celebrant has read the gradual, etc., the deacon *in plano* receives the evangeliarium from the MC. He holds it, closed, before his breast, with both hands, so that the opening of the pages is to his left. He goes to the middle in front of the lowest altar step—having saluted the choir on his way—genuflects on the step and goes up to the altar. He lays the book on the table at the centre and then goes to assist at the putting in of incense at the gospel corner.

Gospel. When the incense has been blessed the deacon kneels on the edge of the footpace and, bowed, says the prayer *Munda cor meum*. Rising, he takes the book, kneels before the celebrant and asks the blessing, saying *Iube, domne, benedicere*. The celebrant turns towards the deacon, gives his blessing, saying *Dominus sit in corde tuo*, etc., and making the sign of the cross over the deacon. The celebrant lays his hand on the top of the closed book and the deacon kisses the hand.

The deacon rises, bows to the celebrant, and comes down the altar steps to the floor of the church where the subdeacon awaits him. He stands here, at the right of the subdeacon, still holding the closed evangeliarium (fig. 11). On a signal from the MC they genuflect on the step, bow to the choir — beginning this time on the epistle side — and go to the place where the Gospel is to be sung. In this procession the deacon walks by the subdeacon's side on his right.[72] When they arrive at the place (fig. 12) — well away from the altar — the subdeacon turns and faces the deacon, who puts the book into his hands,[73] opens it, and with joined hands sings *Dominus vobiscum*. When he sings *Sequentia* (or *Initium*) *sancti Evangelii* he makes the sign of the cross on the book with the thumb of his right hand at the place where the Gospel begins, laying the left hand meanwhile palm downwards on the book; then he lays his left hand on his breast and makes the sign of the cross with the right thumb on his forehead, lips and breast. He now takes the thurible from the MC, and incenses the book with three double swings, in the middle, to his left and to his right, bowing to it before and after. He gives the thurible back to the MC, joins his hands, and sings the Gospel. If required, the MC turns the pages. He bows or genuflects towards the book if any verse is so marked.

At the end of the Gospel[74] he lays the open right hand (palm upwards) at the place where it begins, to show it to the subdeacon. He then follows the MC, thurifer and acolytes back to the foot of the altar and there genuflects on the step at a sign from the MC. After the celebrant has kissed the book he receives the thurible from the thurifer and incenses the celebrant who stands on the footpace with three double swings (fig. 12a), bowing before and after, and gives back the thurible. He then goes and joins the celebrant. If there is to be a homily he goes to the celebrant's right, genuflects with him, and so accompanies him to the sedilia, where they sit in the usual manner. Should the celebrant himself preach, the ministers, having genuflected after the incensation with the celebrant, return to the sedilia.

Creed. If there is no homily, the deacon goes to his place behind the celebrant on the highest step and stands while *Credo in unum Deum* is

---

[72] R., VI, 5. At a pontifical Mass the subdeacon precedes the deacon; C.E., II, viii. 44.

[73] Unless he puts it on the lectern or ambo (p. 128).

[74] *Laus tibi, Christe* is not said.

intoned. He bows at the word *Deum*, goes, without genuflecting, to the celebrant's right, and there joins him in saying the *Credo*. He makes the sign of the cross, bows and genuflects with the celebrant. Then, when they have said the *Credo*, the celebrant and ministers reverence the altar and go to sit at the sedilia in the usual way. If there is no *Credo* the deacon goes to stand behind the celebrant at *Dominus vobiscum* and *Oremus* and all follows as below. He uncovers and bows when the celebrant does so at certain parts of the *Credo*. After the choir has sung the verse *Et homo factus est*, the deacon rises, leaves his biretta at his seat, and receives the burse from the MC. He holds this in both hands at about the level of the eyes, with the opening towards himself, and takes it to the altar. If he passes the celebrant he bows to him, lowering the burse to the level of his chest; he genuflects on the lowest altar step, goes up and puts the burse on the altar. Then he takes out the corporal and puts the burse leaning against a candlestick or the gradine, near the middle on the gospel side. He spreads the corporal before the altar cross, arranges the missal conveniently, genuflects there before the altar, not laying his hands on the table when he does so, and comes back by the shorter way to his seat. Here he takes his biretta, bows slightly to the subdeacon, sits and covers himself. Towards the end of the *Credo*, at the sign from the MC, the deacon, with the others, goes back to the altar by the longer way, with the usual bows to the choir.

Offertory. The deacon stands behind the celebrant while *Dominus vobiscum* and *Oremus* are sung. At the word *Oremus* he bows and goes at once to the celebrant's right. The subdeacon brings the chalice and paten and hands them to the deacon.[75] The deacon takes off the pall and puts it near the corporal. He takes the paten, with the altar-bread on it, hands it to the celebrant, kissing first the paten, then the celebrant's hand. If there is a ciborium with breads to be consecrated he uncovers this and holds it raised a little near where the celebrant holds the paten whilst he offers the bread.[76] When the offertory prayer is ended he covers the ciborium. He takes the chalice in his left hand, receives the wine cruet in his right from the subdeacon and pours in the wine, holding the purifier with the thumb of the left hand against the stem of the chalice. Usually the celebrant gives a sign to show how much wine should be put in. The subdeacon then puts in the water. The deacon wipes away any separate drops on the sides of the chalice, takes it by the stem in his right hand, holding the base in the left with the cross in the base to the front, and so passes it to the celebrant, kissing first the base of the chalice, then the celebrant's hand. As the celebrant lifts the chalice, to offer it, the deacon

---

[75] If there has been no *Credo* the subdeacon brings the burse on the chalice. The deacon then first spreads the corporal, leaning the burse against a candlestick or the gradine. While he does this the celebrant stands away a little, towards the gospel side.
[76] C.E., II, xxix, 2.

also holds it, touching the base with his right hand. He lays his left under his breast. Looking up towards the crucifix, he says the offertory prayer, *Offerimus tibi*, with the celebrant. When the celebrant sets the chalice on the corporal, the deacon covers it with the pall, hands the paten to the subdeacon, and covers it with the right end of the humeral veil. He then lays the purifier, folded in two, to the right of the corporal.

Incensation. He next assists at the blessing of incense in the usual way. He accompanies the celebrant while the altar is incensed, supporting him as before. At the incensing of the *oblata* he places his right hand on the base of the chalice and—if necessary—uses his left to hold back the chasuble. While the altar cross is incensed he moves the chalice to the upper right hand corner of the corporal, and holds back the chasuble if necessary. Then he puts the chalice back in the middle. He genuflects each time the celebrant bows or genuflects supporting the celebrant's elbows. At the end of the incensing of the altar he takes the thurible, goes down and incenses the celebrant as he did at the beginning of Mass, the thurifer standing at his left. Accompanied by the thurifer, he now incenses the choir, if there are clergy[77] present. First they genuflect in the middle, then the deacon incenses the choir on the gospel side.[78] He bows once to all on that side, incenses each cleric with one double swing of the thurible, then bows again.[79] He turns, genuflects at the middle and goes, in the same way, to incense those on the epistle side. On his return to the altar he genuflects, comes to the right of the subdeacon, turns and incenses him with two double swings. He hands the thurible to the thurifer, goes up to his place on the highest step behind the celebrant (not genuflecting again), turns and is himself incensed, bowing to the thurifer before and after. He turns towards the altar and does not genuflect. If he is at his place in time he answers the *Orate, fratres*; otherwise the subdeacon does so. During the preface he stands behind the celebrant. At its final words he goes, without genuflecting, to the right of the celebrant; bowing he says the *Sanctus* with him. He makes the sign of the cross at the word *Benedictus*. Then he goes to the left of the celebrant, genuflecting on the top step as he passes the middle.

Canon. During the canon the deacon stands at the celebrant's left, by the missal, pointing out the places and turning the pages. It is usual that

---

[77] Professed religious not in major orders or seminarians present in choir are treated as clergy in this respect, though they are incensed collectively, not individually (S.R.C. 2791 § 4). The deacon does not incense robed lay singers, or servers, if these alone are present in the choir stalls—the thurifer does this; they, too, are only ever incensed collectively. Cf. O'Connell, *The Celebration of Mass*, 1964 pp. 425ff.

[78] Or the side of greater dignity (see p. 53).

[79] If prelates or canons in chapter be present, the deacon incenses them (each with two double swings) first and bows to each separately before and after incensing him. When the choir is made of clergy of different ranks, divided between the two sides, the dignitaries and canons on *each* side must be incensed before the clergy of lower rank.

he stand back a step or two at the commemorations of the living and of the dead, that he may not hear the names spoken by the celebrant. At the words *Quam oblationem* he goes to the other side of the celebrant, genuflecting in the middle. If there is a ciborium on the corporal he opens it. He kneels (when the celebrant bows down to say the words of consecration) on the edge of the footpace, bowed, during the consecration, and lifts the end of the chasuble at the elevation of the Host (fig. 13). He rises at once, as the celebrant rises after his genuflexion at the end of this elevation, covers the ciborium, if there is one, and uncovers the chalice. Then he kneels, bowed, as before, and again lifts the chasuble as the Chalice is raised. Immediately after the elevation of the Chalice he rises again and covers it with the pall. Then he genuflects with the celebrant. He goes round to the left of the celebrant, genuflecting not in the middle but in the place at which he arrives. Here he stays indicating the places and turning the leaves. He does not strike his breast at *nobis quoque*.

At the words *Per quem hæc omnia* he genuflects and goes to the right of the celebrant again, not genuflecting in the middle. When the celebrant says *præstas nobis*, the deacon uncovers the Chalice, genuflects with the celebrant, and places the index and middle fingers of his right hand on the base of the Chalice. He covers it again after the little elevation when the celebrant has cleansed his fingers over the Chalice and genuflects with the celebrant.

Pater Noster. When the celebrant begins the *Pater noster* the deacon genuflects, turns to the left and goes behind the celebrant, on the highest step. Here he does not again genuflect, but stands there with joined hands during the *Pater Noster*. At the words *Et dimitte nobis* he genuflects with the subdeacon; both go to the epistle side, at the celebrant's right, the deacon nearer to the celebrant. He takes the paten from the subdeacon, cleans it with the purifier and hands it to the celebrant, with the *solita oscula*. He uncovers the Chalice, genuflects, as always, with the celebrant, covers the Chalice again when the Particle has been put into it and repeats the genuflexion. Standing there on the right, he joins in saying the *Agnus Dei*, bowing and striking his breast. When that prayer is ended he kneels on the right of the celebrant. When the celebrant has said the first communion prayer *Domine Iesu Christe, qui dixisti Apostolis tuis,* the deacon rises; with joined hands he kisses the altar at the same time as the celebrant, but outside the corporal; turns to the celebrant, bows, clasps his arms, holding them at the elbows, and receives the pax from him in the usual manner (p. 51). He bows again, genuflects to the Sacred Host, goes to the subdeacon and gives him the pax. According to the general rule, he bows only after having given it. Then — having again genuflected with the subdeacon — he goes up to the celebrant's left. He bows low at the celebrant's communion. If he is to receive Holy

Communion he kneels at the front of the top step (to the right if the subdeacon also communicates) without making any genuflection. He assists with the distribution of Holy Communion to the choir and to the faithful as described in § 12 below.

Postcommunion. After the ablutions the deacon takes the missal to the epistle side, genuflecting in the middle only. He then takes his place on the highest step behind the celebrant for the *Communio*. He follows the celebrant to the middle for the *Dominus vobiscum* and goes behind him to the epistle side for the postcommunions.[80] After these he goes with the celebrant and subdeacon to the middle. The celebrant sings *Dominus vobiscum*. The deacon turns towards the people, with his back to the celebrant, and sings *Ite, missa est*. If he has to sing either *Benedicamus Domino*[81] or *Requiescant in pace,* he does not turn, but sings the versicle facing the altar. When the celebrant has said the prayer *Placeat tibi,* the deacon steps a little towards the epistle side facing the altar and kneels on the edge of the footpace for the blessing.[82] At the blessing he makes the sign of the cross. During the last Gospel he stands at the place where he is with joined hands.[83] He makes the sign of the cross with the right thumb on forehead, lips and breast, and genuflects with the celebrant at the words *Et Verbum caro factum est*. If he is at the right of the celebrant he turns by his left and comes down to the ground with the celebrant and the subdeacon. He genuflects with them, takes the celebrant's biretta from the MC and hands it to him, takes his own, covers himself after the celebrant has done so, and so goes to the sacristy behind the subdeacon, bowing (uncovered) to the choir, if this is to be done, as when they came in. If, on occasion, prayers are said after Mass, he stands with the others before the altar and holds the book with the subdeacon. In the sacristy he takes off the biretta, bows to the cross and to the clergy; salutes the celebrant and takes off the maniple. He assists the celebrant to unvest and then he himself unvests.

§ 11. The Celebrant of Solemn Mass

The priest who is to sing solemn Mass, after having made his preparation, comes to the place of vesting, looks over the prayers and preface, washes his hands saying the appointed prayer, and vests (the ministers having already done so), saying the prayers in the missal as he puts on each vestment. If he is to bless water or if the Asperges takes

---

[80] In Lent when *oratio super populum* is to be sung the deacon turns towards the people by his left when the priest sings *Oremus* for the second or third time and chants *Humiliate capita vestra Deo*. He then turns back to the altar without completing the circle.

[81] This occurs only when a procession is to follow the Mass immediately.

[82] He keeps a little to the right, not to cut off the celebrant from the people he is blessing.

[83] O'Connell holds that he may stand at the right or left of the celebrant; cf. *The Celebration of Mass*, 1964, p. 514. This stance has no basis in the rubrics which are silent on this matter.

place (see § 4 above) he does not put on the maniple until later. He waits there, between the deacon and subdeacon, wearing the biretta, till the MC gives the sign. Uncovering he then bows to the cross in the sacristy, to the deacon and subdeacon, covers again, and follows the rest of the procession in the last place.[84] If the deacon give him holy water on leaving the sacristy, he uncovers to make the sign of the cross. If the procession passes an altar where the Blessed Sacrament is reserved the celebrant uncovers and genuflects to it. If the members of the choir are in their places, and are to be saluted, he uncovers at the entrance of the choir, gives his biretta to the deacon, and bows first to the side of greater dignity. Otherwise he goes straight to the altar steps. Here he uncovers.

If the Blessed Sacrament is reserved at the high altar he genuflects,[85] if not he bows low to the altar. For the Asperges ceremony see p. 108ff.

Voice. At solemn Mass the celebrant sings *Dominus vobiscum* whenever it occurs (except before ascending the altar at the beginning of Mass), the prayers, *Oremus* after the offertory antiphon, *Per omnia sæcula sæculorum* of the secret, the preface, *Per omnia,* etc., at the conclusion of the canon, *Pater noster,* and *Per omnia,* etc., before *Pax Domini.* He intones the *Gloria* and *Credo.*

All other parts that are said by the celebrant aloud *(clara voce)* in low Mass are said softly *(secreto)* in solemn Mass, except the prayers before distributing Holy Communion and the blessing at the end of Mass. The prayers said secretly at low Mass (the offertory prayers, canon, communion prayers, etc.) are said in this same voice at solemn Mass. The parts to which the sacred ministers reply are said in a subdued voice that can be heard by them.

Beginning of Mass. Standing before the lowest altar step, between the ministers, the celebrant begins the Mass. He bows low while he says the *Confiteor.* At the words *vobis, fratres* and *vos, fratres* he turns first towards the deacon, then to the subdeacon. He remains bowed while the ministers say the *Misereatur.* He does not bow to them when they bow to him during the *Confiteor* but he does bow for *Misereatur vestri.* He goes up to the altar saying *Aufer a nobis,* etc., kisses it in the middle and turns right. The deacon presents the spoon saying *Benedicite, Pater reverende* and the celebrant puts incense into the thurible three times, saying as he does so *Ab illo benedicaris / in cuius honore / cremaberis. Amen.* He returns the spoon to the deacon, joins his hands momentarily, and makes the sign of the cross over the thurible. While he puts the incense into the thurible and blesses it — saying nothing — he lays the left hand on the breast. This is the invariable way in which incense is blessed. The deacon hands him the thurible and he proceeds to incense the altar. If the Blessed Sacrament be reserved in the tabernacle, he first genuflects (resting the three

---

[84] If he wears the cope he walks between the ministers, who hold its ends.
[85] *In plano* — all genuflexions henceforth are on the step, save the final one which is *in plano.*

extended fingers of his left hand on the table of the altar), otherwise he
bows low towards the altar cross. He incenses the altar cross with three
double swings. Then he either genuflects or bows, as he did before. If
there are relics or images between the candlesticks he next incenses them,
first those on the gospel side, making two double swings of the thurible
for all of them together, without moving himself from the middle of the
altar, or bowing to them. He again bows to the cross, or genuflects to the
Blessed Sacrament, and incenses in the same way those on the epistle
side. Then, without bowing or genuflecting, he continues the incensing of
the altar (see fig. 4a). He walks before the altar to the epistle side; as he
does so he incenses it over the back part of the mensa or table, with three
single swings of the thurible, one opposite each of the altar candles.[86] At
the epistle corner he lowers his hand and swings the thurible twice along
the side, first low down, then higher up; then he returns to the middle,
again making three single swings along the front part of the table and
bows or genuflects. He now does the same on the gospel side; first three
single swings towards the candlesticks over the mensa, and then two at
the gospel end. Having finished this, he remains standing still at the
gospel end and incenses the front of the table of the altar at that side with
three single swings. Then, still at the gospel corner, he lowers the thurible
and incenses the front of the altar itself three times at the gospel side and
three at the epistle side, meanwhile walking towards the epistle corner
and genuflecting or bowing as he passes the middle. So he arrives at the
epistle end of the altar; here he hands the thurible to the deacon. At the
epistle end of the altar, having given the thurible to the deacon, the
celebrant stands facing him with hands joined and his left side to the altar
and is incensed, bowing slightly before and after.

If the altar be free standing (see fig. 4b), the celebrant — having
incensed the cross and any relics or images as described above — makes
three single swings towards the candlesticks over the near side of the
mensa on the epistle side, and then two at the epistle end, low down and
past the end. He continues around, making the next six swings over the
mensa of the rear side as he walks behind the altar, and making two
swings at the gospel end, low down as before. He then makes three single
swings towards the candlesticks over the mensa on the gospel side. Then,
still at the gospel corner, he lowers the thurible and incenses the front of
the altar itself three times at the gospel side and three times at the front of
the altar on the epistle side, meanwhile walking towards the epistle
corner and genuflecting or bowing as he passes the middle.

Introit. Turning to the altar, on the signal from the MC he says the
introit and *Kyrie, eleison,* the deacon and subdeacon answering. If the

---

[86] The candles are only convenient directions. Not they, but the altar is incensed. It is
incensed three times on either side, whatever the number of candlesticks may be. The
thurible is swung out in a straight line, not in semi-circles.

singing of the *Kyrie* takes much time, so that the celebrant and ministers sit during it, the MC gives a sign. The celebrant goes to the sedilia, without genuflecting or bowing, between the deacon and subdeacon. He sits first, takes his biretta from the deacon, and puts it on. While he sits he lays his hands stretched out, with the palms downwards, on his knees. When they rise, the ministers rise first; the celebrant uncovers, hands his biretta to the deacon, then stands. He goes back to the altar by the longer way, bowing to the choir (first on the epistle side), bows to the altar at the foot of the steps, or genuflects on the step if the Blessed Sacrament be reserved, and from there goes up the steps. This is the invariable rule for sitting at the sedilia and returning to the altar. If the sacred ministers do not sit, on the signal of the MC during the last *Kyrie* he turns by his left to go to the centre of the altar.

At centre of the altar the celebrant intones *Gloria in excelsis Deo*, and then continues with the ministers in a subdued voice, bowing at the appropriate words. At the end he bows, or genuflects, and they go to the sedilia as before. The celebrant uncovers and bows during the sung *Gloria* at the special verses so noted.

Collect(s). When he returns to the altar he kisses it in the middle, turns to the people and sings *Dominus vobiscum*. Then he goes to the epistle side and sings the collect(s).[87] After the last collect he goes to the sedilia and sits to listen to the singing of the Epistle. Where extra lessons are read (on Ember days) he goes to the sedilia with the ministers, returning to the altar for each prayer.

Blessing Subdeacon. After the singing of the Epistle the celebrant returns to the epistle corner of the altar and there blesses the subdeacon, turning to him and laying his right hand on the top of the closed book, the left being placed under his breast. The subdeacon kisses the celebrant's hand; the celebrant makes the sign of the cross over the subdeacon, saying nothing. The celebrant reads the gradual, etc., up to *Munda cor* exclusively.

Gospel. The celebrant then goes to the centre of the altar and, when the subdeacon has moved the missal and the deacon has laid the evangeliarium on the altar, he puts in and blesses incense for the Gospel. Then he blesses the deacon, with the form *Dominus sit in corde tuo*, etc., and puts his hand on the book of the Gospels to be kissed by the deacon. He returns to the epistle corner of the altar and stands there with joined hands, facing the altar, till the deacon sings *Dominus vobiscum*. Then he turns to his left to face the deacon. When the latter sings *Sequentia sancti Evangelii*, etc., the celebrant also makes the sign of the cross with the thumb on forehead, lips and breast. If the Holy Name is sung, or the

---

[87] Should *Flectamus genua* be sung by the deacon the celebrant kneels until *Levate* is sung (R.G., n. 440).

name of the Blessed Virgin or of the saint of the feast, he bows. If a genuflexion is to be made, he faces the altar and rests his hands on it.

At the end of the sung Gospel the subdeacon brings the evangeliarium to the celebrant and shows him the place where it begins. The celebrant, holding the book with both hands, kisses it at this place, saying *Per evangelica dicta,* etc. Standing at the same place, he is then incensed by the deacon, bowing slightly before and after (see fig. 12a).

Homily. If there is a homily he goes to the sedilia in the usual way unless he is himself the preacher; at the end he comes back by the longer way to the altar. If the celebrant himself preaches, he may do so at the altar at the gospel side or he may go to the pulpit (conducted there by the MC). The removal of his maniple or of his chasuble is not required by the rubrics (though customary in some places). The ministers sit at the sedilia. At the end of the homily they join the celebrant when he arrives from the pulpit and go with him, in the usual (longer) way, to the altar. Should another preacher bow to the celebrant before or after the homily, the celebrant uncovers and bows in return.

Creed. Standing at the middle of the altar he intones *Credo in unum Deum,* and continues in the subdued voice with the ministers when they arrive beside him. He genuflects slowly while saying the verse *Et incarnatus est,* etc. At the end of the recitation of the *Credo,* with the ministers, he goes to the sedilia and sits as before. He uncovers and bows at the special verses and at the words *Et incarnatus est,* etc.[88] If there is no *Credo,* as soon as he is incensed after the Gospel he goes at once to the middle and continues Mass, as follows.

Offertory. On returning to the altar after the *Credo* the celebrant kisses it, turns and sings *Dominus vobiscum;* then, turning back, sings *Oremus;* he then reads the offertory antiphon. He takes the paten from the deacon and says the prayer for the offering of the bread, *Suscipe, sancte Pater,* after which he puts the bread on the corporal, in the middle to the front, and puts the paten half under the middle of the right hand side of the corporal. He indicates to the deacon when sufficient wine has been poured into the chalice and then blesses the water, held by the subdeacon, with the usual form, laying meanwhile his left hand on the altar. He continues the prayer with hands joined. The deacon hands him the chalice; holding it up he says the prayer *Offerimus tibi* with the deacon.

At solemn Mass the celebrant never covers nor uncovers the chalice himself.[89] When this is required he usually gives a sign to the deacon by

---

[88] At the three Masses on Christmas Day and at Mass on the feast of the Annunciation (or on the day to which it is transferred) the celebrant and sacred ministers kneel on the lowest step at the epistle side, or in front, and bow during the singing of these words. Cf. p. 123. It may be more convenient to wait until this has occurred before going to the sedilia.
[89] Except the one case when a clerk, not ordained subdeacon, acts as such and the deacon is not at hand (see p. 133).

touching its base. When he has said the prayers *In spiritu humilitatis* and *Veni, sanctificator*, he puts incense into the thurible in the usual way. But here there is a special formula for blessing it, *Per intercessionem beati Michælis*, etc. He takes the thurible and incenses the *oblata*. In doing this he makes the sign of the cross jointly over the bread and chalice three times with the thurible; he then forms two circles round them counter clockwise, and one circle clockwise (see fig. 5). Meanwhile he says the prayer *Incensum istud a te benedictum*, etc., as in the missal. Then he incenses the cross and the altar, as before the introit, this time saying *Dirigatur, Domine, oratio mea*, etc. The celebrant is silent whilst incensing relics or images. At the epistle corner he hands the thurible to the deacon, saying *Accendat in nobis Dominus*. He is himself incensed; then he turns to the acolytes and washes his hands—and not just the tips of his fingers as at Low Mass—saying the *Lavabo*. He comes back to the middle and continues Mass as at low Mass.

Canon. He sings the preface, *Pater noster* and *Pax*. Otherwise there is no difference from low Mass, till the end of the first communion prayer *Domine Iesu Christe qui dixisti*, except that the deacon uncovers and covers the Chalice and presents the paten. The elevation must not take place until the choir has sung the *Sanctus* up to the first *Hosanna in excelsis*—if necessary the celebrant extends the *Memento* or pauses before commencing the *Qui pridie*.[90]

At the end of this prayer the celebrant kisses the altar, and, without genuflecting, turns to the deacon at his right and gives him the pax in the usual form (p. 51). Then, turning again to the altar and bowed as before, he says the second and third prayers before his communion, and so continues.

Holy Communion is distributed to the sacred ministers, to the choir and to the faithful as described in § 12 below.

After communion the celebrant, standing at the centre of the altar, holds out the chalice that the subdeacon may pour in wine, then wine and water for the ablutions. Leaving the chalice (undried), paten, pall and purifier unarranged at the middle, he goes to the epistle side and reads the communion antiphon.

Postcommunion. When the choir has finished the communion antiphon, or any extra singing, he comes to the middle for the *Dominus vobiscum*, then goes back to the epistle side for the postcommunions. He turns by his left and goes to the middle, sings *Dominus vobiscum* and remains facing the people while the deacon sings *Ite, missa est*, but faces the altar if the form be *Benedicamus Domino* or *Requiescant in pace*.[91] Facing the altar and bowing he says the prayer *Placeat tibi*. If there is a last

---

[90] C.E., II, viii, 70.

[91] The celebrant does not say *Ite, missa est* while the deacon sings it; but he does say in a low voice *Benedicamus Domino* or *Requiescant* (S.R.C. 2572 § 22).

Gospel proper to the day, the celebrant should wait before giving the blessing, that the subdeacon may have time to carry the missal across. He turns to give the blessing[92] and says the last Gospel *secreto*. Then he may descend at once to the foot of the altar or he may first go to the middle and bow to the cross. At the foot he bows or genuflects, takes his biretta from the deacon, bows to the choir (if this is to be done), covers himself (when outside the choir if the clergy remain) and follows the procession, himself last, to the sacristy. If prayers are to be said or sung after Mass, the celebrant stands for them and bows or genuflects when they are finished.[93]

In the sacristy he uncovers and with the ministers bows to the cross and then to the clergy, if they are present, on either side, beginning normally with those on the right, and to the deacon and subdeacon, and unvests.

§ 12. The Distribution of Holy Communion

Any Catholic has a right to present himself for Holy Communion at any Mass, on condition that he is in a state of grace and fasting.[94] For the distribution of Holy Communion at solemn Mass (which is required on Maundy Thursday), the following rules are to be observed.

After the *Pax* the MC gives a sign to the members of the choir, if they will receive Holy Communion. Priests and deacons wear a stole of the colour of the Mass or white. Communicants come to the middle of the sanctuary in pairs (higher rank in front), without birettas, their hands joined.

The torch-bearers do not leave after the elevation, but stay kneeling till after the communion.

The members of the choir who do not make their communion kneel during the distribution of Holy Communion. When the celebrant has received the Precious Blood, the subdeacon covers the Chalice and puts it aside towards the epistle side, but not outside the corporal. The deacon and subdeacon genuflect and change places, the deacon going to the right of the celebrant, the subdeacon to his left. The celebrant and ministers genuflect,[95] the deacon opens the ciborium and moves it to the middle of the corporal; all three genuflect.

---

[92] He should wait till the sung response, *Deo gratias*, is finished. He says the formula of blessing just as at low Mass, that is to say, loud enough to be heard by all (R., XII, 1, 7).

[93] Regarding the prayers for the Sovereign, cf. Chapter XIII § 3.

[94] One must abstain for at least one hour before Holy Communion from all food and drink except water and medicine (1983 C.I.C., canon 919 § 1).

[95] Supposing that the ciborium is on the altar, as when the particles have been consecrated at the Mass. If it is in the tabernacle, the deacon first opens the tabernacle, then they genuflect.

Shortly before this the acolytes, or, if they hold torches, the MC and the thurifer, take the communion cloth (should it be used), come with it to the middle before the lowest step, genuflect, separate, each holding one end of the cloth, and go to kneel at the ends of the footpace, facing each other and holding the cloth stretched across between them.

The celebrant takes the ciborium in his left hand, holds a consecrated Particle in the right above it, and says *Ecce Agnus Dei*. Meanwhile the deacon and subdeacon, if they are to receive Holy Communion, come round to the other side of the communion cloth, and kneel there. So the celebrant gives them Holy Communion over the cloth. The deacon and subdeacon, if they receive Holy Communion, always do so before anyone else. The ministers then go to the celebrant's side, the deacon at his right, on the gospel side, the subdeacon at the epistle side. The deacon takes the paten and holds it under the chin of each communicant while Holy Communion is given.[96] The subdeacon stands at the celebrant's left with joined hands.

The members of the choir who are to receive Holy Communion look at the Sacred Host at *Ecce Agnus Dei* and strike the breast at each *Domine, non sum dignus*. After the third *Domine, non sum dignus* the communicants all rise. As soon as the ministers have made their communion, the first two members of the choir genuflect, come forward and kneel on the edge of the footpace, or on the highest step below it. While they are receiving, the second two come to the foot of the altar, genuflect and wait there. When the first two have received Holy Communion, they rise and stand aside to make room for the next two, who then ascend while the first pair descends. The third pair comes forward; all four genuflect together. This is repeated as long as Holy Communion is distributed. Those who have made their communion go back to their places in choir and there kneel, holding their birettas, until *Dominus vobiscum*. The MC and servers receive Holy Communion after the clergy of the choir. If there is no one in holy orders, they do so before the members of the choir. When the torch-bearers are about to come up for Holy Communion they hand their torches to others, to hold till they come back to take them again. If the number of communicants is uneven, at the end three approach together. If there are many communicants, and if there is room, they may approach four at a time, instead of two.

When the members of the choir have done so, the acolytes, or those who hold the communion cloth, come to the middle, fold it, genuflect, and take it back to the credence. The celebrant and ministers then go to the communion rail and give Holy Communion to the people. The deacon may hold the paten under the chin of each communicant; the subdeacon attends as before.

---

[96] Cf. O'Connell, *The Celebration of Mass*, 1964, p. 509.

After communion, if the altar has no tabernacle, the celebrant consumes the remaining Hosts. The ciborium is then purified by the celebrant and wiped by the subdeacon, then the chalice. If there is a tabernacle, the deacon puts the ciborium into it, the celebrant and both ministers genuflecting before and after. The celebrant purifies the paten into the Chalice. The ministers change sides, genuflecting in the middle.

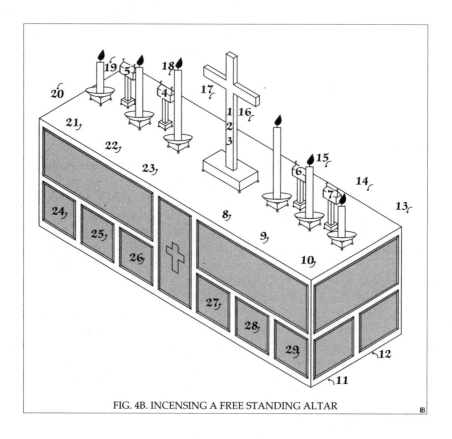

FIG. 4B. INCENSING A FREE STANDING ALTAR

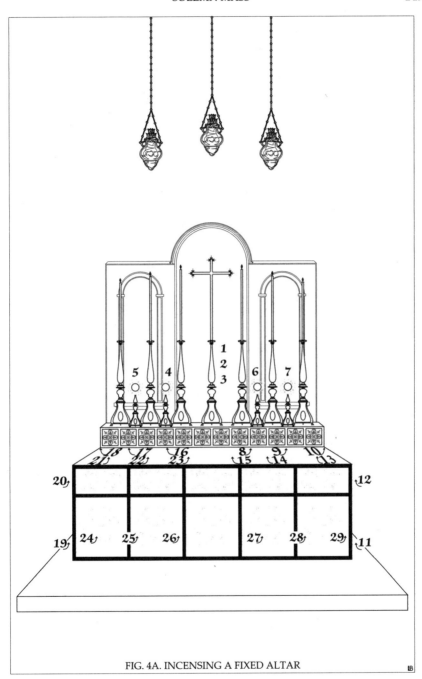

FIG. 4A. INCENSING A FIXED ALTAR

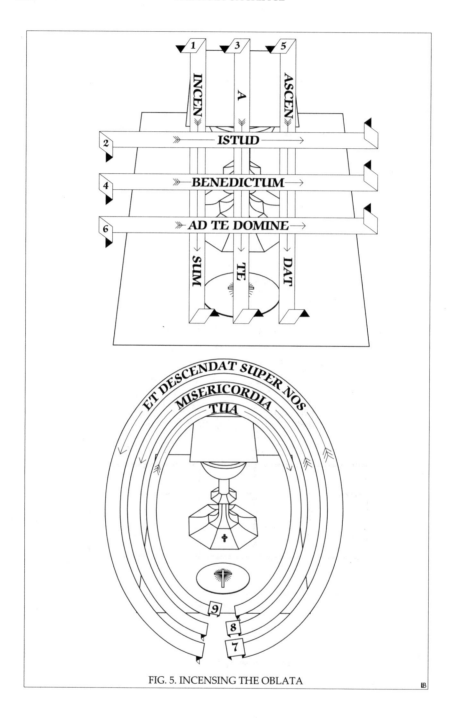

FIG. 5. INCENSING THE OBLATA

Figures
of
Solemn Mass

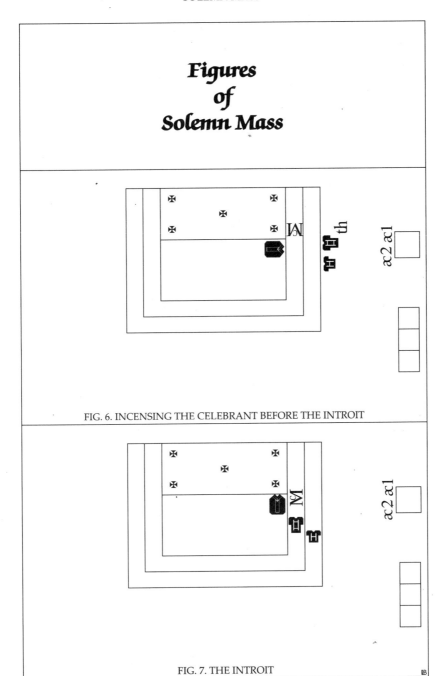

FIG. 6. INCENSING THE CELEBRANT BEFORE THE INTROIT

FIG. 7. THE INTROIT

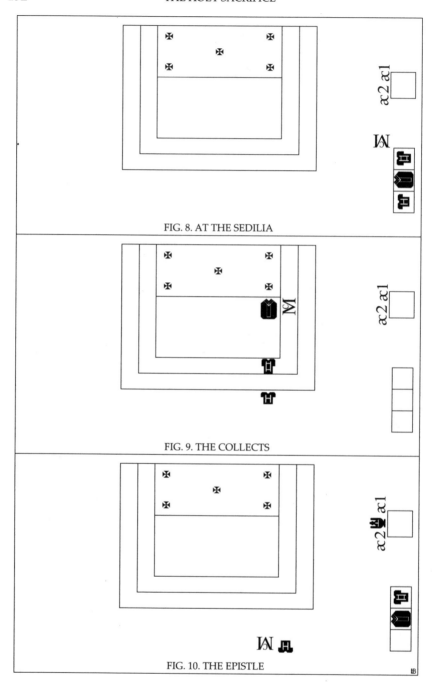

FIG. 8. AT THE SEDILIA

FIG. 9. THE COLLECTS

FIG. 10. THE EPISTLE

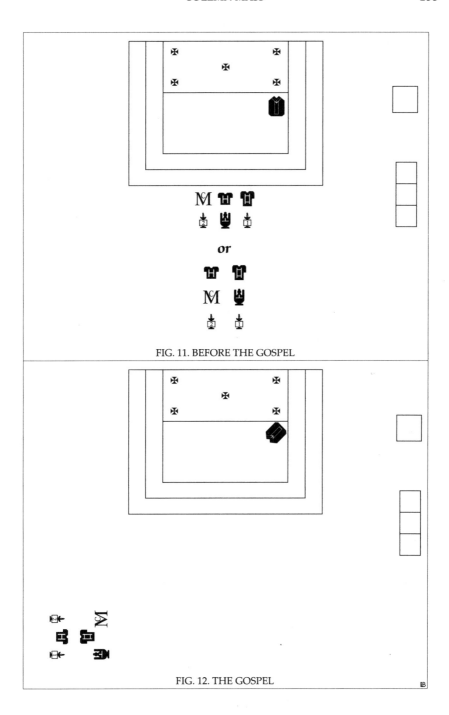

FIG. 11. BEFORE THE GOSPEL

FIG. 12. THE GOSPEL

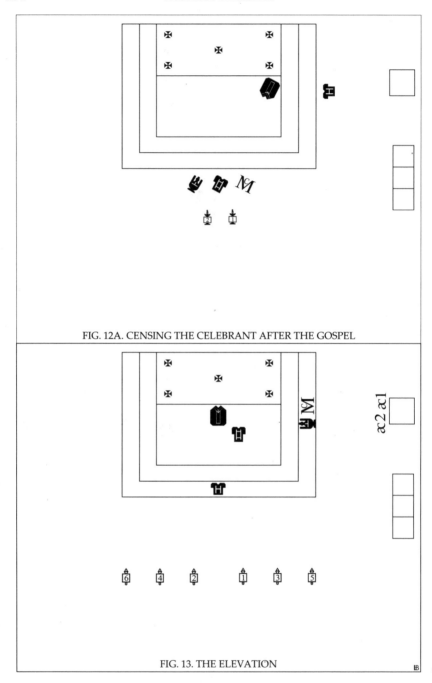

FIG. 12A. CENSING THE CELEBRANT AFTER THE GOSPEL

FIG. 13. THE ELEVATION

Chapter XII

Some Special Forms of Solemn Mass

§ 1. Solemn Mass for the Dead

AT Mass for the Dead certain special rules are observed.[1] The vestments are black. The altar frontal should also be black. If the Blessed Sacrament be reserved on the altar the conopæum of the tabernacle must be violet. (It is never allowed to use a black conopæum on the tabernacle.) The frontal should then be violet also.[2] It is becoming that the altar candles be of unbleached wax. The carpet—which is violet (if the Blessed Sacrament be present) or black—in front of the altar covers only the footpace, not the altar steps. The seats are bare or covered in black or violet. On the credence are placed the chalice, cruets and all that is needed for solemn Mass, also candles to be given to the clergy; and the holy-water vessel and sprinkler, if the Absolution will follow. No humeral veil is required. Incense is not wanted till the offertory.

The prayers are sung in the simple ferial tone.[3] The organ may not be played, except if it be necessary to sustain the chant at Mass, then it should be silent when the singing ceases.

All kisses of hands or of things (handed to or received from the celebrant) are omitted.[4] The salutations to the choir are as usual.

Beginning of Mass. The acolytes carry their candles as usual in the procession to the altar and back to the sacristy, and leave them lighted on the credence during the Mass. The altar is not incensed at the beginning of Mass, but the ministers go up to the altar with the celebrant, as usual, and stand at his sides. They do not genuflect when the celebrant kisses the altar. They go, with the celebrant, to the epistle side for the introit. At the introit the celebrant does not make the sign of the cross on himself. He lays the left hand on the altar and makes the cross over the book with the right. The ministers do not make the sign at all.

During the collects and postcommunion prayers the clergy in the choir kneel and the acolytes at the credence. After the Epistle the subdeacon does not go to be blessed by the celebrant, but returns the book of lessons to the MC or thurifer and joins the deacon.

---

[1] R., XIII; C.E., II, xi.
[2] S.R.C. 3201 § 10, 3562.
[3] Cf. O'Connell, *The Celebration of Mass*, 1964, p. 443.
[4] R., XIII, 2; C.E., I, xviii, 16; II, xi, 5.

After the Epistle, candles may be distributed to the clergy in choir by the acolytes. They light these just before the Gospel, and the clergy hold them lighted during the Gospel, and then extinguish them. They also hold them lighted from the *Sanctus* till the end of the communion.

Sequence. When the celebrant has read the gradual, tract and sequence, if it occurs, should he wish to sit he goes, without a reverence and by the shortest way, with the ministers to the bench. They go back to the altar (by the front) at about the verse *Qui Mariam absolvisti* of the sequence. After the reverence the celebrant goes up to the epistle corner of the altar; the subdeacon remains at its foot. The deacon leaves the book of the Gospels on the table of the altar as usual.

Before the Gospel the deacon kneels as usual to say the *Munda cor meum*, but he does not go to receive the celebrant's blessing.

No incense is blessed before the Gospel, nor is the book incensed. In the procession the order is: the MC, then the deacon, next the subdeacon and last of all the acolytes (not carrying their candles).

After the Gospel the celebrant is not incensed, nor does the subdeacon take him the book to be kissed. Instead he hands it at once to the MC, who takes it later to the credence. The ministers return in procession, in the order in which they came, and go to their places behind the celebrant, genuflect there and stand while he sings *Dominus vobiscum* and *Oremus*.

Offertory. Then the deacon, not genuflecting, goes to the right of the celebrant. The subdeacon genuflects, goes to the credence, takes the chalice covered by the chalice veil and burse (without the humeral veil) and carries it to the altar. The deacon spreads the corporal; the subdeacon uncovers the chalice, handing the chalice veil to the second acolyte. He pours water into the chalice, not asking for the blessing. The subdeacon does not hold the paten at requiem Masses, so he goes at once to the left of the celebrant, genuflecting on the lowest step as he passes the middle. After the offering of the chalice, the deacon puts the paten so that part of it lies under the corporal, as at low Mass; he covers the other part with the purifier. Incense is blessed as usual; the *oblata* and altar are incensed. But then only the celebrant is incensed, not the ministers nor choir. The ministers may wash the celebrant's hands,[5] the deacon taking the hand-towel, the subdeacon the water cruet and dish. Or this may be done, as usual, by the acolytes, in which case the ministers stand in line behind the celebrant as during the collects. In any case they will be in line behind the celebrant after the washing of hands. The deacon answers *Orate, fratres*. If torchbearers are used there are two or four, but no more.[6] At the end of the preface the deacon goes to the right of the celebrant, the subdeacon to his left, to join with him in saying the *Sanctus*, as usual. Then the subdeacon goes down to the middle in front of the lowest step,

[5] Cf. O'Connell, *The Celebration of Mass*, 1964, p. 538 n. 37.
[6] C.E. II, xi, 7.

and stands there with joined hands. The deacon goes to the book and assists the celebrant. At the words *Quam oblationem* the deacon, as usual, goes round to the celebrant's right; the subdeacon, without genuflecting, goes to the epistle side, kneels on the lowest step facing the gospel side of the sanctuary, takes the thurible from the thurifer (who has already had incense put in by the MC) and incenses the Sacred Host with three double swings of the thurible at each elevation. He then rises, hands the thurible back to the thurifer, goes to his place in the middle, genuflects and stands there till *Pax Domini sit semper vobiscum*. The acolytes, or other servers, who have come to kneel with torches before the elevation, stay kneeling until after the communion. The members of the choir kneel from the *Sanctus* to the end of the canon, inclusive.

Pater Noster. Towards the end of the Lord's Prayer (at *Et dimitte nobis*) the deacon genuflects, goes to the celebrant's right and hands him the paten without kissing it. He remains standing there. Just before *Agnus Dei* the subdeacon genuflects and goes to the celebrant's left. They say *Agnus Dei* (in the special form for requiems) with the celebrant, not striking the breast. There is no kiss of peace; so the ministers change their places at once, each genuflecting before and after.

After the last *Dominus vobiscum* the deacon, not turning round, sings *Requiescant in pace* (always in the plural). The celebrant should say this in a low voice. There is no blessing. The subdeacon goes at once to the gospel corner and holds the altar-card for the last Gospel.

If the Absolution follows,[7] the last Gospel is omitted and the thurifer must prepare the thurible during the ablutions and postcommunion.

Homily. If a homily or panegyric about the dead person is preached, it comes at the end of Mass, before the Absolution. The preacher wears no surplice, but only a cassock and "ferraiolo" or his religious habit. A bishop or prelate may wear the rochet and either the mozzetta or the mantelletta according to circumstances.

§ 2. Solemn Mass Before the Blessed Sacrament Exposed

Solemn Mass before the Blessed Sacrament exposed occurs, for example, on the third day of the Forty Hours' Prayer. The Mass will proceed as usual except for the rules given on p. 88ff. and for the following points: If the Asperges be done (*a*) the altar is not sprinkled; (*b*) if the people are sprinkled from the entrance to the sanctuary, the sacred ministers will stand somewhat to the gospel side (not to turn their backs on the Blessed Sacrament).

All who arrive in the sanctuary make a double genuflexion and do the same before departing from it. During the function, within the sanctuary,

---

[7] Cf. Chapter XXXI. There is no law that Absolution at a catafalque must follow a requiem Mass when this Mass is not the exequial one.

all genuflexions are single. The salutations to the choir are omitted (except for the incensation and the kiss of peace). The biretta is not worn and the clergy and sacred ministers sit as little as possible.

The deacon and subdeacon omit such *oscula* as are not inherent in the rite of solemn Mass but are merely acts of ceremonial courtesy towards the celebrant.[8]

They follow these rules for their genuflexions: they genuflect (i) *at the middle* of the altar (only): *(a)* when they arrive there or pass it when not coming from the side of the celebrant; *(b)* when they leave it to go to the side of the celebrant or of the altar; (ii) *on leaving, but not on arriving,* when they leave the side of the altar, or of the celebrant to go to the centre, and vice versa; (iii) *on leaving and on arriving,* when they pass from one side of the altar to the other.

The incensation of the altar and choir is as usual, but *(a)* on each occasion before incensing the altar (after the incensation of the *oblata* at the offertory) the celebrant, kneeling on the edge of the footpace, incenses the Blessed Sacrament (with three double swings), bowing before and after;[9] *(b)* the cross (if there) is not incensed; *(c)* the thurifer stands somewhat to the gospel side to incense the people.

To be incensed and to wash his fingers the celebrant leaves the footpace and stands (on a step or *in plano*) facing the congregation.

The kiss of peace is as usual. The deacon genuflects before turning to sing *Ite,* turns only partly, and genuflects again on turning back to the altar.[10] At the Blessing the celebrant having said *Benedicat...Deus,* genuflects, then partly turns for *Pater,* etc. and turns back the same way. He does not sign the altar at the beginning of the last Gospel if the Blessed Sacrament is on the table of the altar.

---

[8] Hence the kissing of the altar, book, hand of the celebrant after the Epistle and before the Gospel, of the paten and chalice, are *not* omitted.

[9] The clergy in choir need not kneel for this. The subdeacon (holding the paten at the offertory incensation) does not kneel.

[10] For *Benedicamus* he does not genuflect.

Chapter XIII

Sung Mass (*Missa Cantata*)
Without Deacon and Subdeacon

§ 1. The Simpler Form

There are two ways of celebrating a sung Mass without sacred ministers. The rules for the choir are the same as those for solemn Mass in any case.[1]

The first way supposes no servers but two acolytes, or even one. In this case the ceremonies are almost the same as at low Mass (for which see p. 65ff.). The only differences are these: The servers do not say those responses which the choir sings. When the celebrant sits at the seat, that is during the sung *Gloria in excelsis, Credo* (and possibly the *Kyrie, eleison* and sequence) the acolytes go to the middle, genuflect, go to the sedilia. The first acolyte arranges the chasuble over the sedilia then hands the biretta to the celebrant with the usual kisses. They stand on either side of the celebrant, facing each other, with joined hands.[2] The first acolyte takes the biretta from the celebrant before he rises, with the same *solita oscula*, and lifts the chasuble from the seat. They follow him to the altar. At the verses so marked in the sung *Gloria* and *Credo* they bow to the altar. They kneel (if not then sitting), facing the altar, and bow at the verse *Et incarnatus est,* etc.

The ceremonies performed by the celebrant differ but little from those of low Mass. He sings all that is sung at solemn Mass, including the Gospel and *Ite, missa est* or other versicle. He may sit while the choir sings *Gloria, Credo* or sequence. The Epistle may be sung by a cleric[3] (i.e., one who has received at least Tonsure)[4] if such be available. He wears a surplice and stands at the place where the Epistle is usually sung. He does not go to the celebrant for a blessing after the Epistle, but takes the book of lessons back to the credence. If another cleric be not present the celebrant himself reads the Epistle aloud or chants it. There may be torch-bearers (normally two) at the elevation. If so, they observe the rule of solemn Mass. They go to fetch their torches at the preface, come out with them at the *Sanctus*, genuflect in the middle, then kneel, one on either side, in the middle of the sanctuary till after the elevation. They genuflect

---

[1] *Mutatis mutandis,* since there is no kiss of peace and may be no incense.

[2] Or they may sit at a bench different from the celebrant's.

[3] If this is done, the celebrant does not read the Epistle but listens to it.

[4] Or, presumably, when tonsure is not given, by one who is an instituted or ordained lector.

again before the altar and take the torches back to the sacristy. But at Masses for the dead, on fast days and when others besides the celebrant will receive Holy Communion they stay till after the communion.

§ 2. The More Solemn Form

The other form of sung Mass without deacon and subdeacon is more solemn. It supposes an MC,[5] acolytes, thurifer, torch-bearers, and partakes more of the nature of solemn Mass, except for the absence of the sacred ministers. Incense may be used.[6] As a substitute for solemn Mass it has long been the custom to celebrate this kind of *Missa Cantata,* as the principal Mass on Sundays and feasts.

In this sung Mass the same server can perform the function of both thurifer and MC, but it is better to have two persons.

Preparations. The manner of celebration is as follows:[7]

The servers vest in good time in the sacristy. At least four (and not more than six) candles are lighted on the altar. The chalice is placed on the table of the altar (unless there be an assistant who is a cleric, then it will be left on the credence). The missal is left open on the bookstand. Another missal is placed on the credence if a cleric is to sing the Epistle. The MC assists the celebrant to vest. All bow to the cross, at a sign from the MC, and go to the sanctuary in procession, in this order: the thurifer goes first, with joined hands; he is followed by the acolytes carrying their candles, any other servers who may, later, be torch-bearers; the MC, lastly the celebrant wearing the biretta.

Before the altar the celebrant uncovers and hands the biretta to the MC, who receives it with the *solita oscula* and takes it to the sedilia. The acolytes go to the corners of the altar and after the reverence go and put their candles on the credence and stand there. All genuflect when the celebrant genuflects or bows.

---

[5] Cf. S.R.C. 3377 § 1. In addition to his functions as a server at low Mass the chief assistant to the celebrant at a sung Mass may perform the following offices: (i) if he is a layman he may assist at the missal (turning the leaves, etc.) and may hold the hand-candlestick for prelates who are entitled to its use; (ii) if he is a cleric (i.e., a major seminarian initiated by the reception of Tonsure or who has been admitted to candidacy for major orders or one who has been made a lector; or a professed religious of a clerical institute) he may sing the Epistle, and may at the offertory carry the chalice to the altar, and after the ablutions — when it has been wiped by the priest — he may re-veil it and carry it to the credence; (iii) if he is at least a subdeacon he may at the offertory wipe the chalice and pour in the wine and water, he may during the canon remove and replace the pall whenever this is required, and after the ablutions he may wipe the chalice, re-veil and remove it as he would at solemn Mass (S.R.C. 3377 § 1, 4181).

[6] R.G., n. 426. Its use is *ad libitum.*

[7] There is a good deal of difference of opinion among liturgical authorities about the rite of a *Missa Cantata.* One form is given in the text.

Asperges. If the Asperges ceremony is to take place, the celebrant will come from the sacristy in a cope of the colour of the day,[8] the MC or thurifer carries the holy-water vessel and sprinkler. Two servers may hold the ends of the cope, one at either side. At the altar the celebrant and servers kneel. The MC is at the right and hands the sprinkler to the celebrant, with the *solita oscula*. The celebrant takes it, intones[9] *Asperges me, Domine* (or, in Paschal time, *Vidi aquam*) and sprinkles the altar in the middle, on the gospel side, on the epistle side. The celebrant touches his forehead with the sprinkler,[10] then rises and sprinkles the servers on the Epistle and gospel sides. He and the MC reverence to the altar and go to sprinkle the clergy, if there are any in choir, and then to the entrance to the sanctuary, where the celebrant sprinkles the people, in the centre, to his left, and to his right (or he may go down the church).[11] Meanwhile, if there is no choir to sing it, he says the first verse of the psalm *Miserere, Gloria Patri*, etc., and repeats *Asperges me*, etc. On arrival back at the foot of the altar the celebrant and MC reverence to the altar and the celebrant sings the versicles and the prayer .

The celebrant, after the Asperges ceremony, goes to the seat with the MC. The MC puts away the vessel of holy water and the sprinkler. Assisted by him, the celebrant takes off the cope and vests in the maniple and chasuble. The first acolyte takes the cope to the sacristy. If incense is to be used the thurifer should now go to fetch the thurible.

Beginning of Mass. The celebrant and MC come to the foot of the altar and make the proper reverences. Mass begins, the MC answering the preparatory prayers. When the celebrant goes up to the altar, the MC and thurifer come to him. He puts incense in the thurible, and blesses it as at solemn Mass,[12] the MC saying *Benedicite, Pater reverende*. The celebrant incenses the altar.[13] The MC moves the missal when the celebrant is about to incense that part of the altar. Or the MC may accompany the celebrant at his right, the thurifer at his left, while he incenses the altar. In this case the first acolyte removes the missal. When the altar is incensed, the MC takes the thurible from the celebrant, with the *solita oscula*, descends to the floor on the epistle side and incenses the celebrant with three double swings of the thurible. The thurifer meanwhile stands at his left, and both bow before and after. The MC gives the thurible to the thurifer, who takes it to the sacristy. The MC stands by the missal and assists the celebrant, and then answers *Kyrie, eleison*, which the celebrant says at the

[8] In this case the chasuble and maniple must be laid out on the sedilia beforehand.
[9] If there is no choir he says the entire antiphon *Asperges*.
[10] Or he may touch his thumb to it and make the sign of the cross with the thumb.
[11] See p. 109.
[12] P. 141.
[13] P. 141. If incense is used at a *Missa Cantata* it must be used exactly as at solemn Mass. It is not lawful to use it only at the offertory, as in the rite of a requiem Mass.

centre as in low Mass.[14] If the celebrant goes to sit during the sung *Kyrie*, after he has said the *Kyrie* he genuflects or bows at the centre and then goes to the seat; the MC accompanies him, hands the biretta with the *oscula*, arranges the chasuble over the back of the seat and stands at the celebrant's right, facing down the church, with joined hands. This same rule is observed every time the celebrant sits, except during the homily, when the MC sits. If the celebrant has gone to the seat while *Kyrie* is sung, he goes back to the altar towards its end. He gives the biretta to the MC, who takes it, as usual, with the *oscula*, and puts it on the seat. The celebrant goes to the altar by the longer way, bowing low at the foot of the steps or genuflecting on the lowest step. The MC goes back to his place by the missal. He stays there while the celebrant goes to the middle, to intone the *Gloria in excelsis*. Having recited this prayer the celebrant goes to sit as before. At the verses at which everyone is to bow the celebrant uncovers and bows. The MC gives him a sign to do so, by bowing to him; then the MC turns and bows towards the altar. The celebrant comes back to the altar, as before, towards the end of the *Gloria*, at the verse *Cum Sancto Spiritu*.[15] The MC goes to the missal and stands there at the epistle side. If a cleric is to read the Epistle, he takes the book from the credence during the last collect, goes to the middle of the choir, there genuflects, goes to the place of the Epistle (away from the altar) and waits. The celebrant goes to sit at the sedilia as at solemn Mass.

Epistle. When the last collect is finished he chants the Epistle.[16] Then he genuflects in the middle of the choir and takes the book back to the credence. He does not receive a blessing from the celebrant. If there is no cleric to sing the Epistle, the celebrant may chant it or read it in a clear voice at the epistle corner.[17] After the Epistle he reads the gradual, etc.

During the Epistle the thurifer goes to the sacristy to prepare the thurible. If there is a sequence or a long tract the celebrant may go to sit while it is sung, after he has read it himself.[18]

Gospel. The celebrant goes to the centre of the altar towards the end of the sung gradual or sequence. The thurifer and MC come to him; he puts in and blesses the incense. Then he says *Munda cor meum*. Meanwhile the MC moves the missal to the gospel side. The acolytes take their candles from the credence and are led by the thurifer to the middle before the altar. All three genuflect, the thurifer between the acolytes.

---

[14] The *Kyrie* may be recited (it is a Roman usage) at the epistle corner. In this case should the celebrant go to sit he does not first make any reverence to the altar.

[15] If the *Gloria in excelsis* is not sung, immediately after *Kyrie, eleison* the celebrant, at the middle, sings *Dominus vobiscum*, then goes back to the missal (epistle side) for the collects.

[16] R., VI, 8. When the Epistle is chanted the celebrant does not read it and *Deo gratias* is not said at the end of it.

[17] S.R.C. 3350 § 1; R.G., n. 514.

[18] Then the thurifer may go later to prepare the thurible, towards the end of the sequence.

It is convenient so to arrange that their genuflexion should coincide with that of the MC as he carries the missal across the altar. In this case they will genuflect behind him. The acolytes go to the gospel side of the altar and stand on the ground, side by side, facing the epistle side, holding their candles, behind the missal. The MC stands near, at the left of the celebrant when he comes to the missal, the thurifer between the acolytes. The celebrant sings *Dominus vobiscum* and *Sequentia sancti Evangelii.* Then the MC takes the thurible from the thurifer and hands it to the celebrant with the usual *oscula.* The celebrant incenses the missal, as the deacon does at solemn Mass. He gives the thurible back to the MC, who receives it again with the *oscula* and hands it to the thurifer.

At the end of the Gospel *Laus tibi, Christe* is not said nor is the celebrant incensed.[19] The thurifer leads the acolytes to the centre before the altar steps, where all three genuflect. The acolytes carry their candles to the credence, the thurifer his thurible to the sacristy.

If there is a homily the celebrant goes to sit as usual. During the homily all the servers sit in some convenient place. If the celebrant himself preaches he may be accompanied to the pulpit by the MC.

The celebrant intones the *Credo,* at the middle of the altar, and continues it in a low voice. When he genuflects at the words *Et incarnatus est,* etc., all the servers genuflect with him. Then he goes, by the shorter way, to sit. The MC assists him as before. When the verse *Et incarnatus est,* etc., is sung, the MC and all the servers (if standing, otherwise they bow only) kneel at their place. The celebrant uncovers and bows. He goes back to the altar in the usual way.

Offertory. When the celebrant has sung *Oremus* at the altar, the MC, if he is a cleric, will bring the chalice, covered with the veil, to the altar from the credence. Otherwise it should be there before Mass. The celebrant uncovers it and offers the bread. The acolytes bring up the cruets and they or the MC hand them to the celebrant,[20] as at low Mass.

As soon as the *Credo* is finished, the thurifer goes to prepare the thurible. He returns when the celebrant sings *Oremus,* or soon after, so as to be ready after the offering of the bread and wine. The MC and thurifer come to the celebrant after the prayer *Veni, sanctificator;* he prepares incense (the MC assisting), blesses it and incenses the *oblata* and the altar.[21] The thurifer goes to the gospel side to remove the missal when that part of the altar is to be incensed. If the MC and thurifer accompany the celebrant during the incensing, the first acolyte will do this. At the end of the incensing of the altar, the MC takes the thurible from the celebrant and incenses him, as at the introit, the thurifer standing at his left and bowing with him. The MC goes to stand by the missal till the

---

[19] R. VI, 8.
[20] See p. 99.
[21] See pp. 49, 145.

consecration.[22] The thurifer (or the MC) genuflects in the middle and goes to incense the clergy, if any are present. He bows to the choir on the side of greater dignity, or on the gospel side, and incenses those in the farthest row with one double swing for each, bowing at the beginning and end of the incensation of the row. He does the same for the epistle side. He returns to the gospel side and incenses in the same way those in the next row, then those in the corresponding row on the epistle side, and so on, according to the number of rows.[23] Each time, on passing in front of the altar, he genuflects. He next incenses the MC with one double swing; the acolytes, with a double swing for each, bowing once only to the two, before and after (if there is no liturgical choir on either side, he incenses the MC first). Then, genuflecting, he turns and incenses the people. He bows once down the church, makes three single swings (p. 50), one in the middle, one to his left (i.e., the epistle side of the altar), one to his right, then bows. He turns to the altar, genuflects and goes to the sacristy. If there are torch-bearers, they form in line at the middle with the thurifer before he goes out, genuflect and go with him.

As soon as the celebrant has been incensed, the acolytes come to the epistle corner of the altar with the water cruet and bowl, held by the second on the left, the hand-towel by the first on the right. Here they wash the celebrant's hands, as at low Mass. They then stand at their place by the credence. If the acolytes are to bear torches at the elevation they go to fetch them in the sacristy at, or just before, the beginning of the preface. They may join the thurifer, genuflect and go out with him. If the torches are at the credence they take them towards the end of the preface.

Canon. At the *Sanctus* the thurifer comes accompanied by the torch-bearers. All genuflect in the middle together, the thurifer in the middle of the torch-bearers, who genuflect in a straight line across the sanctuary. The thurifer goes to the foot of the steps on the epistle side of the altar. The torch-bearers separate, bow to one another and kneel facing the altar, in line along the middle of the sanctuary. They stay here till after the elevation. The thurifer at the epistle side waits till just before the consecration. After the warning bell the first acolyte puts incense into the thurible. The thurifer kneels on the lowest step on the epistle side, facing the gospel side. At the elevation he incenses the Blessed Sacrament with three double swings at each elevation, bowing once before and after each group of three incensings. It is convenient that he time the incensings so as to correspond with the celebrant's genuflexion, elevation, genuflexion. Before the consecration the MC kneels. He may kneel on the edge of the

---

[22] The MC at the missal turns the pages and assists the celebrant. He may give a sign to the organist (by bowing to him) before the preface and Lord's Prayer. He should stand back a step at the commemorations of the living and of the dead, so as not to overhear their names.
[23] This supposes that each row has clergy of a different order. If only seminarians, or servers, are present in choir, they are incensed collectively, with three single swings, on each side of the choir.

footpace at the celebrant's left, behind him, and raise the end of the chasuble as the celebrant holds up his arms. The first acolyte rings the bell at the *Sanctus;* once when the priest spreads his hands over the *oblata,* and three times at each elevation. After the elevation the MC rises, goes to the celebrant by the book, genuflects and stands there, turning the pages. He will again stand back a step at the commemoration of the dead. The thurifer rises, comes to the middle, genuflects and takes the thurible out. His office is now ended. The torch-bearers, if they are to take the torches to the sacristy, rise and genuflect with him, then follow. But at requiems, on certain fast days, and when people will receive Holy Communion, the torch-bearers stay kneeling till after the communion.

The thurifer and the torch-bearers (unless they are the same as the acolytes) have no more duties after they come back from the sacristy, where they have left the thurible and torches. They go to kneel and stand at some convenient place prepared for them. It may, however, be convenient to delegate other duties, otherwise belonging to someone else, to the thurifer, in order to avoid haste or confusion. This is so especially if there are people other than the celebrant to receive Holy Communion.

The ordinary *Pax* is not given, but the kiss of peace may be given to the clergy present by means of the pax-brede (cf. pp. 42, 51).

Communion. If Holy Communion is distributed either the MC or the thurifer may hold the communion plate.

When it is used the acolytes spread the communion cloth across the front of the footpace (if persons in the choir or sanctuary are to communicate) as described at p. 147. If the acolytes are holding torches, this should be done by the MC and thurifer.

After the communion the first acolyte presents the cruets as at low Mass. The second acolyte carries the missal to the epistle side. As the MC and acolyte cross in front of the altar they genuflect together, the MC passing in front of the acolyte. If the MC has the right to do so,[24] he carries the chalice to the credence. He takes his place at the epistle side by the missal and assists by pointing the place and turning the leaves.

Conclusion of Mass. After the last postcommunion the MC shuts the missal, unless there be a proper last Gospel. In this case he leaves it open and carries it to the gospel side, as soon as the *Ite, missa est* or corresponding versicle has been sung by the celebrant. He may arrange this so that he makes his genuflexion in the middle as the celebrant gives the blessing, and so receive the blessing there. Otherwise (and this is more correct) he will kneel for the blessing at the gospel side. The acolytes and thurifer kneel for it where they are.[25]

During the last Gospel the procession is formed to return to the sacristy. The thurifer goes first (he stands behind the others so as to be in

---

[24] That is, if he is at least a tonsured cleric or its equivalent (as explained above).
[25] The sung *Deo Gratias* should be finished and the choir and organ silent.

front when all turn); the acolytes, with their candles, before him, the torchbearers before them, so that they can take their place behind the acolytes. Meanwhile the MC stands by the altar-card or missal, answers the verses at the beginning of the last Gospel and then goes to fetch the celebrant's biretta and stands at the foot of the altar. At the end of the last Gospel the MC answers *Deo gratias;* the celebrant comes down to before the altar steps. The MC hands him his biretta with the usual *oscula.*

If the prayer for the sovereign, or any prayer ordered by the Bishop, is to be said,[26] the celebrant and the servers stand in their places in front of the altar during the prayer. Then all genuflect, when the celebrant genuflects or bows, and go out as they came in.

If there is no prayer after Mass, as soon as the celebrant comes down before the altar, all reverence to the altar and go out.

§ 3 Prayers for the Sovereign

On Sundays, after the principal Mass — whether sung or not — in all churches and oratories (other than private), in England and Wales it is customary[27] to sing or recite, in Latin, or in the vernacular, the prayers for the Sovereign[28] which are printed in *Ritus Servandus.* If the Leonine prayers are recited, they are to be said first.

---

[26] The prayers in the vernacular ordered by the Pope which are usually said after low Mass are omitted after a sung Mass.

[27] Cf. *Clergy Review* March, 1936, p. 249.

[28] The structure of these prayers is curious; there is no antiphon, but only a versicle and response and prayer. The versicle and response (without the name of the sovereign, of course) form the tenth verse of the nineteenth psalm — a psalm which is a prayer for a king. The versicle is found among those in *Ordo ad Recipiendum Processionaliter Reginam,* in the Roman Pontifical (Part III). The prayer is that *Pro Rege* found among the *Orationes Diversæ* of the Roman Missal (No. 6). with the addition of the words for wartime, and those for the Sovereign's consort and Royal Family. This prayer, which is Gallican in origin, dates from at least the eighth century. It is found (adopted from the missal) in the Roman Pontifical (Part I) for use in the Mass celebrated at the sacring of a Catholic sovereign. The *Gloria Patri* does not form part of the correct text of the Prayers for the Sovereign.

Chapter XIV

The Assistant Priest

§ 1. At Solemn Mass

IT is not lawful for any celebrant—except bishops and other prelates enjoying the use of pontifical privileges—to be assisted by another priest, on the sole ground of honour or solemnity.[1] The canons of certain chapters have this privilege, either by indult or immemorial custom. When a priest says or sings his first Mass, or first three Masses, he may be assisted by another priest. If it is a solemn Mass, the assistant priest may wear a cope. In this case many of the ceremonies performed by the ministers are modified, as follows.

A seat, a stool without a back, is prepared for the assistant priest (AP) near the sedilia, to the right of the deacon's place, facing down the church; or it may be at the left of the subdeacon, so that the AP faces the altar.

The AP wears a surplice, or a rochet (if he have this right). He should also wear the amice over the surplice or rochet and a cope of the colour of the Mass. When he sits he wears his biretta, as do the celebrant and ministers.

Asperges. If the Asperges ceremony is performed before Mass, the AP has no function at that time. He should go to his place in the choir, without the cope, and put on the cope when Mass begins. Otherwise he vests with the celebrant and ministers, putting on the surplice and amice first, the cope when the celebrant has vested.

Beginning of Mass. He comes to the altar at the left but a little in front of the celebrant, the deacon and subdeacon walking, as usual, in front. If there is a choir, when they come to it, the AP passes behind the celebrant, goes to his right and there bows with him. The deacon goes to the celebrant's left, the subdeacon to the left of the deacon. Before the altar they stand in this order.[2] The AP takes the celebrant's biretta (with *solita oscula*) and answers the preparatory prayers with the ministers. When the celebrant goes up to the altar, the AP goes round to the epistle corner, and stands there at the foot during the blessing of incense. When the altar is incensed at that side the AP removes the missal, then replaces it. When

---

[1] C.I.C. 812. Common sense dictates that another priest assist, wearing choir dress (and stole the colour of the day if customary), but no amice or cope, should a priest be infirm or have other need of guidance.

[2] See fig. 14.

the deacon incenses the celebrant the AP stands at the deacon's right and bows with him. Then he goes up to the celebrant's right by the missal and points out the introit. He answers *Kyrie, eleison* with the ministers. If they go to sit during the *Kyrie, eleison* the AP observes the general rule for such occasions, as below, at the *Gloria*.

Gloria. When the celebrant intones *Gloria in excelsis,* the AP may go with him to the middle and point out the intonation in the missal, or on a card which he will bring with him if it be required; then he goes back to the epistle corner, and facing the gospel corner, standing on the top step, he recites the *Gloria* with the celebrant. Or he may stay at the epistle corner while the *Gloria* is intoned. At the end of the *Gloria* he makes the sign of the cross with the celebrant. Then, without genuflecting, he goes straight to his seat by the sedilia, sits here with the others and puts on the biretta. At the end of the sung *Gloria* he rises and uncovers with the others, goes by the longer way to the middle, at the celebrant's right, while the ministers are both at his left.[3] The AP bows to the choir with the celebrant and genuflects when he bows. This is the rule every time they go to sit.

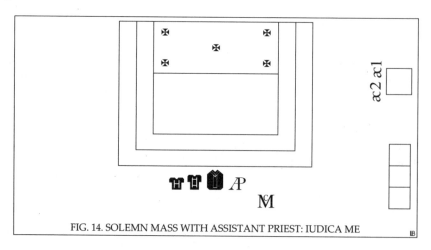

FIG. 14. SOLEMN MASS WITH ASSISTANT PRIEST: IUDICA ME

Gospel. The AP now goes again to the epistle corner and points out all that is to be sung or said and makes the responses not sung by the choir. He stands by the missal between the celebrant and subdeacon while the celebrant reads the gradual, etc., points out the place, turns the pages, and makes the responses. At the celebrant's left he stands facing the deacon while the latter sings the Gospel. When the deacon has incensed the celebrant after the Gospel, the AP may go to the middle, put the missal in its place near the centre of the altar and point out the place for

[3] Whenever both ministers are at the left of the celebrant the deacon stands nearer to him, the subdeacon on the other side of the deacon. The AP accompanies the celebrant to the sedilia for the Epistle.

the celebrant to intone the *Credo*. If this is not necessary, he will stay at the epistle corner. He recites the *Credo* with the celebrant and genuflects with him at the text *Et incarnatus est*, etc. Then he goes to his seat by the sedilia as before. While they sit, the AP does not rise when the deacon carries the corporal to the altar. He goes back to the altar, as after the *Gloria*; but this time he passes behind the celebrant as they go up to the altar, so as to be on his left by the missal. He stays here and moves the book when the altar is incensed. The deacon incenses the AP with two double incensings immediately before he incenses the subdeacon.

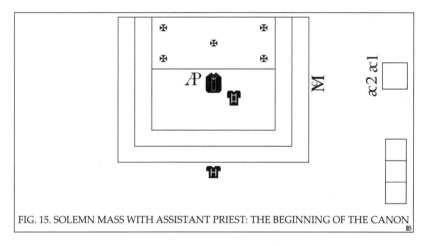

FIG. 15. SOLEMN MASS WITH ASSISTANT PRIEST: THE BEGINNING OF THE CANON

Canon. Since the AP now takes the place of the MC by the missal, the MC must stand away, on the floor at the epistle side. At the *Sanctus* the deacon comes to the right of the celebrant, the AP stays at his left, the subdeacon may remain at the foot of the altar steps. During the canon the AP is by the missal at the celebrant's left. He stands back a step at each *Memento*. The deacon meanwhile stands at the right, behind. At the elevation the AP kneels on the footpace at the gospel side; or he may kneel behind the celebrant at the deacon's left and hold up the chasuble with him. Then he comes back to the book, genuflects and stands there, turning the pages and genuflecting each time the celebrant does so. At the *Agnus Dei* the subdeacon may stay at the foot of the altar steps. The AP and deacon say the *Agnus Dei* with the celebrant. Then they genuflect and change places. The AP genuflects on arriving at the celebrant's right; he rises immediately, kisses the altar (outside the corporal) with the celebrant, not laying his hands on it. He receives the kiss of peace from the celebrant; then gives it to the deacon, who passes it to the subdeacon. The AP next gives the pax to the members of the choir (if clergy). On his return he gives the pax to the MC, then goes to the celebrant's left; the deacon is on his right. They bow low at the celebrant's communion.

Postcommunion. When the time comes, the AP moves the book to the epistle side. He then stands there, by the missal, and assists the celebrant, as before. He shuts the book after the last postcommunion, or moves it to the gospel side, if there is a proper last Gospel. He receives the blessing kneeling alone on the edge of the footpace at the gospel side. He stands there between the celebrant and subdeacon, and assists at the last Gospel. He comes down, so as to be at the right of the deacon before the altar steps. The deacon gives the celebrant his biretta; the AP receives his from the MC. All genuflect together. The AP returns to the sacristy walking on the left of the celebrant, a little in front of him.

§ 2. The Assistant Priest Not in Cope

It may be, especially in the case of the first three Masses of a newly ordained priest, that another priest assists, not wearing the cope. In this case he does not perform all the ceremonies described above. His office is really only to see that the celebrant make no mistake; his ceremonial function is reduced to a very simple one.

The AP wears a surplice only, even if he otherwise has the right to some distinction of dress. If it is a solemn Mass, the AP walks (uncovered) to the altar at the celebrant's left, or he comes to the altar when Mass begins, if it is preceded by the Asperges ceremony. During the prayers before the altar steps he kneels on the ground at the epistle side. He then goes to the epistle corner by the missal and assists the celebrant here, instead of the MC. The MC meanwhile stands aside, near the credence. The AP sits near the sedilia, when the celebrant sits there. At the altar he stands by the celebrant, sees that he make no mistake, turns the leaves of the book and points out the places, as otherwise would be done by the MC. At the offertory he is incensed by the thurifer with one double swing, before the MC. He stands by the book during the canon; the deacon remains behind the celebrant. When the subdeacon carries the missal across before the Gospel, and when the deacon carries it back to the epistle side after the communion, the AP walks with them and genuflects with them in the middle. He does not receive the kiss of peace from the celebrant; instead he goes down to receive it from the subdeacon, after it has been given to the members of the choir. The AP gives it to the MC.

§ 3. The Assistant Priest at Low Mass

The liturgical books give no special directions for this case. It may, however, occur at the first three Masses said by a newly ordained priest, if they are low Masses.

It is not difficult to understand, from the rubrics in general, what the AP has to do. He will accompany the celebrant to the altar, kneel at the epistle side during the preparatory prayers, answering with the server. He will then go to the epistle corner and stand by the book. During all the Mass he stands at the celebrant's side, by the book. Only at the moment of the elevation he steps back and kneels on the edge of the footpace, at the gospel side. His office is only to be near and to guide the celebrant throughout. He must attend to what the celebrant does and says, pointing out places and correcting any serious mistake. A stole is not necessary, but the AP may wear one of the colour of the day—either all the time or from the beginning of the canon to the consumption of the Precious Blood—if it be the custom.[4]

---

[4] S.R.C. 3515 § 7.

Chapter XV

Solemn Mass in the Presence of a Greater Prelate[1]

§ 1. In the Presence of the Bishop in Cope and Mitre

BY a "greater prelate" is meant a cardinal anywhere (outside Rome), a Papal Legate (including a nuncio and apostolic delegate) in the place of his jurisdiction, an archbishop in his province, a bishop within his diocese. A genuflexion is the normal reverence paid to a greater prelate, but canons, prelates and the celebrant of Mass bow to him.

No one ever genuflects to any other bishop, for instance, an auxiliary or an extern bishop; nor to an abbot, except in churches of his jurisdiction. To these one bows.

The first case is when the prelate assists with more solemnity, wearing cope and mitre. The Ordinary should assist in this manner on the chief feasts, if he does not himself celebrate.

Preparations. The following preparations must be made:

If there is a chapel or altar of the Blessed Sacrament, distinct from the high altar of the church, a faldstool or kneeler is prepared in front of the tabernacle. It is draped and has two cushions of the appropriate colour.[2]

By the high altar the Bishop has his throne. In the cathedral this will be a fixed ornament of the church. In other churches a throne is prepared in the sanctuary, normally on the gospel side. Over the seat is a canopy, of which the draperies are, as far as this is possible, of the colour of the Mass. The seat is raised three steps above the floor of the sanctuary. These steps are covered with a carpet and the seat itself is normally covered with silk material. Nearby is a cushion, for use when the prelate kneels or genuflects. All these cloths and coverings should be of the colour of the Mass. On either side of the throne, on its platform, is a stool for the assistant deacons; at the Bishop's right is a third stool for his assistant priest[3] (see fig. 2).

In front of the altar is another faldstool or kneeler—arranged as described above—at which the Bishop prays before Mass.

---

[1] C.E., II, ix, xviii; I, vii, 7; viii, 4.

[2] Red or violet for a cardinal, corresponding with the colour he wears (namely, violet for fast days and mourning); green for a bishop in violet, violet when he wears black (fast days and mourning). One cushion is on the faldstool for his arms, the other to kneel on, on the ground before it. The covering of the kneeler should be of silk for a cardinal, cloth for a bishop. The cushions may be silk for a bishop; for a cardinal they may be fringed with gold.

[3] The place of the AP may be on the other side, facing down the church.

At the entrance of the sanctuary four or six large candlesticks stand, with burning candles.

The Bishop's vestments are spread on the altar. In the middle are the cope (with its morse), stole, pectoral cross,[4] girdle, alb, amice. These are covered with a veil of the colour of the day. On the gospel side stands the precious mitre; the golden mitre is on the epistle side. Both mitres are so placed that their lappets hang over the frontal. The crosier stands near the altar. The chalice with paten, veil, etc., the cruets, bell, book of lessons, humeral veil for the subdeacon and other things needed for Mass, are put on the credence. On this also or on another[5] are prepared the pontifical canon, another missal[6] for the Bishop, the hand-candle, and a book containing the formula of the indulgence, if this is to be proclaimed. A stand for the cross is prepared near the altar on the gospel side, if the prelate who is to assist be an archbishop in his province.

All the vestments for the celebrant, ministers and servers are prepared in the sacristy. The vessel of lustral water and the sprinkler should also be ready.

General Rules. The persons who assist at the ceremony are, besides the ministers and servers required for solemn Mass, an assistant priest and two deacons "at the throne," to wait on the Bishop. These should be, if possible, canons; but others may supply their place. They are dressed in their canonical robes, or choir dress, not in vestments.

A train-bearer[7] and four other servers or chaplains are needed, one to hold the mitre, one for the crosier, one for the book, one for the hand-candle.[8]

There is a first MC to guide the whole service (with particular attention to the Bishop) and a second MC to assist him. Other servers assist at the Bishop's vesting and unvesting. He has an attendant who carries away and brings back the cappa magna. When the Bishop is at the throne, the normal place of the first MC is standing at his left. There is a place for the Bishop's servants and attendants (his 'familiares'), generally east of the throne, or by the (second) credence.

During the ceremony, the celebrant and ministers do not salute the choir, but only the Bishop and the altar.[9] All servers and others who

---

[4] The rubrics speak about preparing the cross with the vestments, but in practice the Bishop arrives wearing his cross.

[5] In practice, the things needed for the Bishop at the throne (missal, canon, hand-candle) are often prepared at a second credence placed near the throne on the gospel side of the sanctuary.

[6] The missals should be covered with a silk covering of the colour of the Mass. The book of lessons has a similar covering (see p. 44).

[7] A train-bearer is needed only when the Bishop is wearing a cappa magna. He wears a violet cassock and a black cloak (ferraiolo), no surplice.

[8] The bearers of mitre and crosier wear silk scarves (vimpæ), through which they hold them. For these four chaplains, cf. Chapter XVI § 2.

approach the Bishop for any purpose make a reverence to him both before and after they bring anything to him.[10] This reverence is a genuflexion, except in the case of canons and the celebrant of the Mass, who bow low.

Whenever the Bishop wears the cope or chasuble and mitre his skull-cap is taken off only when he genuflects or kneels before the Blessed Sacrament, and during Mass from the preface to the communion. At all other times he keeps it on, even when kneeling or bowing. But when he is not in vestments, but wears the cappa, mozzetta or mantelletta and the biretta, he (himself) takes off the skull-cap while the Gospel is sung, when being incensed, and from the beginning of the preface to the communion inclusive.

The first of the assistant deacons always puts on the Bishop's mitre, the second always takes it off. Each takes it from, or gives it to, the mitre-bearer, who holds it through his scarf. Whenever one assistant rises to do anything, the other rises also. Before sitting, they bow the head to each other.

The Bishop reads from the missal four times during Mass, namely, the introit; gradual and other verses; the offertory; the communion. He reads these at his throne; the book-bearer holds the missal before him; when at the throne the bearer of the hand-candle is normally on the book-bearer's right[11] holding it. The missal is not held before the Bishop at the *Kyrie eleison, Gloria in excelsis, Credo, Sanctus, Agnus Dei.* He recites these from memory. Nor is it used in this way at all, if a higher prelate be present.

Four times during the Mass the canons (of the cathedral), if they are present, come to form a circle around the Bishop. These occasions are, when he says the *Kyrie* and *Gloria,* the *Credo,* the *Sanctus,* the *Agnus Dei.* Each time they come from their stalls, those of lesser dignity coming out first; they make the usual reverence (a low bow) to the altar in passing, and to the Bishop. The AP takes his place among them. They stand before the throne in a wide circle (not, however, turning their back to the altar) and say the text with the Bishop. Those of lower rank are before the Bishop somewhat to his left, while those of higher rank are on his right hand. In going back to their stalls these latter go first. When they bow to the Bishop on retiring he gives them his blessing, making the sign of the cross. This circle of the canons is not made in Masses for the dead, nor on Good Friday, nor when a higher prelate is present; and it is made only to the Bishop of the diocese.[12]

---

[9] So most authors arguing from the silence of *Cæremoniale,* e.g., II, v, 5 and 6; II, viii, 40, as compared with its directions when the Bishop is absent, e.g., II, vi, 12 and 14.
[10] Except when the subdeacon brings the book of lessons after the Gospel.
[11] C.E., I, xx, 1.
[12] C.E., I, xxi, 5.

During Mass the deacon *omits*[13] the ceremonial kisses of mere politeness to the celebrant (e.g. of the thurible) but not those that form an intrinsic part of the solemnity of solemn Mass, such as those of the chalice and paten at the offertory, and of the paten and celebrant's hand after *Pater noster*.

At the beginning of the ceremony the celebrant, ministers and servers come to the altar in the usual way and go to the sedilia; the acolytes put their candles on the credence.

Arrival of Bishop. When the Bishop arrives at the church the bells should be rung and the organ sounded.[14] He is met at the door by the highest dignitary of the Chapter or by the rector of the church who offers him holy water. The Bishop signs himself with this, then sprinkles those around. He arrives in rochet, cappa magna[15] and biretta. He goes (uncovered), accompanied by the deacons of the throne and other attendants and servers, his train borne behind, to the chapel of the Blessed Sacrament, if there is one; there, kneeling at the faldstool, he makes a short prayer. The front of the cappa is spread over the faldstool by the MC.[16] His attendants kneel behind him. Then he goes in procession to the high altar. All in choir stand, then kneel to receive his blessing as he passes. The celebrant and ministers stand up at the sedilia. The AP is at the first stall, in choir.[17] When the Bishop arrives at the faldstool or kneeler, before the high altar, he first turns to the celebrant and ministers and blesses them. The celebrant bows low, the others genuflect, unless they are canons. The Bishop bows to the altar, kneels at the faldstool and says a prayer, his attendants kneeling behind him. He then repeats the reverence to the altar and goes to the throne. There he vests. Meantime the celebrant and ministers sit; all others stand.

Vesting. He takes off the biretta and cappa, which are laid aside by his MC or by the Bishop's valet. Servers bring the vestments—handed to them by the second MC—from the altar; the deacons at the throne assist the Bishop to put on these. Finally, the first assistant deacon puts the precious mitre on the Bishop and he then takes the crosier in his left hand. So he goes to the altar, blessing the choir as he passes; the deacons at the throne hold the ends of the cope, the bearers of the mitre and crosier follow.

Asperges. If the Asperges ceremony comes before Mass, the Bishop's mitre is taken off and he stands at his throne. The celebrant sprinkles the altar, then comes to the throne, accompanied by the second MC and the acolyte who carries the aspersory. The celebrant presents the sprinkler to

---

[13] So the majority of rubricians relying on C.E., I, xviii, 16 and S.R.C. 3059 § 2

[14] C.E., I, xv, 4.

[15] If a cappa magna is not available, choir dress (with mozzetta) should be worn.

[16] This is the general rule when the Bishop kneels at a faldstool or kneeler in cappa.

[17] This is his place always when he is not at the throne.

176 THE HOLY SACRIFICE

the Bishop with the usual reverences and *oscula*. The Bishop signs himself, then sprinkles the celebrant and his own assistant deacons. The celebrant having received back the sprinkler and bowed low again to the Bishop returns to the altar. He sprinkles the ministers, then the choir and people, accompanied by his MC and the aspersory-bearer. The ministers stand meanwhile before the altar. The celebrant finishes the Asperges as usual and vests for Mass at the sedilia.

Beginning of Mass. When the Bishop arrives before the altar steps to begin Mass he gives the crosier to its bearer;[18] the second deacon takes off the mitre and all reverence to the altar.

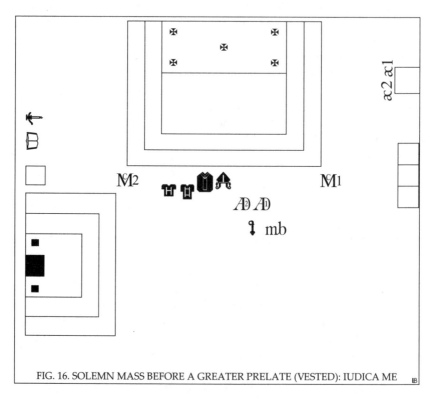

FIG. 16. SOLEMN MASS BEFORE A GREATER PRELATE (VESTED): IUDICA ME

Meanwhile the celebrant of the Mass comes to the altar with his ministers; he stands at the Bishop's left before the steps, a little back. The deacons of the throne stand behind the Bishop, the deacon and subdeacon of the Mass to the left of the celebrant and a little behind him;[19] the other chaplains or servers of the Bishop behind these. The first MC is on the epistle side, the second on the gospel side. The train-bearer

---

[18] The crosier-bearer always receives the crosier directly and — from a "greater prelate" — kneeling.

[19] If the deacon and subdeacon are canons they stand between the deacons of the throne (S.R.C. 1583 § 6), the deacon on the right of the subdeacon.

stands aside on the gospel side. All kneel, except the Bishop, celebrant and canons (including the ministers). The Bishop and celebrant say the prayers at the altar steps, the celebrant answering the Bishop.[20] All the others also say these prayers two and two, according to the usual rule (p. 104). After the prayer *Indulgentiam* the celebrant, having bowed to the Bishop, turns back and stands between the ministers of Mass; the deacons at the throne go and stand on either side of the Bishop. So they say the verses *Deus, tu conversus,* etc. As soon as the Bishop has said *Oremus,* adding no prayer, he bows to the altar; the first assistant deacon puts the mitre on the Bishop, who takes the crosier, blesses the celebrant and his ministers, and goes to the throne, blessing the choir as he passes. The celebrant (having bowed when blessed) then goes up to the altar, kisses it, says the usual prayers, *Aufer a nobis,* etc., and waits there till the thurible is brought to him.

Incensation of Altar. The Bishop lays aside the crosier and sits on his throne. The assistant priest comes from his stall to the throne. The thurifer brings the thurible, hands the incense boat to the AP at the throne, genuflects to the Bishop when the AP bows to him, and kneels before him, holding up the thurible. The AP holds the boat, hands the spoon to the Bishop with the *solita oscula,* and says *Benedicite, Pater reverendissime.* The Bishop puts on the incense and blesses it with the usual formula and one sign of the cross. The thurifer takes the boat, genuflects to the Bishop and to the altar, carries the thurible to the altar and hands it to the deacon, who gives it to the celebrant. The AP returns to his place in choir. The celebrant incenses the altar as usual. When the altar is incensed, the deacon incenses the celebrant with two double swings; then he hands the thurible to the thurifer, who takes it to the throne (genuflecting to the altar on the way) and there meets the AP before the Bishop. The AP and thurifer make the reverences to the Bishop, each according to the general rule for their degree (p. 173). The AP takes the thurible and incenses the Bishop with three double incensings. The Bishop, wearing his mitre, rises to be incensed. When this is done the AP bows, and the Bishop makes the sign of the cross over him, and sits. The AP then goes to his place in choir or joins the canons in the circle. The thurifer takes the thurible to the sacristy.

Introit. The second deacon at the throne now takes off the precious mitre, hands it to the mitre-bearer who puts it on the credence; he takes the golden mitre, brings it to the throne and waits there. The Bishop rising, uncovered, says the introit of the Mass, the book-bearer standing (having on his right the candle-bearer) holds the missal before him. The missal and candle are then taken away; the Bishop says *Kyrie, eleison,* etc., with the canons.

---

[20] The deacon and subdeacon say the prayers to one another; so do the assistant deacons.

Meanwhile, if the Chapter is present, the canons come to form a circle around, as described above. The AP is among them.[21] If the sung *Kyrie* will take some time, the Bishop signs to the canons (blessing them) that they may go back to their stalls; he sits and is covered with the golden mitre by the first assistant deacon. If the *Kyrie* is not long, and if *Gloria in excelsis* follows, the canons do not go to their stalls; they stay, and the Bishop, unmitred, remains standing to recite the *Gloria*. The celebrant at the altar intones the *Gloria* and the choir continues it, as at every solemn Mass. Meanwhile the Bishop and the canons in a circle say it together. Then the Bishop sits and the first assistant deacon puts on him the golden mitre. The canons retire. The deacons at the throne sit in their places; the AP does not return to his place in choir, but sits on the stool placed for him at the throne on the Bishop's right; the servers who carry the mitre, crosier, book and candle sit on the steps of the throne or in some convenient place east of it. During the words *Adoramus te,* etc., the Bishop bows with mitre on, all others uncover and bow.

Collect and Epistle. When the *Gloria* has been sung all (except the Bishop) rise, and the second deacon at the throne takes off the Bishop's mitre. The Bishop stands while the collects are sung. Towards the end of the last collect the subdeacon takes the book of lessons, but does not move from his place. The Bishop sits, the first assistant deacon puts on him his golden mitre. The subdeacon (accompanied by the second MC) comes to the middle, genuflects to the cross, then to the Bishop and going to the usual place for the chanting of the Epistle sings it. He should stand not quite facing the altar, but turned half towards the Bishop. At the end of the Epistle the subdeacon genuflects[22] to the altar, comes before the Bishop, genuflects to him, goes up the steps of the throne and kneels.[23] The Bishop lays his hand on the book, the subdeacon kisses his hand, and the Bishop makes the sign of the cross over him. The subdeacon comes down the steps, again genuflects to the Bishop, then in the middle before the altar, gives the book of lessons to the MC at his side, and waits at the foot of the altar.

Gospel. The AP and assistant deacons stand as the subdeacon comes to the throne; the bearers of the Bishop's missal and hand-candle come to him as the subdeacon leaves. Seated and covered the Bishop reads the gradual and other verses.

Meanwhile the deacon takes the book of lessons and puts it on the altar — genuflecting[24] on his way to the Bishop and altar — and waits at the altar until MC gives him a sign to come to the throne. The celebrant, having read the gradual, etc., stands facing the missal at the epistle

---

[21] It is always supposed that he is a canon.
[22] If he is a canon he bows only.
[23] Ditto.
[24] Ditto.

corner until the deacon sings *Dominus vobiscum*. He then faces the deacon. When the Bishop has read the gradual, etc., the bearers of his book and candle retire.

The deacon, at a sign from the MC, genuflects to the cross, comes to the throne, genuflects[25] to the Bishop, goes up the steps and kneeling[26] kisses the Bishop's hand; coming down the steps he genuflects again to the Bishop, goes to the lowest altar step in the middle,[27] kneels there and says *Munda cor meum*. The thurifer follows the deacon to the throne, so that he is ready there when the deacon comes down. As the deacon genuflects after kissing the Bishop's hand, the thurifer does so too, then he goes up the steps. Here he hands the incense boat to the AP, who comes to the Bishop's right. The Bishop puts on incense and blesses it. The thurifer rises, takes back the boat, genuflects to the Bishop and goes and stands before the altar, waiting till the others come. When the deacon has said *Munda cor meum* he takes the Gospel book, bows to the celebrant, not kneeling for his blessing, and goes with the subdeacon and acolytes to the throne. Before leaving the altar they all genuflect to it. The deacon, preceded[28] by the thurifer, acolytes and subdeacon, goes to the Bishop. Before the throne they form up as at the foot of the altar before going to sing the Gospel, except that the deacon — at the foot of the throne — is in advance of the subdeacon. All kneel before the Bishop; the assistants at the throne stand. The deacon kneeling[29] before the throne says *Iube, domne, benedicere*. The Bishop gives him the blessing with the usual formula (one sign of the cross). Meanwhile the acolytes and the thurifer as well as the subdeacon, kneel.[30] All rise, genuflect again to the Bishop and go for the Gospel to be sung as usual, except that the subdeacon (who precedes the deacon in the procession) must so stand as not to turn his back to the Bishop.

As soon as the deacon leaves the throne, the second deacon takes off the Bishop's mitre. The four chaplains of mitre, crosier, book and candle stand in line facing the deacon (on the east side before the throne). The Bishop stands at his throne and takes his crosier. This he holds with both hands during the singing of the Gospel (except while he makes the small signs of the cross at *Sequentia*, etc., when he holds the crosier in the left hand). If, during the Gospel, a genuflexion is to be made, a server puts a cushion before the Bishop, that he may kneel on that, and the Bishop genuflects towards the book of the Gospels. When the Gospel is finished, the Bishop lays aside the crosier; the subdeacon goes straight to him, without any genuflexion or reverence, holding the open book. The

---

[25] Ditto.
[26] Ditto.
[27] C.E., I, ix, 2; II, viii, 42.
[28] Cf. C.E., I, ix, 2, x, 3; II, xxi, 19; viii, 44.
[29] If he is a canon he bows only.
[30] Ditto.

Bishop lays his hands on it and kisses it, saying *Per evangelica dicta,* etc. The thurifer follows the subdeacon to the throne. The deacon, with the acolytes, goes to the altar, genuflecting to the Bishop, then to the altar. The acolytes put their candles on the credence and stay there. The deacon goes to the celebrant's side. The celebrant is not incensed. The subdeacon leaves the Bishop, with the usual genuflexion, hands the book to the second MC, and goes to the celebrant's left. The AP takes the thurible from the thurifer and thrice incenses the Bishop with the usual reverences. At the end the Bishop makes the sign of the cross over him.[31]

Creed. If the *Credo* is said, the canons (including the AP) come to make their circle around the Bishop, and say it with him. All genuflect at the text, *Et incarnatus est,* etc. The Bishop genuflects on a cushion put before him by a server. Then the canons go back to their stalls, the Bishop dismissing them with a blessing. The AP goes to his place by the throne. The Bishop sits wearing the golden mitre while the rest of the *Credo* is sung. When the words *Et incarnatus est,* etc., are sung, those who are standing kneel; those who are sitting uncover and bow; the Bishop bows, not taking off the mitre. When the deacon goes to spread the corporal, he bows first to the celebrant, then genuflects to the Bishop and to the altar. On going back to the altar the celebrant and his ministers make a reverence to the Bishop and to the altar in the usual way.

Offertory. The second deacon at the throne takes off the mitre, the Bishop rises while the celebrant sings *Dominus vobiscum* and *Oremus.* Standing, he reads the offertory antiphon, the servers holding the book and candle. Then he sits and the first assistant deacon puts on the mitre. The thurifer comes to the throne, genuflecting as always to the Bishop, and hands the boat to the AP. The Bishop puts on and blesses incense with the formula *Per intercessionem.* When the water is to be blessed the subdeacon, at his usual place by the altar, genuflects (or bows if he be a canon) to the Bishop, holds up the cruet and says *Benedicite, Pater reverendissime.*[32] The Bishop at his throne blesses it, saying *In nomine Patris et Filii✠et Spiritus Sancti. Amen.* The celebrant says the prayer *Deus qui humanæ substantiæ,* not blessing the water. The thurifer brings the thurible to the deacon, who hands it to the celebrant. The altar is incensed as usual, then the deacon incenses the celebrant with two swings only. He comes before the throne, where the AP awaits him. He genuflects to the Bishop and hands the thurible to the AP. The Bishop stands, wearing the mitre, and is incensed by the AP with three double swings. Then he

---

[31] For homily and indulgence, cf. Chapter XVI § 5 (including the table). But when the Bishop does not celebrate the Mass *(a) Confiteor* is sung at the foot of the altar (S.R.C. 2682 § 14); *(b)* the prayers, *Precibus,* etc., are said (not sung), *(c)* the book is held by the book-bearer; *(d)* the Bishop stands, mitred, for the *Confiteor;* sits while the indulgence is announced, stands uncovered for *Precibus,* and wears the mitre for *Et benedictio,* etc.

[32] The more correct procedure is to follow the usual order of the Mass, i.e., to bless the water before blessing the incense; most authors, however, suggest the order given above.

blesses the AP, and the latter hands the thurible to the deacon, and goes to his seat by the throne; the deacon (not standing directly before the Bishop) incenses the AP, then the deacons at the throne, each with two double swings, genuflecting to the Bishop when he passes before him. The rest of the incensing proceeds as usual.

Preface. Towards the conclusion of the secret(s) the assistants at the throne all stand; the second deacon takes off the Bishop's mitre, the first his skull-cap. The Bishop stands when the celebrant chants the conclusion of the last secret. The mitre-bearer takes away the golden mitre and brings the precious one. After *Gratias agamus* the canons and the AP form their circle around the throne and at the end of the preface say the *Sanctus* with the Bishop. He dismisses them, as usual, with a blessing and he sits. The AP goes to his stall in choir.

Meanwhile the faldstool, or kneeler, is brought to the middle of the choir before the altar. The first deacon puts on the Bishop's skull-cap and precious mitre. The Bishop rises, takes the crosier in his left hand and comes down from the throne to the faldstool, blessing the choir as he passes. The deacons hold the ends of his cope.

Meanwhile the torch-bearers have taken their torches; they come to the sanctuary, genuflecting to the altar, then to the Bishop (if he is still at his throne). They kneel in two rows, facing each other on either side, the faldstool between them (fig. 17).

Consecration. At the faldstool the Bishop hands his crosier to its bearer and kneels.[33] The second assistant deacon takes off his mitre and skull-cap; the deacons spread out the ends of his cope. They kneel on either side; the mitre and crosier bearers behind. Meanwhile the subdeacon, holding the paten at the foot of the altar steps, moves somewhat towards the epistle side and turns slightly, so as not to stand with his back to the Bishop. When the elevation is over the Bishop rises and genuflects. The two deacons holding the ends of his cope also genuflect, as do all the servers. The first deacon replaces the Bishop's skull-cap and precious mitre; the Bishop takes the crosier in his left hand and goes back to the throne; he does not bless the choir as he passes. As soon as he has left, the faldstool is removed; the subdeacon returns to his place at the centre. At the throne the Bishop hands the crosier to its bearer and sits for a moment while the second deacon takes off his mitre and the first his skull-cap.[34] Then the Bishop stands again, turning towards the altar. At the end of the Lord's Prayer the canons come to form their circle around the Bishop. In the middle they genuflect before the altar. They say

---

[33] When the Bishop, mitred, is to kneel, the mitre is removed after he has knelt (some rubricians say before he kneels—which seems more dignified); but put on when he has risen (C.E., I, viii, 3; cf. II, xviii, 19).
[34] He may, if customary, retain his skull-cap (S.R.C. 3188).

the *Agnus Dei* with the Bishop, then go back, genuflecting before the altar as before.[35]

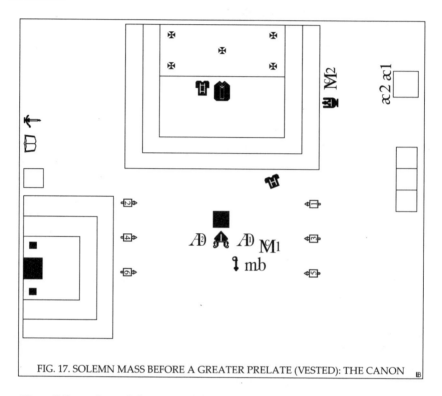

FIG. 17. SOLEMN MASS BEFORE A GREATER PRELATE (VESTED): THE CANON

Pax. When the celebrant and his ministers have said *Agnus Dei,* the deacon goes to stand by the missal, the subdeacon near the AP's place in choir. The AP, as soon as he, with the other canons, has said the *Agnus Dei,* goes to the altar without any genuflexion and kneels there on the footpace, at the right of the celebrant. After the prayer *Domine Iesu Christe qui dixisti* he (instead of the deacon) receives the kiss of peace from the celebrant. He then genuflects to the Blessed Sacrament and goes to the throne. Here, making no reverence to the Bishop, he gives him the pax (placing his arms under those of the Bishop, if this be the custom).[36] Then he steps down, bows *low* to the Bishop and goes to his stall in the choir. The first assistant deacon goes before the Bishop, bows, receives the pax from him, bows low and goes back to his place. Then the second assistant deacon does the same. The AP at his place in the choir gives the pax to the subdeacon. After this he has no further duty. The subdeacon, accompanied by the MC of the Mass, gives it to the first dignitary. Then

---

[35] C.E., I, xxi, 3, prescribes a double genuflexion, but a decision of S.R.C. (4135 § 1) modifies this rubric.

[36] Cf. O'Connell, *The Celebration of Mass,* 1964, p. 429, n. 9.

he gives it to the senior canon on the other side, returns to the altar, gives the pax to the deacon, then to the second ceremoniar (who had accompanied him). The kiss of peace passes through the choir in the usual way.

Postcommunion. After the communion the Bishop sits; the first assistant deacon puts on his skull-cap and the precious mitre. The bearers of the book and hand-candle approach, the Bishop reads the communion antiphon. Then the second deacon takes off his mitre, the Bishop stands while the celebrant sings *Dominus vobiscum,* and the deacon of the Mass sings *Ite, missa est* (or *Benedicamus Domino*). When the celebrant has said the prayer *Placeat tibi* he kisses the altar and goes to stand at the epistle corner, facing the Bishop. The deacon and subdeacon stand on their steps below him, also facing the Bishop. The first assistant deacon puts on the Bishop's precious mitre (the Bishop sits momentarily for this), the bearer of the crosier is at hand, the bearers of the book (who now has the pontifical canon) and of the candle stand before the Bishop. He sings the verses *Sit nomen Domini* (signing his breast)...and *Adiutorium nostrum* (making the sign of the cross)...then *Benedicat vos omnipotens Deus,* extending his arms and looking up. He takes the crosier in his left hand, and with his right, makes the sign of the cross three times as he continues *Pa✠ter et Fil✠ius et Spiritus✠Sanctus.* The assistant deacons standing (being canons) hold the ends of the cope and bow. All present kneel except the bearers of book and candle; and the celebrant and canons, who bow low.

If the pontiff is the Archbishop, the cross-bearer brings the archiepiscopal cross, while the answer to *Ite, missa est* is sung. He carries this before the throne and kneels there on the lowest step, holding the cross so that the figure of our Lord faces the Archbishop. In this case the mitre is not put on; an archbishop blesses without it, because of the cross before him. He bows to the cross after the word *Deus* and before making the first sign of the cross at *Pater.*

Conclusion of Mass. After the blessing the Bishop sits mitred and with his crosier; the celebrant or the AP, turning to the people, announces the indulgence (cf. Chapter XVI § 5), on those occasions it is given, and if it has not already been done by the preacher.[37] The ministers stand on either side of the celebrant while he does so. After the publication the Bishop hands back the crosier to its bearer, and the second deacon takes off the mitre. He stands again for the last Gospel and genuflects, on a cushion, at the text *Et Verbum caro factum est.* The celebrant, ministers and their servers now leave, making the usual reverences, first to the altar and then to the Bishop (who blesses them). The Bishop unvests, assisted by the deacons at the throne. The vestments are carried by servers to the

---

[37] Cf. Chapter XV § 1. The preacher announces the indulgence after he has preached. When the indulgence is imparted at the end of Mass there is no *Confiteor, Precibus,* etc.

altar, laid on it by an MC and covered with a veil, as before Mass. The valet brings the cappa magna, which the Bishop puts on. Meanwhile the faldstool is again put before the altar. The Bishop attended by his deacons and servers (including the train-bearer) comes to it, kneels uncovered and says a short prayer, the others kneeling at his side and behind as at the beginning of the function. He again visits the chapel of the Blessed Sacrament, then leaves the church, blessing the clergy and people as he passes.

§ 2. When the Bishop Assists in Cappa Magna

On less solemn occasions the Bishop may assist at solemn Mass wearing not cope and mitre, but cappa magna.[38]

In this case everything is done as when he presides in vestments (pp. 172ff.), with the exceptions here noted. No vestments are spread on the altar; the Bishop does not vest at the throne nor does he use mitre or crosier. Four or six candles may burn at the sanctuary rails. The celebrant, ministers and servers come to the sanctuary first, and wait there. The Bishop enters wearing rochet, cappa magna, pectoral cross (if customary), skull-cap and carrying his biretta.[39] He wears these latter all the time at the throne, when seated.

He blesses the celebrant and ministers, kneels at the faldstool, or kneeler, rises after a short prayer, reverences to the altar and then goes at once to the altar steps and says the prayers at the beginning of Mass, as described above. Then he goes to the throne. All proceeds as in the last section; the Bishop says the same parts of the Mass from a missal, the servers holding the book and hand-candle. The canons come to form their circles around the throne. The Bishop blesses the incense each time, assisted by his AP. He blesses the subdeacon after the Epistle and the deacon before the Gospel. He kisses the book at the end of the Gospel, as when *paratus*. He receives the kiss of peace from the AP. He comes to the faldstool at the middle for the consecration and elevation. The indulgence, when available, is announced; the Bishop gives the blessing at the end.

Meanwhile two deacons attend him at the throne in choir dress, the assistant priest is by them.

The following further differences are to be noted: The chief is that the Bishop in cappa is incensed (by the AP) only at the offertory, not at any other time. The celebrant is incensed on three occasions (as at any solemn Mass), but with only two double swings each time. Whenever the Bishop stands or kneels he takes off the biretta, except while he gives his

---

[38] C.E., II, ix, 4. The train-bearer wears no surplice, but a *ferraiolo*.

[39] One who is not in sacred vestments (*paratus*) may only wear the biretta in church when seated.

blessing.[40] If he is the Archbishop, he does not wear his biretta at the blessing, because of the cross held before him. He wears the skull-cap all the time, even when he has taken off his biretta, except while the Gospel is sung, while he is being incensed, and from the beginning of the preface to the communion inclusive. At these times he takes off both biretta and skull-cap. The Bishop takes them off himself and hands them to the first assistant deacon. When both are taken off, the skull-cap is held by the deacon on the top of or put inside the biretta. The Bishop puts both on himself, taking them from the first assistant deacon.

§ 3. Solemn Mass for the Dead Before the Bishop

In this case the following special rules are observed.[41]

The Bishop may assist either in a black or violet cope and the simple mitre, or in cappa magna. If he wears the cope and mitre, the vestments are spread on the altar beforehand, the one (simple) mitre stands on the gospel side. The crosier is not used. The throne is covered in violet silk (if the Bishop is in cope), or violet cloth. Its platform may be covered with a violet carpet, like the footpace of the altar. The faldstool or prie-dieu is covered with violet and has violet cushions. The candles are of unbleached wax, except the hand-candle. When the Bishop arrives, the bells are not rung joyfully; they may be tolled. The organ is silent throughout.

The ceremony proceeds as usual (pp. 155, 172), with the following exceptions:

The Bishop gives no blessing (except that of incense) at any time; he does not bless the choir in passing nor the celebrant. According to the rule for all requiem Masses, no blessing is given to the ministers after the Epistle nor before the Gospel, nor does the deacon go to kiss the Bishop's hand. The canons do not come to form a circle around the Bishop.

Towards the end of the singing of the *Kyrie,* the Bishop comes from his throne, wearing the mitre, goes to the faldstool before the altar and kneels there without mitre[42] during the collect. All kneel except the celebrant and ministers.[43] The assistant priest does not go to the throne till the Bishop has returned to it after the collect.

The Bishop puts on incense and blesses it at the offertory; he is incensed by the AP at this point only.

The Bishop kneels at the faldstool from the consecration till *Pater noster* exclusively. Everyone in choir kneels during this time (p. 105). The

---

[40] And except during the chanting of the *Confiteor* before the indulgence, if this be given.
[41] C.E., II, xii. A knowledge of the rubrics which regulate a solemn Mass of requiem and solemn Mass in presence of a greater prelate is presumed.
[42] The mitre is removed after he has knelt (some say before), and put on after he has risen.
[43] If the Bishop is in cope, he wears the mitre while returning to the throne.

Bishop comes again to the faldstool for the postcommunion, as he did at the collect. No blessing is given, no indulgence announced.

If there is a homily after the Mass, the preacher does not ask the Bishop for a blessing. If the Absolution follows,[44] cf. Chapter XXXI §§ 5-6.

If the Bishop wears the cappa, the differences noted above are observed.

§ 4. Solemn Mass Before a Bishop Not in his Own Diocese

When a bishop who has no jurisdiction in the place—and is, therefore, not a "greater prelate" (p. 57)—assists at solemn Mass, he takes no special part in the ceremony. He assists in choir dress, that is, in violet cassock, rochet, mantelletta, pectoral cross, violet biretta, and takes the first place in the choir. The canons are not to go to meet him at the door of the church in full procession, as they meet the Ordinary; but some of them may meet him, of whom the highest in rank offers holy water.[45] The side of the choir on which the bishop sits then becomes that of higher dignity. The celebrant and ministers bow to him at the beginning and end of the Mass. He is incensed (at the offertory *only*) after the celebrant,[46] before anyone else, with three double incensings. He receives the kiss of peace from the deacon before anyone else. He does not give the blessing at the end of Mass, and takes no further part in the function than do others in choir.

---

[44] In this case the last Gospel is omitted.
[45] The bishop takes holy water but does not sprinkle others.
[46] In such a case the celebrant is incensed with the normal three double swings.

Chapter XVI

Pontifical Solemn Mass at the Throne[1]

§ 1. Preparation

A throne is used by a bishop where he has jurisdiction, therefore by the metropolitan throughout his province and the Bishop throughout his diocese (except in the presence of a cardinal), also by a cardinal everywhere outside Rome and in his titular church in Rome.[2]

A chapel—other than that of the Blessed Sacrament—should be set apart (called the secretarium) in which Terce is sung and the Bishop vests.

If the Blessed Sacrament is reserved on the high altar of the church, It should be removed, if possible, before the ceremony to a side chapel or altar. In the chapel of the Blessed Sacrament a faldstool or a kneeler is placed before the altar. This kneeler is covered with a cloth, green or violet according to the occasion (p. 29); either has two cushions of the same colour, one for the Bishop's arms, one on the ground, on which he will kneel. Six candles should be lit on this altar during the time the Bishop is there.

In the Secretarium. There is also an altar in the secretarium. On this are six candles, lit, and the usual altar cross. This altar is vested in the colour of the Mass; on it are laid the Bishop's vestments, namely (inversely to the order in which they are taken): the chasuble, gloves on a salver (to one side), dalmatic, tunicle, the morse of the cope on a plate (small salver), the cope, stole, pectoral cross,[3] girdle, alb, amice. All are covered with a veil of the colour of the Mass. The gremial may be used for this purpose. The precious mitre stands on the altar at the gospel side, the golden mitre at the epistle side. *If the prelate is an archbishop,* on the

---

[1] C.E., II, viii; I, vii, viii, ix, x.

[2] The Ordinary may allow the use of his throne to another bishop, provided this is not his own auxiliary, nor vicar general, nor a dignitary or canon of his cathedral (C.I.C. 337, § 3; S.R.C. 4023 and 4355). A metropolitan may use a throne throughout his province; but in the cathedral of one of his suffragans it is erected, temporarily, on the epistle side of the sanctuary. The same rule holds for an Apostolic Delegate in the place of his legation. A Cardinal, however, occupies the throne of the Bishop on the gospel side (C.E., I, xiii, 4, 9, 10). If the Bishop *pontificates* in presence of a higher prelate he does so at the faldstool.

[3] In practice, normally, the Bishop will use the cross he wears on entering (which should, of course, be suspended on the cord that is part of his choir dress, and not on a chain), taking it off and putting it on again over the alb.

days on which he may use the pallium,[4] this is laid on the altar at the gospel corner, on a salver, and covered with a small veil of the colour of the day. The three jewelled pins to fix it lie on another salver near. The crosier stands near the altar, also the processional cross. But *if he is the Archbishop* he will enter with his cross. In this case there should be a stand for it near the altar on the gospel side. *On the epistle side* is a bench (or stools) for the ministers of the Mass and on it[5] their maniples. A throne with a canopy is prepared in this chapel at either side of the altar according to convenience, normally on the gospel side, and stools at its sides for the AP and the assistant deacons. There is a faldstool before the altar covered in green; and seats for the canons and others in the part of the secretarium that corresponds to the choir.

On the Credence of the Secretarium. The acolytes' candles at the back; the Bishop's ceremonial shoes (with a shoe horn) and stockings, laid on a tray and covered with a silk veil of the colour of the vestments; a book of the Gospels (or a missal), and within its pages, at the Mass to be celebrated, the Bishop's maniple; a breviary, marked for the capitulum of Terce. A lectern, with the antiphonary *(Liber Usualis)* marked for Terce, is at a spot convenient for the cantors. The thurible (with a good supply of lighted charcoal) and incense boat are at hand.

On a Second Credence prepared near the throne of the secretarium are: a pontifical canon, and a breviary (with the prayer for Terce marked); the hand-candle with wax candle; a small salver; the ewer and dish, with two hand-towels, for the washing of the Bishop's hands.

In the Sanctuary. In the sanctuary of the church the high altar is vested for Mass with a frontal of the proper colour. On the table of the altar, in addition to the usual six candles, is a seventh,[6] in line with these. Before this stands the altar cross. The altar cards are not put on. *On the credence at the epistle side* (leaving room at the back of it for the acolytes' candles) are: The chalice prepared for Mass,[7] with its veil folded beside it; the cruets and bell; the pax-brede (if the kiss of peace is to be given to a layman); the ciborium (if Holy Communion is to be given) and the communion cloth (if used). All these are covered over with the humeral veil that the subdeacon will wear; and on top of the chalice, outside this veil, it is convenient to put the burse containing the corporal. On this table also, outside the veil, are the book for the Epistle and Gospel, and

---

[4] The rules about the pallium are in the 1983 C.I.C., canon 437. A list of the days on which the pallium may be worn is given in *Pontificale Romanum* (Part I).

[5] Nearby, if the ministers are to sit before the Bishop's arrival.

[6] C.E., I, xii, 12. The seventh candle is used normally only at pontifical solemn Mass of the living sung by *the* Bishop, i.e., the Ordinary (at his throne or — if circumstances require — at a faldstool).

[7] If the *prægustatio* (cf. Chapter XVI § 5) takes place, two breads are prepared on the paten, and a small bowl is needed for the wine to be pre-tasted.

the ewer and dish[8] for the washing of the Bishop's hands, with three hand-towels.[9] Also the card with the chant of the *Confiteor* and that containing the formula for announcing the indulgence (if this is to be given).

On the Credence near the Throne. The missal on its stand, the pontifical canon,[10] the *Pontificale* (if the Papal blessing is to be given), the hand-candle[11] with a wax candle, the gremial and a small salver.[12] Somewhere on the gospel side, towards the back of the altar, the stand for the processional cross. *If the Archbishop is the celebrant,* his cross is used, and the stand for this is placed on the gospel side of the sanctuary not far from the throne.

The throne in the sanctuary should be covered with cloths of the colour of the Mass; a cushion lies near on which the Bishop will genuflect during the *Credo*. On either side is a bare stool for the deacons at the throne ; on the Bishop's right (or left[13]) a third bare stool for the assistant priest.

East of the throne is the place for the Bishop's attendants *(familiares)*, and there should be a bench (or stools) there for them and for the servers at the throne. Opposite the throne, on the epistle side, are the sedilia for the sacred ministers. At the entrance of the sanctuary, four, six or at most seven candlesticks stand, with burning candles.

In the Sacristy. In the sacristy the vestments for the deacon and sub-deacon (without the maniples) are laid out; also vestments for the canons:[14] copes for the dignitaries, chasubles for the canons who represent priests, dalmatics and tunicles for the canons who represent deacons and subdeacons; two dalmatics for the deacons at the throne,[15] a cope for the AP. Amices are made ready for all these vestments. Four plain copes (if customary) and surplices for the chaplains or servers who will hold the book, hand-candle, mitre and crosier; the veils for the crosier and mitre-bearers (if they do not wear copes); an amice, alb, girdle and tunicle for the subdeacon who will carry the processional cross. All the vestments are of the colour of the Mass. The lustral water, with its

---

[8] Unless there is a duplicate, this must be brought to the sanctuary from the secretarium (after Terce) either by its bearer in the procession, or by the sacristan.

[9] Under the credence or behind the altar is prepared a bowl into which the water used at each washing is poured, that the silver dish may be ready for the next washing.

[10] Unless there is a duplicate, this must be brought to the sanctuary from the secretarium (after Terce) either by its bearer in the procession, or by the sacristan.

[11] Ditto.

[12] Ditto.

[13] The AP may be on the other side, facing down the church.

[14] In some places the canons vest in the secretarium.

[15] These they will wear over surplice (or rochet if they have the right to it) and amice. The AP likewise wears his cope over surplice (rochet) and amice. These ministers wear neither stole nor maniple.

sprinkler, is also prepared for the reception of the Bishop. Torches, at least four and not more than eight, are ready.

§ 2. The Ministers and Servers

The following persons take part in the ceremony:

The deacon and subdeacon of the Mass, who should be canons; two canons (the two senior canons-deacon) who will serve as assistant deacons at the throne;[16] the assistant priest, also a canon, who should be the highest dignitary of the choir (provided he is not a bishop), or the canon who will preach the homily;[17] four chaplains for the mitre, crosier, book and hand-candle; a train-bearer. Six other servers are needed for the vesting of the bishop; these may afterwards serve as torch-bearers. There are also the (second) MC of the Mass, and another (first) MC at the throne, who regulates the whole ceremony. The acolytes and thurifer of the Mass take part as usual. The Ceremonial of Bishops enumerates the servers in this way: first, seven, namely, the bearers of the mitre, crosier, book and candle, then the thurifer and two acolytes. Further, it requires six others: one to have charge of the gremial (in practice the train-bearer can see to this), one of the cruets,[18] the other four[19] assist in cassock, but without surplice, standing by the credence. This makes thirteen servers, besides the two masters of ceremonies, cross-bearer and train-bearer (if the Bishop arrives in cappa magna). Add to these the subdeacon (not a canon) who is to be cross-bearer, the deacon and subdeacon of the Mass, the assistant priest and two deacons at the throne, and we have altogether twenty-three persons in attendance on the Bishop when he sings solemn Mass at the throne. There may be other attendants or servants, such as the Bishop's valet, who wait east of the throne when they are not occupied. The Chapter should be present to sing Terce and assist at Mass; other clergy and seminarians should also attend.

General Rules for Assistants. It will be convenient to give at once some general directions about the functions of these persons.

If the assistants (AP, deacons at the throne, deacon and subdeacon of the Mass) are not members of the Chapter, throughout the function their

---

[16] Whilst it is customary that the Bishop's senior clergy assist him, it is seemly that persons in deacon's or subdeacon's orders only exercise their orders where they are available. If deacons at the throne are not available, the deacon and subdeacon of the Mass may supply their duties (S.R.C. 3114 § 3).

[17] The practice of the major superior of a clerical institute assuming this function during the ordination of his subjects seems particularly apposite.

[18] These two — with the two acolytes — will be needed for the vesting and unvesting of the Bishop.

[19] "Cubicularii sive familiares Episcopi" (C.E., I, xi, 2), i.e., chamberlains and attendants. The ceremonial (I, xi, 11) supposes each of the four to wash the Bishop's hands in turn. In practice, there is generally only one, the Bishop's valet.

reverence to the altar and the Bishop is a genuflexion; for canons it is a deep bow.

During the function the clergy in choir are not saluted, but they are on the arrival of the sacred ministers and before they depart at the end.

The ASSISTANT PRIEST hands the hand-towel whenever the Bishop washes his hands and after the washing (or later) replaces his ring with the *solita oscula*. Hands are washed four times: before Mass, at the offertory, at the *Lavabo*, after the ablutions. The AP holds the boat when the Bishop (at the throne) puts on incense. At the altar he moves the missal. When the Bishop sings anything at the throne the AP holds the book; when he recites, the book-bearer holds it.

Ordinarily the first ASSISTANT DEACON puts on the Bishop's mitre (at the throne,[20] when normally, the deacon of the Mass is not at hand) and gremial, the second takes them off. The Bishop wears the mitre while he walks in procession (e.g., from the throne to the altar, or back), while he sits, while he is incensed (except after the Gospel), while he washes his hands if he is vested at the time, while he gives his blessing.[21] He uses the precious mitre from the beginning to the introit, golden mitre (being lighter) from the introit to the end of the *Credo*, then precious mitre to the end of the whole service. Normally the assistant deacon(s) removes the Bishop's ring when he is about to wash his hands. The AP replaces it.

The gremial is spread over the Bishop's knees while he sits during the sung *Kyrie, eleison, Gloria in excelsis,* Epistle, etc., *Credo.* While he washes his hands at the offertory a towel may be spread.

His crosier is handed to him and taken back directly by the crosier-bearer with *solita oscula*. The Bishop holds it in his left hand in procession (including from throne to altar and back), while the Gospel is sung,[22] while he gives his blessing at the end.

When the Bishop is at the throne, ordinarily the place of the first MC is at his left, standing.

When the Bishop himself celebrates, the canons do not come to form the circle around the throne, as they do when he only presides.

General Rules for Servers. A special feature of pontifical functions is the assistance of four servers (called "capellani" in the Ceremonial), who carry the mitre, crosier, book from which the Bishop reads, and the hand-candle. This is the order of their rank: mitre-bearer, crosier-bearer, book-bearer, hand-candle-bearer. When the bishop has no jurisdiction (therefore in the case of an auxiliary or of an extern bishop) he will not,

---

[20] When the Bishop is *at the altar* the deacon of the Mass puts on and takes off the mitre (unless he be engaged, as after the incensation of the altar — C.E., I, viii, 3).

[21] An archbishop is not covered when he blesses, because of his archiepiscopal cross held before him.

[22] Then he holds it with both hands.

perhaps, use the crosier,[23] so only the three others attend. At solemn functions, when the Bishop and canons are vested, these four chaplains may wear, over their surplices, copes of the colour of the Office. If they do not do this, the mitre and crosier bearers have scarves *(vimpæ)*, with which to hold the mitre or crosier.[24]

The MITRE-BEARER hands the mitre to the deacon (the first assistant deacon or the deacon of the Mass) who puts it on the Bishop. He takes it back from the second assistant deacon or from the deacon of the Mass. In the case of the mitre there are no *oscula*. The mitre-bearer holds the mitre with the lappets towards himself; but when he places it on the altar or credence the lappets are to be turned outwards.

The CROSIER-BEARER always hands the crosier to the Bishop and takes it from him directly, each time with the *solita oscula*. He hands it with the crook towards himself (so that the Bishop may have it facing forward), but carries it with the crook facing forward. He walks, normally, on the left of the mitre-bearer.

The BOOK-BEARER holds the book open before the Bishop (except when the AP does so, see p. 191). He kneels before a "greater prelate" (sitting or kneeling); otherwise he stands. He holds the book at the bottom with both hands, leaning it against his forehead. But when a bishop sits and the book-bearer stands he leans it against the breast. When a bishop uses a book on the altar the book-bearer has no function and stands away, generally on the gospel side, on the ground.

The CANDLE-BEARER holds the candle, lighted, in the right hand by the book. Normally, when at the throne, he should be at the right of the book-bearer.[25] He and the book-bearer genuflect together to a greater prelate, or bow to another bishop, on arriving and retiring. When the Bishop uses a book on the altar the candle-bearer stands at the side of the AP, holding the candle. At the incensing of the altar he stands aside taking the candle with him. When he goes to kneel at the elevation, he leaves the candle on the altar. He stands or kneels as does the book-bearer. When not at the throne his normal place is on the book-bearer's left.

Neither the book-bearer nor the candle-bearer genuflects, even when all others do so, when attending the Bishop with the book or candle.

These four chaplains follow the Bishop in procession. When he is at the altar the mitre-bearer and crosier-bearer are towards the epistle side, for convenience in handing these. The candle-bearer and book-bearer are, normally, by the second credence, on the gospel side (as during the

---

[23] A bishop outside the place of his jurisdiction when he pontificates will use a crosier in functions which require its use (e.g., an ordination) and may use it at any function with the consent of the Ordinary (cf. C.I.C. 337, § 2, and S.R.C. 4355, iii, 3).

[24] C.E. (I, xi, 6) does not suppose a veil used if a cope is worn.

[25] So placed he is not as likely to incommode the AP and is in a more convenient position to hold the candle in the right hand.

prayers at the foot of the altar). When the Bishop is at the throne these two are nearby. From the offertory, the candle-bearer is on the footpace on the gospel side; the book-bearer stands away on the ground, on that side, not holding a book.

A "greater prelate" has a TRAIN-BEARER to carry the train of his cappa magna. Other bishops (an auxiliary or visitor) do not use a train;[26] so this server does not attend them. Whenever the Bishop with train goes in procession, even from one part of the sanctuary to the other, the train-bearer goes behind him holding the train with both hands. When the Bishop does not go in procession, the train-bearer stands or kneels aside, but near. His place then is at the east side of the throne; or near the (second) credence, when the Bishop is at the altar.

Choir Ceremonies. In addition to the ordinary ceremonial at solemn Mass, the clergy in choir at a pontifical function kneel, momentarily, when the Bishop arrives in or departs from the choir, and whenever he passes from the altar to the throne or *vice versa*. Prelates and canons bow low. The clergy kneel while the Bishop prays for a brief space (at the faldstool) on his arrival and before his departure at the beginning and end of the function. While he is at his throne, vested, they stand or sit according as the Bishop does. They stand while the Bishop unvests.

§ 3. The Vesting of the Bishop

The service begins while the canons sing Terce (on great festivals) in the choir of the secretarium. First, the bells of the church are rung, the organ is played. The canons proceed in choral dress to meet the Bishop. The ministers of the Mass who are canons go also to meet the Bishop or they may vest beforehand in the sacristy and then await the Bishop in the secretarium.[27] The bearers of the mitre and crosier wait near the credence; the bearers of the book and candle near the throne in the secretarium.[28] The cross-bearer and other servers are there too, vested; the train-bearer is with the Bishop.

---

[26] A bishop in the place of his jurisdiction may wear his cappa magna even in the presence of his superior. In deference to the latter he does not allow the train to flow but carries it folded up. He will, however, allow it to flow if he is about to pontificate, but even then not when he walks with his superior or performs any act of deference towards him (S.R.C. 4355, II, 2).

[27] C.E. (I, ix, 1) says the deacon is to assume his vestments in the same place as the other canons, i.e., *extra secretarium* (II, viii, 4). Though C.E. supposes him and the subdeacon to vest at the same time as the other canons, some authors (e.g., Martinucci, Schober) advise that they vest beforehand and at the sedilia await the arrival of the Bishop in the secretarium. This is more convenient.

[28] The mitre and crosier bearers may be in cope from the beginning of the function; the book and candle bearers may put on their copes after the Bishop has read the prayers of preparation. Or all four may put on the cope (in the sacristy) after the Bishop has vested for Mass.

Arrival of Bishop. The Bishop arrives in the church in rochet and cappa. He receives the *aspergillum* from the senior canon, signs himself and then sprinkles (thrice) the canons, and after them all present (thrice). Accompanied by his attendants, and by the canons (who follow him), he goes first to the chapel of the Blessed Sacrament, removes his skull-cap, genuflects and kneels at the faldstool[29] or prie-dieu prepared there and says a short prayer. Then he rises, genuflects, replaces his skull-cap and goes to the secretarium, bows to the altar cross, kneels at the faldstool there again for a few moments. Then he goes to the throne, sits, and puts on his biretta. Here the deacons assisting and the AP await him, in choir dress. Meanwhile the canons (except those assisting at the throne) vest in the secretarium or in the sacristy or other convenient place and then return to their places in the secretarium. The chaplains of the book and candle take these from the credence and come before the Bishop.

Beginning of Terce. When the canons return to their places after vesting, the Bishop takes off his biretta, hands it to the first assistant deacon, rises, and intones *Deus in adiutorium meum intende* (signing himself). The canons answer; the hymn *Nunc Sancte nobis Spiritus* (intoned by cantors) is sung, the antiphon intoned and the psalms of Terce begin. Then the Bishop sits, puts on his biretta; the book and candle bearers come before him and he begins the prayers before Mass, *Ne reminiscaris* and the psalms. The assistant priest and deacons (standing uncovered) may say these with him. The canons sit at their places and continue Terce slowly, so as not to finish before the Bishop is vested.[30]

The subdeacon goes to the credence and takes the Bishop's shoes and stockings, on their tray covered with a veil. With this veil he also covers his hands, and carries the tray with both hands and raised to the height of his eyes. He comes to the throne and kneels before the Bishop; assisted by the Bishop's servant (who removes the Bishop's ordinary shoes and afterwards takes them away hidden under his cloak) he puts on the liturgical shoes and stockings, beginning with the right foot. The subdeacon then takes the tray back to the credence, and goes to the sedilia, where he waits by the deacon.

Prayers of Preparation. Meanwhile, the Bishop says the prayers of preparation.[31] When he arrives at *Kyrie, eleison,* he uncovers, rises and finishes the prayers facing the altar. He then sits and puts on his biretta. Meantime the servers receive the vestments from the second MC at the altar and bring them near the throne. An attendant (usually the Bishop's valet) takes off the cappa, the first assistant deacon having removed the

---

[29] The MC spreads the front of the cappa over the faldstool and sets it free when the Bishop rises. This is the rule always when a bishop in cappa kneels at a faldstool or kneeler.
[30] If necessary the organ may play between the psalms (C.E., II, viii, 8).
[31] A bishop who is about to celebrate pontifical Mass satisfies the obligation of the canonical hour (Terce or None) by reciting these prayers which are prescribed by the Ceremonial (S.R.C., 9 April 1921).

pectoral cross,[32] if the Bishop wears it over the cappa, and laid it aside. The deacon and subdeacon of the Mass come to the throne; the assistant deacons (the first one having removed the Bishop's ring[33] for the washing of the hands) retire (usually to the sacristy, if nearby) put on their amices and dalmatics, return and stand back, so as not to hinder the others. The Bishop, with his biretta on, now washes his hands. The AP spreads one of the hand-towels over the Bishop's knees. An attendant,[34] kneeling before the Bishop, holds the dish and pours the water, the AP hands the second hand-towel.[35] He then goes to put on his amice and cope, and comes back to the throne when vested.

Vesting the Bishop for Terce. The servers who hold the vestments now come to the throne; the Bishop's biretta is taken away and put with his cappa. Meanwhile the other persons in choir, canons, prebendaries or chaplains, continue Terce. The Bishop vests in order, saying each prayer assisted by the deacon (the subdeacon aiding when necessary). The pectoral cross is put on after the cincture and the deacon kisses it before presenting it to the Bishop to kiss. When the cope is put on the morse is added (for the Ordinary). Lastly the Bishop sits and the deacon puts on him the golden mitre. The ministers of the Mass go to the sedilia and are replaced by the assistant deacons.

Conclusion of Terce. When the psalms of Terce are finished, the subdeacon of the Mass (aided by the second MC) takes a breviary, goes to the place at a distance from the foot of the altar where the Epistle is read and chants the Chapter, taking care not to turn his back to the Bishop, who rises, not taking off the mitre; all rise with him. After the Chapter the subdeacon returns to his place at the sedilia. Cantors (in the middle of the choir) sing the short responsory and the versicles of Terce. The acolytes (directed by the second MC) bring their candles to the throne and stand at the bottom of its steps, on either side facing each other. The chaplains of the book and candle approach. The Bishop may sit while the second assistant deacon takes off his mitre.[36] Then he rises and sings *Dominus vobiscum* and the prayer *(in tono festivo)*, the AP holding the book before him. He repeats *Dominus vobiscum,* the acolytes and chaplains retire; the cantors sing *Benedicamus Domino.* The verse *Fidelium animæ* is not sung,

---

[32] The MC or a server will keep it on a salver until it is put on after the cincture.

[33] (C.E. II, viii, 10). Kissing both the hand and the ring, as always. The ring is not replaced until after the vesting for Mass, when the precious mitre has been put on (S.R.C. 3747 § 1 and cf. C.E., II, viii, 22; § II of C.E. does not refer to the pontifical ring, but to other rings, no longer worn by bishops). The MC will have at hand a salver (held by a server) to receive the pectoral cross or the ring when they are taken off momentarily.

[34] For a cardinal the nobleman and chamberlain in attendance wash his hands (C.E., I, xi, 12; II, viii, 11); for the Bishop it is usually one of the servers.

[35] While the Bishop washes his hands those ministering near the throne (except canons) kneel; but if a prelate of higher rank be present, they do not kneel (C.E., II, viii, 10).

[36] The mitre-bearer takes away this golden mitre and gets the precious one. He keeps with him, however, the golden one to bring to the high altar in the procession.

since Mass will follow at once. The deacons at the throne stand aside. The deacon and subdeacon of the Mass come again to the throne.

Vesting the Bishop for Mass. The servers return to the throne, bringing the Mass vestments (the tunicle, dalmatic, gloves and chasuble) handed to them by the second MC. The deacon takes off the Bishop's morse and cope, which the MC or a server takes away. The Bishop puts on the tunicle and dalmatic. Then he sits while the deacon puts on the right glove, the subdeacon the left, each kissing first the Bishop's hand and then the glove. Then the Bishop rises and puts on the chasuble. Meanwhile the thurifer prepares the thurible. *If the prelate is the Archbishop,* and if it is a day on which he wears the pallium, this is brought by a subdeacon-canon from the altar, handed to the deacon of the Mass, who puts it on the Bishop and fixes the pins, assisted by the subdeacon.[37] The Bishop sits and the deacon puts on the precious mitre, the subdeacon aiding by lifting the lappets.[38] The ministers of the Mass go to the sedilia and put on their maniples; the assistant deacons take their place beside the Bishop. The AP, with the *solita oscula,* puts on the Bishop's ring over the glove. The subdeacon takes the evangeliarium— with the maniple between its leaves—and carries it leaning against his breast, the opening towards his left.

Procession to the Sanctuary. The thurifer comes to the throne, the Bishop puts on incense and blesses it, the AP assisting.[39] Meanwhile the thurifer, as always in such cases, kneels. The subdeacon who carries the cross[40] now takes it and is joined by the two acolytes carrying candles. The crosier-bearer brings the crosier to the Bishop. The Bishop rises and bows to the cross on the altar of the secretarium; the Archbishop bows to the metropolitan cross; the second MC forms the procession.[41] The thurifer goes first (often preceded by the second MC to clear the way), unless there are servants of the Bishop in lay dress to go in front of all. Then comes the subdeacon with the cross between the acolytes. He holds the cross so that the figure of our Lord is turned forward, in the direction of the procession. The clergy follow in order, two and two (juniors first), then the canons (wearing their birettas, as they are vested); subdeacons,

---

[37] C.E., II, viii, 20, gives detailed instruction about the arrangement of the pallium and the pins.

[38] C.E., II, viii, 21.

[39] The AP uses the form *Benedicite, Pater reverendissime;* for a cardinal *Benedicite, eminentissime et reverendissime Pater.* The Bishop blesses incense with the usual words and *one* sign of the cross (C.E., I, xxiii, 2).

[40] Not, of course, the subdeacon of the Mass. The subdeacon cross-bearer is vested in amice, alb, cincture and tunicle.

[41] If Terce is sung in choir and the Bishop vests in the sanctuary, incense is not put in and there is no procession (C.E., II, viii, 25; S.R.C. 3228 § 1). In going from the throne to the foot of the altar the subdeacon (with the book) precedes the AP and deacon (on AP's left); the Bishop, between the assistant deacons, follows them and last of all come the bearers of the Bishop's mitre and crosier.

deacons, priests and dignitaries. The subdeacon of the Mass follows, holding before his breast the evangeliarium closed and containing the Bishop's maniple; then the AP with the deacon of the Mass at his left; then the Bishop between his two assistant deacons. As he passes he blesses the people, holding the crosier in his left hand. The four chaplains of the mitre (carrying the golden mitre), crosier, book (with the pontifical canon) and candle follow. Lastly, the Bishop's attendants, or servants in livery.

If the Bishop is the metropolitan, the subdeacon of the cross carries it between the acolytes immediately before the canons;[42] he holds it so that the figure of our Lord is turned towards the archbishop. In this case no cross is carried at the head of the procession unless it be a very long one. Then the cross of the Chapter may be carried at the head by a cleric wearing a surplice.

Arrival in the Sanctuary. When the procession arrives at the sanctuary of the church, the attendants or servants remain outside; the subdeacon cross-bearer puts the processional cross in a stand prepared for it on the gospel side of the sanctuary and stays by it;[43] the thurifer goes to the epistle side; the acolytes to the credence and deposit their candles there. The clergy genuflect and bow to one another; the canons bow to the altar cross, then bow to each other, two and two, and go to their places; the subdeacon of the Mass goes to the altar steps at the gospel side and hands his biretta and the book to the second MC; the deacon goes to the right of the subdeacon and slightly in front of him; the AP to the epistle side before the steps. The Bishop on arriving in the sanctuary, wearing his mitre, salutes with a slight bow of the head the canons (who respond by a low bow)[44] and then goes to the middle between the AP and the deacon, who stand a little back. His assistant deacons stand behind him; behind these the mitre and crosier bearers.[45] The first MC is on the epistle side (and takes the AP's biretta), the second on the gospel side (and he takes the deacon's biretta). The Bishop, arriving before the altar, hands his crosier to its bearer; the deacon (of the Mass) takes off the mitre and hands it to the mitre-bearer. The Bishop bows low to the altar; all the others genuflect, except canons. So Mass begins.

---

[42] Whenever the Chapter is present the canons — if preceding — and they alone, go between the archiepiscopal cross and the Archbishop. Otherwise the cross is carried immediately before the Archbishop.

[43] His task is finished (and he may go and unvest) unless (i) the celebrant is the Archbishop; or, (ii) at the end of the function, the celebrant will return *paratus* (vested) in procession to the sacristy.

[44] If there is a "greater prelate" present, the Bishop (mitred), and his assistants, salute him on their way to the altar (C.E., II, viii, 29).

[45] While the mitre and crosier bearers kneel behind the Bishop during the preparatory prayers, because they will be needed after them, the book and candle bearers, on arrival in the sanctuary, go to their places east of the throne and there kneel for the opening prayers.

§ 4. From the Beginning of Mass to the Gospel

In all that follows, the usual ceremonies of solemn Mass are supposed, except where a difference is noted.

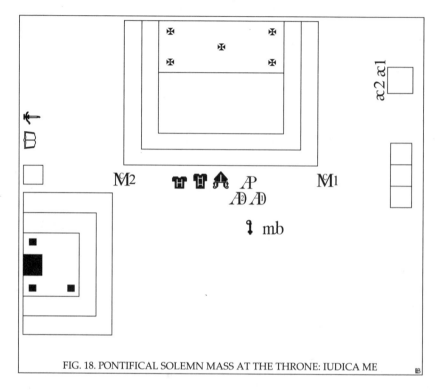

FIG. 18. PONTIFICAL SOLEMN MASS AT THE THRONE: IUDICA ME

The Bishop says the preparatory prayers at the foot of the altar, as usual.[46] The AP, the deacon and subdeacon answer him.[47] When he begins the prayer *Indulgentiam,* the deacon steps back, the subdeacon takes the Bishop's maniple (from the second MC) and when he has finished the prayer puts it on his left arm, kissing first the maniple (at the side), then presenting the cross on the top to be kissed by the Bishop, and lastly kissing the Bishop's hand. When the Bishop goes up to the altar the AP passes behind him to his left, the deacon goes to his right. The subdeacon, taking the book of Gospels (from the second MC), goes up to the altar with the Bishop on the left of the AP. The assistant deacons remain where they are *in plano*. The Bishop kisses the altar, then the Gospel book presented by the subdeacon open at the Gospel of the Mass

---

[46] One of the MC's must see that the pontifical canon (open at *Oramus te, Domine*) is on the table of the altar at the centre. If a second pontifical canon is used, it may be placed so ready before the function begins.

[47] In the *Confiteor* AP, deacon and subdeacon say, as usual, *tibi Pater* and *te Pater*, bowing towards the Bishop.

(the beginning of which AP will indicate to the Bishop), laying both his hands on it. The subdeacon hands it to the second MC or the book-bearer; the AP goes down and stands *in plano* at the gospel corner during the incensation.[48] The thurifer comes up and kneels and the Bishop puts on and blesses incense as usual, the deacon handing the spoon and saying *Benedicite, Pater reverendissime*. The Bishop incenses the altar, assisted by the deacon and subdeacon (each placing the nearer hand to him under his arm).

The deacon takes the thurible from the Bishop. The first deacon of the throne comes and puts the precious mitre on the Bishop. The deacon of the Mass, with the subdeacon at his left, standing at the foot of the altar on the epistle side, incenses the Bishop with three double swings, bowing deeply before and after. When he has done so the Bishop gives him a blessing.[49]

Bishop goes to the Throne. The Bishop from the epistle corner bows, with all his assistant sacred ministers, to the altar-cross, takes his crosier from its bearer, and accompanied by the two assistant deacons, with the AP before him, goes directly to the throne, blessing the choir as he passes. The mitre and crosier-bearers follow him. The ministers of the Mass go to the sedilia. They stand whenever the Bishop stands.

At the throne the Bishop hands his crosier to its bearer, and sits momentarily while the second assistant deacon takes off the mitre. The chaplains of the book (missal) and candle come to the throne, genuflect to the Bishop and hold the book and candle. The Bishop, still without the mitre, stands, makes the sign of the cross, and reads the introit. The bearer of the mitre puts the precious mitre on the credence near the throne, and takes the golden mitre. The Bishop says *Kyrie, eleison* with those around him; the deacon and subdeacon say it to one another.

Gloria. If the sung *Kyrie* will take a long time, the Bishop may now sit, with mitre and gremial (put on by the first assistant deacon), as he will at the *Gloria*. When *Kyrie, eleison* has been sung, the AP holds the book (the pontifical canon—if the Bishop wishes to use it), and the Bishop standing—without mitre or skull-cap[50] and facing the altar—intones *Gloria in excelsis Deo* (if it occurs), disjoining and elevating his hands at *Gloria*, joining them and bowing his head at *Deo*. The book-bearer takes it from the AP, who goes back to his stool. The Bishop recites the hymn with his assistants, the deacon and subdeacon say it at the sedilia. When the Bishop has finished saying the *Gloria* the bearers[51] of book and hand-

---

[48] C.E., I, vii, 4. Some authors direct him to stand between the assistant deacons.

[49] The Bishop answers all incensing and reverences made by the canons or sacred ministers by making the sign of the cross over them.

[50] C.E., II, viii, 37; the second assistant deacon removes the gremial (which a server may hold momentarily) and mitre, the first the skull-cap.

[51] They do not come to the throne at all for the *Gloria* if the Bishop intones and recites it by heart.

candle take these to the credence, leave them there and come back. The Bishop sits; the first assistant deacon puts on the skull-cap and the golden mitre, then takes the gremial from the server who has brought it and spreads it on the Bishop's knees. The assistants at the throne sit on their stools, the four bearers[52] on the steps of the throne or on a seat to the east of the throne (genuflecting first to the Bishop), the ministers of Mass at the sedilia. When the words *Adoramus te*, etc., are sung the Bishop, with mitre on, bows; all others uncover and bow. Towards the end of the *Gloria* sung by the choir, all stand, except the Bishop.

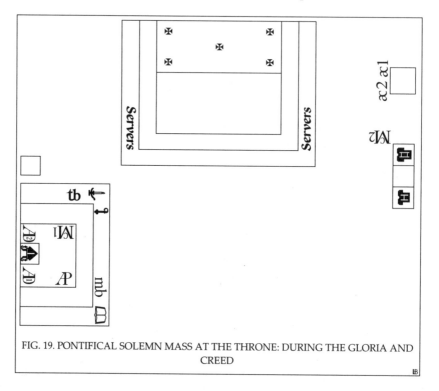

FIG. 19. PONTIFICAL SOLEMN MASS AT THE THRONE: DURING THE GLORIA AND CREED

Collect(s). The bearers bring the book (missal) and candle, the second assistant deacon removes the gremial and hands it to a server, then he takes off the mitre.[53] The AP holds the book, the Bishop stands, turns towards the people, sings *Pax vobis*; then turned to the altar he sings the collect or collects with the usual gestures. He sits again and is covered with the golden mitre, and the gremial is laid over his knees. The subdeacon sings the Epistle as usual, a distance away from the altar, making first the reverences to the altar and Bishop, and standing so that he does not turn his back to the Bishop. The Epistle may be sung from the ambo,

---

[52] Having laid aside the candle, book, etc.

[53] This is always the order. The mitre is put on before and taken off after the gremial.

if the church has one, or a folding lectern may be brought out, erected at the place required, later taken away. After the Epistle all those around the Bishop stand; the subdeacon, accompanied, as usual, by the second MC, reverences to the altar, comes to the throne, reverences to the Bishop, goes up the steps, and bowing profoundly (or kneeling, if he is not a canon) lays the book of lessons on the Bishop's knees, kisses his hand placed on the book and receives his blessing. He goes away with the same reverences, gives the book to the second MC, bows to the deacon and sits by him at the sedilia. The thurifer prepares his thurible.

The book-bearer kneels before the Bishop, holding the missal open; the Bishop (seated, mitred) reads the gradual, *Alleluia* verse, tract, sequence or whatever occurs in the Mass between the lessons; the hand-candle is held near.

The Bishop does not read those parts of the pre-Mass which are sung by the deacon or subdeacon.[54]

Gospel. Towards the end of the gradual (tract or sequence) sung by the choir, the deacon of the Mass, having made the proper reverences to the Bishop and the altar, lays the Gospel book on the altar, reverences to the altar, goes *per breviorem* to kiss the Bishop's hand (making a reverence to him before and after), then goes to the lowest altar step, kneels and says the *Munda cor meum*. Then he gets the book from the altar, holds it before his breast, and waits standing *in plano* at the epistle corner until incense has been put in and blessed; then he goes to the centre, at the foot of the altar steps, and is joined by the subdeacon, on his left. The acolytes, with their candles, stand behind them.

The thurifer goes to the throne. The Bishop puts on and blesses incense as usual, the AP assisting. The thurifer comes to the middle and there joins the deacon, subdeacon and acolytes. Towards the end of the last verse of the gradual (or tract or *Alleluia* or sequence), all reverence to the altar and go to the throne in the same order (the subdeacon preceding the deacon) in which they go to form the Gospel group. At the throne the deacon (a little in advance of the subdeacon) bows low[55] and asks the Bishop's blessing with the usual form *Iube, domne, benedicere.* Meanwhile the subdeacon bows;[56] all others kneel. When the Bishop has given the blessing,[57] all who are kneeling rise; the deacon and subdeacon bow low to him, the others genuflect. All go to the place where the Gospel is sung, first the MC of the Mass, then the thurifer, the acolytes together, then the subdeacon, and after him[58] the deacon holding the Gospel book. The

---

54 R.G., n. 473.
55 If he is not a canon he kneels.
56 Ditto.
57 He does not present his hand to be kissed as the deacon has already given this mark of respect.
58 C.E., I, ix, 2; II, viii, 44.

Gospel is sung as usual. The four bearers stand in line before the throne on the east side facing the place where the Gospel is sung.

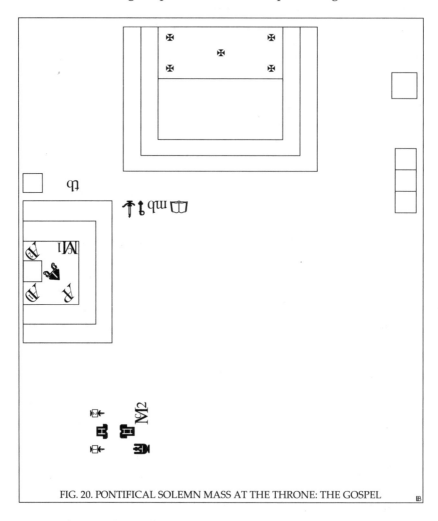

FIG. 20. PONTIFICAL SOLEMN MASS AT THE THRONE: THE GOSPEL

The ambo may be used as at the Epistle, or the lectern brought out and set up.[59] Before the deacon sings *Dominus vobiscum* the mitre and gremial are taken from the Bishop, he stands (retaining his skull-cap), takes his crosier in his left hand, makes the sign of the cross on his forehead, lips and breast as the deacon does so, and stands holding the crosier in both hands while the Gospel is sung. Then he lays it aside. The subdeacon

---

[59] If there is an ambo, the subdeacon stands at the deacon's right, hands him the thurible, turns over the pages. If there is a portable lectern (which should be ornamented and have spread over it a covering of cloth of gold or of silk of the colour of the vestments) the subdeacon stands behind it, resting his hands on the edges of the book, as if he were holding it.

goes to the Bishop with the book open at the page of the Gospel, making no reverence either to him or the altar, and points the place of the Gospel. The Bishop Says *Per evangelica dicta,* etc., laying both hands on the book, and kisses it. The subdeacon goes down, making the proper reverence to the Bishop and altar and gives away the book to the second MC. The AP, standing before the throne, incenses the Bishop (who remains without his mitre). The thurifer stands by the AP and holds the end of his cope meanwhile; when he has been incensed the Bishop blesses the AP. In the meantime the deacon, second MC and acolytes return in procession to the altar (in the order in which they came and saluting the Bishop on the way), reverence it, and go to their places.

§ 5. From the Gospel to the Communion

Homily. If the Bishop preaches, he does so vested and mitred. He may preach from the throne, or from a faldstool placed for him before the altar, facing the people. If at the faldstool placed on the footpace the AP sits at his right meanwhile; behind the AP sit the deacon of the Mass (and deals with the Bishop's mitre) and first assistant deacon, the subdeacon and second assistant deacon at the Bishop's left (a little behind him). If the homily is preached by a canon or priest,[60] he wears his choir dress; if he be a religious, his habit. It is customary (outside Rome) to wear a stole of the colour of the Mass. Before the homily the preacher, accompanied by the second MC, comes to the throne, genuflects, kneels before the Bishop (a canon bows only), kisses his hand and says *Iube, domne, benedicere.* The Bishop answers *Dominus sit in corde tuo et in labiis tuis, ut digne et fructuose annunties verba sancta sua. In nomine Patris*✠*et Filii et Spiritus Sancti. Amen,* making the sign of the cross (once) over him. Then, if the occasion is such that an indulgence may be granted,[61] the preacher asks for the indulgence, saying *Indulgentias, Pater reverendissime.*[62] The Bishop answers *Consuetas.*[63] Without again kissing the Bishop's hand, the preacher rises, genuflects (or bows) to the Bishop and goes to the pulpit or place where he will preach, making the proper reverence to the altar as he passes it. When he enters the pulpit he kneels towards the altar and recites aloud the *Hail Mary,*[64] then he rises, puts on his biretta and begins.

---

[60] C.E., II, viii, 48 prefers that the Bishop preach himself. If not, the preacher should be a canon and he should be AP for the occasion (C.E., I, xxii, I). But this rule is often not observed. If the AP does preach he retains his cope. It would seem incongruous for a priest acting as subdeacon to preach wearing a tunicle.

[61] For the occasions, such as the pastoral visitation of the Bishop, the day of the dedication of a church or an altar, particular jubilees, etc., on which indulgences may be granted, and for their conditions, see the *Enchiridion Indulgentiarium.*

[62] To a cardinal he says: *Pater eminentissime ac reverendissime.*

[63] Either plenary or partial indulgences are granted.

[64] C.E., I, xxii, 3. The preacher says the entire prayer himself.

Should he address himself to the Bishop during his discourse he uncovers and bows to the prelate.

Indulgence. At the end of the homily the preacher kneels in the pulpit (a canon bows) towards the altar for *Confiteor*. The deacon of the Mass comes before the throne[65] (with the proper reverences to the altar and the Bishop) and bowing his head chants the *Confiteor*. At the words *tibi Pater* and *te Pater* he genuflects to the Bishop (a canon bows). Meanwhile the Bishop rises and stands at the throne wearing the mitre, and all in choir kneel. The deacon goes back to the sedilia. The Bishop sits (all others stand) and the preacher stands and reads the form of indulgence,[66] as it is in the Ceremonial (I, xxv, I; II, xxxix). The Bishop then comes down from the pulpit. The bearers of the book and candle come to the throne; the Bishop rises, the mitre having been taken off, and chants the prayers *Precibus et meritis* and *Indulgentiam*, the book being held by the AP. All kneel, except canons and prelates, who bow standing. The Bishop sits for a moment while the mitre is put on; then he stands and gives the blessing, holding the crosier.[67] *If he is the Archbishop,* the subdeacon cross-bearer comes and kneels before him, holding his cross with the figure towards him, and the Archbishop does not wear the mitre. Then Mass continues.

Creed. The Bishop, uncovered, turned towards the altar, intones the *Credo* (if it occurs), the AP holding the book. Then the book is handed back to its bearer, who continues to hold it before the Bishop while he says the *Credo*. The deacon and subdeacon recite the *Credo* at their places. When the Bishop says the words *Et incarnatus est,* etc., he genuflects on a cushion placed before him by the MC. All genuflect with him, except the bearers of book and candle. Then the Bishop sits, is covered with the golden mitre and gremial. When the choir sings the verse *Et incarnatus est,* etc., the Bishop bows towards the altar, still covered; all the others who are sitting bow also, while those who are standing kneel and bow according to the rules (cf. p. 105.)

On Christmas Day and the Annunciation the Bishop kneels at the throne wearing the mitre, and bows.

After *Et incarnatus* the deacon takes the corporal to the altar, as usual, genuflecting (or bowing low, if he be a canon) to the Bishop and the altar on his way.

---

[65] C.E., II, xxxix, 1. Should the Bishop have preached from the footpace the deacon, for the *Confiteor,* stands on the highest step (to the Bishop's left) (C.E., I, xxv, 1; ix, 3).

[66] If the Bishop himself has preached, the form of indulgence is read by the AP, and it is he who holds the book for the Bishop to sing the absolution and blessing.

[67] The form is given in C.E., I, xxv, 3 (cf. Chapter XXIX § 3). If there is no homily the indulgence is announced after the blessing at the end of Mass (C.E., I, xxv. 8). If the Bishop is to give the Papal Blessing with plenary indulgence at the end of Mass (cf. Chapter XVI § 9) the partial indulgence and blessing are not given after the homily (S.R.C. 2682 § 14).

The Episcopal Indulgence at Solemn Mass

Case	Announcement of Indulgence	Confiteor sung by deacon of the Mass	Precibus
(1) Bishop (Ordinary) pontificates at the throne and preaches there.	By AP (C.E., I, xxv, 2; II, viii, 50). Bishop sits covered; all others stand.	At foot of throne (C.E., II, xxxix, 1; S.R.C. 2682 § 14 [1]). Bishop stands covered (cf. 2682 § 14 [3]). All others kneel.[68]	Sung *in tono orationis* (C.E., I, xxv, 2, II, xxxix, 3). AP holds book. Bishop stands uncovered. All kneel.[69]
(2) Bishop pontificates at throne, preaches from faldstool on footpace.	Ditto.	At Bishop's left on top step (C.E., I, xi, 3; cf. II, viii, 50).	Ditto.
(3) Bishop pontificates at throne; AP (or another priest) preaches.	Preacher, even if AP or an extern bishop (C.E., I, vii, 4; II, viii, 51; S.R.C. 4355 § 111 [8]).	As for case (1) (cf. C.E., I, ix, 3).	Ditto.
(4) Bishop assists at Mass in cope and mitre or in cappa;[70] AP (or another priest) preaches.[71]	Ditto.	At foot of altar (S.R.C. 2682 § 14 [1]; cf. C.E., I, xxv, 1) turned towards Bishop. Preacher and all others kneel.[72] (Cf. C.E., I, xxii, 4; xxv, 1; II, xxxix, 2).	Said, not sung (C.E. I, xxv, 2; cf. II, xxxix, 3). Book-bearer holds book. All kneel.[73]
(5) If there is no homily.	AP if Bishop pontificates; Celebrant[74] if Bishop assists—both after Blessing of the Mass (C.E., I, xxv, 8; II, viii, 80).	None.	None.

Offertory. When the *Credo* is over, the Bishop's gremial is removed and his mitre taken off. He stands, turns towards the people, sings *Dominus vobiscum* and—turned to the *altar*—*Oremus*. He reads the offertory antiphon, the book-bearer holding the book. He sits and the first deacon puts on him the precious mitre. A server comes with the salver for the ring and gloves. The assistant deacons take off the Bishop's ring and gloves, putting them on the salver. The servers approach with the

---

[68] Except prelates and canons.

[69] Ditto.

[70] Or in a mozzetta should a cappa not be available.

[71] Should the Bishop preach in this case, the AP announces the indulgence; the deacon sings the *Confiteor* at the foot of the altar (S.R.C. 2682 § 14).

[72] Except celebrant, prelates and canons.

[73] Ditto.

[74] But if an extern bishop be the celebrant, the AP of the Ordinary announces it.

ewer, dish and hand-towels. The assistant deacons spread one towel over the Bishop's knees, the AP holds the other. The servers kneel while the Bishop washes his hands. Those near the throne kneel too, except canons, who stand. The Bishop makes the sign of the cross over the servers; they go away. The AP replaces the ring on the Bishop's bare hand, with the *solita oscula*.[75]

The AP takes the missal on its stand,[76] and—accompanied by the (second) MC[77]—goes to the altar and arranges it there on its stand or cushion, and then at the gospel side of the footpace awaits the arrival of the Bishop. The bearers of book and candle follow him. The subdeacon goes to the credence; the acolytes put on him the humeral veil; he takes the chalice to the epistle corner at the same time as the Bishop arrives at the altar, and is followed by the acolyte carrying the cruets, and the bowl for the pre-tasting of the wine (if this takes place). The thurifer prepares his thurible.

Bishop goes to Altar. The Bishop rises at the throne, takes his crosier and goes to the altar, blessing the choir as he passes. He is followed by the mitre and crosier bearers. At the foot of the altar he gives up the crosier; the mitre is removed by the deacon of the Mass; the Bishop bows low to the cross and goes up to the footpace. The AP is then on his left[78] the deacon of the Mass comes to his right. The assistant deacons go on either side of the Bishop as he goes to the altar, they stand on the ground before it, at the foot of the steps, the bearers of crosier and mitre stand behind them. The candle-bearer goes up to the foot-pace and stands there at the left of the AP.[79] This is now his place while the Bishop reads. He stands aside at the censing of the altar, taking the candle with him. All in choir sit. The Bishop kisses the altar. The subdeacon brings up the chalice and consigns it to the deacon of the Mass. The latter takes the chalice, uncovers it, takes one of the two altar breads, touches with it the other bread, the paten, and the chalice within and without, and gives it to the sacristan (or to the acolyte who brings the cruets) who eats it.[80] The other altar bread on the paten he gives to the Bishop, who offers the bread as usual and then puts the paten under the corporal. The deacon pours a

---

[75] The gloves are not worn after this.

[76] Or AP may send the book-bearer, immediately after the Bishop has read the offertory, to the altar with the missal (C.E., II, viii, 57). In this case AP will accompany the Bishop (on his left) to the altar. Some authors say that AP is also to take the pontifical canon to the altar. C.E. is silent about this, and so the (second) MC may see to it (placing it, open at the offertory, against the cross or tabernacle).

[77] C.E., II, viii, 57.

[78] From the offertory to the *Agnus Dei* the AP is at the Bishop's left, by the book (and turns the pages), except at the lavabo and elevation.

[79] Or he may leave the candle on the altar near the missal, and stand at the foot on the gospel side with the book-bearer.

[80] This is the *prægustatio* ceremony, a curious relic of early times. It is obviously a precaution against poison. The ceremony is often omitted. It does not break the Eucharistic fast.

little of the wine and water into the vessel prepared and gives it to the sacristan to drink.[81] The deacon[82] wipes the chalice and pours in the wine, the subdeacon—having held up the water cruet to the Bishop and asked his blessing, saying *Benedicite, Pater reverendissime* – pours in the water. Meanwhile the Bishop recites *Deus, qui humanæ*, etc. The deacon hands the chalice to the Bishop who offers it assisted, as usual, by the deacon.

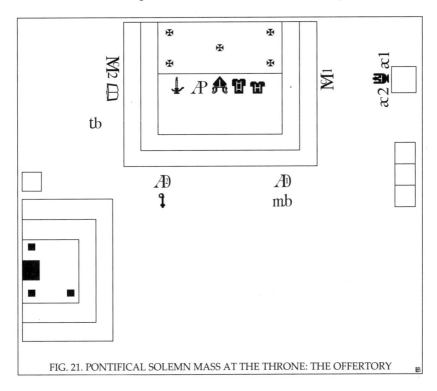

FIG. 21. PONTIFICAL SOLEMN MASS AT THE THRONE: THE OFFERTORY

Incensation. The deacon, having given the paten to the subdeacon, assists at the putting in of incense and incensation, as usual. The Bishop incenses the *oblata* and the altar; the AP removes the missal, descending from the footpace on the gospel side; and, having replaced it after the incensation of the gospel side, goes to the epistle side for the washing of the hands. When the Bishop has incensed the altar, the first assistant deacon comes to him, at the epistle side, with the bearer of the mitre, and puts the precious mitre on the Bishop; the Bishop is incensed by the deacon of the Mass and blesses him. The Bishop washes his hands,[83] the AP presenting the hand-towel and the servers kneeling. The pontifical canon, taken from the centre of the altar, is held before the Bishop (if

---

[81] Ditto.

[82] Not the subdeacon (C.E., II, viii, 62).

[83] No rubric prescribes the removal of the ring for this washing.

necessary) by the MC or book-bearer while he recites the *Lavabo* psalm. The second assistant deacon (or the MC) takes off the Bishop's mitre before he says *Gloria Patri* at the end of the psalm. The deacon of the Mass, when he has incensed the Bishop, incenses the AP and the two deacons of the throne, each with two double swings. Then he incenses the prelates and canons and the sub-deacon as at solemn Mass. He then goes up to stand behind the Bishop, and is himself incensed by the thurifer (who then incenses the rest of the clergy, the MC's, servers and people).

Preface. Meanwhile the Bishop continues Mass as usual. After the secrets the AP changes the missal for the pontifical canon (open at the preface) on the stand or cushion.[84] Before the Bishop sings *Per omnia sæcula sæculorum* the MC takes off his skull-cap and hands it to the mitre-bearer. The deacon of the Mass stands on the right and the AP on the left side of the Bishop, to say the *Sanctus* with him; the subdeacon does not go up to the footpace. All this time, unless they are otherwise occupied, the two assistant deacons stand on the ground before the altar steps, the subdeacon standing between them.

The torch-bearers[85] come before the altar, genuflect, and kneel, either behind the subdeacon or at the sides of the altar, holding their torches. All in choir and sanctuary kneel, after the singing of *Sanctus*, except the AP, MC, assistant deacons, deacon and subdeacon, thurifer, bearers of book, candle, mitre and crosier. The subdeacon has received the paten from the deacon at the offertory; he stands holding it before the altar steps. The deacon (once he has recited the *Sanctus*) is on the top step behind the Bishop, the AP at the Bishop's left.

Consecration. Before the elevation, incense is put in the thurible by the second MC (or by an acolyte); the MC or the thurifer incenses the Blessed Sacrament, kneeling on the lowest step at the epistle corner. At the words *Qui pridie* the deacon and AP kneel at the edge of the footpace, the others at their places; at the elevation they hold the end of the chasuble. The deacon uncovers the chalice, as at every solemn Mass.[86] After the elevation the deacon stands behind the Bishop, the AP is at the book, the torch-bearers retire unless Holy Communion is to be given. The AP and deacon genuflect with the Bishop whenever he genuflects during the canon.[87] The deacon comes to the Bishop's right to uncover the Chalice at *benedicis et præstas nobis* and to put his hand on it at *Per ipsum*, etc. He then returns to his place behind the Bishop. Towards the end of the *Pater*

---

[84] He hands the missal to the MC or book-bearer who lays it on the credence till it is wanted again after the ablutions. It is rubricians who direct the AP to replace the missal by the pontifical canon for the preface. C.E. is silent on the point.

[85] There should be four, six, or at most eight torches (C.E., II, viii, 68).

[86] The bell should be rung as usual at the *Sanctus,* before the consecration, and at each elevation (S.R.C. 4377).

[87] C.E., I, vii, 5; II, viii, 69.

noster the deacon comes to the Bishop's right, the subdeacon to the deacon's right (each having first genuflected); the paten is handed to the Bishop as usual, the subdeacon has the humeral veil taken off by the second MC or an acolyte, genuflects to the Blessed Sacrament and goes to the foot of the altar steps in front.

Agnus Dei and Pax. At the *Agnus Dei* the deacon is at the Bishop's right; the subdeacon does not go up to the altar. The deacon and AP say the *Agnus Dei* with the Bishop. They then genuflect and change places; the deacon goes to the missal and assists there; the AP to the Bishop's right. When the Bishop has recited the prayer *Domine Iesu Christe*, the AP (who will have just arrived) genuflects, rises at once and, with the Bishop, kisses the altar, not laying his hands on it. The Bishop gives the kiss of peace to the AP. He genuflects and goes to give it to the dignitaries and canons in choir, accompanied by the second MC. The first and second assistant deacons, the deacon and subdeacon (if not going to Holy Communion) of the Mass, now come up in turn to the Bishop's right, each (genuflecting before and after, but not kissing the altar) receives the pax from him. The subdeacon stands at the Bishop's right and uncovers the Chalice at his communion, the deacon is by the book, till the AP returns from giving the pax. When the AP comes back to the altar he gives the pax to the MC who had accompanied him (and he in turn goes to give it to the clergy in choir who are not canons, to the first MC and to the servers). Then he stands at the Bishop's left and the deacon at the Bishop's right. The subdeacon now goes down to his place at the foot of the altar.

If the ministers receive Holy Communion, they do not take the kiss of peace from the Bishop before his communion but later, immediately after their own. They make their communion kneeling, first kissing the Bishop's hand, then they rise and kiss his left cheek, while he says *Pax tecum.* They answer *Et cum spiritu tuo.*[88]

§ 6. From After Communion Until the End of Mass

As soon as communion is over the MC replaces the Bishop's skull-cap. The deacon[89] pours in the wine, and the wine and water for the ablutions (at the centre of the altar); the subdeacon goes up to the gospel corner of the altar, wipes and veils the chalice (an acolyte bringing him the veil from the credence) and takes it to the credence. The AP puts the pontifical canon in the middle of the altar, replaces the missal (brought to

---

[88] The C.E., II, xxxi, 5 says that it is "very becoming" that the deacon and subdeacon make their communion at the Bishop's Mass on Sundays (cf. *Conc. Trid.,* Sess. XXIII. cap. xiii). Indeed C.E., I, ix, 6 says the sacred ministers are to communicate, when they are not priests desirous of saying Mass. For the rite see C.E., II, xxix, 3 (cf. p. 146).

[89] Not the subdeacon (C.E., I, ix, 5).

him by the book-bearer) on its stand, moves it across, opens it at the *Communio*, then stands at the epistle corner ready for the washing of hands. The precious mitre is put on the Bishop by the deacon of the Mass. Standing at the epistle corner the Bishop washes his hands,[90] the AP presenting the hand-towel. The Bishop blesses the servers, the precious mitre is taken off by the deacon.

Postcommunion. The Bishop reads the communion antiphon, says *Dominus vobiscum*, sings the postcommunion(s), as the celebrant at every solemn Mass. The deacon sings *Ite, missa est,* as usual. When the Bishop has said the prayer *Placeat tibi,* the deacon of the Mass puts on the Bishop's precious mitre. Facing the altar the Bishop sings the versicles (from the pontifical canon), *Sit nomen Domini,* etc. As he sings the end of the formula of blessing, before the word *Pater,* he turns, takes the crosier in his left hand and gives the blessing, making the three signs of the cross. All kneel, except canons and prelates, who bow. *If he is the Archbishop,* the subdeacon who carries the cross brings it before him, and kneels with the cross facing him. An archbishop is uncovered when blessing, but holds his crosier.

If the indulgence has not been announced after the homily it is announced now. The AP, standing at the epistle corner—having by a bow asked the Bishop's leave—reads the form appointed,[91] while the Bishop, mitred, remains standing, facing the people before the altar, holding his crosier.

Then the procession is formed, by the second MC, in the same order as at the beginning, but without the thurifer. The Bishop gives up the crosier, his mitre is removed by the deacon of the Mass. *If it is the Archbishop* who has worn the pallium this is now taken off by the deacon, aided by the subdeacon, laid on the salver on which it was brought at the beginning, covered with its veil and placed on the altar.

Last Gospel. The Bishop, at the centre turned towards the gospel corner, says in a low voice *Dominus vobiscum,* and signs the altar and himself saying *Initium sancti Evangelii secundum Ioannem.* He is then covered with the precious mitre by the deacon, takes the crosier, descends, reverences to the altar, and follows the procession out, continuing slowly the last Gospel as he goes.[92] The procession goes to the secretarium,[93] where the canons and others take their places. The Bishop,

---

[90] No rubric orders the removal of his ring for this, nor do most rubricians.

[91] *Confiteor* and prayer *Precibus* are not said.

[92] If there are any special prayers to be said after Mass (e.g., for the Sovereign) they are said by the Bishop standing at the throne (at the foot of the altar, if he unvests in the secretarium) immediately after Mass (cf. S.R.C., 6 July 1929).

[93] C.E., I, xvii, 8; II, viii, 80. Some authors direct the Bishop to unvest at the throne (cf. C.E., I, xv, 11) and Vavasseur-Stercky (I. 122) says this is the usage of Rome. If he does he goes to the throne between the assistant deacons preceded by the subdeacon, whom the AP with the deacon on his left follow, and followed by the mitre and crosier bearers.

entering the secretarium, blesses the choir as he passes. He bows to the altar, goes to the throne, and the deacon of the Mass takes off his mitre. Genuflecting at the throne on a cushion, towards the altar, he says the verse *Et Verbum caro factum est*, and so finishes the Gospel. He then hands his crosier to its bearer and sits.

Unvesting. The deacon and subdeacon of the Mass take off their maniples, which are carried away by a server. The subdeacon takes off the Bishop's maniple, hands it to a server, who lays it on the altar. The rest of the Bishop's vestments are taken off in order, by the deacon and subdeacon, as they were put on. They are all laid on the altar (by the second MC) and covered with a veil. He does not take off the ceremonial shoes and stockings in the church.[94] Meanwhile the AP and assistant deacons unvest and then return to the throne when the deacon and subdeacon leave it. The four bearers go to the sacristy, take off their copes and return. The canons in vestments take these off and resume choir dress. The ministers of the Mass, having unvested the Bishop, go to sit at the sedilia. The Bishop's attendant brings the cappa and puts it on him. The bearers of the book and candle come to the throne. Sitting, the Bishop reads the thanksgiving psalms; he stands for the versicles and prayers. Meanwhile the second MC puts the faldstool (with its cushions) in the middle of the sanctuary. Having finished his thanksgiving, the Bishop (followed by the train-bearer) goes to the faldstool, kneels and says a short prayer. He then visits the Blessed Sacrament at Its altar and departs. The canons may accompany him (following him). Afterwards they return and sing Sext and None.

§ 7. If the Bishop Does Not Vest in the Secretarium

If there is no chapel that can be used as a secretarium, or if for any reason the Bishop does not wish to use it, there are two other ways in which he may vest before Mass: at the throne in the sanctuary,[95] or in the sacristy. Neither case presents any special difficulty:

(1) If he vests at the throne in the sanctuary, he will come to the church in rochet and cappa (wearing his ceremonial shoes and stockings), visit the Blessed Sacrament, then kneel at a faldstool in the sanctuary, go to the throne and do everything as described above. But when he has vested at the throne there will not be the great procession from the secretarium.

---

[94] If he unvests there (S.R.C., 4 December 1952).

[95] In this case: (i) the Bishop's vestments are laid on the high altar; (ii) those for the AP and assistant deacons are prepared somewhere behind the altar; (iii) the maniples for the deacon and subdeacon may be put on the credence near the throne; (iv) the vestments for the canons may be prepared at their places in choir; (v) what was prepared at the credences in the secretarium (p. 187) is now prepared at the credences in the sanctuary.

Instead, the Bishop, in precious mitre and holding his crosier, goes from the throne to the altar,[96] blessing the clergy in choir as he passes.

(2) If he vests in the sacristy, a faldstool will be prepared in the middle for him. The vestments will be laid out on a vesting table. At this faldstool the Bishop vests in the same way as at the throne. Then the procession (with incense) is formed to the church and altar.

§ 8. If the Chapter is Not Present

The Ceremonial supposes, as the normal custom, that the Ordinary sings solemn Mass in his Cathedral, his Chapter assisting.

It may, however, frequently happen that he sings Mass in another church of his diocese, where the Chapter is not present. In this case a temporary throne is erected beforehand, on the gospel side, and is vested in the colour of the Mass. Terce is not said beforehand; the secretarium is not used. The Bishop vests either in the sacristy or at the throne. The ministers of Mass and assistants at the throne need not be canons. If they are not, they genuflect to the altar and to the Bishop and kneel for all blessings. All else proceeds as described above, except, of course, that there may be no clergy to be incensed or to receive the kiss of peace.

§ 9. The Papal Blessing

On Easter Sunday and on two other solemn feasts of the year chosen by him the Bishop of the diocese may impart, after solemn Mass (either celebrated by him or at which he has presided), the Papal blessing, which carries with it a plenary indulgence.[97]

The form of blessing is that found in the Roman Pontifical, a slight change being made in the words of the announcement,[98] given that the faculty to give the blessing is granted by common law. The reading of the "Litteræ Apostolicæ" is omitted.

At the end of Mass the Bishop goes to his throne, gives away the crosier, and sits mitred. The deacon takes off the Bishop's maniple, and he and the subdeacon take off their own maniples. A server brings the Bishop's gloves on a salver. The deacon removes the Bishop's ring and puts on the glove on the Bishop's right hand; the subdeacon puts the other on the Bishop's left hand, both with the usual *oscula*. The AP replaces the ring. The deacon and subdeacon go to the sedilia; the assistant deacons are by the Bishop and the AP.

---

[96] Between the assistant deacons preceded by the subdeacon, whom the AP with the deacon on his left follow, and followed by the mitre and crosier bearers.

[97] S. Penitentiary, 20 July 1942; *Enchridion Indulgentiarum*, norm 7 § 2.

[98] E.g. "Attentis facultatibus in Iuris Codice expressis, Revmus. Dominus, Dominus N., Dei at Apostolicæ Sedis gratia hujus sanctæ N. Ecclesiæ Antistes, dat et concedit, etc."

The MC or some other priest may now usefully tell the congregation (if this has not been previously done) about the plenary indulgence, and the conditions for gaining it (confession, Holy Communion, prayer for the Pope's intentions—a *Pater* and an *Ave*—and being free from all attachment to sin, including venial sin).

The book-bearer (with the pontifical or a card containing the formula) and candle-bearer come to the throne. The AP holds the book for the Bishop. He rises, without the mitre, and, with hands joined, chants, *in tono orationis, Precibus, Misereatur* and *Indulgentiam.* All kneel, except prelates and canons, and answer *Amen* to each prayer. Before the blessing the Bishop sits and receives the mitre from the first assistant deacon. The Bishop rises, faces the congregation, raises his eyes and hands to heaven, and gives the blessing with the triple sign of the cross. After *omnipotentis* he takes the crosier in his left hand. After the blessing the Bishop gives away the crosier and sits, mitred.

If the Archbishop gives the blessing, he wears the pallium, if he has worn it during Mass.[99] His cross is held before him, and—with head uncovered —he bows to this before giving the blessing.

The MC (or some priest, in surplice) reads the announcement of the blessing, in Latin and then in the vernacular.

The deacon and subdeacon return to the throne and help to unvest the Bishop.

If the Bishop has not sung the Mass, but only presided at it: (i) if he presided in cope and mitre, he gives the Papal Blessing so vested (and the gloves are not worn), (ii) if he presided in cappa, he must vest in amice, pectoral cross, stole, and cope; and use mitre and crosier.

---

[99] He may not put it on just for the blessing on a day when it may not be used at Mass (S.R.C. 3605 § 8).

Chapter XVII

Pontifical Solemn Mass at the Faldstool

§ 1. Preparation

EXCEPT for a "greater prelate," every other bishop (an extern bishop or auxiliary) uses, not the throne, but a faldstool in front of the altar.[1] It may also happen that the Ordinary uses this faldstool, instead of his throne, as when, for example, a cardinal is present.[2] For Mass at the faldstool the following alterations are made in the ceremony.[3]

The bishop may begin his preparation for Mass in the sacristy. If he does so, the usual vestments for the deacon and subdeacon are laid out there, but not their maniples, which are put on the sedilia in the church. A carpet is laid in the middle of the sacristy with a chair on it. The bishop makes his preparation there. The pontifical canon and hand-candle are at hand; and the bishop's liturgical shoes and stockings are laid out in the sacristy near the chair.

Preparations. At the high altar of the church the Blessed Sacrament should be removed, if It is reserved there. Six candles are lighted, not seven. There are no altar-cards. The bishop's vestments are laid on the altar as for pontifical solemn Mass at the throne.[4] His gloves lie on a salver. All are covered with a veil, which may be the gremial. The precious mitre stands on the gospel side, by it the mitre-bearer's veil. The golden mitre is on the epistle side; their lappets hang over the frontal.[5]

On the credence the two acolytes' candles burn. Between them the following are placed: the chalice and paten, prepared as usual for Mass, the cruets and bell, all covered by the humeral veil. The evangeliarium (missal), with the bishop's maniple between the leaves at the place of the Gospel of the day, the Epistolarium or book of lessons,[6] the missal on its stand, the ewer, basin and hand-towels for washing the bishop's hands, a small salver, and the gremial (if it is not covering the vestments). If there is not room for all this on the credence, another table should stand by its

---

[1] In general, this Mass is celebrated as a pontifical Mass at the throne except for the changes expressly ordered in C.E.

[2] This case lies outside the scope of this book. The description of Mass at the faldstool given in this chapter does not suppose the presence of a prelate superior to the celebrating bishop; nor that the crosier is used; or that the ministers are canons.

[3] C.E., I, vii, 4; viii, 2; ix, 3, 4; xi, 12; xii, 10, 11; xix, 4, 5; xxiii, 24; II, viii, 41, 56.

[4] Unless the celebrant be the Ordinary the morse is not used.

[5] If the bishop uses the golden mitre only, this stands on the gospel side.

[6] The books should be covered with silk of the colour of the day.

side. On the ministers' bench are left amice and cope for the AP, and the maniples of the deacon and subdeacon.

The Roman books suppose that the thurible, incense boat, the fire and charcoal and the torches for the elevation all stand in the sanctuary near the credence. It may, however, be more convenient to prepare these in the sacristy.

On the epistle side at the foot of the altar, a little away from the bottom step, is placed the faldstool.[7] It is covered with cloths of the colour of the Mass. On the epistle side of the sanctuary — on the right of the faldstool and nearer 'to the nave of the church — is the sedilia. In the centre of the lowest step of the altar is a cushion (of the colour of the Mass) on which the bishop will kneel to pray before Mass.

§ 2. The Ministers and Servers

The following persons assist the bishop: an assistant priest, the deacon and subdeacon of the Mass, two Masters of Ceremonies, the three servers who carry the mitre, book and hand-candle,[8] the thurifer and acolytes, four or six torch-bearers, who will also assist at the vesting. The bearers of mitre (who wears a vimpa), book and candle do not wear copes. There are no assistant deacons. The deacon and subdeacon supply their places.[9] No one genuflects to the bishop in the course of the function; one bows only.

§ 3. The Beginning and the Vesting of the Bishop

The bishop arrives in the sacristy and sits (with biretta on) on the chair prepared, the AP, in surplice, standing on his right. The book-bearer stands before the bishop, holding the pontifical canon open at the preparation for Mass. The bearer of the candle stands on the book-bearer's right,[10] holding it lighted. The bishop begins to say the psalms appointed for the preparation.[11] While he does this a servant takes off his ordinary shoes and puts on the liturgical shoes and stockings, kneeling before him to do so. The bishop finishes the preparation standing,

---

[7] The faldstool may be placed on a raised platform covered with a carpet (cf. C.E., xii, 11), when the celebrant is a "greater prelate."

[8] There is no crosier-bearer, since the crosier is not, ordinarily, used in this case. However, if it is, the crosier-bearer should carry out his function *mutatis mutandis* as at solemn pontifical Mass at the throne.

[9] C.E., I, viii, 2. When they are not free the MC attends to the bishop's mitre.

[10] Cf. C.E., I, xx, 1.

[11] *Should a bishop celebrate Mass in presence of the Ordinary or his superior*, the bishop vests in the sacristy and goes (between the AP and deacon) to the sanctuary. There, seated at the faldstool, he awaits the arrival of the presiding prelate (unless he be already at his throne).

uncovered, and turned towards the cross of the sacristy. The pontifical canon and hand-candle are then taken to the credence in the sanctuary.

Meanwhile the deacon and subdeacon vest, assisted by the acolytes. Vested, but without maniples, they bow to the cross in the sacristy and to the bishop. They go to the church, the second MC before them, followed by the acolytes and other servers.[12] In church they all salute the clergy in choir and genuflect to the altar, the acolytes and servers stand aside near the credence, the ministers give away their birettas to the MC and stand behind the faldstool facing the people, the deacon on the gospel side, the subdeacon on the epistle side.

Arrival of Bishop. Then the bishop comes from the sacristy. He wears the rochet and mantelletta,[13] and holds his biretta in his hand. The first MC goes in front of him, the AP at his left. At the entrance to the church the AP presents the sprinkler, which the bishop touches and then signs himself but does not sprinkle anyone. They come before the altar, the deacon and subdeacon bow to the bishop; he bows to the clergy in choir and to the altar. Then he kneels for a short prayer on the cushion at the foot of the altar. When he rises, this cushion is taken away.

The bishop, rising, again bows to the altar and to the choir and goes to the faldstool. Here he sits. The deacon takes off the pectoral cross, then holds it to the bishop, that he may kiss it, and hands it to the MC. He removes the mantelletta and gives this, too, to the MC. The bishop puts on his biretta. The deacon removes the bishop's ring. A server comes with the ewer, basin and hand-towel. Standing before the bishop the server pours water over his hands. The AP hands the hand-towel to the bishop and then returns to his place at the sedilia.

Vesting. The vesting now begins.[14] The second MC goes to the altar and there hands each vestment to a server, who will bring it to the bishop. If there are not enough servers, they may, after having handed a vestment to the ministers, return to the altar to bring another. The bishop stands and the book-bearer stands before him, still holding the book. The bishop takes off his biretta before rising and hands it to the MC, who puts it with the mantelletta. The deacon vests the bishop, the subdeacon assisting. The pectoral cross (first kissed by the bishop) is put on after the cincture. When the bishop has put on the dalmatic he sits, the ministers put

---

[12] The bishop (having had the liturgical footwear put on) may go to the altar in this procession. If so, the AP, on the right of the first MC, precedes him; and the bishop walks between the deacon and subdeacon.

[13] If the bishop does not possess a mantelletta, the use of a mozzetta may be tolerated.

[14] As the bishop should put on the buskins and sandals in the sacristy (S.R.C., 4 December 1952) he may complete his vesting there. In this case the celebrant's vestments; a second ewer, basin and hand-towel; the acolytes' candles and the book containing the celebrant's maniple are all prepared in the sacristy; and there is a solemn procession to the altar as for solemn pontifical Mass at the throne (but the cross is carried by a server and the bishop walks between AP on his right and the deacon on his left).

on his gloves (each one glove, kissing first his hand and then the glove) and the chasuble. The deacon puts on him the precious mitre, bowing before and after. The ministers then retire to put on their maniples. The AP at the sedilia[15] puts on amice and cope (over a rochet or surplice); he comes to the bishop, carrying the ring on a salver, and puts it on the bishop's finger, kissing first the ring, then the hand. He bows before and after doing this, then stands at the bishop's right. When all the vestments are taken from the altar the second MC removes the golden mitre and the veil which had covered the vestments and puts them on the credence. He places the pontifical canon — open at *Aufer a nobis* — at the centre of the table of the altar leaning against the cross or tabernacle, and gets the evangeliarium (containing the bishop's maniple).

The bishop rises and goes to the altar; the AP is at his right, the deacon at his left; the subdeacon, at the deacon's left. The mitre-bearer and Masters of Ceremonies follow. All reverence to the choir (if the clergy are there) on the way.

§ 4. The Mass

At the altar the deacon takes off the mitre and hands it to the mitre-bearer (who then retires to the credence); the bishop bows low, the others genuflect. Mass begins as usual. The AP is at the bishop's right, the ministers at his left. After the prayer *Indulgentiam,* the subdeacon puts the maniple on the bishop's arm as described above (p. 198). After *Oremus* the AP and deacon change places. When they go up to the altar, the subdeacon gets the missal from the second MC and holds it open at the Gospel of the day; the AP points out the beginning of the Gospel;[16] the bishop, having kissed the altar, kisses the page. The AP descends *in plano* and stands (facing the altar) near the faldstool to the right of it. The altar is incensed as usual, except that the thurifer does not kneel when presenting the thurible. The bishop gives the thurible to the deacon, the subdeacon or MC puts on the bishop's precious mitre.

The deacon, with the subdeacon at his left, goes down the altar steps, and incenses the bishop. The bishop goes *per breviorem* to the faldstool, bowing first to the cross. The deacon on his right and the subdeacon on his left accompany him. Before the faldstool the AP (on the right), the deacon (in the centre) and the subdeacon on his left face the bishop. He sits on the faldstool and the deacon removes the mitre. The bishop rises and turns to the altar by his left.[17] The book-bearer, standing before the bishop, holds up the missal, the candle-bearer is at the book-bearer's

---

[15] When he has nothing special to do during the vesting he sits, covered, at the sedilia.

[16] Some authors (e.g., Martinucci, Vavasseur-Stercky) say that it is the subdeacon who does this at Mass at the faldstool.

[17] As the celebrant does at the altar. Cf. C.E., I, xix, 4, 5.

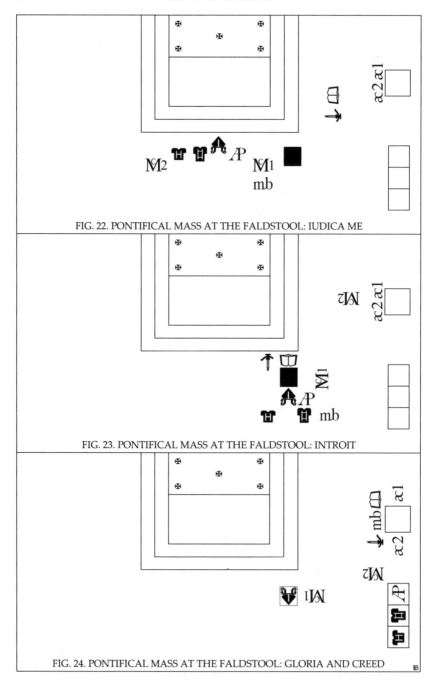

FIG. 22. PONTIFICAL MASS AT THE FALDSTOOL: IUDICA ME

FIG. 23. PONTIFICAL MASS AT THE FALDSTOOL: INTROIT

FIG. 24. PONTIFICAL MASS AT THE FALDSTOOL: GLORIA AND CREED

right, the AP at the bishop's right points to the places. The deacon is at the bishop's right (behind the AP), the subdeacon at his left, but a little back. The bishop reads the introit, then says the *Kyrie, eleison* with the ministers. If the sung *Kyrie* takes much time he may now sit (with mitre and gremial on), as he will at the *Gloria*.

Gloria. The bishop (uncovered), facing the altar, intones the *Gloria in excelsis*; the AP at his right, partly facing him, holds the book for the intonation,[18] then hands it to the book-bearer; the book-bearer and candle-bearer stand before the bishop. While the bishop intones the hymn the ministers stand behind him in line; then they come one on either side and say the *Gloria* with him. When he has said the *Gloria*, the bishop—turning by his right—sits on the faldstool; the deacon puts on the golden mitre and spreads the gremial[19] over his knees. All then bow to him[20] and go to sit at the sedilia in this order: the deacon is in the middle, the AP at his right, the subdeacon at his left.[21] They receive their birettas from the second MC and cover themselves. The second MC stands near the seat at the usual place, as at every solemn Mass. The first MC stands behind the bishop at his left. The servers sit on the step at the epistle side of the altar, if there is no bench for them near the credence.

Towards the end of the *Gloria in excelsis* the ministers rise, come before the bishop, stand in line and bow to him. The deacon removes the gremial and hands it to a server, who puts it on the credence. He then removes the mitre. The bishop stands facing the people and sings *Pax vobis*; the deacon and subdeacon stand between him and the people in line, the AP is at his side (on the epistle side) facing the altar.

Collect(s). Then the bishop turns to the altar and sings the collect(s), the AP holding the book, with the candle-bearer at his right.[22] The Ministers stand one after the other behind the bishop. The first MC stands by the AP, the second is at the credence by the acolytes. During the last collect the subdeacon takes the book of lessons, goes, with the second MC, to the centre, genuflects to the altar, bows to the choir (gospel side first), then goes to the place of the Epistle,[23] away from the altar. When the collects are finished, the bishop sits again, and receives the mitre and gremial from the deacon, as before. The AP and deacon bow to him and go to sit. The subdeacon bows to the bishop, and standing before him a suitable distance away, sings the Epistle. Then he goes to the middle, genuflects to the altar, bows to the choir, comes to the bishop, bows, kneels,[24] kisses his hand and receives his blessing. He then rises

---

[18] Cf. C.E., I, vii, 4.

[19] Some authors say the subdeacon is to look after the gremial.

[20] Whenever the AP, deacon, and subdeacon stand before the bishop seated on the faldstool, the deacon is in the centre, the AP on his right, the subdeacon on the deacon's left.

[21] The AP will sit nearest the bishop (cf. C.E., I, vii, 4); therefore whether he will be on the right or left of the deacon will depend on the position of the sedilia.

[22] So placed he is not as likely to incommode the AP and is in a more convenient position to hold the candle in the right hand.

[23] See O'Connell, *The Celebration of Mass*, 1964, p. 473 n. 29.

[24] Obviously the usual rule, not to kneel except to a greater prelate, does not apply to the blessing at Epistle and Gospel, when the ministers would kneel before a priest.

and holds the missal, that the bishop may read the gradual, *Alleluia* verse or other texts which occur between the lessons, sitting on the faldstool. The AP rises and comes to the bishop's left to assist him as he reads. The Bishop does not read the parts of the pre-Mass which are sung by the deacon or subdeacon.[25] Meanwhile the bearer holds the hand-candle, at the bishop's left. After the bishop has read the gradual, etc., the AP stays where he is. The subdeacon hands the missal to a server and stands opposite the bishop, at a little distance from him.

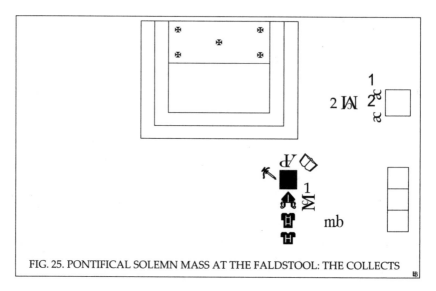

FIG. 25. PONTIFICAL SOLEMN MASS AT THE FALDSTOOL: THE COLLECTS

Gospel. Towards the end of the sung *Alleluia* verse (or whatever chant may take its place) the deacon, who has been sitting at the sedilia, rises, takes the evangeliarium (or missal) and carries it to the altar closed. He bows to the clergy on the epistle side, then to the bishop in passing, then to the clergy on the gospel side and genuflects to the altar before and after laying the book on it; then comes straight to the bishop's right, where he assists at the imposition and blessing of incense. For this the thurifer approaches, bows and stands before the bishop. The deacon ministers the incense. Meanwhile the acolytes take their candles from the credence and led by the second MC come and stand before the bishop at some distance.

When the incense is blessed the deacon goes to say the prayer *Munda cor meum*, kneeling on the lowest step at the centre of the altar;[26] the thurifer stands before the acolytes with the second MC on his left. The deacon then takes the missal from the altar, genuflects, comes to the

---

[25] R.G., n. 473.

[26] Cf. C.E., I, ix, 2; II, viii, 42. Some authors say that the deacon is to kneel on the edge of the top step in the centre of the footpace.

bishop (a little in advance of the subdeacon), bows, kneels and says *Iube, domne, benedicere.* The bishop blesses him (one sign of the cross) and he kisses the bishop's hand in the usual way. Then he stands before the bishop, in front of the second MC and the thurifer; the subdeacon is at his left. All bow to the bishop, go to the centre, genuflect, bow to the choir (first on the epistle side) and go to the place where the Gospel is sung. As soon as they have gone, the first MC removes the bishop's gremial and mitre; the AP stands a little behind the bishop at his left. The bishop stands and faces the deacon. The deacon should be careful not to begin to sing the Gospel till the bishop is thus ready.

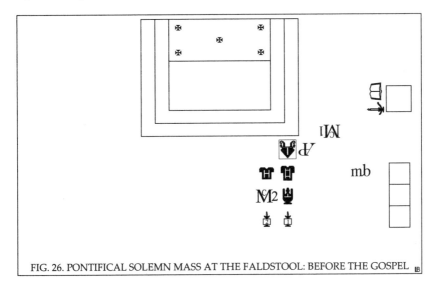

FIG. 26. PONTIFICAL SOLEMN MASS AT THE FALDSTOOL: BEFORE THE GOSPEL

If a genuflexion is to be made at any text in the Gospel, the MC places a cushion, on which the bishop genuflects, towards the Gospel book.

After the Gospel the subdeacon comes up immediately and brings the book to the bishop, making no genuflexion nor inclination to him. He points to the beginning of the Gospel text, which the bishop kisses, saying *Per evangelica,* etc., and laying both hands on the text. He then shuts the book, bows to the bishop, hands the book to the first MC and stands at the left of the AP. As soon as the Gospel is finished the second MC leads the deacon, followed by the thurifer and acolytes, back in procession to before the faldstool. They genuflect to the altar as they pass the centre. The deacon takes the thurible and incenses the bishop (still unmitred) with three double swings; he, the thurifer at his side, and the second MC bow before and after. The thurifer takes the thurible to the sacristy or other place where it is kept. Meantime the acolytes go and place their candles on the credence.

If there is a homily at this point, the ministers form in line before the bishop, bow to him, and go to sit at the sedilia. The bishop sits at the

faldstool. If he preaches himself, he may do so standing before the faldstool, or sitting on it, or he may go to the pulpit, conducted by the first
MC. The ministers do not sit nor cover themselves until the bishop is
ready to begin the homily.

Creed. When the *Credo* is intoned the deacon and subdeacon stand in
line behind the bishop. He stands uncovered facing the altar; the
pontifical canon is held by the AP, with the candle-bearer on his right.
After the intonation the AP hands the book to the book-bearer. The
deacon and subdeacon come to the bishop's side and say the *Credo* with
him, as at the *Gloria*. The MC places a cushion for the bishop to genuflect
at *Et incarnatus.*[27]

The bishop then sits, the deacon puts on the gremial and golden mitre;
the ministers bow to the bishop and go to sit, as at the *Gloria*. At the
words *Et incarnatus est,* etc., the bishop bows, wearing the mitre, the
ministers uncover and bow; and the others kneel, unless they are sitting,
when they only bow.

On Christmas Day and the Annunciation the bishop kneels on a
cushion at these words before the faldstool, not uncovering; the ministers
kneel at the sedilia.

After this text the deacon rises, takes the burse from the credence, and
spreads the corporal on the altar, making the usual inclination to the AP
(who does not stand), to the bishop, to the clergy on the epistle side, and
to the clergy on the gospel side and genuflexions to the altar. He goes
back to his place by the shortest way, bowing to the other ministers
before he sits again. The second MC or book-bearer places the missal-
stand on the altar in position for the offertory.

Offertory. Towards the end of the sung *Credo* the ministers come
before the bishop, stand in line and bow to him, the deacon takes off the
gremial and mitre; the deacon and subdeacon form in line *(unus post
alium)* between the faldstool and the people, the AP stands at the side on
the epistle side. The bishop rises, sings *Dominus vobiscum* facing the
people, then turns by his left to the altar, sings *Oremus* and reads the
offertory. The book-bearer and candle-bearer stand before him, the
ministers at his sides (after *Oremus*).

The bishop sits again, the deacon puts on his precious mitre, the three
ministers bow to the bishop, the AP and the deacon go to his right, the
subdeacon to his left. Servers bring a salver to hold the ring and gloves,
and the vessels and hand-towel to wash his hands. The deacon takes off
the ring and right glove, the subdeacon the left glove, with the usual
oscula. The ring and gloves are put on the salver. The servers who hold
the ewer and dish come before the bishop and bow. He washes his
hands, the AP presents the hand-towel and then puts the ring on the
bishop's bare hand, again with the *solita oscula*. The subdeacon brings the

---

[27] The book- and candle-bearers do not genuflect.

chalice from the credence and carries it to the altar as the bishop goes up to the altar.

After the bishop has washed his hands, the AP takes the missal from the credence, and the pontifical canon, and carries them to the altar.[28] The second MC goes with him, and the server bearing the candle. They bow to the clergy on the epistle side, to the bishop in passing, to the clergy on the gospel side, genuflect before the altar steps and the AP arranges the missal and the pontifical canon[29] on the altar and places the hand-candle near them. He then stays by the book. The bishop rises and goes to the altar between the deacon (on his right) and the MC, the mitre-bearer following; all salute the choir on the way. Before the altar the deacon takes off the mitre, the bishop bows low, the others genuflect. The bishop, with the deacon on his right, goes up to the altar and kisses it. The AP meets the bishop on the footpace; the subdeacon has gone to the credence to bring the chalice.

From now to the end of Mass everything continues as in the case of solemn pontifical Mass at the throne, except that (a) the deacon incenses the AP and the subdeacon (each with two double swings) *after* the incensation of the choir, (b) in the case of a bishop not in his own diocese, no indulgence is announced, (c) the bishop recites the last Gospel at the gospel corner. The subdeacon holds the pontifical canon. The candle-bearer holds the candle at the left of the AP (who stands between the bishop and the subdeacon).

Conclusion of Mass. At the end of Mass the bishop may go with the ministers and servers in procession[30] to the sacristy and there unvest. Or he may go to the faldstool (having saluted the altar and clergy) and unvest there. In this case, when he arrives at the faldstool, he sits and the three ministers bow to him, go to the sedilia, where the AP takes off the cope, the others their maniples. The deacon and subdeacon come back to the bishop; the subdeacon takes off the bishop's maniple, the deacon his mitre. Then they assist him to unvest, handing each vestment to a server who carries it to the altar and consigns it to the second MC. The mantelletta is put on, the deacon hands him the pectoral cross to kiss and puts it on him and then hands him his biretta. The deacon and subdeacon now bow to the bishop and retire to the sacristy. The bishop sits at the faldstool and says the prayers after Mass (uncovering and rising and turning to the altar for *Kyrie* and the subsequent prayers), the book-

---

[28] Or this may be done by the book-bearer (accompanied by the candle-bearer). Then the AP accompanies the bishop (on his left) from the faldstool to the altar. Some say that the AP takes the pontifical canon to the altar; others that MC2 does this.

[29] Leaning against the cross or gradine. If this is not convenient the pontifical canon is put on the missal-stand and the missal laid on the altar until it is needed for the secret(s).

[30] The acolytes with their candles will be at the head (having got into place for the departure during the last Gospel); the subdeacon precedes the bishop, who walks between the AP (on his right) and the deacon (all vested and covered).

bearer holding the book standing before him, the candle by the book.[31] Finally, after a concluding prayer said kneeling in the centre on the lowest step of the altar (on a cushion placed for him by the MC), the bishop retires, accompanied — as at his coming — by the AP and MC.

---

[31] Or the bishop may read these prayers in the sacristy during the removal of his ceremonial shoes and stockings. This latter may not be done in the church (S.R.C., 4 December 1952).

Pontifical Mass at the Throne and at the Faldstool [32]

	At the throne	At the faldstool
Assistants	Two assistant-deacons at the throne.	Deacon (D) and Subdeacon (SD) replace assistant-deacons.
Reverences	(i) Non-canons genuflect to salute the Bishop (B). (ii) Thurifer, book and candle-bearers, and those who wash his hands kneel.	All salute B. by a bow only.
Salutations to Choir	Omitted (except at beginning — if clergy already in choir — and end).	Not omitted.
Vesting	(i) B. vests in secretarium during and after Terce. (ii) SD puts on B.'s ceremonial shoes and stockings during Terce in secretarium.	(i) B. may vest in sacristy, or at the faldstool in the chancel. (ii) Server (or servant) puts them on B. in sacristy.
Procession to the high altar	B. goes vested — preceded by second SD (in tunicle) as cross-bearer, by SD, Assistant Priest (AP) and D — between the assistant deacons.	B. *if vested* — preceded by a server as cross-bearer, and by SD — goes between AP (on his right) and D. *If not vested:* — (a) goes between D and SD preceded by AP, or, (b) in a separate procession, with AP on his left, after D and SD have gone to the altar.
Incensation	(i) AP assists B. at throne in putting in incense for Gospel and incenses B. after the Gospel. (ii) At offertory incensation AP is incensed immediately after B.	(i) Deacon does this at faldstool. (ii) AP is incensed after[33] the incensation of the clergy by D.
Gospel	D goes to the throne and kisses B.'s hand before saying *Munda cor meum.*	D kisses B.'s hand after having received the blessing before the Gospel.
Last Gospel	Recited by B. as he leaves the altar. [34]	Recited by B. at the gospel corner of the altar.

[32] This table deals only with those points in which pontifical Mass at the throne and at the faldstool differ.

[33] Some rubricians say before the incensation of the choir.

[34] A few rubricians say that: (i) D and SD do not receive the pax directly from B. at Mass at the faldstool, and (ii) that at this Mass B. recites the last Gospel, while leaving the altar.

Chapter XVIII

Pontifical Solemn Mass for the Dead[1]

§ 1. Preparation

WHEN a bishop sings Mass for the dead, whether he does so at the throne or at a faldstool, the following changes must be made. The Bishop uses neither crosier, gloves, nor ceremonial shoes and stockings. He has the gremial, of black silk. He wears only the simple mitre, of white linen, with ruddy fringes to its lappets.

The vestments are kissed during the vesting and unvesting; there are no *solita oscula* during Mass. The Bishop gives no blessing to anyone. The Blessed Sacrament should not be at the high altar, according to the general rule for pontifical Mass.

Preparations. In the chapel of the Blessed Sacrament a kneeler or faldstool is prepared, as usual. Its coverings and cushion are in violet.

In the sacristy are prepared the vestments (black) for the deacon and subdeacon; on the benches of the choir are laid the vestments for the canons, including the black dalmatics (with amices) for the two assistant deacons.

If torches are used there are two or four, but no more.[2]

On the altar of the Blessed Sacrament six candles are lit, at least during the time the Bishop kneels there, before and after the ceremony. On the high altar are six candles (never seven) of unbleached wax, and the altar cross. The candlesticks should be sombre (e.g., bronze, or of dark wood); not gilt nor of silver. No other ornament should stand on the altar or retable. The frontal is black.[3] The footpace is covered with a violet (or black) carpet, the rest of the sanctuary is bare. The Bishop's vestments, black—the maniple included—are laid out on the altar as usual. The simple mitre, only, stands on the gospel side. Before the altar is the faldstool on a small violet carpet (for the Bishop to kneel on his arrival). It is covered with violet and furnished with two violet cushions.[4] The usual vessels are put on the main credence, namely, the acolytes' candles (lighted and of unbleached wax), the chalice prepared (with two breads

---

[1] C.E., II, xi, xii. This chapter presupposes a knowledge of the ceremonies of a non pontifical solemn Mass of the dead, and of a pontifical Mass not for the dead.

[2] C.E. II, xi, 7.

[3] Should the Blessed Sacrament be present the frontal and the conopæum should be violet (cf. S.R.C. 3035 § 10, 3201 § 10, 3562).

[4] For Mass at the throne. But for requiem Mass at the faldstool it is covered in black.

and two purifiers),[5] the cruets, bell, the ewer, dish and hand-towels for washing hands, the Epistolarium (book of lessons). The missal on its stand, the pontifical canon which should be covered with black, the hand-candlestick with a candle of white wax, and the gremial are on the credence near the throne. At the sedilia an amice and black cope for the assistant priest, the maniples for the ministers. A black cope with simple morse (formale) is prepared nearby for the Bishop, if he will give the Absolution. In this case the pontifical (part III) will also be wanted. Candles of white wax to be distributed to the clergy, if this is the custom, are made ready and tapers to light them. The four torches are of unbleached wax. Four or six candles of unbleached wax may burn at the entrance to the chancel.

If the Absolution is to follow, the processional cross should be ready near the credence and the aspersory and sprinkler at hand.[6] *If the celebrant be the Archbishop* within his province, the processional cross will not be needed, but a stand for the Archbishop's cross should be prepared.

The sedilia are bare or covered in black or violet. If there is a throne it is covered in violet cloth and may have a violet carpet; the stools for the assistants are bare. If the Absolution is to be given at the catafalque, this stands before the sanctuary, outside the chancel; surrounded by candles of unbleached wax, which are lighted for the Mass and Absolution. At its foot is another faldstool (covered in black), if available.

§ 2. Requiem Mass at the Throne

The same ministers, assistants and servers attend as at all such Pontifical Masses, except that there is no crosier-bearer. When the Bishop enters the church the bells are not rung joyfully. They may be tolled. The organ is not used at all.[7]

All proceeds as is usual in pontifical Mass at the throne, except the following points:

The deacon and subdeacon, having vested in the sacristy, go, with the servers, to the sanctuary and, at the sedilia, await the Bishop's arrival.

The Bishop vests at the throne. He omits the prayers of preparation; he says the vesting prayers (beginning with *Exue me, Domine*), omitting those for the ceremonial shoes and for the gloves. The maniple is put on him after the girdle, before the pectoral cross.[8] An archbishop does not wear the pallium at requiem Masses. When the Bishop is vested, the AP

---

[5] If the *prægustatio* takes place.

[6] These will be needed at the church door if the Bishop is to be received ceremonially.

[7] C.E., I, xxviii, 13; S.R.C. 4265 § 2. In case of necessity, the organ may be used to sustain the singing, and so must not be played by itself.

[8] Because of the practical difficulty it may be put on immediately after the dalmatic.

puts on his ring; the deacon and subdeacon put on their maniples, brought to them by the second MC.

Beginning of Mass. All then go to the altar as at a pontifical Mass not for the dead, the Bishop with joined hands, since he does not use the crosier. The subdeacon does not bring the Gospel book with him. After the prayers at the foot of the steps the Bishop, between the deacon and subdeacon, goes up and kisses the altar, not the Gospel book. The deacon puts on the Bishop's mitre. The altar is not incensed; the Bishop (having bowed to the cross) preceded by the AP and accompanied by the assistant deacons, goes back to the throne at once. The deacon and subdeacon go to the sedilia. After the sung *Kyrie, eleison* the Bishop sings *Dominus vobiscum,* not *Pax vobis.* During the collects (which are sung in the simple ferial tone) all in choir kneel except the sacred ministers and the candle-bearer. After the Epistle the subdeacon reverences to the altar and to the Bishop, but is neither blessed nor kisses the Bishop's hand. During the sequence, candles (if they are to be used) are given to all in choir by servers and are lit by them.[9] They hold these burning during the Gospel, and then again from the *Sanctus* to the ablutions. During the last verse of the *Dies iræ* the deacon carries the book to the altar,[10] but does not kiss the Bishop's hand nor seek a blessing. He says the *Munda cor meum* kneeling on the top step. The procession to the place of the Gospel proceeds in this order: first the MC, then the deacon followed by the sub-deacon, lastly the acolytes.[11] If it passes the throne, all (except canons) genuflect to the Bishop. At the Gospel there is no incense, nor do the acolytes hold their candles. They stand on either side of the subdeacon with joined hands.

Offertory. After the Gospel the subdeacon does not take the book to be kissed by the Bishop, but hands it at once to the second MC. Those taking part in the Gospel group return to the altar in the same order in which they came. The Bishop goes to the altar, having read the offertory and washed his hands. At the foot of the altar the deacon takes off the mitre. The subdeacon brings the *oblata* (with the burse containing the corporal), not wearing the humeral veil. The water is not blessed. The Bishop blesses incense and incenses the altar as usual; then he alone, wearing the mitre, is incensed by the deacon. The deacon removes the mitre after the Bishop has washed his hands. The torch-bearers (four in number) kneel before the altar till the ablutions; and all in choir kneel until the conclusion of the canon.[12] The subdeacon does not hold the paten. He assists the Bishop (on his left) during the incensation. Then he

---

[9] Candles are not handed to the assistant deacons as they could not conveniently hold them and assist the Bishop. It is a moot point as to whether the Bishop himself holds one at the Gospel.
[10] C.E., II, xi, 6.
[11] Ibid.
[12] R.G., n. 521 c.

returns to his place at the foot of the altar. He incenses the Blessed Sacrament at the elevation (the second MC having put incense into the thurible) with three double swings at each elevation,[13] kneeling on the lowest step at the epistle side. The kiss of peace is not given, nor do the sacred ministers strike their breasts at *Agnus Dei*. When the deacon, facing the altar, sings the verse *Requiescant in pace* the Bishop does not say it himself.[14] There is no blessing at the end of Mass, nor is an indulgence announced. The Bishop begins the last Gospel at the altar, continues it as he goes back, wearing his mitre, to the throne, and ends it there, genuflecting at the throne at the words *Et Verbum caro factum est*. He then sits, and the ministers take off their maniples; the AP takes off his cope.

The Bishop is unvested by the deacon and subdeacon at the throne.[15] They then depart and are replaced by the two assistant deacons (who meantime—with all the other canons in choir—have taken off their vestments) for the Bishop's thanksgiving. If the Absolution follows at once,[16] the assistant deacons and all the canons remain vested, the deacon and subdeacon aid the Bishop to vest in cope and mitre, when the chasuble, dalmatic and tunicle have been taken off. The subdeacon then departs to act as cross-bearer and the deacon (with the AP) takes his part in the Absolution.

§ 3. Requiem Mass at a Faldstool

No special directions for this are necessary. All is done according to the normal rules for pontifical solemn Mass at the faldstool with the exceptions and particular rules for requiems in general and those noted in the above section for pontifical requiems. The faldstool is draped in black. The Bishop wears only the simple mitre; he gives no blessing (except that of incense), the altar is incensed only at the offertory and so on, as already explained.

---

[13] The Sacred Host is not elevated until the singing of the *Sanctus* has concluded (S.R.C. 4364).

[14] R.G., n. 473.

[15] If there is a homily, it is preached after Mass.

[16] Then there is no last Gospel. For the Absolution, cf. Chapter XXXI.

Chapter XIX

The Faithful at Mass

§ 1. Rules for the Laity at Mass

(A) At a 'Private' Mass[1]

IN accordance with a rubric of pre-1962 missals (*Rubricæ Generales Missalis*, xvii, 2), now obsolete, those present at a Mass in which they are taking no active part are accustomed to kneel except at the Gospels, when they stand, and during the offertory and ablutions, when they sit.

In addition those present should at least make certain liturgical gestures with the priest:

(a) the sign of the cross whenever he makes it during the Pre-Mass, and at the Blessing:

(b) striking the breast at *mea culpa* of the *Confiteor,* and at Agnus Dei (the communicants strike their breast also at *Domine, non sum dignus* before their own communion):

(c) making the small sign of the cross on the forehead, lips, and breast at the beginning of each Gospel.

Those attending a private Mass stand as the celebrant comes to the altar and while he departs.

(B) At Solemn or Sung Mass

For a solemn or sung Mass the General Rubrics give no rules for the laity present. They are supposed to take an *active* part in the ceremony with the sacred ministers and clergy, and so the rubrics assume that, as far as possible, the laity will conform to the rules laid down for the clergy when they are present in choir. Accordingly:

1. All stand when the procession to the altar makes its appearance from the sacristy, and remain standing until the Mass is begun, even though the Asperges takes place.

2. Each person bows and makes the sign of the cross when sprinkled at the Asperges.

---

[1] By a private Mass is meant one at which there is no congregation or in which those present take no active part. For a Dialogue Mass, see § 2 below.

3. All kneel for the prayers of preparation (up to *Oremus*), unless they sing the introit, and stand when the celebrant ascends the altar steps.

4. All remain standing for the introit, *Kyrie,* and the *Gloria in excelsis,* while they are recited by the celebrant.

5. When the celebrant has sat down for the singing of the *Gloria,* all sit. If the people join in the singing—which is highly desirable—they may stand while they sing *Gloria, Credo,* etc. They rise when the celebrant rises towards the end of this chant.

6. All stand for the singing of the prayers (except at penitential Masses celebrated in violet vestments, and at a requiem Mass, when they kneel), and sit for the chanting of the Epistle and what follows.

7. When *Dominus vobiscum* is sung before the chanting of the Gospel all stand. They remain standing during the recitation of the *Credo,* genuflecting with the celebrant at the words *Et incarnatus est,* etc.

8. All sit when the celebrant has sat down for the singing of the *Credo.* While the words *Et incarnatus,* etc., are sung all bow. Only those who are *standing* at the time when these words are begun then kneel; those seated bow only. They rise when the celebrant rises towards the end of the *Credo,* remain standing while he sings *Dominus vobiscum* and *Oremus,* and then sit.

9. All rise for the incensation of the clergy; bow to the thurifer when he bows to them before and after he incenses them, and, having been incensed, they sit.

10. When the celebrant begins to sing *Per omnia sæcula sæculorum* before commencing the preface, all rise and remain standing until the *Sanctus* has been recited (or sung, if the people sing it). Then all kneel.

11. All bow down during the consecration but look up for a moment at the Sacred Host, (silently saying "My Lord and my God" is praiseworthy) and at the Chalice, when they are elevated. After the elevation all stand (except at penitential Masses celebrated in violet vestments and a requiem Mass, when they remain kneeling until the end of the canon, when they stand). They bow while the celebrant receives the Sacred Host and drinks the Precious Blood. Then all sit.

12. Those who are to receive Holy Communion come to the altar immediately after the warning bell has been rung. All others kneel during the distribution of Holy Communion and remain kneeling until the door of the tabernacle has been closed, if a ciborium is to be replaced therein.

13. All stand for the singing of *Dominus vobiscum* before the postcommunion prayers, and remain standing during these prayers (except at penitential Masses celebrated in violet vestments and at a requiem Mass, when they kneel).

14. All kneel for the Blessing and make the sign of the cross.

15. All stand for the last Gospel (genuflecting with the celebrant, if he genuflects during its recitation) and remain standing until the procession has returned to the sacristy.

(C) Other Rules

1. On Palm Sunday and at Candlemas, palms and candles respectively, may be distributed liturgically to the laity before the procession in which they take part. This is done with the *oscula*, whereby the person first kisses the celebrant's hand then palm or candle, before taking the palm or candle from him.
2. When receiving Holy Communion from a bishop or from another prelate entitled to the pontifical ring (e.g. an abbot), the communicant kisses the pontifical ring before receiving the Sacred Host.

§ 2. Dialogue Mass

An instruction of the Sacred Congregation of Rites, *De Musica Sacra* (3 September 1958), lays down rules[2] for the direct, active participation of the people, by gesture[3] and voice, in a solemn, sung or low Mass. There are three degrees of participation in a solemn or sung Mass:[4] (i) chanting the liturgical responses; (ii) singing, in addition, these parts of the Ordinary of the Mass: *Kyrie, eleison; Gloria in excelsis; Credo; Sanctus-Benedictus; Agnus Dei;* (iii) chanting also the proper parts of the Mass.

Similarly, there are four degrees of direct liturgical participation by the congregation in low Mass:[5] (i) answering aloud the short responses; (ii) saying aloud all the responses made by the server, and the triple *Domine, non sum dignus* before their communion; (iii) reciting, in addition, with the celebrant, these parts of the Ordinary: *Gloria in excelsis, Credo, Sanctus-Benedictus* and *Agnus Dei;* (iv) saying aloud with the celebrant these four parts of the proper of the Mass: introit, gradual, offertory and communion antiphons. In a low Mass also the faithful may recite the *Pater noster* aloud, with the celebrant and in Latin—all answering *Amen* at the end.[6] All these texts recited in this direct participation in the Mass must be in Latin.[7] Certain things are, however, prohibited for the congregation: (i) to *alternate* with the celebrant in the recitation of the *Gloria in excelsis, Credo, Sanctus-Benedictus* and *Agnus Dei;*[8] (ii) to recite

---

[2] Instruction, Chap. III.
[3] Ibid., cf. § 22b.
[4] Ibid., § 25.
[5] Ibid., § 31.
[6] Ibid., § 32.
[7] Ibid., § 14b.
[8] Cf. S.R.C. 3248 § 5.

aloud any part of the Mass not permitted by the above rules; (iii) to say *aloud* at the elevation the ejaculation "My Lord and my God".[9]

To aid the people in taking an active part more easily in liturgical actions a commentator may give brief, appropriate explanations and directions.[10] If possible he should be a priest, or at least a cleric, vested in choir dress; if not a suitable layman may be chosen (a woman is not admissible). A cleric may stand in the sanctuary or at the altar rail, or in the pulpit or ambo; a layman takes his place outside the sanctuary and pulpit. The commentary should be prepared in writing, be brief and temperate, and spoken in a moderate voice at appropriate moments, and never when the celebrant is praying aloud. Silence is kept from the consecration to *Pater noster*.[11] On Sundays and feast days, at low Masses, a reader may read the Epistle and Gospel in the vernacular.[12]

To aid in achieving the purpose of the Dialogue Mass—to influence the congregation to take an *active* part in the sacrifice as a communal act—it is desirable to adopt for it a form of congregational ceremonial akin to the correct ceremonial for solemn Mass.[13] Accordingly, those taking part should (i) stand when the celebrant goes up to the altar after the prayers of preparation; (ii) sit for the Epistle, gradual, *Alleluia* or tract; (iii) stand for the Gospel, *Credo* and *Oremus;* (iv) sit until *Orate, fratres;* (v) stand for the preface and *Sanctus;* (vi) kneel for the canon;[14] (vii) stand for *Pater noster* and prayers before communion; (viii) kneel for the communion; (ix) sit for the ablutions;[15] (x) stand at *Dominus vobiscum;* (xi) kneel for the Blessing; (xii) stand for the last Gospel (cf. Chapter XIX § 1). Those who take part in the Mass should, in addition to observing the correct postures, carry out the correct liturgical gestures (genuflecting or bowing, making the sign of the cross, striking the breast, etc., at the proper moments).

Vernacular hymns that are approved by the Ordinary may be sung at low Mass with his permission; not, however at high or sung Mass.[16]

§ 3. Civil Dignitaries at Mass

In different parts of *Cæremoniale Episcoporum* and in a number of replies to queries proposed to S.R.C., directions are given for the liturgical

---

[9] S.R.C. 4397 § 1.
[10] Instruction, § 96.
[11] Ibid., § 14c, cf. § 27f.
[12] Ibid., § 14c. If all have printed missals or leaflets this is not necessary.
[13] Cf. O'Connell, *Sacred Music and Liturgy* (1959), p. 38.
[14] Strictly speaking they should stand after the consecration.
[15] Those who have received Holy Communion continue kneeling.
[16] Cf. Instruction, § 13-14; S.R.C. 31 March 1909.

honours to be given to Catholic civil dignitaries, when they are present in an official capacity at Mass or Vespers.[17]

In addition to a king or queen, or president of a State *(princeps magnus* or *maximus),* C.E. speaks of "magistratus," "gubernatores," "officiales civitatis," "barones," "nobiles" and others — in fact it provides for a series of public personages from the head of the State to the mayor of a town.

Reception. A form of solemn reception of a king or queen, or great prince (and so, presumably, the president of a republic) is provided in *Pontificale Romanum* (Part III). Other distinguished persons are received at the door of the church by one of the Chapter (at the cathedral), or by the rector of the church, in choir dress, who presents lustral water with the *aspergillum* (or may sprinkle the official),[18] and then conducts him to his special place outside the chancel.

If the dignitary should enter with the Bishop, he will be sprinkled by him with lustral water after the canons,[19] and immediately precede the Bishop[20] (in choir dress) in the procession to the altar.[21]

Place in Church. A king by Apostolic privilege occupies a throne adorned in silk — on the gospel side of the chancel; a president a special place on the gospel side. Before him is placed a prie-dieu, draped and with cushions of silk of the colour of the Mass.[22] Other officials (even if they are ministering to the Bishop pontificating[23]) occupy a special place,[24] but *outside the chancel.*[25] The seat for them — not on a platform,[26] not canopied[27] — may have a covering,[28] not silk; the prie-dieu is to be undraped, but may have cushions (not silk).[29]

Arrival in Church. If the dignitary arrives after the function has begun, before going to his place he kneels facing the altar and says a short prayer, genuflects to the altar and to the Bishop, and bows to the

---

[17] Dignitaries who are not Catholic, including clergy of other denominations, who may be present may not be accorded any of the following liturgical marks of distinction. It is appropriate that, before the liturgical rite commences, a cleric of suitable rank greet the dignitary upon his arrival and escort him to his place outside the chancel. Those responsible for organising the ceremony should ensure that the visiting non-Catholic dignitary is briefed about the protocol of not receiving Holy Communion.

[18] Cf. S.R.C. 911, 2483 § 2, 2638 § 6, 2753. *If the Asperges precedes the Mass:* (i) lustral water is not then presented at the door of the church; (ii) the head of a State is sprinkled — with a bow before and after — before all others in choir; lesser dignitaries are sprinkled after the clergy in choir but before the congregation.

[19] S.R.C. 2638 § 6, 911.

[20] C.E., I, xv, 2.

[21] The dignitary's attendants precede him in the procession to the altar.

[22] Cf. C.E., I, xiii, 13; S.R.C. 2621 § 10.

[23] C.E., I, xi, 12.

[24] C.I.C. 1263; S.R.C. 2007.

[25] C.E., I, xi, 12; xiii, 13; S.R.C. 1792, 1838 § 1, 1849, 1910 § 2, 2036.

[26] S.R.C. 1830 § 3, 2753 § 2.

[27] S.R.C. 1792.

[28] Cf. C.E., I, xiii, 13; S.R.C. 2753 § 2.

[29] S.R.C. 1830 § 3, 2462 § 4, 2753 § 2.

canons and to other persons of equal rank that may be present.[30] When canons on their way to choir pass the dignitary they may bow to him; so may the sacred ministers (covered) going to, or returning from, the high altar.[31]

Incensation. At solemn Mass (of the living[32]) and Vespers distinguished laymen are incensed. A king is incensed before the Bishop (presiding, not pontificating); a president, a viceroy, a governor of a State, immediately after the Bishop[33] and his immediate ministers (AP and assistant deacons). Each of these is incensed by the deacon (the AP at Vespers) with three double swings.[34] High officials (e.g., a minister of State) are incensed before the canons, if these are not in vestments (after them, if they are); officials of the next rank (e.g., a Lord Mayor) are incensed after prelates and canons, but before the rest of the clergy.[35] Each of these personages is incensed by the deacon (the AP at Vespers) with two double swings. Lesser officials are each incensed after all the clergy in choir and by the thurifer,[36] with two double swings.

The Kiss of Peace. A king or president (or anyone who is incensed before canons) receives the kiss of peace by embrace, given him by the AP, before he gives the pax to the Bishop in the case of a king; after, in the other cases. All other distinguished persons receive the pax by means of a pax-brede,[37] and in the same order in which they were incensed. In a pontifical Mass the brede is kissed by the AP.[38] (immediately after receiving the pax from the celebrant); and is carried by him to the official(s) who had been incensed by the deacon, carried by an MC or server to all others.[39] In a solemn Mass *coram Episcopo* the brede is kissed by the AP (after having given the pax to the subdeacon), and conveyed by the subdeacon to all who had been incensed by the deacon, by an MC or server to the rest. In a solemn Mass at which the Bishop is not present, the brede is kissed by the deacon (after he has given the pax to the subdeacon) and conveyed by the subdeacon. In a sung Mass (or low Mass) if the pax-brede is used, it is kissed by the celebrant; presented by a server. In the private Mass of a bishop,[40] if a very high official is present,

---

[30] C.E., I, xviii, 5.

[31] S.R.C. 2753 § 3, 1279, 1837 § 1, 2231 §6, 2753 § 4.

[32] S.R.C. 690.

[33] C.E. I, xxiii, 30.

[34] C.E., I, xxiii, 32.

[35] C.E., ibid; S.R.C. 281, 1078, 2132 § 9.

[36] C.E., ibid; S.R.C. 497, 1187, 1192, 1290 § 2, 1898, 2175, 3264 § 3. All officials (except a king) receive one swing fewer if a cardinal be present.

[37] C.E., I, xxiv, 6; S.R.C. 1830.

[38] C.E., I, xxiv, 6.

[39] C.E., I, xxv, 7; S.R.C. 3780 § 9.

[40] C.E., I, xxiv, 12; xxix, 8. In this Mass a missal (not the one used by the celebrant) is brought to the dignitary at the end of the Gospel by a server, and he kisses the text of the Gospel of the Mass (ibid. 9).

the brede is kissed by the celebrant and presented to the official by the first assisting chaplain.[41] The pax-brede is presented, unveiled—at the time of giving the pax in Mass—by an MC or server to the person who is to convey the kiss of peace "from the Sacrifice of the altar"[42] (the AP, deacon, celebrant); he kisses it, saying *Pax tecum.* The person holding the brede answers *Et cum spiritu tuo.* The person who is to present the pax-brede takes it to each person who is to receive the pax and presents it to him to be kissed, saying *Pax tecum;* the other replies *Et cum spiritu tuo.* The person receiving the pax bows before and after; the person giving it, after only.[43] A small linen towel is carried with the pax-brede and the person who presents the brede wipes it after it has been kissed by one person before presenting it to another .

In Processions. In a procession of the Blessed Sacrament (e.g., at Corpus Christi)[44] dignitaries go after religious, and before the cross that heads the secular clergy. The chief ones carry the canopy over the Sacred Host outside the church when the procession is going out, and inside the church on its return.[45] The most distinguished among the dignitaries holds the end of the Bishop's cope as he carries the Sacred Host.

---

[41] C.E., I, xxix, 8.
[42] Ibid.
[43] Ibid.
[44] C.E., II, xxxiii, 5; cf. S.R.C. 330.
[45] C.E., II, xxxiii, 13, 23. Cf. S.R.C. 3024. The order of their precedence is laid down in C.E., I, xiv, 2, 3.

Part III

Evening Services

Chapter XX

Vespers

§ 1. General Directions

ALTHOUGH the Ceremonial of Bishops is intended primarily for pontifical functions, its directions and rubrics apply, with the necessary modifications, for all celebrations of the services it contains. For Vespers, therefore, the Ceremonial, Lib. II, cap. i-iii, and the other places at which Vespers are described, forms the final standard, as far as its directions go.

In the descriptions of the ceremony which are given here, account is taken of the different circumstances which are likely to arise. The rubrics of the Ceremonial have been followed as closely as possible. Necessary modifications have been made and details added in accordance with the decisions of the Congregation of Sacred Rites and the opinions of the best rubricists, and account has been taken of local usages which are not contrary to the rubrics.

General Rules. Vespers may be solemn or not solemn. On weekdays which are not great feasts the celebrant uses no cope, the altar is not incensed, there are practically no ceremonies. On Sundays and feasts the Vespers should be solemn, that is, with cope, incense, acolytes. There should further be assistants to the celebrant (who must always be a priest), who wear copes. On ordinary Sundays there should be two such assistants, in some sort corresponding to the deacon and subdeacon at Mass. On greater feasts there may be four or six. Since they wear the cope, according to the general rule these assistants should be at least tonsured. They must not be canons. In addition to the assistants in cope there should be (on greater days) two cantors, in surplice. They may sit with the other clergy in choir (on either side or on the same side) or have a place behind the assistants in cope in the sanctuary, near its entrance. Their business is to intone the psalms, the *Magnificat*, and (if the choir does not do it) the antiphons for the commemorations (if any). If there are only two assistants in cope, the cantors will also sing the versicles and *Benedicamus Domino*, and will pre-intone the antiphons to the clergy in choir. If there be no assistants in cope, the cantors will, in addition, pre-intone to the celebrant the first antiphon, the hymn, and the antiphon of the *Magnificat.*

It is supposed, normally, that where Vespers are sung there is a liturgical choir placed in seats or stalls on either side of the altar, though it is possible to celebrate Vespers without such a choir.

Preparations. In the sacristy a cope of the colour of the Office and a surplice are prepared for the celebrant,[1] surplices and copes for the assistants, surplices for the cantors, the MC, and servers. The acolytes' candles are ready. The thurible will be needed towards the end of the chanting of the psalms.

In the sanctuary the sedilia or bench on the epistle side is ready for the celebrant.[2] In front of it is laid a carpet, and a lectern (covered with a silk cloth of the colour of the Office, and having on it a vesperal or breviary — also covered in silk) may be placed there or off to one side. Near the sedilia, on the right, is put a stool for the MC. For the assistants in cope, benches (covered in green) or stools in the middle of the choir, on the side, facing the altar.[3] If it is customary another lectern may be placed in the middle of the choir, at which the cantors will intone the psalms. On it a vesperal (covered in silk of the colour of the Office) should lie.

The cover which protects the altar cloths may remain on the table of the altar (as it does for pontifical Vespers), or it may be removed — the latter is appropriate if the altar is to be incensed (and therefore kissed). If Benediction follows Vespers the cloth ought to be removed, but candle branches and flowers (if permitted and used) should be kept as far as possible off the table of the altar, leaving it unencumbered for the incensation. The frontal and conopæum (if the Blessed Sacrament be present) are of the colour of the Office. For solemn Vespers on greater days the six large candles are lighted: four suffice on ordinary Sundays. If other altars are to be incensed (cf. § 4 below), at least two candles should be lighted on them.

§ 2. Rules for the Choir

Whether Vespers be celebrated solemnly or simply the rules for the liturgical choir are the same. Its members generally enter the church in procession following the acolytes, unless they are already in their places for some preceding service. They come in pairs, genuflect to the altar, bow to each other, and go to their places in the stalls, as at solemn Mass. Here they stand till the celebrant and his assistants come before the altar.

---

[1] If he has the right to wear the rochet he will use it instead of the surplice and wear over it an amice.

[2] He may, however, sit in the first stall of the choir (on either side, according to custom). If he does, there is practically no difference in the ceremony, the assistants and acolytes will go to him there as they would to the sedilia. In this case a cushion is placed on the seat of the stall and one on the kneeler in front, which should be covered with a (green) cloth.

[3] The first two assistants generally sit beside the celebrant on the sedilia (or on stools, if the sedilia be short) and the first, on his right, ministers to the celebrant.

When the first psalm has been intoned they sit (at the asterisk of the first verse).

They uncover and bow (towards the altar, if standing) at the verse *Gloria Patri* at the end of each psalm, at the Holy Name, the name of Mary,[4] of the Saint of the Office[5] or commemoration, or at the names of the three Divine Persons, at the last stanza of hymns when this stanza is a real doxology, at *Oremus,* and, if it is customary, at verse 2 *(Sit nomen Domini benedictum)* of Psalm 112 *(Laudate pueri).* As each antiphon is intoned all stand meanwhile.[6] All stand during the chapter, hymn and to the end of Vespers.

They kneel if the *Preces feriales* are said and at the prayer when the rubric so directs. They kneel during the anthem of the Blessed Virgin, at the end of Compline except on Saturdays, Sundays and during all Paschal time. They kneel during the entire first stanza of the hymns *Ave maris stella* and *Veni, Creator,* during the entire stanza *Tantum ergo* of the *Pange lingua,* if the Blessed Sacrament is present on the altar,[7] during the whole stanza *O crux ave spes unica* in the hymn *Vexilla regis.* At the *Magnificat,* when they are incensed, they bow as at Mass.

§ 3. Solemn Vespers with Two Assistants in Cope

We shall first describe what should be the normal ceremonies on Sunday, when clerics in cope *(pluvialistæ)* assist the celebrant, then add what modifications should be made, when the rite is more solemn or when it is impossible to carry out the whole of this rite.

Vesting. In the sacristy the celebrant vests in a surplice (or rochet with amice), and over it a cope of the colour of the day.[8] On Sundays he should have two assistants who wear surplice and cope also, copes which are less ornate than the celebrant's, or at most ones which are identical to his. They and the celebrant wear the biretta. The first assistant or the MC helps the celebrant to vest. The procession is formed and all (uncovered) bow to the cross in the sacristy. The acolytes holding their lighted candles go first, then the members of the choir (lay members if in cassock and surplice, and the clergy after them), the cantors, the MC[9] and the

---

celebrant between the two assistants who hold the edges of his cope, turning in the orphreys. The acolytes go to the foot of the altar and turn out and go to stand one at each corner before the steps facing each other. The members of the choir genuflect in pairs, salute one another and go to their places; so do the cantors. The MC stands aside at the epistle side, and the celebrant and assistants go to the foot of the altar. There they bow profoundly[10] (or genuflect *in plano* if the Blessed Sacrament is reserved there); the MC and acolytes genuflect. The acolytes go to the sides of the altar, set down their candles (on the ground or on the lowest step) at each side, and extinguish them (unless the Blessed Sacrament be exposed). Then they go to their places at the credence or in choir, genuflecting at the centre as they pass.

Beginning of Vespers. The celebrant and the assistants bow to the choir on either side, first to the side opposite the place to which they will now go. They go to the sedilia. The assistants stand here, facing each other, on the floor of the sanctuary or go to the sides of the celebrant; the MC is at his right, having, if necessary, moved the lectern in front of the celebrant. The first assistant (or MC) lifts the right end of the celebrant's cope; he makes the sign of the cross, singing *Deus in adiutorium meum intende*. All in choir make the sign of the cross with him. The choir continues, answering the verse. At the words *Gloria Patri*, etc., all bow towards the altar.

While the *Sicut erat* is sung, the first assistant (accompanied by the MC) comes before the celebrant, facing him, bows and pre-intones the first antiphon to him, i.e., sings in a low tone the opening words (as far as the asterisk). The celebrant repeats the same notes in a louder tone, and the choir continues the antiphon, so that the antiphon is sung in full before as well as after the psalm. When the celebrant has intoned the antiphon the first assistant bows again and returns to his place at the celebrant's right, or, if the first two assistants are seated at the front of the sanctuary, they bow to the celebrant, go to the foot of the altar, genuflect, and go to sit on their stools.[11]

Psalms. Meanwhile the cantors come to the middle of the sanctuary (before the lectern, if there is one), bow to each other, genuflect, and when the antiphon ceases, intone the first psalm. They sing either the whole first verse or up to the asterisk only, according to custom, and then

---

[10] When the assistants *in cope* reverence to the altar (at which the Blessed Sacrament is not reserved) with the celebrant they bow profoundly, but when not with the celebrant they genuflect *in plano*. If the Blessed Sacrament be present all three genuflect *in plano* at each arrival at and before each departure from the foot of the altar.

[11] If the two assistants sit in the centre of the sanctuary (and this they must do if the celebrant is not at the bench, but in the first stall in choir) both will go before the celebrant for the pre-intonation, genuflecting as they go and return.

bow to that side of the choir that is to continue the psalm;[12] they
genuflect, bow to each other, and return to their places.

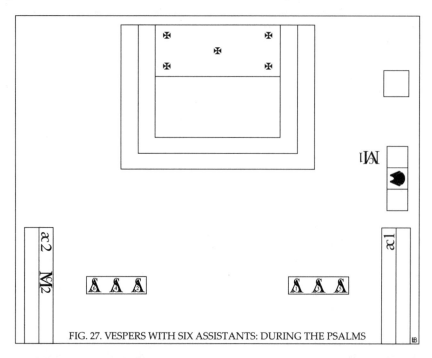

FIG. 27. VESPERS WITH SIX ASSISTANTS: DURING THE PSALMS

In figures 27 & 28 the first two assistants may also be at the celebrant's side.

When the psalm has been intoned (at the asterisk of the first verse, to
secure uniformity) all sit and put on their birettas, the first assistant[13]
hands his biretta to the celebrant with the *solita oscula*. The choir
continues the psalm. At the last verse of each psalm the MC rises and
bows to the celebrant to uncover. All uncover and bow (the MC towards
the altar since he is standing) for *Gloria Patri*. After this verse the MC
bows to the celebrant to resume his biretta and sits. After *Sicut erat* the
whole choir sings the entire antiphon. During this the cantors again come
to the middle, genuflect, and go to stand before the person of highest
rank in the choir (no matter what side he be on), to pre-intone the next
antiphon to him. If there is no person of higher rank, they go to him
whose place is nearest the altar, in the farthest row, on the gospel side.
They pre-intone the antiphon to him as before, singing its first words in a
low voice. He repeats what they have sung, the choir continues. The

---

[12] Cf. Chapter XX § 5. In some churches the rule is that the second verse of this psalm is to
be sung by the side on which the first dignitary or the hebdomadarian sits. If the entire
antiphon, or its beginning, consist of the opening words of the psalm, the intonation of the
psalm will begin where the antiphon terminated.

[13] The MC, if the assistant does not sit beside the celebrant.

cantors go back to their places, again genuflecting before the altar. The same process is repeated at the antiphon of each psalm; the cantors go then to the person of next highest rank (on the opposite side to the person to whom they had intoned the second antiphon), or to the one nearest the altar on the epistle side, then to the second on the gospel side and so on. When they come before him who is to intone and bow to him, he rises, and all the choir with him,[14] but not the celebrant nor the assistants in copes.

Hymn. Towards the end of the fifth psalm the acolytes go to the altar, light their candles and stand by them. During *Sicut erat* they come before the altar, with their candles, genuflect, go before the celebrant, where they are joined by the assistants, bow in a line with them to the celebrant, and then go and stand at each side of the lectern that is before the celebrant, and facing each other. The assistants come before the celebrant, bow with the acolytes, and stand before him.[15] When the last antiphon is finished, the celebrant rises, and all the choir with him. He first hands his biretta to the MC, who receives it, as always, with the *solita oscula*. Standing he sings the chapter; the choir answer *Deo gratias*. The first assistant bows and pre-intones the hymn to the celebrant, singing its first line in a low tone. The celebrant repeats this in a louder tone and the choir continues it.[16] The assistants and acolytes (who come into line with them) bow to the celebrant, and the assistants return to their places beside the celebrant (if in the sanctuary, they go with the acolytes genuflecting on the way). The acolytes set down their candles at the sides of the altar as before, not extinguishing them, and stand before them, until the end of the *Magnificat*.[17]

Magnificat. During the hymn the thurifer goes to the sacristy and prepares the thurible, comes out with the thurible and incense boat, genuflects to the altar, bows to the celebrant, and waits standing in the sanctuary by the altar at the epistle side. While the last verse of the hymn is sung the cantors come to the middle, salute each other, genuflect, and, when the hymn is finished, sing the versicle of the Office, the choir answering. They go back to their places, the first assistant comes to the celebrant, bows to him and pre-intones the antiphon of the *Magnificat*. The celebrant intones the same words, then sits and puts on his biretta.

---

[14] Or only those on the side where it is intoned (S.R.C. 3781 § 2).

[15] If the assistants do not sit beside the celebrant, but in the middle of the sanctuary, they will join the acolytes before the middle of the altar, genuflect with them and go to the celebrant.

[16] If alternate stanzas are sung by each side of the choir, that on which the celebrant is will take up the first stanza of the hymn when it has been intoned by the celebrant. If the first verse be *Veni, Creator* or *Ave maris stella*, all (except the acolytes carrying candles) kneel in their places until the end of the first stanza.

[17] The altar table should not be covered: before Vespers begins the cover should be removed.

All sit with him; the choir continues the antiphon and the assistant returns to his place; the MC may move the lectern to one side. The cantors come to the middle and sing the first verse of the *Magnificat*. As soon as they begin, the celebrant and all in choir rise and may make the sign of the cross. The celebrant goes to the altar, accompanied by the assistants and the MC. If the assistants are not at the sedilia the MC holds the celebrant's cope. If other altars are to be incensed, the MC brings the celebrant's biretta. On their way to the altar they bow to the choir on either side, beginning on the epistle side. The celebrant and assistants bow to the altar (or genuflect *in plano* if the Blessed Sacrament is reserved there); the thurifer also comes up, he and the MC genuflect in any case. The assistants on either side of the celebrant hold the ends of his cope; between them he goes up to the altar, kisses it, turns to the epistle side, puts on and blesses incense. The first assistant holds the incense boat and says *Benedicite, Pater reverende,* ministering the spoon, as the deacon at Mass, with the *solita oscula.* The second holds aside the right end of the cope. The celebrant blesses the incense with the usual form *Ab illo benedicaris,* etc. He incenses the altar as at Mass, the assistants on either side holding back the cope and supporting him when he genuflects. At the epistle corner he hands the thurible to the first assistant, who receives it with the *solita oscula* and hands it to the thurifer. The celebrant comes to the middle, bows, descends between the assistants, bows or genuflects with them at the foot, and goes back to his seat, bowing to the choir first.[18] The assistants follow him and stand facing him, the first takes the thurible and incenses the celebrant with three double swings, bowing before and after. He gives the thurible back to the thurifer; both assistants go to their places. If necessary, the MC moves the lectern back in front of the celebrant. The thurifer incenses the choir as at Mass, then the assistants, giving two double swings to each, the acolytes, and lastly the people, as at Mass.[19] The singers must take care not to end the *Magnificat* too soon. For this reason, if the incensing takes long (and especially if other altars are incensed), the organ should play when permissible — between the verses, or at the end of the last verse, before the *Gloria Patri.* The *Gloria Patri* of the *Magnificat* should not begin till the thurifer has incensed the people. While it is sung, unless he has already finished and has gone back to the sacristy, he will stand facing the altar and bowing, at the place where he has last incensed. Then he genuflects and goes to put away the thurible in the sacristy. He comes back to his place, and has no

---

[18] Beginning with the side opposite to the one to which he is to return.

[19] Rubrical authorities are not in agreement about the order of the incensation. That most commonly adopted by them is: (1) canons, (2) the clergy, (3) the assistants, (4) the M.C, and acolytes, (5) the people. Some prescribe the incensation of the assistants before that of the clergy in choir.

further duty. After the verse *Sicut erat* has been sung, all sit during the repetition of the antiphon.

Prayer. Meanwhile the acolytes take up their candles and go to the altar, the assistants in copes also rise and go to the place just before the acolytes (unless the assistants are already by the celebrant). All genuflect to the altar, come to the celebrant, and bow to him. The acolytes again stand one on either side as before, the assistants are by the celebrant. When the antiphon is ended the celebrant uncovers, rises and all rise with him. He sings *Dominus vobiscum,* and the collect of the Office in the solemn tone (as at Mass). If there are commemorations, the cantors go to the middle, at the lectern. The choir sings the antiphon of each commemoration, the cantors the versicle, the celebrant the collect (each preceded by *Oremus,* the last alone with its conclusion). Then the celebrant sings *Dominus vobiscum,* and the cantors *Benedicamus Domino.* While they sing this the acolytes bow to the celebrant, go to the altar (not genuflecting this time) and stand there on either side.[20] When the choir has answered *Deo gratias* to the verse *Benedicamus Domino,* the celebrant in a lower voice says *Fidelium animæ,* etc. The choir answers *Amen.*

Unless another service follows, all form in procession before the altar, make the usual reverence to it, and go out, as they came. If Benediction is to follow the acolytes may place their candles upon the altar.

§ 4. Incensing Other Altars at Vespers

If the Blessed Sacrament is exposed on the altar of the choir where Vespers are sung, no other altar may be incensed. Otherwise, if the Blessed Sacrament is reserved at another altar, this altar must be incensed first, before that of the choir. If it is the custom, other altars in the church (e.g., an altar dedicated to a saint whose feast occurs) may then be incensed also. If the Blessed Sacrament is not at the altar of the choir, this latter is incensed last. Candles (six, or at least two) should be lit on each altar, at least for the time while it is incensed. The celebrant puts on and blesses the incense once only, at the first altar incensed. The thurifer may afterwards add more incense himself if this is necessary.

In going to incense other altars the celebrant may be accompanied by some canons or members of the choir if this is the custom. In this case the MC must give them a sign in time, so that they come out from their places and form in the procession. In going to the other altars (all having first formed up before the high altar and reverenced to it) the thurifer leads; the acolytes follow with their lighted candles (all three having gone to the entrance of the choir during the antiphon preceding the

---

[20] If no other service is to follow they may go and stand at the entrance of the sanctuary.

Magnificat), next the MC and then the celebrant between the assistants,[21] who hold the ends of his cope. The accompanying canons or clergy follow him. The celebrant and assistants wear their birettas while going from one altar to the other. At each altar they uncover and make the usual reverences; the celebrant kisses the altar and incenses it, as already described in the case of the high altar. When all have been incensed the procession comes back to the choir, all go to their places, and the celebrant is incensed.

§ 5. Vespers with More than Two Assistants in Cope[22]

The Ceremonial orders that Vespers should be celebrated with two assistants (as described above) on Sundays and feasts observed by the people. It adds that on certain greater days there should be four to six assistants. Naturally this is possible only when a number of clerics (i.e., men who are at least tonsured[23]) are available.

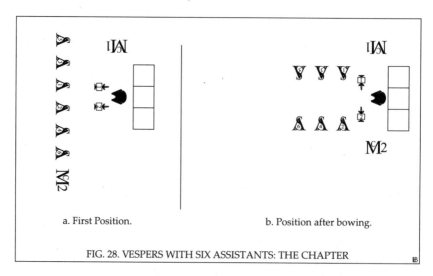

a. First Position.   b. Position after bowing.

FIG. 28. VESPERS WITH SIX ASSISTANTS: THE CHAPTER

On the following feasts six assistants take part: Christmas, Epiphany, Easter Sunday, Ascension Day, Whit Sunday, Corpus Christi, the feast of the Sacred Heart and of Christ the King; the Immaculate Conception and Assumption of Our Lady; the feasts of St Joseph; SS Peter and Paul; All

---

[21] Should there be several assistants in cope they — except the first and second who are with the celebrant — walk in pairs before the celebrant.

[22] The function of Vespers has been described above in detail (§ 3), only the differences when more than two assistants in cope take part are described here. There may be a second MC to direct the assistants in cope, and accompany the person who pre-intones.

[23] In modern terms this means having been through the rite of Admission to Candidacy for major orders or having made simple religious profession.

Saints; the Titular of the church; the Patron of the place; the Dedication of the church.

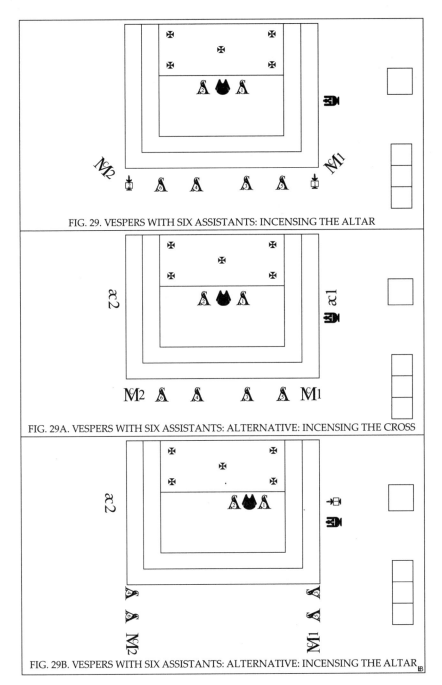

FIG. 29. VESPERS WITH SIX ASSISTANTS: INCENSING THE ALTAR

FIG. 29A. VESPERS WITH SIX ASSISTANTS: ALTERNATIVE: INCENSING THE CROSS

FIG. 29B. VESPERS WITH SIX ASSISTANTS: ALTERNATIVE: INCENSING THE ALTAR

Four assistants take part on the three days following Christmas; on the two days following Easter and Whit Sunday; on 1 January and Candlemas; on Trinity Sunday; the Annunciation and Our Lady's Birthday; on the Birthday of St John the Baptist and on the Dedication of St Michael, Archangel.[24]

Rules for Assistants. The first two assistants may sit at each side of the celebrant (when he is at the bench) or with the others in the middle of the choir.[25] The position of the assistants is indicated in fig. 27.

The first two assistants are with the celebrant when he walks and raise the edges of his cope. The first of them pre-intones to the celebrant the antiphon of the first psalm,[26] the hymn and the antiphon of the *Magnificat,* and incenses the celebrant. The last of the assistants (the fourth or sixth) announces the antiphons to the clergy in choir[27] (accompanied by an MC), and incenses the clergy and the other assistants (accompanied by the thurifer). He is himself incensed by the thurifer, who then incenses the MC, the acolytes and the people. The two last assistants (standing before the altar in the middle and genuflecting before and after) sing the verse after the hymn, the verses of the commemorations, and *Benedicamus Domino.*

Rules for Cantors. Two cantors (who occupy convenient places in choir, either together or on opposite sides), in surplice, should intone the psalms (the entire first verse of each or as far as the asterisk only, according to custom), the *Magnificat,* and the antiphons of the commemorations.[28] They go to the centre of the choir, near the entrance (behind the assistants in cope), bow to one another, genuflect, and intone. At the end of the intonation they bow to the side of the choir that is to continue the psalm (i.e., to the side opposite to that to which the antiphon was intoned if they intone the entire first verse of the psalm; to the same side, if they intone the first verse of the psalm only to the asterisk). They then repeat the genuflexion and the salutation and retire to their places.

Ceremonies of Assistants. All the assistants in copes come before the celebrant for *(a) Deus in adiutorium* and the intonation of the antiphon of the first psalm; *(b)* the capitulum and the intonation of the hymn;[29] *(c)* the incensation of the celebrant; *(d)* the prayer of the Office, and the commemorations (if these occur the two last assistants go to the foot of the altar to sing the antiphons, the versicles and *Benedicamus Domino,* they

---

[24] Cf. C.E., II, iii, 16, 17.

[25] In this case it is the MC who will assist the celebrant at his place.

[26] This is the usual practice. C.E., II, iii, 6 says, "unus ex dictis presbyteris paratis."

[27] "Canonicis ab utraque parte chori per ordinem, incipiendo a dignioribus" (cf. § 3 above). Or this pre-intoning may be done by the two cantors (C.E., II. iii, 8).

[28] When these are not intoned by the choir.

[29] If the hymn be *Veni, Creator* or *Ave maris stella,* they kneel where they are by the celebrant until the end of the first stanza, and only then depart.

then return to before the celebrant). They genuflect before the altar,[30] coming and going, and—in a line—bow to the celebrant on arrival and before departing. The positions which they occupy when bowing and subsequently are shown in fig. 28.

Magnificat. The first assistant alone (except for the MC) comes before the celebrant to intone the antiphon of the *Magnificat*.

After the intonation of the *Magnificat* all the assistants join the celebrant at the foot of the altar and on arrival there bow with him to the cross (or genuflect *in plano* if the Blessed Sacrament be present) and to the clergy. During the incensation of the altar the first two assistants accompany and aid the celebrant, the others remain standing at the foot of the altar[31] (fig. 29).

Alternatively, after the intonation of the *Magnificat*, the two acolytes go and stand by their candles, facing each other across the predella; assistants 3, 4, 5, and 6, and the two MC's line up in front of altar, and all stand as shown in diagram 29a while AS1 and AS2 assist at the censing of the cross and relics as usual. When the celebrant and AS1 and AS2 genuflect and start towards the epistle side, AS3-6 and the two MC's turn to face each other, arranging themselves as shown in diagram 29b. The acolytes lift their candles while their sides of the altar is being censed: so A2 will lift his candle while the epistle side of the altar is being censed; when C, AS1 and AS2 genuflect, A2 puts his candle down, while A1 picks his up and holds it while the gospel side is censed. After the gospel side has been censed, A1 puts his candle down, and the MC's and AS3-6 turn back to face the altar, once again arranging themselves as in diagram 29a.

After the incensation of the altar, the assistants reverence with the celebrant to the altar and choir, and accompany him to his place. They stand in line before him while the first assistant incenses him (bowing when the first assistant bows) and then return to their places, the last of them[32] taking the thurible from the first and going to incense the clergy, and afterwards the other assistants in the order of their rank (two double swings for each).

When the celebrant has sung *Dominus vobiscum* (the second time), after the final prayer, the two last assistants sing *Benedicamus Domino* at the foot of the altar and then rejoin the other assistants before the celebrant. He recites *Fidelium animæ* in a low tone and Vespers end. If Compline follows, the celebrant and his assistants with the MC and acolytes, having saluted the altar and clergy, depart in procession as they entered.

---

[30] If the first two assistants are beside the celebrant they do not go to the centre to genuflect but take their place in the middle of the others when these arrive before the celebrant.
[31] If other altars are incensed all the assistants go in procession with the celebrant for the incensation.
[32] Or the thurifer (C.E., II, iii, 12).

§ 6. Vespers Without Ceremonies

During the week, on weekdays and lesser feasts, there are no assistants; the celebrant sits at the first place in the choir, he wears no cope; there are neither acolytes nor thurifer, the altar is not incensed. There are no ceremonies at all, except observance of the rules for the choir as to rising, bowing, and so on. There may be cantors or precentors. The Office is sung straight through, as, for instance, Compline.

§ 7. Vespers Before the Blessed Sacrament Exposed[33]

If the celebrant is to expose the Blessed Sacrament immediately before Vespers he will put on a stole with the surplice and cope, and he may retain it during Vespers, if Benediction will immediately follow.[34] But if the Blessed Sacrament be already exposed, it is more correct not to use the stole at Vespers, but to put it on after Vespers if Benediction follows.[35] If another priest exposes the Blessed Sacrament he wears a stole, only while so doing.

In the case in which the Blessed Sacrament is exposed immediately before Vespers, two torch-bearers at least will come out in the procession. They kneel before the altar. The thurifer carries the thurible with lighted charcoal. The acolytes place their candles, as usual, on the lowest step but leave them lighted.

The Blessed Sacrament is exposed on the throne and incensed as usual (cf. Chapter XXIII § 2). On arriving before the altar, the celebrant genuflects on both knees on the floor and then goes to his seat. The acolytes leave their candles burning on the lowest step before the altar. The thurifer and torchbearers, having made a double genuflexion, go back to the sacristy.

If the Blessed Sacrament is already exposed, the procession comes out without incense or torches. As soon as they are in sight of the throne of exposition all uncover. All make a double genuflexion on both knees on the ground before the altar. Vespers proceed as usual. But the acolytes leave their candles burning before the altar; all kisses and reverences to persons are omitted, even to a bishop if he be present. All should stand the whole time. If this is found too fatiguing, at least no one when seated covers his head during any part of the service.[36] At the *Magnificat* the celebrant, having kissed the altar, puts on incense and blesses it standing on the footpace a little towards the gospel side. Then without

---

[33] This case will occur especially on Corpus Christi and during the Forty Hours' Prayer.
[34] S.R.C. 3593 § 2, 4269 § 12.
[35] S.R.C. 4084 § 2.
[36] C.E., II, xxxiii, 33.

genuflecting he comes down to the second altar step and kneeling on the edge of the footpace incenses the Blessed Sacrament with three double swings, bowing low before and after. He incenses the altar, but not the cross (if it be there). He and others are incensed as usual; but no one should turn his back to the altar. No other altar may be incensed.[37]

§ 8. Solemn Vespers for the Dead[38]

Solemn Vespers for the dead (for one deceased person, or for many or for all the faithful departed) may be sung the evening before any day on which a requiem Mass is allowed, under the same conditions. Naturally this Office is not permitted if the Blessed Sacrament is exposed.

The altar is clothed in black, but if the Blessed Sacrament be present the conopæum and the frontal should be violet. The celebrant wears a surplice and a black cope—with or without a black stole.[39] There are no assistants in copes and incense is not used, but (if possible) there will be two cantors, and the acolytes will have their candles, as usual, but of unbleached wax. They place them at the sides of the altar at the beginning as usual and extinguish them, as they are not needed until after the *Magnificat*. The salutations to the choir are not omitted,[40] but the *solita oscula* are. The antiphons are not pre-intoned but are sung straight through by the choir. The cantors intone the psalms. After the intonation of the first psalm all sit and remain seated until the *Magnificat*, when they stand. The altar is not incensed. All sit again while the *Magnificat* antiphon is repeated. Meanwhile the acolytes light their candles and come to stand beside the celebrant.[41] When the antiphon is finished all kneel for the *Pater noster*, etc., sung by the celebrant. He alone rises for *Dominus vobiscum* and the prayer. This will be selected for the occasion from the prayers given in the breviary or Roman Ritual, will be sung to the simple ferial tone (without inflexion) and will have the long conclusion.

The *Requiem æternam* at the end of each psalm and of the *Magnificat*, and that which follows the prayer are always to be in the plural, even

---

[37] S.R.C. 2390 § 6.

[38] The Office of the Dead and the rubrics for it are to be found not only in the breviary, but also in the Roman Ritual (Tit. VII, cap. 4).

[39] "Aut saltem stola nigra" (C.E., II, x, 10; S.R.C. 3029 § 8).

[40] S.R.C. 3059 § 27.

[41] Some authors (e.g., Vavasseur-Haegy-Stercky, Britt, Callewaert, Stappen-Croegaert) follow Martinucci's view (which, it would seem, was based on the Roman usage of his day) that the acolytes do not take part in Vespers for the Dead. But for pontifical Vespers of the Dead, C.E. (II, x, 4) expressly speaks of them, and there seems to be no sufficient reason for departing from its directions when the Vespers, though not pontifical, are solemn. This is the view of such good authorities as *Caeremoniale Romano-Seraphicum*, de Amicis, Baldeschi, Augustine, Hébert, Vismara.

where the Office is for one person; but the versicles between the *Pater* and the prayer will be in the singular, if the Office is for one person only.

After the prayer the celebrant chants *Requiem æternam* and the cantors *Requiescant* (both in the plural, because these last prayers are for the souls of all the faithful departed).

§ 9. Vespers in Small Churches

In many churches it is not possible to provide a liturgical choir on each side of the altar, nor assistants in copes. In this case Vespers should be celebrated with as much of the ceremonies of the Ceremonial as possible.

A simple ceremony is given here[42] which supposes the presence of two acolytes and a thurifer. Generally it will be possible to add an MC and sometimes two cantors. In the absence of assistants in cope the cantors will not only intone the psalms but one of them will pre-intone the first antiphon, the hymn, and the antiphon of the *Magnificat* to the celebrant. If no cantors are available the celebrant himself may intone the antiphons and psalms and sing the versicle and *Benedicamus Domino*.

In the procession out the cantors may accompany the celebrant, holding the ends of his cope. If there are no cantors the MC and thurifer may do this.

Beginning of Vespers. On arrival before the altar the celebrant bows low (genuflects, if the Blessed Sacrament be present), his assistants all genuflect. The acolytes place their candles at the sides of the altar and extinguish them. The MC will accompany the celebrant to the sedilia and there assist him (taking his biretta, etc.). The celebrant intones *Deus in adiutorium,* etc., and the choir continues. The antiphons are sung by the singers, wherever they may be placed. If there are no cantors to intone them, it will be convenient if one or two leaders in the choir begin them (as far as the asterisk). If there are cantors they will sit, one at each side, in the sanctuary facing the altar, go to the celebrant for the pre-intonations, and to the centre for the intonation of the psalms, etc; they genuflect together in the middle each time, going and coming. If there are no cantors the choir will begin the psalms (one or two leaders may intone each one, up to the asterisk). A good arrangement is that the special singers chant alternately with the whole congregation.

The celebrant uncovers and bows at the verse *Gloria Patri* each time, also (if it is the custom) at the verse *Sit nomen Domini benedictum* in the psalm *Laudate servi,* at the Holy Name, the name of Mary and of the saint of the Office or commemoration.

Chapter. Towards the end of the fifth psalm the first acolyte lights the acolytes' candles; during the last antiphon the acolytes come to the

---

[42] For a more detailed treatment of the ceremony, see §§ 3 and 5 above.

middle, take their candles, genuflect together before the altar, come to the celebrant, bow to him, then stand one on either side, facing one another. The celebrant uncovers, gives his biretta to the MC, who lays it on one side, then rises and standing at his place chants the chapter. The acolytes then bow to him, go to the altar, genuflect and set down their candles on the lowest altar step, one on each side, not extinguishing them. They stand before the candles.

At the first stanza of the hymns *Veni, Creator* and *Ave maris stella* the celebrant, MC and servers in the sanctuary kneel. In this case the acolytes do not kneel, but stay standing on each side of the celebrant till the stanza is ended. All kneel also during the stanza *Tantum ergo* in the hymn *Pange lingua,* if the Blessed Sacrament is exposed, or if It is reserved in the tabernacle;[43] also during the stanza *O Crux ave spes unica* in the *Vexilla regis.* In these two cases, since the acolytes are before the altar, they kneel there. The cantors, or the celebrant, sing the versicle after the hymn.

Magnificat. The altar must be incensed when the celebrant wears the cope, even if there be no assistants in copes.[44] The thurifer goes out towards the end of the hymn and prepares the thurible. He comes back with it, genuflects and stands waiting in the sanctuary at the epistle side. As the antiphons are doubled the celebrant sits while the antiphon of the *Magnificat* is sung first. Then he rises and makes the sign of the cross (all in the sanctuary doing the same) as the initial words of the canticle are sung. He goes to the altar, genuflects or bows (according to the usual rule), goes up and kisses the altar. The thurifer and MC join him here. He puts on and blesses incense as usual.

Incensation. While the celebrant incenses the altar the MC may hold the end of the cope on his right and the thurifer on his left. He returns the thurible to the MC, bows to the cross at the centre, descends to the foot of the altar, reverences there to the Blessed Sacrament or to the cross and goes to the sedilia. The MC incenses him with three double swings, bowing before and after. The thurifer incenses the clergy (if any are present), the singers (if present in surplice in the sanctuary),[45] the MC (who has gone to his place by the celebrant's side), the acolytes and people. The clergy, the MC and acolytes receive each one double swing; in incensing the people the thurifer bows, incenses with one simple swing straight down the church, then with one swing to his left, one to his right, then again bows, turns round, genuflects to the altar and goes out. He comes back without the thurible and takes his place in the sanctuary.

[43] S.R.C. 1280 § 2 allows standing should the Blessed Sacrament be present but not exposed.
[44] S.R.C. 3844 § 2.
[45] As described in Chapter XI. The singers are incensed in a body (like the people) with three simple swings for each side.

Prayer. When the *Magnificat* is finished, the celebrant sits and puts on his biretta. The acolytes again come to him and stand on each side as before; after the repetition of the antiphon he uncovers, rises and sings *Dominus vobiscum* and the collect. If there are commemorations, the cantors may sing the versicle for each, or the celebrant may do so himself. The cantors (or the celebrant) may sing the verse *Benedicamus Domino;* the acolytes go back to the altar and set down their candles. The celebrant, still standing, says "in a lower tone" *Fidelium...* He then takes his biretta, goes to the altar, bows or genuflects, and all go out as they came in, unless Benediction or some other service follows immediately.

Chapter XXI

Pontifical Vespers

§ 1. Vespers in the Presence of the Bishop at the Throne

THERE is a difference between Vespers celebrated by a bishop and Vespers celebrated by a priest when a bishop is present.

The first case is when a bishop assists at Vespers celebrated by a priest, and uses the throne.[1] It is supposed in this case, first that the Bishop is the Ordinary or other greater prelate since these alone have, normally, the right to use a throne;[2] secondly, that the Bishop will the next morning, in the same way, assist at solemn Mass.

Preparations. The church and altar are prepared as usual for Vespers, except that no lectern is placed before the seat of the celebrant. Further the throne is covered with a canopy and cloths of the colour of the Office. A faldstool or kneeler is prepared in the middle of the sanctuary, and another in the chapel of the Blessed Sacrament.[3] These are adorned as always in such cases (cf. Chapter XV § 1). Near the throne are the three stools for the assistant deacons and priest. Four or six candles stand lighted at the entrance of the sanctuary. The liturgical books suppose that the Chapter is present, as when the Ordinary assists at solemn Mass.

The celebrant (supposed to be a canon) vests in the sacristy, wearing on this occasion an amice (over his rochet) under his cope;[4] his assistants wear only surplice and cope. The servers are those for solemn Vespers. All go in procession to the sanctuary, and, having saluted the altar, go to their places to await the Bishop. The celebrant goes to the sedilia. His assistants in copes stand on either side of him, not facing him, lest they turn their back to the throne, but looking in the same direction as he does.

Arrival of Bishop. Meanwhile the canons go to the door of the church to receive the Bishop. The Bishop wears cappa magna and biretta.[5] The senior canon offers him holy water, and he signs himself and sprinkles

---

[1] C.E., II, ii, 4-11.

[2] But the Ordinary may allow the use of his throne to certain other bishops (cf. Chapter XVI § 1).

[3] The Blessed Sacrament should not be reserved at the high altar during pontifical functions.

[4] C.E., II, ii, 4.

[5] If the Bishop assists in mozzetta he may not (apart from special indult) use the throne. He occupies the first place in choir and the only difference that his presence makes is that he is incensed (by the first assistant of the celebrant) with three double swings after the celebrant has been incensed with two.

the canons. He goes to the chapel of the Blessed Sacrament and there prays for a short time. He comes to the sanctuary and kneels again at the faldstool or kneeler. Two canons in choir dress serve as his assistant deacons. They kneel one on either side of him, rather behind the faldstool.

As the Bishop enters the sanctuary the celebrant and his assistants stand. He blesses them; according to the general rule the assistants genuflect, the celebrant bows low. While the Bishop kneels at the faldstool those in choir and sanctuary (except the celebrant and his assistants) kneel too.

Beginning of Vespers. The Bishop rises, bows to the altar, blesses the celebrant and his assistants and goes to the throne. Here he sits for a moment and puts on his biretta. All in choir sit at the same time, the assistant deacons on either side of the throne on the stools prepared for them. Then the Bishop rises and all rise with him. He hands his biretta to the first assistant deacon, who receives it with the *solita oscula*. Vespers then proceed as usual. The celebrant bows to the Bishop and intones *Deus in adiutorium meum intende*. All the pre-intonation of antiphons and so on is as usual for solemn Vespers. The Bishop takes no part in this. The first and second assistants in copes sit one on either side of the celebrant, the others (if there are others) at the benches or stools in the middle of the sanctuary. In going to and fro in the sanctuary everyone genuflects to the altar, then to the Bishop, except the celebrant and canons, who bow to him. As soon as the first psalm is intoned the canon who is to be AP (i.e., the highest of the presbyteral canons) comes from the choir to his place by the Bishop.

Chapter. The chapter is not read by the celebrant, but by a member of the choir invited for that purpose by the MC.[6] He comes out, makes the usual reverence to altar and Bishop and sings the chapter at the place where the subdeacon at Mass sings the Epistle. Meanwhile the Bishop and all others uncover and stand. The hymn and antiphon for the *Magnificat* are intoned by the first assistant in cope to the celebrant as usual. During the antiphon before the *Magnificat* the thurifer brings the thurible to the throne, genuflecting as usual first to the altar, then to the Bishop, then kneeling.

Incensation. The Bishop puts on and blesses the incense, the AP presents the boat *(Benedicite, Pater reverendissime)*. The celebrant with all the assistants in copes goes to the altar, making the usual reverence to the Bishop on the way. The thurifer brings him the incense here; he incenses the altar as usual, having first kissed it. He is then incensed with two double swings by the first assistant in cope, while he stands, not at the sedilia but at the epistle corner of the altar. The thurifer takes the thurible to the AP, who incenses the Bishop with three double swings. The AP

---

[6] "Ab aliquo cantore" (C.E., II, ii, 7).

then returns to his place in choir. All (including the incensation of the assistants at the throne and the choir) proceeds as usual[7] to the versicle *Benedicamus Domino*. The verse *Fidelium animæ* is not sung. The chaplains with book and hand-candle come to the throne, the Bishop wearing his biretta gives his blessing in the episcopal form, singing first the verses *Sit nomen Domini*, etc. If he is the Archbishop, his cross is held before him (the cross-bearer kneeling) and he is uncovered.[8] The faldstool is brought again to the middle. The Bishop goes to it and prays there for a little time, all in choir kneeling too, except the celebrant and his assistants, who stand and bow. The Bishop, accompanied by canons, goes to the chapel of the Blessed Sacrament and then leaves the church. As soon as he has left the sanctuary, the celebrant and the rest go to the sacristy.

§ 2. Vespers in the Presence of a Bishop who is not the Ordinary or a Greater Prelate

Except in the case of the Ordinary or a greater prelate (occupying the throne), there is no special ceremony when a bishop assists at Vespers. A bishop other than the Ordinary, dressed in rochet and mantelletta,[9] has the first place in choir. He is treated as the person of greatest dignity, incensed first, after the celebrant, with three double swings (in the absence of a greater prelate), and so on.

§ 3. Vespers Celebrated by the Bishop or a Greater Prelate When He is to Sing Mass the Following Day

This is the case of greatest solemnity.[10] It is supposed that the whole celebration of a feast is one thing, beginning at the first Vespers the evening before. If then the Bishop of the diocese, or other greater prelate, intends to celebrate all the feast himself, there are special ceremonies at the first Vespers. There is another rite, slightly modified, if the Bishop celebrates Vespers on other occasions, not as the first part of a solemnity to be continued by his solemn Mass the next morning.[11] This will be described below (§ 4). The Ceremonial says: "If the Bishop will solemnly celebrate Mass the following day, Vespers are carried out with more solemnity than if he were not to do so."[12] There follows a list of feasts on which this connected celebration of Vespers and Mass should especially

---

[7] As there is no lectern a cleric holds the book for the celebrant when he sings the prayer "stans versus Altare a latere Epistolæ" (C.E., II, ii, 10).

[8] The Bishop will give the blessing at the throne "if from there he can be seen by the people," otherwise at the altar (C.E., II, ii, 11).

[9] Or, if a mantelletta cannot be had, his mozzetta.

[10] C.E., II, i.

[11] Namely in the same church and at the same altar.

[12] C.E., II, i, 2.

be carried out.[13] But the Bishop may use the same solemnity at the second Vespers, if he has sung the solemn Mass in the morning, at least on certain greatest days of all.[14]

Preparations. The things to prepare beforehand are much the same as those for pontifical solemn Mass at the throne, except that the secretarium is not needed, and the vestments are different. It is supposed that the Blessed Sacrament is not reserved at the time on the high altar .

In the chapel of the Blessed Sacrament the frontal and conopæum are of the colour of the Office; before its altar a kneeler or faldstool is prepared, arranged as for pontifical solemn Mass, six candles on the altar are lit, at least for the moments when the Bishop comes here, before and after the ceremony.

The high altar has a frontal of the colour of the Office, and six (not seven) candles are lit on it. The Bishop's vestments are laid out on the altar. They lie on a veil or altar cover spread over the linen altar cloths. The vestments in order are: a cope and stole of the colour of the Office, the pectoral cross,[15] girdle, alb, amice and, near by, the Bishop's morse *(formale)* on a salver. All are covered with a veil of the colour of the Office. The precious mitre stands on the gospel side, the golden mitre on the epistle side. The crosier is near the altar. The veils for the mitre-bearer and crosier-bearer are on the altar near the precious mitre. On the main credence are placed the acolytes' candles lit, and the book for the subdeacon who pre-intones the antiphons. On a credence near the throne the hand-candle, a vesper book *(vesperale, antiphonarium)* for the Bishop's use, which is covered with silk of the liturgical colour; the pontifical canon, if it will be needed for the blessing.[16]

In middle of the sanctuary a faldstool stands with cushions, as described in Chapter XVI § 1. The throne is covered with hangings of the liturgical colour; if the Bishop will kneel at the throne[17] there must be a cushion there for him to kneel on. On either side of the throne is a stool, of plain wood, for the assistant deacons, on the Bishop's right a third stool for the assistant priest. On the opposite side of the sanctuary is a stool for the subdeacon who will pre-intone and will sing the chapter. On the canon's stalls their vestments are prepared; namely, copes for the dignitaries, chasubles for the canon priests, dalmatics for the deacons, tunicles for the subdeacons. Near at hand are two dalmatics for the deacons at the throne, and a cope for the AP. On each vestment an amice is laid.

---

[13] Christmas, Epiphany, Ascension, Pentecost, SS Peter and Paul, Assumption, All Saints, Dedication and Titular of the church, Patron of the city (ibid.).
[14] Easter, Christmas, Titular of the church and Patron of the city (C.E., II, i, 3).
[15] But generally the Bishop will use over the alb the same pectoral cross that he wears on arriving. In this case it is taken off before he vests and put on again after the alb and girdle.
[16] If the celebrant is the Archbishop a stand for his cross is prepared near the throne.
[17] In the case of stanzas in certain hymns noted below.

At the entrance of the choir are large candles burning, either four, six or at most eight, according to the feast.

In the sacristy are prepared four copes, less adorned than the others, for the chaplains who will bear the mitre, crosier, book and hand-candle; the thurible and incense boat. If the prelate is the Archbishop, the amice, alb, girdle and tunicle for the subdeacon who will bear his cross are laid out in the sacristy, or behind the choir.

Assistants and Servers. The persons who assist at this ceremony are (besides the Bishop himself) the Chapter, arranged in orders as dignitaries, priests, deacons and subdeacons; two assistant deacons at the throne, who on this occasion wear dalmatics; an assistant priest, who should be the canon first in rank, and who wears a cope. A canon subdeacon who will pre-intone. He will be the subdeacon of the Mass on the following day or another canon, according to the custom of the church. There are two Masters of Ceremonies, two acolytes, a thurifer, two cantors (who wear copes or cottas according to custom) and other servers to bring the vestments to the throne. There are also the four chaplains or servers who carry the mitre, crosier, book and candle; they may wear copes. There are no other assistants in copes (*pluvialistæ*). A train-bearer in *ferraiolo*.

General Rules for Assistants. Before going through the ceremony in detail it may be useful to note in general the office of each assistant and server.

The function of the AP is to hold the book whenever the Bishop sings from it, to offer the incense boat and spoon, incense the Bishop and present the ring. He intones the third antiphon.

The assistant deacons vest and unvest the Bishop; the first puts on the Bishop's mitre, the second takes it off. They walk on either side of the Bishop, holding the ends of his cope (with the orphreys turned in), when he incenses the altar, and every time he goes from one place to another; they hold back the cope when he blesses, puts on incense, or performs any other action at which it would otherwise be inconvenient.

When they are not occupied these three have their places on the stools by the throne.

The subdeacon pre-intones the antiphons and sings the chapter. He should be one of the canons of that order, vested in tunicle. However, the Ceremonial does not require absolutely that this function be performed by the subdeacon of the Mass on the following day. It says, "the subdeacon, or other person, according to the custom of the church,"[18] from which it appears that he may be another canon or dignitary.

The first MC stands near the throne at the Bishop's left, and sees that all is done rightly; the second looks after the inferior ministers,

[18] C.E., II, i, 7.

accompanies the subdeacon at the pre-intoning, and stands by his stool, at his right, when he sits there opposite the Bishop.

General Rules for Servers. The four servers of the mitre, crosier, book and hand-candle have much the same functions as at pontifical solemn Mass. The book-bearer will bring the antiphonary to the throne when it is wanted, and hand it to the AP. Afterwards he takes it away and holds it till it is wanted again, or he puts it on the credence if there is a long interval. The bearer of the candle attends and holds it by the Bishop, on the book-bearer's right, when he sings or reads. The bearers of mitre and crosier come to the throne and hand these when they are wanted. These four sit on the bottom step of the throne, or aside, without their burdens, while the psalms are sung.

The acolytes and thurifer have the same office as always at Vespers, with the changes that follow from the special ceremonies of a pontifical Office. The acolytes stand on each side of the throne before the Bishop at the collect and commemorations only. They do not put their candles on the altar step nor extinguish them. The candles are left lighted on the credence before the function and when they are not in use. While the psalms are sung they, and all other servers, sit on the altar steps at the epistle side, if no special seats are provided for them.

The Bishop wears the golden mitre only while he sits during the five psalms. At all other times the precious mitre is used.

Once for all—whenever anyone goes from one part of the choir or sanctuary to another, normally[19] he genuflects first to the altar, then to the Bishop. Everyone who comes up to the throne for any purpose genuflects to the Bishop, at the foot of its steps, before going up. The exception is that canons bow, instead of genuflecting, to the Bishop. The assistant deacons and priest are canons, according to the Ceremonial.

Arrival of Bishop. The Bishop (in rochet and cappa[20] with biretta) is received at the door of the church by the canons in their robes. He uncovers, takes holy water himself and sprinkles those around, goes (uncovered) to the chapel of the Blessed Sacrament and says a prayer (first removing his skull-cap), then to the faldstool in the middle of the choir, all as in the secretarium before his Mass. While the Bishop is received by the canons the four servers of book, hand-candle, mitre and crosier put on their surplices and copes in the sacristy. So does the subdeacon who will carry the Archbishop's cross, if there is one. These then come and wait at the credence.

While the Bishop prays at the faldstool in the sanctuary, the canons go to their stalls and put on the vestments, each according to his order. The AP and the assistant deacons also vest at the stalls, then go to wait by the throne. The AP at first waits at the stall nearest to the throne on that side.

---

[19] Cf. C.E., I, xviii, 13.

[20] Or mozzetta if a cappa not be available.

The MC frees the Bishop's cappa from the faldstool;[21] the Bishop bows to the altar, goes to the throne and sits there, blessing the choir as he passes. The faldstool is then put aside until it is wanted again at the end.

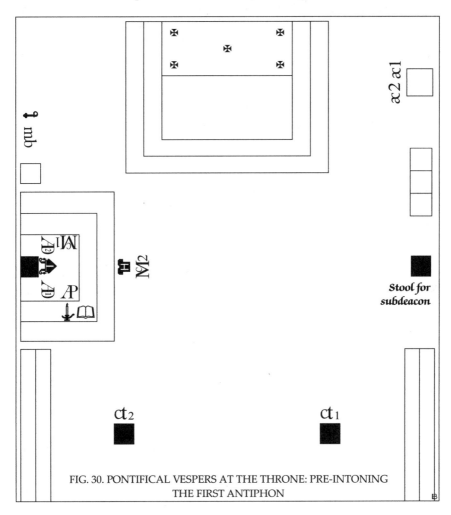

FIG. 30. PONTIFICAL VESPERS AT THE THRONE: PRE-INTONING THE FIRST ANTIPHON

Vesting of Bishop. The precious mitre and crosier are taken by their bearers, with the veils. They come and stand by the throne aside. The Bishop takes off his biretta, handing it to the first assistant deacon, and stands. The deacons take off his pectoral cross (if he is wearing it) and cappa. They hand the cappa to the servant or a server, who lays it aside.

The servers (directed by the second MC) bring each vestment to the deacons. They aid the Bishop to put on the amice, alb, girdle, pectoral cross,[22] stole, cope, morse. The Bishop sits and the first deacon puts on

[21] While the Bishop kneels before the faldstool his cappa is spread over it.
[22] The first deacon first presents the cross to be kissed by the Bishop.

the precious mitre. The AP puts on the ring, if the Bishop is not already wearing it.[23] The Bishop, seated, rests a little.[24] The AP now goes to his stool by the throne.

The second assistant deacon takes off the mitre, hands it to the bearer, who carries it to the altar, here changes it for the golden mitre, and comes back to the throne. During all this time, since the Bishop entered the church, the organ is played.

Beginning of Vespers. The Bishop rises, and the organ is silent. The Bishop intones *Deus in adiutorium meum intende*, he and all making the sign of the cross. While the choir sings *Gloria Patri*, etc., all bow towards the cross on the altar. Meanwhile the subdeacon who is to pre-intone comes from his stool, accompanied by the second MC, who hands him an antiphonary or other book containing the music (if necessary), and goes to the middle of the sanctuary. He comes to the Bishop with the usual reverences and pre-intones to him the first antiphon, singing its text, as far as the asterisk, in a low voice. The AP (if necessary)[25] holds the book and the Bishop intones this antiphon. The AP returns to his stool. The subdeacon and second MC now go to their place opposite the Bishop. The cantors come to the middle and intone the first psalm, singing its first verse. They then bow to that side of the choir which will sing the second verse. The Bishop sits when the first psalm has been intoned, the first deacon puts on him the golden mitre. The Bishop remains seated during the five psalms. All sit in their places after the Bishop. Vespers proceed as usual. The subdeacon pre-intones the antiphons. The first is pre-intoned to the Bishop, as already said, the second to the first assistant deacon, the third to the assistant priest, fourth to the first canon in choir, fifth to the second assistant deacon. When one of the assistants intones an antiphon his co-assistants and they alone rise with him; when the canon in choir does so the members of the choir rise.[26] At the verse *Gloria Patri* the Bishop bows, wearing the mitre; all others uncover and bow. The same rule applies to the verse *Sit nomen Domini benedictum* in the psalm *Laudate servi*. During the last antiphon, after the fifth psalm, the bearers of book, candle, mitre and crosier rise and genuflect to the Bishop. Those of the book and candle go to fetch these from the credence; the mitre-bearer and the crosier-bearer stand east of the throne. The servers who sat on the altar steps also rise and go to the credence. The Bishop rises, and all with him. He stands wearing the mitre, the others uncover before standing. The subdeacon, at the place (at a distance from the altar steps) where the

[23] The Bishop does not wash his hands at Vespers.
[24] C.E., II, i, 5.
[25] Cf. C.E., I, xx, 4, and II, i, 7. As the antiphon is pre-intoned, the Bishop will not, ordinarily, need the book to intone it.
[26] All the choir, according to C.E., II, i, 10. But S.R.C. 3781 § 2 allows only the side where it is intoned to stand.

Epistle is read, chants the chapter; the second MC hands him the book, conducts him, and stands at his side.

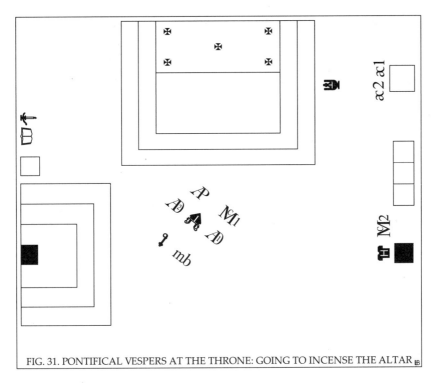

FIG. 31. PONTIFICAL VESPERS AT THE THRONE: GOING TO INCENSE THE ALTAR

Hymn. The subdeacon then comes to the Bishop and pre-intones the hymn. The Bishop sits and the second assistant deacon takes off the mitre. The Bishop rises; the AP holds the book (if necessary), the Bishop intones the first line of the hymn. At the first stanza of the hymns *Veni, Creator* and *Ave maris stella* all kneel when he intones, and the Bishop himself kneels after he has sung the first line. For this a cushion is placed before the throne, and the first deacon takes off the Bishop's skull-cap. The mitre-bearer takes the golden mitre to the altar and brings back the precious mitre. If necessary, the acolytes go to uncover the table of the altar.[27] During the doxology stanza of the hymn all bow towards the altar.

Magnificat. The cantors come out and sing the versicle. The subdeacon pre-intones the antiphon of the *Magnificat* to the Bishop. The Bishop intones it, then sits and is covered with the precious mitre. All in choir sit. Meanwhile the thurifer has come with the thurible and the crosier-bearer

---

[27] This cover is supposed by C.E., II, i, 13, which directs that the acolytes before the incensation fold it back on the table of the altar ("illamque conduplicant usque ad medium") and afterwards spread it again. However it may be more dignified to uncover the altar after the vesting of the Bishop and to cover it again after Vespers.

with the crosier; they stand near. Sitting, the Bishop puts on and blesses incense, the AP assisting, the thurifer kneeling. The cantors intone the *Magnificat*. At once the Bishop rises, wearing his mitre, and makes the sign of the cross (all do so too); he takes the crosier from its bearer and goes to the altar. He is preceded by the AP, the assistant deacons go on either side holding the ends of his cope; lastly, the bearers of mitre and crosier. The first MC goes by the AP and signs to the choir (except the dignitaries and canons) to kneel. As the Bishop passes he blesses the clergy.

Incensation. Before the altar the Bishop gives his crosier to its bearer, and the second assistant deacon takes off the mitre. The Bishop and assistants bow low to the altar, and go up to it; the Bishop kisses the altar. He takes the thurible from the AP and incenses the altar in the usual way, reciting meantime with his assistants the *Magnificat*, if this is the custom.[28] The assistant deacons hold the cope on either side, the AP goes to stand at the epistle end, on the ground. Then the Bishop gives the thurible back to the AP (who goes up to receive it and then hands it to the thurifer), again takes the mitre[29] and crosier at the epistle corner, reverences to the cross at the middle, and goes back to the throne by the shorter way (preceded by the thurifer and AP), blessing the clergy as before. At the throne he gives away the crosier and is incensed by the AP (with three double swings). The assistant deacons hold the cope. The Bishop blesses the AP and sits. The second deacon takes off the Bishop's mitre; he rises, takes again the crosier and stands, holding it with both hands, as at the Gospel of Mass, while the rest of the *Magnificat* is sung. The subdeacon has come to the side of the AP. He now takes the thurible and incenses the assistant priest and deacons at their place by the throne, bowing and making two double swings to each. He then incenses the canons, each in order and with two double swings, bowing to each separately before and after. He hands the thurible to the thurifer, who incenses him (with two double swings), the rest of the choir and the people as usual. The singers should not begin the *Gloria Patri* till this is ended. The organ may be played between the verses of the *Magnificat*, or at the end of the verse *Sicut locutus est*, etc. While the antiphon is sung after the canticle the Bishop hands the crosier to its bearer, and sits wearing the mitre. All sit with him.

Collect. The acolytes now bring their candles to the throne;[30] the AP takes the antiphonary from its bearer. The second deacon takes off the mitre. The Bishop rises, turns towards the people, sings *Dominus vobiscum*, and—having turned to the altar—the collect, while the AP holds the book and the candle—bearer the candle on his right. If there are

---

[28] Other altars are not incensed when the Bishop sings Vespers (S.R.C. 3110 § 6).

[29] It is put on by the first assistant deacon.

[30] C.E., II, i, 17 directs the (second) MC to conduct the acolytes to and from the throne.

commemorations, the AP hands the book to its bearer till the time comes for the Bishop to sing each collect. The cantors in the middle sing the versicles. Then they sing *Benedicamus Domino*. Meanwhile the acolytes go back to the credence during the second *Dominus vobiscum* after the prayer or prayers.

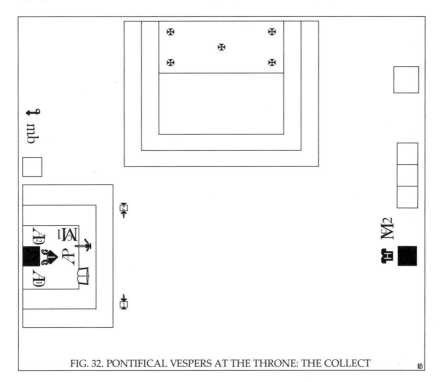

FIG. 32. PONTIFICAL VESPERS AT THE THRONE: THE COLLECT

Pontifical Blessing. The pontifical blessing follows. The Bishop sits to be covered with the precious mitre. The book-bearer brings the pontifical canon (or the antiphonary, if it contains the form) to the AP; the crosier-bearer is at hand. The AP holds the book before the Bishop; he rises and the assistant deacons hold the ends of his cope. He sings the verses *Sit nomen Domini*, etc., then lifts his hands and eyes, joins the hands, takes the crosier in his left hand (after the words *Benedicat vos omnipotens Deus*) and makes the sign of the cross thrice over the people, singing the form *Benedicat vos*.[31] All kneel, except the canons in their places, the assistant deacons and priest. If the celebrant is the Archbishop, the subdeacon of the cross brings this and holds it, kneeling before him, so that the figure of our Lord is turned towards the Archbishop. He does not wear the mitre when blessing and bows to his cross before he blesses.

---

[31] If the Bishop cannot well be seen at the throne, he may go to the altar to give the blessing (C.E., II, i, 18). He then gives it as he would at Mass, kissing the altar first. The indulgence is not given at Vespers.

Unvesting. The verse *Fidelium animæ* is not said. After the blessing the Bishop unvests at the throne, assisted by the deacons. Servers take each vestment and put it back on the altar, as at the beginning directed by the second MC. The AP goes back to his place in choir. The canons unvest and put on their robes again. Meanwhile the organ is played. The four bearers of mitre, crosier, book and candle go to the sacristy and there unvest. The faldstool is brought back to the middle of the sanctuary. The cappa is put on the Bishop. He goes to the faldstool and prays there. Meanwhile the assistant deacons take off their dalmatics at the stalls. The Bishop goes to the chapel of the Blessed Sacrament, prays there, then leaves the church accompanied by the canons (who follow him).

§ 4. When the Bishop Does not Sing Mass the Next Day

In this case the following changes are made in the ceremony:[32]

The assistant priest and deacons wear their usual choir dress. Only four or six canons in choir will wear copes, the others have choir dress. The canons who are in vestments will occupy the first stalls near the throne and remain there all through the ceremony. The clerics who act as mitre-bearer, etc., do not wear copes.

The antiphons are not pre-intoned by a subdeacon, but by a canon or other person (in choir dress), according to the custom of the church. The first is pre-intoned to the Bishop and intoned by him, the others to the canons who are vested, in order of dignity (beginning with the highest).

The chapter is read by one of the cantors, at his place in choir, or at the usual place, according to custom. The AP does not hold the book, but its bearer does so. The AP incenses the Bishop; a cleric who is not a canon incenses all others. All the rest is as above (§ 3).

§ 5. Pontifical Vespers at the Faldstool

As at Mass, a bishop who is not the Ordinary of the diocese, that is, an auxiliary or extern bishop, does not use the throne.[33] If he celebrates Vespers, he does so at a faldstool on the epistle side of the sanctuary, and the whole ceremony is considerably modified.[34]

Preparations. The preparations to be made in this case are the following: The altar is arranged as for Vespers at the throne. It has a frontal of the colour of the Office; the Blessed Sacrament should not be reserved at the high altar .

---

[32] C.E., II, ii. These Vespers are sometimes called semi-pontifical.
[33] But see Chapter XVI § 1.
[34] There is much diversity of opinion among authors on many points of detail regarding Vespers at the faldstool; hence there is room for approved local custom in this ceremony.

On the altar the bishop's vestments are laid out in the middle, namely, the cope (no morse), stole, pectoral cross,[35] girdle, alb, amice. These are covered with a veil of the liturgical colour. The precious mitre stands on the gospel side, the golden mitre on the epistle side. The crosier is not used. The six candles are lit.

On the credence the acolytes' candles stand (unless the bishop is to vest in the sacristy), lighted, also the hand-candle, an antiphonary, which may be covered with silk of the liturgical colour, and the pontifical canon for the blessing at the end.

In the sanctuary, at the foot of the altar, there is a cushion, of the colour of the Office, on which the bishop will kneel before Vespers begin. On the epistle side of the sanctuary the faldstool is placed. It should be covered with the colour of the Office.[36] At the end of the choir nearer the altar[37] are two benches covered with green for the assistants in copes, one on either side, so that they sit facing the altar; or they may have two rows of stools. There must be benches or seats for the other servers, either on each side after the manner of choir stalls, or in some other convenient place.

In the sacristy the copes for the assistants are laid out; a faldstool or a chair is prepared in the middle, on which the bishop will sit on arriving, if he is to vest in the sacristy.

Assistants. The following persons assist at the ceremony, besides the bishop himself. There are always two assistants in copes, who attend the bishop, one on either side, as do the deacons when Vespers are sung at the throne. Besides these there may be two or four others, in copes, according to the feast.[38] All the copes are of the colour of the Office. Those who wear copes also have the biretta. There are two cantors in surplice. There is no assistant priest.

There are, further, two Masters of Ceremonies, two acolytes, a thurifer, three servers who bear the book, hand-candle and mitre and, if possible, other servers, who assist at the vesting of the bishop.

It may be that the bishop vests in the sacristy.[39] In this case, having vested and wearing the precious mitre the bishop goes into the church between the first two assistants, at the end of the procession. The golden mitre alone stands on the altar. The acolytes' candles are prepared in the sacristy; they go at the head of the procession, following the thurifer. Before the altar the bishop's mitre is removed (by the first assistant) and he kneels there for a moment's prayer, then goes to the faldstool.

---

[35] Unless the same cross will be used that the bishop wears on arriving.
[36] For the arrangement of the faldstool, see above, Chapter I and Chapter XVII § 1.
[37] These benches are sometimes some distance back. Separate stools are more convenient (see fig. 27). Domestic chairs are not allowed.
[38] Cf. Chapter XX § 5.
[39] Ordinarily the bishop will vest in the sanctuary; in churches where there is a Chapter, or if he is to officiate in presence of a greater prelate, he vests in the sacristy.

Procession to Sanctuary. If he vest at the faldstool, the following order is observed:

The assistants put on their surplices and copes in the sacristy: all the others vest in surplice. The bishop comes to the sacristy, bows to the cross there and sits on a chair till the procession is ready. He wears rochet and mantelletta. When the assistants are vested they come before the bishop, form in a straight line and bow to him. The first and second stand at his side, right and left. The procession goes to the sanctuary, first the thurifer, with hands joined, then the acolytes, also with joined hands, the choir, the first MC, assistants in copes, if there are more than two, the bishop between the first and second assistants.[40] Then follow the three bearers of book, hand-candle and mitre.[41] The second MC walks at the side of the first assistant or may lead the procession. Before leaving the sacristy all bow to the cross there. At the door all take lustral water, uncovering at the time; the first assistant offers it to the bishop. In the sanctuary all take off the biretta again, the assistants form one line, with the bishop in the middle. Before the altar the bishop bows,[42] all the rest genuflect. The bishop kneels on the cushion prepared and says a short prayer; the assistants kneel on each side. All then rise, bow or genuflect, as before, bow to the choir (first to the gospel side), and go to the faldstool. The bishop sits covered, facing the people; the assistants stand before him and bow. The first two go to his sides, facing the people, the others to the bench near the entrance of the sanctuary. The second MC takes the assistants' birettas. The bishop uncovers and hands his to the first assistant, who receives it with the *solita oscula* and gives it to the first MC. The birettas are put aside, on the credence or other convenient place.

Vesting of Bishop. The bishop takes off the pectoral cross, helped by the first assistant, and the mantelletta. Now the first assistant vests the bishop in amice, alb, girdle, pectoral cross, stole and cope, the other assistant helping. Each vestment is brought from the altar, where the second MC hands them to servers. The other assistants (if there are more than two) come to the bishop, genuflecting first to the altar; they stand in line before the faldstool, and bow, then form in two lines before him as at a procession.

---

[40] Menghini thinks it unsuitable that the bishop in mantelletta should come in procession with assistants in copes. He notes that at Rome the assistants and acolytes come first to the sanctuary and await the bishop there (Martinucci, II, ii, p. 548, n. 1). De Herdt, Favrin, Saraiva, Le Vavasseur and others are of the same opinion. If this is done the second MC heads the procession to the sanctuary. The first and second assistants in cope follow him, then the other vested assistants, the acolytes, and lastly the other servers. On arrival the first and second assistants take their places at each side of the faldstool. All the others go to their seats in the sanctuary.

[41] The mitre-bearer wears the veil *(vimpa)* to hold the mitre.

[42] If the Blessed Sacrament is there reserved he genuflects.

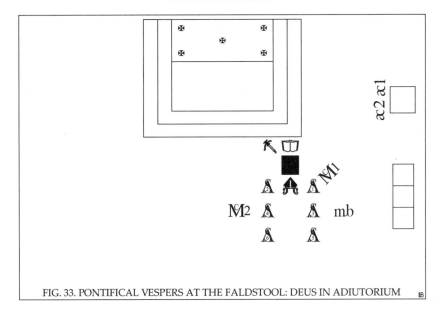

FIG. 33. PONTIFICAL VESPERS AT THE FALDSTOOL: DEUS IN ADIUTORIUM

Beginning of Vespers. The bearers of book and candle must now be at hand. The mitre-bearer gets the gold mitre from the altar and waits near the faldstool. The bishop stands and faces the altar; all in choir uncover and stand too. The first two assistants change places and stand at the bishop's sides (the first on his right), the others behind him (he has turned his back to them). The bishop makes the sign of the cross as he sings *Deus in adiutorium meum intende;* the assistants holding the ends of the cope. The candle and book (if necessary[43]) are held before him by their bearers, on the other side of the faldstool. When the choir has ended the response to this, the first assistant comes to the bishop, bows and pre-intones the antiphon of the first psalm.[44] The bishop then intones it; the assistant bows again, and returns to the bishop's right. The cantors stand in the middle and intone the first psalm. They then take their place in the choir stalls at the end near the people, so that they can easily come forward each time to intone the psalms. The bearers of book and candle retire and put these on the credence.

As soon as the psalm is intoned the bishop turns by the right towards the people and sits on the faldstool; the first assistant puts on the golden mitre. All the assistants in copes (the first and second having come before the bishop in front of the others) bow to the bishop, genuflect at the middle to the cross, salute one another and go and sit at the stool or benches prepared for them (the first assistant occupying the inmost one on the epistle side; the second the inmost on the gospel side) facing the

---

[43] Cf. C.E., I, xx, 4; II, i, 7.

[44] The bishop is standing facing the altar across the faldstool. The first assistant comes before him, on the other side of the faldstool, a little to his left and faces him.

bishop.[45] They sit and cover themselves. All in choir sit. At the *Gloria Patri* all, except the bishop uncover and bow; he bows wearing the mitre. The last of the assistants in cope pre-intones the second and remaining antiphons to members of the choir beginning with the highest in rank. The cantors intone the first verse of each psalm. In going to the middle they genuflect each time before the altar and bow to the bishop.

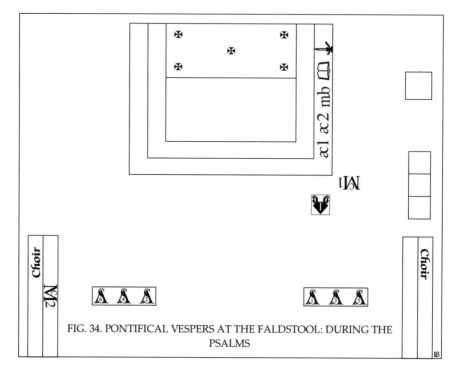

FIG. 34. PONTIFICAL VESPERS AT THE FALDSTOOL: DURING THE PSALMS

Chapter. At the end of the fifth psalm all the assistants in copes come to the bishop (first genuflecting to the altar), bow to him, and stand before him in time, except the first two at his sides. The bishop rises (mitred) and all in choir rise with him.[46] The first cantor reads the chapter, at his place. When *Deo gratias* has been answered the first assistant pre-intones the hymn to the bishop. Immediately afterwards the latter sits for a moment and the first assistant takes off the mitre. (The mitre-bearer takes this to the credence and exchanges it for the precious mitre. The golden mitre will not again be used.) The bishop stands, turns to the altar and intones the first line of the hymn. The book and candle

---

[45] Or the first and second assistants may sit at the sedilia on the epistle side, the first being nearer the bishop.

[46] Most authors direct the bishop to turn to the altar for the chapter, but De Herdt (*Praxis Pont.* III, 437)—with whom Ab Appeltern and Moretti agree—says that he does not turn to the altar "because he is not about to read or sing anything."

are held by their bearers before him. While the hymn is sung the bishop stands towards the altar, the first two assistants are at his sides, the others go to stand before their benches. If a stanza occurs at which all kneel a cushion is placed for the bishop to kneel on, before the faldstool; the first assistant removes the bishop's skull-cap and replaces it at the end of the stanza.

Magnificat. During the hymn the thurifer prepares the thurible, comes back with it and waits in the sanctuary. After the hymn the two last assistants in cope sing the versicle in the middle of the choir. When the response to the versicle has been sung the first assistant pre-intones the antiphon of the *Magnificat* to the bishop, which he intones, still standing towards the altar. He turns and sits while the antiphon is continued by the choir; the first assistant puts on him the precious mitre. The other assistants go to their place, except the cantors, who intone the first verse of the *Magnificat* in the middle. While the antiphon is sung all sit. Before the *Magnificat* is begun the thurifer comes to the bishop, bows and stands before him. Sitting, the bishop puts on and blesses the incense, while the first assistant holds the boat, asks the blessing *(Benedicite, Pater reverendissime)* and hands him the spoon with the *solita oscula*. Meanwhile the acolytes take their candles from the credence, and go to stand before the altar, bowing to the bishop as they pass. If the first altar to be incensed is not the high altar the acolytes stand near the entrance of the sanctuary. As soon as the cantors begin the *Magnificat* the bishop rises (mitred) and makes the sign of the cross. All in choir do so with him. The cantors, when they have intoned, genuflect and go to their place. The bishop comes to the altar between the first assistants, saluting the clergy on the way. The others join the first two on either side, making one long line with them and the bishop, then form, two and two, as in processions.

Incensation. If the Blessed Sacrament is reserved at the high altar this alone is incensed. The bishop's mitre and skull-cap are taken off, he genuflects with all the others, goes up, kisses the altar, takes the thurible from the first assistant and incenses the altar as usual. But if, as should be, the Blessed Sacrament is reserved at another altar, that altar is incensed first. In this case the bishop and the assistants in cope bow to the high altar, the others genuflect; all then go in procession to the altar of the Blessed Sacrament. If it is the custom, some of the principal members of the choir may accompany this procession. The thurifer goes first with the thurible and boat, then the acolytes, first MC, assistants in copes, except the first two, the bishop between the first assistants, the mitre-bearer follows, lastly the members of the choir who accompany the bishop. The bishop wears the mitre; those in vestments wear the biretta on leaving the chancel.

At the altar of the Blessed Sacrament six candles burn, at least for this time of incensing; the altar is uncovered. On arriving before the altar all take off the biretta. The acolytes stand right and left, the assistants part on either side to allow the bishop, with the first two, to come before the altar. The first of these takes off the mitre and skull-cap. The bishop genuflects, goes up to the altar between the assistants, kisses it, then incenses it as at Mass. The procession is formed again; all genuflect, the skull-cap and mitre are put on the bishop and the procession returns to the high altar. On the way the biretta is worn by those in vestments.

If other altars are to be incensed this is done, in the same way (except the reverence to the altar will be a bow and the skull-cap is not removed), before they come back to the high altar. The bishop always incenses without the mitre. When they come back to the high altar the acolytes go to put their candles on the credence. The bishop kisses and incenses the high altar. He gives the thurible to the first assistant, who hands it to the thurifer. At the epistle corner the mitre is put on the bishop. He bows to the altar, and goes directly to the faldstool. He stands here facing the people. All the assistants stand before him facing him; the first takes the thurible and incenses him with three double incensings. The thurifer holds back the right end of this assistant's cope meanwhile. The bishop then sits, the first two assistants come to his sides, the first takes off his mitre; he stands and faces the altar for the rest of the *Magnificat*.

The other assistants return to their bench, except the last assistant in cope who now incenses the canons in choir, next the assistants beside the bishop, then the others, with two double swings for each, bowing before and after. Then he finishes the incensation of the clergy in choir who are not canons. He gives the thurible to the thurifer, who incenses him, the servers at the credence and the people as usual. The choir must take care that they do not sing the *Gloria Patri* verse of the *Magnificat* till the incensing is finished. The organ may be played between the verses, or after the verse *Sicut locutus est ad patres nostros*. As soon as the verse *Sicut erat in principio* is finished the bishop turns and sits and is covered with the mitre. All in choir sit with him. But the first two assistants stand, one on either side of the faldstool. Towards the end of the antiphon after the *Magnificat* the other assistants rise, come to the middle, genuflect, then go to stand in line before the bishop.

Collect. The acolytes, at the same time, take their candles from the credence and come to stand at each side of the faldstool. The bearers of book and candle also come to the bishop. Then the first assistant takes off the mitre, the bishop rises and faces the altar.

The first assistants should now change places behind the bishop, so that the first is on his right. The others are in two lines behind him. The book-bearer holds the antiphonary before him; the candle-bearer holds the candle at the book-bearer's left. Both are on the other side of the faldstool, between the acolytes. The bishop, standing and facing the altar, with joined hands, sings *Dominus vobiscum* and the Collect. If there are commemorations the choir sings the antiphon of each; meanwhile the last two assistants in cope go to the middle, genuflect, and standing there sing each versicle. The bishop then sings the prayer. When the commemorations are finished he again sings *Dominus vobiscum;* the last two assistants in the middle sing *Benedicamus Domino.* The acolytes go back to the credence and put down their candles; the bearers of book and candle go with them. The second MC takes the pontifical canon and puts it in the middle of the altar, with the hand-candle by it, for the blessing which will now follow. The verse *Fidelium animæ* is not sung. The bishop sits and the first assistant puts on his mitre. The first two assistants again change places; the others go to their bench. The bishop goes to the altar, bowing to the choir on the way.

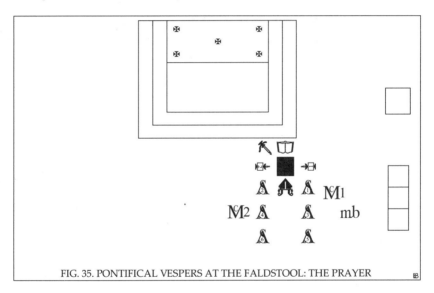

FIG. 35. PONTIFICAL VESPERS AT THE FALDSTOOL: THE PRAYER

Pontifical Blessing. The assistants at his sides hold the ends of his cope. In front of the altar, with mitre on, he and the assistants in copes bow;[47] the others genuflect. The bishop goes up to the altar, kisses it, and sings the verses *Sit nomen Domini,* etc. He turns to the people and blesses them with the form *Benedicat vos omnipotens Deus.* The first and second assistants stand at his sides holding the cope while he sings the verses, then kneel in front of him (unless they are canons) on the edge of the footpace, as he gives the blessing. The other assistants in cope kneel at the foot of the altar. All in choir kneel too, except canons, who bow low. Then the bishop comes from the altar between his assistants (having turned at the foot and, with his assistants, bowed to it), bows again to the choir in

---

[47] Supposing the Blessed Sacrament not to be reserved there.

passing and goes back to the faldstool. A server takes the book and hand-candle to the credence.

Unvesting. The bishop sits between the assistants at his sides. He now unvests, the first assistant taking off his mitre and the other vestments in order, while the second helps. The cushion is placed in the middle of the lowest altar step. An attendant brings the mantelletta; it is put on the bishop and his pectoral cross over it. He goes before the altar, bowing to the choir on his way, there bows to the altar, while the others genuflect and kneel; he kneels there on the cushion for a short time. The first two assistants kneel at his sides. All the servers kneel behind the bishop.

The bishop rises, all make the usual reverence to the altar and the choir, and the procession goes out in the order in which it came.[48]

If the bishop unvests in the sacristy, the procession is formed as soon as he has given his blessing. In this case the acolytes go first with lighted candles.

In the sacristy the bishop (all having, as usual, bowed to the cross) either sits for a moment while the assistants bow to him, or he unvests at the chair there prepared.

---

[48] If the bishop unvests at the faldstool, it is better that he return to the sacristy accompanied only by the MC, and that the assistants who are still in vestments should retire in a separate procession after the bishop has left in the order in which they came.

Chapter XXII

Other Evening Services

§ 1. Compline[1]

COMPLINE is the simplest and, therefore, in many ways, the best liturgical evening service for a small church having but one priest. While the prayers of Compline are most suitable for evening devotion, and the chants are both beautiful and easy to sing, it has hardly any ceremonies.

The rules for Compline are simply one particular case of the Divine Office sung in choir without solemnity. However great the feast, there are never solemnities at Compline, as at Vespers. It is one of the lesser hours, of the same rank as Prime, Terce, Sext and None.

Two candles may be lighted on the altar, when Compline is sung in a public church; on a great feast even four may be used. If Compline immediately follows Vespers, the candles lit for that office remain lighted for Compline.

The altar is not incensed nor otherwise used. It may, however, be uncovered, especially if Benediction follows at once.

Assistants. The persons who take part in the Office are the celebrant (called *hebdomadarius*),[2] a reader *(lector)*, two cantors and a choir. But it is possible to reduce the number if necessary. The reader may be one of the cantors; if there is no liturgical choir (in surplices, before the altar), Compline may be sung by singers in other parts of the church, or the verses of the psalms may be sung alternately by trained singers and the congregation. If there are no cantors before the altar, the responsory, versicle and so on may be sung by one or two singers away from the sanctuary .

Beginning of Compline. The only vestments worn are cassock and surplice, except that the celebrant and clergy present wear the biretta when seated. The celebrant is not to wear a cope.[3] He comes to the altar, in choir dress, behind the cantors, followed by the others. All genuflect before the altar if the Blessed Sacrament is there reserved, otherwise the celebrant bows low. All kneel for a moment's prayer. They rise, make the

---

[1] Cf. C.E., II. iv. The text with a translation and helpful notes may be found in the recent publication *Ad Completorium* (ed. Finnegan & Paver, 2000).

[2] This is the name for the officiating priest at the Divine Office. It is, however, convenient to use the general name celebrant for all functions.

[3] C.E., II., iv, 4.

same reverence to the altar as before, and go to their places, the reader to the middle of the choir. The celebrant goes to the first place in the choir, or to the sedilia. If there is no liturgical choir and no stalls, benches are prepared for the reader and cantors on either side.

All stand at their places. The reader stands in the middle before the altar. He turns to the celebrant, bows towards him and sings *Iube, domne, benedicere.* He stays bowed while the celebrant gives the blessing, *Noctem quietam et finem perfectum,* etc. The choir answers *Amen.*[4] Then the reader sings the short lesson, *Fratres, sobrii estote,* etc. As he chants the last words of this, *Tu autem, Domine, miserere nobis,* he genuflects, bows to the choir and goes to his place. The celebrant sings the verse *Adiutorium nostrum in nomine Domini;* as he does so, he and all make the sign of the cross. All say *Pater noster* silently right to the end or pause silently to examine their consciences. The celebrant, bowing straight before him, says the *Confiteor,* not singing it, but reciting on one note.[5] He strikes his breast thrice at the words *mea culpa, mea culpa, mea maxima culpa.* He turns towards the choir at *vobis, fratres* and *vos, fratres.* The choir answer *Misereatur,* while the celebrant still bows. Then he stands erect; the choir together say the *Confiteor,* they turn to the celebrant and bow as they say *tibi, pater* and *te, pater;* they strike the breast at *mea culpa,* etc. The celebrant answers *Misereatur vestri,* etc. The choir do not stand erect till he has finished this. Then he says *Indulgentiam,* etc., all making the sign of the cross. If there is no choir before the altar, the part of the choir may be taken by the cantors or by the reader. If the reader takes this part he should stay at the middle till the end of the prayer *Misereatur.* The celebrant sings the verse *Converte nos, Deus, salutaris noster,* he and all making the sign of the cross with the thumb on the breast. Then, making the sign of the cross in the usual way, he sings *Deus in adiutorium meum intende.* The choir or singers answer.

Psalms. The cantors sing in full the antiphon assigned for the day and the first verse of the first psalm. If there are no cantors this may be sung by the reader or by one or two persons among the singers. At the end of the first half of this verse the choir takes up the psalm and all sit; those who wear the biretta cover themselves. They remain seated till the end of the antiphon after the three psalms. The first half of the first verse of each psalm is intoned by the cantors. At the verses *Gloria Patri,* all uncover and bow.

Hymn. After the repetition of the antiphon, all uncover and rise. They now stand to the end, except during the prayer when the Office is ferial. The hymn is sung, having been intoned by either the celebrant or the cantors. All bow to the altar at its last verse. The celebrant sings the chapter, and the choir answers *Deo gratias.* The cantors come to the

---

[4] C.E., II, iv, 3 says that the organ is not played, "unless in some churches it is the custom to celebrate this Office more solemnly, in which case the organ may be used."

[5] "Voce recta et paulisper depressa" *(Cantorinus,* 1912).

middle and sing the verses of the short responsory *In manus tuas,* the choir or people answering. The reader may take the part of cantor, or the verses may be sung by one or two among the singers. The versicle *Custodi nos, Domine, ut pupillam oculi* is sung by those who sang *In manus tuas.* The cantors (or other persons, as before) sing the part of the antiphon *Salva nos,* and the first part of the first verse of the canticle *Nunc dimittis,* etc. It is usual to make the sign of the cross at the opening words of this.

Prayer. The celebrant sings *Dominus vobiscum* and the prayer.[6] He sings again *Dominus vobiscum,* the cantors sing the verse *Benedicamus Domino,* the celebrant says the blessing *Benedicat et custodiat nos.*[7] He makes the sign of the cross on himself as he sings the names of the Divine Persons: all do so with him. He begins the anthem of the Blessed Virgin. This is said standing on Saturdays and Sundays, and during Paschal time; otherwise kneeling. According to the Ceremonial the anthem should be recited in a low voice;[8] it is, however, generally sung, and this practice is allowed. There is no rule that the celebrant should stand before the altar during the anthem, but it is a common and lawful custom. The celebrant sings (or says, if the anthem were recited only) the versicle and prayer of this anthem. He says the collect standing. Then he says,[9] the verse *Divinum auxilium*[10] at which all make the sign of the cross.

§ 2. Matins and Lauds[11]

The general rules for Matins sung in choir are these.[12] The persons who take part are the celebrant, two cantors, lectors for the nine lessons. There may be an MC to supervise the whole ceremony. All wear only cassock and surplice (with biretta if clergy) during the first part of Matins. The celebrant puts on a cope of the colour of the Office before the ninth lesson. This cope should therefore be laid out beforehand on the credence or other convenient place. There should be a lectern in the middle of the choir and before this the lessons are sung.

The ceremonies are those of every part of the Divine Office sung in choir, adapted to the special form of Matins. The procession should come in this order: MC, cantors, celebrant (in choir dress), clergy; those of higher rank before the others.[13]

---

[6] To the simple ferial tone, without inflection.
[7] "Recta sed gravi et protracta voce" *(Cantorinus).*
[8] C.E., II, iii, 15.
[9] "Voce recta et paululum depressa" *(Cantorinus).*
[10] Compline has a slightly different form during the Triduum Sacrum (when it is without lights and without chant), the Easter octave (cf. Roman Breviary) and on 2 November.
[11] Included here under "Evening Services" because of the (now obsolete) practice of anticipation on the previous evening.
[12] C.E., II, vi.
[13] C.E., II, vi, 2.

Beginning of Matins. All kneel during the words *Venite, adoremus et procidamus, et genua flectamus Domino* in the Invitatory psalm, and during the verse *te ergo quæsumus,* etc., in the *Te Deum.* All stand during the Invitatory and hymn till the first verse of the first psalm; also during the versicle, the Lord's Prayer and absolution in each nocturn after the psalms. The choir should also stand during the blessing given before the first lesson of each nocturn and before the ninth lesson, and sit during others. They stand while the fragment of the Gospel is read at the beginning of the seventh lesson (on Christmas night also before the eighth), and during the *Te Deum.* All the rest of the time the choir sit. The rules for bowing and uncovering are those usual in the Divine Office, namely, at the *Gloria Patri,* the last verse of the hymn (Doxology), the Holy Name and so on.

The celebrant has his place at the chief stall in choir, or at the sedilia. He intones the hymn and the first antiphon (both being pre-intoned to him by the first cantor). He always stands to bless, even when the others sit. The sign of the cross is not made at the blessings before the lesson.

Psalms and Lessons. The cantors sing the Invitatory (before the lectern). One of them pre-intones the hymn and first antiphon to the celebrant and each succeeding antiphon to a different cleric in choir (beginning with the person of highest rank). Both cantors intone each psalm, in the middle of the choir, before the lectern. The first eight lessons are chanted by eight members of the choir. If there are not eight the same person may chant several. The cantors sing the versicles after the psalms of each nocturn. During the eighth responsory the celebrant puts on the cope. The cantors may also put on copes at this time.[14] The acolytes should light their candles before the ninth lesson. They come and stand on either side of the celebrant, facing one another. He chants this lesson at his place. If other priests are present, before the ninth lesson the celebrant turns and bows to one of them (the first in rank) and asks him for the blessing. Otherwise (without bowing) he says *Iube, Domine, benedicere,* and gives the blessing himself. No one who is not a deacon may read the Gospel at the beginning of lessons. If the lector is not ordained deacon the celebrant supplies this part. The celebrant intones the words *Te Deum laudamus,* pre-intoned to him by the first cantor.

At Lauds the ceremonies are the same as at Vespers. There are the same distinctions as to assistants in copes and so on. The altar is incensed during the *Benedictus.* But at Lauds only the altar of the choir is incensed.

---

[14] C.E., II, vi, 15.

§ 3. Non-Liturgical Services

In many churches it is the custom to form the service on Sunday evening of vernacular prayers, or the Rosary, and vernacular hymns, followed by a homily, and then Benediction. Since such prayers and hymns are not liturgical services, but private devotions, there are no liturgical rules for them, except negative ones. The priest who conducts such services is free to arrange them in any way he likes, as long as he violates no general rule or local legislation (e.g., synodal law). He will, naturally, continue the custom of the church, unless he has good reason to change it.

He must, however, observe the rules which forbid certain ceremonies used only at liturgical functions. There are other points that may be noticed, since they make for reverence and decorum.

At non-liturgical services the priest who conducts them does not wear a stole or other vestment, except cassock and surplice, with the biretta under the usual conditions. He may light some candles on the altar, though there should not be as many as at Benediction or during Exposition of the Blessed Sacrament. Two are generally sufficient.

He may conduct the prayers from a stall in the choir or kneeling before the altar. He may kneel at a desk there. The Rosary and prayers in general are said kneeling; hymns are usually sung standing.

In the case of vernacular devotions only approved forms may be used;[15] and hymns approved by the Ordinary.

§ 4. Sermons

In preaching members of religious orders which have a distinct dress wear their habit. Other priests or deacons wear a surplice. It is the custom to preach in a stole of the colour of the day.[16] If the homily comes between vernacular prayers or hymns the stole should be put on immediately before it begins and taken off again as soon as the homily ends. The preacher may wear a biretta, which he will take off if he mentions the Holy Name and under the usual other conditions. In quoting the Bible he should use an approved translation.[17]

---

[15] Cf. C.I.C. 1259. A mere *imprimatur* for the book in which they recur is not sufficient. For England the *Manual of Prayers* is approved. The prayers in the various editions of the *Garden of the Soul* are also approved by the bishops. The prayers in the collection *Enchiridion Indulgentiarum* (Vatican Press) are approved by the Holy See.

[16] There is no authority for the stole, except recognised custom. (Cf. S.R.C. 2682 § 21, 3157 § 6, 3185).

[17] C.I.C. 1327-1348, contains important rules as to the duty of, and faculties for preaching. Regarding a sermon before the Blessed Sacrament exposed, cf. Chapter XXIII § 5.

§ 5. The Way of the Cross

Though the pious exercise of the Way of the Cross is not a liturgical function, it is described by Pius XII in *Mediator Dei* as one of those practices "that enjoy a special importance and dignity" and may be regarded "as raised to liturgical rank." It is popular, and so below we give the correct method of carrying it out.

When the Stations of the Cross are made privately all that is required is that the person making them should move from Station to Station and meditate, even briefly, on the Passion of our Lord. No vocal prayers are necessary, though they may be used, but meditation on the Passion in general or on some part of it is essential.

When the Stations are made publicly in a church or public oratory those taking part should, if possible, follow the priest from Station to Station. This, however, is almost always impossible in our churches which are filled with seats, and so it is permitted[18] that the people remain in their places, answering the prayers, kneeling, standing and genuflecting when the priest does so, and that only the priest and his assistants need move from Station to Station.

If, in a large church, those present could not hear the prayers if recited before each Station, they may be recited by a priest in the pulpit, but another must (with his assistants) move from Station to Station.[19]

If *in the semi-public oratory* of a religious house of men or women, or of a college, hospital, etc., the Stations are made in common by a number of those living there, it suffices if one person (man or woman) moves from Station to Station and recites the prayers, while the others answer, stand, kneel and genuflect in their places.[20]

The outline of the form which is to be followed when the Stations are made in public is indicated by Pope Clement XII in the instruction (§ 5) which he issued on 3 April 1731 on the exercise of the Way of the Cross. At each Station a cleric or a priest is to "read aloud the consideration corresponding to each mystery and Station and having recited a *Pater* and *Ave* and made an act of contrition he continues his way, and from one Station to another the *Stabat mater* or another prayer is sung."

Following this instruction the usual way of making the Way of the Cross solemnly, according to Roman usage and the practice of the Franciscan Fathers, is as follows: The priest, vested in surplice and violet stole, is accompanied by two acolytes in surplice, carrying the usual acolytes' candles, and a cross-bearer.[21] Having bowed to the sacristy cross

---

[18] The Sacred Penitentiary, 14 December 1917.

[19] Rescript of S. Cong. Propaganda, 1 March 1884.

[20] Penitentiary, 20 March 1946.

[21] The Roman practice is to use a large cross made of wood, painted black and having no figure.

they go in procession to the altar. The priest goes to the foot of the altar, the cross-bearer stands in the middle of the sanctuary between the acolytes. The priest bows low to the cross or genuflects to the Blessed Sacrament and kneels on the lowest step; the acolytes and the cross-bearer remain standing.[22] The priest recites the preparatory prayers of whatever form of the Stations is followed. The priest then rises, reverences once more and then all go in procession to the first Station. There they stand in a line, the cross-bearer between the acolytes, the priest nearest the altar and directly in front of the Station (or, if room permits, the priest may stand before the acolytes). The priest, having bowed or genuflected to the cross of each Station, says the versicle "We adore thee, O Christ, and praise thee," to which his assistants and the people answer, "Because by thy holy Cross thou hast redeemed the world." The priest then reads the consideration which is proposed for the particular Station. If a prayer based on the consideration follow he and his assistants (but not the acolytes and cross-bearer) may kneel for it. In any case he kneels for the *Pater, Ave* and short act of contrition which follow the meditation. In some places the *Gloria Patri*[23] is added and the prayer for the dead ("May the souls of the faithful departed, through the mercy of God, rest in peace. ℟ Amen."). Between the Stations the hymn *Stabat Mater* is usually sung. This hymn consists of ten stanzas of two strophes each. As the stanzas ought not to be broken up the best arrangement is to sing one entire stanza after each two Stations (beginning after the first Station). The seventh stanza is then sung after the thirteenth Station and as the priest returns to the foot of the altar the remaining stanzas — or the last (tenth) only — may be sung. If there are concluding prayers in the form of the Way of the Cross which is used the priest recites them kneeling at the foot of the altar. He then rises, receives the cross from the cross-bearer, ascends to the footpace and with the cross blesses the people,[24] saying the usual form *Benedictio Dei*, etc. He descends to the foot of the altar, restores the cross to the cross-bearer and, having reverenced to the altar or the Blessed Sacrament, returns in procession to the sacristy.

---

[22] The priest may be accompanied by two assistants. They stay with him, one on each side.

[23] It should be omitted during the Triduum Sacrum.

[24] This is the Roman practice.

Chapter XXIII

Exposition
and Benediction of the Blessed Sacrament

§ 1. General Rules

THE part of Benediction which begins at the *Tantum ergo Sacramentum* and ends with the actual benediction is found in the liturgical books, i.e., in the Ceremonial of Bishops (II, xxxiii, 24 *seq.*), in the Roman Ritual at the end of the procession of the Blessed Sacrament (X, v; cf. V, vii), and in the Clementine Instruction which regulates the Forty Hours' Prayer (xxxi), and is a strictly liturgical function. The part preceding the *Tantum* is not found in the liturgical books and, accordingly, is regulated by decisions of S.R.C., by the directions of the Ordinary and by local usages which are in accordance with the general principles of Sacred Liturgy and with the rubrics concerning Exposition of the Most Holy Sacrament.

According to the 1917 Code of Canon Law,[1] permission must be obtained from the Ordinary for Benediction given in its solemn form (i.e., with the monstrance). It is not lawful to give it on any day, at the discretion of the rector of the church. Canon 1274 gives the general law about Benediction (which in its solemn form involves "exposition" in the sense of c. 1274):[2] "In churches which have the faculty of reserving the most holy Eucharist...public exposition, i.e., with the monstrance, may take place on the feast of Corpus Christi...during Mass[3] and at Vespers; at other times, however, only for a just and grave cause, especially a public one, and with the permission of the Ordinary of the place, even though the church belongs to an exempt religious order." When leave is given by the Ordinary the days on which this service may be held are specified. They usually include Sundays and holy days of obligation. No permission is needed for Exposition for the October devotions, since these are prescribed by the Holy See. The 1983 Code of Canon Law, c. 941 § 1 permits Exposition (and Benediction) "either with the ciborium or

---

[1] For the regulations of the 1983 Code see canons 941-944.

[2] Pontifical Commission for the Authentic Interpretation of the Code (6 March 1927).

[3] The correct interpretation of this is disputed; the better interpretation seems to be that the Exposition begins from the communion time of the last Mass celebrated at the altar of Exposition (cf. C.E., II, xxxiii, 17; R.R., X, v, 2). When a Host consecrated prior to this Mass is used for Exposition (outside Corpus Christi or Forty Hours' Prayer) It may not be exposed until after the last Gospel (S.R.C. 4629 §§ 10, 11).

282

with the monstrance" without the above restrictions in all churches or oratories permitted to reserve the Blessed Sacrament.

Since the first part of Benediction is not a strictly liturgical service, there are, naturally, considerable local differences in its forms in different countries. For England there are authoritative rules made by the Hierarchy,[4] which must be observed[5] exactly in England, as far as they go. They still allow some latitude as to the details of what is sung, and in the ceremonies.

Preparations. The first preparation is that a throne, with a canopy over it, must be placed on or near the altar; generally it is placed in a high position over the altar but it should be easy to approach. On this throne the monstrance will stand. The throne should be, ordinarily, a movable structure. A fixed throne is not a part of a correctly built altar, and is forbidden if it interferes with the correct rubrical construction of the altar. Hence it may not be permanent if it is erected on or too near the tabernacle, or if it prevents an altar cross of proper size from standing in front of it.[6] The throne should not as a rule be *on* the tabernacle; but it must not be too distant from the altar. If it is placed behind the altar, it must appear to be joined to it, so as to form one moral whole with the altar.[7] If there is a permanent canopy (civory or tester) over the altar, then there need not be a throne[8] for Benediction. The monstrance is placed on the table of the altar[9] which is the most hallowed place in the church.

At least twelve[10] wax candles must burn on the altar during Benediction. More are allowed. In Paschaltide the Paschal candle is not to be lighted.[11] The veil which covers the altar cloths during the day should be removed. The altar frontal and conopæum are white, unless Benediction *immediately* follows another function requiring a different colour. For exposition of some length it is better to remove the altar cross; for short exposition this is not necessary unless the position of the throne should require it.[12] It is not allowed to place a cushion on the lowest altar step, unless a bishop or prelate gives Benediction.[13] Still less is a kneeler

---

[4] These rules are contained in the *Ritus Servandus in Solemni Expositione et Benedictione SS. Sacramenti* (Burns and Oates, 1963, pp. vii to xiv).
[5] The ceremonial part of the *Ritus Servandus* was submitted for approbation to S.R.C., and though its directions in some details go beyond the common law, it was formally approved in these words: "Præsens Cæremoniale legibus liturgicis conforme est; ideoque approbari potest et observandum est" (S.R.C. 29 March 1912).
[6] The cross may not stand in the throne. Cf. S.R.C. 3576 § 3, 4136 § 2, 4268 § 4.
[7] S.R.C. 4268 § 5. "The most holy Sacrament ought never to be placed outside the hallowed altar, which represents Christ himself" (R.S. § 1).
[8] Cf. R.S., p. xi, §§ 1-2.
[9] Cf. C.E., II, xxxiii, 22, 24, 33; R.R., X, v, 5; I.C. § xxxi.
[10] Cf. S.R.C. 3480, 4257 § 4; R.S. § 3.
[11] S.R.C. 3479 § 3. If Benediction immediately follows Vespers at which the Paschal candle was lit it may remain lighted for Benediction (S.R.C. 4383).
[12] Cf. I.C. § 5; S.R.C. 2365 § 1. R.S. § 3, however, directs that the cross be removed.
[13] S.R.C. 4268 § 9.

allowed. The monstrance may stand (sideways) on the altar before Benediction begins. It should be covered with a white veil while not in use.[14] It is preferable to place the extra candlesticks (and *a fortiori* flowers, if they are used) off the table of the altar as far as possible (i.e., right at the back of the table, or on a gradine, if there is one).

On the throne a corporal is placed, on which the monstrance will stand. The interior of the throne may not be lit up by electric light.[15] The burse (of the colour of the vestments) and tabernacle key (which must, however, be kept under careful supervision) are on the altar.

In the sacristy cassocks and surplices must be ready for the servers; the charcoal[16] is lighted before Benediction and the thurible made ready. Torches are prepared, according to the number to be used, as indicated below.

Assistants. The persons who take part in Benediction are the following: the celebrant,[17] at least one assistant, who will bring the humeral veil, ring the bell, etc. (MC),[18] at least two torch-bearers and a thurifer.

It is good, if possible, that another priest or deacon expose the Blessed Sacrament.[19] The celebrant may be further assisted by a deacon and subdeacon; but there may not be assistants in copes, except when Benediction immediately follows Vespers in which these assistants took part. Various combinations are possible. There may be one priest who will give Benediction, and one priest or deacon to expose the Blessed Sacrament, or there may be a priest, deacon and subdeacon. In this case the deacon exposes the Blessed Sacrament. Or there may be a celebrant, deacon, subdeacon and a priest to expose.

Two torch-bearers suffice; on more solemn occasions the number of torch bearers may be increased. There may be four, six, or, on an exceptional occasion, even eight.

Vestments. The celebrant at Benediction wears a surplice, stole and cope.

The colour for Benediction is white. But if it follows a liturgical Office immediately and the celebrant does not leave the altar, if he is already wearing a cope of the colour of the Office, he may give Benediction in this (unless the colour of the Office be black).[20] But he must put on a stole under the cope, which will be of the same colour. In any case the humeral

---

[14] S.R.C. 4268 § 7.

[15] Cf. S.R.C. 4275, 2613 § 5.

[16] A good quantity of well lighted charcoal should be used, otherwise the incense — the smoke of which is a symbol of prayer — will not burn properly and is wasted.

[17] Canon 943 of the 1983 C.I.C. gives the faculty of giving Benediction to deacons.

[18] It is difficult to dispense with this server (here called MC), since neither a torch bearer can leave his torch, nor the thurifer conveniently leave his thurible to bring the humeral veil to the celebrant, ring the bell or take the biretta.

[19] It is actually prescribed in England in a church served by several priests (R.S., *Præmonenda*, § 3).

[20] S.R.C. 1615 § 6, 2562, 3175 § 3, 3799 § 2, 3949 § 7, 4269 § 13.

veil is always white. The celebrant may wear amice, alb, girdle, stole and cope; this should be his dress, if there are assistants in dalmatic and tunicle or if there is a procession.[21] These assistants wear amice, alb, girdle and dalmatic or tunicle. The deacon wears also a stole, diagonally, from the left shoulder to under the right arm. The priest or deacon who exposes the Blessed Sacrament, if he is not one of the two assistants, wears a surplice, and, at the moment of opening the tabernacle and exposing, as also when he replaces the Blessed Sacrament, a stole. He may carry the stole, over his arm, to the altar or it may be left on the credence beforehand. This stole will be of the colour worn by the celebrant.[22]

§ 2. The Rite of Benediction

The servers come to the sanctuary holding their torches, preceded by the thurifer with burning charcoal, but without incense in the thurible. They are followed by the MC, the priest who exposes (if he assists), then the celebrant (covered) who, if he has two assistants, walks between them, while they hold the ends of his cope, turning in the orphreys so that the lining does not show unduly.

Before the altar the torch-bearers part on either side to allow the celebrant to pass them, the thurifer goes over to the epistle side of the sanctuary and stands before the credence. The celebrant with his assistants comes before the altar. On entering the sanctuary, if there are clergy in choir, otherwise at the foot of the altar, all take off the biretta. The MC takes the birettas and hands them back at the end. The deacon, if there is one, takes the celebrant's biretta (with the *solita oscula*) and then hands it to the MC. The birettas are put aside (on the sedilia) till the end. Before the altar all genuflect on the ground, then kneel in silent prayer for a moment.

Exposition of Sacred Host. The priest who exposes the Blessed Sacrament now does so. He may be the celebrant himself; if another priest or a deacon, he now puts on his stole (first kissing the cross on it). He goes up to the altar, takes the corporal from the burse, puts this aside, and spreads the corporal on the mensa as at Mass. Next he unveils the monstrance and places it on the corporal towards the gospel side. He takes the tabernacle key, opens the tabernacle and genuflects on one knee. If the celebrant himself exposes, he genuflects straight in front of the tabernacle door, placing his hands on the table of the altar. If it is another priest or deacon, he should stand back a step towards the epistle side, so as not to turn his back to the celebrant; then he genuflects

---

[21] S.R.C. 3201 § 6, 3799 § 1, If the celebrant has a right to the rochet, he wears it and an amice under the cope.
[22] S.R.C. 4268 § 8.

towards the tabernacle. No one else makes any reverence at this moment, since they all already kneel.[23] The priest who exposes takes the little vessel which contains the Blessed Sacrament (the *lunula*) from the tabernacle, puts it on the corporal, shuts the tabernacle door, opens the *custodia* (pyx) and places the Blessed Sacrament in the monstrance. He closes the *custodia* and places it aside on the corporal. If the monstrance is to remain on the mensa he places the monstrance in the middle of the corporal and genuflects again to the Blessed Sacrament. If the monstrance is to be put into a throne over the altar, a stand or small ladder (if necessary) is brought forward by a server and put in position (in some churches there are steps behind the altar leading to the throne). The priest genuflects, takes the monstrance, carries it to the throne and places the monstrance on the corporal which lies there. He descends, once more genuflects, and returns (not turning his back directly on the Blessed Sacrament) to his place at the foot of the altar. When the Blessed Sacrament is in position, an assistant priest or deacon in stole and surplice takes off the stole[24] and puts it somewhere near, till he uses it again later.

Incensation. As soon as the Blessed Sacrament is exposed, It is incensed. The celebrant and his assistants bow,[25] rise, the thurifer comes forward and hands the incense boat to the deacon, or to the MC. The celebrant — turned towards the epistle corner — puts on incense as usual, but nothing is kissed; nor does he bless it, because the Blessed Sacrament is now exposed. The celebrant kneels, takes the thurible from the deacon or MC and incenses the Blessed Sacrament three times with the double swing, bowing before and after. He hands the thurible back to him from whom he received it. All remain on their knees, for prayers, and for hymns of adoration to the Blessed Sacrament (e.g., *O Salutaris, Tantum ergo*); for other hymns all stand (kneeling, however, for the first stanza of *Veni, Creator;* and of *Ave, Maris stella;* for *O crux, ave* of *Vexilla regis;* for *Te, ergo, quæsumus* of *Te Deum*). The thurifer stands before the credence, gently swinging the thurible, open (at his side), with the right hand, to keep the charcoal alight.

Hymns and Prayers. While the Blessed Sacrament is being exposed the hymn *O Salutaris* is usually sung. This custom, not usual in Rome, is to be maintained in England.[26] When that hymn is finished, and before the *Tantum ergo Sacramentum* is begun, any approved hymn,[27] litany or

[23] Cf. S.R.C. 4179 § 2.

[24] Whether he then kisses the cross on it or not depends on local usage (S.R.C. 2990 § 1).

[25] "Inclinatio mediocris" (S.R.C. 4179 § 1).

[26] R.S. § 6.

[27] For England and Wales, see *Ritus Servandus,* p. ix.

antiphon[28] may be sung either in Latin or in the vernacular. Liturgical texts, however—such as *Te Deum, Lauda Sion,* an introit or communion antiphon and (it would seem) the liturgical litanies—may be *sung* only in Latin.[29] Prayers (provided they have ecclesiastical approbation) may be recited aloud; these may be in the vulgar tongue. This is the moment (and not after *Tantum ergo*) at which special prayers ordered by the Bishop of the diocese to be said at Benediction occur. Throughout England at the principal Benediction on Sundays and holy days of obligation the prayer *O blessed Virgin Mary, Mother of God,* initiated by Pope Leo XIII, is to be said after the *O Salutaris,* or at latest before the *Tantum ergo.* But on the second Sunday of each month, instead of this, the *Hail Mary,* Cardinal Wiseman's prayer *O merciful God, let the glorious intercession of thy saints assist us,* and *O most loving Lord Jesus,* are said here. In Wales at every Benediction a prayer for the conversion of that country is prescribed. Prayers directly addressed to our Lady or the saints (such as novenas) are better said before the Blessed Sacrament is exposed.[30] If several prayers are recited their order should be that of the dignity of the person addressed (e.g., a divine Person before our Lady; a saint after her).

Second incensation. Then follows the hymn *Tantum ergo.* This may be intoned by the celebrant. As the words of the second line, *Veneremur cernui,* are sung, all bow moderately. At the beginning of the second verse, *Genitori Genitoque,* the Blessed Sacrament is incensed, as before.[31] After this hymn the versicle *Panem de cælo præstitisti eis* is sung by one or two cantors, or by the celebrant. The choir answers. The celebrant stands, without first bowing.[32] With joined hands and bowing his head at *Oremus,* he sings the prayer of the Blessed Sacrament, *Deus qui nobis sub Sacramento mirabili,* etc. on one note, with a fall of a minor third (d'l) on the last syllable of the prayer and of the conclusion. Meanwhile the assistants hold the book before him, or he may sing the prayer from memory. No other prayer may be added after the *Tantum ergo*[33] unless this be prescribed by the Holy See (as at the Forty Hours' Prayer).

---

[28] *Alleluia* is not to be added to antiphons or versicles (outside the Divine Office) in Paschaltide, except where it is expressly prescribed (e.g., after *Panem de cælo; Gaude et lætare*) (S.R.C. 1334 § 6, 3764 § 18).

[29] S.R.C. 3124 § 7, 3537 § 3, 4235 § 8, 4268 § 10, and cf. 3496 § 1). For England the Præmonenda of *Ritus Servandus* (§ 5, p. ix) regulates the singing to be used at Benediction. The better practice is not to sing hymns in English in presence of the Blessed Sacrament exposed, but before or after the exposition.

[30] This is the practice of Rome.

[31] This second incensation is prescribed even though the first has taken place but a short time before. In this case incense is not again put into the thurible (unless this be necessary) but the priest immediately receives the thurible and incenses the Blessed Sacrament (S.R.C. 4202 § 1). When incense is to be put in a second time, the correct moment to commence doing it is between the two stanzas of *Tantum ergo.*

[32] S.R.C. 4179 § 3.

[33] S.R.C. 4194 § 10, 4350 § 2.

Benediction. When the prayer is finished, the priest or deacon who exposed the Blessed Sacrament puts on the stole again. He goes to the throne, genuflects *in plano,* takes the monstrance and puts it on the corporal on the altar. The celebrant receives the humeral veil from a server (the MC). He goes up to the altar, making no reverence first. Here he (with his hands on the table of the altar) with the priest who exposes, genuflects on one knee. Then the priest who exposes hands the monstrance to him, both standing; or the celebrant may take the monstrance from the altar having first turned it around.[34] The other priest or deacon then goes back to kneel at his place. If there is no second priest or deacon, the celebrant himself goes to the throne and takes the monstrance, putting it on the altar. Then he kneels on the edge of the footpace and so receives the humeral veil.

In giving Benediction the celebrant holds the monstrance through the ends of the humeral veil, turns by his right to the people, and makes the sign of the cross once over them, not lifting the Host above the level of his own eyes and not moving his feet.[35] Meanwhile he neither sings nor says any words aloud.[36] He then turns back to the altar by his right so as to complete the circle. Either the assistant priest or deacon comes to him, receives the monstrance, standing, then both genuflect; or the celebrant himself places it on the altar, then genuflects.

While the celebrant gives Benediction nothing may be sung (it may immediately after), but the organ may be played gravely and reverently.[37] The Sanctus bell may be rung. It is usual to ring the bell three times, once as the celebrant turns to the people, once in the middle of the blessing, once as he turns back to the altar. It is not necessary to ring the bell if the organ is played meanwhile, though this may be done. Instead of the Sanctus bell, or together with it, the bell of the church outside may be rung in the same way.[38]

If deacon and subdeacon assist at Benediction they should go up to the footpace with the celebrant, kneel on its edge, bowing on either side before him, and hold the ends of his cope while he gives the blessing. If the deacon has exposed the Blessed Sacrament he may hand the monstrance to the celebrant and take it back (both standing while doing so). He will then genuflect with the celebrant when the monstrance is replaced on the altar. All then come down (the celebrant keeping a little towards the gospel side) avoiding turning their back on the Blessed Sacrament and kneel again on the lowest step. The humeral veil is

---

[34] S,R.C. 3975 § 4.

[35] Cf. S.R.C. 1562 § 2. The cross is made within the limits for correctly blessing with the hand at Mass.

[36] S.R.C. 2464, 2722 § 3.

[37] S.R.C. 2464, 3058 § 2; cf. C.E., II, viii, 70.

[38] There is no rubric requiring the incensation of the Blessed Sacrament by the thurifer during the act of benediction. If it be the custom it may be done (S.R.C. 2956 § 9, 3108 § 6).

removed. The Divine Praises may then (if it is the custom) be said in English.

Conclusion of Benediction. Afterwards the priest who has exposed — having resumed his stole, if he had not handed the monstrance to the celebrant — or the deacon, or the celebrant himself, goes to the altar, genuflects, takes the Blessed Sacrament from the monstrance, replaces it in the *custodia* and then in the tabernacle, genuflects, shuts and locks the tabernacle, removes the monstrance from the corporal, covers it with its veil, folds the corporal, replaces it in the burse, puts the burse flat on the centre of the altar, comes back to his place and takes off the stole. When he genuflects the others, who are kneeling, do not bow.[39] While the Blessed Sacrament is put back in the tabernacle the antiphon *Adoremus in æternum Sanctissimum Sacramentum,* with the psalm *Laudate Dominum omnes gentes* (Ps. 116) may, if customary, be sung. The antiphon is sung before and after the psalm. But any other text, a hymn or suitable anthem may take the place of this.

When the tabernacle is closed all stand. All bow at the *Gloria Patri* of the psalm (if it be sung). When the singing ends all genuflect on one knee, on the ground, and go back to the sacristy as they came.

In Rome for Benediction it is the custom that a priest in surplice and stole should come first, carrying with him the burse and tabernacle key, preceded by thurifer and two torch-bearers. He opens the tabernacle, exposes the Blessed Sacrament on the throne and incenses it. Hymns and litanies or such chants are sung. At the end of all that the celebrant in a cope with assistants and torch-bearers comes from the sacristy, the *Tantum ergo* is sung, and all proceeds as above.

§ 3. Benediction by a Bishop

In this case there should always be deacon and subdeacon, also, if possible, a priest or other deacon to expose and replace the Blessed Sacrament; and a number of attendants to act as bearers of mitre, crosier (wearing *vimpæ*), book and hand-candlestick. A cushion (white) is placed for the bishop on the lowest step of the altar. The bishop will use his precious mitre and (if customary) his crosier. He will, normally, vest in the sacristy (but may vest at his throne).

The bishop's mitre is taken off before the altar (by the deacon),[40] his skull-cap (by the MC) as soon as the tabernacle is opened. The bearer of the hand-candlestick may hold it near the bishop when he reads or sings anything from a book. The thurifer does not kneel when presenting the

---

[39] S.R.C. 4179 § 2.
[40] If the Blessed Sacrament is already exposed, the ministers uncover when they come in sight of the Blessed Sacrament, and the deacon removes the bishop's mitre and skull-cap. All make a double genuflexion before the altar.

thurible to have incense put in.[41] The bishop gives the blessing, making the sign of the cross thrice with the monstrance in the same way as when he blesses with his hand. There is no other difference. The skull-cap is replaced when the tabernacle has been shut at the end, the mitre (by the deacon) after the final genuflexion.

If the Bishop assists at Benediction wearing his cappa magna, he kneels in the centre of the sanctuary, or to one side, at a faldstool or at a kneeling desk (covered and with cushions, as usual). Assisted by the senior of the presbyteral canons he puts in incense and going to the foot of the altar incenses the Blessed Sacrament at the usual times and then returns to his place. The celebrant — not the Bishop — sings the prayer and gives Benediction.

If the Bishop assists in rochet and mozzetta he kneels at the first place in choir or at a kneeler and takes no special part in the function.

§ 4. Benediction with the Ciborium

This is a little ceremony which may be held any day for a just cause.[42]

The priest who celebrates it wears only surplice and stole. He may, however, wear a cope. He may give this Benediction immediately after Mass, wearing the Mass vestments except the maniple, which he takes off first. At least six candles[43] should be lit on the altar. There is no throne; the altar cross remains. If possible there should be two torch-bearers. If not, it is laudable to light two candles in the sanctuary before the altar on the lowest step at each side. On arriving at the altar, after the usual genuflexion, the priest spreads the corporal, opens the tabernacle, genuflects again and leaves it open, so that the people may see the veiled ciborium. He may bring this forward in the tabernacle, that it may be better seen. He must not place it on the altar table.

The usual hymns may be sung; the *Tantum ergo* with the versicle and prayer must be either sung or recited. If incense is used,[44] the priest incenses as soon as he has come back to his place after having opened the tabernacle ; and again at the verse *Genitori Genitoque*. For the blessing, the priest receives the humeral veil, goes up to the altar, genuflects, takes the ciborium and places it on the corporal before the tabernacle. He takes it with the left hand covered by the veil, and arranges the other end of the

---

[41] If Benediction immediately follow pontifical Vespers, the AP from his place in choir comes to assist the Bishop to put in incense and at each incensation. He then returns to his place in choir (S.R.C. 4302 § 2).

[42] Permission of the Ordinary is not required for this simplest form of Benediction.

[43] Congreg. Epis. et Regul. 9 December 1602. Nowadays four wax candles are certainly sufficient (cf. S.R.C. 18 August 1949).

[44] The Blessed Sacrament may be incensed; but this is not necessary, nor does the S.R.C. appear to desire it: "The omission of incensing is more conformable to the practice of the Church in Benediction with the sacred pyx" (= ciborium) (2957 cf. 4202 § 1).

veil over it with the right and so holds the ciborium with both hands. He turns and gives the blessing with one sign of the cross, saying nothing. He replaces the ciborium momentarily on the corporal (until he has freed his hands from the veil), or directly in the tabernacle, and genuflects. He comes down to say the Divine Praises (if customary). Then he goes up to the altar, genuflects, moves the ciborium farther into the tabernacle, closes its door, and replaces the corporal in the burse, etc., as at Benediction given with the monstrance.

§ 5. Exposition of the Blessed Sacrament

The best known case of exposition is that of the Forty Hours' Prayer, for which see cf. Chapter XXVIII. But it may happen, on other occasions, that the Ordinary allows or commands exposition for some space of time, that the people may have this opportunity of paying special honour to the Blessed Sacrament.[45] When the exposition lasts for some hours the Blessed Sacrament should not remain in the tabernacle at the altar of the exposition. If this is its customary place, it should be removed, temporarily, to another altar.

For exposition of some hours the Blessed Sacrament should be placed in a throne above the altar. It is better that any fixed image over the altar should be veiled; other images are to be removed, and relics may not be put on. The altar and tabernacle are vested in white, and it is better to remove the cross.[46] Twenty wax candles, or at least twelve,[47] are to burn during the exposition. Flowers may be used, but with great restraint. Neither they nor the candles should be near the throne; the Sacred Host ought to stand out in a detached manner.

The ceremonies are the same as those of Benediction. Indeed this exposition may be considered as one long Benediction service, with an interval between the exposing of the Blessed Sacrament and the blessing and reposition at the end. During this interval the priest who has exposed and his servers may go away.

The Blessed Sacrament is exposed by a priest or deacon in surplice and white stole. If the exposition begins immediately after Mass[48] the celebrant of Mass may place the Blessed Sacrament on the throne. In this case he wears the Mass vestments, except the maniple, which should be first taken off. If possible, two priests or clerks in surplices should watch

---

[45] Cf. C.I.C. 1275.

[46] R.S. (§ 3) prescribes this for England.

[47] Local legislation (e.g., synodal law) may prescribe a greater number. But a decision of S.R.C. 18 August 1949, requires nowadays only four wax candles, where these are difficult to obtain.

[48] Only for the Corpus Christi procession and Forty Hours' Prayer may the Sacred Host (consecrated at the Mass immediately preceding the Exposition) be put into the monstrance immediately after the communion (S.R.C. 4269 § 11).

kneeling in the sanctuary all the time of exposition. Priests and deacons should wear a white stole. It will not always be possible to observe this. But someone should be in the church, kneeling before the Blessed Sacrament all the time outside the sanctuary. People may relieve one another at intervals.

While the Blessed Sacrament is exposed *O Salutaris* may be sung.[49] As soon as It is placed on the throne It is incensed. The priest who exposed will now generally retire, making a double genuflexion. This rule is observed by everyone who comes to the church, passes before the altar, or rises to leave. But, according to the general rule, if someone is occupied in the sanctuary he will make the double genuflexion only on entering and leaving. While passing, during the time he is there, he genuflects on one knee only. No one should enter the sanctuary unless vested in surplice; women may not enter it at all.

During all the time of exposition the Sanctus bell may not be rung except at a Mass *coram Sanctissimo.* Holy Communion should not be given from the altar of exposition, unless there is no other way.[50] No one may wear a biretta or skull-cap. No one bows to the choir, but its members are incensed as usual.

All the *solita oscula* of mere courtesy are omitted, but not those inherent in the rite of the Mass (e.g., at the Epistle, Gospel and for the altar, the paten and chalice). The hours of the Divine Office may be said or sung, but not the Office for the dead. If, during the Office, a veil is placed in front of the Blessed Sacrament,[51] the members of the choir may cover when seated; but, even then, it is better not to do so.[52] Homilies may be preached, but only on the subject of the Holy Eucharist. During a homily (unless it be only a short *fervorino*) a veil must be placed over or a screen placed before the Blessed Sacrament; the preacher may not cover his head.[53] No one should sit with his back to the altar.

During the time that no liturgical function is celebrated private prayers may be said aloud and hymns may be sung. Either may be in Latin or in the vulgar tongue. The texts must be approved. Translations of liturgical texts are not allowed, since these must be sung in Latin.

While the Blessed Sacrament is exposed, even more than at any other time, reverence should be shown by everyone in church.

---

[49] This does not seem of obligation. Neither the decrees of the S.R.C. nor Roman books on ceremonies say anything about a hymn or prayer at the time of exposition, though they require the *Tantum ergo* at the end. The rule of the *Ritus Servandus* (§ 6) is for Benediction. Therefore, at the beginning of exposition any approved Latin hymn may be sung; or it may be begun in silence.

[50] S.R.C., 3448 § 1, 3482, 4353, and cf. S.R.C. 27 July 1927.

[51] This is generally a little banner of white silk on a staff.

[52] S.R.C. 2552 § 1.

[53] Cf. S.R.C. 1352. He should wear a surplice even if a Regular, and, outside Rome a (white) stole.

When the time of exposition is over Benediction is given. The celebrant enters, with or without deacon and subdeacon or assistant priest, to put back the Blessed Sacrament. All make a double genuflexion before the altar, then kneel. The usual form of Benediction may be used (without, of course, the rite of taking the Blessed Sacrament from the tabernacle, since It is already exposed), or only the latter part, from the *Tantum ergo*. The Blessed Sacrament will not be incensed on the arrival of the celebrant, but only at the verse *Genitori Genitoque*.[54] The closing of the tabernacle after Benediction ends the exposition.

§ 6. The Removal of the Blessed Sacrament

If, for any reason, the Blessed Sacrament is to be carried from one altar to another[55] (which may not be done in the monstrance), this is done by a priest or deacon[56] in surplice and white stole. He is accompanied by three servers, of whom two carry torches,[57] the third the small canopy (umbella) used on these occasions.[58]

A corporal must first be spread on the altar to which the Blessed Sacrament will be brought (this may be done by the sacristan) and the tabernacle key in readiness. On the altar from which It is taken there is another corporal, unless the priest or deacon brings this with him with the tabernacle key. By this altar a white humeral veil and the umbella are made ready. On both altars two candles should be lighted. The torch-bearers may come from the sacristy holding their torches, or these may be ready for them to take at the altar to which they first go. The bearer of the canopy goes first, then the torch-bearers, then the priest or deacon.

At the altar from which the Blessed Sacrament will be taken all genuflect, then kneel for a moment. The priest goes up to the altar, spreads the corporal, opens the tabernacle, genuflects, takes out the ciborium or pyx and places it on the corporal, closes and locks the tabernacle, if it still contains the Blessed Sacrament. Then he kneels and receives the humeral veil from a server. With this he holds the ciborium or pyx, covering it with the veil and carrying it breast high. The torch-

---

[54] S.R.C. 4202 § 2.

[55] The rubrics do not contemplate the taking of the Sacred Host to another place outside the church in which It is reserved (e.g., to give Benediction), except in public procession, or to the sick. It seems, however, that the Ordinary may grant this permission for a sufficient reason. (Cf. Mahoney, *Questions and Answers,* I, Q. 178; *Irish Ecclesiastical Record,* May 1947, p. 439.)

[56] A deacon may always do so, even if priests are present (S.R.C. 4194 § 3; cf. C.I.C. 1274, § 2.)

[57] In case of necessity one torch-bearer is sufficient. (Cf. Instruction of the Congregation of the Sacraments, Ascension Day, 1938.)

[58] Cf. Chapter III § 2. The umbella is always used at Rome. If the church does not possess one, it may be dispensed with. But, where the Blessed Sacrament is reserved not on the high altar, this umbella becomes a necessary article of furniture, which should be procured.

bearers go in front with the torches, the other server walks behind the priest, holding the canopy open over him.

On the way to the other altar the priest should recite psalms.[59] On arrival he goes straight up to the altar and places the ciborium or pyx on the corporal there and genuflects. The torch-bearers kneel some little distance from the altar steps; the umbella is closed and put aside. Then the priest kneels on the edge of the footpace and the veil is taken from him. He opens the tabernacle, puts the ciborium or pyx in it, genuflects again and closes the tabernacle. The servers rise; the torches are extinguished. The priest comes down the steps and all genuflect together and go back to the sacristy.

---

[59] The psalms are not specified. Ps. 115 (Confisus sum), 147 (Lauda Jerusalem), 121 (Lætatus sum), 112 (Laudate servi), 116 (Laudate Dominum), or others from the office of Corpus Christi are suitable. They are recited with the servers, if these are clerics who know them.

Part IV

The Liturgical Year

Chapter XXIV

Advent to Holy Week

§ 1. Advent

THE colour of the season in Advent is violet. The *Gloria in excelsis* at Mass and *Te Deum* at Matins are not said, except on feasts. But *Alleluia* is said in the Office, as usual, and on Sundays at Mass. From 17 December (*O Sapientia*) to Christmas, votive Masses of the fourth class and requiem Masses of the fourth class are not allowed.

During Advent (and Lent) the altar is not to be decorated with flowers or other such ornaments; nor is the organ played at liturgical Offices. But the organ may be played at Benediction,[1] and it is tolerated, even at Mass, if the singers cannot sing correctly without it. In this case it should be played only to accompany the voices, not as an ornament between the singing.

The exceptions to this rule are the third Sunday of Advent—mid-Advent, "Gaudete"—and the fourth Sunday of Lent—mid-Lent, "Lætare." On these two days in the year the liturgical colour is rose (*color rosaceus*).[2] On both these Sundays the altar may be decorated as on Sundays outside Advent and Lent, and the organ may be played.

§ 2. Christmas and Epiphany

Christmas eve is a vigil of the first class; its colour, violet. Should it fall on the fourth Sunday of Advent the Office is entirely of the vigil—at Matins invitatory *Hodie*, hymn *Verbum*, nine antiphons and psalms of the Sunday, then three lessons of the homily of the vigil with their responsories and no *Te Deum*—without any commemoration of the Sunday. The Mass is of the vigil, no *Gloria*, *Alleluia* and verse after the gradual, preface of the Trinity, *Ite missa est*. As the vigil of Christmas, should it fall on the fourth Sunday of Advent, replaces the Sunday, the latter is not commemorated.

The feast of Christmas has an octave of the second class, the days within the octave are liturgical days of the second class and are regulated in a special way (see *infra*); the octave-day itself (1 January) is a liturgical

---

[1] There is no law requiring the organ at any time. If a priest thinks well to mark the season by complete silence of the organ at all services during this time he may do so, and does well.

[2] For want of rose vestments the usual violet may be used (violet dalmatic and tunicle).

day of the second class and is called "the Octave-day of the Lord's Birth." The days within the octave of Christmas are regulated in this special way:

On 26 December is the feast of St Stephen, Protomartyr (II class);

On 27 December is the feast of St John, Apostle and Evangelist (II class);

On 28 December is the feast of the Holy Innocents, Martyrs (II class);

On 29 December commemoration is made of St Thomas, Bishop and Martyr;[3]

On 31 December commemoration is made of St Silvester, Pope and Confessor.

Of particular feasts only those of the first class and in honour of saints who are on these days inscribed in the universal calendar, though only by a commemoration, are admitted; others are transferred to after the octave.

The Office of the Sunday within the Christmas octave occurring between 26 and 31 December is always celebrated, with the commemoration of a feast falling by chance on that date, in accordance with the rubrics. However, if the Sunday falls on a feast of the first class, then the feast is celebrated with a commemoration of the Sunday.

Christmastide runs from the first Vespers of Christmas to 13 January inclusive. This period comprises: (a) the Christmas season proper, which is from the first Vespers of Christmas to None inclusive of 5 January; (b) the Epiphany season, which runs from the first Vespers of the Lord's Epiphany to 13 January inclusive.[4]

The colour for Christmas is white. On that day (beginning at midnight) every priest may say Mass three times. No special privilege is needed for this (C.I.C. 806 § 1). Three Masses are provided in the missal, one for the night, one for dawn, one for the day. If a priest says Mass once only, he should choose the one which best corresponds to the hour at which he says it. The same rule will apply to a priest who says two Masses. If he says three he must say the three provided, in their order, at whatever time he says them.[5]

It is not allowed (without special indult) to say a purely private Mass on this night.[6] One Mass only is allowed at midnight, the conventual or

---

[3] As St Thomas is in England and Wales the Patron of the pastoral clergy, the Holy See (at the request of the English hierarchy) raised the rank of the feast for England and Wales to a feast of I class, enabling it to be celebrated on its proper date. The ordering of the Divine Office within the Christmas octave is dealt with in R.G.(B.), nn. 175, 176 and 161c.

[4] R.G., nn. 68-69, 72.

[5] But if he sings the third Mass, he may say the first and second later.

[6] C.I.C. 821 § 2. By a private Mass here is meant one that is neither a sung nor a conventual Mass, nor a Mass said at a fixed hour in a public church for the people (a "parochial" Mass).

parochial one.[7] It should be, if possible, a solemn Mass: but a Sung, or even a low Mass is allowed, if it is the one which the people attend, and is said in default of solemn Mass. It may not begin before midnight. People are allowed to receive Holy Communion at the midnight Mass, unless the Bishop, for some reason, forbids this.[8] If they do so they must fast from solid food and alcoholic drinks for three hours, from other liquids (except water) for one hour, before communion.[9]

If Matins are said or sung in church before midnight Mass, see the rules in cf. Chapter XXII § 2. The celebrant, when he intones the hymn *Iesu redemptor omnium* at Matins, should extend, raise and join the hands, bowing towards the altar.[10]

At all sung Masses on Christmas Day the celebrant and his ministers kneel on the lowest step in front of the altar or at the epistle side (or they may kneel before the sedilia) and bow while the choir sings the words *Et incarnatus est de Spiritu Sancto ex Maria Virgine: et homo factus est.* If they have not yet left the altar they descend a step, kneel on the edge of the footpace and bow.

A special clause is inserted in the *Communicantes* prayer of the canon.

In this clause the celebrant says *noctem sacratissimam celebrantes* at the first Mass (at whatever hour he may celebrate); at the second and third Masses and during the Christmas octave he says *diem sacratissimum.* At the second Mass, even if a solemn Mass, there is a commemoration of St Anastasia.

At the Gospel of the third Mass the deacon who reads it, and all, except the subdeacon who holds the book and the acolytes, genuflect at the words *Et Verbum caro factum* est—the deacon towards the book, all others towards the altar. The last Gospel at the third Mass is omitted.

There is a special arrangement for the period from 2 January to 5 January. The Office (unless a feast occurs) is of a feria of the fourth class. The *Te Deum* is said at Matins. The conclusion of hymns and the verse of the short responsory at Prime are of the Nativity. The Mass is that of 1 January but without the *Credo* and with the common *Communicantes.* During the period requiem Masses of the fourth class are prohibited.

Epiphany. The Epiphany is, liturgically, one of the great feasts of the year. It has no vigil or octave. Its colour is white. Matins of the Epiphany begins with a special form. The Invitatory is not said, nor *Domine, labia mea aperies,* nor *Deus in adiutorium.* The Office begins at once with the first

---

[7] *In all religious or pious houses* having an oratory with the faculty of keeping habitually the Blessed Eucharist one priest may celebrate up to three Masses on the night of the Nativity. Those present satisfy the precept of hearing Mass, and Holy Communion may be given (C.I.C. 821 § 3).

[8] Cf. C.I.C. 821 § 3; 867 § 4; 869.

[9] Canon 919 § 1 of the 1983 C.I.C. stipulates one hour's fast from everything except water and medicine before receiving Holy Communion.

[10] C.E., II, xiv, 5.

antiphon. In the Mass a genuflexion is made at the words of the Gospel *procidentes adoraverunt eum.*

In cathedrals and the principal church of each place, after the Gospel the movable feasts of the year are announced. If this is done, a white cope is prepared in the sacristy for the priest or deacon who will do so. A lectern stands on the gospel side of the choir, or the pulpit may be used. The lectern or pulpit is covered with a white veil. The priest or deacon who will announce the feasts goes to the sacristy during the gradual and puts on the cope over his surplice. He comes out, makes the usual reverences to altar, celebrant and choir, and announces the feasts. The form for doing so, with the chant, is in the pontifical at the beginning of its third part.

From 7 January to 12 January the Office is of the feria of Epiphanytide. The antiphons and psalms, and the verse of the one nocturn of Matins, are of the current feria; the rest of the Office is as on the feast of the Epiphany except the lessons which are of the occurring Scripture with its responsories (formerly used during the octave). The *Te Deum* is said at Matins. The Mass is that of the Epiphany until the first Sunday after Epiphany, thereafter of that Sunday, without the *Credo* and with the common *Communicantes.* During the period requiem Masses of the fourth class are prohibited.

§ 3. Candlemas

Candlemas (the Purification of the Blessed Virgin Mary, 2 February) is a feast of the Lord of the second class. On this day candles are blessed and distributed, and a procession is made with them before the principal Mass. The colour of the day is white, also for the blessing of candles and procession.

Supposing first the normal conditions, that is, that solemn Mass will be celebrated with deacon and subdeacon, the ceremony is arranged in this way:[11]

Preparations. On the credence, all required for solemn Mass, as usual; covered with a white veil, also the holy water and sprinkler, and a basin of water, basin, soap and a hand-towel for the cleansing of the celebrant's hands after the distribution of the candles; two tapers. Near by is the processional cross. If another priest will assist to give out the candles a white stole is required for him. On the sedilia the white chasuble, and three maniples are laid out. Near the altar a table stands at the epistle side, so that the celebrant standing there can easily sprinkle and incense the candles on it. This table is covered with a white cloth, on which the

---

[11] Cf. C.E., II, xvi, xvii; M.R., I.

candles lie. They are then covered with a white cloth.[12] The altar is prepared for Mass, the six candles are lit. The frontal and conopæum (if the Blessed Sacrament be in the tabernacle) are white. The altar-cards are better not placed on it till the beginning of Mass. The missal, covered with white,[13] stands open at the epistle side. Following the usual procession of servers,[14] the celebrant comes from the sacristy in amice, alb, girdle, white stole and cope, between the ministers, who wear dalmatic and tunicle (no maniples), the deacon with his stole. If it is a Sunday the usual Asperges ceremony is first carried out, in white vestments. The celebrant and ministers bow, as usual, to the choir, bow or genuflect to the altar, go up to it; the celebrant kisses it (the ministers do not genuflect while he does so); then they stand at the epistle side, the ministers on each side of the celebrant, not holding the cope.

Blessing of Candles. The MC uncovers the candles. With joined hands all the time (even at *Oremus*, at which, however, the celebrant bows to the book) the celebrant sings *Dominus vobiscum* and the prayers provided in the missal for the blessing of candles, all in the second ferial tone.[15] As he signs the cross over the candles he lays his left hand on the altar and the deacon raises the right side of the cope. While these prayers are said all in choir stand; the thurifer goes to prepare the thurible, if he has not brought it at the beginning. When the fifth prayer is ended, the thurifer approaches, with (on his right) the first acolyte who carries the holy water and sprinkler. The celebrant puts on and blesses incense as usual, the deacon assisting and holding the incense boat. Meanwhile the subdeacon raises the right end of the cope. When the incense is blessed the deacon hands the sprinkler to the celebrant (*solita oscula*). He sprinkles (in the centre, to his left and to his right) the candles, saying in the subdued voice the entire antiphon *Asperges me, Domine* only (not the psalm). Then he incenses the candles with three simple swings — towards the centre, to his left and to his right — saying nothing. The thurible and the holy water are put back in their places.

Distribution of Candles. The celebrant and ministers go to the middle of the altar, turn to the people, not changing their places. The deacon remains at the celebrant's left. The priest highest in rank — even a bishop, if he be not a "greater prelate" — comes to the altar (not wearing a stole). The MC hands him a candle, which he gives to the celebrant, both

---

[12] "Aliqua mappa munda" is the direction of M.R., I, i. The table may also be set in the middle of the sanctuary.

[13] The Roman texts always suppose that books are covered in the colour of the Office (cf. C.E., I, xii, 15). This is often not observed; a veil to cover the missal stand is sometimes used instead.

[14] An MC, thurifer and acolytes at least are required. There may be others, and clergy. The subdeacon will carry the cross at the procession of candles.

[15] On the last syllable of the end of the prayer and of the conclusion there is a fall of a minor third; cf. O'Connell, *The Celebration of Mass*, 1964, p. 443.

standing. The celebrant gives this candle to the subdeacon, who lays it on the altar or gives it to the MC to put on the credence. The celebrant now receives another candle from the deacon and hands this to the priest from whom he received his own.[16] This priest kneels to take it, kissing first the celebrant's hand, then the candle. If he is a prelate he stands and kisses only the candle. He then goes back to his place. The ministers kneel before the celebrant, who gives them candles in the same way. The ministers hand their candles to an acolyte, who puts them on the credence.

The clergy in choir now come up in order and kneel on the footpace. The celebrant hands to each a candle in the same way. Canons and prelates do not kneel to receive theirs.[17] If canons are present the ministers (unless they, too, are canons) receive their candles after them. The servers and singers also come up to take their candles. This should be arranged so that the singing is not interrupted. The MC must see that the candles are brought from the table to the celebrant and handed to him by the deacon.

If the people receive candles, the celebrant, with his ministers, goes to the communion rail or entrance of the choir and distributes them. Another priest, in surplice and white stole, may assist in distributing the candles.

During the distribution, beginning as soon as the celebrant has received his candle, the choir sings the antiphon *Lumen ad revelationem gentium,* etc., with the canticle *Nunc dimittis*[18] as in the missal and gradual. Towards the end of the distribution the candles of those in choir are lighted by the acolytes. After the distribution the celebrant washes his hands at the epistle side of the altar *in plano;* the acolytes serve him, as at Mass, the ministers holding the ends of the cope. Then, ascending by the shorter way and standing at the epistle side as before, he sings *Oremus* (with hands joined) and the collect *Exaudi, quæsumus Domine* as in the missal. Meanwhile the MC or servers light the candles of the celebrant and deacon.

Procession. The procession follows:[19] If the thurifer has laid aside the thurible he takes it again during this last prayer. The celebrant, still standing at the epistle corner, puts on and blesses incense, assisted by the deacon. Then the subdeacon goes to the credence and takes the processional cross; the acolytes, carrying their candles, go with him and stand at his side by the entrance of the choir, facing the altar. The thurifer

---

[16] In no case may the deacon or subdeacon give the celebrant his candle. If no other priest is present, a candle is laid on the altar by the MC. The celebrant takes this from the altar himself, standing.

[17] C.E., II, xvii, 2.

[18] This is repeated as long as the distribution goes on. *Gloria Patri* is said as a conclusion.

[19] If the blessing of the candles is carried out the procession may *not* be omitted. The arbitrary mutilation of a rite is quite unlawful.

goes to stand behind the subdeacon, so as to be first in the procession. The MC hands the celebrant's candle to the deacon, who gives it (*solita oscula*) to the celebrant. The celebrant and deacon, at his right, turn towards the people. The deacon sings *Procedamus in pace;* the choir answers *In nomine Christi. Amen.* The celebrant and deacon come down the altar steps, all genuflect;[20] the celebrant and deacon put on their birettas. The procession goes in this order: first, the thurifer, then the subdeacon bearing the cross between the acolytes, the choir, clergy, celebrant, with the deacon at his left holding the cope (all, except the deacon, carrying their lighted candles in the outside hand). The MC may walk at the right of the celebrant (holding the cope) or in front of him. The procession passes around the church, or goes outside,[21] according to the custom of the place. Meanwhile the choir sings the antiphons *Adorna thalamum tuum Sion,* and *Responsum accepit Simeon,* from the gradual.[22] One of these may be omitted, if there is not time for both. During the procession the church bells should be rung. On entering the church, if the procession has gone without, the choir sings the responsory *Obtulerunt pro eo Domino par turturum.* If the procession has not left the church this is sung as it comes back to the sanctuary.[23] The sacristan puts on the altar-cards and may put on flowers (if their use is customary). When the procession returns to the sanctuary the clergy genuflect, two and two, bow to each other, and go to their places. The celebrant and deacon come before the altar (MC takes the celebrant's candle) and make the usual reverence. The thurifer goes to the sacristy to prepare the thurible for Mass, the acolytes put their candles on the credence, the subdeacon puts the cross near, and goes to the celebrant's left. The celebrant and ministers then go to the sedilia and vest for Mass, assisted by the MC and acolytes. They come to the altar and begin Mass.[24]

Mass. During Mass—at which the psalm *Iudica* and the Confession, *Aufer* and *Oramus* are omitted—the candles are held lighted by those in choir during the Gospel, and from after the *Sanctus* to the end of the communion.[25] The MC will see that they are lit in time, first during the Epistle or gradual, the second time after the choir is incensed at the offertory. At the sung Gospel the celebrant also holds his candle lit. The MC hands it to him (*solita oscula*), after he has signed himself, at the

---

[20] Except the subdeacon with the cross and acolytes. The celebrant, canons and prelates bow only, if the Blessed Sacrament is not reserved on the altar.

[21] In the first case it turns to the right outside the sanctuary, goes around and returns to the altar; in the second case it goes down the church directly to the door (M.R. I, II, § iii, 5).

[22] The singers need not carry lighted candles if they cannot conveniently hold them with their books.

[23] "In ipso cancellorum presbyterii ingressu" says M.R., I, II, § iii, 7.

[24] The same priest who blesses the candles must celebrate the Mass. Only the Bishop of the diocese may bless the candles and not celebrate the Mass that follows.

[25] It is preferable to extinguish them before the Pax (cf. Gromier, p. 363).

words *Sequentia sancti Evangelii*. Each time, when the period in question is ended, everyone blows out his candle and lays it down. After the Gospel the celebrant gives his candle back to the MC. The preface is that of the Nativity.

If the Forty Hours' Prayer should be in progress on 2 February, the Blessed Sacrament is transferred to another altar where the adoration can continue without disturbing the piety of the faithful, or the adoration is interrupted and resumed after the blessing and procession of candles and Mass.

§ 4. Candlemas in Small Churches[26]

The following preparations must be made beforehand:

On the credence the chalice, with its ornaments, are prepared for Mass.[27] The Mass vestments are made ready at the sedilia. The holy water and sprinkler are on the credence, the cruets for Mass, a plate with soap, with which to cleanse the celebrant's hands after the distribution of candles, and another vessel of water with a dish and hand-towel for this purpose; a taper. All on the credence is covered with a white veil.

The altar is covered with a white frontal. The tabernacle is covered with a white conopæum, and the missal-stand has a white cover. Four or six candles are lighted. At the epistle corner of the altar is a table with a white cloth, on which are the candles to be blessed, covered with a clean cloth ("aliqua mappa munda"). The processional cross and flowers (if customary to use them) are near. In the sacristy are the surplices for the servers, the amice, alb, girdle, white stole and cope for the celebrant, the thurible and incense boat.

If it is a Sunday the Asperges ceremony is held first, in white vestments.

Blessing of Candles. The simple form, with or without chanting, may be used when the solemn form is not possible, if at least three servers are available. Of these three one, the first, brings the thurible when it is required at the blessing; he then lays it aside and, in due time, takes the processional cross and goes in front of the procession. The other two stand on either side of the celebrant during the blessing (the second uncovers the candles at the beginning of it), answer the prayers, hand him the sprinkler for the holy water, assist when he puts on and blesses incense, and finally walk on each side of him, presumably holding the ends of his cope, in the procession and recite the chants with the celebrant, if there are no singers.

If no other priest is present the first server after the blessing lays a candle on the altar at the centre; the celebrant goes there, standing takes

---

[26] Cf. rubric of the missal at the end of the blessing and M.R., Tit. I.

[27] If one of the servers is not at least tonsured the celebrant himself must see to this.

it, and then gives it to the server to keep, till he requires it again for the procession. If a priest is present, he gives the candle to the celebrant, who receives it before the altar, facing the people, both standing. This second priest receives his candle from the celebrant kneeling.

There is no difficulty about the blessing. The celebrant — with hands joined — says all the prayers in order, as they are in the missal, the servers at his side answer. M.R. says that, when the candles are blessed, the celebrant sitting with his head covered at the gospel side of the footpace may preach to the people about the meaning of the ceremony. When he has taken his own candle, he stands before the missal at the epistle side and there recites with the servers the antiphon *Lumen ad revelationem* with the *Nunc dimittis*,[28] etc. Then he gives the candles to the people (having, with the servers, reverenced to the altar before going to the communion rail).[29] The servers accompany him, right and left, and hand him the candles to distribute. The first brings them from the table. The celebrant then goes back to the altar, washes his hands — the first server pouring the water, the others handing the hand-towel. Then, returning to the missal, he says *Oremus* and the prayer.

Procession. Finally, taking at the epistle corner his lighted candle from a server, he turns to the people and says or sings *Procedamus in pace.* The servers (or singers) answer *In nomine Christi. Amen.* The celebrant and servers descend and reverence to the altar. The celebrant puts on his biretta, then carries his candle in the right hand. So the little procession goes, the cross before, borne by the first server.[30] During the procession (unless there be cantors to sing them) the celebrant recites with his assistants the antiphon *Adorna;* and, as the procession re-enters the church (if it remains inside, then as it re-enters the sanctuary), *Responsum.* When it comes back to the altar, all make the usual reverence, the celebrant goes to the seat, gives away his candle and takes off the cope and stole, putting on Mass vestments, assisted by the second and third servers. While he does this the first server puts vases of flowers on the altar, if their use be customary.[31] Mass (sung if possible) follows, at which the preparatory prayers are omitted.

---

[28] If there are singers they chant these. The celebrant does not then read them but at once distributes the candles (cf. M.R., I, II, § ii, 3).

[29] M.R., I, II, § ii, 6 says first to the men, then to women. This is not usual now. If there be clerics present they receive their candles — those of higher rank first — before the people and kneeling on the footpace.

[30] The cross-bearer — who does not genuflect before the altar before leaving — leads the procession either without or within the church, according to custom. In the first case he leads it straight down to the door; in the second he turns to the right outside the sanctuary and going around returns to the altar (M.R., I, II, § iii, 5). If the people take part in the procession they follow the priest.

[31] If he be at least tonsured he arranges the chalice on the altar, otherwise the celebrant must take it with him when he is vested for Mass.

During Mass the servers (and presumably the people) hold the candles lighted during the Gospel, and from after the *Sanctus* to the communion (inclusive).

More Solemn Form. To this simple ceremony it is possible to make the following additions: There may be an MC, thurifer, cross-bearer and two acolytes. These acolytes cannot well be the two servers who stand at the celebrant's side (his assistants), because these should walk on either side of him in the procession, whereas the acolytes go in front on either side of the cross. Other servers in surplices may attend, to carry blessed candles and make a longer procession. They may come out from the sacristy in the usual order and stand in the sanctuary during the blessing. All receive candles, but the acolytes, thurifer, cross-bearer and two assistants cannot carry theirs in the procession. The acolytes hold, not the blessed candles, but those of their office, in candlesticks. Incense will be put on and blessed by the celebrant before the procession begins.

All may be sung as when there are deacon and subdeacon. The celebrant in this case will sing the prayers,[32] the choir answering. He will sing *Procedamus in pace* before the procession. During the procession the choir sings the antiphons provided in the gradual.

If the procession is not made, the candles should not be blessed; it is not lawful to mutilate a rite to suit one's own convenience. They are blessed and distributed primarily in order to be held during the procession. Indeed, in many countries the candles are given back to the church afterwards. In others people keep them for use at when Holy Communion is brought to the sick, or to burn by the bed of a dying person.

It is customary that other candles be blessed at the same time, not distributed, but used in the course of the year at the altar .

§ 5. Septuagesima and Lent

The time from Septuagesima to Ash Wednesday partakes in many ways, but not in all, of the character of Lent. The colour of the season is violet from Septuagesima to Easter.[33] The *Te Deum* is not said at Matins, nor the *Gloria in excelsis* at Mass, except on feasts. At the end of Mass *de tempore* the deacon (or celebrant) says *Ite, missa est*. In no case is the word *Alleluia* used at all from Septuagesima till it returns at the first Easter Mass. On all days (except in the ferial Masses of Tuesday, Thursday and Saturday), even feasts, a tract takes the place of the *Alleluia* and its verse after the gradual. In the Office at the end of the response to *Deus in adiutorium* –

---

[32] The prayers have a short conclusion and are sung to the second ferial or semi-festal tone (a drop of a minor third at the end of both the prayer and its conclusion).

[33] Except on Mid-Lent Sunday (rose), Maundy Thursday (white for Mass), Good Friday (black), and Holy Saturday (partly white), as will be noted.

Laus tibi, Domine,· rex æternæ gloriæ is said instead of *Alleluia*. The playing of the organ is allowed from Septuagesima to Ash Wednesday (exclusive).

In all liturgical functions, except Benediction, all instrumental music[34] is forbidden from Matins of Ash Wednesday to *Gloria in excelsis* of the solemn Easter Vigil Mass, except on the fourth Sunday of Lent and on greater feasts.

From Ash Wednesday to the Wednesday of Holy Week there is a special prayer called *Oratio super populum* added in ferial Masses after the post communion prayers. The celebrant sings *Oremus* with the usual gestures. The deacon turning to the people sings *Humiliate capita vestra Deo,* and the celebrant, turned to the altar, and with hands extended, sings the prayer, in the simple ferial tone. In low Masses the celebrant says *Oremus* and *Humiliate,* etc., bowing once towards the missal.

On Ash Wednesday and the three following days the Office is said as on other ferias of the year, though they have special prayers, antiphons at the *Magnificat* and *Benedictus* and ferial *Preces* on Wednesday and Friday. The Lenten order of the Office does not begin till the first Sunday of Lent.

During Lent votive Masses of the fourth class and requiem Masses of the fourth class are not allowed.

On mid-Lent Sunday, the fourth of Lent *(Lætare)*, rose-coloured vestments are used, the altar is decorated as for Sundays outside Lent, the organ is played.[35]

Passiontide. During the last fortnight of Lent, from First Passion Sunday, the verse *Gloria Patri* in the Office of the season is omitted at the invitatory of Matins, at all responsories, at the Asperges and at the introit and lavabo of Mass *de tempore*. The psalm *Iudica me* in Masses *de tempore* is not said. Before the first Vespers of Passion Sunday all statues and images (including crucifixes) in the church which are objects of veneration and not merely ornamental, are to be covered with a plain opaque violet veil. No figure or ornament is allowed on these veils. The images are not to be uncovered for any reason (except the crosses on Good Friday) till the veils are removed at the *Gloria in excelsis* at the first Easter Mass. But the Stations of the Cross may remain uncovered.

At solemn Mass on the Annunciation (25 March or the day to which the feast may be transferred) the celebrant and ministers come to kneel before the altar, on the lowest step at the epistle side (facing north) or at the centre, and bow while the choir sings *Et incarnatus...et homo factus est,* as at Christmas.

---

[34] It may be played during *Gloria in excelsis* on Maundy Thursday.
[35] The rule is the same as for mid-Advent.

§ 6. Ash Wednesday

Ash Wednesday is a feria of the first class. The rite of blessing the ashes is similar to that of blessing candles at Candlemas.[36]

Preparations. The colour is violet for both blessing and Mass. The frontal and conopæum are violet. Flowers are not used. The altar-cards are better put in their place only before Mass begins. The missal, covered with violet, stands open on the epistle side; near it, between the book and the end of the altar, is a vessel containing the ashes (finely powdered and dry) made by burning palms or other foliage blessed on last Palm Sunday. This vessel—"of silver or other ornamental material"[37]—is covered with a lid of similar material or with a violet veil. On the sedilia are the three maniples, and a chasuble for the celebrant. At the credence everything is prepared for Mass, as usual. There is, moreover, the vessel of holy water and sprinkler, water in a vessel, a basin, hand-towel and soap, that the celebrant may wash his hands after the distribution of ashes. If another priest will assist in distributing the ashes, a violet stole and a second vessel for ashes are made ready for him.

In the sacristy everything is prepared for Mass as usual, except the maniples and the celebrant's chasuble, which are at the sedilia. The celebrant vests in violet stole and cope; the deacon in stole and violet dalmatic, the subdeacon in violet tunicle.

The function takes place before the principal Mass.[38]

Blessing of Ashes. The procession comes to the sanctuary as usual. The celebrant, between the ministers, goes up to the altar and kisses it in the middle. The ministers do not genuflect. All three go to the missal at the epistle side and stand there, the celebrant between the ministers, who do not hold the ends of his cope. The ashes are uncovered by the MC. While the choir sings the antiphon *Exaudi nos, Domine,* etc., the celebrant reads it in a low voice, with joined hands. Meanwhile those in choir sit. Then all stand and remain standing while the ashes are blessed. The celebrant sings the four prayers, as in the missal. He chants them in the ferial tone,[39] with joined hands, and does not turn to the people at *Dominus vobiscum.* At the word *Oremus* he bows to the missal. The

[36] C.E., II, xviii, xix; M.R., Tit. II.

[37] M.R. (cf. C.E., II, xviii, I).

[38] For the convenience of the people it is permitted to bless the ashes early in the morning, with or without Mass, before the solemn blessing takes place. A priest vested in surplice and violet stole does this, using the blessing found in the missal without any chanting. These ashes may be distributed at any time by a priest vested in surplice and violet stole, or in Mass vestments if the distribution is immediately before or after a private Mass. In churches where evening Mass is usually celebrated with a crowded congregation the Ordinary may allow the solemn blessing of ashes to be repeated.

[39] All the prayers have the short conclusion and so are sung to the second ferial or semifestal tone (an inflection of a minor third at the end of the prayer and of the conclusion); cf. O'Connell, *The Celebration of Mass,* 1964, p. 443.

ministers are at his sides. Meanwhile the thurifer goes to prepare the thurible, and returns with it. When the celebrant blesses the ashes, he lays his left hand on the altar and makes the sign of the cross over them with the right. The deacon holds back the cope. Incense is put on and blessed — the deacon, as usual, saying *Benedicite, Pater reverende* — the ashes are sprinkled thrice (in the centre, to the celebrant's left and to his right) with holy water, then incensed with three simple swings, as always on such occasions. While sprinkling the ashes the celebrant says the entire antiphon *Asperges me, Domine,* without the psalm. He incenses them, saying nothing. The thurible is taken back to the sacristy. While the ashes are distributed the choir sings the antiphons appointed in the missal and gradual.

Distribution of Ashes. If another priest is present he gives the ashes to the celebrant. In this case he does not wear a stole. He comes to the altar when the blessing is finished. The celebrant, with the ministers, also comes to the middle and turns to the people; the ministers turn also, so that the deacon is on his left, the subdeacon on his right as they face the people. The MC gives the vessel with ashes to the deacon to hold. The priest who gives the ashes to the celebrant takes some from the dish between the forefinger and thumb of his right hand, and sprinkles them in the form of a cross or with his thumb dipped in them makes the sign of the cross on the celebrant (standing bowed). The rubrics do not define exactly the place where the ashes are put.[40] It is usual, in the case of priests and of all who are tonsured, to put the ashes at the place of the tonsure. Lay people receive them on the top of the head or on the forehead. In the case of women they should be put on the hair or forehead (when this can be conveniently done), not on the headdress. In making the cross with ashes the verse *Memento homo quia pulvis es et in pulverem reverteris* is said.

If no other priest is present the celebrant stands[41] facing the altar, and puts the ashes on himself, in the form of a cross, saying nothing. Neither of the ministers may give the ashes to the celebrant. The celebrant next gives the ashes to the priest from whom he himself received them. This priest kneels on the edge of the footpace (if he is a prelate or canon he stands and bows). The deacon hands the dish to the MC, and kneels before the celebrant; he and the subdeacon receive the ashes. If prelates or canons are present they receive ashes before the ministers, unless these, too, are canons.

The ashes are then distributed to the clergy in choir, in order. They come before the altar two by two (if their number is unequal the last group is of three). They kneel on the footpace — unless they are prelates or

---

[40] The missal simply says "cineres imponit in capite"; M.R. says "in modum crucis imponit in capite."

[41] S.R.C., 1 November 1931.

canons, in the dress of their rank, when they stand on the step below the footpace, bowed — while the celebrant puts the ashes on their tonsure or forehead, in the form of a cross, saying to each *Memento,* etc. The deacon holds the vessel of ashes meanwhile at the celebrant's left.

Ashes are then given in the same way to the servers. Lastly they are given to the people at the communion rail. To do so the celebrant goes there between the ministers, having first reverenced at the foot of the altar. The Roman books direct that men should kneel separate from women.[42] This is not the usage in many countries. When the distribution begins and as long as it continues the choir sings the antiphons (repeating them if necessary) and responsory which are given in the missal.

While the ashes are distributed the clergy in choir sit as soon as all in their order have received them. If another priest assists, or alone gives the ashes to the people, the MC must put some ashes into a vessel for his use, and he will wash his hands after the celebrant.

Final Prayer. When the distribution is over the celebrant goes to the epistle corner of the altar, and there *in plano* washes his hands. The first acolyte holds the plate with soap, the second the water and dish, with the hand-towel over his arm. The ministers at the celebrant's sides hold the ends of his cope. Then ascending by the shorter way to the epistle corner of the altar, the celebrant sings (with joined hands) *Dominus vobiscum* and the last prayer, as in the missal. The ministers stand at his side as before. All three then go straight to the sedilia, without a reverence to the cross, and there the celebrant takes off the cope, putting on the maniple and chasuble; the ministers put on their maniples. The MC and acolytes assist them.

Mass. Mass follows as usual and must be celebrated by the priest who blessed the ashes.[43] The *Iudica* psalm, Confession, *Aufer* and *Oramus* are omitted. When the celebrant reads the verse *Adiuva nos* in the tract he does not genuflect. Instead he kneels on the footpace, between the ministers, while the choir sings the entire verse *Adiuva nos...nomen tuum.*

After the last postcommunion the celebrant sings *Oremus,* the deacon, with joined hands, turns to the people, sings *Humiliate capita vestra Deo,* then turns back to the altar. The celebrant sings the *Oratio super populum.*

If the Forty Hours' Prayer is in progress, see the directions given for 2 February (Candlemas) above.

§ 7. Ash Wednesday in Small Churches

The *Memoriale Rituum* (Title II) in its description of this ceremony has almost the same account as is already given above, and this simpler form (that is, without sacred ministers or singers) is allowed wherever the

---

[42] M.R., II, II, § ii, 4.
[43] Only the Bishop of the diocese may bless ashes and not celebrate the Mass that follows.

solemn form is not possible.[44] The ministers have so little to do on Ash Wednesday that the description above will do for this case too, with the obvious exception that their part is left out. The servers assist at the incensing and sprinkling of ashes. A server holds the vessel of ashes by the celebrant while he distributes them. According to the *Memoriale Rituum* the celebrant, with the servers, recites the antiphons, if there is no one to sing them, as soon as he himself has received the ashes. If there is a choir they will sing the same parts as when there are deacon and subdeacon.

---

[44] The rubrics of the M.R. are very detailed and speak for themselves.

Chapter XXV

The First Part of Holy Week

§ 1. General Rules

THE rites for Holy Week were reformed by a general decree of S.R.C. of 16 November 1955 *(Maxima Redemptionis Nostræ Mysteria),* with its accompanying Instruction. The official text, *Ordo Hebdomadæ Sanctæ Instauratus* (OHS), was issued on 30 November 1955. On 1 February 1957 came Ordinations and Declarations of S.R.C. making some changes in the rubrics.

Obligation and Rite of Holy Week. The functions of Holy Week are of obligation in cathedral, collegiate and parish churches. When possible they should be carried out according to the solemn rite in such churches, and they may be so performed in all churches and public or semi-public oratories. In churches and oratories where the solemn rite cannot be carried out the ceremonies may be done in the manner set forth in OHS *Ritus Simplex* (1957) provided that (a) a minimum number of clerics or servers is available (i.e., three for Palm Sunday and Maundy Thursday, four for Good Friday and Holy Saturday); (b) servers are duly trained to do their part correctly.[1] If the ceremony of carrying the Blessed Sacrament to the place of repose is carried out after the evening Mass on Maundy Thursday, the Good Friday service must be performed in that church or oratory. The Easter vigil (Holy Saturday) ceremonies may be done even in churches or oratories where those of Maundy Thursday and Good Friday were not carried out; and they may be omitted in churches or oratories where these functions were performed.

In Mass during Holy Week all commemorations and *orationes imperatæ* are excluded.

When the Blessed Sacrament is present on the altar all salute It by a genuflexion. When It is not present the celebrant, prelates and canons salute the altar and its cross by a low bow, all others by a genuflexion during a function. When not even the cross is on the altar (as at the first part of the service on Good Friday) all salute the altar, during a function, by a bow of the head only.

In the services of Holy Week, two ferial tones are used for prayers. In the first or simple ferial tone — normally used for prayers with a long conclusion — the prayer is chanted from beginning to end on the same note

---

[1] These two conditions are insisted upon in a declaration of S.R.C. of 15 March 1956.

311

recto tono; there is no inflection, but at the colon, at the semi-colon, and at the end of both the prayer and its conclusion, the note is prolonged a little and softened. In the second or semi-festal tone—normally used for prayers with a short conclusion—the prayer is sung on one note, but on the last syllable,[2] at both the end of the prayer and of its conclusion, there is a flex, a fall of a minor third (d'l).

§ 2. Palm Sunday

On the Second Passion Sunday or Palm Sunday the solemn blessing of, and procession[3] with, palms in honour of Christ, the King, takes place, normally, in the morning after Terce. The Asperges is omitted. In addition to the celebrant, deacon and subdeacon, there should be two masters of ceremonies (MC1 and MC2), a thurifer, two acolytes, a cross-bearer (subdeacon or server) and torch-bearers. If the Passion is to be sung, three singers who are at least deacons will be needed.[4]

Preparations. The *high altar* is clothed in a violet frontal and over it a red[5] one; the tabernacle veiled in violet, and over this a red conopæum;[6] altar cross veiled in violet; branches of palm or other shrubs may be placed in vases between the candlesticks.

On the footpace or *in plano* in the sanctuary (to the epistle side if the Blessed Sacrament is present) a table—so placed that the people may easily see the blessing being done—covered with a white linen cloth. On it branches of palm,[7] olive, or other trees in a container, covered with a red veil; a copy of OHS or of the missal (on a lectern, if this is used); the aspersory and sprinkler. *The credence* holds all that is necessary for solemn Mass, covered with a violet humeral veil. *On an extra table* the missal-stand and altar-cards; a ewer of water, basin, soap and hand-towel for the washing of the celebrant's hands after the distribution of the palms. *On the sedilia* violet solemn Mass vestments for the sacred ministers.

On the gospel side of the sanctuary, three unveiled lecterns (their backs turned to the north wall) for the singing of the Passion.

In the sacristy: amices, albs, cinctures and birettas for the sacred ministers, red stole and cope for the celebrant, red stole and dalmatic for the deacon, red tunicle for the subdeacon. If the cross-bearer is a subdeacon, a red tunicle, amice, alb and cincture; if not, a surplice.

---

[2] On the last syllable but one in a word which is accented on the antepenult.

[3] If palms are blessed it is unlawful to omit the procession.

[4] If two any of the sacred ministers perform this function, see below note 13 below.

[5] Removed before Mass begins.

[6] Ditto.

[7] There must be at least sufficient for all those ministering and any clergy who may be present. Branches for the people may be brought by them or made available to them as they enter the church.

For the deacons of the Passion: amices, albs, cinctures and violet stoles; and the books containing the text of the Passion. Surplices for MC's and servers. The processional cross unveiled; thurible with good supply of well-lit charcoal and incense-boat; acolytes' candles and torches.

Note. If the blessing of palms takes place outside the church, as is recommended, in an adjoining building, from which the procession will start, or even in the open air, all that is necessary for the blessing is prepared there, and then the high altar and tabernacle of the church are covered in violet only and set up for Mass as usual.

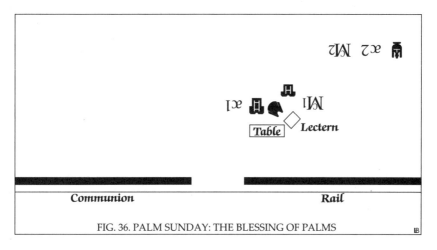

FIG. 36. PALM SUNDAY: THE BLESSING OF PALMS

Blessing of Palms. The celebrant, having washed his hands, vests, assisted by the deacon and subdeacon, already vested. Maniples are not worn. In the procession to the altar the celebrant walks between the deacon and subdeacon, who hold back the edges of his cope. The procession is led by MC2 and the thurifer, followed by the acolytes carrying candles. All salute the altar, genuflecting to the cross (except the celebrant).[8] The acolytes place their candles on the credence and stand before it; the thurifer stands near them. The sacred ministers go to the table on which the palms are prepared and stand facing the people. Meantime the choir sings the antiphon *Hosanna*. The first acolyte (or MC2) brings the aspersory. MC1 unveils the palms and holds the book and the celebrant, with hands joined, sings the *Dominus vobiscum* and the prayer of blessing, in the (second) ferial tone.[9] All make the responses. At the end of the prayer the celebrant sprinkles the palms with lustral water in silence, the deacon presenting the aspergil with the *solita oscula*. If the people are holding their own palms the sacred ministers go to the altar rail and from there the celebrant sprinkles the palms,[10] cross-wise (i.e.,

---

[8] He genuflects, too, if the Blessed Sacrament is present.

[9] A fall of a minor third (d'l) on the last syllable of the prayer and of its conclusion.

[10] The people hold up their palms for the sprinkling and incensation.

before him, to his left, to his right). Or the sacred ministers may go around the church, the celebrant sprinkling the palms all the while, the deacon and subdeacon holding the edges of the cope, and accompanied by MC1. Having sprinkled the palms the celebrant puts[11] in and blesses incense, and incenses the palms (with three single swings). He similarly incenses the people's palms either from the altar rail or walking around the church accompanied by the deacon and subdeacon as before.

Distribution of Palms. The celebrant goes to the altar, makes due reverence, ascends, kisses the altar and begins to distribute the palms to the deacon and subdeacon, any clergy who may be present and to the servers. Each one kneels on the footpace for this. Each genuflects at the foot of the altar before and after and kisses the palm and then the celebrant's hand. MC1 puts aside a palm for the celebrant in the procession.

If palms have to be distributed to the people, the celebrant does this at the altar rail. Each person kisses the palm and then the celebrant's hand. During the entire distribution the choir sings the appointed antiphons and psalms, repeating them, if necessary; they finish with *Gloria Patri* and the repetition of the antiphon, if the distribution ends earlier .

The Gospel. After the distribution the celebrant, at the extra credence, washes his hands, assisted by the acolytes. MC2 removes the table and the lectern. Accompanied by the deacon and subdeacon he salutes the altar, ascends, kisses the table, and, on the footpace, puts incense into the thurible. The deacon gets the book from MC2 and places it on the altar. Kneeling on the edge of the footpace he says *Munda cor meum.* Then he takes the book, kneels before the celebrant and asks his blessing. The celebrant gives it, all as at solemn Mass. Meanwhile the subdeacon goes to the foot of the altar and is there joined by MC2, the thurifer and acolytes. The deacon comes down. All genuflect to the cross (or to the Blessed Sacrament) and go to form the Gospel group, as at solemn Mass. The deacon sings the Gospel, the celebrant standing on the footpace at the epistle corner, facing him. After the Gospel all return to the foot of the altar, the subdeacon takes the Gospel text to the celebrant, who kisses it saying *Per evangelica dicta,* etc. The celebrant is not incensed, but goes at once to the middle of the footpace, where he is joined by the deacon and subdeacon.

The Procession. Towards the end of the Gospel the cross-bearer enters the sanctuary. MC2 leads him (with unveiled cross) and acolytes (with candles) to the entrance to the sanctuary. On the footpace the thurifer presents the thurible and incense is put in—in good quantity—for the procession; he then takes his place behind the cross-bearer to lead, with

---

[11] Whenever incense is put into the thurible (except when the Blessed Sacrament alone is to be incensed) it is blessed, the deacon saying *Benedicite, Pater reverende,* and the celebrant: *Ab illo benedicaris in cujus honore cremaberis.*

MC2, the procession. The deacon, facing the people, sings *Procedamus in* *pace;* all reply *In nomine Christi. Amen.* The sacred ministers descend to the foot of the altar and receive their birettas from MC1, and the celebrant takes his palm. Meantime MC2 starts the procession and directs the surpliced singers and the clergy into it, the juniors first. On a signal from MC1 the sacred ministers salute the altar and join the procession, the celebrant walking between the deacon and subdeacon, all three wearing their birettas. The people — carrying their palms — walk in the procession after the sacred ministers. When the procession does not come from another building, it should be a longish one and — when possible — go outside the church. During it the choir and the people sing the appointed seven antiphons, the hymn *Gloria laus* and Psalm 147 — or some of these according to the time occupied by the procession — and the people may add the hymn *Christus vincit* and other hymns in honour of Christ, the King.[12] As the procession re-enters the church, when the celebrant crosses the threshold the last antiphon *Ingrediente* is begun. On arriving in the sanctuary, the thurifer — having saluted the altar — and the cross-bearer and acolytes, lay aside what they are carrying and stand near the credence. If he was vested the cross-bearer goes to the sacristy and unvests. The sacred ministers give away their birettas, to MC1 and MC2, and their palms also, at the foot of the altar, salute this and go up to the footpace. The first acolyte brings the book and holds it before the celebrant, who, facing the people and with hands joined, sings *Dominus* *vobiscum* and, in the (second) ferial tone, the prayer that terminates the procession. All make the responses. The sacred ministers salute the altar and go *per breviorem* to the sedilia, where they exchange their red vestments for violet ones for the Mass, aided by the masters of cere-monies. MC1 removes the red conopæum and frontal. MC2 and the acolytes go to the sacristy.

The Mass. The preparatory prayers are omitted, and so the sacred ministers — having saluted the clergy in choir and the altar — go up at once to the altar; and the celebrant, having kissed the altar, at once incenses it. Meantime the choir sings the introit, which the celebrant recites after he has been incensed. With the deacon he genuflects towards the book, at the epistle corner, as the subdeacon sings *ut in nomine Iesu,* etc. Having blessed the subdeacon, he reads the gradual and tract. The celebrant does not read the Passion. Having, from the centre of the footpace, blessed the three deacons, who kneel at the foot of the altar, he goes to the epistle corner and stands there facing the deacons while they chant the Passion, the deacon on his left on the top step, the subdeacon on his left on a lower step or *in plano.*[13] If the Passion is not sung, the

---

[12] These may be in the vernacular, but they may not be translations of liturgical hymns.
[13] If the celebrant has to supply the place of a deacon for the chanting of the Passion, he sings the *Christus* part in chasuble standing at the gospel corner of the altar using the missal

celebrant recites *Munda cor meum, Iube, Domine,* etc., bowed at the centre of the altar, and then reads the Passion at the gospel corner, the deacon on his right, the subdeacon on his left.

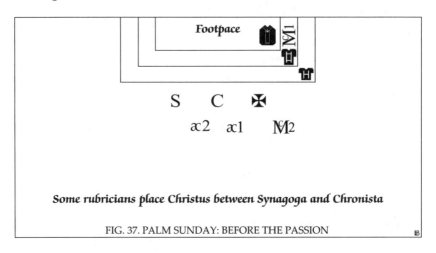

FIG. 37. PALM SUNDAY: BEFORE THE PASSION

The Passion. During the singing of the gradual and tract the three deacons who are to sing the Passion—assisted by MC2 and two servers— vest in the sacristy in amice, alb, cincture and violet stole (worn over the left shoulder) and biretta. When the chanting of the tract is finished MC2 leads out the deacons—each carrying a book—in this order: the narrator *(Chronista),* then the deacon who is to sing the parts of individuals other than our Lord *(Synagoga),* followed by the deacon who is to sing the part of our Lord *(Christus),*[14] lastly come the two servers, walking abreast and without lights. At the entrance to the choir the deacons give away their birettas to the servers, salute the clergy in choir, genuflect before the altar and kneel on the lowest step. Bowed, they recite *Munda cor meum* in a low tone, and then—in the medium voice—ask the celebrant's blessing, saying *Iube, domne, benedicere.* The celebrant, facing the deacons, gives the blessing, in the medium voice *(Dominus sit in cordibus vestris,* etc.) and makes the sign of the cross over them. They answer *Amen,* rise, genuflect and go to the lecterns on the gospel side; S. goes first, then C. and lastly ✠. Before the lectern and facing north—C. stands in the middle, with ✠ on his right. The servers may stand behind the lecterns facing the deacons. The latter do not sign the book or themselves, but C. immediately begins the Passion. After the words *emisit spiritum* the deacons kneel facing the lecterns; the celebrant, deacon and subdeacon

stand, which is moved there by the subdeacon as usual. If the deacon or subdeacon (provided the latter is at least in deacon's orders), must do so, they remove the dalmatic or tunicle and wear the diaconal stole; cf. O'Connell, *Ceremonies of Holy Week,* 1959, p. 12.

[14] In the text their parts are indicated by C., S. and ✠. The crowd parts may be sung by the choir.

kneel where they are facing the deacons. On a signal from MC1, all rise and the Passion is continued. When it is finished the deacons, led by MC2, and followed by the two servers, go to the foot of the altar, genuflect, receive their birettas, salute the clergy in choir and return to the sacristy. The celebrant does not kiss the book at the end of the Passion; nor is *Laus tibi, Christe* said. MC1 moves the missal to the gospel side, near to the centre.

Continuation of Mass. The rest of the Mass follows the ordinary rite of solemn Mass except that (a) *Orate, fratres* is said in the clear voice, (b) *Ite, Missa est* is said, (c) there is no last Gospel.

Note. If a priest celebrates a second or third Mass on Palm Sunday he is not obliged to repeat the Passion. Instead he may say the special Gospel (Matt. 27, 45-52) provided in § 11 of OHS. In all Masses at which the liturgy of the day does not take place the ordinary rite of Mass must be followed, and the last Gospel will be that used at the blessing of the palms (*Cum appropinquasset*). The rectors of churches are to have a supply of blessed palms at hand, so that persons who have not been able to be present at the blessing and procession may obtain a palm to take home with them if they so desire.[15]

§ 3. Palm Sunday in Small Churches

The rite of Palm Sunday in small churches or oratories, where only three servers, and possibly no choir, are available is set forth in the *Ordo Hebdomadæ Sanctæ Instauratus, Ritus Simplex*,[16] issued by S.R.C. on 5 February 1957. This book replaces the *Memoriale Rituum* of Benedict XIII —dealing with the functions of six days in the year, in small parish churches—for the ceremonies of Holy Week and may be used not only in parish churches, but also in public and semi-public oratories, where it is not feasible to follow the solemn rite. The Mass may be a sung one or a low Mass.

Preparations. On the *high altar*, the cross veiled in violet; a red frontal over a violet one; on the tabernacle a red conopæum over a violet one. Palm or other branches may be placed between the candlesticks.

In the sanctuary, at a spot—either *in plano* or on the footpace (to the epistle side if the Blessed Sacrament is present)—where the people can see the blessing, a table covered with a white cloth, and on it palms or other greenery; and a lectern.[17] *On the gospel side, in plano*, a lectern, covered with a red veil and facing north for the Gospel. *On the epistle side*, the processional cross, unveiled; the sedilia, and on it the violet

---

[15] S.R.C., 1 February 1957, § 7.
[16] Cited as "R.S."
[17] At least sufficient for all in the sanctuary, if the people have their own.

vestments for Mass.[18] *On the credence,* the chalice prepared for Mass, with violet veil and burse;[19] a ciborium with breads for Holy Communion; the communion plate; cruets, hand-towel and bell; OHS or missal containing the rite;[20] ewer of water, basin, soap and hand-towel for the washing of the priest's hands after the distribution of the palms; books for the servers if, in the absence of a choir, they are to recite the antiphons, etc., with the celebrant. If extra servers are available, acolytes' candles to be carried beside the cross in the procession.

In the sacristy: Amice, alb, cincture, red stole and cope[21] for the celebrant; cassocks and surplices for the (three) servers; a ritual or *Ritus Servandus* for the blessing of lustral water, aspersory of water with sprinkler, and some salt; thurible with well-lit charcoal and incense-boat; torches (if the Mass is to be sung and extra servers are available).

Note. If there is a suitable place adjoining the church and the blessing of the palms is to take place there, all that is necessary for the blessing and procession is prepared there; and at the high altar the frontal and conopæum will be violet from the beginning.

Blessing of Palms. The celebrant, having washed his hands, vests in amice, alb, cincture and red stole, assisted by the second and third servers (S.2, S.3). The first server (S.1) lights the altar candles. The celebrant then vests in red cope, if available. S.1 takes the aspersory to the credence in the sanctuary. The celebrant, having bowed to the sacristy crucifix and put on his biretta, goes between S.1 and S.2—holding back the edges of his cope—to the altar; S.3, with the thurible and boat, leads the way. Surpliced singers or extra servers follow S.3. On arrival at the altar the celebrant gives away his biretta to S.1 and all salute the altar.[22] The celebrant goes to the table and stands facing the people; S.1 gets the aspersory from the credence and stands on his right; S.2 gets the book (if it is not on a lectern) and holds it towards the celebrant's left. S.3 stands on the celebrant's left. Meanwhile the antiphon *Hosanna* is sung; if there is no choir, the assisting clergy recite it or the celebrant says it with the servers. With hands joined the celebrant says[23] *Dominus vobiscum* and, in the (second) ferial tone,[24] the prayer. All make the responses. After the prayer the celebrant sprinkles the palms with lustral water, in silence. If the people already have their palms,[25] the celebrant goes to the altar-rail

---

[18] Unless it is found more convenient to prepare these in the sacristy.
[19] Unless one of the servers is a (tonsured) cleric, the chalice must be made ready on the altar by the priest.
[20] If a lectern is used the book will be on this, to the left of the table with the palms.
[21] If a red cope is not available he ministers in alb and stole.
[22] The celebrant with a deep bow (a genuflexion if the Blessed Sacrament is present), the others with a genuflexion.
[23] "Says" means "recites" or "sings" as the case may be (as R.S. uses *dicit*).
[24] A fall of a minor third (d'l) on the last syllable of the prayer and of its conclusion.
[25] They may bring them with them or receive them at the door of the church as they enter.

and sprinkles them cross-wise (before him, to his left and to his right); or he may go around the church, sprinkling continuously as he proceeds — S.1 holding the aspersory and cope on his left, S.2 holding back the cope on his right. After the sprinkling incense is put in the thurible held by S.3,[26] S.1 presenting the boat. The celebrant incenses the palms on the table with three single swings, crosswise. He then similarly incenses the people's palms at the altar rail, or continuously while walking around the church accompanied by S.1 and S.2 who hold back the edges of the cope. After the incensation S.3 takes the thurible to the sacristy; S.1 lays aside a palm for the celebrant to carry in the procession.

Distribution of Palms. The celebrant goes to the altar, makes due reverence, ascends, kisses the altar and begins to distribute the palms to any clergy who may be present, and at least to the servers. Each one kneels on the footpace for this. Each genuflects at the foot of the altar before and after and kisses the palm and then the celebrant's hand.

If the people do not already have their palms, the celebrant, assisted by the servers, distributes them at the altar rails; the people kiss the palm and then the celebrant's hand. During the distribution the choir sings — or assisting clergy recite — the appointed antiphons and psalms. If there are no singers or assisting clergy, the celebrant, before the distribution, recites with the servers the two antiphons *Pueri Hebræorum,* without the psalms. After the distribution the celebrant, assisted by the servers, washes his hands, standing at the sedilia. The servers move aside the table and lectern that were used for the blessing.

The Gospel. If the function is sung the celebrant, standing at the sedilia, puts incense into the thurible. Taking the book he goes, with the servers, before the altar, kneels on the lowest step and, bowed, says, in a low voice, *Munda cor meum, Iube, Domine, benedicere,* and *Dominus sit in corde meo,* etc. He rises, salutes the altar, goes to the lectern *in plano* on the gospel side of the sanctuary, places the book on it, incenses it as in a sung Mass, and sings or says the Gospel *Cum appropinquasset.* The servers stand behind him facing north. At the end of the Gospel the celebrant kisses the book saying *Per evangelica dicta* and the servers reply *Laus tibi, Christe.* The celebrant returns, with the servers, before the altar, makes due reverence to it and puts incense in the thurible for the procession.

The Procession. Facing the people the celebrant says *Procedamus in pace,* and all answer *In nomine Christi. Amen.* S.1 hands the celebrant his biretta, his palm, and — if necessary — the book for the texts to be sung or recited in the procession.[27] The cantors, or assisting clergy, begin the antiphon *Occurrunt turbæ;* if none are present the celebrant recites it and

---

[26] Each time incense is put into the thurible, S.1 asks a blessing *(Benedicite, Pater reverende)* and the celebrant blesses the incense, saying *ab illo benedicaris,* etc., and making the sign of the cross.

[27] He will also hand a book to S.2 and take one himself if they need them in the procession.

the other texts during the procession with the servers. The people should join in as much as possible, especially in the repetition of the refrain of the hymn *Gloria laus*. They may also sing *Christus vincit* and other hymns in honour of Christ the King, even in the vernacular (though not vernacular translations of liturgical hymns). S.3 leads the procession, carrying the cross; S.1 and S.2 accompany the celebrant who wears his biretta (S.1 and S.2 do not carry palms but hold back the celebrant's cope). They are followed by the people, bearing their palms. If, however, extra servers are available, S.3 will head the procession carrying a smoking thurible; S.4 will carry the unveiled cross, at his sides S.5 and S.6 with lighted candles; and these are followed by any clergy or other servers who may be present. The procession should not be a short one and should, if possible, go outside the church. The better way is to bless the palms in some adjoining suitable place (or even in the open air, before a shrine or even before the processional cross) and thence lead the procession to the church. As this enters the church, while the celebrant crosses the threshold, the Responsory *Ingrediente Domino* is begun. When the procession arrives before the altar S.3 (or S.4) puts aside the cross (the extra servers their candles, on the credence) and fetches the book for the concluding prayer. At the foot of the altar the celebrant gives away his biretta and palm to S.1, salutes the altar, goes up to the footpace, and standing between S.1 and S.2, facing the people with hands joined, he says *Dominus vobiscum*, and—in the second ferial tone—the prayer. S.3 holds the book. All make the responses. Then, having saluted the altar, the celebrant, with S.1 and S.2, goes *per breviorem* to the sedilia, and puts on the violet vestments for Mass assisted by S.1 and S.2. S.1 puts the book on the altar at the epistle corner .

The Mass. If S.1 is a cleric he should bring the chalice up to the altar. Otherwise the celebrant should himself take it from the credence to the altar. The celebrant then goes to the foot of the altar, salutes it, ascends at once—there are no preparatory prayers—saying nothing, kisses the table, and says the introit.[28] Having read the gradual and tract,[29] the celebrant, bowed at the centre of the altar, says *Munda cor meum, Iube, Domine, benedicere, Dominus sit in corde meo,* etc. Meanwhile one of the servers moves the book to the gospel corner of the altar. There the celebrant, without signing the book or himself, nor saying an introduction, says the Passion.[30] The book is not kissed and *Laus tibi...* is not said.

If there are three deacons to sing or read the Passion, after having read the tract, the celebrant, at the epistle corner, facing the deacons—who,

---

[28] If the Mass is a sung one, incense is used, and the altar is first incensed, exactly as at solemn Mass.

[29] If the Mass is sung, and a lector is available, he—in choir dress—chants the Epistle, and the celebrant does not then read it.

[30] If on Palm Sunday a priest has to celebrate a second or a third Mass, he is not obliged to repeat the Passion, but may say instead the Gospel provided in OHS, § 11.

kneeling on the lowest step, have recited *Munda cor meum* and asked his blessing—gives them the blessing *(Dominus sit in cordibus vestris,* etc.). In this case he does not himself read the Passion, but listens to it, standing at the sedilia. If only two deacons are available to sing or read the Passion, the celebrant standing on the footpace at the gospel corner, and retaining his chasuble takes the *Christus* part. In this case *Munda cor meum* is said by the celebrant, in a low voice, bowed at the middle of the altar on the footpace, while the two deacons are reciting it, kneeling, bowed, on the lowest step. All three say in a low voice *Iube, Domine, benedicere,* and *Dominus sit in corde meo,* etc., like the celebrant in low Mass.

Palms are not held by anyone during the Passion, and at its close the celebrant does not kiss the book; nor is *Laus tibi, Christe* said. At the end of Mass *Ite, missa est* is said and the last Gospel is omitted.[31]

§ 4. The Passion on Tuesday and Wednesday

The Passion is sung or read in the same manner on Tuesday and Wednesday of Holy Week as on Palm Sunday. On Wednesday it is the deacon who, before the first prayer, is to sing *Levate*—after some moments of prayer following *Flectamus genua*—in a solemn Mass; the celebrant in a low Mass.

---

[31] In Masses at which the liturgy of the day does not take place, the last Gospel will be *Cum appropinquasset* from the blessing of the palms.

Chapter XXVI

The Sacred Triduum

§ 1. The Divine Office (in Choir)

DURING the Triduum Sacrum (Maundy Thursday, Good Friday and Holy Saturday) the rules for the Divine Office sung in choir, or recited in common, are these: (1) Matins and Lauds are not anticipated, but said in the morning at the appropriate hour. But in churches where the Mass of the Chrism takes place on Maundy Thursday morning, Matins and Lauds may be anticipated on Wednesday evening. (2) The Small Hours are said at the normal hour. (3) On Thursday and Friday Vespers are omitted, being replaced by the liturgy of the afternoon or evening, and on Saturday Compline is omitted.

The private recitation of the Office on these three days[1] follows the rubrics of the breviary (care should be taken that the edition used conforms to the code of rubrics for the breviary issued by Blessed John XXIII in 1960).

Tenebræ [2]

This Office is simply Matins and Lauds of each day of the Sacred Triduum. This Office may not be anticipated (and so recited at night) except in a church in which the Mass of the Chrism is to be celebrated on Maundy Thursday morning. There Matins and Lauds may be anticipated on Wednesday evening.

Preparations. The six candles on the altar should be of unbleached wax; the candlesticks the plainer ones used for Good Friday. On Thursday the altar cross is veiled in violet as during Passiontide; on Friday the altar is completely bare; on Saturday the unveiled cross and candlesticks, but no altar cloths. The frontal is violet on Thursday; there is none on Friday or Saturday. The Blessed Sacrament should be removed. On the epistle side of the choir, at about the place where the Epistle is read, the hearse[3] stands, bearing fifteen candles of unbleached wax.[4] An

---

[1] But a priest who has taken part in the liturgy of the day may omit the private recitation of Vespers on Thursday and Friday, and Compline on Holy Saturday.

[2] C.E., II, xxii.

[3] The hearse is a tall staff supporting a triangle on which are fifteen spikes or sockets for candles. Originally the word meant a harrow (a triangle with spikes). The Tenebræ hearse is so called because it looks like a harrow. Such triangles of candles were erected on the stand where a coffin rests in church; so this too is still called a hearse.

extinguisher should be near or, if convenient, one at each side. In the middle of the choir a lectern stands, uncovered, facing east, with a breviary for the lessons. At Tenebræ on Thursday the altar carpet may be violet. In the other two cases there should be no carpet before the altar at all. The candles on the altar and all those of the hearse are lighted for the function.

The procession to the choir should proceed in this order: the MC, the server, the two cantors, celebrant, the choir, those of greater dignity before the others. All wear choir dress (cassock and plain surplice, except for prelates or canons). The person who presides has neither stole nor cope. He occupies the first place in choir. At Tenebræ on Friday and Saturday no reverences are made to the choir.[5] All salute the bare altar with a bow on Friday; all genuflect to the cross on Saturday. If a server is present he should sit on a stool near the hearse.

The singing of Tenebræ may not be accompanied by the organ.

Matins. The Ceremonial (II, xxii, 6) does not suppose that the antiphons be pre-intoned at Tenebræ. The first antiphon is intoned by the cantors and sung by the choir. The cantors intone the first psalm either at their places or in the middle of the choir; all sit, put on the biretta, and continue it. Everything proceeds as usual at Matins (cf. Chapter XXII § 2) except that the verses *Gloria Patri* and *Sicut erat* are not sung at the end of the psalms.

At the end of the first psalm the MC, or a server appointed for this purpose, goes to the hearse and—having reverenced to the altar if necessary and, on Thursday, to the clergy in choir—extinguishes the lowest candle on the gospel side. At the end of the second psalm he extinguishes the lowest candle on the epistle side. So he extinguishes a candle after every psalm, going to alternate sides to do so. There are fourteen psalms in Tenebræ, nine at Matins and five at Lauds. When the last psalm of Lauds is finished, he will have extinguished all the candles, except the one in the middle at the summit of the triangle. This remains alight until the service ends.

At the end of the third psalm of each nocturn of Matins the versicle and response appointed are sung, the versicle by the cantors. Then all stand and say the Lord's Prayer silently. All sit again and put on the biretta. The lessons are sung at the lectern in the middle. The MC should go to each lector, beginning with those of lower rank, accompany him to the lectern (having made due reverence to the altar and—on Thursday—to the clergy) and stand at his left behind while he chants, holding his biretta. The lessons are chanted without asking first for a blessing, and without the final clause *Tu autem, Domine, miserere nobis.* While chanting

---

[4] All the candles should be unbleached. There is no authority for using a white candle in the centre.

[5] Cf. S.R.C. 3059 § 27.

the lector lays his hands on the book. There should be nine lectors chosen beforehand. The celebrant does not sing the last lesson. The lessons of the first nocturn (Lamentations of Ieremias) have a special tone. Any or all of these may be sung by the choir, in which case no one goes to the lectern. At the end of each lesson the lector and MC repeat the reverence to the altar—and, on Thursday, to the choir—and the MC conducts the lector back to his place.

Lauds. Lauds follows immediately after the ninth responsory; all rise for the intonation, sitting after that of the first psalm. All stand when the *Benedictus* is begun. The *Benedictus* has twelve verses. During the last six of these (beginning with *Ut sine timore*) the same server who put out the candles on the hearse puts out one of the six candles on the altar, beginning with the farthest candle on the gospel side. Next time he puts out the farthest on the epistle side, and so on alternately; or the MC and server may, taking up positions on the Gospel and Epistles sides, extinguish candles on their sides. As soon as the last candle on the altar is extinguished, all lights in the church are put out by a sacristan, except those which burn before the tabernacle. The lamps are not lit again till after the third singing of *Lumen Christi* on Holy Saturday night.

While the antiphon at the end of the *Benedictus* is sung, all in choir sit.

Christus Factus Est. As soon as the antiphon *Christus factus est* is begun, all kneel; *Pater noster* is said silently; he who presides says the prayer *Respice,* the conclusion silently. Then all rise, salute the altar and depart in silence, seniors first.

§ 2. Maundy Thursday

The Mass of the Chrism is celebrated in the morning after Terce. The Mass of the Lord's Supper is to be celebrated in the evening, at a suitable hour, but not before 4 p.m. or after 9 p.m.[6] Where pastoral needs so require, the Ordinary of the place may permit one or two low Masses in each church or public oratory, one Mass only in semi-public oratories. These Masses must be said not earlier than 4 p.m. nor later than 9 p.m., and follow the normal rite of low Mass.[7] On this day Holy Communion (except for the sick[8]) may be given only within the evening Mass, or immediately after it and in connection with it.

Those taking part in the evening Mass on Maundy Thursday are the celebrant, deacon and subdeacon, two MC's, a cross-bearer (a subdeacon in alb and white tunicle, or a server in surplice), two thurifers, two

---

[6] S.R.C., 1 February 1957, § 8.

[7] The Leonine prayers may be omitted.

[8] To them Holy Communion may be given at any hour of the day (S.R.C., 1 February 1957, § 12).

acolytes, torch-bearers (four or six), canopy-bearers according to the number of poles.

Preparations. *The altar* is adorned soberly, and clothed in white; the altar cross is veiled in white. *The tabernacle* is empty,[9] unveiled, half open; its key at hand. OHS or a missal is placed at the epistle corner of the altar. *On the credence* the chalice[10] prepared for Mass; ciboria with sufficient breads for Holy Communion on Thursday and Friday, with their veils; communion cloth (if used); Gospel book; cruets with bowl and hand-towel; bells to ring during *Gloria in excelsis,* if this is customary; clappers (if used). All the things on the credence are covered with a white humeral veil. *Aside in the sanctuary,* the processional cross veiled in violet.[11] Outside the altar rail a canopy (to be carried over the Blessed Sacrament in procession), or a white umbella; candles for the clergy distributed on the choir stalls.

If the washing of feet is to take place: on a second credence, a large ewer of water, basin and twelve towels; an apron for the celebrant;[12] ewer of water, basin, soap and a towel for the washing of the celebrant's hands. At the west end of the sanctuary seats or one or two benches placed in front of the choir stalls for the twelve men whose feet are to be washed.

In the sacristy: white solemn Mass vestments for the three sacred ministers; a white cope;[13] violet stoles for the celebrant and deacon (for the stripping of the altars); surplices for MC's and servers; two thuribles, charcoal, incense; acolytes' candles; torches (four or six); white stoles[14] for priests or deacons who may be present in choir.

The rites of Maundy Thursday and Good Friday require two places to be prepared for the Blessed Sacrament: (i) the "place of repose" *(locum repositionis),* where one ciborium of Sacred Hosts for Holy Communion on Friday is kept after the evening Mass of Thursday; (ii) the "place of reservation," where older Hosts from before that Mass are kept, extra ciboria (if necessary) for Friday, and all Hosts after the communion service on Friday until after the Easter Vigil Mass. The former should be some chapel (or altar) of the church—with a lockable tabernacle (or casket) to contain the ciborium—soberly adorned with precious hangings and lights (at least four wax candles with other lights), but no images or relics. It is becoming to adorn the altar or table with a white frontal over which an altar cloth is spread; a corporal is spread in the tabernacle (or casket) and another before it (the burse placed aside as at Mass). The key

---

[9] Except it should have a corporal in it.

[10] With one bread only.

[11] Or this may be prepared in the sacristy.

[12] An amice serves the purpose.

[13] Or this may be made ready near the sedilia, on a cope-stand or draped over a lectern, preferably out of view.

[14] They wear these from the beginning of the function until the stripping of altars, exclusively.

should be at hand, and a conopæum to cover the tabernacle while the Blessed Sacrament is in it, as well as the lamp to be lighted after the public veneration of the reserved Sacrament ends.[15] The place of reservation—where the Blessed Sacrament is kept for Holy Communion of the sick, but not for public veneration—is some suitable place, outside the church, if possible,[16] containing a tabernacle for the safe custody of the Blessed Sacrament. This should be covered with a white conopæum, have a corporal within, and its key at hand. Before it a corporal is spread; two candles are prepared (to be lighted when the Blessed Sacrament is to be brought there or removed), and the lamp to be lit while the Blessed Sacrament is present.

Beginning of Mass. During the procession through the church to the altar the introit is sung, and may be prolonged by singing verses of psalm 66, repeating the antiphon after each verse or two. The *Iudica* psalm is omitted (as always during Passiontide). The celebrant having incensed the altar and recited the introit and *Kyrie, eleison,* intones the *Gloria.* The church bells are rung and the organ played;[17] if customary, small bells may also be rung in the sanctuary until the recitation finishes. The celebrant sits to listen to the subdeacon chanting the Epistle, and then returns to the epistle corner on the footpace to bless the subdeacon and to read the gradual. The celebrant blesses incense and the deacon as usual.

Washing of Feet. The washing of feet (the Mandatum) may take place within Mass, after the short homily, but is not of obligation. Twelve men—clerics or laymen—are chosen for the ceremony. At the sedilia the celebrant removes his maniple and chasuble and is girded with an apron. The deacon and subdeacon take off their maniples. The first acolyte gets the ewer of water, the second the basin and towels. Meanwhile the deacon and subdeacon, led by MC2, conduct the men, two by two, to the places prepared for them in the sanctuary. On their way they genuflect to the altar and bow to the celebrant. The choir (or clergy present) begin the chanting or recitation of the prescribed antiphons, etc., and continue these while the washing lasts. Towards its close they begin the antiphon *Ubi caritas,* with its verses, which must never be omitted. The sacred ministers, with the thurifer and acolytes behind them, salute the altar and go in procession, led by MC2, to the first man.[18] They all kneel before him thus: the celebrant immediately before him, having the deacon on his right and the subdeacon on his left; the first acolyte is on the deacon's right a little in front of him; the thurifer behind the deacon, on his left; the second acolyte to the left of the subdeacon. As the procession approaches

---

[15] It is useful to have a second incense-boat in this chapel.

[16] If a chapel of the church must be used, a curtain should be drawn across to cut it off.

[17] It may accompany the chant of the entire *Gloria* but must then be silent until the *Gloria* of the Easter Vigil Mass.

[18] The one nearest the altar on the epistle side.

him each man removes his shoe and sock from his right foot.[19] The subdeacon raises the man's foot and the first acolyte pours a little water over it,[20] the second acolyte holding the basin underneath. The celebrant washes the foot a little with his right hand and then dries it with a towel handed to him by the deacon. When the washing has been completed the sacred ministers and servers salute the altar and go to the epistle side of the sanctuary. Near the credence the celebrant—assisted by the acolytes, who have laid aside the vessels used for the Mandatum, and by the deacon—washes his hands, and then removes his apron. He resumes his maniple and chasuble, and the deacon and subdeacon put on their maniples. The sacred ministers, having saluted the altar, go up to the footpace, and, facing the people, the celebrant sings *Pater noster*, the versicles, and—in the second ferial tone—the prayer. One of the acolytes holds the book. After the prayer, the men are conducted by the deacon and subdeacon back to their places in the church, having first genuflected to the altar and bowed to the celebrant. If the men are clerics, they sit in choir. The offertory follows, the *Credo* is not said.

If the Mandatum takes place outside of Mass, it is carried out as described above, in some suitable place in the church away from the altar of repose, or outside the church. White vestments are used, the celebrant wearing a white stole and cope—the latter of which he removes for the actual washing—and no maniple. At the beginning of the service, however, the Gospel *Ante diem festum Paschæ* (from the Mass of Maundy Thursday) is sung by the deacon, exactly as at solemn Mass. The deacon and subdeacon, who are in white dalmatic and tunicle, do not wear maniples.

Continuation of Mass. *Orate, fratres* is said in a clear voice that all may reply. If customary, the clappers may be used where the bell would, normally, be rung, at *Sanctus*, etc. Otherwise the bells are left silent. There is a proper *Communicantes, Hanc igitur* and *Qui pridie*. The reply to the third *Agnus Dei* invocation is *Miserere nobis*. The kiss of peace is not given, and the first prayer after *Agnus Dei, Domine Iesu*, is omitted. For the communion of the clergy and servers on the footpace, the acolytes hold the communion cloth (if used). The deacon holds the paten under the chin of each communicant. Extra priests or deacons—in choir dress and white stole—may aid the celebrant to distribute Holy Communion. During the communion the choir may sing the communion antiphon, and may chant psalms 22, 71, 103, 150, repeating the antiphon after each psalm (but no *Gloria Patri*). After the communion the ciborium is left on the corporal[21] and Mass is finished with the ceremonial of Mass *coram*

---

[19] He replaces them after his foot has been dried.

[20] Or the celebrant may do this.

[21] If there are extra ciboria they may be moved to the place of reservation immediately after communion, if there is a priest or deacon available to do this, or else they are put into the tabernacle and removed before the stripping of the altars (Cf. R.S., II, II, iv, 7).

Sanctissimo.[22] *Benedicamus Domino* is sung by the deacon, instead of *Ite*, and the celebrant recites *Placeat* and kisses the altar, but there is no blessing or last Gospel.[23] The sacred ministers make a double genuflexion at the foot of the altar, and go to the sedilia. Meanwhile MC1 fetches the cope and then, if necessary, lights the candles of the senior clergy in choir. There they remove their maniples and the celebrant exchanges his chasuble for a white cope, each taking care not to turn his back on the Blessed Sacrament. Meanwhile MC2 marshals those who are to take part in the procession to the altar of repose: two thurifers, the cross-bearer[24] and acolytes (with candles), a banner if carried, the torch-bearers,[25] the clergy who carry lighted candles and the canopy-bearers.

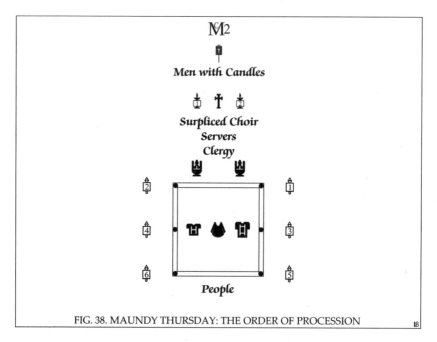

FIG. 38. MAUNDY THURSDAY: THE ORDER OF PROCESSION

Transfer of the Blessed Sacrament. When all is ready for the procession, the sacred ministers go to the foot of the altar, make a double genuflexion *in plano*, kneel on the lowest step and say a brief prayer. Then the celebrant puts incense — which he does not bless — into two thuribles, and with one incenses the Blessed Sacrament. He then receives the humeral veil from MC1, and the three sacred ministers rise and go up to the footpace and genuflect there. The deacon hands the ciborium to the celebrant, standing, and arranges the ends of the humeral veil over it. The

[22] O'Connell, *The Celebration of Mass*, 1964, p. 561.
[23] Extra low Masses allowed by the Ordinary end in the normal way.
[24] If he is a subdeacon he vests in amice, alb, cincture and white tunicle in the sacristy during the communion.
[25] They remain in the sanctuary after the communion.

celebrant faces the people, the deacon and subdeacon change places behind him, and are at his sides holding the cope for the procession. MC1 holds the umbella over the celebrant until he passes under the canopy waiting outside the altar rails. The procession is led by MC2, followed by the standard usually carried in processions—if carried; men[26] carrying candles (in the outside hand); the cross-bearer and acolytes, the surpliced choir, servers, the clergy[27] (each carrying a lighted candle in the outside hand), the two thurifers—walking forward but slightly turned towards the Blessed Sacrament, swinging their thuribles at the inside continuously—and, under the canopy, the sacred ministers. When the procession begins, the *Pange lingua* is begun by the cantors, and is sung by all up to *Tantum ergo* exclusively. If the length of the procession requires it the strophes are repeated—beginning always at the second verse—or other hymns or psalms may be sung.

At the Altar of Repose. On arrival at the chapel of the reposition, the cross-bearer and acolytes move to one side, the choir and clergy take up their positions at each side (the seniors nearer the altar). The torch-bearers go near to the altar and kneel immediately. MC1 goes to the right and kneels. The thurifers keel on either side a few feet back from the step. The sacred ministers pass from under the canopy and go to the altar, where the celebrant, aided by the deacon, places the ciborium on the corporal spread before the tabernacle. The sacred ministers genuflect and then kneel on the lowest step. An MC removes the humeral veil. *Tantum ergo* is sung. The other MC assists as the celebrant places incense into the thurible of the first thurifer when *Genitori Genitoque* is sung—again, not blessing it—and incenses the Blessed Sacrament. The deacon puts the ciborium into the tabernacle or casket—genuflecting before and after, standing back a little from the table—closes and locks the door. He then folds the corporal and replaces it in the burse, placing the burse flat on the middle of the altar. The clergy extinguish their candles, the torch-bearers their torches. After some moments of prayer, on a signal from MC1, all stand, and make a double genuflexion (except the cross-bearer and acolytes). The clergy are conducted by MC2 back to the choir for the stripping of the altars. The cross-bearer and acolytes, followed by the torch-bearers and MC1, lead the sacred ministers back to the sacristy; when out of sight of the Blessed Sacrament the sacred ministers out on their birettas (which will have been brought by a sacristan). In the sacristy they take off their white vestments, and the celebrant and deacon don violet stoles.[28] Any extra ciboria should now be removed by a priest

---

[26] While OHS does not expressly mention laymen in this procession, R.S. does (*sodales vel pii viri*).
[27] All make a double genuflexion (except the cross-bearer, acolytes and thurifers) before departing from the sanctuary.
[28] The celebrant, being in an alb, wears the stole crossed.

or deacon—vested in surplice and white stole and with the humeral veil—to the place of reservation. Candles should be extinguished.

Stripping of altars. The sacred ministers, covered, preceded by MC2 with the OHS, the acolytes and MC1, go to the high altar, saluting the clergy as they enter the choir. The celebrant bows to the altar whilst all others genuflect. The celebrant, standing, says aloud the antiphon *Dividunt* and the opening words of Psalm 21. The clergy (seated) continue the psalm until the stripping ends. If there are no clergy in choir, the celebrant recites the Antiphon and the first verse only of Psalm 21. The sacred ministers go up to the altar and carry out the stripping, assisted by the MC's and the acolytes. Everything is removed without ceremony—including carpets—except the cross and candlesticks.[29] The sanctuary lamp is extinguished and the tabernacle door is left open. Having stripped the high altar, the sacred ministers, with their attendants, strip all other altars—except, of course, the altar of repose—beginning with the altar nearest the high altar on the gospel side. Should they pass the altar of repose, all make a double genuflexion. When the stripping is finished they return to the high altar and there the celebrant repeats the antiphon. Then all salute the cross and depart to the sacristy.[30] Compline in choir, soon after,[31] is recited only, and without lighted candles.

Adoration of Blessed Sacrament. Public adoration of the Blessed Sacrament at the altar of repose goes on until midnight. After that it suffices to have one lamp burning there, and flowers (if used) should be removed, as the commemoration of the Passion has begun.

§ 3. Maundy Thursday in Small Churches

The Mass of the Lord's Supper is to be celebrated in the evening between 4 p.m. and 9 p.m. and may be a sung Mass (when the use of incense is allowed[32]) or a low Mass. Normally, only one Mass will be celebrated, at which all—clergy and laity—go to Holy Communion, but if pastoral reasons so demand, the Ordinary of the place may permit one or two extra low Masses in any church or public oratory, one extra only in a semi-public oratory. Any extra Mass must be celebrated within the specified times. Holy Communion may be given—except for the sick—only within Mass, or immediately after Mass and in connection with it. At least three servers are needed for Mass, and a fourth for the

---

[29] The candles are extinguished before the stripping begins.
[30] Lustral water is removed from the church stoups after the evening Mass. Some must be kept in the sacristy for the blessing of the new fire on Saturday.
[31] In religious houses it may be recited later (S.R.C., 23 July 1956).
[32] Then it is used exactly as at solemn Mass.

procession; a fifth will be needed to carry the umbella (if there are no canopy-bearers); if possible, two more to carry candles by the cross.

Preparations. *The altar* is adorned soberly, with a white frontal and the cross veiled in white;[33] the tabernacle empty (except for a corporal), unveiled, half-open, the key at hand; OHS or missal at the epistle corner of the altar; altar cards. *On credence 1*, the chalice[34] prepared for Mass (one bread only); ciboria with sufficient breads for Holy Communion at this Mass and on Good Friday, and veil(s) ; communion plate;[35] cruets and hand-towel, bells to ring during *Gloria in excelsis* (if customary); clappers;[36] acolytes' candles (if extra servers are available to carry them beside the cross in the procession after Mass).[37] *On credence 2* (if washing of feet takes place), ewer of water, basin and 12 towels; apron for celebrant (an amice); water, soap and hand-towel to wash the celebrant's hands. *Aside in the sanctuary,* on the sedilia, a white humeral veil; processional cross veiled in violet.

Outside the altar rail, the canopy or umbella, to be carried over the Blessed Sacrament in procession.

The places of repose and reservation are prepared as described above.

In the sacristy, amice, alb, cincture, white maniple, stole and chasuble for the celebrant; cassocks and surplices for the servers, and books for them, if there are no singers present; white cope;[38] violet stole (for the stripping of the altars); thurible with charcoal and incense; torches or candles — which may be placed in the choir stalls — for the procession;[39] white stoles if there are priests or deacons present.[40]

First Part of Mass. The celebrant, having washed his hands, vests for Mass, assisted by S.2 and S.3, while S.1 lights the altar candles. The celebrant, having bowed to the sacristy cross, preceded by the clergy and servers (if the Mass is sung, by S.3 with the thurible, and S.4 and S.5 — if available — with lighted candles), goes, covered, to the altar, passing, if possible, through the church.[41] At the foot of the altar he gives away his biretta to S.1, and, all having saluted the altar, the Mass begins. Being Passiontide the psalm *Iudica me* is omitted. The altar is incensed, if the Mass is sung. At *Gloria in excelsis* the church bells are rung, and, if the Mass is sung, the organ is played. If customary, small bells are rung by the servers. The bells and organ are then silent until the *Gloria* of the

---

[33] For Mass only.

[34] Unless one of the servers is a (tonsured) cleric it must be prepared on the altar by the priest.

[35] Communion cloth also if there are clergy for Holy Communion.

[36] To replace bell at *Sanctus,* etc., if customary.

[37] They are also carried, if extra servers are present, in the procession to the altar at the beginning of Mass, if this is a sung Mass.

[38] Or this may be prepared at the sedilia.

[39] If there are clergy present, or men who will take part in the procession.

[40] These they wear during the function until the stripping of the altars (exclusively).

[41] Meanwhile, in a sung Mass, the introit may be sung.

Easter Vigil Mass. If the Mass is sung and a suitable lector is available (who may be one of the servers), he, in surplice, sings the Epistle, while the celebrant, at the altar, listens. The lector is not blessed after the Epistle. A homily is recommended. The celebrant preaches fully vested. There is no *Credo*.

Washing of Feet. If the washing of feet takes place,[42] the celebrant, having saluted the altar, goes to the sedilia and sits. Meanwhile S.1 and S.2 bring the twelve men whose feet are to be washed to the places prepared for them at the west end of the chancel or at the front of the choir stalls.[43] The celebrant removes his chasuble and maniple and girds himself with the apron. At credence 2, S.1 gets the towels, S.3 the water and basin. With the celebrant and S.2 they salute the altar and go to the man closest to the altar at the gospel side. They kneel before him.[44] S.2 holds the right foot of the man and the celebrant washes it—S.3 handing him the water and holding the basin under the foot—and dries it with a towel presented by S.1. This is repeated for each man. Cantors, or the clergy, sing the appointed antiphons, etc., as long as the washing goes on.

If there is no one else to do this, the celebrant, after the washing of feet, cleanses his hands and resumes his maniple and chasuble. Standing, facing the people, *in plano*, before the altar, in the middle, he recites aloud antiphon 8 (*Ubi caritas*) with its verses, and then continues as below.

When the washing is coming to a close the singers begin antiphon eight, which must never be omitted. Having completed the washing, the celebrant returns to credence 2 and washes his hands, aided by the servers. He then takes off his apron and resumes his maniple and chasuble. Going to the middle, before the altar, facing the people, he says—from the book held by S.3—the concluding verses and prayer. All make the responses. S.1 and S.2 then conduct the twelve men back to their places in church.

Continuation of Mass. At the offertory S.1, if he is a (tonsured) cleric, brings the chalice and the ciboria to the altar. *Orate, fratres* is said in the clear voice that all may answer. There is a proper *Communicantes, Hanc igitur* and *Qui pridie*. To the *Agnus Dei* said the third time the response is *Miserere nobis*.

The first prayer before Holy Communion is not said; nor is the kiss of peace given. If there are clergy for Holy Communion they kneel on the footpace and two servers hold the communion cloth (if used) before them. If the Mass is sung the communion antiphon may be chanted by the choir during the communion; and if this continues for a long time

---

[42] Described above.

[43] On arrival in the sanctuary they genuflect to the altar and bow to the celebrant. They do the same before returning to their places after the washing.

[44] While the rubric directs only the celebrant to kneel, it is more becoming and convenient if his assistants kneel also.

they may add psalms 22, 71, 103 and 150—or some of them—repeating the antiphon after each psalm. When the communion is over the veiled ciborium is left on the corporal, and from this point on Mass is celebrated as *coram Sanctissimo*. If there are extra ciboria they are put into the tabernacle before the ablutions, and are transferred, after Mass, before the stripping of the altars, to the place of reservation. If S.1 is a cleric he veils the chalice and takes it to the credence after the ablutions, without the corporal and burse; otherwise it is put aside on the altar. The candles at the place of repose are lighted by the sacristan, and candles are distributed to the clergy, or to men who will take part in the procession, and lighted. The celebrant says *Benedicamus Domino* (not *Ite*) and *Placeat*, and kisses the altar, but there is no blessing or last Gospel. The celebrant and servers genuflect on both knees at the foot of the altar and go to the sedilia. There the celebrant—without turning his back on the Blessed Sacrament—takes off the chasuble and maniple and dons a white cope, assisted by S.1 and S.2. S.4 gets the processional cross and stands near the entrance to the sanctuary.[45] S.3 brings the thurible and incense boat.

Transfer of Blessed Sacrament. The celebrant, with S.1 and S.2, makes a double genuflexion *in plano* before the altar and kneels on the lowest step. After a short prayer he puts incense into the thurible, not blessing it, and incenses the Blessed Sacrament. He receives the humeral veil from S.1, ascends to the altar, genuflects, and takes the ciborium, covering it with the ends of the veil. He faces the people, and *Pange lingua*—which should be sung by all, up to the strophe *Tantum ergo*, during the procession—is intoned by the cantors. If there are no cantors the celebrant begins the hymn. The order of the procession is: the standard usually carried in processions—if carried; men carrying candles (in the outside hand); S.4 with the cross flanked by servers with candles, if available; cantors (if in choir dress); clergy, carrying candles; S.3 with smoking thurible;[46] the celebrant, between S.1 and S.2, holding back the edges of his cope, walking under a canopy, held by four men (in choir or confraternity dress), or under an umbella carried by a server.

At the Place of Repose. At the place of repose all laymen remain outside the chapel; the thurifer goes to the right in the chapel, the cross-bearer to the left; the celebrant, with S.1 and S.2, goes to the altar. All kneel as the Blessed Sacrament passes by (except the thurifer, cross and candle-bearers). The celebrant places the ciborium on the corporal spread before the tabernacle (or casket), genuflects, and kneels at the foot of the altar. S.1 removes the humeral veil. The celebrant puts incense into the thurible, not blessing it, and incenses the Blessed Sacrament, while *Genitori Genitoque* is sung. He then ascends the altar, genuflects, puts the

---

[45] He is accompanied by two acolytes carrying candles, if extra servers are available.
[46] Walking forward, but slightly turned toward the Blessed Sacrament, continually swinging the thurible. The boat must be brought unless there is another at the altar of repose.

ciborium into the tabernacle, genuflects, closes and locks the tabernacle.[47] All adore the Blessed Sacrament for a few moments and then stand. The celebrant, with S.1 and S.2, makes a double genuflexion *in plano,* and, preceded by S.4 with the cross and S.3, returns to the sacristy.[48] He puts on his biretta (previously moved by the sacristan from the sanctuary to the place of repose) when out of sight of the Sacrament. In the sacristy he takes off his white stole and cope and puts on, cross-wise, a violet stole. S.1 extinguishes the altar candles.

The Stripping of Altars. The celebrant preceded by S.1 — with OHS — and S.2 goes, with joined hands and wearing his biretta, to the high altar. There he bows low, while the servers genuflect. Standing at the foot of the altar he says aloud the antiphon *Dividunt* and the first words of Psalm 21. Cantors or clergy in choir (seated) recite the psalm.[49] The celebrant goes up to the altar and begins the stripping with the altar cloths, assisted by the servers. Everything is removed except the cross and candles. If this cannot be conveniently done then the stripping is begun by the celebrant and finished later by the sacristan without ceremony. If there are other altars, the celebrant and servers strip these (except, of course, the altar of repose), beginning at the one nearest the high altar on the gospel side of the church. The sanctuary lamp is extinguished and the tabernacle door is left open. They then return to the high altar where the celebrant repeats the antiphon *Dividunt.* They then salute the cross (the celebrant bows, the servers genuflect) and return to the sacristy.[50]

S.1 replaces the violet veil on the altar cross.

At the place of repose the veneration of the Blessed Sacrament continues until midnight. Then all lights (except one lamp) are extinguished, and flowers (if used) are removed, as the remembrance of the Passion has begun.

§ 4. Good Friday

The solemn liturgy of the day — the liturgy of the Passion and Death of the Lord — is to be commenced in the afternoon, about 3 p.m. For pastoral reasons, however, it may be begun at any hour between midday and 9 p.m. Except for those in danger of death, Holy Communion may be given

---

[47] He takes the key away with him unless there are other ciboria to be removed now to this tabernacle, for want of another suitable place.

[48] Extra ciboria should now be moved to the place of reservation, by the celebrant wearing white stole and humeral veil. He is accompanied by two servers with candles and a third who carries the umbrella.

[49] If there is no one present who can do this, the celebrant, with the servers, says the antiphon and first verse of the psalm before the stripping of the high altar; and after the stripping of the last altar, repeats the antiphon standing before the high altar.

[50] Lustral water is removed from the church stoups after Mass. Some must be kept in the sacristy for the blessing of the new fire on Saturday.

only within the afternoon liturgy. In addition to the celebrant, deacon and subdeacon, a lector is needed to read the first lesson. There should be two MC's and at least four acolytes.[51] If the Passion is to be sung there must be three singers who are at least deacons. The *solita oscula* are entirely omitted on Good Friday; and so are all salutations to the clergy in choir.

Preparations. *The altar* is entirely bare without frontal, cloths, cross or candlesticks; the tabernacle empty (except for a corporal), unveiled, half open, the key at hand. On the uncarpeted altar steps three violet cushions are laid.

Credence 1, with linen cloth covering the top only: one altar cloth; violet burse with corporal; paten (held by deacon for Holy Communion),[52] and communion cloth (if this is used and if there are clergy to communicate); purification bowl and hand-towel; OHS on an unveiled missal-stand, a book for the Lessons and a wooden clapper. Nearby stands a lectern for the lessons.

Credence 2: vestments, i.e., violet chasuble and stole, and over them, black cope for the celebrant; violet dalmatic and stole, and, over them, black dalmatic for the deacon; violet tunicle, and, over it, black tunicle for the subdeacon. *Aside*: violet stoles for priests or deacons who are to receive Holy Communion; base for the cross;[53] near the sedilia, a shoe horn; seats for the servers.

On the gospel side of the sanctuary: three unveiled lecterns (facing north) for the Passion.

In the sacristy: a large crucifix veiled[54] in violet; two candlesticks with candles of unbleached wax; vestments, i.e., amices, albs, cinctures and birettas for the sacred ministers; black stoles for the celebrant and deacon; amices, albs, cinctures, black stoles and books for the three deacons of the Passion.

At the place of repose: corporal spread on the table before the tabernacle (or casket) and its key; two candlesticks[55] with candles of unbleached wax, standing on the table or on the floor at each side. Aside, a white humeral veil and the umbella.

At the place of reservation: a corporal spread before the tabernacle; its key; two candlesticks with candles of bleached wax.[56]

First Part of the Liturgy. The sacred ministers vest in albs, the celebrant and deacon wearing stoles. The procession to the altar — through the church, if possible — is in silence, and is led by MC2 and the

---

[51] A thurifer is not needed on Good Friday.

[52] The communion plate will be needed if another priest or deacon gives Holy Communion.

[53] Or this may be placed in position at the back of the table of the altar (behind the tabernacle, if there is one).

[54] The veil must be easily removable.

[55] To be carried before the Blessed Sacrament when it is borne to the high altar.

[56] To be lighted when the ciborium is brought thither at the end of the service.

acolytes (without cross or candles). Then come the clergy, juniors first. Lastly, the sacred ministers, covered, *unus post alium.*

All bow (only) to the high altar. MC1 takes the birettas to the sedilia and brings the OHS from the credence, kneeling to the right of the deacon. The sacred ministers prostrate themselves, leaning their faces and arms on the cushions set on the altar steps. All others kneel, bowed, and remain for some time in prayer. After about the length of a *Miserere,* on a signal from MC1, all rise to a kneeling posture, while the celebrant stands and — facing the altar and with joined hands — sings, in the second ferial tone, the prayer *Deus, qui peccati.*[57] All answer *Amen.* The deacon and subdeacon then stand, and with the celebrant bow to the altar. They then go to the sedilia and sit, covered, to listen to the Lessons. A server removes the cushions from the altar steps, and the sacristan or MC2 places the lectern in the middle of the choir.

The Lessons. MC2 may present the book to the lector, who, having bowed to the altar, goes to the lectern and, facing the altar,[58] reads the first Lesson *in tono prophetiæ*[59] with no introductory title, and no *Deo gratias* at its close. After the Lesson the Responsory is sung by the choir or recited by the clergy, while the lector, having bowed to the altar, returns to his place. When it is finished all rise. The celebrant, at the sedilia, chants *Oremus,* the deacon *Flectamus genua,* and all kneel for some time in prayer. Then the deacon sings *Levate,* all rise, and the celebrant, with hands joined, sings the prayer in the first ferial tone. An acolyte holds the book. All sing *Amen* and sit. MC2 presents the book to the subdeacon. He bows to the altar, goes to the lectern, and chants the second Lesson *in tono lectionis.*[60] There is no introductory title and no response at the end. The subdeacon salutes the altar, returns the book to MC2, and sits again at the sedilia. MC2 goes to the sacristy. The choir sings the second Responsory, or it is recited by the clergy. MC1 removes the lectern.

The Passion. Led by MC2, the deacons of the Passion, having vested in the sacristy during the Lessons, come (covered) to the sanctuary and bow to the altar. MC2 takes their birettas. The ceremonial for the singing of the Passion is the same as on Palm Sunday, except that the deacons do not say *Munda cor meum,* but go at once to the celebrant, before whom, standing, they bow low. He says *Dominus sit,* etc., aloud and the deacons, standing erect, answer *Amen,* and go and sing the Passion. After the words *tradidit spiritum* all kneel in their places until MC1 gives the signal to rise. At the end of the Passion MC2 returns their birettas to the deacons

---

[57] MC1 holds the book before him.

[58] Or, by analogy with Holy Saturday (OHS § 15) the lector may face northwards, partly turned to the people.

[59] Cf. *Graduale Romanum,* p. 113*.

[60] Ibid.

and leads them to the sacristy to unvest. If a homily is given it is after the Passion.

The Solemn Prayers. At the sedilia the celebrant puts on a black cope, the deacon a black dalmatic, the subdeacon a black tunicle, assisted by the MC's and the two acolytes. Meanwhile acolyte 1 spreads the single cloth on the altar table and acolyte 2 places the missal-stand, with OHS, in the centre of the altar. The sacred ministers bow to the altar and ascend. The celebrant kisses the altar, and—with the deacon at his right and subdeacon at his left, assisting him—chants the nine solemn prayers.[61] With joined hands he sings the intention for each prayer and then *Oremus.* The deacon sings *Flectamus genua,* and all kneel for a little while in prayer. The deacon then sings *Levate,* all rise, and the celebrant, with hands extended, sings the prayer in the first ferial tone. He joins his hands at the conclusion of each prayer, as at Mass. At the end of the prayers, the sacred ministers bow to the altar, and go by the shorter way to the sedilia. Acolyte 1 removes the missal-stand and book to the credence. At the sedilia the celebrant takes off his cope, the deacon his dalmatic and the subdeacon his tunicle assisted by MC1 and the acolytes.

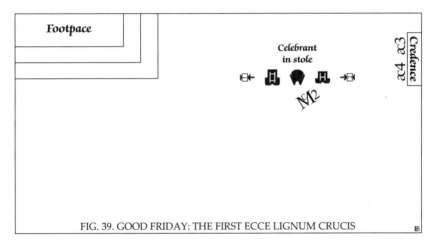

FIG. 39. GOOD FRIDAY: THE FIRST ECCE LIGNUM CRUCIS

The Unveiling of the Cross. While the celebrant and subdeacon remain standing at the sedilia, the deacon, preceded by MC2 and four acolytes, in pairs, goes to fetch the large veiled crucifix from the sacristy. The return procession is led by MC2, followed by two acolytes, and then comes the deacon carrying the cross, walking between the other two acolytes carrying lighted candles. As they approach, MC1 takes the book and goes with the celebrant and subdeacon to meet them, and in the middle of the sanctuary the celebrant bows to the cross and receives it from the deacon facing away from himself. The celebrant goes around to

---

[61] The word "perfidis" is omitted from the eighth prayer; S.R.C. 19th March 1959.

the epistle corner of the altar, *in plano*, followed by the deacon and subdeacon and the acolytes with the candles. The other acolytes stand before the credence. The celebrant faces the congregation, having the deacon on his right, the subdeacon on his left, both facing the people. The first acolyte stands on the deacon's right, the second on the subdeacon's left, both facing towards the cross. MC2 or a server holds the book before the celebrant, not directly in front of him. Lifting the cross up, but not too high—about the height of his eyes—the celebrant unveils the top of it assisted by the deacon (not exposing the face of the figure) and chants *Ecce lignum crucis* by himself. The deacon and subdeacon continue with him *in quo...pependit*. All then sing *Venite adoremus*. When this is finished all, except the celebrant and the acolytes holding candles, kneel on both knees in worship. The celebrant with his attendants then goes up to the footpace and stands there at the epistle corner. He unveils the right arm of the figure, raises the cross a little higher, and, at a higher pitch, sings again *Ecce lignum crucis*. The deacon and subdeacon join in at *in quo,* etc., all answer *Venite,* and then kneel as before. Finally the celebrant moves to the middle of the altar, unveils the cross completely—giving the veil to MC1, who takes it to the credence and returns with the acolytes, acolyte 1 bringing a purifier—raises it still higher and at a higher pitch sings *Ecce lignum* for the third time, all the others acting as before. The two acolytes come forward, genuflect, and take the cross from the celebrant. Standing near the front edge of the footpace, facing the people, they hold the cross erect by its arms, resting the foot on the ground. The other two acolytes place their candlesticks on each side of the cross, and kneel on the top step at each side of the altar, facing the cross. The MC's and sacred ministers go down, genuflect, and return to the sedilia. If convenient, the sacred ministers, at the sedilia, and the clergy and servers, remove their shoes for the veneration of the cross.

Veneration of the Cross. The celebrant, followed by the deacon and subdeacon, goes some distance away from the altar and advances towards the cross, making a simple genuflexion, three times, at intervals. Kneeling, or standing, he kisses the feet of the Crucified, and, without any further genuflexion, returns to the sedilia and puts on his shoes. The deacon and subdeacon, *unus post alium*, do the same. The acolyte with the purifier wipes the feet each time they are kissed. On their return to the sedilia the sacred ministers, with the celebrant, wearing their birettas, sit and listen to the *Improperia*. The clergy line up in the sanctuary and venerate the cross in the same manner as the sacred ministers. They are followed by the servers. In the meantime the choir, divided into two parts, sings the *Improperia*, in the manner indicated in OHS, as long as the veneration of the cross continues. The chant is always to be concluded with the doxology *Sempiterna* (if the hymn *Crux fidelis* is sung). When the veneration of the servers is finished, the acolytes holding the cross—

accompanied by the two who carry candles—carry it to the communion rail, and there, resting the foot on the rail or on a platform prepared for it, present it for the veneration of the people. The acolytes with candles place them at each side of the cross, and stand facing it. The people approach in single file, genuflect once only, and, standing, kiss the feet of the Crucified. They do not genuflect again but return at once to their places in church.[62] Should a large number of people be venerating the cross, additional acolytes may relieve those holding the cross and candles. When the veneration is finished, the acolytes—accompanied by the candle-bearers, who place their candles on the altar table at each side of the cross and then retire to the credence—take the cross to the altar, and there set it on the base provided for it, so that it may be visible to all, without impeding the celebrant during the communion.[63] All stand while this is done.

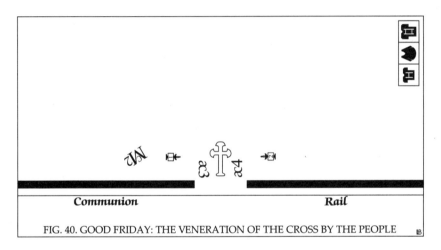

FIG. 40. GOOD FRIDAY: THE VENERATION OF THE CROSS BY THE PEOPLE

The Blessed Sacrament Procession. At the sedilia the celebrant and deacon take off their black stoles; the former puts on a violet stole and chasuble, the latter a violet stole and dalmatic. The subdeacon dons a violet tunicle. They are assisted by MC1 and acolytes 1 and 2. The celebrant and subdeacon may then sit. MC1 takes the burse from the credence and presents it to the deacon who genuflects on the lowest step of the altar, goes up, and spreads the corporal on its table. Meanwhile, one acolyte puts the purifying bowl and hand-towel on the altar, to the

---

[62] If the number of persons taking part in the ceremony is so great that the worship of the cross could not be properly carried out in the manner described above, after its veneration by the clergy and servers, the celebrant—accompanied by the deacon, subdeacon and candle-bearers—on the footpace, holds up the cross before the people and briefly invites them to venerate it, kneeling for a few moments in one silent collective act of homage (S.R.C., 1 February 1957, § 17). Alternatively, four different acolytes may take two different crosses to either end of the altar rails or to side altars.

[63] Crosses throughout the church are now unveiled by the sacristan.

right of the corporal; another places the missal-stand, with OHS, to the left of the corporal, at an angle as at the canon of Mass. MC2 leads three acolytes to the middle of the sanctuary, the deacon descends and stands before them, all genuflect to the cross and go in procession to the place of repose. There they all make a double genuflexion and kneel in prayer for a moment. The deacon then unlocks the tabernacle (or casket), genuflects, and places the ciborium on the corporal. MC2 puts the white humeral veil on the deacon, while two acolytes take the candlesticks prepared on the altar, or standing on the ground, and the third gets the umbella. The deacon genuflects, takes the ciborium and wraps the veil around it. Preceded by MC2 and between the candle-bearers, with the third server holding the umbella over the Blessed Sacrament until the sanctuary is reached, the deacon carries the ciborium to the sanctuary and places it on the corporal on the altar. MC1 sounds the clapper when the Blessed Sacrament enters the sanctuary, and all in choir kneel. As the Blessed Sacrament approaches the sanctuary the celebrant and subdeacon stand, and he and the subdeacon genuflect as It passes. The deacon then genuflects and MC2 removes the humeral veil. The candle-bearers put their candles on the table of the altar (so that there are now four candles there), genuflect, and kneel on the lowest step at each side of the altar. During the procession the choir sings—as long as it lasts—the three antiphons appointed in OHS.

The Communion. The celebrant and subdeacon make a double genuflexion at the foot of the altar and ascend. The three sacred ministers genuflect. With hands joined the celebrant recites aloud *Oremus. Præceptis ...dicere.* Then all present say in Latin the *Pater noster,* reciting it "solemnly, gravely and distinctly." They end with *Amen.* Then the celebrant alone, with hands extended, recites aloud the embolism *Libera.* He does not make the sign of the cross at *da propitius.* All answer *Amen.* In a low voice, bowed, and with joined hands laid on the edge of the altar, the celebrant says the prayer *Perceptio.* The deacon removes the veil and the celebrant uncovers the ciborium. The sacred ministers genuflect. The celebrant takes a Host in his right hand, passes It into his left, and holds It over the ciborium. Bowing, he recites in the medium voice, thrice, *Domine, non sum dignus,* striking his breast each time as the MC sounds the clapper. He then passes the Host into his right hand, signs himself with It, saying, in a low voice, *Corpus Domini,* etc., and receives the Host. With hands joined before his face he spends a few moments in meditation on the Sacrament. The deacon, standing bowed on the top step at the epistle side, facing the celebrant, recites *Confiteor;* the subdeacon standing bowed on the top step at the gospel side. The celebrant genuflects, and, facing the people, says *Misereatur* and *Indulgentiam.* All answer each *Amen.* Two acolytes hold the cloth for the communion of the clergy. The celebrant, holding aloft a Host, says, as usual, *Ecce Agnus Dei* and *Domine, non sum dignus*. If it be customary, the clapper may be sounded as a signal to the people. He then gives Holy Communion to the clergy,[64] servers, and people, the deacon holding the paten under the chin of each communicant. During the communion, Psalm 21 (without *Gloria Patri*) and any of the Responsories of the Matins of Good Friday may be sung.

If an extra priest or deacon also gives Communion, wearing a surplice and violet stole, he goes, preceded by MC2, and two servers, to the place of reservation.[65] There he puts on the humeral veil and brings a ciborium — accompanied by the servers carrying candles and MC2 holding the umbella over the Blessed Sacrament — to the high altar. Having doffed the humeral veil, he goes at once to distribute Holy Communion without any preliminary prayers. He should begin the distribution after the celebrant does and finish before him. He may then take his ciborium back to the place of reservation or leave it in the tabernacle of the high altar to be removed after the liturgy.

The End of the Liturgy. When the communion is finished the paten (and communion plate, used for Holy Communion distributed by an extra priest) is purified into the ciborium or into the purifying bowl; and in this the celebrant, in silence, washes his fingers. The deacon covers and veils the ciborium, and replaces it in the tabernacle. He then folds the corporal and puts it in the burse.[66] The subdeacon places the book in the middle of the altar, parallel to its edge. Standing in the middle, with the deacon and subdeacon at his sides, the celebrant, with joined hands, sings, in the second ferial tone, the three prayers of thanksgiving. All stand — MC1 obtains the birettas — and answer each *Amen*. The sacred ministers descend, receive their birettas from MC1; MC2 assembles the four acolytes behind them, all genuflect to the cross, and, led by MC2, return to the sacristy. Vespers are not said, and Compline is recited — not sung — in choir, without lighted candles. At a convenient time all ciboria are removed from the high altar and from the place of repose to the place of reservation.[67] This is done by a priest or deacon, in surplice, violet stole and white humeral veil, accompanied by lights and the umbella. When the ciborium has been removed from the high altar, this is stripped by the sacristan, without ceremony, leaving only the cross and the four candlesticks.

From the unveiling of the cross on Good Friday to Vespers of Holy Saturday (inclusive) it is saluted by all with a genuflexion during a function.

---

[64] Priests and deacons wear violet stoles. MC2 sees to the provision of these.
[65] The sacristan must see that the humeral veil, two candles and the umbella are there for the transfer of the ciborium.
[66] MC2 or a server then carries this to the credence.
[67] Two candles must be lighted for the arrival of the Blessed Sacrament, and a lamp then kept burning there.

§ 5. Good Friday in Small Churches

The solemn liturgy of the day is to be started in the afternoon about 3p.m. For pastoral reasons, however, it may be begun at any hour between midday and 9p.m. Except for those in danger of death, Holy Communion may be given only within the afternoon liturgy. At least four servers are required.[68] If the Passion is to be sung there must be three singers who are at least deacons. If the function is a sung one, and a suitable lector is available (he may be one of the servers) he — in choir dress — reads the Lessons.

Preparations. *The altar* completely bare, without frontal, cloths, cross or candlesticks; the tabernacle empty (except for a corporal), unveiled, half open, the key at hand; a base for the cross (normally behind the tabernacle). A violet cushion on the uncarpeted second step of the altar. *On the credence* (covered with a linen cloth that does not hang over), one altar cloth; unveiled missal-stand with OHS; violet burse with corporal; purifying bowl and a hand-towel; communion plate(s); wooden clapper.

On the epistle side, the sedilia (uncovered); on or near it, violet chasuble and stole, and over them a black cope. *Aside,* an unveiled lectern for the reading of the Lessons. If the Passion is to be sung, three unveiled lecterns on the gospel side of the sanctuary, facing north. Seats for the servers. A shoehorn may be near the sedilia.

At the place of repose, a corporal spread on the altar table; key of the tabernacle, two candlesticks with candles of unbleached wax (for the procession of the Blessed Sacrament); white humeral veil and the umbella. *At the place of reservation,* the tabernacle key;[69] corporal spread before the tabernacle; two candlesticks with candles of bleached wax.

In the sacristy, amice, alb, cincture and black stole for the celebrant; cassocks and cottas for the servers, and books for them, if there is no choir; a large crucifix veiled in violet (the veil easily removable); two candles of unbleached wax to be carried in procession beside the cross; violet stoles for the communion of priests or deacons, if any.

For the deacons of the Passion, three amices, albs, cinctures, black stoles, birettas and books.

The First Part of the Liturgy. The celebrant washes his hands, and vests in amice, alb, cincture and black stole (crossed). Having bowed with the servers to the (covered) sacristy cross he goes with them, preceding him in pairs, to the altar (passing, if possible, through the church). On arrival there he gives away his biretta, salutes the altar and prostrates, leaning on the cushion set on the altar step. The servers kneel beside him

---

[68] S.R.C. 15th March 1956, no. 2. A fifth (and a sixth) server are desirable for the unveiling of the cross.
[69] To be brought after the service.

in plano and bow. After about the time required for *Miserere* the celebrant stands, all others kneeling erect, and—facing the altar and with joined hands—says[70] in the (second) ferial tone the prayer *Deus, qui peccati veteris.* S.2 holds the book for him. All answer *Amen.*

The Lessons. The celebrant and the servers bow to the altar and the former goes to the sedilia, sits, covered, and listens to the Lesson. If the function is sung S.2 places the lectern in the middle of the choir; S.1 presents the book to the lector, salutes the altar and then the celebrant with him and conducts him to the lectern. There, facing the altar,[71] he sings the first Lesson *in tono prophetiæ;*[72] there is no introductory title or *Deo gratias* at its close.

If the function is not sung, or a suitable lector is not available, the celebrant, standing at the lectern himself chants the Lesson, while all sit and listen. After the Lesson the Responsory is sung by the choir, or recited by the clergy, or, in default of these, read by the celebrant (seated) with the servers. After the Responsory all stand. The celebrant, at the sedilia, says *Oremus. Flectamus genua.* All, including the celebrant, kneel for a few moments in prayer. The celebrant says *Levate* and all stand. With joined hands he says the prayer in the (first) ferial tone. All answer *Amen.* The second Lesson is said in *tono lectionis* at the lectern.[73] The second Responsory follows, during which the lectern is removed by S.3. After that, the Passion is said or sung. An unveiled lectern is placed on the gospel side of the sanctuary, facing north. The celebrant, accompanied by S.1 and S.2, goes to the middle of the choir and, bowing low, says aloud *Dominus sit...meis.* They salute the altar and go to the lectern. The celebrant, facing north, with S.1 and S.2 at his sides, reads or sings the Passion. *Laus tibi, Christe* is not said at its conclusion.

If there are three deacons they sing the Passion as described above for Palm Sunday and for the solemn rite for Good Friday. The celebrant, standing at the sedilia, listens. If there are only two deacons available the celebrant may sing or read the Christus part. In that case he[74] joins the two deacons before the altar, standing between them. All three, deeply bowed, say *Dominus sit in corde meo et in labiis meis,* in a low voice. Then, erect, they salute the altar, and go to the lecterns. There the celebrant stands on the right of the narrator,[75] and they sing or read the Passion.

The Solemn Prayers. After the Passion, the celebrant at the sedilia, with the assistance of S.1, dons a black cope. Meanwhile S.2 and S.3

---

[70] "Says" is used all through this book for either chanting or merely reciting a prayer, according to circumstances, as the rubrics use *dicit.*

[71] Or, by analogy with Holy Saturday (OHS § 15) the lector may face northwards, partly turned to the people.

[72] Cf. *Graduale Romanum,* p. 113*.

[73] Ibid.

[74] Retaining his stole worn cross-wise.

[75] And so nearest the altar.

spread the single altar cloth on the table of the altar and place the book-stand, with OHS, at the centre, parallel to the edge of the altar. The celebrant, accompanied by S.1 and S.2, salutes the altar, ascends, kisses the altar just to the left of the missal, and begins the solemn prayers, the two servers at his sides holding back the cope. He chants the introduction to each prayer with hands joined. Then he sings *Oremus. Flectamus genua,* and, with all present, kneels on both knees for some moments in prayer. Then he chants *Levate* and all arise. With hands extended he sings each prayer in the (first) ferial tone. All answer *Amen* each time.[76]

Unveiling of Cross. After the solemn prayers, the celebrant and servers salute the altar and go, by the shorter way, to the sedilia, where the celebrant removes his cope. Then, with four servers, having saluted the altar, he goes to the sacristy to fetch the cross. In the procession back S.1 and S.2 lead; and the celebrant bears the veiled cross, walking between S.5 and S.6, carrying lighted candles. Meanwhile S.3 gets the book for the unveiling. The celebrant, with S.1 and S.2 and the candle-bearers, goes to the epistle corner, *in plano,* and faces the people, S.1 and S.2 at his sides; S.5 and S.6 stand beside S.1 and S.2, but facing towards the cross. S.3 holds the book for the celebrant, who unveils the top of the cross (not exposing the face of the figure) and holds it up. In a grave voice he says (or chants to the music of OHS) *Ecce lignum crucis,* etc. All answer *Venite adoremus,* and then (except the celebrant, S.5, S.6 and S.3) kneel and silently venerate the cross for a little while. The celebrant, with the five servers, then goes up to the footpace, and, at the epistle corner, unveils the right arm of the figure. Raising the cross a little higher than before he says (or sings at a higher pitch), *Ecce lignum,* etc. All answer and kneel as before. Finally, the celebrant moves to the middle of the altar, unveils the cross completely (giving away the veil to S.2), holds it up still higher, and repeats at a higher pitch, *Ecce lignum,* etc. All answer and kneel as before.[77]

After the unveiling, the celebrant hands the book to S.2 and the cross to S.3 and S.4. They stand on the footpace towards the front edge, and hold the cross by its arms facing the people, resting its foot on the footpace. S.5 and S.6 put their candles on the footpace, at each side of the cross, not too close to S.3 and S.4 ; and go and kneel on each side on the top step, facing the cross.[78]

Veneration of the Cross. The celebrant goes to the sedilia and, if convenient, removes his shoes. Accompanied by S.1 he goes some distance down the sanctuary, makes three simple genuflexions, at intervals, as he

---

[76] The word "perfidis" is omitted from the eighth prayer; S.R.C. 19th March 1959.

[77] Crucifixes throughout the church are now unveiled by the sacristan.

[78] If only four servers are available S.1 and S.2 carry the candles in the procession with, and unveiling of, the cross; set them down after the unveiling beside the cross (held by S.3 and S.4) and then descend to the sedilia with the celebrant.

approaches the altar, and kneeling or standing, kisses the feet of the Crucified. Without any further genuflexion he returns to the sedilia, resumes his shoes, sits, covered, and listens to the *Improperia.* The clergy and servers having, if convenient, removed their shoes—go, one after the other, to venerate the cross. Each makes a simple genuflexion, three times, while approaching, kisses the feet of the Crucified, and returns at once to his place. The cross is then taken by S.3 and S.4 to the altar rail for the veneration by the people. They rest the foot of the cross on the rail, or on a platform prepared for it. S.5 and S.6 accompany the cross, place their candles at each side of it, and stand facing it. The people approach in procession, men first.[79] Each makes one simple genuflexion, kisses the cross, standing, and at once moves on and returns to his place.[80] While the veneration is in progress the choir, if possible divided into two parts, sings or recites the *Improperia* in the manner indicated in OHS. These are ended when the veneration finishes, but, if the hymn *Crux fidelis* is sung, they must be concluded by the doxology *Sempiterna.* If there is no choir the celebrant, seated, recites aloud parts I and IV of the *Improperia* with S.1 and S.2 or with the clergy, as indicated in the text.

The Blessed Sacrament Procession. When the veneration of the cross is ended all stand and S.3 and S.4—accompanied by S.5 and S.6 with their candles—take it to the altar and set it in its base. It should be so placed as to be easily seen by the congregation but not interfere with the communion service. S.5 and S.6 place their candles on the altar, at each side of the cross and retire to the credence. The celebrant takes off his black stole and dons a violet stole and chasuble, assisted by S.1. The latter brings the burse from the credence to the celebrant, and with S.2, genuflects with him at the foot of the altar. The celebrant spreads the corporal on the altar, while S.1 brings up the purifying bowl and hand-towel and places them to the right of the corporal; and S.2 arranges the book, at an angle, on the left of the corporal. The celebrant descends to the foot of the altar, genuflects, with S.1, S.2 and S.3 behind him, and, preceded by them, goes to the place of repose to fetch the ciborium. On arrival there all make a double genuflexion and kneel for a moment in prayer. The celebrant takes the ciborium from the tabernacle, receives the humeral veil from S.1 and covers the ciborium with it. S.1 and S.2 take a candle each, while S.3 gets the umbella. S.1 and S.2 walk at each side of the celebrant, while S.3 holds the umbella over the Blessed Sacrament, and they go to the high altar. As they pass all kneel. S.4 sounds the clapper as the Blessed Sacrament enters the Sanctuary. Meanwhile the choir sings the three antiphons appointed in OHS. If there are no singers the celebrant recites them aloud with the servers, kneeling on the lowest

---

[79] This may not be feasible, where the sexes are not separated in church.
[80] If the crowd is so great that it is impossible for the worship of the cross properly to be carried out, one collective silent act of homage is permitted (S.R.C., 1 February 1957 § 17).

step at the altar of repose, before he takes the ciborium from the tabernacle. On arrival at the high altar, the celebrant ascends, accompanied by S.1 and S.2. He places the ciborium on the corporal, S.1 and S.2 put their candles on the altar, and all three genuflect. S.1 takes the humeral veil from the celebrant. S.1 and S.2 descend and stand before the altar in front of the lowest step.

The Communion. With joined hands, the celebrant recites the introduction to the Lord's Prayer (*Oremus. Præceptis*, etc.). All, standing, then recite with him aloud, in Latin, *Pater noster,* "solemnly, gravely, and distinctly." All add *Amen* at the end. The celebrant alone, with hands extended, says aloud the prayer *Libera.* At its conclusion all answer *Amen.* The celebrant, bowed and with joined hands laid on the altar, recites, in a low voice, the prayer *Perceptio.* He then uncovers the ciborium, genuflects, takes a sacred Particle with his right hand, and passes It into his left, with which he holds It over the ciborium. Bowed, he says thrice, in the medium voice, *Domine, non sum dignus,* while striking his breast. S.3 sounds the clapper three times. Then, he passes the Host into his right hand, signs himself with It, saying *Corpus Domini,* etc., in a low voice, and receives the Host. He meditates for a short time on the Sacrament. At once the servers, kneeling, and all who are about to communicate, recite the *Confiteor.* The celebrant, having genuflected, gives the absolution, says *Ecce Agnus* and *Domine, non sum dignus* as usual—S.3 sounding the clapper—and distributes Holy Communion. If there are priests (or deacons) present they wear a violet stole for communion. If there is a large number for communion extra priests—in surplice and violet stole— may distribute Holy Communion at the altar rail, or in any other suitable place in the church. While this is going on, Psalm 21 (without *Gloria Patri*) or any of the Responsories from Matins of Good Friday may be sung.

The Conclusion of the Service. When the communion is finished, the celebrant washes his fingers in the purifying bowl, in silence. He puts the ciboria into the tabernacle, and replaces the corporal in the burse (which S.1 takes to the credence). Standing in the middle of the altar, with the book before him, with joined hands, he sings in the second ferial tone, or says, the three prayers of thanksgiving. All stand for them and answer *Amen* to each. The celebrant descends, receives his biretta from S.1, genuflects *(in plano)* with the servers, and follows them to the sacristy. There he unvests and makes his thanksgiving.

At a suitable moment the ciboria in the tabernacle—and any extra ones that may be at the place of repose—are moved, in the simple form (two servers with lights, and one with the umbella) to the place of reservation,[81] where a lamp must then burn. The high altar is stripped,

---

[81] Cf. § 2 above. There two candles are lit for the arrival of the Blessed Sacrament.

without ceremony, by the servers or sacristan, leaving only the cross and the four candlesticks.[82]

§ 6. Holy Saturday

The Divine Office. The choral recitation[83] of Matins and Lauds may not be anticipated on Good Friday evening, but takes place at the proper hour[84] on Saturday morning. At Lauds and for the Small Hours, after the antiphon *Christus factus est,* and *Pater noster* (said silently), the psalm *Miserere* is omitted, and a new prayer *Concede* (with its conclusion recited silently) replaces the prayer *Respice.* At these Hours nothing more is added after the prayer.

Vespers on Holy Saturday — sung after midday — are those of Maundy Thursday except for the first antiphon *(Hodie),* and the antiphon at the *Magnificat (Principes).* After the repetition of this, *Christus factus est, Pater noster,* and the *Miserere* are omitted, and the prayer is the one as at Lauds (with a silent conclusion). Nothing else is added.

Compline is omitted on this night.

In the rite for Holy Saturday, Matins of Easter Sunday (one nocturn) is omitted, and a shortened form of Lauds is incorporated into the end of Mass. The Easter Sunday Office, as found in the breviary, begins, then, at Prime.[85]

The Paschal Vigil

The solemn Easter Vigil service is to commence at an hour that will enable solemn Mass to begin about midnight. The Ordinary of the place may, however, for good reasons to be approved for each church, allow the service to begin earlier, but not before twilight and certainly not before sunset. Priests who *celebrate* midnight Mass may again celebrate Mass on Easter Sunday (and twice or three times, if they have the faculty to binate or trinate). Holy Communion — except to those in danger of death — may be given only during the Mass, or immediately after and in connection with it.

Preparations. *At the high altar,* a violet frontal over a white one; three altar cloths; six unlit festal candlesticks; cross unveiled; the tabernacle empty (except for a corporal), unveiled, half-open, the key at hand.[86]

---

[82] Even these may be removed if neither Compline nor Tenebræ takes place.

[83] The private recitation of Matins may be anticipated for a just cause.

[84] OHS, Holy Saturday, n. 1.

[85] In the private recitation of the Office all is said as in the Roman Breviary, except for the changes (two antiphons and a prayer) noted above. At Compline, having recited the *Confiteor* and absolution, the psalms (of Sunday) are begun at once. After them come *Nunc dimittis, Pater noster* and the prayer *Visita,* omitting everything else.

[86] A white conopæum and a lamp must be prepared aside for use after Mass.

On the gospel side of the sanctuary: The Paschal candlestick, suitably adorned. In the middle of the sanctuary a temporary stand for the candle, adorned.

On the epistle side: For the Præconium, a lectern, covered with an ornamental white veil, facing north. *Aside* (out of sight), a festive carpet for the altar steps, with relics and flowers (if used) for solemn Mass. The sedilia shows its violet covering; its white covering being underneath.

Credence 1: What is necessary for solemn Mass, i.e., the chalice prepared for Mass with white burse and veil; ciboria containing sufficient breads, and veils to be put on them; communion cloth (if used); intonation card; evangeliarium; cruets; bell(s) — all covered with a white humeral veil and over it a violet one.

Credence 2: A second copy of the *Ordo Hebdomadæ Sanctæ* (or missal); missal-stand and altar cards; English version (approved by the Ordinary) of the form for the renewal of the baptismal promises; candles for the deacon and subdeacon for this renewal; tapers.

Credence 3 (on the epistle side at the front of the Sanctuary): All that is required for the blessing of baptismal water and the administration of baptism if these are to take place, i.e., a vessel to receive some of the blessed water before the holy oils are put into it to be used for sprinkling; a jug or ladle to put the water into this vessel; vials containing the Oil of Catechumens and Chrism on a salver; cotton wool; ewer of water and basin, with slices of lemon and breadcrumbs, and hand-towels[87] for the washing of the celebrant's hands; empty aspersory and sprinkler.[88] *For baptism:* ritual; ladle or shell to pour water and a basin to catch it; holy oil stocks with cotton wool on a salver; white robe(s); candle(s); taper.

Near credence 3: A large vessel of water to be blessed, suitably adorned, on a stand or table that can be easily moved. *At the sedilia:* the sub-deacon's biretta.

Nearby: White cope and stole; a stool (or prie-dieu) at which the celebrant kneels for the Litanies, etc.; seats for the servers.

In the sacristy: White chasuble, dalmatic, tunicle etc., for solemn Mass; amices, albs, cinctures for the sacred ministers (with birettas for the celebrant and deacon); a violet cope and stole for the celebrant; violet dalmatic and stole for the deacon; violet tunicle for the subdeacon;[89] cassocks and surplices for MC's and servers; processional cross; acolytes'[90] unlit candles; torches (two, four or six).

---

[87] One of these will be needed to wipe the Paschal candle.

[88] Unless a second one is available this will have to be brought (having been emptied of the old lustral water) from the porch, after the blessing of the new fire, etc.

[89] If there is a second subdeacon to act as cross-bearer, amice, alb, cincture and violet tunicle.

[90] These are needed only for solemn Mass, unless water is to be blessed in a baptistery *apart from the church.* Then they are made ready on one of the credences for use in the procession to that baptistery.

In the porch (or before the church door or at the west end of the church, wherever the people can best see the ceremony): A brazier with coals, previously lit by a spark struck from a flint,[91] charcoal and tongs; and, on a table, the Paschal candle; [92] the five grains of incense[93] on a small silver salver; a stylus; incense-boat and empty thurible; aspersory of lustral water and sprinkler; lectern with *Ordo Hebdomadæ Sanctæ* (or missal); candles for the celebrant, clergy and servers;[94] long tapers. *Aside,* white stole and dalmatic for the deacon.

In the baptistery: The font, cleaned and adorned, with the plug in, ready to receive the newly blessed baptismal water.

In the church: There must be no votive candles burning and only the minimum of necessary lighting. It is better that the Church be in complete darkness, at least when the ceremony has begun, and that those who need to do so use a small torch discreetly. After the third *Lumen Christi* the full lighting will be put on.[95]

The Assistants. For the rite of Holy Saturday there are needed the celebrant, deacon, subdeacon; two MC's; a thurifer and two acolytes; torchbearers for Mass, who can also help as extra servers for other parts of the service; cantors.

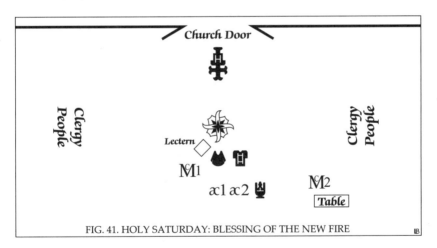

FIG. 41. HOLY SATURDAY: BLESSING OF THE NEW FIRE

Blessing the New Fire. Over the amice, alb and cincture the celebrant vests in violet stole and cope, the deacon in violet stole and dalmatic, the subdeacon in violet tunicle. In the procession to the porch MC2 and the thurifer lead, then come the acolytes (not carrying candles), next the sub-

---

[91] Such as a cigarette lighter.

[92] Which may be marked beforehand so that the celebrant may more easily draw the lines with the stylus, and which may be decorated with paint or other markings, but which should have nothing attached to it.

[93] These are renewed each year.

[94] The people should have candles before the ceremony begins.

[95] If practicable, it may be preferable to delay switching on electric lighting until the *Gloria*.

deacon (with the processional cross), then other servers, next the clergy, and finally the celebrant with the deacon on his left and MC1 on his right, both holding the edges of the cope. After the reverence to the high altar (all, except the celebrant and subdeacon, genuflect to the cross) they go outside the church, or into the porch, or stay inside the church near the door—whichever is the best place for the people to see the ceremony. On arrival where the fire is prepared, the subdeacon stands with his back to the church door, or to the high altar, the celebrant faces him, with the fire between them, the deacon on his right. The servers stand around in places convenient for their office, and the clergy encircle the ministers (those of highest rank nearest the celebrant). The celebrant, uncovered, blesses the fire with *Dominus vobiscum* and one prayer *Deus qui per Filium tuum*,[96] the first acolyte holding the book before him (unless there is a lectern). MC2 brings the aspersory and the celebrant sprinkles the fire thrice (centre, to his left and right) saying nothing. The thurifer transfers some lighted charcoal from the blessed fire into the thurible. The celebrant puts in (thrice) and blesses incense in the usual way and censes the fire with three single swings.

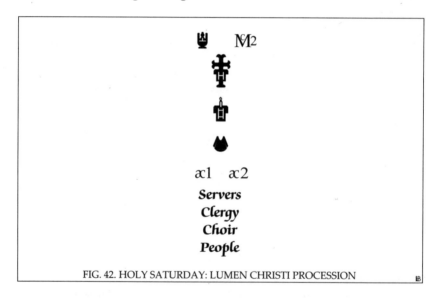

FIG. 42. HOLY SATURDAY: LUMEN CHRISTI PROCESSION

Blessing the Paschal Candle. MC2 brings the candle. The celebrant with the stylus draws a cross between the points where the grains of incense will be inserted, and traces the first and last letters of the Greek alphabet, and the date, in the form and with the words prescribed in the text of OHS (acolyte 1 holding the book before him, or it may be on a lectern). The deacon presents the grains of incense, and the celebrant

---

[96] The first of the three prayers in the missal.

blesses them[97] by sprinkling them thrice with lustral water (saying nothing), and then censes them (three simple swings). The celebrant then inserts the grains into the candle, with the prescribed words. Next the deacon presents a taper lit from the new fire and the celebrant with it lights the candle, saying aloud the prescribed words. Then the celebrant blesses the lighted candle saying *Dominus vobiscum* and the prayer *Veniat.*[98]

Solemn Procession. The deacon takes off the violet dalmatic and stole[99] and dons a white stole and dalmatic and then assists in the preparation of incense. Incense is put in the thurible, for the procession, and blessed by the celebrant. Candles are distributed to the celebrant, servers, clergy and people. The deacon takes the Paschal candle and the procession is formed: MC2 and thurifer, then the subdeacon with the cross, next the deacon with the candle, followed by the celebrant and MC1 and after him the acolytes and other servers, the clergy and the people. The candles remain unlit. Inside the church the celebrant takes off his biretta; the deacon holds up the candle and standing, chants in a low key *Lumen Christi,* all (except the deacon, subdeacon and thurifer) genuflect towards the candle and reply *Deo gratias.* The celebrant lights his candle from the Paschal candle. The procession goes on until the deacon is at about the middle of the church. He chants a second time, at a higher pitch, *Lumen Christi,* and all genuflect and answer as before. The acolytes light their candles from the Paschal candle and then light the candles of the other servers and clergy. The procession continues to the chancel. Meanwhile the sacristan (or MC2) places in the middle of the sanctuary (if it is not already there) the stand to hold the Paschal candle during the *Præconium,*[100] etc., and to the right of it (facing north) the lectern[101] on which the book for the *Præconium* will be put by the deacon. When the procession arrives in the chancel the thurifer stands to the right of the lectern facing the cross held by the subdeacon; the subdeacon passes to the gospel side and stands facing the lectern (his right hand side being towards the nave). The deacon, standing in the middle of the choir, before the stand in which the Paschal candle is to be placed, sings for the third time, in a still higher pitch, *Lumen Christi.* All genuflect and reply *Deo gratias* as before. The deacon puts the candle into the base provided for it and goes to assist the celebrant putting incense in the thurible. The celebrant and MC1 go to the sedilia, the acolytes to the credence, the clergy and people to their places. All sit. Meanwhile—after the third

---

[97] If they were blessed previously, they are not to be blessed again.

[98] This is the prayer formerly used to bless the grains of incense, with the word *cereum* added; and *intende* replaces *accende.*

[99] Which a server or the sacristan takes to the sedilia in the sanctuary.

[100] The candle should be raised on high, so as to be distinctly visible to the congregation.

[101] The lectern must be so placed as to allow room for the deacon to go around the candle when censing it.

Lumen Christi – servers light the people's candles with tapers lit from the Paschal candle; and the lamps all through the church are lit. Incense is put in the thurible by the celebrant at the sedilia.

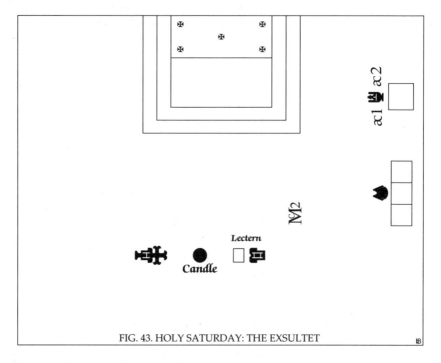

FIG. 43. HOLY SATURDAY: THE EXSULTET

Præconium Paschale (*Exsultet*). The deacon receives the book for the *Præconium* from MC2 and, accompanied by him, goes to the celebrant, kneels before him and asks the blessing, saying aloud *Iube, domne, benedicere*. The celebrant gives the blessing *Dominus sit...suum paschale præconium: in nomine,* etc., and lays his hand on the book. The deacon answers *Amen*, kisses his hand, rises, bows to the celebrant, goes to the centre, genuflects with MC2, bows to the choir and goes to the lectern, on which he sets the book. He incenses it, as at solemn Mass; then walking round the Paschal candle he censes it continuously with single swings. The thurifer takes the thurible to the sacristy as it will not be wanted again until the procession to the baptistery. All stand holding their lighted candles. The deacon sings the *Præconium* facing north (i.e., the candle before him, the altar to his right) as when singing the Gospel. Should the Holy See or the diocese be vacant at the time the respective clauses are omitted. That for the local Ordinary is sung by all, including exempt religious.

The Lessons. When the *Præconium* is finished, all extinguish their candles and sit; the subdeacon gives away the processional cross to a server to be put aside and, with the deacon, goes to the sedilia. There the deacon takes off the white vestments and resumes the violet stole and dalmatic. MC2 removes the white veil from the lectern, and there the chanting of the four lessons is done by readers[102] (each, conducted by MC2, genuflecting in the centre of the choir west of the candle and saluting the choir before and after). They stand facing north (with the candle before them, the altar to their right). For this all remain seated and simply listen. Each lesson is begun without any title and *Deo gratias* is not said at the end. At the conclusion of the first lesson, and after the chant *canticum* that follows each of the other three lessons, all stand. Acolyte 1 holds the book. The celebrant at the sedilia sings *Oremus,* the deacon *Flectamus genua,* and all (including the celebrant) kneel for a little time in prayer. The deacon then chants *Levate* and all rise. The celebrant, hands joined, sings[103] the prayer and all answer *Amen.*

First Part of the Litanies. When the fourth prayer has been concluded all kneel (the celebrant at a prie-dieu or stool before the sedilia). Two cantors, who may be in copes, are led in by MC2 and kneel in the middle of the choir, before the Paschal candle. They chant the Litanies of the Saints up to *Omnes sancti* inclusive. All answer, not repeating the invocations. Meantime the MC's and servers see to the preparations for the blessing of the baptismal water in the middle of the choir, in sight of the congregation.[104] After *Omnes sancti et sanctæ Dei* all stand.

Blessing the Baptismal Water. The celebrant and ministers come from the sedilia, and stand before the table with the vessel of water, etc. — now placed in the sanctuary towards the epistle side. They stand facing the congregation, so that the people can see the ceremony, having the Paschal candle on their right. A server holds the processional cross (facing the celebrant, on his left) as set out in fig. 44.

With joined hands, the Celebrant sings *Dominus vobiscum* and, in the first ferial tone, the prayer. All sing the responses. The Celebrant sings the last words of the conclusion of the prayer *(Per omnia)* in the form that introduces a preface, and chants this special one of blessing in the ferial tone. After the words *de Spiritu Sancto,* the celebrant, holding his right hand extended, divides the water, tracing on it a cross with his little finger. He wipes his finger — the deacon handing him a towel brought by MC2 (or the thurifer). After *corrumpat* the celebrant touches the water, laying the palm of his right hand on it; he dries his hand. Three crosses — traced with the little finger — are made with the extended right hand over the water, not touching it, at the point marked in the text. After *ferebatur* he scatters with his right hand a little of the water towards the people, towards himself, to his left and to his right, and dries his hand. The words *Haec nobis...aspira* are sung in *tono lectionis.* The celebrant breathes

---

[102] If no clerics are available, suitable laymen, in choir dress, may (it would seem) do this.

[103] The tone will be the simple ferial one; cf. O'Connell, *The Celebration of Mass,* 1964, p. 443.

[104] If there is no font in the church, the renewal of the baptismal promises follows immediately the first part of the Litanies.

(halat) thrice cross-wise over the water, pronouncing in the same tone the words *Tu has*, etc. MC2 (or the thurifer) brings the Paschal candle, and the deacon hands it to the celebrant. He puts the end of it a little way into the water and resumes the preface tone for *Descendat*, etc. He takes the candle out of the water, plunges it in again a little lower than before while singing, at a higher pitch, *Descendat*, etc. He repeats all this for the third time, plunging the candle to the bottom of the water, and singing in a still higher pitch *Descendat*, etc. The celebrant, still holding the candle in the water, bending down, breathes three times, in the form of a trident or of the Greek letter psi, over the water between the candle and the edge of the vat. Then, erect, he chants *Totamque...effectu*. He withdraws the candle. The deacon hands it to MC2 who dries it with one of the towels and returns it to its place in the stand in the middle of the sanctuary. The celebrant continues the preface, the conclusion of which is recited. All answer *Amen*. Using a jug or ladle, the sacristan (or the thurifer) takes some of the water and pours it into *(a)* the aspersory, *(b)* the vessel made ready for it on credence 3 (for the Easter supply of lustral water). MC2 brings the deacon the salver with the vials of holy oil and cotton wool. The deacon hands the vial of oil of Catechumens to the celebrant who pours some into the water, cross-wise, saying aloud *Sanctificetur*, etc. All answer *Amen*. The deacon removes any drops of oil from the outside of the vial with cotton wool and replaces it on the salver. He presents the Chrism to the celebrant who pours some, cross-wise, into the water, saying *Infusio*, etc. All answer *Amen*. The celebrant, retaining the Chrism receives from the deacon the Oil of Catechumens and pours a little from both vials together, cross-wise, on to the water, saying *Commixtio*, etc. He does this three times at the words *Patris*, etc. He returns the vials to the deacon who wipes them, and replaces them on the salver. MC2 returns this to credence 3. The celebrant mixes the oil and water with his right hand. The celebrant wipes his hand with cotton wool. MC2 and thurifer bring the ewer, basin, bread, lemon and hand-towel; the celebrant washes his hands.[105]

If baptism be administered the preliminary rites (exorcisms, anointing with the Oil of Catechumens, etc.) may be carried out earlier in the day (and by a different priest), and the celebrant—having changed into a white stole and cope—then begins at the queries *Credis in Deum? (Quis vocaris?* for an adult). He need not change back again into violet vestments for the procession to the baptistery with the blessed water.

The chant *Sicut cervus* and the prayer *Omnipotens...respice* occur when the blessed water is being carried to the baptistery; and the people are not sprinkled with the newly blessed water until after the renewal of the baptismal promises.

---

[105] O'Connell, *Ceremonies of Holy Week*, pp. 61-62.

If there is a baptistery which is *separate from the church,* the baptismal water may be blessed there. Then after the invocation *Sancta Trinitas, unus Deus, miserere nobis* of the Litanies, the sacred ministers go there in procession, led by MC2. Then comes the Paschal candle borne by a server, followed by a server with the cross and acolytes with their (lighted) candles, the clergy, MC1 and the sacred ministers. On the way the canticle *Sicut cervus* is sung, and the celebrant sings the prayer *Omnipotens...respice* before entering the baptistery. Some cantors and the people remain in their places in church and continue the Litanies, until the return of the procession, repeating the Litanies, if necessary (recommencing at *Sancta Maria*). After the blessing of the water the sacred ministers and those who accompany them return in silence to the sanctuary.

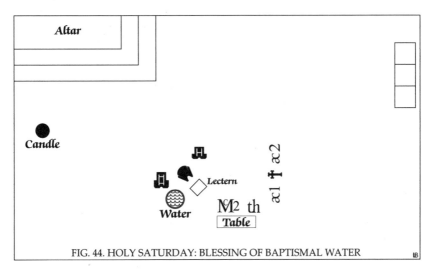

FIG. 44. HOLY SATURDAY: BLESSING OF BAPTISMAL WATER

Procession to the Baptistery. When the baptismal water has been blessed it is carried in solemn procession to the baptistery. The thurifer[106] — having had incense put in and blessed by the celebrant — heads the procession with MC2. They are followed by the cross-bearer carrying the cross, the clergy, servers, the deacon carrying the vessel of blessed water,[107] and the celebrant accompanied by MC1. During the procession *Sicut cervus* (which had been omitted before the blessing of the water) is sung. In the baptistery the thurifer passes to the right, the cross-bearer and servers to the left, the celebrant stands before the font. The blessed water is poured into this by the deacon (or by the acolytes, if they had carried it), or, if the vessel belongs in the font, it is placed back in it.

---

[106] He gets his thurible towards the end of the blessing of the water.

[107] Or this may be carried by a server (or servers); then the deacon accompanies the celebrant on his right; the subdeacon on his left.

The celebrant says (sings) *Dominus vobiscum, Oremus* and the prayer, with hands joined. Then he censes[108] the font, with three single swings. All return in the same order and in silence to the choir. The cross-bearer puts aside the cross. The celebrant, at the sedilia, takes off the violet vestments and puts on a white stole and cope. Servers light candles for the deacon and subdeacon, and for the people, from the Paschal candle.

Renewal of the Baptismal Promises. The celebrant, accompanied by the deacon and subdeacon, goes before the Paschal candle. He puts incense into the thurible, blesses it, and censes the candle, with single swings, while walking round it. The clergy and people (standing) hold lighted candles. The celebrant, standing by the candle, turns to the congregation (or addresses them from the pulpit or ambo, the deacon and subdeacon remaining at the foot of the pulpit, if there is not room for them beside the celebrant) and carries out the renewal of the baptismal promises in the form prescribed. For this the vernacular may be used, in a translation approved by the local Ordinary. The text should be printed and circulated among the congregation beforehand. At the end of the renewal the celebrant sprinkles the people (in front of him, to his left and right, or continuously going around the church) with the lustral water, taken from the baptismal water when this was being blessed.[109] The clergy and people extinguish their candles, and kneel.

Second Part of the Litanies. MC1 marshals the thurifer, acolytes and sacred ministers into processional order. They all (except the celebrant, who bows) genuflect in the centre and salute the choir, and then go to the sacristy, and vest there in white for Mass. When they have left the sanctuary two cantors, kneeling in the middle of the choir, sing the second part of the Litanies of the Saints *(Propitius esto* to *Christe, exaudi nos)*. All sing the responses. During this, under the direction of MC2 servers remove the Paschal candle to its candlestick on the gospel side, take off the violet frontal and all violet veils, spread the carpet, and prepare the altar for the Easter Mass. The altar candles are lit.

The Easter Vigil Mass. While the cantors sing *Kyrie, eleison,* or, in a large Church, *Agnus Dei,* the sacred ministers—preceded by MC2, thurifer, and acolytes with their candles—go to the altar and reverence it and bow to the choir. The sacred ministers ascend at once—the preparatory prayers and Confession (with *Aufer* and *Oramus*) being omitted—the celebrant kisses the altar and censes it in the usual way. Meanwhile—immediately after *Christe, exaudi nos*—the choir sings the *Kyrie, eleison* (unaccompanied). There is no introit. The celebrant recites *Kyrie, eleison* with his ministers (on his right) at the epistle corner and then, at the middle, intones *Gloria in excelsis.* The bells of the church,

---

[108] If fresh incense is needed in the thurible the celebrant puts it in and blesses it, as usual.
[109] With ordinary lustral water, if baptismal water was not blessed.

great[110] and small, are rung during the *Gloria*, the singing of which is accompanied by the organ. The images of the church are unveiled. The differences in this Easter Mass from an ordinary solemn Mass are: (i) Having given the blessing to the subdeacon at the end of the Epistle, the celebrant—with the deacon and subdeacon in a semicircle to his right—sings the triple *Alleluia* at a higher pitch each time, and all repeat it in the same pitch each time; (ii) at the Gospel the acolytes assist without their candles, but the book is censed as usual; (iii) there is no *Credo* or offertory antiphon; (iv) at the *Lavabo*, *Gloria Patri* is said; (v) *Orate, fratres* is said in the clear voice; (vi) The preface is the Easter one *(in hac...nocte)*, the *Communicantes (noctem)* and *Hanc igitur* are proper; (vii) *Agnus Dei*, the first prayer before communion and the kiss of peace are omitted. If ciboria are put back into the tabernacle the veil is put on and the sanctuary lamp should be lit.

Lauds of Easter Day. Immediately after the communion and ablutions the choir sings, for Lauds, the antiphon *Alleluia* (thrice), Psalm 150 with *Gloria Patri,* and repeats the antiphon. Meanwhile the thurifer prepares the thurible. The celebrant, having taken the ablutions, goes with the deacon to the missal at the epistle corner. The subdeacon stands at the deacon's right—as at the introit—when he has veiled and removed the chalice to the credence. All stand. A chapter, hymn and verse are not said. The celebrant intones the antiphon to the canticle *Benedictus (Et valde mane)* and the choir continues it, and then sings the *Benedictus* (with *Gloria Patri* at the end of it). All make the sign of the cross at the first words of the *Benedictus.* Meanwhile the celebrant puts incense into the thurible, blesses it, and censes the altar. He is censed by the deacon, and then the clergy and subdeacon are censed by the deacon; the deacon, MC, servers and people by the thurifer, in the usual way. When the choir has repeated the antiphon, the celebrant goes to the middle of the altar (the deacon and subdeacon behind him), kisses it and sings *Dominus vobiscum.* He then sings the postcommunion *(Spiritum)* at the epistle corner and *Dominus vobiscum* at the middle, as usual. The deacon adds *Alleluia* twice to *Ite, missa est.* The blessing is given, but there is no last Gospel.[111]

The celebration of the Easter Vigil Mass alone, without the preceding ceremonies, is forbidden.

---

[110] In places where there is only one church, its (exterior) bells are rung when the *Gloria* is begun. Where there are several churches the bells of all are rung together when the *Gloria* is begun at the principal church and no sooner. (In case of doubt about which is the chief church the local Ordinary is to be consulted.)

[111] The ciborium used for Holy Communion is put in the tabernacle after the communion; the Blessed Sacrament reserved elsewhere is brought back to the tabernacle after Mass, or, if required for Holy Communion, may be brought in after the consecration by another priest or deacon.

§ 7. Holy Saturday in Small Churches

The solemn Easter Vigil service is to be begun at an hour that will allow Mass to be celebrated about midnight. The Ordinary of the place may, for local reasons, allow the service to begin earlier, but not before twilight, and certainly not before sunset. The priest who celebrates the midnight Mass may again celebrate Mass on Easter Sunday (and twice or three times, if he has the faculty to binate or trinate). Holy Communion may be given only during the Mass, or immediately after and in connection with it (except for those in danger of death). At least four servers are needed on Holy Saturday.

Preparations. *Outside the church door,* or in the porch, or within the church (wherever the ceremony can best be seen by the people), on a table covered with a white cloth: OHS or a missal with the rite;[112] a salver with the five grains of incense; an empty thurible (for which a stand is useful) and the incense-boat; aspersory with lustral water[113] and sprinkler; white stole and dalmatic; tapers; stylus (to trace the characters on the Paschal candle). *Aside:* a brazier with coals previously lit from a spark struck from flint (such as a cigarette lighter) and charcoal, and a tongs; the Paschal candle with the characters marked out on it; candles for the celebrant, servers, and people;[114] clappers to call the people.

In the sanctuary: high altar, with three altar cloths, unlit feast day candles and unveiled cross; violet frontal over a white one; tabernacle empty (except for a corporal), unveiled, half open, the key at hand, a white conopæum and lamp prepared. Lamp(s) ready to be lit. *In the choir:* temporary stand for the Paschal candle in the centre; lectern,[115] covered with a white veil, for the *Præconium,* on the epistle side, facing north; on the gospel side the Paschal candle candlestick, adorned; the sedilia in its usual place, uncovered or with a violet cover over a white one; seats for the servers.

Credence 1: OHS or missal for the *Præconium* and the lessons;[116] missal-stand and altar cards; chalice prepared for Mass,[117] with white burse and veil; ciboria with altar breads and veil(s) for communion; cruets and hand-towel; bells to ring at *Gloria,* if customary ; communion plate;[118] English version of the form for the renewal of the baptismal promises approved by the Ordinary; tapers. *Aside:* White stole and cope; stool (or prie-dieu) for the celebrant to kneel at for the prayers and Litanies.

---

[112] Or this may be prepared on a lectern.

[113] Some should have been kept when the stoups were emptied on Maundy Thursday.

[114] The people should have candles before the ceremony begins.

[115] The same lectern, unveiled, may be used for the lessons.

[116] Or this may be brought by the sacristan from the porch after the ceremony there.

[117] Unless one of the servers is a (tonsured) cleric this must be brought by the priest to the altar for Mass.

[118] And a communion cloth if there are clergy for Holy Communion.

Credence 2: If baptismal water is to be blessed and baptism is to be administered: (cf. § 6 above — credence 3). *Aside:* A vat of water.

In the sacristy: Amice, alb, cincture, violet stole and cope for the celebrant; cassocks and cottas for the (four) servers, and books for them if there are no cantors or clergy in choir; white vestments for Mass; processional cross (unveiled); relics and flowers to adorn the altar for the Easter Mass.

At the place of reservation: White humeral veil; two candles (or torches) and a taper; the umbella, for the transfer of the Blessed Sacrament back to the high altar after Mass.

At the baptistery: The font, cleaned and adorned ready to receive the newly blessed baptismal water, with the plug in.

Blessing the New Fire. The celebrant, having washed his hands, vests in amice, alb, cincture, violet stole and cope.[119] With the servers he bows to the sacristy cross and, wearing his biretta, goes to the altar, in this order: S.4 with the processional cross, S.3, the celebrant between S.1 and S.2 who hold back the edges of his cope. On passing the high altar all genuflect to the cross, except the celebrant, who bows and S.4, who makes no reverence. When they arrive outside the church S.4 stands with his back to the door (to the altar, if the ceremony takes place within). The celebrant stands before the fire, facing the cross, with the three servers at his sides. He takes off his biretta and hands it to S.1, who puts it aside and returns with the aspersory and sprinkler. S.2 holds the book, unless a lectern is used. With joined hands the celebrant says or sings *Dominus vobiscum,* and (in the second ferial tone[120]) the prayer. All make the responses. He then sprinkles the fire (centre, to his left and right) in silence. S.1 puts aside the aspersory and brings the Paschal candle. S.3 transfers some of the blessed burning charcoal to the thurible (with the tongs) held, momentarily, by S.2. The celebrant puts in incense, blesses it as at Mass and incenses the fire. S.3 puts aside the thurible and gets the grains of incense on a salver .

Blessing the Paschal Candle. S.2 presents the stylus to the celebrant, who traces out on the candle the characters illustrated in OHS, saying aloud the formulæ given therein. S.3 presents the grains of incense, and — if they have not previously been blessed — the celebrant blesses them by sprinkling them and incensing them thrice in silence, S.2 presenting the aspersory and thurible. The celebrant fixes the grains into the candle, saying aloud the words given in OHS. S.3, having put aside the salver, presents a taper to the celebrant, and from the blessed fire he lights the candle with it, saying aloud *Lumen,* etc. Then he blesses the candle saying (or singing in the second ferial tone) *Dominus vobiscum* and the prayer

---

[119] If a violet cope is not available he remains in alb and stole.
[120] On the last syllable of the end of the prayer and of the conclusion there is a fall of a minor third; cf. O'Connell, *The Celebration of Mass,* 1964, p. 443.

Veniat. All make the responses. Meanwhile all of the lights of the church are extinguished, and candles are distributed to the clergy (if any), to any extra servers, and to the people for the procession, if they have not already got them.

Procession with Candle. The celebrant — aided by S.2 — takes off his violet vestments, and puts on a white stole and dalmatic. S.3 presents the thurible and the celebrant puts in incense and blesses it, and then receives from S.1 the Paschal candle. A procession is formed: S.3 with the smoking thurible and carrying the incense-boat leads, then comes S.4 with the cross, next the celebrant with the Paschal candle, and lastly S.1, with the celebrant's (small) candle,[121] still unlit, and S.2 with OHS.[122] Finally come any extra altar servers, the clergy and the people, all with unlit candles. Having entered the church (a little way up, if the ceremony was begun inside the church) the celebrant stops and all turn to face him. He raises the candle a little and sings the first *Lumen Christi*. All (except the celebrant, S.3 and S.4) genuflect towards the candle and answer *Deo gratias*. S.1 then lights the celebrant's candle from the Paschal candle. In the middle of the church the celebrant sings at a higher pitch *Lumen Christi*; all genuflect and reply as before; and from the Paschal candle the candles of any extra servers and of the clergy are lighted. In the middle of the sanctuary the celebrant sings for the third time, in a still higher pitch, *Lumen Christi*, all genuflecting and replying as before, The candles of the people are then lighted.[123] The sacristan lights the church lamps and — if this is not done at the *Gloria* — switches on the lights. In the sanctuary S.3 stands by the credence, S.4 on the gospel side facing the lectern; the celebrant puts the Paschal candle into the stand prepared for it in the centre, and goes to the credence, accompanied by S.1 and S.2. Incense is put in, S.2 presenting the boat.

The Præconium Paschale (*Exsultet*). S.1 then brings the book to the celebrant, who, kneeling on the lowest step at the epistle side, says, in a low voice, *Iube, domne,* etc., as indicated in OHS. With S.1 and S.3 (carrying the thurible), the celebrant goes to the lectern, puts the book on it, and incenses it with three double swings. He then incenses the Paschal candle, going around it. S.3 takes the thurible to the sacristy. All stand holding their lighted candles and the celebrant sings or reads the *Præconium*, having in front of him the Paschal candle and the cross; on his right the altar, on his left the congregation. Should the Holy See or the diocese be vacant at the time the respective clauses are omitted. That for the local Ordinary is sung by all, including exempt religious.

---

[121] So the rubric, though the celebrant never uses this candle.

[122] Unless there is a second copy in the sanctuary.

[123] A few are lighted by S.1 and S.2 with tapers lit from the Paschal candle and the light then passed on to all the others.

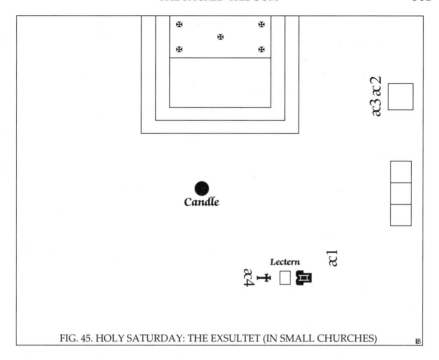

FIG. 45. HOLY SATURDAY: THE EXSULTET (IN SMALL CHURCHES)

The Lessons. After the *Præconium* the celebrant goes to the sedilia, takes off the white dalmatic and stole, and resumes the violet stole and cope. S.4 lays aside the processional cross, while S.3 removes the veil from the lectern. If there is a lector available, vested in cassock and cotta, he — having saluted the altar and the celebrant — may sing the lessons in the correct tone,[124] or read them. He may be one of the servers. The celebrant, seated at the sedilia, listens to them. If there is no lector, the celebrant himself reads the lessons at the lectern. They have no title and *Deo gratias* is not said at the end. The canticle after lessons 2, 3, 4 is said or sung by cantors or clergy present. If there are none, the celebrant says it with the servers. At the end of the first lesson — after the canticle that follows the others — all stand and the celebrant standing at the lectern (or sedilia) says *Oremus. Flectamus genua.* All, with him, kneel and pray for a short time. He then says *Levate,* all rise, and, with joined hands, he says, or sings in the first ferial tone,[125] the prayer. All answer *Amen.*

First Part of the Litanies. After the fourth prayer all kneel — the celebrant at a stool or prie-dieu placed before him at the sedilia and the Litanies of the Saints are sung, without doubling the invocations, as far as *Propitius esto* exclusively, by two cantors kneeling in the middle of the choir. All make answer. If there are no cantors, the celebrant — kneeling

---

124 Cf. *Graduale Romanum,* p. 113*.

125 A fall of a minor third (d'l) on the last syllable of the prayer and of its conclusion (cf. O'Connell, *The Celebration of Mass,* 1964. p. 444).

with the servers on the lowest step at the epistle side, facing northwards—says them (but does not sing them). If there is a baptismal font in the church, the blessing of the baptismal water follows; if not the renewal of the baptismal promises takes place at once.

Blessing of Baptismal Water. During the Litanies S.3 and S.4 (aided by the sacristan) prepare for the blessing of the water. For the blessing[126] — which is done as described in detail in § 6 above—S.4 acts as cross-bearer, S.3 holds the book (unless a lectern is used), while S.1 and S.2 assist the celebrant.

Procession to the Font. When the blessing of the water has been completed the larger vessel is carried to the font in the baptistery. The celebrant puts incense into the thurible, presented by S.3, S.1 handing the incense. Then a procession is formed: S.3, with smoking thurible and boat, leads the way; then S.4 with the cross; after him S.2 with the vat of water (aided, if necessary, by S.1); at the end the celebrant, covered, with S.1 holding the edge of his cope. The Paschal candle is not carried in the procession. As the procession wends its way the canticle *Sicut cervus* is sung, if there are singers; or recited by any clergy present. Otherwise the celebrant recites it aloud. On arriving in the baptistery S.3 passes to the right, S.4 to the left. S.2 (aided by S.1) pours the water into the font.[127] Then the celebrant, with hands joined, says—or sings in the first ferial tone—*Dominus vobiscum* and the prayer. All make the responses. The celebrant then incenses the font with three single swings.[128] All return to the sanctuary in the order in which they came[129] and in silence. There S.4 puts aside the cross and stands, with S.3, at the credence. The celebrant having, with S.1 and S.2, saluted the altar, goes to the sedilia.

Renewal of Baptismal Promises. There he exchanges his violet vestments for a white stole and cope. Meanwhile S.4 lights the candles of all present from the blessed candle. If there had been no blessing of baptismal water, S.3 brings the thurible from the sacristy. S.1 gets the aspersory,[130] S.2 the form for the renewal of the baptismal promises. The celebrant puts incense in the thurible, presented by S.3, and, with the servers, goes before the altar and salutes it. He incenses the Paschal candle, walking around it.[131] Standing near the candle (or in the ambo or pulpit) he carries out the renewal of the promises. All stand, holding their lighted candles in the right hand. The celebrant gives the address, using the approved vernacular text, and puts the queries to the people. They make answer, from the forms provided for them, and recite the *Our*

---

[126] The rite is the same as was formerly in the missal. See O'Connell, *Ceremonies of Holy Week*, p. 107.

[127] Or replaces the vessel of water in the font, if it is part of the latter.

[128] If the thurible is not smoking properly, he first puts in incense.

[129] S.2 may now walk on the celebrant's left.

[130] If baptismal water had not been blessed ordinary lustral water is used for the renewal.

[131] S.3 then takes the thurible to the sacristy and renews the charcoal for Mass.

Father. When the renewal is finished the celebrant sprinkles the people, cross-wise, from the entrance to the sanctuary; or by going around the church, sprinkling continuously as at the Asperges. The people extinguish their candles.

Second Part of the Litanies. If there are cantors,[132] they kneel once more in the middle of the sanctuary and continue the singing of the Litanies from *Propitius esto,* while the celebrant and servers, having saluted the altar, go to the sacristy to prepare for Mass. If there are no cantors, the celebrant kneels on the lowest step at the epistle side, and, with the servers, kneeling beside him, finishes the Litanies. The people make the responses. In the sacristy the celebrant, aided by S.3 and S.4, puts on white vestments for Mass, while S.1 and S.2 and the sacristan prepare the altar. They remove the violet frontal and sedilia cover, put on the missal-stand with the book and the altar cards, adorn the altar with relics and flowers, and light the altar candles. The Paschal candle is removed to its candlestick on the gospel side of the sanctuary. The temporary candlestick is removed.

The Easter Vigil Mass. The celebrant comes to the altar, with the servers walking in pairs before him,[133] while the cantors (if the Mass is sung) begin the solemn chant of *Kyrie, eleison.* There is no psalm or confession, and so the celebrant, having saluted the altar, goes up at once, saying nothing, and kisses it. Standing in the middle he says *Kyrie, eleison,* as usual. There is no introit. After the recitation or singing of *Kyrie,* the celebrant begins *Gloria in excelsis.* The church bells are rung, and—if the Mass is a sung one—the organ is played, and (if customary) small bells are rung by the servers until the celebrant has finished saying the hymn. Images throughout the church are unveiled by the sacristan. After the Epistle (which in a sung Mass may be chanted by a lector, in choir dress, and then the celebrant listens to it, seated) the celebrant says aloud, or sings, thrice—each time at a higher pitch—the *Alleluia.* All repeat it each time. The cantors then sing the verse and psalm or the celebrant reads them aloud. Candles are not carried for the Gospel. There is no *Credo,* no offertory antiphon.[134] *Gloria Patri* is said at the lavabo. *Oratre, fratres* is said in the clear voice. The Easter preface is used *(in hac...nocte)* and there is a proper *Communicantes* and *Hanc igitur. Agnus Dei* is omitted and so is the first prayer following it. After the communion the ablutions are as usual. If ciboria are reserved in the tabernacle the conopæum is put on and the lamp is lit.

---

[132] If there are no singers, any assisting clergy may finish the litanies.

[133] If the Mass is a sung one and incense is used S.3 leads the procession carrying the thurible. The altar is incensed by the celebrant the moment he arrives. Incense is used during the rest of the Mass exactly as at solemn Mass.

[134] One of the servers if a cleric brings the chalice and the ciboria to the altar.

Lauds. Lauds of Easter Day are said or sung. The antiphon *Alleluia* (thrice) is sung, then Psalm 150, and the antiphon is repeated. There is no chapter or hymn, but at once the celebrant, standing at the epistle corner, intones the *Benedictus* antiphon *Et valde mane.* This is continued by the cantors, who then intone the *Benedictus*. This is sung by the choir, during which the altar is censed. S.3 acting as thurifer then incenses the celebrant, clergy, servers and people. The antiphon is repeated. If there are no cantors, the celebrant, standing at the epistle corner of the altar, recites aloud all this (antiphon, psalm and canticle) with the servers, who recite every other verse of the latter. After the repetition of the antiphon the celebrant goes to the middle of the altar, kisses it, says (sings) *Dominus vobiscum,* facing the people, and, going to the epistle corner, says (or sings in the solemn tone) the prayer, which is the postcommunion. To *Ite, missa est* and *Deo gratias, Alleluia* is added twice. The blessing is given as usual, but there is no last Gospel.

Removal of the Blessed Sacrament. At a convenient moment the celebrant, wearing a white humeral veil over an alb (surplice) and white stole — accompanied by S.3 with the umbella and S.1 and S.2 with candles — brings the ciboria from the place of reservation to the tabernacle of the high altar.

§ 8. The Semi-Solemn Rites of Holy Week

In churches or oratories where the Holy Week ceremonial is carried out according to the simple (sung) rite, if an extra priest or deacon is available he may — vested as a deacon — perform the functions of a deacon as described below.[135]

PALM SUNDAY

The preparations are the same as for the solemn rite, above, omitting what is proper to the subdeacon. All is carried out as described for the solemn rite except what is noted here.

Procession. The deacon, having vested in a red dalmatic, assists the celebrant in vesting and accompanies him on his left to the altar, holding the edge of the cope. He assists the celebrant during the blessing of the palms (handing the aspersory and thurible, etc.), and at their distribution. After the celebrant has washed his hands the deacon goes up to the altar with him and assists while incense is put in. He then gets the book for the Gospel, says *Munda cor meum* kneeling, receives the blessing, and goes to sing the Gospel. The book is held by a server or put on a lectern. After the Gospel the deacon carries the book to the celebrant to kiss the text, then

---

[135] S.R.C., 1 February 1957, § 3. This form of semi-solemn rite was already in use in certain religious orders for some functions.

gives it to the MC or a server, and assists the celebrant putting incense in for the procession. He then hands the celebrant the palm reserved for him, turns to the people and sings *Procedamus in pace*. During the procession he walks at the celebrant's left holding back the cope. After the return of the procession he goes up to the altar with the celebrant and faces the people while the celebrant sings the closing prayer. He then goes to the sedilia with the celebrant and both change their vestments.

Mass. The Epistle is read by a lector or by the deacon. If there are no extra deacons to sing the Passion, it is sung or read by the celebrant and deacon[136] – each retaining his vestments – the former taking the Christus parts, the latter those of the Narrator and the Synagogue. *Munda cor meum, Iube, Domine, benedicere,* and *Dominus sit in corde meo* are said by each in a low voice; by the celebrant standing, bowed at the centre of the altar on the footpace, by the deacon kneeling on the lowest step. During the Passion the celebrant remains at the gospel corner on the footpace; the deacon stands at the gospel side, *in plano,* facing north, the book on a lectern. At the offertory the deacon brings the chalice to the altar and pours in the wine and water; the paten is put under the corporal as at low Mass. If necessary, the deacon may help in distributing Holy Communion. After this he ministers the ablutions, rearranges the chalice and carries it to the credence.

MAUNDY THURSDAY

The preparations are the same as for the solemn rite (above), omitting what is proper to the subdeacon.

Mass. Up to the Gospel the ceremony is as at solemn Mass. The Epistle is read by a lector or by the deacon. After the homily the deacon leads to their places the men whose feet are to be washed. At the sedilia he takes off his maniple, helps the celebrant to take off his chasuble and maniple and accompanies him for the washing of the feet as described above. After this, when the celebrant resumes his maniple and chasuble the deacon resumes his maniple. Both go to the middle for the concluding prayer, during which the deacon is on the celebrant's left. At the offertory the deacon brings the chalice to the altar and serves the wine and water. After the communion (at which he may help, if necessary) he serves the ablutions, rearranges the chalice and carries it to the credence.

Procession to Altar of Repose. After Mass the deacon, at the sedilia, takes off his maniple and helps the celebrant unvest and put on the cope. He assists at the incensation and helps the celebrant take the ciborium and cover it with the humeral veil. During the procession he is on the celebrant's left, holding back the cope. At the altar of repose he helps the celebrant put the ciborium on the altar, assists at the incensation, and,

[136] There is no authority for anyone below the rank of deacon to sing the Passion.

after *Tantum ergo,* puts the ciborium into the tabernacle or casket — genuflecting before and after, standing back from the altar — and locks it. Having made a double genuflexion with the celebrant he accompanies him, on his left, back to the sacristy, takes off his white dalmatic and stole (unless there is an extra ciborium to be moved to the place of reservation) and puts on a violet stole to help at the stripping of the altars.

GOOD FRIDAY

The preparations are the same as for the solemn rite (above), omitting what is proper to the subdeacon.

First Part of the Afternoon Service. The deacon wears amice, alb, cincture and black stole. At the altar — whither he precedes the celebrant — he prostrates himself on the left of the celebrant. For the lessons he sits at the sedilia beside the celebrant. If there is no lector the deacon reads the two lessons. He says *Flectamus genua* and *Levate* before the prayer between the lessons. If there are no deacons for the Passion the celebrant takes the part of Christus, the deacon that of the Narrator and of the Synagogue. Each retains his stole. Both, bowed before the altar, say in a low voice *Dominus sit in corde meo et in labiis meis.* The Passion is read or sung *in plano* on the gospel side facing north, the books on lecterns. After the Passion, at the sedilia, the celebrant puts on a black cope, the deacon a black dalmatic. During the solemn prayers the deacon stands on the celebrant's left, and says each *Flectamus genua* and *Levate.*

Veneration of the Cross. After the prayers the deacon takes off his dalmatic at the sedilia and goes to fetch the cross. During its unveiling, he assists the celebrant, standing on the latter's left, and joins in the chant at *in quo.* He venerates the cross after the celebrant. If the veneration by the faithful is carried out collectively, the deacon stands for it on the celebrant's left on the footpace.

The Communion. After the veneration of the cross the deacon puts on a violet stole and dalmatic at the sedilia, and spreads the corporal on the altar table. He then brings the ciborium from the altar of repose as in the solemn rite. He assists the celebrant during the communion rite, and may help in distributing Holy Communion, if necessary. At the thanksgiving prayers he stands at the celebrant's left on the footpace. After the service he carries the ciborium to the place of reservation, wearing a white humeral veil over surplice and stole.

HOLY SATURDAY

The preparations are the same as for the solemn rite above, omitting what is proper to the subdeacon.

First Part of the Ceremony. For the blessing of the fire and the Paschal candle the deacon — in violet stole and dalmatic — is at the celebrant's side to assist him. After the blessing of the candle the deacon changes into a white stole and dalmatic, assists at putting incense into the thurible, and takes the Paschal candle. He then acts as in the solemn rite for the procession to the sanctuary and the singing of the *Exsultet*. After that he resumes his violet vestments and is by the celebrant at the sedilia for the lessons, etc., for which he says *Flectamus genua* and *Levate*. He kneels beside the celebrant for the Litanies; sing them with him if there are no cantors.

Blessing of Baptismal Water. During the blessing the deacon ministers to the celebrant. For the transport of the water to the baptistery he acts as in the solemn rite. If servers carry the vessel of water, the deacon walks on the celebrant's left, holding the cope. During the renewal of the baptismal promises he stands on the celebrant's left, having assisted at putting in incense and the incensation of the candle. After *Pater noster* he passes to the celebrant's right and carries the bucket, accompanying the celebrant for the sprinkling of the people. During, or — if there are no cantors — after, the singing of the second part of the Litanies he accompanies the celebrant to the sacristy and vests in white for Mass.

Easter Mass. At the Mass he sings the Gospel — and if there is no lector, the Epistle — brings the chalice to the altar and ministers the cruets; re-veils the chalice and carries it to the credence; sings *Ite* with double *Alleluia*. He may help in distributing Holy Communion.

Chapter XXVII

Easter to Advent

§ 1. Eastertide

EASTERTIDE *(Tempus Paschale)* begins with the first Easter Mass and ends after None and Mass on the Saturday before the feast of the Blessed Trinity, which feast is kept on the first Sunday after Pentecost.

Eastertide Office. Eastertide has its own hymns at Matins, Lauds and Vespers. In all hymns of the common (iambic dimeter) rhythm the last verse is changed to:

> *Deo Patri sit gloria*
> *Et Filio qui a mortuis*
> *Surrexit, ac Paraclito,*
> *In sempiterna sæcula.*

To all versicles in the Divine Office and to *Panem de cælo præstitisti eis* at Benediction, and to their responses, *Alleluia* is added. But *Alleluia* is never added to *Adiutorium nostrum in nomine Domini; Domine, exaudi orationem meam; Dominus vobiscum;* or to their responses.

In the responsories after the lessons at Matins *Alleluia* is added after the first part (the response) each time it is said, not after the versicle. At Prime, Terce, Sext, None and Compline the short responsories are changed, so that the whole first part (the response), normally divided by an asterisk, is put before that asterisk. The second part consists of *Alleluia, Alleluia.* This second part *(Alleluia, Alleluia)* alone is repeated after the versicle. The versicle which follows the short responsory obeys the usual rule for this time, having *Alleluia* at the end, as also its response. At Prime the versicle of the short responsory is *Qui surrexisti a mortuis* (except at Ascension and Pentecost).

During Eastertide *Alleluia* is added to all antiphons of the Office, if they do not already so end, also to the Invitatory at Matins. At the end of Matins *Te Deum* is said on ferias.

Eastertide Mass. At Mass the Sundays of the season have their own proper, interspersed with *Alleluia*. In these the introit has *Alleluia* in the middle of the antiphon and again two or three times at the end. The offertory has *Alleluia* at the end once; the communion antiphon twice.

If a Mass such as may occur either in Eastertide or not (such as the Masses of commons of saints)[1] is said in this season, at the end of the antiphon of the introit *Alleluia* is added twice, and once at the end of the offertory and communion antiphon.[2]

During Eastertide in all Masses (except those for the dead), instead of the gradual and *Alleluia,* the Great Alleluia is said. This is formed thus: *Alleluia* is said twice. When it is sung the second time it has the Iubilus[3] at the end. Then follows an Alleluiatic verse. The tone changes. *Alleluia* is said again with a Iubilus, a second Alleluiatic verse, then *Alleluia* with its Iubilus as before this verse.[4] In Masses which may occur in Eastertide a form of the Great Alleluia is provided to take the place of the gradual.

The hymn *Gloria in excelsis Deo* is said throughout Eastertide, even on weekdays, except in the Rogation Masses, requiems, and certain votive Masses.

During this season (to Whit Sunday inclusive) the chant for the sprinkling of holy water before Mass is *Vidi aquam* instead of *Asperges me.* On Easter Day, if the church has a font, the Asperges is done with water from the baptismal font kept from the day before.

Lighting of Paschal Candle. During Eastertide — until after the Gospel of the chief Mass on Ascension Day — the Paschal candle is lit at solemn or sung Mass and at sung Vespers; it may be lit also at low Mass celebrated with some solemnity and at other liturgical functions.[5] It is also to be lighted at solemn Mass or solemn Vespers which are celebrated in the presence of the Blessed Sacrament solemnly exposed during Paschaltide.[6] It is not lit at requiems, nor at the Office for the dead, nor at any service held with violet vestments (as Rogation Masses), nor at Mass on the vigil of Pentecost, nor at Benediction.[7]

After Ascension Day (see below) the Paschal candle is not again used, and is removed from the sanctuary.

§ 2. The Easter Octave

The first week of Paschaltide is the Easter octave, which has its own further rules. This octave begins at the first Easter Mass and ends after None and Mass on the Saturday after Easter day *(sabbatum in albis).* Low Sunday, although it is the octave day of Easter, conforms to the normal rules of Eastertide.

---

[1] Apostles and martyrs have a special common for Eastertide.

[2] *Alleluia* is added twice to the offertory and communion antiphons in the first Mass of Martyrs in Paschaltide; and twice to the offertory antiphon of the second Mass.

[3] The long neum on the syllable "a" at the end of "alleluia."

[4] But see *infra* for the Easter octave.

[5] OHSI *(Ritus Simplex),* IV, II, ix, 15.

[6] S.R.C. 4383 § 2.

[7] Unless Vespers immediately preceded and it was lit at that Office (S.R.C. 4383 § 1).

Easter Day is the greatest feast of the year.[8] Each day of the octave is of the first class. No feast may be kept on it or during its octave; nor may there be any commemoration (except of the Greater Litanies in Mass) or any *oratio imperata,* or any votive Mass.

During the Easter octave there is only one nocturn at Matins. There are no versicles except at Matins. There are no chapters nor short responsories, nor hymns in any part of the Office. There are no antiphons to the psalms at Prime, Terce, Sext, None. At Compline there is no antiphon at the beginning of the psalms; at the end *Alleluia, Alleluia, Alleluia, Alleluia* is sung. After the psalms of each Office the antiphon *Hæc dies quam fecit Dominus,* etc., is sung, all standing. At Lauds and Vespers this is intoned by the celebrant. The first assistant, in cope, pre-intones it to him.

At the end of Lauds and Vespers *Alleluia, Alleluia* is added to the verse *Benedicamus Domino.*

At Mass (till Friday) there is a gradual, formed in the usual way, the first verse being *Hæc dies.* After the Alleluia verse the sequence *Victimæ paschali* follows.

At the end of Mass *Alleluia, Alleluia* is added to *Ite, missa est* and to its response.

§ 3. Greater and Lesser Litanies

On four days in the year there are special supplications to beg God's blessing on the fruits of the earth. On each of these days there is, normally, a procession during which the Litanies of the Saints (as given in the Roman Ritual, Title X, chap. iv), with certain prayers, are sung, followed by the Mass of Rogations (a votive Mass of the second class).

These days are 25 April (feast of St Mark),[9] and the three days preceding Ascension Day; on the first day the Litanies are called *Greater,* on the other three days they are called *Lesser* Litanies or Rogation Days.

Should Easter Sunday or Monday fall on 25 April, the Greater Litanies are transferred to Easter Tuesday.

The local Ordinary may appoint three other successive days for the Lesser Litanies if the days preceding Ascension Day are not suitable.

There is nothing concerning these four days in the Divine Office, only in Mass.

---

[8] It may fall on or between 22 March and 25 April.

[9] There is no inherent connection between St Mark and the procession. 25 April (vii kal. maias) was the date of a pre-Christian procession of the same kind at Rome (the so-called Robigalia). That day occurs at just the time when the harvest (in Italy) should ripen. The pagan procession was replaced by a Christian one before the feast of St Mark began to be kept on that day. The Rogation days are later and originally Gallican. They are said to have been introduced by St Mamertus, Bishop of Vienne, about the year 470. They were not kept at Rome till the time of Leo III (795-816).

When the procession for the Greater Litanies is not feasible the local Ordinary is to see that a special service of supplication takes its place and at this the Litanies and other prayers are said. These may then be in the vernacular. Afterwards it is becoming that the Mass of Rogations be celebrated, if the date allows a votive Mass of the second class.

Clerics bound to the Divine Office, if they do not take part in the procession or special service of supplication, must say (privately) the Litanies on the day of the Greater Litanies; this is not so for the Lesser Litanies.

The Greater Litanies must be commemorated in every Mass—it is a privileged commemoration—which is not the Mass of Rogations or a requiem Mass.

Procession of the Rogations. Normally on these four days the procession should be made, if possible to another church, where the Rogation Mass is sung. But on St Mark's feast, if the procession ends at a church where his feast is of the first class, the Mass of his feast is said there. If it is not possible to end the procession at another church it may come back to the one from which it set out.

There should be only one general procession in each place, at which all the clergy, secular and regular, take part.[10] It sets out from the principal church of the place. If a general procession through the town is not possible, each church may make its own procession inside the building.

The same priest should, if possible, preside at the procession and sing the Mass which follows it. However, in case of real difficulty, this rule is not urged.

The rules for the procession are these.[11]

Preparation. At the church from which it sets out all is provided for a procession, with violet[12] vestments, that is: the processional cross, acolytes' candles, surplices as required, vestments for the celebrant and ministers, namely, amice, alb, girdle, stole, violet dalmatic and tunicle for the ministers, violet stole and cope for the celebrant. A book containing all that the celebrant will chant must be provided. The high altar is vested in violet.

At the church at which the procession will arrive all is prepared, as usual, for solemn Mass with violet vestments (the chasuble and three maniples). If the priest of the procession will sing the Mass (as he should), he and the ministers vest for Mass at the sedilia. In this case the maniples and his chasuble will be laid out there. On St Mark's feast, if it be of the first class, the frontal and vestments will be red.

---

[10] For the order of the procession, cf. § 7 below.

[11] Cf. C.E., II, xxxii; R.R., X, iv.

[12] The colour for the procession is always violet, whatever be the colour for the Mass that follows (cf. R.R., X, iv, 1).

Beginning of Procession. The procession takes place after None.[13] If None is said publicly,[14] the celebrant and ministers go meanwhile to the sacristy to vest for the procession. Otherwise they and the clergy come out at the appointed time, following the cross-bearer and acolytes. The cross-bearer and acolytes do not genuflect before the altar, they go to stand at the gospel side of the sanctuary facing the epistle side. All the members of the choir (the clergy) genuflect as usual, and go to their places. They stand till the celebrant is before the altar. The celebrant and ministers wear the biretta, but uncover as they enter the choir. They bow to the choir on either side, and genuflect at the foot of the altar (the celebrant bows low if the Blessed Sacrament is not at the altar). They kneel on the lowest step; all kneel with them.

A short prayer is said in silence. Then all stand and the cantors begin the antiphon *Exsurge, Domine;*[15] it is continued by the choir. The psalm verse is sung with *Gloria Patri* and *Sicut erat;* the antiphon is repeated. Meanwhile the cross-bearer and acolytes go to stand at the entrance of the choir, facing the altar. All the others kneel again as soon as the antiphon has been repeated.

Two cantors—kneeling in the middle of the choir—begin the Litanies of the Saints. The invocations are not doubled.

When *Sancta Maria, ora pro nobis* has been sung, all rise; the procession sets out. The cross-bearer goes in front between the acolytes. The cantors follow, then come the clergy, the MC, and the celebrant between the ministers, who hold his cope. The celebrant and ministers wear the biretta during the procession outside the choir; all the clergy, outside the church. The MC, or a server, carries the book from which the celebrant will chant the prayers. The church bells are rung as the procession starts.

If the Litanies are finished (exclusive of the prayers) before the procession arrives at its final place, they may be repeated, beginning again at *Sancta Maria, ora pro nobis.* Or penitential and gradual psalms may be sung. It is not allowed to sing joyful chants. The prayers which follow the Litanies must not be sung till the procession arrives at the church where it ends.

Visit to Churches on the Way. The procession may visit other churches on the way. In this case, it is received by the clergy of each church. The rector (in choir dress, without stole) may offer holy water to the celebrant and ministers at the door. The procession will go up the church till it arrives in the choir and the celebrant is before the altar. All then kneel awhile in silent prayer. The celebrant rises and all rise with him. The cantors sing the antiphon for a commemoration of the Titular of

---

[13] In cathedral or conventual churches; in other churches at any convenient hour, but in the morning.

[14] *Fidelium,* etc., is not added when the procession follows.

[15] R.R., X, iv, l.

the church; the corresponding versicle and response are sung. The celebrant sings in the second ferial tone[16] the prayer of that saint, ending in the short form, *Per Christum Dominum nostrum*. Since it is Eastertide, *Alleluia* is added to the antiphon, versicle and response. Meanwhile the singing of the Litanies is interrupted. The Litanies are then resumed, and the procession proceeds.

Conclusion of Procession. At the church at which the procession is to end it is received by the clergy, and holy water is offered at the door to each member of the clergy on the side near the rector as he passes in (who in turn passes it to the person beside him) and to the celebrant and ministers, as above. All come to the choir, the celebrant and ministers before the altar. The usual reverence is made. The cross-bearer puts aside the cross near the credence; the acolytes put their candles on it. All kneel. If the Litanies are not finished they are sung to the end. Then, all kneeling, the celebrant sings *Pater noster*, etc. The cantors intone the psalm, which is sung alternately by the choir. The celebrant sings the versicles, as in the text, the ministers holding the book before him. He alone rises, sings *Dominus vobiscum* and the prayers. Then he kneels and sings again *Dominus vobiscum*. He adds the verses *Exaudiat nos omnipotens et misericors Deus,* and in a lower tone *Et fidelium animæ per misericordiam Dei requiescant in pace.* The choir answers *Amen* each time.

The celebrant and ministers go to vest for Mass at the sedilia or sacristy. Mass of the Rogations[17] follows.[18] It has no preparatory prayers,[19] nor *Gloria in excelsis,* nor *Credo* (except on a Sunday). The prayers are sung in the (simple) ferial tone. The preface is, normally, of Eastertide, but sung in the ferial tone. At the end of Mass the deacon sings *Ite, missa est.*

Everyone who is bound to say the Divine Office is bound to say the Litanies of the Saints, with the following psalm and prayers, on the days of the Greater Litanies, if he does not take part in the procession or other special service. They should be said after Lauds and may not be anticipated the day before. They should follow *Benedicamus Domino* at the end of Lauds. The verse *Fidelium animæ* is then not said.

In churches where the procession cannot be held, it is recommended that the litanies be said or sung before the chief Mass, all kneeling. The invocations are not doubled.

---

[16] Cf. O'Connell, *The Celebration of Mass,* 1964, p. 443.
[17] It is—even if it be the only Mass celebrated that day—the Mass of the Rogations, except on a day of the first class. Then the Mass is of the feast, with a commemoration of the Rogations under one conclusion.
[18] The Paschal candle is not lighted.
[19] Even if the Mass is not of the Rogations.

§ 4. Ascension Day

On Ascension Day the Paschal candle is lit for the principal Mass. It is extinguished by a server after the first Gospel and taken away after Mass.

§ 5. Pentecost

This is a feast of the first class with an octave. No other feast may displace it, nor be celebrated during the octave. Each day of the octave is of the first class. No commemoration or *oratio imperata* is allowed.

The colour of the feast and octave is red.

At the verse of the Great Alleluia, *Veni, Sancte Spiritus, reple tuorum corda fidelium,* etc., all genuflect. At low Mass the celebrant genuflects as he says these words. At solemn or sung Mass he does not genuflect then, but goes to kneel (between the ministers) on the edge of the footpace while they are sung by the choir. The sequence *Veni, Sancte Spiritus* follows.

Matins has only one nocturn. At Terce the hymn *Veni, Creator Spiritus* is said, instead of *Nunc Sancte nobis Spiritus.*[20] The hymn *Veni, Creator Spiritus* is also the Vesper hymn. Whenever this is sung, all kneel during the first stanza. The hymn should be intoned by the celebrant.[21]

§ 6. Time After Pentecost

This season occurs from 14 January to None of the Saturday before Septuagesima Sunday and from first Vespers of Trinity Sunday to Advent. Its second period contains at least twenty-three Sundays, and may have as many as twenty-eight.[22] The Offices for twenty-four are provided in the breviary and missal. If Easter falls early, so that there are more, the Offices for these are taken from those which were omitted after Epiphany. But, in every case, the Mass and Office of the twenty-fourth Sunday (containing the Gospel about the day of Judgment) is said on the last Sunday after Pentecost.

The colour of this season is green. It has no liturgical peculiarities; but many great feasts occur during it.

---

[20] Because it was at the third hour that the Holy Spirit came down on the Apostles, the hour of Terce (Acts, ii, 15).

[21] This hymn keeps its Paschal doxology (last stanza) whenever it may be sung or said.

[22] There are twenty-three Sundays after Pentecost when there are only fifty-two Sundays in the year and Septuagesima falls on the seventh Sunday after Epiphany. There are twenty-eight Sundays after Pentecost when Septuagesima falls on the third Sunday after Epiphany.

§ 7. Corpus Christi

The Thursday after the feast of the Blessed Trinity is Corpus Christi. It will occur between 21 May and 24 June. On Corpus Christi *Alleluia* is added to the versicle *Panem de cælo præstitisti eis* and to its response, whenever they are sung or said.

The full solemnity consists of the Mass of the feast and one general procession of the Blessed Sacrament.[23] Canon 1274, § 1, of the Code gives permission for all churches (in which the Blessed Sacrament is reserved) to have public exposition on the feast of Corpus Christi. The authority of the Ordinary is not necessary for this.

General Rules for the Procession. The procession should be a general one for the whole town. That is to say, there should be only one in each town, setting out from the principal church and returning to it, in which the clergy of all the other churches, secular and regular, take part. It should go out from the church into the streets, the houses in which are to be ornamented with draperies and sacred images.

In some countries is generally not possible to carry the Blessed Sacrament through public streets; nor may this be done without special leave of the Ordinary. Each church will have its own procession inside the church. Where a large garden or private grounds belonging to a religious house or to a Catholic can be used the procession may be made through these grounds.

The procession normally should be held in the morning, immediately after the Mass, with a Host which has been consecrated at the solemn Mass.[24] It is, however, allowed, and it is not unusual, to put it off till the afternoon, for reasons of convenience.

Route of Procession. It should be held with every possible solemnity. The Corpus Christi procession is the chief public joyful solemnity of the kind in the year. If the procession passes over much ground, there may be one or two places (not more) of repose, arranged like altars,[25] at which it stops. According to the Ceremonial of Bishops the Blessed Sacrament should be placed on these "altars" and incensed, the *Tantum ergo* sung, with the usual versicle and response and prayer, but, strictly, Benediction should not be given. However, the Congregation of Rites allows

---

[23] C.I.C. 1291.

[24] C.E., II, xxxiii, 15, 17, and all rubricians suppose this.

[25] C.E., II, xxxiii, 22. The purpose of the stops is not to give Benediction, but to rest the celebrant. Over these "altars" — which are decorated with wax candles and flowers (with no statues or relics) — there should be some form of canopy or throne under which the monstrance will be placed and a corporal spread on which to stand it.

Benediction to be given at altars of repose (not more than twice) if such is the ancient custom.[26]

The route over which the procession passes should be ornamented with flowers and greenery; draperies, banners and pictures may be hung along the way.[27] In the procession itself there may be no scenic representations or people dressed in fancy costumes to represent saints or angels, nor anything theatrical or profane.[28] Nor may relics and statues be carried.[29] Not more than two thurifers are allowed.[30] The Congregation of Rites tolerated — in two special cases[31] — the custom that children scatter flowers on the way; but it is a very undesirable practice. They may not walk among the clergy nor between the clergy and the celebrant carrying the Blessed Sacrament.

Dress of Clergy. The secular clergy should wear the surplice only, regulars wear the habit of their order, prelates their robes. If the cathedral Chapter assists, the canons ought to wear vestments of their three orders, that is subdeacons in tunicles, deacons in dalmatics, priests in chasubles; dignitaries in copes.[32] These are put on after the communion of the Mass and should be worn immediately over the rochet and an amice, without stole or maniple, as when the Ordinary sings solemn Mass. The colour of the vestments is white. If the cathedral Chapter is not present the clergy may be divided into groups wearing these vestments.[33] If the clergy are so vested the processional cross is borne by a subdeacon in amice, alb, girdle and tunicle; otherwise by a server in surplice only. If the canopy is borne within the church[34] by four, six or eight of the clergy — as the Ceremonial directs — these wear white copes in a cathedral church, in other churches they wear choir dress. The Host borne in the procession should be consecrated at the preceding Mass. The celebrant of Mass[35] should carry it all the time, without giving place to another priest. He must carry the monstrance in his hands, walking. No other manner is allowed.[36]

Preparations. In the church and sacristy all is prepared for solemn Mass, with white vestments, as usual. The church should be adorned as

---

[26] S.R.C. 2609, 3086 § 4, 3448 § 10, 3621 § 3. The custom of giving Benediction at the door of the church if the crowd was so great that many could not get into the church for the Benediction there, may be followed (S.R.C. 4257 § 8).

[27] C.E., II, xxxiii, 2.

[28] Ibid., 12.

[29] S.R.C. 1361 § 7.

[30] Ibid., 3448 § 9.

[31] Ibid., 3324, 3935 § 1

[32] C.E., II, xxxiii, 5.

[33] Cf. S.R.C. 2362 § 1.

[34] Outside it is borne by laymen of distinction (cf. C.E., II, xxxiii, 13, 21).

[35] The only exception is if the Bishop of the place should himself carry the Blessed Sacrament.

[36] Cf. S.R.C. 4389.

sumptuously as possible. In the sacristy two thuribles are prepared, torches (4 or 6) for torch-bearers who take part in the procession. At the credence, beside all that is needed for Mass, another white humeral veil, more adorned, may be laid out for the celebrant in the procession. There will be a white cope (not a heavy one) for him; the monstrance (light in weight) covered with a white veil; a second altar bread (in the lunette) to be consecrated at Mass and carried in the procession; the book with prayers for Benediction;[37] if necessary, cords of white silk to put around the celebrant's shoulders, by which the weight of the monstrance may be relieved while he holds it. In the sanctuary, the processional cross is by the credence. In the choir, or by the communion rails, is the canopy for the procession. There may be 4 or 6 lanterns, containing candles, to carry on either side of the canopy. Candles are prepared for the clergy and others who walk in the procession. Cards containing the psalms and hymns that will be recited by the deacon and subdeacon with the celebrant during the procession.

The Ceremony.[38] Solemn Mass begins as usual. The colour is white; there is a sequence, *Lauda Sion*. At the offertory the second altar bread is brought in the lunette. The torch-bearers remain kneeling after the elevation. After the communion the monstrance is brought to the altar. When the subdeacon has covered the chalice the celebrant and ministers genuflect; they change places behind him and genuflect again. The deacon puts the Blessed Sacrament into the monstrance[39] and stands it on the corporal. The celebrant and ministers genuflect again; they change places, as before. The rest of Mass is celebrated as before the Blessed Sacrament exposed (cf. Chapter VI § 8 & Chapter XII § 2) except *Benedicamus Domino* at the end of Mass and no blessing or last Gospel. Towards the end of Mass all is prepared for the procession. Candles are given out to the clergy and others and lighted.

After Mass. After Mass the celebrant and ministers come down the steps, make a double genuflexion and go to the sedilia. Here, not turning their back to the Blessed Sacrament, they take off the maniples; the celebrant also takes off the chasuble and puts on the white cope. They are assisted by the MC and acolytes. They come back to the altar, prostrate on both knees and kneel there for a short time in prayer. Meanwhile the missal and altar-cards are removed from the altar.

---

[37] The *Ritus Servandus,* in England.
[38] C.E., II, xxxiii; R.R., X, v. For this ceremony—especially if many are to take part in the procession—at least two MC's. will be needed. The formation and direction of a procession needs the attention of more than one MC. There should be several stewards to help the MC.
[39] He should not touch the Blessed Sacrament: if he does, he must at once wash his fingers in the little vessel, by the tabernacle.

The cross-bearer takes the cross and goes to stand at the entrance of the choir, between the acolytes with their candles. Those who will carry the canopy stand by it outside the choir.[40]

Incensation of Blessed Sacrament. The celebrant bows, rises and puts incense on the two thuribles (not blessing it), assisted as usual by the deacon who omits the *solita oscula*. With one thurible the celebrant incenses the Blessed Sacrament. If necessary, a scarf or cord is now arranged by the MC around the celebrant's neck to help him to sustain the monstrance.

If there is room in the sanctuary and choir it is best that the clergy now come out from their places and kneel before the altar, in the inverse order of the procession, so that they can rise, prostrate, turn round and go at once in the procession. (Should the number taking part be large the MC or one of his assistants will begin the formation of the procession before the end of Mass.) The celebrant receives the humeral veil from the deacon or MC. He and the ministers rise and go to the edge of the footpace. He and the subdeacon kneel here. The deacon goes to the altar, takes the monstrance, and hands it to the celebrant, who receives it kneeling and bowing. The deacon then genuflects. The celebrant and subdeacon rise. The ministers change places behind him. The cantors intone the hymn *Pange lingua* (if there are no cantors the celebrant intones it), and the procession sets forth, all rising and prostrating first (except the cross-bearer and acolytes). It should go in this order:

Order of Procession. First a banner of the Blessed Sacrament[41] may be borne by a clerk in surplice. Then religious associations *(piæ uniones)*, confraternities[42] and Tertiaries[43] in that order. After them lay religious (i.e., Brothers). Then come clerical religious (members of a congregation), then regulars, next monks, and finally Canons Regular.[44] Next the processional cross of the secular clergy between the acolytes with their candles; the choir of singers; seminarians; assistant priests and parish priests; the Chapter and dignitaries; the two thurifers, swinging their thuribles;[45] then the celebrant, holding the monstrance under the canopy. He goes between the ministers, who hold his cope. At the sides of the

[40] The person of highest rank holds the first pole on the right of and before the celebrant; the second in rank the first on the left; the third the second pole on the right, and so on.

[41] No other image may be carried in a procession of the Blessed Sacrament (except the processional cross).

[42] In processions of the Blessed Sacrament confraternities of the Blessed Sacrament have precedence over other confraternities in the procession itself, in carrying the canopy and in bearing torches beside the Blessed Sacrament (C.I.C. 701, § 2; S.R.C. 4143).

[43] These three classes enjoy precedence in a liturgical procession only when walking as a body, behind their own cross or banner, and in the dress and insignia of their society (C.I.C. 701).

[44] C.I.C. 106, 491; C.E., II, xxxiii, 5.

[45] It is better to walk straight, not backwards or sideways. Each thurifer swings his thurible by the inside hand. From time to time an MC puts in fresh incense.

canopy go the torch-bearers. Lanterns with candles may be carried at the sides of the canopy, if the procession goes outside the church. Prelates, if any are present, follow the canopy; those of highest rank nearest the Blessed Sacrament. At the end of the procession come such laymen as are not members of any of the religious societies who are taking part officially in the procession.[46]

All go bareheaded and all carry lighted candles (in the outside hand); those who have birettas carry them in their hands. The masters of ceremonies must see that good order and decorum are observed by all who take part in the procession.[47]

During the procession hymns and canticles (in Latin) to the Blessed Sacrament and suitable psalms are sung.[48] The same hymn may be repeated. The celebrant and ministers recite psalms or hymns, in the subdued voice.

Benediction on the Way. At the places of repose the deacon takes the monstrance and sets it on the altar, observing the usual rules. The celebrant (having taken off the humeral veil) puts incense in one thurible and incenses the Blessed Sacrament. Meanwhile the *Tantum ergo* is sung. The versicle *Panem de cælo*, etc., with its response, and the prayer *Deus, qui nobis sub Sacramento mirabili* follow. If Benediction is to be given at these places of repose, it follows as usual. The celebrant resumes the humeral veil and procession sets out again.

Return of Procession. Finally it arrives back at the high altar of the church from which it set out. At the foot of the altar the celebrant standing gives the monstrance to the deacon—who first genuflects and then receives it standing—and then genuflects to the Blessed Sacrament; then the deacon sets the monstrance on the altar. The *Tantum ergo* is sung with versicle, response, and prayer. The Blessed Sacrament is incensed and Benediction is given as usual.[49] The Blessed Sacrament is put in the tabernacle (unless Exposition follows), and then all who carry candles extinguish them.

---

[46] The rubrics do not suppose women to take any part in a procession of the Blessed Sacrament. If women do—by legitimate custom—they should come at the very end (after the Blessed Sacrament). If a band is tolerated by the Ordinary it must go at the head of the procession and may not play in the church. If soldiers in arms take part as a guard of honour to the Blessed Sacrament they walk *at the sides*, not in the procession (Cf. S.R.C. 1633).

[47] Cf. O'Connell, *Rubrics of the Forty Hours' Exposition*, pp. 29ff.

[48] The Roman Ritual (X, v) gives as suitable after the *Pange lingua*: (a) *Sacris solemniis*, (b) *Verbum supernum*, (c) *Salutis humanæ Sator*, (d) *Æterne Rex altissime*, and then *Te Deum*, *Benedictus*, *Magnificat*. The cantors will see that the strophe *Tantum ergo Sacramentum* of *Pange lingua* is not sung when the procession is moving, but is reserved to be sung when it stops.

[49] Even if Exposition follows, Benediction is given at the end of the procession. For the Exposition the deacon places the monstrance in the throne after the Benediction.

Special exercises of piety that used to be carried out with a crowded church during the days of the former octave of Corpus Christi may be observed. When there is a procession on these days two votive Masses of the Blessed Sacrament,[50] as votive Masses of the second class, may be celebrated. If the procession follows Mass immediately, *Benedicamus Domino* replaces *Ite, missa est,* and the blessing and last Gospel are omitted.

§ 8. All Souls

The Office of All Souls, said on 2 November (or 3 November if All Saints fall on a Saturday), is the Office of the day, having all the normal parts. The colour of the day is black.

On All Souls every priest may say three Masses for the dead.[51] The text of these Masses is provided in the missal under the date.

If a priest is saying only one Mass he will say the first one, for this is the Mass of the day; if he is *singing* a Mass he will use the formulary of the first Mass and may in this case anticipate the second and third Masses. The missal in a rubric at the end of the first Mass explains about the purification of the chalice at the time of the ablutions in the first and second Masses; and in a rubric given after the offertory verse of the second Mass it directs what is to be done in putting in the wine and water at the second and third Masses.

The priest who says three Masses may accept a stipend for only one (whichever one he wishes), applying this Mass according to the will of the donor, the second he must apply for all the faithful departed and the third for the intentions of the Pope.

If the three Masses are non-public low Masses and are said immediately one after another the prayers in the vernacular are said after the last Mass only.

---

[50] The formulary is the votive Mass of the Blessed Eucharist, not the Mass of Corpus Christi.
[51] C.I.C. 806. The *Editio Typica Tertia* (2002) of the post-conciliar missal states that this concession is current (cf. p. 859).

Part V

Occasional Functions

Chapter XXVIII

The Forty Hours' Prayer

§ 1. General Directions

O NE of the best known popular devotions in Catholic churches is exposition of the Blessed Sacrament, lasting part of three days, which we call the devotion of the Forty Hours' Prayer.[1] It is to be held yearly—on days appointed by the Ordinary—with the greatest possible solemnity, in all parish churches and in those in which the Blessed Sacrament is habitually reserved (C.I.C. can. 1275).

The laws which regulate this devotion were promulgated finally in 1731, but the devotion itself is older. Going back, it seems, in its first origin to mediaeval customs, such as watching by the Easter sepulchre, then later connected with special prayers of expiation at Carnival time, it was begun in Milan in 1527 and ten years later revived in that city by the preaching of a Capuchin friar, Padre Giuseppe da Ferno. It was then that the two special notes of this devotion were instituted, namely, that it should last, as nearly as possible, for forty consecutive hours, and that it should begin in another church at the exact moment when it ended in one, and so be kept up all the year round.[2] The idea of exposing the Blessed Sacrament for forty consecutive hours has been variously explained, for instance, as a memory of our Lord's forty days' fast. But the common explanation is that it is in memory of the forty hours during which His body lay in the tomb, between His death and resurrection.[3]

Clementine Instruction. In 1575 St Charles Borromeo issued a detailed instruction for the due ordering of the Prayer in Milan. On 25 November 1592 Clement VIII (1592-1605) issued his constitution *Graves et diuturnæ*, formally recognising the devotion and ordering the practice of it in Rome. On 21 January 1705 Clement XI (1700-1721) published directions for its observance in the churches of Rome. They were republished by Clement XII (1730-1740) on 1 September 1731. This document, written in

---

[1] "Oratio (Supplicatio) Quadraginta Horarum." Not uncommonly called by the Italian form "Quarant' Ore."

[2] An excellent account of the history of the devotion will be found in H. Thurston, S.J., *Lent and Holy Week* (Longmans, 1904), chap. iii, pp. 110-148.

[3] Neither in the period commemorated nor in the period of the exposition is the number forty hours exact. From three in the afternoon of Good Friday to sunrise (conventionally 6 a.m.) on Easter Day is thirty-nine hours. But St Augustine calls it forty, counting in the ninth hour (2-3 p.m.) of Friday *(De Trinitate,* iv, 6; Migne, P. L., xlii, 894-895).

the Italian language, is the *Instructio Clementina*, by which the Forty Hours' Prayer is still largely regulated.[4]

The Clementine Instruction, in itself, applies only to churches in the city of Rome. It was published for them, and has strict force of law only in their case. However, as always happens, other dioceses follow the example of the mother Church. Several times the Congregation of Rites has expressed its wish that in the arrangements of this devotion, wherever held, the Instruction should be observed as far as possible and any bishop may order its observance in his diocese.[5] The indulgences attached to the Prayer are to be gained only on condition that at least the substance of that Instruction remain, though later popes (e.g., St Pius X in 1914) have conceded modifications of the law of the Instruction in several points without loss of the *spiritual* privileges.[6]

The essence of the devotion was originally that the Blessed Sacrament remain exposed day and night for about forty hours without interruption, that is to say, from solemn Mass on one day until after solemn Mass on the third day. The three Masses for the Prayer must be solemn Masses. These Masses are votive Masses of the second class.[7]

At the beginning and end of the exposition there should be a procession of the Blessed Sacrament. On the second day of exposition there is to be a votive solemn Mass, at another altar in the same church. This votive Mass may be that of the Blessed Sacrament or any other votive Mass suitable for the special needs of the place. It is a votive Mass of the second class with its privileges.

Modifications of Clementine Instruction. Only in few places does the exposition begin at another church immediately it ends in the former one, so as to continue in some church of the city or diocese all the year round. In others arrangements are made by the Ordinary by which the Forty Hours' Prayer is held at different churches at such intervals as are possible and convenient throughout the year. There is no longer any special connection between this devotion and the time of Carnival immediately preceding Lent.

A further concession is that the Blessed Sacrament may be exposed, not continuously day and night for forty hours, but by day for three days,

---

[4] The *Instructio Clementina*, in Italian with a parallel Latin translation and a long commentary by A. Gardellini, is contained in vol. iv of the Decrees of S.R.C. It was brought into line with the Pian reform of the Roman Missal by an Instruction of S.R.C. of 27 April 1927. It must be corrected in accordance with the general rubrics of the 1962 missal (R.G., nn. 348-355). The Instruction is cited in here as I.C. The 1952 edition of R.R., V, vii, gives — with the musical text of the Litanies — brief directions for the first and third days.
[5] S.R.C. 2403, 3049 § 4, 3332 § 1-3, 4105 § 5.
[6] In accordance with the 1962 rubrics (R.G., n. 348) even an interrupted Forty Hours' Prayer — where the exposition does not continue during the night — shares the full privileges of the Prayer. Cf. also *Enchiridion Indulgentiarum*, conc. 7.
[7] I.C., § XV; cf. S.R.C. 4268 § 1; R.G., nn. 348-349.

being put in the tabernacle at night. This arrangement may be followed whenever there is grave difficulty in watching through the night.

General Directions for the Prayer. The general instructions of Clement XII's document for the Forty Hours are these: A sign (e.g., a shield) or banner should be placed over the door of the church, bearing a symbol of the Blessed Sacrament, that people may see that the Forty Hours are being held there. The exposition should be made at the high altar of the church. If there is a picture over the altar it is to be covered with a red or white hanging. In the same way all images close to the altar are to be covered. No relics or statues of saints are to be placed on the altar. Over the altar in a prominent place is prepared a throne draped in white, according to the usual rule for Exposition. If the altar has a permanent civory or tester over it, a canopy is not necessary over this temporary throne. Around the throne or place where the monstrance will stand, wax candles are to burn continually during the time of exposition. At least twenty such candles should burn all the time. Flowers may be placed on and around the altar[8] (but they should not be too near the place where the monstrance will stand). While Mass is said at the altar of exposition an altar cross is not necessary, but is allowed. No light may be placed behind the monstrance, so as to shine through the Blessed Sacrament.[9]

The windows near the altar may be darkened to foster recollection in prayer. Whatever colour may be required for the Mass of Exposition, the altar frontal is to be white. A bench is prepared, which will be placed near the lowest step of the altar after the first Mass, at which priests and clerics kneel during the exposition. This bench may be covered with red or green. Clerics wear cassock and surplice while watching; priests and deacons a white stole also, if customary. If possible two priests or clerics should watch all the time. Lay people who watch do so outside the sanctuary. During the exposition, if anyone has duty in the sanctuary, he must wear a surplice. Women (even religious) are not to go into the sanctuary at all. The Blessed Sacrament reserved in the tabernacle should be removed, if possible, to another altar, so that people may make their communion there. They should not receive Holy Communion from the altar of exposition unless this is unavoidable. Masses said in the church where the Prayer is going on may not be celebrated at the altar of Exposition. If the day be one on which a votive Mass of the fourth class is allowed, it is becoming to say the votive Mass of the Blessed Sacrament (no *Gloria* or *Credo*, and one or two occurring commemorations are made). If the Mass of the day is celebrated, the prayer of the Blessed Sacrament is not added. This is done only at a Mass said at the altar of

---

[8] In Rome they are not used for the Prayer. The floral decoration is often overdone. Sometimes it is difficult to see where the Sacred Host is in an overcrowded altar.
[9] I.C., § VI; S.R.C. 2613 § 5. Electric light is forbidden on the altar or within the throne of exposition (S.R.C. 4086, 4097, 4206, 4210 § 1, 4275).

Exposition by indult; then it is added, under one conclusion, to the prayer of the Mass, and this prayer of the Blessed Sacrament is excluded on a Sunday or on a day on which a feast or commemoration of the Second Divine Person occurs.[10] At Masses celebrated at an altar other than that of the Exposition the bell is not rung during the Prayer.[11]

Homilies are discouraged during the Forty Hours. But homilies about the Holy Eucharist are tolerated. The preacher wears a surplice (even if a Regular), and, outside Rome, a (white) stole; he preaches bareheaded. He must stand near the altar of exposition, so that no one shall turn his back to it.

Should the Exposition be in progress on 2 February, Ash Wednesday or Palm Sunday, during the blessing and procession of candles or palms and the imposition of the ashes the Blessed Sacrament is either transferred to another altar, or the Exposition is interrupted and resumed after the Mass. The Forty Hours' is not allowed during the Sacred Triduum.[12]

The day before exposition begins the church bells should be rung, with special solemnity, at the Angelus, and again half an hour before sunset and at the first hour of the night. During the exposition the bells should be rung every hour day and night.[13]

§ 2. The First Day

The Mass is, normally, a high votive (of II class) Mass of the Blessed sacrament with *Gloria in excelsis*, only one occurring commemoration, no *oratio imperata*, no *Credo* (unless an occurring Sunday or octave should require it), the seasonal or common preface. This votive Mass is excluded on any Sunday or feast of the first class, Ash Wednesday, the eve of Christmas or Pentecost, during Holy Week and the octaves of Easter and Pentecost, and on 2 November.[14] On these days the Mass of the day is sung with a commemoration under one conclusion of the Blessed Sacrament. This latter is, however, excluded on the days given under nn. 1, 2, 3 and 8 of the table of precedence of liturgical days,[15] or if the Office of the day be of a mystery identical with the Blessed Eucharist.[16]

---

[10] R.G., n. 355.
[11] On All Souls' Day the votive Mass of the Blessed Sacrament for the Exposition should follow the chief Mass of the day, for the Reposition it should precede this. Low Masses are of the day, in violet vestments and not at the altar of Exposition.
[12] S.R.C. 1190, 3574 § 5.
[13] So I.C. (§§ X, XI) for Rome.
[14] It may also be excluded on certain days if only one Mass is celebrated in the church in question (R.G., nn. 317, 326).
[15] R.G., n. 91.
[16] R.G., n. 112.

Preparations. All is made ready for the exposition, as described in the former paragraph. The altar picture is covered, the candles are arranged at the sides of the throne, but are not yet lighted (except the six altar candles for Mass). A corporal is laid on the throne. The altar cross is in its place. Whatever the colour of the Mass may be, the altar is vested in white. The usual preparations for solemn Mass are made, according to the colour that will be used. Beside these, a cope of the colour of the chasuble is laid out near the credence; and a white humeral veil, even if the colour of the Mass is not white; also the monstrance, covered with a white veil, and a book containing the prayers to be sung at the end (the *Ritus Servandus*) are made ready. A second large altar bread is laid on the paten.[17] The bench at which the priests and clerks who watch will kneel is ready, but is not put before the altar till the end of the ceremony. White stoles for priests and deacons are prepared.

The canopy to carry over the Blessed Sacrament is made ready near the altar rails. The processional cross is by the credence. In the sacristy provision should be made for two thurifers and as many torches or lanterns as will be used in the procession. Candles to be held by the clergy in the procession will be at hand, either in the sacristy or at some convenient place in the church.

Besides the celebrant, ministers and servers for solemn Mass, a cross-bearer will be required,[18] two thurifers, a number of torch-bearers, men to hold the canopy.

The Mass of Exposition. Solemn Mass[19] is celebrated as usual, to the communion. Two Hosts are offered and consecrated. After the communion, when the subdeacon has covered the chalice, the ministers genuflect, change places behind the celebrant and genuflect again. The MC brings the monstrance to the altar. The celebrant, aided by the deacon, puts the Blessed Sacrament in the monstrance. He stands it on the corporal (unveiled). From now Mass continues as before the Blessed Sacrament exposed (cf. Chapter VI § 8 & Chapter XII § 2). *Benedicamus Domino* is said, and there is no blessing or last Gospel.

Towards the end of Mass the other candles on the altar are lighted, and candles are given out to the members of the choir (the clergy), and are lighted.

After Mass the celebrant and ministers, having genuflected at the altar in the centre,[20] come down the altar steps, make a double genuflexion and go to the sedilia[21] Here, assisted by the MC and acolytes, they take off their maniples, the celebrant exchanges the chasuble for a cope. In so

---

[17] It is supposed that the Host to be exposed will be consecrated at the Mass.

[18] Not a subdeacon, but a server in surplice (I.C., § XX).

[19] The solemn tone is used for the prayers, etc.

[20] Or they may descend to the foot of the altar *per breviorem* from the gospel corner.

[21] It is the celebrant of the Mass who is to carry the Sacred Host. Only a Cardinal or the Bishop of the diocese may do so, if he has not celebrated the Mass of Exposition.

doing they should not turn their backs to the altar. The altar cross, cards and missal are removed.

Meanwhile two thurifers bring thuribles from the sacristy, leading out a procession of the torch or lantern bearers. On entering the sanctuary, or before leaving it, everyone prostrates before the Blessed Sacrament exposed according to the usual rule.

Incensation of Blessed Sacrament. At the sedilia,[22] when he is vested, the celebrant puts incense on the two thuribles, not blessing it. He does so facing the Blessed Sacrament; he is assisted, as always, by the deacon (who omits the *solita oscula*), while the subdeacon holds the cope.

The celebrant and ministers then come to the altar and prostrate. The celebrant incenses the Blessed Sacrament, using the thurible of the first thurifer.

Procession. Meanwhile the procession is formed in the sanctuary or choir.[23] The men who are to carry the canopy stand by it outside the sanctuary.

When the Blessed Sacrament has been incensed, the MC puts the white humeral veil on the celebrant, the subdeacon ties it. All go up to the footpace, the celebrant and subdeacon kneel on its edge, the deacon genuflects (a little towards the epistle side), takes the monstrance, and hands it to the celebrant. He receives it kneeling, first bowing. When he has handed the monstrance, the deacon genuflects. The sacred ministers stand, the celebrant turns towards the people, the ministers change places behind him, so that the deacon shall now be on his right. The cantors intone *Pange lingua*. The celebrant descends at once and goes under the canopy. The MC sees that the deacon and subdeacon have their cards with the psalms, etc., to be recited during the procession.

As soon as the celebrant and ministers have gone to the altar, the cross-bearer takes the cross and goes to stand at the farther end of the choir. The acolytes with their candles stand at his sides. The members of the choir should already be kneeling in the centre (if there is room there). All now rise, prostrate (except the cross-bearer and acolytes), turn, and so the procession begins. It goes in this order:

First, confraternities of laymen, then the cross-bearer between the acolytes, then the (surpliced) singers, and lastly the clergy,[24] all holding lighted candles in the outside hand. The thurifers go immediately in front

---

[22] I.C., § XIX (cf. C.E., II, xxxiii, 19).

[23] The procession must be held unless it be quite impossible to carry it out or its omission is permitted by Papal indult. If the procession is to be a large one, an assistant MC should begin its formation earlier — any time after the consecration of the Mass. When a procession is held within the church, normally it turns to the right outside the sanctuary, goes down the church on the gospel side and returns by the centre passage.

[24] For details of the order of the procession, see the directions for Corpus Christi given above, and O'Connell, *Rubrics of the Forty Hours' Exposition*, pp. 29ff.

of the canopy,[25] the torch-bearers at each side of it.[26] At the entrance of the sanctuary the celebrant goes between the ministers under the canopy; they hold the ends of his cope. During the procession they should recite suitable psalms and hymns together in the subdued voice.

Unlike the procession on Corpus Christi this procession is not to go outside the church, unless the church is very small. In this case it may go round the square or place just outside.[27] Meanwhile the *Pange lingua* is sung; the church bells are rung.[28]

Return of Procession. When the procession comes back to the high altar the cross-bearer and acolytes enter the sanctuary, put aside the cross and the candles (on the credence), and kneel before the credence when the Blessed Sacrament arrives. The choir and clergy — without a reverence to the altar — go to their places. As the Blessed Sacrament passes, all fall on their knees. The canopy remains outside the sanctuary.

Before the altar *(in plano)* the deacon kneels,[29] bows and takes the monstrance from the celebrant, and waits standing while the celebrant genuflects. The celebrant then kneels on the lowest step — the subdeacon on his left — and the deacon puts the monstrance on the throne. The deacon may place the monstrance on the altar, and another priest or deacon in surplice and white stole may put it on the throne.

The subdeacon unfastens the celebrant's humeral veil; the MC takes it from him. Now (not before) the stanzas *Tantum ergo* and *Genitori Genitoque* are sung. At this last stanza the celebrant incenses the Blessed Sacrament, as at Benediction. The two thurifers may now go to the sacristy.

Litanies. Meanwhile two cantors come to kneel in the middle of the choir or sanctuary. They begin the Litanies of the Saints.[30] These are sung through, the choir answering each petition. The petitions are not sung twice. The cantors sing the first half (e.g., *Sancta Maria*), the choir answers the second half *(Ora pro nobis)*. After the Litanies the celebrant, still kneeling, intones *Pater noster*. It is continued silently; he sings *Et ne nos inducas in tentationem;* the choir answers *Sed libera nos a malo.* The cantors intone the psalm *Deus in adiutorium meum intende,* which is continued by the choir, each side singing an alternate verse. The celebrant, still kneeling, sings *Salvos fac servos tuos,* and the verses which follow.

---

[25] See fig. 38. It is better to walk straight, not backwards or sideways. The MC puts in more incense when this is necessary.

[26] I.C. (§ XX) directs that eight priests (in surplice) carry torches, walking before the thurifers.

[27] I.C., § XXI.

[28] I.C., § XX.

[29] I.C., XXXIV.

[30] The Litanies (of which there is a special form for the Prayer) and the following prayers for the Forty Hours are in the Roman Ritual (V, vii) and in the English *Ritus Servandus,* pp. 16ff.

He stands and sings *Dominus vobiscum,* and the prayers, to the simple ferial tone.[31] The ministers hold the book. Then, kneeling again, the celebrant sings *Domine, exaudi orationem meam.* The cantors sing *Exaudiat nos omnipotens et misericors Dominus.* The celebrant sings on one note, *Fidelium animæ per misericordiam Dei requiescant in pace. ℟. Amen.*

The clergy extinguish their candles. All remain for a short time praying silently. They rise, prostrate and go to the sacristy (the sacred ministers remaining uncovered until they are at a distance from the altar).

The Blessed Sacrament remains exposed. There must always be people who watch in the church, taking hours, or shorter periods, by turn. If possible there should be two priests, deacons, clerics or male religious who kneel at the bench in the sanctuary. Priests and deacons wear surplice and white stole, others surplice only.

§ 3. The Second Day

On this day, at an altar other than that of the Exposition, a solemn Mass is celebrated as a votive Mass of the second class. It may be the votive Mass of the Blessed Sacrament, or any other votive Mass suitable for the special needs of the place. There will be a *Gloria* (unless the Mass be in violet vestments) and one occurring privileged commemoration is allowed; no *oratio imperata.* There is no added prayer of the Blessed Sacrament. The *Credo* is not said unless an occurring Sunday or octave should require it. The preface will be the seasonal one or the Common preface.

§ 4. The Third Day

Solemn Mass of Deposition follows the general rules of that of exposition on the first day. It is a high votive Mass of the Blessed Sacrament sung at the altar of exposition. All must be prepared beforehand for the Mass and procession, as on the first day. The rules for days on which the votive Mass may not be said are the same as on the first day. On these days the Mass of the day is said, with the collect, secret and postcommunion of the Blessed Sacrament, after those of the Mass, under one conclusion.[32] The chief difference is that this Mass of Deposition is all sung before the Blessed Sacrament exposed. Therefore, during the whole Mass the rules for that are to be observed (cf. Chapter VI § 8 & Chapter XII § 2).[33] Since a procession is to follow the Mass *Benedicamus Domino* replaces *Ite, missa est,* and there is no blessing or last Gospel.

---

[31] A fall of a minor third (d'l) on the last syllable of the prayer and of its conclusion.

[32] Except on certain days, as noted in the rules given for the first day, above.

[33] In this Mass such *solita oscula* as are merely marks of reverence to the celebrant, but not part of the rite itself, are omitted. Hence, e.g., the kissing of the paten and chalice at the offertory, of the paten and the celebrant's hand after the *Pater noster,* are not omitted.

The procession follows at the end of Mass. But this time the Litanies are sung before the procession.

Litanies. At the end of Mass the celebrant and ministers go to the sedilia, to change their vestments, as on the first day. Meantime the crucifix (if used), the missal and altar cards are removed; a corporal spread on the altar; the tabernacle key and monstrance veil put near it. The sacred ministers come back to the altar, prostrate and kneel on the lowest step. The cantors, kneeling in the middle of the choir, begin the Litanies of the Saints. They are sung as on the first day. The prayers follow as before, down to the versicle *Domine, exaudi orationem meam* and its response (inclusive).

Towards the end of the Litanies, the two thurifers go to the sacristy and return with thuribles. They make the usual double genuflexion before going and on returning. The cross-bearer gets the cross, the acolytes their candles and stand at the entrance to the sanctuary. The torch-bearers and canopy-bearers make ready. Candles are distributed to the clergy and others. The procession is formed. When the response to *Domine, exaudi orationem meam* has been sung, the celebrant rises and puts incense in both thuribles, not blessing it. Taking the first thurible he incenses the Blessed Sacrament. He receives the humeral veil and goes up the steps with the ministers. Here the deacon gives the celebrant (kneeling)[34] the monstrance, as on the first day.

Procession. The procession goes round the church singing *Pange lingua*. The celebrant and ministers recite suitable psalms and hymns meanwhile. They come back to the altar, the deacon puts the monstrance on the corporal on the table of the altar. The stanzas *Tantum ergo* and *Genitori Genitoque* are sung. The Blessed Sacrament is incensed at this last stanza. The cantors sing the versicle *Panem de cælo*, etc. Then the celebrant, standing, sings (without *Dominus vobiscum*) the prayer *Deus qui nobis sub Sacramento mirabili,* and adds at once the other prayers, which on the first day are sung at the end of the Litanies (including the verse *Fidelium*). The celebrant gives Benediction according to the usual rules. The Blessed Sacrament is put back in the tabernacle by the deacon or by an assistant priest. The clergy who hold lighted candles extinguish them. All rise, genuflect and go to the sacristy as after every Benediction.

---

[34] I.C., XXX.

Chapter XXIX

Canonical Visitation and Confirmation

§ 1. General Principles

ONE of the chief duties of a diocesan bishop is to know his clergy and people, to see that everything concerning the worship of God in his diocese is in order, to decide disputed matters, and correct any possible abuses. The opportunity for all this is his Canonical Visitation of churches, parishes and religious institutions.[1]

The Council of Trent explains the purpose of Canonical Visitation: "The chief object of all Visitations is to maintain right and orthodox doctrine, to drive out heresies, defend good and correct bad manners, to incite the people to religion, peace and innocence by homilies and warnings, to arrange all things according to the need of the place, time and occasion by the prudence of the Visitor, for the good of the people."[2]

The Ordinary should make the visitation himself,[3] or (if he is legitimately prevented) by a delegate. There is no special law as to who this delegate shall be. The Ordinary may send any priest he chooses to appoint, his vicar-general, a rural dean, or another. But, since in most countries the opportunity of the visitation is used for the administration of Confirmation, either the Ordinary will come himself or he will send an auxiliary bishop.

The Council of Trent desires the visitation to be made once a year, or (in the case of a large diocese) once every two years.[4] The 1917 Code of Canon Law says that the Bishop is to visit yearly his diocese, either completely or in part, so that at least every five years he shall have visited the entire territory. The Ordinary may, however, visit more often and at any time that he thinks fit.

All persons, places and objects belonging to the diocese are visited; that is, the clergy and Catholics who live in each parish, all churches and chapels, including the churches of regulars, as far as they do diocesan work. The Code[5] says: "to the ordinary episcopal visitation are subject persons, things and religious places, although exempt, which are

---

[1] C.I.C. 343-346. References here are to the 1917 C.I.C. Cf. also canons 396-398 of the 1983 C.I.C.

[2] Conc. Trid. Sess. XXIV, de Reform, c. 3.

[3] In default of the Ordinary, the Metropolitan. C.I.C. 274, 5°.

[4] Conc. Trid., Sess. XXIV, de Ref., c. 3; C.I.C. 343 § 1.

[5] Canon 344. Regarding the visitation of religious, see canons 512, 513, 631, 690, 1261, 1491. Cf. also canon 628 § 2 & § 3 of the 1983 C.I.C.

contained within the ambit of the diocese, unless it can be proved that a special exemption from the visitation had been granted them by the Apostolic See. The Bishop may visit exempt religious, however, only in cases laid down in law." The Ordinary also visits all convents of nuns,[6] religious and pious institutions, such as schools, orphanages, almshouses and so on. He examines the objects of divine worship, the furniture of the church, vessels and vestments.

He inquires into the conduct of services, the administration of sacraments, administration of ecclesiastical property in all its forms. He examines the books of the parish, the register of baptisms, marriages, confirmations and funerals. He makes any inquiries that seem opportune to him concerning the life of the clergy and people. He allows the people an opportunity of speaking to him, that they may expose any question or make any complaint.

The entertainment of the Bishop and those who accompany him and the travelling and other expenses are to be provided for in accordance with legitimate local usage.

The Ordinary may bring other co-visitors with him, to whom he delegates part of the duty.

There is no suspensive appeal (*appellatio suspensiva*) from any decision made by the Ordinary in those matters which concern the object and end of the visitation; that is to say, no such appeal as can impede the execution of what he decides. But a devolutive appeal (*appellatio devolutiva*) is allowed, namely, the decision may be deferred to a higher court, after it has been obeyed. The Bishop must proceed, even at the time of the visitation, in accordance with law.

There are differences in the ceremony of visitation, according to whether it is made by the Ordinary or by his auxiliary bishop. There are further modifications according to the rank of the Ordinary. In the first place we consider the visitation of the church of the parish, next that of convents and institutions, lastly that of the churches of exempt regulars.[7]

§ 2. Before the Visitation

Notice of the visitation will be sent in due time to the rector of the church and he may be sent a questionnaire to answer about the affairs of his parish. In most cases the day and hour of the function are arranged by

---

[6] All convents of religious women are subject to visitation by the Ordinary, whether they have a regular Superior or not. But those under regular Superiors are examined by him for certain specified matters only (cf. canon 512).

[7] The ceremonies for Canonical Visitation are in the pontifical ("Ordo ad visitandas parochias" in Part III). There is a booklet in use in England entitled *Order of the Episcopal Visitation of Parishes, with the Rite of Confirmation* (Burns and Oates, 1931). It is an excerpt from the Roman Pontifical giving the prayers in Latin and English, with the rubrics in English.

agreement with him, so that both may be convenient for the people who will attend and the candidates for Confirmation.

. According to custom the visitation is announced to the people beforehand, generally on the Sunday before it takes place, if not earlier. Notice is given that the faithful will have an opportunity of seeing the Bishop privately in the sacristy or other convenient place. The hymn *Veni Creator* is sung or recited, with the versicle *Emitte Spiritum tuum,* its response and the prayer *Deus qui corda fidelium,* after the chief Mass on the Sunday before the visitation.

§ 3. Visitation by the Ordinary

Supposing the Ordinary to be a bishop[8] the following are the ceremonies of his visitation.

The general order is always the same, namely, reception of the Bishop at the doors of the church, procession to the altar, prayers for him, his blessing (possibly Mass), his sermon to the people, announcing the indulgence, prayers for the dead, visitation of the tabernacle and altar (possibly Benediction), Confirmation, visitation of the church and its furniture, of the sacristy (its vessels, holy Oils, relics and vestments), the opportunity for the faithful to speak to the Bishop, examination of the mission books and accounts, instructions to the clergy, last visit to the Blessed Sacrament.

In the details, the vestments worn and so on, greater or less solemnity may be used.[9] If the visitation takes place in the morning, either the Bishop himself may say or sing Mass, or the rector of the church may do so in his presence. In this case the Mass is said after the Bishop has given his blessing. His address to the people is normally made after the Gospel of the Mass.

The Preparations. The following preparations are made:

The church and high altar are decorated as for a feast. If Mass will be celebrated the altar is vested in the colour of the day; otherwise it is vested in white for the Benediction (if this should take place) and Confirmation. At the epistle corner of the altar, facing that corner, a pontifical (or other book) open at the prayers for the reception of the Bishop is ready on the missal stand.[10] The pontifical canon — open at the form for a bishop's blessing — is placed at the centre of the altar, leaning against the tabernacle or cross. The altar cards are not put on.

---

[8] For the changes in the rite when he is an archbishop, see § 4 below.

[9] For example, in the more solemn form the Bishop puts on amice, stole and cope (with morse) for the Absolution and for the visitation of the tabernacle; in the simpler form he uses a stole only, worn over the rochet.

[10] With it a card containing the prayer of the Titular of the church.

At the door of the church a small carpet is laid, and on it a prie-dieu with a (green)[11] cushion is placed for the Bishop. If there are not enough servers to make a procession to the door, a table must stand there, on the right just inside the door, on which are placed the incense boat, a crucifix (covered with a white veil) which the Bishop will kiss, the vessel of lustral water and sprinkler.

In the sanctuary a carpet is laid before the altar steps. On it is a kneeling-stool covered with a cloth and with two cushions, one on which the Bishop will kneel, the other on which he will rest the arms. The colour of this covering and the cushions is green for a bishop, red for a cardinal.

If Mass is not to be said, a faldstool (covered in white) or chair is placed on the footpace on the gospel side, where the Bishop will sit while preaching.

On the ordinary credence are prepared: a white burse (containing a corporal), the tabernacle key, a white stole for the rector, the bell.

If *Mass is to be celebrated by the Bishop:* on the credence, in addition, are made ready the chalice prepared for Mass, the Bishop's maniple, and the cruets. Vestments (amice, alb, cincture, stole and chasuble) are prepared near the credence (they will later be transferred to the table of the altar).

If *Mass is to be said in the Bishop's presence,* the cruets are made ready with the things on the credence; and the vestments and chalice for the celebrant are prepared in the sacristy. The missal and altar cards are ready near the altar.

At an extra credence (near the ordinary one) are laid out the special requisites for the Bishop:[12] his mitres, the hand-candle, a small salver, the pontifical (Part III), a book for the Absolution for the dead, the form for announcing the indulgence, a card or book containing the music of the *Confiteor,* if this is to be sung. Nearby (at the sedilia or other convenient place) are an amice, white stole, cope and morse for the Bishop (stole only, if he will follow the simpler rite); a black stole, cope and simple morse (or stole only) for the Absolution; a white humeral veil.

Aside in the sanctuary is a black cloth (or a catafalque) for the Absolution for the dead.

If *Confirmation is to be administered* the following additional things are put on either credence: the *Pontificale,* Part I (or *Ritus Servandus*); the Chrism, a supply of cotton wool, the ewer and basin (with some lemon and dry bread) with towels, and a linen gremial veil (for which an amice serves). Nearby is the crosier.

In the sacristy: a white cope for the rector (if the rite will be the more solemn one), the aspersory, the thurible and boat, the processional cross, and a small crucifix on a salver and covered with a white veil.

---

[11] Violet on a penitential day.

[12] Normally the pontifical ornaments and vessels, etc., will be brought by the Bishop and arranged beforehand by his chaplain or by the MC.

For the Bishop's visitation, towards the end of the function, the keys of the baptistery, of the aumbry for the Holy Oils, and of any reliquaries that are to be inspected, are at hand.

The vessels, vestments and furniture that the Bishop will examine must be ready for this purpose; also whatever books he will see, either in the sacristy or the priest's house.

Assistants. All the clergy of the church go to the door to receive the Bishop. There should also be a thurifer, cross-bearer and acolytes, two other servers to carry the holy water and crucifix, four servers to hold the book, candle, mitre and crosier (these last two wearing white *vimpæ*), torchbearers.[13] The rector of the church wears a surplice; or he may, for greater solemnity, go to the door in surplice, and white cope. He does not wear a stole.

The procession may go to the house where the Bishop awaits it and conduct him thence to the church. Meanwhile the canticle *Benedictus* may be sung.

Reception of the Bishop. The Bishop, with his chaplain, is usually received at the door of the church. The Ordinary wears rochet and mozzetta, or the cappa magna. The rector, clergy and servers go to meet him at the door.[14] The cross-bearer and acolytes stand on the left of the entrance, the thurifer, aspersory-bearer, and crucifix-bearer on the right. The rector holds the small crucifix for the Bishop to kiss. Meanwhile the Bishop, without biretta and skull-cap, kneels on the kneeling-stool there prepared. The Bishop rises and resumes his skull-cap. The rector hands him the sprinkler, kissing it first, then the Bishop's hand. The Bishop sprinkles himself on the forehead with holy water, then sprinkles the rector and those who are around. All genuflect (except the cross-bearer and acolytes) and make the sign of the cross. The rector receives back the sprinkler. The thurifer kneels before the Bishop, holding up the thurible. The rector takes the spoon and hands it (with the *solita oscula*), saying *Benedicite, Pater reverendissime* (to a cardinal *Benedicite, eminentissime ac reverendissime Pater*). The Bishop puts on incense and blesses it (one sign of the cross). The thurifer rises; the rector takes the thurible and incenses the Bishop (covered) with three double swings, bowing low before and after.

The procession now goes up the church. The thurifer goes first, then the cross-bearer between the acolytes, then the choir, servers, clergy, the Bishop's chaplain, the rector of the church, lastly, the Bishop himself

---

[13] If the Bishop wears the cappa, a train-bearer will be needed.

[14] They may go in this order: The crucifix-bearer having on his left the thurifer, and on his right the aspersory-bearer. These are followed by the cross-bearer between the acolytes (with their candles). Then come the singers (if robed); next the servers; then the clergy and lastly the rector .

(uncovered).[15] If the Bishop is in cappa his train is held by a server. As the Bishop goes up the church he blesses the people, who kneel as he passes. Meanwhile the antiphon *Sacerdos et Pontifex,* or the responsory *Ecce Sacerdos magnus,* is sung or recited.

Prayers for the Bishop. Before the altar the Bishop kneels at the faldstool. The cross and acolytes' candles are put aside in the usual place. The aspersory-bearer leaves the aspersory on the credence. The thurifer goes to the sacristy and makes ready the thurible for the Absolution (unless Mass intervenes). All kneel, except the rector, who—if he is not already in cope—puts on a white stole and stands at the epistle corner of the altar (on the top step), facing the gospel side. He then sings or says the following versicles, the choir singing the answers, or the servers and congregation saying them:[16]

℣. *Protector noster aspice Deus,*
℟. *Et respice in faciem christi tui.*[17]
℣. *Salvum fac servum tuum.*
℟. *Deus meus, sperantem in te.*
℣. *Mitte ei, Domine, auxilium de sancto,*
℟. *Et de Sion tuere eum.*
℣. *Nihil proficiat inimicus in eo.*
℟. *Et filius iniquitatis non apponat nocere ei.*
℣. *Domine, exaudi orationem meam,*
℟. *Et clamor meus ad te veniat.*
℣. *Dominus vobiscum.*
℟. *Et cum spiritu tuo.*
Oremus.
Deus, humilium visitator, qui eos paterna dilectione consolaris, prætende societati nostræ gratiam tuam, ut per eos in quibus habitas tuum in nobis sentiamus adventum. Per Christum Dominum nostrum.
℟. *Amen.*

The rector takes off his cope if he has worn one, and lays it aside.

The Bishop goes up to the altar[18] and kisses it in the middle. He says or sings the form for his blessing, the clergy or choir answering:

---

[15] If he has co-visitors they (in cassock and ferraiolo unless they are entitled to any special dress) follow him.

[16] The text is given, since there may be difficulty in finding it. It is found in Part III of the Roman Pontifical.

[17] The "christus" is the (anointed) bishop. The prayer—*Deus humilium*—is sung in the second ferial tone: a fall of a minor third (d'/l) on the last syllable of the prayer and of its conclusion.

[18] The *Pontificale* makes no special mention in the rite of Visitation of the singing by the choir of the antiphon, versicle and response of the Titular of the church (from Lauds in the forenoon; from Vespers in the afternoon) and of his (her) prayer by the Bishop, at the epistle

℣. *Sit nomen Domini benedictum.*
℟. *Ex hoc nunc et usque in sæculum.*
℣. *Adiutorium nostrum in nomine Domini,*
℟. *Qui fecit cælum et terram.*
Benedicat vos omnipotens Deus, Pa✠ter et Fi✠lius et Spiritus ✠Sanctus.
℟. *Amen.*

Meanwhile the rector and all in church kneel.

Mass and Sermon. If Mass is to be said, it follows now. If the Bishop will say Mass, he is vested before the altar.[19] If it is to be said in his presence, the celebrant goes to the sacristy to vest. The Bishop kneels at the kneeling-stool in the centre of the sanctuary or on the gospel side of it (unless there is a throne for him).

For the ceremonies of low Mass by a bishop see Chapter IX above. For low Mass in his presence see Chapter VIII.[20]

After the Gospel of the Mass the faldstool or a chair is placed on the footpace at the gospel side. The Bishop sits there and addresses the people.[21] Meanwhile the celebrant sits at the sedilia. After the address the indulgence is announced, as below.

If Mass is not said, as soon as the Bishop has given his blessing he sits on the faldstool or chair on the footpace and addresses the people. After the address a priest or server stands before him, below the altar steps, and (moderately bowed) sings or says the *Confiteor*. This may be done by the rector of the church. No change is made in the text of the *Confiteor;* but he who says it genuflects to the Bishop as he says *tibi, pater* and *te, pater*. The Bishop stands during the *Confiteor*, then sits for the announcement of the indulgence.

The Indulgence. The rector then, standing near the Bishop, bows to him and reads the formula of indulgence, first in Latin, then in English:

Reverendissimus in Christo Pater et Dominus, Dominus N.[22] Dei et Apostolicæ Sedis gratia huius sanctæ N.[23] Ecclesiæ Episcopus, dat et concedit omnibus hic præsentibus indulgentiam plenariam suetis conditionibus lucrandam. Rogate Deum pro felici statu sanctissimi Domini nostri N.[24] divina providentia Papæ N.,[25] Dominationis suæ reverendissimæ et sanctæ Matris Ecclesiæ.

---

corner. It does prescribe this at the reception of a Prelate, and some authors prescribe it here at the Visitation, as it is really the completion of the Bishop's ceremonial reception.
[19] While he reads the psalms of preparation at the prie-dieu the (second) MC arranges the vestments on the altar and servers prepare to bring them from there for the vesting.
[20] If solemn Mass is to be sung in his presence, or if he will himself sing solemn Mass the rules for these functions may be found above, Chapters XV and XVI.
[21] Or the Bishop may defer his address until after Mass. In either case it is after the homily that the indulgence will be imparted.
[22] The Bishop's Christian name only.
[23] The Pope's name only (genitive).
[24] The name of the diocese in adjectival form (genitive singular).
[25] The Pope's number (genitive case).

The Right Reverend Father and Lord in Christ, N. by the grace of God and of the Apostolic See, Bishop of this holy Church of N., gives and grants to all persons here present a plenary indulgence to be gained on the usual conditions. Pray to God for the good estate of His Holiness N.[26] by Divine Providence Pope, of His Lordship the Bishop, and of holy Mother Church.

For an ARCHBISHOP:

Reverendissimus in Christo Pater et Dominus, Dominus N. Dei et Apostolicæ Sedis gratia huius sanctæ N. Ecclesiæ Archiepiscopus, dat et concedit omnibus hic præsentibus indulgentiam plenariam suetis conditionibus lucrandam. Rogate Deum pro felici statu sanctissimi Domini nostri N. divina providentia Papæ N., Dominationis suæ reverendissimæ et sanctæ matris Ecclesiæ.

The Most Reverend Father and Lord in Christ, N. by the grace of God and of the Apostolic See Archbishop of this holy Church of N. gives and grants to all persons here present a plenary indulgence to be gained on the usual conditions. Pray to God for the good estate of His Holiness N. by Divine Providence Pope, of His Grace the Archbishop and of holy Mother Church.

For a CARDINAL ARCHBISHOP:

Eminentissimus et reverendissimus in Christo Pater et Dominus, Dominus N. Tituli sancti N. sanctæ Romanæ Ecclesiæ (presbyter) Cardinalis N. [et Archiepiscopus N.] dat et concedit omnibus hic præsentibus indulgentiam plenariam suetis conditionibus lucrandam.[27] Rogate Deum pro felici statu sanctissimi Domini nostri N. divina Providentia Papæ N., Dominationis suæ eminentissimæ ac reverendissimæ et sanctæ Matris Ecclesiæ.

The Most Eminent and Right Reverend Father and Lord in Christi N.[28] Cardinal (priest) of the holy Roman Church, of the title of Saint N. [and Archbishop of N.] gives and grants to all persons here present a plenary indulgence to be gained on the usual conditions. Pray to God for the good estate of His Holiness N. by Divine Providence Pope, of His Eminence the Cardinal and of holy Mother Church.

Meanwhile two servers take the pontifical and candle, they genuflect before the altar, then before the Bishop, and stand by him. The Bishop, standing uncovered, reads or sings the form *Precibus et meritis*, etc.; then *Indulgentiam, absolutionem*, etc. Lastly, *Et benedictio Dei* – with his biretta on (unless he be an archbishop, when his cross will be held before him) – *omnipotentis Pa✠tris et Fi✠lii et Spiritus✠Sancti descendat super vos et maneat*

---

[26] The Pope's name and number.

[27] The faculty to give a plenary indulgence to those who, on the occasion of the Bishop's visitation of a church or oratory, visit there and pray for the Pope's intentions, having confessed and communicated, is given in the quinquennial faculties of bishops (Formula III, cap. 6, S. Pœnitentiaria No. 10). Concession 32 of the 1999 *Enchiridion Indulgentiarum* grants a plenary indulgence to all who assist at a sacred function associated with the visitation.

[28] It is usual to say the cardinal's Christian name first, then, after "Cardinalis" his surname.

semper. To each form the answer is *Amen.* All kneel during the prayers and blessing.

Absolution for the Dead. The prayers for the dead follow[29] even on a feast which is of the first class.

If the church has no churchyard or cemetery immediately around it, the following form of the Absolution is used.[30]

A catafalque is set up in the church, or a black cloth is spread on the ground in the middle of the choir. The Bishop, having put on a black stole over his rochet (or vested in amice, black stole, cope, simple morse and simple mitre), stands *in plano* somewhat to the epistle side, facing the cloth, or goes to the catafalque. The servers hold the book and hand-candle before him. Others have lustral water and incense at hand.

The responsory *Libera me* is sung by the choir (or sung or recited by the clergy or servers, if there is no choir). During its repetition the Bishop puts in and blesses incense. After the *Libera* the Bishop uncovers (if mitred) and says the following versicles and prayers. Those around answer them:

℣. *Kyrie, eleison.*
℟. *Christe, eleison.*
℣. *Kyrie, eleison. Pater noster* (continued silently).

During *Pater noster* the rector presents the sprinkler and the Bishop, remaining in his place, thrice sprinkles the black cloth or catafalque with lustral water and incenses it thrice.[31] He continues:

℣. *Et ne nos inducas in tentationem.*
℟. *Sed libera nos a malo.*
℣. *In memoria æterna erunt iusti,*
℟. *Ab auditione mala non timebunt.*
℣. *A porta inferi,*
℟. *Erue, Domine, animas eorum.*
℣. *Requiem æternam dona eis, Domine,*

---

[29] If there is a cemetery adjoining the church, for the rite of the Absolution there, see *Pontificale,* Pars III, or *Order of the Episcopal Visitation of Parishes,* pp. 15ff.

[30] The form of Absolution given in the latter book *(Order)* derives from a reply of Cardinal Barnabo (1866). This form combines into one the two absolutions given in the *Pontificale.* The *Pontificale* supposes an absolution for *dead bishops* (presumably buried in the church, and so this absolution would be omitted where there are none such) given in the church, and one for deceased priests and people given in the adjoining cemetery. When there are no bishops buried in the church and no cemetery near by, an absolution is given over a black cloth (or a catafalque). In this case it would seem that the *De profundis* with its antiphon, and the Responsory *Qui Lazarum* should be omitted, but that the Responsory *Libera* should be sung, as is normally done at an absolution for the dead. (Cf. Nabuco, III, pp. 244, 246, 257.)

[31] He sprinkles in the centre, to his left and to his right. He incenses in the same way with simple swings of the thurible.

℟. *Et lux perpetua luceat eis.*
℣. *Domine, exaudi orationem meam.*
℟. *Et clamor meus ad te veniat.*
℣. *Dominus vobiscum.*
℟. *Et cum spiritu tuo.*

Oremus:
Deus qui inter apostolicos sacerdotes...[32]
Deus veniæ largitor et humanæ salutis amator...
Deus cuius miseratione animæ fidelium requiescant,...[33] and he recites these three prayers under one conclusion *(Per eundem Dominum nostrum. ℟. Amen.)*
℣. *Requiem æternam dona eis, Domine.* (While saying this Bishop makes the sign of the cross over the catafalque or cloth.)
℟. *Et lux perpetua luceat eis.*
The cantors :
℣. *Requiescant in pace.*
℟. *Amen.*

This is the end of the prayers for the dead in churches which have no cemetery attached. The catafalque or cloth is removed.

Visitation of the Blessed Sacrament. The Bishop, standing before the altar, is vested in white stole and cope (with precious morse),[34] and kneels on a cushion at the foot of the altar before the tabernacle, with head fully uncovered. If the Blessed Sacrament is reserved in a side chapel, the Bishop (mitred) is conducted thither.

The rector of the church puts on a white stole, and takes from the credence the burse and tabernacle key. He goes up to the altar, spreads the corporal, opens the tabernacle, genuflects, and pulls aside the curtains of the conopæum that the ciborium may be visible. He again genuflects, descends, and takes off the stole.

The Bishop—assisted by the rector—puts incense into the thurible and incenses the Blessed Sacrament, as usual. The *Tantum ergo* is then begun. After the words *veneremur cernui* the Bishop goes up to the altar, genuflects, takes out the ciborium and other vessels containing the consecrated Particles, uncovers them, inspects them and the inside of the tabernacle. He re-covers the vessels, genuflects, leaves them on the corporal and comes back to kneel before the altar or on the edge of the footpace, receives the humeral veil and gives Benediction (a triple

---

[32] In this combined form of the absolution the words *Pontificali seu Sacerdotali* are used to include both deceased bishops and priests in this prayer.
[33] In this case, if no one has been buried in the church, the words *hic et* (before *ubique*) are omitted in this prayer as given in the pontifical.
[34] Or he may wear only a white stole, if he is following the simpler form of the ceremony.

blessing) with the ciborium,[35] while *Genitori,* etc., is sung, and then descends *in plano.* The rector resumes the stole, puts the vessels back into the tabernacle, making the usual genuflexions, shuts the tabernacle, folds the corporal, and puts aside his stole. The Bishop resumes his skull-cap.

Visitation of Church and Sacristy. The Bishop is then unvested. In rochet and mozzetta (or cappa) he now goes round the church, attended by the rector and other clergy. He examines the chapels, altars, ornaments, confessionals, pulpit, font, the seats for the people, the notices at the church doors, and any other article of furniture or ornament he may wish to inspect. He is conducted to the sacristy and here examines the relics, stocks of holy Oils, vestments, vessels and furniture;[36] and he may bless vestments,[37] etc. Then he may administer the sacrament of Confirmation (see below), or this may be done immediately after the visitation of the Blessed Sacrament.

The Bishop will then give an opportunity to the people to speak to him privately, either in the sacristy or other convenient place.

Generally in the presbytery the Bishop examines the books of the church. He writes the word *Visum* with his signature and the date at the last used page of the registers. He examines the account books and others concerning the mission or school. He asks any questions he may think fit. Then the rector and clergy receive his instructions.

Finally the Bishop, in private dress, is conducted to the church again that he may make a visit to the Blessed Sacrament before his departure.[38]

§ 4. Visitation by an Archbishop

If the Ordinary is an archbishop, the following alterations in the ceremony must be made. The processional cross is not used; instead of it the archiepiscopal cross is carried before the Archbishop. If he does not bring this archiepiscopal cross with him, the processional cross of the church may take its place.

It is not carried before the procession on the way to the door to meet the Archbishop. It should be placed by the door beforehand. As the procession comes up the church, the cross is carried immediately before the rector of the church and the chaplain, who walk in front of the Archbishop. It is always carried so that the figure of our Lord shall face the Archbishop. Acolytes do not go on either side of the cross.

---

[35] The verse *Panem,* etc., and the prayer *Deus qui nobis* are not sung.

[36] A list of all objects and persons examined at the Visitation, drawn up originally by Pope Benedict XIII (1724-1730), is printed in Schulte-O'Connell, *Benedicenda,* pp. 213ff.

[37] Or he may do all this at another time.

[38] The pontifical directs the Bishop at this last visit to stand at the epistle corner of the (high) altar, and say — with the clergy — *De profundis, Pater noster,* the versicles and prayer *Deus cujus miseratione* for the dead.

While the Archbishop gives the first blessing (after the prayers for him at the altar) the cross-bearer holds the cross before him, facing him. The bearer kneels on the lowest altar step. This is done again while he gives the indulgence, namely, while he says the prayers *Precibus et meritis,* etc. The cross is borne in the same way before the Archbishop if he goes to the cemetery, and in other processions. The form for proclaiming the indulgence is slightly modified, as also for a cardinal (above).

§ 5. Visitation by an Auxiliary Bishop

The auxiliary bishop wears rochet and mantelletta[39] when he arrives at the door of the church. He does not kiss a crucifix, nor is he incensed. The rector of the church offers him holy water, handing him the sprinkler, with which he signs himself only.

In the rest of the ceremony the following changes occur: The prayers for the Ordinary are not said by the rector. The bishop kneels for a short time at a faldstool or kneeler (undraped) before the altar. Then, if Mass is said, it follows at once. Otherwise the bishop, standing or sitting, addresses the people. No indulgence is announced.[40] The prayers for the dead follow, either in the cemetery or before a catafalque or black cloth in the sanctuary, as above. For the examination of the vessels containing the Blessed Sacrament, the bishop puts on a white stole over his rochet (if he does not wear amice, stole and cope), then he kneels before the tabernacle, the rector opens it, the bishop examines the vessels and tabernacle (as above) and gives Benediction with the ciborium. The bishop unvests; wearing rochet and mantelletta, he goes round the church inspecting everything. He inspects the sacristy and its furniture, and gives the people an opportunity of speaking to him, all as above. Confirmation may follow (at which the crosier is used). He examines the books and gives instructions to the clergy. He signs the books in the same way as the Ordinary.

§ 6. Visitation of Other Buildings and Institutions

After the visitation of the church, the Bishop, if he desire to do so, may inspect the school, orphanage, or any other religious institutions in the parish. He may inspect the buildings, interview the teachers or officials, examine the account books and other documents, and so satisfy himself as to the good state of the school or institution in every respect.

---

[39] If the bishop does not possess a mantelletta, the use of a mozzetta may be tolerable.
[40] Unless the Ordinary commissions the bishop to impart it. Then it is announced in the Ordinary's name.

§ 7. Visitation of Convents

All convents of religious women are subject to visitation by the Ordinary.[41] The visitation of a convent may, or may not, take place at the occasion of the visitation of the church. Notice of it will be given to the Superior beforehand, and prayers will be said by the nuns for the blessing of God. Unless the order is subject to a Regular Superior, a copy of the rules and constitutions is sent to the Ordinary before the visitation.

At the convent the Bishop may, if he think fit, carry out the ceremonies used at the visitation of churches. He may say or assist at Mass, address the nuns, and give the Absolution for the dead. He will inspect the tabernacle and ciborium, if the chapel has the right of reserving the Blessed Sacrament. The convent chaplain will attend as the rector of the church.

The Bishop will then interview each member of the community in order, beginning with the youngest. If the community is enclosed, a table with a crucifix, writing materials and a list of the nuns will be placed before the grating of the enclosure. Here the Bishop will sit and will see each nun separately and privately. He will ask any questions he thinks fit as to the manner in which the rule is kept and the lives of the nuns, and will give such advice as he thinks needed.

The Bishop then visits the buildings, beginning with the outer premises. If the community is enclosed, the Bishop enters the enclosure.[42] The community of an enclosed order receives the Bishop at the door of the enclosure. At the entrance a kneeling-stool is placed, on which the Bishop kneels to kiss a crucifix handed to him by the Superior. The nuns then form a procession, with their processional cross, to conduct him to their choir, singing meanwhile *Veni, Creator*. In the choir the versicles and prayers are said as at the visitation of a church (if the visitor is the Ordinary). The Bishop may then address the nuns and give them his blessing. The nuns go to their cells, except the Superior and four others, chosen by the Chapter, or appointed by the Bishop, to accompany him. He inspects every part of the convent. The books and accounts are presented outside the enclosure, and are examined by the Bishop or by someone appointed by him. The whole community assembles at the end to receive his final address and blessing.

---

[41] Cf. C.I.C. 344, 512, 513.

[42] C.I.C. 600 says that at least one cleric or religious man of mature age should accompany him.

§ 8. Visitation of the Churches of Exempt Regulars

When the Ordinary or his delegate visits the church of a religious order exempt from his jurisdiction,[43] all the ceremonies are carried out as above with the following exceptions:

The Ordinary visits the church, clergy, objects, services, only in so far as they concern the people living around, and so the diocese. If the church has the rights and duties of a parish, the Bishop examines all that concerns these. If it is not a parish church and has no parochial rights or duties, it is not subject to episcopal visitation. In a parish church or public oratory served by regulars he does not inspect every altar, but only that at which the Blessed Sacrament is reserved. He visits the confessional, pulpit, font (if there is one), because these are used for the parish or people. He examines in the sacristy all that is used for public or parochial functions and services. He visits the schools, in the same way as those of the diocesan clergy, the property of the parish (not that of the order). He makes a personal visitation of those members of the order who are engaged in parish work, not with a view to see whether they are faithful to their rule (for this is the business of their Regular Superiors), but to see whether they fulfil faithfully the duties they owe to the people, and so to the diocese. From this point of view the Ordinary may inquire into the life and manners of these priests, since that affects the parish as well as their rule. The Bishop examines the parish registers and signs them, as in the case of other churches.

"In one word, whatever the bishop may inquire and demand of a secular parish priest, all that he must inquire and demand of a Regular parish priest, excepting only what belongs to the observances of his religious order."[44]

§ 9. The First Visitation of the Ordinary

The first visitation of the Ordinary should be held with more pomp. The following additions to the ceremony may be made where possible:

If there is a separate chapel of the Blessed Sacrament, a draped kneeling desk is prepared there, and a faldstool at the epistle side at which the Bishop will unvest. In the sanctuary on the gospel side of the high altar a throne is prepared covered with white hangings.

The Bishop wears the cappa on arriving, and has a train-bearer. He is received at the door of the church, or gate of the churchyard, by all the clergy, the rector wearing surplice and white cope. He is escorted to the altar under a canopy held by servers in surplice, or distinguished male

---

[43] Cf. C.I.C. 344, § 2; 512; 513; 1261, § 2.
[44] Const. *Firmandis* of Benedict XIV (1744), § 11.

members of the congregation. The rector takes off his cope after the versicles and prayer for the Bishop before the altar.

The Bishop goes to the throne to preach, or, if this is not convenient,[45] to the altar, where the indulgence is announced and he gives the blessing *Precibus et meritis*. He is assisted by two deacons in choir dress, who then vest him, at the throne, in black stole and cope and white mitre. He comes down between them and performs the Absolutions either at the cemetery or in the middle of the choir. The rector now acts as assistant priest and (without the *solita oscula*) hands him the lustral water sprinkler and incense spoon, holding the boat. Going back to the throne he there changes his vestments to a white stole and cope and golden mitre. He goes with the assistants to the altar of the Blessed Sacrament, the tabernacle is opened by the AP (the rector), who then assists at the incensing. The Bishop examines the tabernacle. He may give Benediction according to the special form for visitation (above).

If the Blessed Sacrament is reserved at the high altar the Bishop goes to the throne to be unvested. If it is in aside chapel he unvests at a faldstool there. He continues the visitation in cappa. The canopy is not used as he departs.

Confirmation may be administered after the prayers for the dead and the general inspection, as above. The four chaplains of mitre, crosier, book, candle assist throughout; the train-bearer while the Bishop wears the cappa magna.

§ 10. The Sacrament of Confirmation

In most parish churches Confirmation[46] is administered by the Ordinary, or his auxiliary bishop, on the occasion of the canonical visitation. But this is not always the case.

Preparations. The following preparations are made:

Each person to be confirmed should have a card on which are written his name and the name he will take in Confirmation[47] (in Latin, in the nominative case). A godfather is required for men, a godmother for women. Only one sponsor is to stand for each person confirmed; and each sponsor is to stand for only one or two persons, unless the minister decide otherwise for a just cause.[48] The sponsors must be themselves confirmed, and fulfil the other conditions laid down in the Code of

---

[45] The difficulty of preaching from the throne is that it faces sideways across the church, so that the people often cannot well see or hear the Bishop.

[46] The rite is in the pontifical (Part I, first chapter), and in the English *Ritus Servandus*, pp. 72-74. Cf. C.I.C. 780-800.

[47] It is a general usage to take an extra name of a saint at Confirmation and the usage is approved by S.R.C. 2404 § 7. There is no rubric which prescribes it.

[48] C.I.C. 794.

Canon Law (cc. 795 and 796).[49] They will contract spiritual relationship with their godchildren. The sponsor stands during the Confirmation behind the candidate.

The Bishop may confirm with simple rite—in the church or, for a reasonable cause, in any becoming place[50]—wearing only a white stole over his rochet[51] and surplice and the mitre. In solemn administration he wears amice, pectoral cross,[52] white stole and cope, and cloth of gold mitre. The Bishop will use the crosier and, if he is the Ordinary, the morse also. The vestments are laid on the centre of the altar in the inverse order, namely, cope,[53] stole, amice. The golden mitre is placed on the gospel side. But if the Bishop also uses the precious mitre (for other ceremonies at the visitation), this is put on the gospel side, the golden one on the epistle side.

Before the ceremony the crosier—in a stand or leaning against the wall—is on the epistle side of the sanctuary. Near by are prepared the veils for the bearers of mitre and crosier. The altar is vested in white (unless Mass is to be celebrated and the colour of the Office is not white). The six candles are lit.

On the credence are the hand-candle, the vessel of water, basin and hand-towels to wash the Bishop's hands, a plate containing bread and lemon, a plate with cotton wool,[54] the pontifical (or *Ritus Servandus*), the stock of Chrism, a linen gremial.[55]

A faldstool or chair is placed either in the middle of the footpace or on the ground before the middle of the altar steps, and is covered in white.

Assistants. The following persons assist the Bishop: two priests, of whom one stands at his right, takes the cards[56] and tells the Bishop the Confirmation names and wipes off the Chrism from the forehead of the confirmed; the other, on his left, holds the Chrism. Three servers are required to hold the mitre, book and hand-candle. If the Bishop uses the crosier a fourth is required to carry this.[57] If he is the Ordinary a fifth will carry his train if he wears the cappa magna. The two acolytes wash the

---

[49] Cf. canon 874 of the 1983 C.I.C.

[50] C.I.C. 791.

[51] A stole should never be worn over the mozzetta or mantelletta (cf. S.R.C. 4355, I, ad 4). At private Confirmation, for a just cause, the mitre need not be used.

[52] Usually the Bishop's pectoral cross is taken off before he vests and is put on again over the alb before the stole.

[53] If the Bishop is the Ordinary the morse, on a salver, will be placed on the altar near the vestments.

[54] This should be prepared in balls, one for each confirmand (or for each two or three if they are numerous) and there should be a (silver or glass) dish to receive the balls after use.

[55] An amice may be used for this.

[56] There should be a basket or some other receptacle to hold these cards when received from the confirmands.

[57] The bearers of mitre and crosier wear white veils (*vimpæ*) over their shoulders through which they hold these ornaments.

Bishop's hands. Afterwards they aid the assistant priests, one receiving the cards after use, the other holding a bowl for the cotton wool used in wiping the foreheads of the confirmed. The godparents must be ready somewhere near the altar rails.

No one who has been confirmed may leave the church till the Bishop has given his blessing at the end.[58]

Arrival of Bishop. The Bishop, when he arrives at the church for the Confirmation, will wear rochet and mozzetta or mantelletta. If Confirmation takes place during the Visitation it may follow at once after the Absolution for the dead and the visitation of the Blessed Sacrament.

If Confirmation does not follow Visitation the Bishop on arrival will kneel in prayer for a short time before the altar at the faldstool (or at a kneeling-stool) prepared there.

Address to Candidates. He rises and is vested for Confirmation as above. Wearing the golden mitre he sits on the faldstool (or chair) and addresses or catechises the candidates. He holds the crosier in his left hand while so doing. When finished he hands the crosier to its bearer,[59] who takes it with the *solita oscula*. The Bishop washes his hands[60] (the acolytes kneeling if he is the Ordinary), the priest at his right hands him the hand-towel and when he has dried his hands, takes off the mitre. The Bishop stands facing the candidates and joins his hands. The book-bearer holds the book before him (standing), the other server holds the candle at the Bishop's left. The Bishop says the first versicle *Spiritus Sanctus superveniat in vos et virtus Altissimi custodiat vos a peccatis*. ℟. *Amen*. The other versicles and the prayer follow, as in the pontifical. The assisting priests answer. During the prayer the Bishop stretches his hands over the candidates. Meanwhile the candidates kneel in places in front of the church, or at the communion rails. After the prayer the Bishop sits and the mitre is put on by the first assistant priest. A linen gremial veil is placed on the Bishop's lap and fastened. The vessel with Chrism is brought to the Bishop and held by the second assistant priest at his left.

The Confirming. Each candidate now comes forward, genuflects and kneels before the Bishop.[61] The godparent lays his right hand, ungloved, on the candidate's right shoulder.[62] The candidate hands his card to the

---

[58] There is a special rubric in the pontifical to this effect. It is to prevent any doubt as to the integrity of the sacrament.

[59] The crosier-bearer always receives the crosier (kneeling, if the prelate be the Ordinary or a higher prelate) directly from the Bishop, and directly hands it to him, with the usual ceremonial kisses. He holds the crosier with both hands, the crook turned forward (except when handing the crosier to the Bishop).

[60] So the rubric of the pontifical. In practice, the Bishop follows the normal rule of washing his hands before he vests.

[61] If there are many candidates, they may kneel at the communion rail. The Bishop then confirms, standing, passing along the rail between the two priests.

[62] The pontifical says that the candidate puts his foot on the right foot of the godparent. This is obsolete. It supposes that they stand to receive the sacrament (cf. S.R.C. 2404 § 6).

priest at the Bishop's right, who says the Confirmation name to the Bishop.[63] The Bishop, holding the crosier in his left hand (if he wishes)[64] dips the thumb of the right hand into the Chrism, makes the sign of the cross once with it on the candidate's forehead, laying the hand on his head, and says the form of Confirmation, making the sign of the cross three times over the person confirmed at the words *In nomine Patris*, etc. He then lightly strikes the candidate on the left cheek saying *Pax tecum*. There is no answer to this. The candidate rises, giving place to the next. He passes to his left and stands before the priest on the Bishop's right, who wipes away the Chrism from his forehead with cotton wool.[65] The candidates pass before the Bishop from his left to his right. When the Chrism has been wiped off, each person who has been confirmed genuflects and returns to his place.

After the Confirming. When all are confirmed the Bishop gives away his crosier and washes his hands, using bread and lemon. The acolytes who bring the water and these, kneel. Meanwhile the choir sings (or the assistant clergy say) the antiphon *Confirma hoc*, with the *Gloria Patri*, etc., and antiphon repeated. The gremial is removed and the mitre is then taken off by the priest at the Bishop's right. The Bishop rises, turns towards the altar, and sings or says, with hands joined, the versicles *Ostende nobis, Domine, misericordiam tuam*, etc. (the book-bearer and candle-bearer standing before him). The choir sings the responses, or those around say them. The persons confirmed remain on their knees till the end of the service. The Bishop, with hands still joined, says or sings in the second ferial tone the prayer *Deus qui apostolis tuis*. ℟. *Amen*. Then *Ecce sic benedicetur omnis homo qui timet Dominum*. He turns, receives the crosier and makes the sign of the cross (once) over the confirmed, saying *Bene✠dicat vos Dominus ex Sion*, etc. The Bishop sits, receives the mitre, and addresses the sponsors on their duties to their spiritual children. Usually he recites the *Credo*, Lord's Prayer and "Hail Mary" with the confirmed. He may, in conclusion, give a simple blessing[66] to all those present with his right hand, saying nothing; or use the usual form *Sit nomen Domini*. The parish priest notes the confirmations in a special book, and also in his Baptism register.[67]

Confirmation Administered by a Parish Priest.[68] When a bishop is not available, a parish priest may[69] give Confirmation to any person

---

[63] In what case? The Bishop uses the vocative. Usually the priest says the name in the nominative and leaves the Bishop to decline it.

[64] The pontifical makes no mention of the crosier in the form (Part I) for the confirmation of many, but prescribes it in the form (Appendix) for the Confirmation of one person.

[65] Only a cleric in major orders may do this.

[66] The pontifical says nothing of this blessing, but some rubricians mention it.

[67] C.I.C. 798.

[68] Canon 884 § 1 of the 1983 C.I.C. allows the Bishop to grant a priest the faculty of administering Confirmation to persons not in danger of death. Canon 883 concedes this

within his parish who is in real danger of death from a grave illness. The form of administration is given in the 1952 Roman Ritual (III, ii).[70] The priest will need a server to hold the book during the prayers (said with joined hands) and at the imposition of hands and anointing. The Chrism is carried in a white silk bag. The P.P. wears a surplice (if possible) and white stole. He begins by telling those present that a bishop is the ordinary minister of Confirmation, and that a priest administers by virtue of special delegation. All the prayers are said facing the sick person. For the prayer *Omnipotens,* the verses, and the prayer *Adimple,* the priest extends both hands towards the sick person. During the anointing the sponsor puts his right hand on the right shoulder of the invalid. The priest anoints the latter on the forehead[71] with the thumb of the right hand and at the same time places this hand on the head of the invalid. He makes the triple sign of the cross over the latter at *In nomine,* etc., and then strikes him lightly on the left cheek. He then wipes the Chrism from the invalid's forehead with cotton wool; cleanses his own hand with bread crumb and water (all these are later disposed of in the sacrarium);[72] and continues *Confirma,* etc. Later he enters the particulars of the administration in the parochial Confirmation register — adding "Confirmatio collata est ex Apostolico indulto, urgente mortis periculo ob gravem confirmati morbum" — and in the baptismal register. He is to notify the diocesan Ordinary at once, explaining the circumstances of the case. If the invalid was from another parish, the P.P. of this is to be notified also. If Confirmation be given with the last sacraments, it follows confession and precedes Holy Viaticum.[73]

---

faculty to priests who baptise those no longer infants, or who receives such persons into full communion with the Church.

[69] S. Cong. Sacr., 14 September 1946. Cf. *Excerpta,* p. 35.

[70] The new form issued by the Congregation simply adapts the rubrics of the form of the pontifical and R.R. to the case of one sick person.

[71] Using his new name, if he takes one in Confirmation.

[72] If this be inconvenient, they may be disposed of in the fire at the house of the sick person

[73] If several sick persons be confined at the same time, the form of the sacrament and *Pax tecum* are said in the singular to each one; the other prayers are said in the plural.

Chapter XXX

The Ceremonies of the Ritual

§ 1. The English Ritual

B Y ritual in this case is meant the book, the *Rituale*. There is a *Rituale Romanum*, published (after there had been many books of the same kind) by Pope Paul V (1605-1621) in the constitution "Apostolicæ Sedi" of 17 June 1614. It was revised and published again in 1752 by Benedict XIV (1740-1758) and has had further revisions by Leo XIII (1878-1903) in 1884, under St Pius X (1903-1914) in 1913, under Pius XI in 1925, bringing it into conformity with the Code of Canon Law (1917) and the rubrics of the missal (1920); and under Pius XII in 1952. The ritual contains the texts and ceremonies for all sacraments administered by a priest, the rite of funerals, blessings, liturgical processions, the liturgical litanies, exorcism, and the forms for keeping parish registers. This book is used exclusively in many dioceses. It forms the ultimate standard for all rituals. But it is not imposed by law on all dioceses of the Roman rite. In many parts of the Church local rituals are still allowed and used. This is the case in England. In this country we have had our own ritual with the title: *Ordo Administrandi Sacramenta et Alia Quædam Officia Peragendi* and we have *Excerpta e Rituali Romano* (1961).[1] This is the book we use ordinarily. A priest in England may, and indeed should, possess a copy of the *Rituale Romanum* to supplement *Excerpta*. He will normally administer sacraments and sacramentals from the English *Ordo Administrandi* or from *Excerpta* which may be imposed on him by the authority of his bishop. However, to a great extent, the difference is merely theoretical; for our books are conformable to the Roman Ritual throughout, except that, in one or two ceremonies, such as particularly the marriage rite, we have some forms peculiar to English dioceses. Otherwise the differences between our rituals and the Roman book are rather of the nature of additions to it (as the title page of the *Ordo* states). In any case in practice the immediate norm and standard for England is this English book.

The ceremonies of the ritual here discussed are those of Baptism, Penance, the receptions of converts, Holy Communion, sick calls,

---

[1] The full title of this book is *Excerpta e Rituali Romano pro Diœcesibus Anglice et Cambriæ edita*. It is published with the permission of the Holy See (Decree of S.R.C., 14 January 1959). Ireland has its own trilingual ritual, *Collectio Rituum* (1960), in use in Scotland also. For the U.S.A., see the Appendix.

Extreme Unction and the last rites, Marriage, churching of women, and various blessings. The funeral rites are described in the next chapter. No detailed description of these ceremonies is necessary. They are all exceedingly simple; the ritual gives exact rubrics throughout. From these rubrics alone it is possible to perform the ceremonies correctly. However, some notes about the necessary preparations and certain special points will be found useful.

§ 2. Baptism[2]

The common case is that of the solemn[3] Baptism of infants. Children should be brought to church to be baptised as soon after birth as possible, i.e., as is safe and reasonably convenient. Unless there is grave danger to the child's life, it is to be brought to the church and there baptised solemnly by the parish priest of the place in which it is born, or a priest authorised by him or by the Ordinary.[4]

Sponsors. The child should have one godparent; or at most a godfather and a godmother. Not more than two are allowed. To act validly as a sponsor the person must be a Catholic (in good standing with the Church)[5] appointed by the parents or guardians of the child (or, failing them, by the priest who baptises), intending to act as sponsor and must at the actual baptism touch the child physically. To act lawfully the sponsor must be at least fourteen years of age and know the rudiments of the faith.[6] Members of religious orders may not without express leave from their Superior be godparents lawfully; nor priests, unless they have leave from their Ordinary; nor the child's parents. The godmother (ungloved) holds the child during the whole ceremony. The godfather stands by her side, answers the questions in the child's name, touches the child physically (generally by putting his hand on its shoulder) at the moment when the priest pours the water, and holds the lighted candle given (theoretically) to the child at the end. If there is only one godparent, he or she must do all that otherwise is done by either. In our time the duties of the godparent towards the child are much reduced from what they were in the Middle Ages.[7] There remains a general duty of looking after the child's spiritual welfare, especially in default of its parents.

---

[2] R.R., Tit. II; C.I.C. 737-779; *Excerpta,* 2-30. For the U.S.A., see the Appendix (below).

[3] Solemn Baptism means with all the ceremonies of the ritual; private Baptism is the essential matter and form, with or without some of the ceremonies prescribed by the ritual. C.I.C. 737, § 2.

[4] The Ordinary may allow Baptism in a house for very special reasons (cf. R.R., II, i, 45). A deacon may baptise solemnly, by leave of the Ordinary or of the parish priest of the place; but then the salt and baptismal water that are used must have been blessed by a priest (R.R., II, i, 15; ii, 27).

[5] See C.I.C. 765 § 2, 766 § 2.

[6] The sponsor must be able to recite the Creed and *Our Father* during the ceremony.

[7] These duties are given in R.R., II, i, 38.

Place of Baptism. It is usual to fix a time for solemn Baptisms, generally on Sundays after noon. But the priest will be ready to baptise at other times, if the request is reasonable. Solemn Baptism is a public ceremony of the Church, at which anyone may be present; indeed it should be of interest to the entire parish. It supposes three distinct places, the narthex or porch of the church, in which the first part of the rite takes place (till the priest lays his stole on the child and says *N. ingredere in templum Dei,* etc.); the nave or other part of the church, outside the baptistery, where the ceremony continues till he has changed the stole; the baptistery, where it is concluded. The baptistery should be either a separate chapel, or it should at least have a railing round it. If there is no visible distinction (as there ought to be) between these three places, the priest and godparents must move nearer to the font each time, crossing an imaginary line of division.

Preparations. Near the font there should be a table covered with a white cloth, unless the font is so made that the necessary objects can be placed on it. Here are prepared: the stocks containing Oil of Catechumens and Chrism,[8] a vessel with the salt, the shell or ladle used for pouring the water, a towel to wipe the child's head after Baptism, cotton wool to use after the anointings, the white robe (Chrism), a wax candle,[9] the white stole, a vessel of water and a hand-towel, with bread (or soap) on a plate, for cleansing the priest's hands after Baptism.

There ought to be at least one server, to hand the things and especially to answer; but often the priest has to baptise without one, answering the versicles and saying *Amen* himself. In the baptistery or sacristy the register of Baptisms must be ready to be filled up immediately afterwards.

At the Church Door. The priest first washes his hands in the sacristy, then vests in cassock, surplice and violet stole; he carries the ritual with him. The server or servers vest in cassock and surplice. The priest with them goes to where the godparents wait with the child, in the porch or narthex. The child should be borne by the godmother[10] on her right arm. The priest must first ascertain the child's name; it should be the name of a saint.[11] He then begins the rite, as in the ritual.

---

[8] R.R. (II, i, 53) directs that the Oils be kept in the church in a special place, which is to be decent, clean, safe and locked. It is best to have an aumbry (with a white and violet curtain hung before it) and marked clearly "Olea Sacra." A distinct aumbry should contain the other requisites for Baptism. The font should be kept locked (R.R., II, i, 46).

[9] No rubric orders this candle to be lighted till it is given to the godfather. It may, however, very suitably stand in a candlestick and burn during the whole ceremony.

[10] Usually the godmother carries the child throughout the entire ceremony. She need not, however, do so, except at the actual baptism.

[11] If it is not, the priest should himself add the name of a saint and enter both names in the register (R.R., II, i, 30; cf. no. 70).

The questions may be asked and answered, and some parts of the rite said, in the vernacular. The priest may have to prompt the godparent as to the answers. If the child receives several Christian names, all may be said at the first question and at the actual baptism. Otherwise the first name is sufficient. The gender of all prayers is changed, according to the sex of the child, except in the exorcism *Exorcizo te, omnis spiritus immunde,* where all is neuter, agreeing with *plasma.*

The priest blows gently—not merely breathes—on the child at *Exi ab eo.* The sign of the cross (and the imposition of the hand) is to be made by physically touching the child (or its dress), when the part of the body to be signed is definitely mentioned (e.g., the head); otherwise the sign is made *over* the child.

The salt may have been already blessed. In this case it is not blessed again. But it must have received the special blessing for baptism.

Entering the Church. After the prayer *Æternam ac justissimam pietatem,* the priest lays the left end of his stole momentarily on the child as he says *N. ingredere in templum Dei,* etc. and introduces him into the church. Walking by the side of the child and godparents or before them, he says with them the *Credo* and Lord's Prayer in Latin or English. Standing near, but outside the baptistery, with his back to it, he says the exorcism *Exorcizo te, omnis spiritus immunde.* He then moistens his own right thumb with his tongue, and with the thumb touches the lobes of the ears and the nostrils of the child, saying the forms *Ephpheta,*[12] etc. There is no direction to make the sign of the cross here. He wipes his thumb with a towel. For the anointing with Oil of Catechumens the godmother uncovers the child's breast and loosens its dress behind.[13] All anointing is done on the bare skin and in the form of a cross; but it is not necessary to open the dress very far down. After the anointing the priest wipes the child and his own thumb with cotton wool. He then changes the violet stole for a white one; he enters the baptistery, followed by the godparents and child. The interrogations about belief follow.

The Baptism. At the moment of pouring the water and baptising, the godmother holds the child's head over the font,[14] the godfather lays his right hand, bare, on the child. The child is better held with its face sideways, so that the water flows over its bare skin, and yet is not poured over its features. The priest pours[15] three distinct times in the form of a cross, as he says the words marked with a cross in the book. There is no *Amen* to the form. The priest must see that the water touches the skin of the child and flows. He, or one of the godparents, wipes the child's head

---

[12] For a good reason—for cleanliness' sake, or if there is danger of contracting or spreading disease—this use of saliva is omitted, but the touching, with its form, is retained (R.R., II, ii, 13).

[13] It is advisable to warn the godmother or nurse about this before the ceremony begins.

[14] Over that part of it into which the water when it has been used is to flow.

[15] "Abluenda est pars capitis superior" (*Ordo,* p. 7).

with a towel, used for this purpose only. If Baptism is given under condition, he uses the form *N. si non es baptizatus (a)*, etc., as in the ritual.

Anointing with Chrism. The anointing with Chrism follows. The child is anointed at the top of the head (on the skin) in the form of a cross (at the words *ipse te liniat);* then the priest wipes the place and his thumb with cotton wool. Instead of a complete white garment, it is now usual to lay a white cloth on the head of the child, as the rubric implies.[16] The priest gives the candle, lighted, to the godfather. If there is no godfather the godmother holds the candle. Lastly, he dismisses the child with the form *N. vade in pace,* etc. He wipes his thumb with bread, and washes his hands. The entry in the Baptism register is made at once, in the baptistery or sacristy.[17] If the child belongs to another parish the priest who has baptised it is to inform the child's parish priest as soon as possible of the Baptism. A note of the Baptism must be made in the child's parish also.[18] The priest is to warn the sponsors of the (diriment) impediment to marriage that spiritual relationship creates. The water used for the Baptism and that used to wash the priest's hands is poured into the sacrarium and all is put away.

§ 3. Baptism of Several Children Together

The ritual gives the forms for this. The boys are to be placed on the right of the girls[19] and the priest begins each action with the boys. The book gives plainly the forms to be said in the plural for all, and those said in the singular to each child separately. If boys and girls are addressed together, the masculine plural is used, according to the normal rule of Latin grammar. When the priest has to lay his hand on them, he does so, for a moment, on each; then says the prayer with hand outstretched, but not touching any one child. For the entry into the church the stole is laid on the first child only, the others follow in.

---

[16] "Linteolum candidum loco vestis albæ" (R.R., II, ii, 24), though there is no reason why the baptised cannot be clothed in a white garment.

[17] If the child be illegitimate, C.I.C. 777, § 2 directs how the entry is to be made.

[18] Congregation of the Sacraments, 29 June 1941.

[19] This is the better interpretation of the rubric (R.R., II, ii, 28). The priest is to begin each action with the boys, and he will more naturally move from left to right along the row or circle of children.

§ 4. Baptism Administered by a Bishop[20]

In general a bishop baptises in the same way as a simple priest, but the ceremony is carried out with greater pomp, the bishop uses cope, mitre and crosier, and he is seated for much of the time.

Preparations. *In the sacristy* the vestments for the bishop are laid out: amice, alb, cincture, violet stole and cope, simple morse (if he is the Ordinary), gold mitre.[21] At hand is the crosier (if the bishop is the Ordinary). Surplices are made ready for the assistants and servers; vimpae for the mitre and crosier-bearers; the ewer and tray for the washing of the bishop's hands, with a hand-towel; a small salver (to hold his biretta and his pectoral cross). A faldstool or armchair for the bishop.

In the baptistery: all that is normally prepared for Baptism. In addition, the ewer and basin,[22] with its tray containing cubes of dry bread and slices of lemon (for the washing of the bishop's hands after the anointings) and a towel; a basin to hold the water that will flow from the baby's head, and a linen gremial (an amice).

Outside the entrance to the baptistery: a credence and on it a white stole and cope;[23] the precious mitre; the Oil of Catechumens on a salver and some cotton wool; a towel (for the bishop to wipe his thumb after the *Ephpheta*).

In the narthex of the church: On a carpet a faldstool—covered in violet over a covering of white—is so placed that the bishop will sit with his back to the (inner) door of the church. A credence is prepared with the vessel of salt and a towel on a salver; the hand-candle (with a lighted wax candle) and book *(Pontificale,* appendix); a card with the names to be taken by the child, and one (if necessary) with the prayers to be recited by the godfather (or godmother).

Assistants. For the ceremony two priests will assist the bishop (in the cathedral, two canons, in rochet and surplice); and six servers at least will be needed, i.e., the bearers of the mitre and crosier[24] (wearing vimpae); of the book and hand-candle; a fifth server to present the salt, and a towel whenever needed, and to take away the violet vestments when the bishop changes into white outside the baptistery; a sixth server to see to the faldstool (transferring it from the narthex to the entrance to the

---

[20] R.R., II, vii; *Pontificale Romanum* (Appendix).

[21] R.R., II, vii, 3.

[22] If a second bacile is not available, the one used in the sacristy at the beginning of the ceremony must be transferred (with the addition of the bread, lemon and a fresh hand-towel) to the baptistery.

[23] And the precious morse, if the bishop is the Ordinary.

[24] The crosier is used by the Bishop (if the Ordinary) while going from the sacristy to the narthex; from the narthex to the entrance of the baptistery; possibly, from there to the font; and finally, while returning from the font to the sacristy.

baptistery, and thence[25] — in due time — to the baptistery itself). A master of ceremonies directs the entire function. If the Archbishop is the officiant, a cross-bearer will be needed. The first assistant priest will hand things to the bishop with the *solita oscula*, and see to the mitre (putting it on when the bishop has sat down, removing it before he rises).

The godfather (or godmother) waits in the narthex for the arrival of the bishop. He makes the responses to the queries on behalf of his godchild and to any formulae directed to the baby; the bishop's assistants make the other responses (e.g., the *Amen* to the prayers). When presenting the baby before the bishop for any rite, or presenting any object to the bishop (e.g., the salt to be blessed), if the bishop is the Ordinary the person who does so kneels.

The Ceremony. The rubrics of the *Pontificale* indicate clearly, at each step in the rite, when the bishop sits or stands; when he is mitred, when uncovered.

In general: the bishop sits for all the interrogations; and for all the ritual actions, except the blowing on the infant's face, both impositions of hands (each of which is accompanied by a prayer), the second signing with the cross (on the forehead), and the *Ephpheta*. He is always mitred when sitting; and mitred when standing for the *exsufflatio*, for all exorcisms (unmitred for all prayers),[26] for the second signing with the cross, at the moment of entering the church *(Ingredere)*, and at the *Ephpheta*. All prayers and exorcisms are said standing, with hands joined.[27]

The bishop is received at the church door by the rector, and by his assistants, in the ordinary way, and lustral water presented to him. He vests (over his rochet) at the faldstool or chair in the sacristy — having washed his hands — assisted by the two priests. He then goes in procession to the narthex — preceded by servers and clergy — between his two assistants, who hold back the edges of his cope. He is followed by the bearers of mitre, crosier, book and candle. During the ceremony these stand in convenient positions near the bishop, as directed by the MC.

The rite proceeds as at Baptism by a priest, except for the points mentioned above (the use of the mitre and the faldstool), and is fully and clearly set forth in the *Pontificale*.

The bishop carries out the actual Baptism sitting. Just before it the linen gremial is placed on his lap and fastened. A basin is held by a server under the infant's head, to catch the water.[28] At each anointing the first assistant priest wipes off the oil with cotton wool, and presents

---

[25] Having removed the outer violet covering.
[26] Including the recitation of *Credo* and *Pater noster*.
[27] Regarding the possible abbreviation of the rite when a bishop officiates, see R.R., II, vii, 5.
[28] This water is afterwards thrown into the sacrarium.

cotton wool to the bishop to cleanse his thumb. At the end of the rite the bishop washes his hands, using the bread and lemon to cleanse them.[29]

The rector of the church will see to the registration of the Baptism.

§ 5. Baptism of Adults

The Roman Ritual has a much longer form for the solemn Baptism of grown-up people, but the Ordinary for a grave and reasonable cause may permit the form for infants to be used in the Baptism of adults. In addition, for the *conditional* Baptism of adult *heretics*, the Ordinary may permit the form of private Baptism to be used.[30] The only differences in the Baptism of adults according to the form for infants are that the catechumen answers the questions with his godparents (and says the *Credo* and *Our Father* with them), stands between his godparents, and lays his head over the font. While the priest pours the water the godparents lay their right hands on his shoulder. It is recommended that the minister and subject be fasting. The neophyte should then (unless there are urgent and grave causes to the contrary) hear Mass and receive his first Holy Communion.[31]

In response to the request of some bishops, particularly in missionary territories, a decree of the Sacred Congregation of Rites (16 April 1962) published an order of the Baptism of adults arranged in seven degrees through which adult catechumens may, in the course of appropriate intervals of time, proceed to receive the sacrament of Baptism. Norm I of the *ordo* concedes to all local Ordinaries the faculty to permit or to prescribe the use of this rite in the Baptism of adults.[32]

§ 6. Private Baptism

In case of danger of death anyone may baptise, even a heretic or pagan. It is sufficient that he administer the essential matter and form and have the implicit intention of doing what Christ instituted. Naturally a Catholic should be preferred, if possible. A man is preferred to a woman; but anyone else to the parents.[33] A priest may administer private Baptism (i.e., Baptism without the full rite) as well as a layman; indeed, if he is at

---

[29] The water should afterwards be poured into the sacrarium and the bread and lemons buried.

[30] R.R., II, i, 26, 28. In England the conditional Baptism of converts is carried out privately, with lustral water and without ceremonies (First Synod of Westminster, D. XVI. 8°).

[31] C.I.C. 753. Baptism of adults is, when convenient, to be announced to the Bishop beforehand, that Baptism may, if he wishes, be more solemnly administered by himself or his delegate. R.R., II, iii, 2.

[32] The rite is published in C. Braga C.M., (ed.), *Documenta ad Instaurationem Liturgicam Spectantia 1903-1963*, Centro Liturgico Vincenziano, Rome 2000, pp. 1180-1200.

[33] R.R., II, i, 16.

hand the priest should obviously be preferred. If possible, a priest or deacon should wear a surplice and a white stole. Private Baptism may be given only in the case of real necessity, i.e., if the child (or adult) is in danger of dying before the full rite is completed. If it were possible to go through the whole rite, the case would not be one of necessity at all, and so there would be no excuse for private Baptism. But it may well happen that, after the essential matter and form, the child still survives, at least for a time. In this case, if a priest or deacon baptises, and if he has the Chrism, white robe and candle at hand, he should go on with the ceremonies to the end, anointing with Chrism, giving the robe and the candle.[34] Obviously these ceremonies are not repeated, if there is a later supplying of ceremonies. For private Baptism any natural water may be used validly, and lawfully in case of need. But baptismal water is to be preferred, if it is at hand. There may be a godparent; but it is not necessary.[35] All the ceremonies that precede the actual Baptism are omitted. Private Baptism should be entered in the register as such.

§ 7. Supplying the Ceremonies of Baptism

After private Baptism, administered in case of urgent danger, the child, if it survives, must later be brought to the church that the ceremonies may be supplied. The form for doing this is in the ritual.[36] There must be a godparent, as at Baptism; but he does not contract the spiritual relationship unless he had been sponsor at the actual Baptism. Everything is done as at Baptism, except, of course, the interrogation *Vis baptizari* and the Baptism itself. The three places are used for the three parts of the rite. All follows as at Baptism, with certain verbal alterations (noted in the ritual) necessary to the circumstance. After the questions about faith, which, normally, come immediately before the actual Baptism, the priest simply omits the Baptism and goes on at once to the anointing with Chrism, unless this has already been performed.

§ 8. Conditional Baptism

In this case, the normal rite is exactly the same, with the one exception of the sacramental form, which becomes *N. si non es baptizatus (baptizata) ego te baptizo,* etc. But in the case of grown-up converts from heresy, conditional Baptism may, with the permission of the Ordinary, be given privately without ceremonies,[37] as noted below.

---

[34] R.R., II, ii, 29.
[35] R.R., II, i, 31. There should be two witnesses or at least one (n. 16).
[36] R.R., II, v; *Excerpta,* p. 21
[37] R.R., II, i, 26, 28. In England this form of Baptism is of obligation *in casu.*

§ 9. Blessing the Font

If it is necessary to bless baptismal water[38] in the course of the year, not on Holy Saturday, the priest uses the short form in the ritual (R.R., II, viii). The font must be filled with clean water beforehand, the stocks of Oil of Catechumens and Chrism placed near it. A hand-towel will also be needed, a vessel of water and basin, with bread, to wash the priest's hands afterwards. There should be a cross-bearer, two acolytes and thurifer. It will be well to have two other servers also, if possible, to answer, assist and hand things to the priest. The priest wears surplice and violet stole.

The procession goes to the baptistery in the usual order. Here the cross-bearer and acolytes stand opposite the priest, as on Holy Saturday. The thurifer is by his side. The priest and all[39] kneel, facing the altar of the baptistery, if it have one, or the high altar of the church. The priest says the Litanies of the Saints, either in the usual form, or the shorter form of Holy Saturday (not doubling the petitions). He rises and makes the sign of the cross over the water as he says twice *Ut fontem istum*, etc.[40] He kneels again till he has said the final *Kyrie, eleison*. Then all rise. The priest recites aloud the *Pater* and *Credo* and then the verses, prayer and exorcism. The ceremonies which follow are described clearly in the rubrics.[41] After he has breathed on the water the priest puts on and blesses incense *(Ab illo,* etc.), then incenses the water thrice with three simple swings (in the centre, to his left and to his right).[42] The holy Oils are poured into the water[43] and mixed, as on Holy Saturday. At the end he washes his hands, using bread to cleanse them from oil; and the water in which he has washed them is poured into the sacrarium.

§ 10. The Sacrament of Penance[44]

There should be, at each church, fixed days and hours at which confessions are heard. The clergy wait at these times so that people know that, coming then, they can make their confession without special appointment.[45] But at other times, too, priests who have care of souls

---

[38] Ordinary water may be added (in less quantity) to baptismal water, even many times (R.R., II, i, 6).

[39] Except, of course, the cross-bearer and acolytes.

[40] This is the special petition inserted twice, before: "Ut nos exaudire digneris."

[41] And compare the rite of Holy Saturday (Chapter XXVI).

[42] Incense is not used at the solemn blessing on Holy Saturday; it may seem strange that it be used now. The usual explanation is that it is a substitute for plunging the Paschal candle.

[43] If he has but little Oil he may dip his thumb or a silver rod into it and therewith make the sign of the cross in the water *(Ordo Adm.,* no. 6, p. 63).

[44] R.R., IV; *Ordo Administrandi*, Tit. III; *Excerpta*, p. 37.

[45] Conc. prov. Westm., I, Decr. xix, no. 8, p. 23.

must be ready to hear the confession of those who demand this reasonably.

Normally the proper place for hearing confessions is the confessional in the church. Confessions of men may be heard anywhere for a reasonable cause. The confessions of women are not to be heard outside the confessional, except in case of sickness or other real necessity.[46]

To administer the sacrament of Penance the priest wears a surplice and violet stole. (Regulars wear the stole only, over their habit.) This is the normal dress for confessions heard in church. In other cases the priest should wear at least the stole.[47] In case of necessity, naturally, he may hear confessions in any dress. Penance is the only sacrament administered sitting by a priest. He sits as a judge at his tribunal.

In many countries it is usual for the penitent to begin by asking the priest's blessing. The Roman Ritual speaks only of the penitent making the sign of the cross and says nothing about seeking a blessing. The English *Ordo Administrandi* says that he should do so, and suggests the form of blessing *Dominus sit in corde tuo,* etc., or a similar one.[48] It is also usual for the penitent to say either the *Confiteor,* or some similar prayer, before telling his sins. The ritual suggests the *Confiteor* or the short form *I confess to almighty God and to you, Father.*[49] Normally, the confessor gives the penitent his penance before pronouncing absolution. The form of absolution is given in the ritual. The prayers *Misereatur* (with hands joined) and *Indulgentiam* (without any sign of the cross) before the absolution and the prayer *Passio* after it may be omitted for a just cause.[50] From the beginning of *Indulgentiam* till he makes the sign of the cross at the end of the absolution form (or, if he does not say *Indulgentiam,* from *Dominus noster Iesus Christus*) the priest holds the right hand raised, palm towards the penitent.[51] This is the remnant of the old imposition of hands at Penance. He makes the sign of the cross over the penitent where the cross is marked, at the invocation of the Holy Trinity; then continues *Passio Domini nostri,* etc., with hands joined. In the form the word *Deinde*

---

[46] R.R., IV, i, 9.

[47] R.R., IV, i, 10 says: "Superpelliceo, et stola violacei coloris utatur, prout tempus vellocorum feret consuetudo." In Ireland the usage is to wear the stole only. There can be no question other than that the cassock or religious habit is worn to hear confessions.

[48] *Ordo Adm.,* Tit. III, cap. ii, § 13, p. 67. At the end of the telling of their sins penitents should say at once: "For these and all my sins, I am truly sorry," or some such words, thus indicating in a becoming way that they have finished and giving external expression to their sorrow (which is part of the matter of the sacrament).

[49] R.R., IV, i, 15.

[50] R.R., IV, ii, 4.

[51] If the confessor wears the biretta in the confessional he should be uncovered for *Misereatur, Indulgentiam* and *Passio Domini.*

is part of it;[52] the word *suspensionis* is used only when the penitent is tonsured. A bishop makes the triple sign of the cross when absolving.

In case of urgent necessity, in danger of death, the short form of absolution is *Ego te absolvo ab omnibus censuris et peccatis, in nomine Patris, et Filii +et Spiritus Sancti. Amen.*

§ 11. Reception of Converts in England[53]

There are two very different cases of reception of a convert into the Church, according as he is already baptised or not (and about this careful preliminary investigation must be made). A third case is if he has received doubtful Baptism in some heretical sect.

Theoretically there is all the difference in the world between the first and second cases. If a man has never been baptised, is a Jew, Moslem or Unitarian,[54] he has never been a member of the Catholic Church. So he becomes a Catholic in the normal way, by Baptism. It would seem that nothing more is needed. He must, of course, be instructed first. He must, when receiving the sacrament, have the necessary intention and dispositions, faith and repentance for his sins. Otherwise it should suffice that he be baptised, since really he is in the same state as the infant presented for baptism. He makes his profession of faith by saying the Apostles' Creed in the Baptism ceremony, which is exactly the purpose for which it is put there. The Baptism should be in the form for adults unless the Ordinary for a grave and reasonable cause permits the use of the infant form.[55]

But in England we have a law modifying this simple position in two ways. First, we may always (in this case), by privilege, use the form of Baptism for infants;[56] secondly, independently of the Creed said at the baptismal ceremony, a grown-up convert must make the usual profession of faith, as do those already baptised.[57]

The case of a convert already baptised differs entirely in principle. He has once been a Catholic. He became so when he was baptised, no matter who baptised him or where. But since then he may have incurred excommunication for frequenting the conventicle of an heretical sect. All

---

[52] It is printed as part of the form in the typical editions of the Roman Ritual of 1913, 1925, 1952.

[53] *Excerpta*, p. 38. For Ireland, see § 12 below; for U.S.A., see the Appendix.

[54] Some Unitarians do baptise, with the form of Matt. xxviii, 19. Supposing they pour water and have the implicit intention of doing what the Church does, their Baptism is valid.

[55] R.R., II, i, 26.

[56] Cf. the general law of R.R., II, i, 28, which allows the Ordinary to permit private Baptism (i.e., Baptism without the full ceremonies) in the case of an adult *heretic* who is to be baptised *conditionally*. This private Baptism is of obligation in England (I West., xvi, 8).

[57] *Ordo Adm.*, Tit. III, cap. iv, no. 1, following the Instruction of the Holy Office, 20 July 1859, p. 72. There is a modified form of the profession, *Excerpta*, p. 40.

that is needed then, in principle, is that he now be absolved from that excommunication. The process of his reception is a negative rather than a positive one. The priest who receives him takes away the censure of excommunication, and so restores him to the rights given, all unconsciously, by the heretical minister who baptised him. In England there is no supplying the ceremonies for adult converts validly baptised outside the Church.

In the case of a man doubtfully baptised no one of course can say which of these two processes really takes place. We baptise again conditionally as a precaution for the one case, and absolve him from excommunication and hear his confession for the other.[58]

In the case of all adult converts (those over seven years old) the priest who will receive them must first report the case to the Ordinary of the place where the person is to be received, using the form provided for that purpose, and must obtain leave and faculties to receive the convert.

(i) **Convert not already baptised.** If the convert is CERTAINLY NOT BAPTISED he has not incurred any censure; he makes no abjuration of heresy, but (in England) he does make the public profession of faith, if he is grown up. Then he is baptised publicly with the full form used for children. He has, of course, no confession to make, since sins committed before Baptism are not valid matter for the sacrament of Penance, but are remitted in Baptism. Children, in this case, are simply baptised.

(ii) **Convert already baptised.** If the convert is CERTAINLY ALREADY BAPTISED, there can be no question of baptising him again. It would be a grave sacrilege to attempt to repeat Baptism. In this case he makes his profession of faith, abjures heresy, is absolved *(in foro externo)* from excommunication and other censures which he may have incurred. Then he makes his first confession (in which he is absolved absolutely) and Holy Communion.

(iii) **Convert doubtfully baptised.** The commonest case is that of converts DOUBTFULLY BAPTISED. Such a convert makes his profession of faith and abjures heresy. He is then baptised conditionally (the condition is expressed), privately, with lustral water (not baptismal water) and without ceremonies. Then comes the (conditional) absolution from excommunication. Then the convert makes his first confession and is absolved conditionally.[59]

In all cases the reception of a convert is to take place before a priest appointed by the Ordinary, and at least two witnesses (in order that the abjuration may be juridical, which is required by C.I.C. 2314, § 2). These

---

[58] Both sacraments, Baptism and Penance, are given conditionally, and one of the two is certainly invalid. No one can say which.

[59] Conc. prov. Westm., I, Decr. xvi, § 8, pp. 15-16; *Ordo Adm., loc. cit.,* nos. 1, 3, 5, pp. 72-74. The confession must be made in the case of conditional Baptism (Conc. prov. Westm., I).

must also be present at the Baptism (even private), unless, for a grave reason, the Bishop dispenses.

Children[60] who are received from heretical sects, and are either certainly or doubtfully baptised, do not make any abjuration, nor are they absolved from censures, which they cannot have contracted. They make a simple profession of faith, either the Apostles' Creed or the form used for adults, without the abjuration. If necessary they are then baptised conditionally.[61]

In the case of babies who cannot speak or understand even the simplest profession of faith,[62] if they are certainly baptised, there is nothing to do but to see that henceforth they are brought up as Catholics and in due time receive the sacraments. Such children have never ceased to be Catholics since they became so at their Baptism.

The Ceremony Preparations. Two candles are lighted on the altar. Before it (on the epistle side if the Blessed Sacrament is present) is placed a stool for the priest; near by is the book of the Gospels (a missal will serve the purpose). In the sacristy a surplice, violet stole and ritual for the priest; white stole and cruet of lustral water, if Baptism is to be given privately, a basin to catch the water used and a towel to dry the convert's head. For public Baptism the usual preparations are made.

(1) **The ceremony** for the reception of a convert NOT BAPTISED previously is very simple.[63] In the presence of the priest and that of two witnesses the convert makes his profession of faith (in England), as in the ritual.[64] Then (having reminded him to make an act of at least attrition for his sins), he is baptised publicly using (by privilege) the rite for the baptism of children.

(2) The other two cases (of CONDITIONAL Baptism, or NONE) may be described together.

"Veni, Creator" and Profession of Faith. The priest, vested in surplice and violet stole,[65] sits before the altar facing the convert kneeling before him. With head covered he addresses the convert, exhorting him to thank God for the gift of faith, which in future he is to show forth by deed. Then the priest rises and kneels before the altar; all present kneel with him. So they say (or sing) the hymn *Veni, Creator* alternately. The priest (alone) stands to say the prayer after the hymn. He sits again and puts on the

---

[60] In regard to Baptism a person under seven years old is a "child;" in regard to censures "children" are boys under fourteen, girls under twelve (or, probably, fourteen). Regarding the baptism of children being received into the Church, see Canon Mahoney's *Questions and Answers*, I, Q. 9.

[61] *Ordo Adm., loc. cit.,* no. 2, pp. 72-73.

[62] Such a case may occur when a whole family joins the Church.

[63] In this case, too, the *Veni, Creator* may precede and the *Te Deum* follow the reception, but the psalm *Miserere,* etc., are not recited—it would seem—since these form part of the rite of absolution from censure (cf. R.R., IV, iii).

[64] In 1945 a simpler form was authorised. See *Excerpta,* p. 40.

[65] Instruction of Holy Office of 20 July 1859.

biretta; kneeling before him the convert reads the profession of faith,[66] as in the *Ordo Administrandi* or ritual.[67] The priest holds a book of the Gospels open on his knees, which the convert meanwhile touches.[68] They remain in the same position while the priest says the psalm *Miserere* or *De profundis,* at his discretion. He then takes off his biretta, stands facing the convert, and says *Kyrie, eleison* and the versicles and prayer which follow. The convert or people present should answer; if no one can, the priest himself answers.

Conditional Baptism. After this prayer is the right time for conditional Baptism (in England, according to the *Ordo Administrandi*), if it is to be administered. The priest goes with the convert to the sacristy, the two witnesses following. There, in their presence[69] (having reminded the convert to make at least an act of attrition for his sins), he baptises the convert, pouring lustral water over his head into a vessel, and saying the form *Si non es baptizatus, N. ego te baptizo in nomine Pa✠tris et Fi✠lii et Spiritus✠Sancti.* For this the priest wears a white stole.

Absolution from Censure. Returning to the church the priest (having resumed the violet stole) sits at the seat having his back to the altar, with head covered. The convert kneels before him. So he absolves him from excommunication,[70] using the form in the book *Auctoritate apostolica,* etc. In case of doubts as to whether the convert has incurred excommunication by professing heresy, the priest inserts the word *forsan* after *incurristi,* as directed in the note. He then imposes a penance for this absolution.

Te Deum. The convert may make his confession now or after the *Te Deum,*[71] All standing, the priest says *Te Deum laudamus,* alternately with the convert and those present. They kneel, as always, at the verse *Te, ergo,*

---

[66] If the convert cannot read the priest slowly reads for him the profession of faith so that he may understand it and may be able to pronounce it distinctly with the priest *(Ordo).* As the form is a very difficult one the priest who instructs the convert should coach him in it before the day of his reception.

[67] There is a booklet – *Form for the Reception of a Convert* – published (1947) by C.T.S. containing the entire rite in Latin and English.

[68] There is no direction to kiss the book at the end.

[69] One of them may act as sponsor, for the convert. There is no spiritual relationship except as in C.I.C. can. 763 § 2.

[70] This absolution in the external forum is valid in the internal forum as well. Once absolved from censure in the external forum, the convert can be absolved from sin in the internal forum by any confessor (C.I.C. can. 2314 § 2).

[71] There is a practice that the convert should make his confession, then receive conditional Baptism, then make a general statement repeating that he wishes to confess all the sins he has already told, then be absolved (cf. *Ordo,* p. 73, n. 3). If so, the priest must, of course, be the same throughout. But there is no necessity to confess before Baptism. It is often better that the convert should make his confession last of all, partly because he need not confess to the priest who receives him (there is, indeed, no general law of the Church commanding him to go to confession at once), partly because the witnesses and other people may then go away before his confession.

quæsumus, etc. Still standing, while the others kneel, the priest says the verses and prayer that follow. He turns to the convert and makes the sign of the cross over him, as he gives the blessing at the end. He sits and again speaks to the convert about his duties as a Catholic, as is directed in the rubric.

Confession. Lastly, if he has not already done so, the convert makes his confession. Since it is his first, it will be a general confession of his whole life. If the convert has just received conditional Baptism, the absolution will be conditional also; but this condition is not expressed in words.

The convert will attend Mass and receive his first Holy Communion immediately, if possible, after his reception and Baptism, or confession,[72] and receive Confirmation as soon as this is feasible.

If several converts are being received at the same time, it suffices if one of them pronounces the profession of faith for all, but each one must make the abjuration at the end of it ("So help me God," etc.). The priest says his formulae in the plural.

Résumé of Rite of Reception of a Convert

Whose baptism is:	Abjuration or profession of faith:	Absolution from Censures	Baptism	Ceremonies
Valid.	Abjuration, unless under age of puberty.	Yes, unless under age of puberty.	No.	By custom not supplied (except for an infant)
Doubtful.	Abjuration, unless under age of puberty.	Yes, unless under age of puberty.	Yes, conditionally, with lustral water.	Private baptism; no ceremonies.
Invalid.	Profession of faith.	No.	Yes (absolutely).	Public baptism with rite of infant baptism (by privilege).

§ 12. Reception of Converts in Ireland

In Ireland the form used for the reception of converts is derived from the common law of the Code (canons 744, 753, 7552, 759) and some decisions of the Holy Office. See *Collectio Rituum,* pp. 65-77.

It differs from the form used in England, and commented on above (§ 10), only in the following points: (1) not lustral water, but baptismal water (or, in case of necessity, ordinary water) is used for the conditional baptism of a convert; (2) when the baptism is absolute, no profession of faith is prescribed other than that contained in the actual rite of baptism.

---

[72] C.I.C. 753, § 2. In some dioceses, after his reception the convert must sign a declaration of his submission to and reception into the Church.

§ 13. Reconciliation of a Dying Non-Catholic

If a priest is called to a dying non-Catholic the procedure to be followed will differ with the various cases that may occur. As the person is in danger of death it is not necessary to approach the Ordinary beforehand for permission to receive him into the Church; nor does the need for the faculty to absolve from censure arise, since in danger of death any priest can absolve from censures.

Case 1: the person is conscious and desires to be received into the Church. First inquiries must be made about his baptism. (A) If it is certain that he was not previously baptised, a brief instruction is given, if time permits, on the main points of the faith;[73] the necessary dispositions for the reception of baptism validly and fruitfully (intention, acceptance of the Catholic faith, and, at least, attrition for sin) are seen to; baptism with the short form (using ordinary water, unless baptismal water be easily available) is given absolutely. If possible, the ceremonies that follow baptism are carried out.[74] (B) If previous baptism is doubtful, the steps in reconciliation are these:

(i) a brief instruction followed by a profession of faith, using some short form,[75] such as the Apostles' Creed;

(ii) conditional baptism (having seen to the dispositions of the dying person) with lustral water (in England), or with ordinary water;

(iii) conditional absolution from censure (using the form given in the *Ordo* or ritual; or, if necessary, the short form given at the end of that book).

(iv) confession, with conditional absolution;

(v) as the person is now a Catholic, the last sacraments and last blessing are administered (and, perhaps, Confirmation).[76]

If no baptism is to be given, because previous baptism is certain, then the absolution in confession is given absolutely.

Afterwards notice of the reception of the convert is given to the Ordinary, the baptism (if conferred) entered in the baptismal register, and the signed declaration of the convert (if it be possible to obtain this) sent to the Ordinary.

---

[73] See the short profession of faith suggested, *infra*.

[74] Cf. C.I.C. can. 759 § 1.

[75] The following brief profession of faith has been approved for use in Ireland: "I firmly believe that there is one God in three Divine persons, who will reward the good and punish the wicked. I firmly believe that God the Son became man, that he died on the cross to redeem and save us, and that he arose the third day from the dead. In a word, I firmly believe all that the holy Roman Catholic Church believes and teaches, because thou, my God, the infallible truth, hast revealed it, and in this faith I firmly resolve, by thy holy grace, to live and die. Amen."

[76] If the priest has the faculty to administer it and may lawfully use it.

Case 2: at the arrival of the priest the patient is unconscious: (i) if he had given any indication of willingness to receive the ministration of the priest, baptism with the short form is given (unless it is certain that the person had been already baptised), conditional absolution (*si es capax*), and conditional[77] Extreme Unction; (ii) if he had given no indication of wanting the ministration of a priest, the sacraments may be administered conditionally to him, if there is a presumption of his good faith and *secluso scandala;* (iii) if he had definitely excluded the help of a priest while conscious, even then some theologians allow the priest to give conditional baptism to the dying man, and conditional absolution and Extreme Unction—the condition in each case being *si capax es*—provided there is no danger of giving scandal by doing so.

§ 14. Holy Communion Outside of Mass

The normal time for distributing Holy Communion is at the moment appointed in Mass.[78] The rite in this case is described above.

But no priest may make any difficulty against giving people Holy Communion at other times, if their request is reasonable, that is if they have a serious (not necessarily a very grave) reason, and if they satisfy the law, being in a state of grace and fasting according to law.[79]

The rite of distributing Holy Communion out of Mass is this:[80]

A server is needed to say the *Confiteor.* If possible, he should wear cassock and surplice and kneel in the sanctuary; but often it is necessary that someone in the church (a man rather than a woman) should say the prayers. Two candles are lighted on the altar; the dust-cloth is removed; the communion plate[81] is made ready on the credence; the purifying bowl on the altar near the tabernacle.

The priest washes his hands, and vests in surplice and white stole or stole of the colour of the day.[82] He comes from the sacristy (following the server), covered, with hands joined or carrying the burse (of the same colour as the priest's stole) "ante pectus," containing a corporal, and the tabernacle key. Obviously, communion in this way can be given only from an altar where the Blessed Sacrament is reserved. At the foot of the altar the priest uncovers and he and the server genuflect and kneel for a

---

[77] In the case of a person who had desired to become a Catholic but was unconscious when the priest arrived Extreme Unction is administered without any condition.

[78] Regarding a second priest assisting, see R.G., n. 502.

[79] Cf.R.R.,V,i,13, 16.

[80] R.R., V, ii; *Excerpta*, p. 45.

[81] An Instruction of the Congregation of the Sacraments (26 March 1929) directs that a plate—of silver or of metal gilt, and entirely smooth on its inner surface—be used, in addition to the cloth, for the communion of the people. It is held by each communicant (or it may be carried by a server) and afterwards purified by the priest into the chalice or (outside Mass) into the ciborium.

[82] On All Souls' Day white or violet is used instead of black.

moment's prayer. The server puts the biretta on the credence and then kneels at the epistle side and says *Confiteor.* He then carries the communion plate to the first communicant (unless he himself is to receive Holy Communion, or hold the plate for the communicants). Meanwhile the priest goes up to the altar, spreads the corporal, opens the tabernacle, genuflects (with his hands laid on the altar, outside the corporal), takes the ciborium and places it on the corporal. He closes the tabernacle unless it is now empty. He uncovers the ciborium — laying the veil outside the corporal, the lid within it — genuflects again, partly turns to the people, not turning his back to the Blessed Sacrament, and says *Misereatur.* The server answers *Amen.* Then, making the sign of the cross over the people, he says *Indulgentiam,* to which the server again answers *Amen.*[83] Both these prayers are said in the plural even if there be only one communicant. The priest turns to the altar, genuflects, takes the ciborium in his left hand; with the thumb and forefinger of the right he takes a consecrated Particle and holds it over the ciborium held breast high. So he turns to the people, this time with his back to the middle, and says aloud *Ecce Agnus Dei,* etc., and *Domine, non sum dignus,* etc., three times. The form is always masculine *(dignus),* even if only women are present. Carrying the ciborium and Particle in the same way, he goes to the communion rail and gives each person Holy Communion with the usual form *(Corpus Domini nostri,* etc.), said aloud for each communicant, beginning at the epistle end. He makes the sign of the cross with each sacred Particle, held over the ciborium, before placing it on the tongue of the communicant. When all have received, he takes the communion plate from the last communicant (unless the server has charge of it),[84] goes back to the altar, places the ciborium and the plate on the corporal, genuflects (with at least the right hand within the corporal) and then says aloud at once *O sacrum convivium,* with its versicle, response and prayer, the server answering. In Eastertide and on Corpus Christi *Alleluia* is added to the antiphon, versicle and response; the prayer is *Spiritum nobis, Domine* in Paschaltide. Each prayer has the long conclusion; and the Easter one *(Spiritum)* has *ejusdem,* since the prayer makes reference to the Holy Ghost. While saying these prayers, the priest purifies the thumb and index of his right hand and the communion plate (if he sees any particles of the Sacred Species on it) into the ciborium, and then puts the plate outside the corporal to be removed by the server. He then washes the thumb and index of the right hand in the little vessel for that purpose by the tabernacle, and wipes them on the purifier by it. He covers and

---

[83] If there is no server one of the communicants should say the *Confiteor* and answer the prayers. If there is no one who can do this the priest — standing bowed, at the foot of the altar or on the footpace — must himself say the *Confiteor* and the responses. He omits *tibi, Pater* and *te, Pater.*

[84] He then carries it back to the altar and places it on or near the corporal to be purified.

veils the ciborium (or he may do this before washing his fingers), puts it in the tabernacle, genuflects, closes and locks the tabernacle. Then he gives the blessing. He says *Benedictio Dei omnipotentis,* facing the altar (but not kissing it) raising his eyes to the cross and extending, raising and joining his hands; he bows his head to the cross at the words *Dei omnipotentis,* then turns fully to the people and makes the sign of the cross over them as he continues: *Patris et Filii✠et Spiritus Sancti.*[85] The server answers *Amen.* The blessing is always in the plural.[86] The priest turns back to the altar by the same way, not completing the circle, folds the corporal and puts it back in the burse. He takes the burse and key, comes down the steps, genuflects with the server, puts on the biretta and goes back to the sacristy.

Communion may be given in this way either entirely apart from Mass or immediately before or after (even evening) Mass. In this case the priest wears all the Mass vestments. If they are black he does not give the blessing. Nor, if he says Mass with black vestments in Eastertide, does he add *Alleluia* after the antiphon or versicle, but he does say the prayer *Spiritum* at Easter.

When evening Mass is not celebrated the local Ordinary may permit Holy Communion to be given immediately before or after another evening function approved by him (Holy Office, 21 March 1960).

§ 15. Matrimony[87]

The ideal, when Catholics marry, is that they should receive the Nuptial Blessing. This blessing is always given in the Nuptial Mass (or other Mass which takes its place, on days when a Nuptial Mass may not be said; see *infra*). It is not allowed to give the Nuptial Blessing without Mass.[88] The parties are to be strongly urged to go to confession beforehand and receive Holy Communion at the Nuptial Mass.

General Rules for Nuptial Blessing. The Nuptial Mass is permitted whenever a marriage is allowed, either outside the forbidden period or within it if the local Ordinary, for a just reason, allows the solemn blessing of marriage. It is a votive Mass of the second class and so forbidden on days on which such a Mass is not allowed,[89] and also on any Sunday and whenever the Nuptial Blessing may not be given. When

---

[85] When a bishop gives Holy Communion outside Mass, he gives the blessing in the usual episcopal way, saying *Sit nomen Domini,* etc., and making the triple cross.

[86] If a priest, having distributed Holy Communion outside Mass, is to go, with the ciborium, to communicate the sick, he still gives (as usual) the blessing with his hand (but only partly facing the congregation, not to turn his back on the ciborium) to those present in the church, before going to the sick (S.R.C. 5 February 1946).

[87] *Excerpta,* p. 89; R.R., VIII, ii. For U.S.A., see the Appendix.

[88] For the special blessing when Mass is not celebrated, see "Blessing Outside Mass" below.

[89] For the days on which a votive Mass of II class is excluded (R.G., n. 341), see p. 385.

the special Mass but not the Blessing is forbidden, the Mass of the day is said and to its prayer is always added, under one conclusion, the prayer from the Nuptial Mass, and the Blessing is given in this Mass of the day. The Blessing must be given by the celebrant of the Mass, even if another priest and not he had assisted at the marriage.

The Blessing may not be given at a mixed marriage, nor unless both parties are present, nor if either party has already received it at a previous marriage.[90]

On 2 November and during the Triduum Sacrum both the Mass and Blessing are excluded.

When both the Nuptial Mass and Blessing are prohibited, they may be transferred to a convenient day, not impeded, after the marriage.

Banns. The banns of marriage are to be proclaimed beforehand at Mass, or at other services which are well attended, on three successive Sundays or on a holy day of obligation, should it occur (or the Ordinary may, instead, allow a notice to be hung in the porch for eight days, which must include two days of obligation). The form is given in the ritual.[91] If the persons live in different places the banns must be announced in both. For mixed marriages the banns are not called without the authority of the Ordinary.[92] It is possible, for a sufficient reason, to obtain dispensation from the proclamation of banns from the Ordinary. Marriage should take place in the parish church; in other churches or oratories (public or semi-public) only by leave of the Ordinary of the place or of the parish priest. The Ordinary may allow it to be celebrated in a private chapel or house only in an extraordinary case and always for a just and reasonable cause. Marriages may be allowed by the Ordinary in the churches or oratories attached to seminaries or convents only in case of necessity and with due precautions.

Form of Marriage. Besides the priest two witnesses must be present. In England we must also obey the law of the land which requires the presence of the government official (registrar) and the declarations made afterwards before him and two witnesses.[93] Sometimes the registrar is present in the church during the ecclesiastical function, sometimes he waits in the sacristy. The witnesses of both declarations, those made in the church during the marriage, and those made before the registrar, should be the same persons. The priest who marries the people must be the same who presides at the civil declarations afterwards.

---

[90] If only the man had previously received the Blessing it may be repeated for the benefit of the woman if this is customary.

[91] R.R., VIII, i, 8; *Ordo Adm.*, p. 197.

[92] C.I.C. 1026.

[93] By order of the bishops (in England) the religious ceremony must precede the civil one. In Ireland and in Australia there is only one ceremony, the religious one, as the priest acts as registrar for the State.

Rite of Marriage. The essential rite is the same in all cases:
The priest wears surplice and white stole.[94] If he is to celebrate Mass *immediately* afterwards, he should wear the vestments, except the maniple. There should be a server in surplice who carries the lustral water. On the credence, or on a small table near the entrance to the sanctuary, a salver or plate is laid, on which the ring (with the gold and silver) will be placed while it is blessed.

The priest stands with his back to the altar at the entrance of the sanctuary or choir. The man and woman to be married kneel[95] (outside the sanctuary)[96] before him, the man at the woman's right. The witnesses stand behind, or on either side. The priest first asks the question of the man: N., *wilt thou take N.,*[97] *here present,* etc., as in the ritual. The man answers *I will.* The priest asks the question of the woman, and she answers. The man and woman then join right hands.[98] If the woman is a widow she wears a glove on her right hand, otherwise not. The man first says the form, *I, N., take thee, N., to my wedded wife,* etc., repeating it in short phrases after the priest.[99] He then releases her hand. She takes his hand in her right and makes the declaration in the form appointed for her. They then join their hands while the priest makes the sign of the cross over them, saying *Ego coniungo vos in matrimonium, in nomine Patris✠et Filii et Spiritus Sancti. Amen.* He then sprinkles them thrice with lustral water (in front, to his left and to his right).

The husband or best man puts the ring, a piece of gold and a piece of silver[100] on the salver or plate held by the server. The priest blesses the ring with the form in the ritual[101] and sprinkles it once with lustral water.

---

[94] Whilst use of the cope for marriage ceremonies outside of Mass is strictly a pontifical privilege, it is permitted in the U.S.A. (cf. the Appendix) and customary in others.
[95] So a new rubric of R.R. of 1925.
[96] A number of rubricians, while teaching that the correct thing is that lay persons should not enter the sanctuary during any liturgical function (except when this is permitted, temporarily, by the rubrics) allow the parties to do so for the few moments of the actual marriage, where this is a long-established usage. Scarcely any of them, however, will permit the parties to be placed within the sanctuary for Mass, if it follows the marriage. They should remain *outside the chancel,* but may have special places, e.g., prie-dieux (undraped), just outside the altar rails.
[97] The Roman Ritual by the single letter N. seems to indicate that only the Christian name is used. It is, however, permissible to use both the Christian name and surname and this is the practice in many places.
[98] In some places the person who "gives the bride away" places her right hand in her husband's at this moment. The rubric of the English ritual speaks of the "giving away." In some places it is also customary that the priest circles their joined hands with the ends of his stole whilst they pronounce the form.
[99] In this formula the words "if holy Church will it permit" have been withdrawn in England, and in Ireland in its new ritual (1960).
[100] Generally gold and silver coins, but other objects (e.g., a cross or medal) may be used.
[101] The ritual assumes only a single ring but many priests are happy to bless two. The pluralised form is: Béne✠dic, Dómine ánulos hos, quos nos in tuo nómine bene✠dícimus: ut,

The husband takes the ring from the priest, gives the gold and silver to the bride (who puts them away or gives them to someone to hold for her) and says, in short phrases after the priest, *With this ring I thee wed,* etc.[102] Then the husband puts the ring on the woman's left hand. He puts it first on the thumb, saying *In the name of the Father,* takes it off and puts it on the forefinger, saying *and of the Son,* takes it off again and puts it on the second finger, saying *and of the Holy Ghost,* putting it on the third *Amen,* and leaves it there. If the woman places a ring on her husband's hand she does so at this point in the same way.

The priest says the versicles *Confirma hoc Deus,* etc., and the prayer, the server (or if present, a choir,) answering.[103] That ends the essential rite.

Civil Declaration. Usually the priest, husband, and wife, with the witnesses, now (or after Mass) go to the sacristy, to make (in England) the civil declarations. The priest takes off the stole. Before the registrar they each make two declarations, repeating the words in short clauses after the priest. First the man says:

I do solemnly declare that I know not of any lawful impediment why I, N.N., may not be joined in matrimony to N.N.[104]

The woman makes the same statement, in the same way.

Then the man says: *I call upon these persons, here present, to witness that I, N.N., do take thee, N.N., to be my lawful wedded wife.* The woman says the same, changing the word *wife* to *husband.* The book kept by the registrar is then filled up and signed by the priest among others.

For a mixed marriage all sacred rites are forbidden and the marriage must take place outside the church, unless the Ordinary permit it to be held therein.[105] The Ordinary may also allow some of the usual ecclesiastical ceremonies,[106] but never Mass. Even a private Mass (not the Nuptial one) is forbidden if in the circumstances it could be regarded as part of the marriage service.[107] As the essential rite of marriage requires only the expression of consent in the presence of proper witnesses, the civil ceremony (which is conducted by the priest), would suffice at a mixed marriage.[108]

---

qui eos gestáverint, fidelitátem íntegram suis sponsis tenéntes, in pace et voluntáte tua permáneant, atque in mutuáli caritáte semper vivant. Per Christum Dóminum nostrum.

[102] In Ireland the words "with my body I thee worship" are omitted.

[103] When more than one pair are married at the same time, having first received the consent of each pair and duly celebrated their union, and having said to each pair *Ego conjungo vos,* etc., the priest blesses the rings and carries out the other blessings once for all in the plural.

[104] Christian names and surnames (the wife's maiden name).

[105] R.R., VIII, i, 20.

[106] C.I.C. 1102, § 2.

[107] Commission for Interpretation of the Code, 10 November 1925.

[108] In Ireland *Collectio Rituum* provides a form for a mixed marriage. It is much more brief than the ordinary rite.

Nuptial Mass. If Nuptial Mass is to follow, the priest puts on the maniple and Mass begins. The newly-married kneel close to the altar, but outside the sanctuary.[109]

The Nuptial Mass is the votive Mass *Pro sponsis* in the missal. It is a votive Mass of the second class and so it is celebrated with *Gloria*, no *Credo*, one commemoration at most, no *oratio imperata*, the seasonal or common preface. If the Mass is sung the solemn tone is used for the prayers, preface and *Pater noster*. The vestments are white.

The rubrics of the missal suppose that the husband and wife make their communion at this Mass.[110] It is celebrated as usual, with two exceptions. After the *Pater noster*, before the prayer *Libera nos*, the priest genuflects, goes to the epistle corner and turns to the husband and wife, who remain kneeling. The server holds a missal (or other book containing the form of blessing) before the priest. With joined hands he says the two prayers *Propitiare Domine* and *Deus, qui potestate virtutis tuæ*, as in the missal. He returns to the centre of the altar, genuflects and goes on with Mass. The server puts the book back on its stand (or on the credence). Again after *Ite, missa est* the priest turns, this time at the middle of the altar. The husband and wife remain kneeling and the priest says the prayer *Deus Abraham* in the missal. The server again holds the book before him. The server puts back the book and brings the lustral water. The priest now addresses the husband and wife on the duties of married life.[111] Then he sprinkles them with lustral water (thrice, i.e., in the centre, to his left and to his right), turns to the altar and ends Mass as usual. The Leonine prayers may be omitted after this Mass.[112]

Blessing Outside Mass. In England by special indult of the Holy See, (or by centenary custom)[113] if both husband and wife are Catholics, if it is a day on which the Nuptial Blessing is allowed but Mass is not celebrated, the other form of blessing in the English ritual may be used. It consists of the psalm *Beatus quicumque; Kyrie, eleison,* etc., *Pater noster, Domine, exaudi orationem meam,* etc., and two prayers.[114] This form may be used before the civil declarations are made in the sacristy.

---

[109] Cf. C.E., I, xiii, 13; S.R.C. 157,175,1258 § 2, 1288, etc. The best plan is to arrange a kneeling bench or prie-dieux for them just outside the altar rails. If they cannot kneel near the sanctuary during Mass they should come forward and kneel at the altar rails for the prayers of the Blessing.

[110] It is a praiseworthy practice to place on the paten, with the bread for Mass, two small breads to be consecrated for their communion.

[111] The rubric at the end of this Mass in the missal says he should do so. The English ritual supposes that an instruction on marriage is given before the ceremony and *Excerpta* gives a specimen (p. 88).

[112] The Blessing may be given to more than one pair at the same time. In that case no change—it would seem—is to be made in the prayers (S.R.C. 3 March 1936). Some rubricians, however, think the prayer *Deus, qui potestate* is to be said in the plural.

[113] Cf. *Clergy Review,* May 1942, p. 228 (Mahoney, *Questions and Answers* I, Q. 322).

[114] R.R., VIII, iii; *Ordo Adm.,* Tit. VII, cap. ii, pp. 204-206; *Excerpta,* p. 92.

Again, in England by special indult, if the woman is a widow who had already received the Nuptial Blessing, or if the marriage takes place within the forbidden times and the Ordinary does not give permission for the Nuptial Blessing, a special form of prayer for the wedded pair may be used.[115]

The rector of the church or whoever takes his place (even though the parties were married in presence of another priest) must at once enter the marriage in the register, and add a note about it to the entry of baptism of each person in the baptismal register; or, if they were not baptised in his church, he must send a statement to the rector of the church where they were baptised, that he may make this entry.[116]

Blessing for a silver or golden wedding anniversary. The Roman Ritual of 1952 gives (Appendix, Pars II, p. 15*)[117] a special form of blessing for married people on the twenty-fifth or fiftieth anniversary of their wedding. The priest, vested for Mass, gives a short address to the happy couple. He then celebrates Mass for them. This Mass may be the votive Mass of the Most Holy Trinity or of our Lady. It may not, however, be the Nuptial Mass, but it has the same liturgical privileges[118] as this Mass, being a votive Mass of the second class. The prayer of thanksgiving[119] is added to that of the votive Mass under one conclusion.[120] After the last Gospel the priest removes his maniple, and, turning towards the married couple, gives them the blessing as set forth in the ritual. Before the final form of blessing *(Benedictio)* he sprinkles the couple with lustral water. If a votive Mass be impeded by the Office of the day, the prayer of thanksgiving is added, under one conclusion, to the Mass of the day.[121]

§ 16. Marriage Blessed by a Bishop

Preparations. *At the high altar:* the frontal and conopæum are white; of the colour of the Mass, if this follows the marriage and is the Mass of the day, and not the Nuptial Mass. On the altar are laid the vestments for the bishop: amice, alb, cincture, white stole and cope (with the precious morse, if the bishop is the Ordinary). These are covered with a white veil.

---

[115] R.R., VIII, iv; *Ordo Adm.,* Tit. VII, cap. ii, pp. 207-208; *Excerpta,* p. 94.

[116] R.R., VIII, ii, 7.

[117] In the 1953 edition of the Roman Ritual, the blessing is incorporated into the body of the ritual, as Chapter vii of Title VIII ; *Excerpta,* p. 100. A rubric concerning a votive Mass (no.12) is given in the 1962 missal.

[118] See "Nuptial Mass" above.

[119] This prayer is in the missal at the end of the votive Masses, and immediately preceding *Orationes Diversæ.*

[120] The two prayers are regarded as one in enumerating the prayers.

[121] Ditto.

The golden mitre is also on the altar, and near by the crosier (if the bishop is the Ordinary). Six or four candles are lit.

On the credence: the aspersory, a small salver, the book *(Ordo Administrandi* or *Excerpta)*[122] and the hand-candlestick with a wax candle, a card with the names of the parties to be married. If Mass is to follow, the requisites for a bishop's Mass[123] — including the maniple and the pontifical canon, the ewer and basin *(bacile)* with hand-towels, a book for the Nuptial Blessing,[124] and the pax-brede (with a towel to wipe it after use), if the kiss of peace is to be given to the newly-wed, or if the bishop is not to celebrate Mass but assist at it.

On the sedilia: the stole and chasuble of the colour of the Mass.

At the foot of the altar: a cushion (white) on the lowest step; the faldstool, draped in white, at the epistle corner.

For the parties: two undraped prie-dieux (or a kneeling bench) which may have a cushion to kneel on, but not one on the top to lean on — and two chairs. These prie-dieux are to be placed outside the sanctuary.[125] In the sacristy are prepared surplices for the assistants and servers, and vimpae for the mitre and crosier-bearers.

Assistants. The Bishop is assisted by two priests (in the cathedral by two canons in rochet and surplice), the first seeing to the mitre, putting it on when the Bishop has sat down, taking it off before he rises. Six servers will be needed; book and candle-bearers, mitre[126] and crosier[127] bearers, and two others to assist at the vesting of the Bishop, to wash his hands (if he says Mass), to see to the aspersory (which will be needed three times (i) to sprinkle the parties after *Ego coniungo vos,* and (ii) after the Bishop's address to them at the end of the marriage service, if no Mass follows, or at the end of the Nuptial Blessing; (iii) at the blessing of the ring), to move the faldstool, to present the pax-brede to the bishop and the parties (if the pax is to be given), and to hold the communion cloth (if necessary) before the newly-wed, when they receive Holy Communion. There will

---

[122] The outlines of the marriage rite are in the *Pontificale* (Appendix) and are slightly different from those in the Roman Ritual but in England or Ireland the local ritual is needed to give the English formulae and the local additional rites.

[123] On the paten two small breads (or more, if the witnesses and others are to communicate — in which case a ciborium may be preferable) for the communion of the parties.

[124] Given also in missal and *Pontificale.*

[125] The rubric of the *Pontificale* directs the parties to come to the foot of the altar, and even mount the steps, for the rite of the actual marriage. It does not direct them to remain in the sanctuary (which is contrary to liturgical law) for the Mass; nor even to enter it for the Nuptial blessing, but some authors allow this latter. The parties are to be *genuflexi ante altare (coram altari)* and this direction of the rubrics is fulfilled when their prie-dieux are just outside the altar rail.

[126] The mitre is used during the marriage ceremony, but not during a subsequent low Mass.

[127] The Bishop uses the crosier on the way to and from the altar, if he vests and unvests in the sacristy, and when going from the foot of the altar to, or returning from, the faldstool.

be an MC to direct the whole function. A cross-bearer will be needed, if the Archbishop officiates.

The Ceremony. The parties and witnesses should be coached beforehand about the rite. The bridegroom kneels on the right of the bride, at their prie-dieux, and on the top step of the altar for the marriage itself;[128] the witnesses stand behind them at the marriage. The newly-wed may — if their prie-dieux are a long distance from the altar — come nearer (twice) for the Nuptial Blessing, and kneel at the foot of the altar. Before the ceremony the MC gets the ring and the pieces of money, and puts them on the salver at the credence.

The Bishop is received in the usual way by the rector of the church, the assistants and the MC (one of the servers will have the aspersory ready at the church door). He kneels for a moment in prayer at the foot of the altar, goes to the faldstool, and there vests assisted by the two priests (having first read the prayers of preparation and washed his hands, if he is to celebrate Mass). Mitred and carrying the crosier he ascends to the footpace, gives away the crosier, kisses the altar, and sits at the faldstool, placed in the middle.[129] The MC brings forward the bridegroom and bride (ungloved), followed by the witnesses. The groom and bride genuflect at the foot of the altar, and then kneel on the top step before the Bishop; the witnesses remain at the foot of the altar. After *Ego coniungo vos*[130] the Bishop rises (mitred) and sprinkles the newly-wed, in the form of a cross (i.e., centre, to his left, to his right). He then turns towards the altar and (unmitred) blesses the ring, held on a salver before him, sprinkling it after the prayer. He then sits (mitred) for the giving of the coins and the putting on of the ring, which he hands to the groom. Afterwards *Confirma hoc,*[131] etc., is sung, or is said by the Bishop. He then rises (unmitred) and, turned towards the parties, recites the concluding prayers *(Kyrie, eleison,* etc.), with joined hands.

The Mass. If Mass, with Nuptial Blessing, is to follow, the Bishop - mitred and carrying his crosier — descends to the faldstool and vests for Mass. If Mass is not to be celebrated, or is celebrated by another, the bishop (mitred) remains at the faldstool on the footpace, and from there makes his address to the newly-wed (before Mass) and at its conclusion sprinkles them (thrice) with lustral water.

The Mass is celebrated according to the rite for the low Mass of a bishop. The Nuptial Blessing is given at the usual time, the Bishop standing at the epistle corner for the first part of it, and at the centre of the footpace (unmitred) for the second part. If it is the local usage, the

---

[128] A rubric added in R.R. of 1925 directs the parties to kneel all the time for the marriage.
[129] To one side if the Blessed Sacrament is behind him.
[130] It is the Bishop who says *Amen* at the end of this formula (R.R.).
[131] In the *Pontificale* (not in R.R.) *Gloria Patri* is added and the antiphon is repeated.

kiss of peace is given to the newly-wed by means of the pax-brede.[132] After the Nuptial Blessing the Bishop sits (mitred) and addresses the parties;[133] and then, standing (still mitred), sprinkles them. The Leonine prayers are omitted after Mass. The Bishop unvests at the faldstool (and there reads the prayers of thanksgiving) or in the sacristy. Here the civil declaration and the registration of the marriage take place.

§ 17. Churching[134]

Only the mother of a child which has been born in legitimate wedlock has a strict right to receive the blessing after childbirth. The imparting of this blessing is not reserved to the parish priest. It is not of obligation. The mother comes to the church at a convenient time after the birth of the child. The priest wears a surplice and white stole. There should be a server carrying lustral water. The mother holds a lighted candle. She kneels in the porch or by the door of the church.[135] The priest, standing before her, sprinkles her thrice (centre, to his left, to his right) with lustral water, then says the prayers in the ritual. After the psalm *Domini est terra* and its antiphon, the woman rises and he gives her the left end of his stole to hold and introduces her into the church saying *Ingredere,* etc. The woman—who may hold the stole until she arrives at the altar—goes to the altar (that of the Blessed Sacrament or of the Lady Chapel—or another according to custom—where a prie-dieu and a candlestick have been made ready) and kneeling there gives thanks to God for the favours bestowed on her. Standing with his back to the altar (inside the rails or on the footpace at either corner) the priest continues the prayers. Finally he sprinkles the woman again thrice with lustral water, saying the blessing *Pax et benedictio,* etc.

When more than one woman is churched at the same time the stole is handed to the first, the others follow her and the priest into the church; the formula of introduction *(Ingredimini)* and the subsequent prayers and the blessing are all said in the plural.

§ 18. Blessings[136]

There are blessings which any priest may use; others, called consecrations, used only by a bishop; and a third class which may be

---

[132] As described in Chapter VIII.
[133] This is the moment to announce the Papal Blessing, if it has been granted to the newly-wed.
[134] R.R., VIII, vi; *Excerpta,* p. 98.
[135] "Poris ad limina genuflectentem" (R.R.).
[136] R.R., IX, normally, things to be blessed must not be put on the altar but on a table (cf. R.R., IX, i, 9).

given by a priest if he has permission from the Ordinary or has an apostolic indult.[137] To this third class belongs the blessing of vestments.[138]

The general rule for blessings is that the priest wears a surplice and a stole of the colour of the day unless another colour is expressly prescribed (e.g., if there is an exorcism the colour will be violet). The priest stands uncovered while blessing; he nearly always uses the form *Adiutorium nostrum, Dominus vobiscum* and a prayer or prayers, and he ends by sprinkling the person or thing thrice (i.e., in the form of a cross) with lustral water. Sometimes incense is also used.

The blessing of lustral water[139] (with salt) should normally be made on Sunday before the chief Mass. Then follows the Asperges ceremony.

§ 19. Sick Calls[140]

The ceremonies to be noted in connection with sick calls are those of the sacraments then administered.[141]

If there is time, a dying man will receive the sacraments of Penance, Holy Eucharist and Extreme Unction; and, perhaps, Confirmation.

Preparations. If these sacraments are to be administered in one visit,[142] the priest will take with him the Blessed Sacrament in the small pyx used for this purpose, the Oil of the Sick in its stock. By the sick man's bed (in a position where the patient can easily see it) a table is prepared, covered with a white cloth, having on it two wax candles burning, lustral water and a sprinkler,[143] a wineglass with a *little* water to drink. It is suitable that a crucifix also stand on the table; it is needed if Extreme Unction is to be given. If Extreme Unction will be administered at the same visit, a plate with cubes of dry bread, water to wash the priest's hands, a hand-towel and cotton wool[144] should be on the table. A communion cloth (a clean napkin or handkerchief will do) should be spread under the chin of

---

[137] C.I.C. 1147. Canon 1169 § 3 of the 1983 C.I.C. states that "A deacon can impart only those blessings which are expressly permitted to him by law."

[138] The forms for blessing vestments are also in the missal among the blessings which follow the Masses and prayers for the dead. C.I.C. 1304, 3°, gives the faculty of blessing vestments, etc., to parish priests for the churches and oratories within their parish and to rectors of churches and religious superiors for their own churches. Other priests (who are not religious) require a special faculty from the Ordinary.

[139] In the missal: *Ordo ad Faciendam Aquam Benedictam,* first among the blessings: also in R.R., IX, ii; *Ordo Adm.,* Tit. XI, cap. i, pp. 240-244; *Excerpta,* p. 103.

[140] For U.S.A., see the Appendix.

[141] For prayers, advice and help in general to be given to the sick, see R.R., VI, iv; *Ordo Adm.,* Tit. V, cap. iv, pp. 125-137. Cf. *Excerpta,* pp. 167-176.

[142] The liturgical books suppose that Extreme Unction is not given at the same time as Holy Communion. It is, however, often necessary to do so.

[143] Unless the priest brings holy water with him. The best kind of sprinkler is a small branch of box, yew, or some such plant.

[144] The priest usually brings this with him in the bag containing his oil stock. It is useful to have a small plate or glass dish ready to hold it.

the sick person at the moment of communion. It is rarely possible to carry the Blessed Sacrament to the sick publicly[145] (except, of course, in a religious house or a Catholic institution having an oratory). In a small, quiet district, where the house is not very far from the church, the priest may be able to wear his cassock, surplice, stole and a cloak covering all. In many large towns, and where the distance is great, he must take the Blessed Sacrament in his usual dress, with no external sign. He wears at least a (white) stole,[146] and if he cannot wear cassock and surplice he takes them with him to be put on when he arrives in the house of the sick person.[147] He carries the little bag which contains the pyx concealed within his coat, hanging by its strings round his neck.[148] The Oil of the Sick is carried in another bag;[149] also a little vessel of lustral water is brought, unless it is already prepared at the house. When the Blessed Sacrament is carried privately the little bag which contains the pyx should also contain a small corporal (in which the pyx may be wrapped up) and purifier, such as are used for sick calls.

Communion of a Sick Person. In the church two candles are lighted on the altar. The priest (in surplice and white stole) spreads the corporal, opens the tabernacle, takes a consecrated Particle and lays It in the pyx, arranges the pyx as he will carry it, and, having washed his fingers, replaces the ciborium in the tabernacle. He then changes into his outdoor dress. He goes directly to the sick man's house, speaking to no one on the way, reciting the psalm *Miserere* and other psalms and canticles. At the door of the house (unless people carrying lights had accompanied him) he is met by a person who holds a lighted candle and who genuflects as the door is opened. Entering the sick-room the priest says *Pax huic domui,* to which the answer is *Et omnibus habitantibus in ea.* He first sees that the candles on the table are lighted, then spreads the corporal on the table, puts the pyx on it and genuflects. If Extreme Unction is to be administered, he lays the Oil and cotton wool on the table also. If he has brought the Blessed Sacrament privately he now vests in surplice and

[145] The rubrics of the ritual suppose, normally, a public procession to take the Blessed Sacrament to the sick, with torches, the priest in surplice, stole (even cope) and humeral veil, under a canopy (R.R., V, iv, 6, 12, 13). But the note on p. 102 of *Ordo Administrandi* says that this public procession may not be held (in England) without leave from the Bishop. It is held, however, in religious houses, and in Catholic hospitals and institutions.

[146] A stole white on one side and violet on the other (for confession and Extreme Unction) is useful.

[147] Only a most urgent reason would allow of his giving Holy Communion in his outdoor dress.

[148] The usage of putting the pyx also into an inside pocket for greater safety seems permissible.

[149] The rubric (R.R., VI, ii, 2) supposes the Oil of the Sick to be carried in a little bag of violet silk, and that a server, with crucifix, lustral water and ritual, accompanies the priest. Normally, this is scarcely feasible. It does not suppose that the Blessed Sacrament is carried at the same time. If It is and a cleric accompanies the priest, the former carries the Oil.

white stole. All present in the room kneel. He sprinkles the sick man and the room,[150] saying (even in Paschaltide) *Asperges me, Domine,* etc., with the versicles and prayer in the ritual, genuflecting before and after. If no one else can answer, the priest must answer himself. If the sick man will now make his confession,[151] the other people leave the room, genuflecting to the Blessed Sacrament when they rise from their knees. The priest changes his stole to violet, genuflects and goes to hear the sick man's confession, sitting so as not to turn his back to the Blessed Sacrament. On returning to the table he genuflects again. The friends of the sick man may and ought now to return. Either the man himself or someone else in his name says the *Confiteor* in Latin or in English (otherwise the priest himself must say it in Latin); the priest changes his stole to white, stands before the table, opens the pyx. He genuflects, turns partly and says *Misereatur* and *Indulgentiam* in the singular. He genuflects again, takes a Sacred Particle in the right hand, holding It over the pyx held in the left, turns and says *Ecce Agnus Dei* (showing the Host to the patient) and *Domine, non sum dignus,* thrice.[152] The sick man says the same words (in Latin or English) in a low tone at least once. Meanwhile the cloth is spread on the bed beneath his chin.[153] The priest gives him Holy Communion, saying either the usual form, *Corpus Domini nostri,* or, if Holy Communion is given as Viaticum, the form *Accipe frater* (or *soror*) *Viaticum Corporis Domini nostri Iesu Christi, qui te custodiat ab hoste maligno et perducat in vitam æternam. Amen.*[154]

Returning to the table the priest genuflects (if a Particle remains in the pyx) covers the pyx and washes (in silence) the forefinger and thumb of the right hand in the water there provided and dries them with the purifier. If the pyx is empty he may purify it into the water. This purification is in due time put into the sacrarium or, if this be not convenient, into the fire; or it may be given to the patient to drink. He then says *Dominus vobiscum* and the prayer *Domine sancte, Pater omnipotens,* in the ritual. If any Particle remains in the pyx[155] he

---

[150] The rubric in the administration of Extreme Unction (R.R., VI, ii, 4) says that the priest sprinkles the patient, room and those around, and in the form of a cross (i.e., straight in front, to his left and to his right). He avoids turning his back fully on the Blessed Sacrament.
[151] If possible, the confession should be heard at another visit beforehand. The ritual supposes this, and it prevents the danger that the man may be unfit to receive the Holy Eucharist when It has been brought to him.
[152] If death were imminent and delay be dangerous the priest may omit some or all of the prayers preceding *Misereatur,* etc. (R.R., V, iv, 21) and need not supply them later, if the patient survives.
[153] If the patient is a bishop, priest or deacon he wears a surplice (if feasible) and white stole to receive Holy Communion.
[154] This form is used whenever Holy Communion is given as Viaticum, that is, as long as the sick person is in danger of death from any cause, external or internal.
[155] R.R., V, iv, 12, 23, 27 says that more than one Particle ought to be taken to the house of the sick person unless the journey thither be too long or too difficult. This rubric, however, supposes that the Blessed Sacrament is carried publicly in procession.

genuflects, takes the pyx in both hands, blesses the man with it, saying nothing. If no Particle remains he gives the blessing with his hand, using the form *Benedictio Dei omnipotentis,* etc., in the singular (unless more than one had received) and with the usual gesture. If Extreme Unction, etc., immediately follows, the blessing (with the Blessed Sacrament or the priest's) is postponed until the end of the whole ceremony.

Public Procession of the Blessed Sacrament. When Holy Communion is carried publicly to the sick[156] (e.g., in a college or convent) the priest wears surplice, white stole and humeral veil, and a small canopy (umbella) should, when possible, be carried over the Blessed Sacrament. The ciborium itself may be carried or some Particles (one more than the number required for the sick) may be transferred to a veiled pyx. R.R. supposes an acolyte to lead the procession, one to carry the aspersory and the burse (containing a corporal and a small purifier), a third to carry the ritual and ring a bell all the time, and torch-bearers. Usually, however, the holy water will be made ready on the table in the sick room, and the corporal (spread), purifier and book put there also beforehand, and one server will precede the priest carrying a light and ringing the bell to mark the passing of the Lord, while a second carries the canopy. In convents should a server not be able to accompany the priest, two of the sisters may carry lights, but they must *follow* the priest (a third sister may precede the little procession if it is necessary to guide it to the rooms of the sick). The priest carries the pyx held before his breast. In the sick room the priest puts off the humeral veil on his arrival and resumes it before blessing the patient at the end of the ceremony.

Return to the Church. When the Blessed Sacrament is carried back publicly to the church the priest on the way recites the psalm *Laudate Dominum de cælis* and other psalms and hymns. On arrival he places the pyx or ciborium on the altar, genuflects, kneels on the foot-pace or on the lowest step, and says *Panem,* etc., then rising says *Dominus vobiscum* and the prayer *Deus, qui nobis* (with the short conclusion), even in Paschaltide.[157] Then he genuflects and blesses those present with the pyx wrapped up in the humeral veil, saying nothing. He then replaces the Blessed Sacrament in the tabernacle, genuflecting before he closes the door.

If the Blessed Sacrament has to be carried back privately the priest may laudably recite the psalms on the way, and it would seem that he should say *Panem de cælo* and the prayer before closing the tabernacle

---

[156] If this should take place immediately after the distribution of Holy Communion *(extra Missam)* the priest completes the rite of distribution by blessing the congregation with his hand (withdrawing towards the gospel corner a little, and not turning fully to the people, because of the ciborium on the table of the altar), and only then puts on the humeral veil to carry the Blessed Sacrament to the sick.

[157] *Alleluia* is added to the verse and the response in Paschaltide and on Corpus Christi.

door. If anyone had accompanied him he may bless him with the Blessed Sacrament before replacing it.

Communion of Several. If Holy Communion is given to several people in one room, the words are said once only for all *(Misereatur, Indulgentiam* and the prayer *Domine sancte* being said in the plural), except the actual form of administration *(Accipe frater* or *Corpus Domini)* said to each. If Holy Communion is distributed to several sick people who are in the same house or hospital but in different rooms,[158] the greeting, the sprinkling and the prayers before communion are recited (in the plural) once only, viz., in the first room. In all the other rooms the priest says only *Misereatur tui...Indulgentiam...Ecce Agnus Dei...Domine, non sum dignus* (once only)...*Accipe frater (soror)*...or *Corpus Domini*...and in the last room he adds the versicle *Dominus vobiscum* with its response and the prayer *Domine sancte*...said in the plural. In the last room also, if a consecrated Particle be left, he imparts the Eucharistic blessing. He then completes the prayers in the church in the usual way.[159]

With the Ordinary's or parish priest's leave, granted for a grave cause, a deacon may give Holy Communion, using all the forms and blessing as above; in case of necessity the permission may be presumed.

Evening Communion of the Sick. A sick person—even if not confined to bed or in danger of death—may be given Holy Communion even after noon. The hour and frequency of this communion are to be determined by the priest, and the rules for the Eucharistic fast *for the sick* are to be observed.[160]

Communion of the Sick in Holy Week. During the Triduum Sacrum when the Blessed Sacrament is reserved in a private place for the communion of the sick only, for the removal and replacement (in surplice and white stole; and white humeral veil, if used) of the pyx to give Holy Communion to the sick (on Maundy Thursday) or Viaticum the usual procedure is followed. *Gloria Patri* is said at the end of the psalms, but the prayer (on returning to the church) is *Respice,* there is no blessing of the people, no bell is rung. (Cf. S.R.C. 2383).

§ 20. Extreme Unction[161]

Normally this sacrament will be administered after confession and Holy Communion. But the Roman Ritual does not suppose that it be given usually at the same visit as when the sick man receives Holy

---

[158] It will be necessary to have a table with two lighted candles and a corporal spread on it in each room; and also the vessel for the purification of the priest's fingers, unless a server carries this from one room to another.

[159] S.R.C., 9 January 1929; cf. *Excerpta,* p. 51.

[160] Holy Office, 21 Oct. 1961.

[161] R.R., VI, i, ii; *Excerpta,* pp. 53 *seq.*

Communion. The ideal is that the three sacraments be administered at three successive visits, though it is provided that the man "if he wish to confess" should do so again, immediately before the anointing. Extreme Unction may be given to those who are unconscious or delirious, if there is no fear of profaning the sacrament. It may not be given to those who are manifestly impenitent, or excommunicate, nor to children under the age of reason, nor to any who are not in danger of death at the time through sickness or old age. It is not given more than once in the same danger of death. It may be given again, if the person has partly recovered, and then again falls into danger.

Preparations. If, then, Extreme Unction be given at a separate visit, a table is prepared near the bed, covered with a white cloth, on which are placed a crucifix, a candle, lighted, and held by a server during the anointing[162] (if its light be necessary); also cotton wool divided into six swabs on a plate or in a glass dish; cubes of bread, water to wash the priest's hands, and a hand-towel; lustral water and a sprinkler. The priest arrives in cassock, surplice and violet stole, bearing the Oil of the Sick in a violet silk bag (which, for greater safety, may be suspended from his neck, and should be concealed under his surplice, if he is wearing one). He may also bring the lustral water and cotton wool. He generally comes in outdoor dress and vests at the house.

Arrival of Priest. Arriving at the sick-room he says *Pax huic domui,* etc., lays the stock of holy Oil on the table, vests if he is not already vested, gives the sick man a crucifix to kiss, performs the Asperges ceremony (sprinkling the patient, room, and those around in the form of a cross), saying Asperges,[163] etc., but not *Miserere* nor *Gloria Patri.* Then, if necessary, he hears the confession, instructs the man about the sacrament, encouraging him, and finds out his baptismal name (which is to be mentioned in one of the prayers after the anointing). He then begins the rite of Extreme Unction, saying *Adiutorium nostrum.* If there is no one to answer, the priest himself must do so.

But often it will be necessary to give Extreme Unction immediately after Viaticum, at the same visit. In this case, having finished the prayer *Domine sancte,* the priest puts on a violet stole, and, omitting the greeting and sprinkling, at once presents the cross to the patient to kiss.

Opening Prayers. The priest says the opening prayers facing the sick man, and makes the sign of the cross[164] in the first prayer where it is

---

[162] If there is no server the candle may stand in a candlestick on the table. If Extreme Unction is given immediately after Holy Communion a third candle is not needed, the two used during communion continue burning; and the greeting and Asperges are not repeated.

[163] Even in Paschaltide, and without then adding *Alleluia.* It is disputed whether it is made over the sick person only (as in the later prayer) or over the place and all present also as the words seem to require.

[164] It is disputed whether it is made over the sick person only (as in the later prayer) or over the place and all present also as the words seem to require.

marked in the book. When he has said the prayer *Exaudi nos, Domine sancte*, the sick man, server, or other person says the *Confiteor* in Latin or the vernacular.[165] In case of necessity the priest must say it himself. The priest, turned towards the sick man, says *Misereatur* and *Indulgentiam* in the singular. He then tells those present to pray for the sick man. They may say the seven penitential psalms and Litanies, or other suitable prayers, while the priest administers the sacrament. He says *In nomine Pa✠tris et Fi✠lii et Spiritus✠Sancti*, etc., making the sign of the cross over the man, and then holds his right hand extended over the patient's head during the remainder of this prayer.

The Anointings. He then dips the thumb of the right hand into the stock of Oil of the Sick (preferably after the anointing of each organ). If there is a server in holy orders present he will wipe away the Oil after each anointing. Otherwise the priest does so himself. The most convenient way (unless there is someone to hold the plate containing the wool) is to hold a small piece of cotton wool between the forefinger and second finger of the right hand, and wipe the place anointed each time immediately with it.[166] Only in case of grave necessity (e.g., in the case of contagious disease of a serious character) is it allowed to anoint with an instrument. This may be a small pencil of wood, or piece of cotton wool. There must be a separate pencil or piece for each anointing, lest the infection return to the vessel of oil. These pieces of wood or wool are burned afterwards and the ashes thrown into the sacrarium.

The priest makes the sign of the cross with the Oil on each organ and limb, saying the form once only for the pairs of organs (spreading it out over the two anointings). According to the rite the eyes (closed), the ears (the lobes), nostrils, mouth (with closed lips),[167] hands and feet are anointed. The right organ or limb is anointed first. For any reasonable cause the anointing of the feet may be omitted. For each organ the priest says the form in the ritual at the same moment (morally) as he does the anointing; *Amen* is part of each form, and is said by the priest himself. He ought to know these forms by heart. The hands of priests are anointed on the back, those of laymen on the palms. The nostrils are anointed either with one anointing on the tip or preferably with two on the sides; the feet preferably above,[168] not on the soles. If any organ is not anointed it is not lawful to anoint another part of the body instead. If a limb or organ is mutilated or wanting, the nearest part of the body to it is anointed, with the form for that limb. The priest then wipes his fingers with dry bread

---

[165] The *Confiteor* with *Misereatur* need not be repeated if they had been recited a short time previously for the communion.
[166] The cotton wool used for this must later be burned and the ashes thrown into the sacrarium.
[167] If it is not feasible to anoint both lips, it suffices to anoint either.
[168] The English *Ordo* in a note to the rubric (p. 110) says: "Ad nares Unctio fit in parte inferiore: ad pedes, in parte superiore."

and washes them (the bread and water are later to be thrown into the sacrarium or into the fire). He continues the prayers in the ritual, facing the sick man. He should then address the man, saying suitable words to prepare him for death if death is imminent, or urging him to bear his sickness patiently. The ritual instructs the priest to see that the sick man has a crucifix (to look at and to kiss from time to time) and holy water at hand.

If Extreme Unction immediately follows Viaticum, and a Sacred Particle remains in the pyx, the priest puts on a white stole, resumes the humeral veil, and gives the blessing with the Blessed Sacrament. If no Particle remains, without changing his stole, he gives his own blessing.

Anointing in Immediate Danger of Death. If there is immediate danger of death, the priest, omitting vesting and all that goes before the anointing, at once anoints the organs; then if the person remains alive he says the preliminary prayers which had been omitted. If the danger is very urgent he anoints one of the senses, or preferably the sick man's forehead, saying the one formula, *Per istam sanctam Unctionem indulgeat tibi Dominus quidquid deliquisti. Amen;* afterwards he must supply (unconditionally) the anointings of each of the senses and the prayers of the rite, if the person still lives.[169] In doubt whether the man is still alive he begins with the condition *Si vivis.*

Extreme Unction to Several. If Extreme Unction be given to more than one person at the same time the prayers which precede and follow the anointings are said once in the plural. The crucifix is given to each person to kiss[170] and the anointings (with their forms) are, naturally, done for each one. In the second prayer which follows the anointing, at N. the names may be omitted.

§ 21. The Apostolic Blessing for the Moment of Death

Every priest who attends a dying person has the faculty and the duty to impart to him the Apostolic Blessing,[171] which will enable him to gain a plenary indulgence at the moment of death. The form given in the ritual is used. The blessing may be given to anyone in danger of death from any cause. It may be given even to those who are unconscious (and then nothing need be done by the person to whom it is imparted) or delirious or insane. It may not be given to the excommunicated, the impenitent or those who die in manifest mortal sin.

---

[169] R.R., VI, i, 20, 12.

[170] In such a case, it would seem lawful first, to sprinkle all the patients with one common sprinkling and then go to each with the crucifix to kiss and with the offer of confession, if desired.

[171] Cf. R.R., VI, vi, 2; *Excerpta,* p. 59, *Enchiridion Indulgentiarum,* conc. 12.

The priest wears a surplice and violet stole. The sprinkling (with *Asperges*, etc., but without the psalm and *Gloria Patri*) is done unless it had been carried out for Viaticum or Extreme Unction immediately before. If the sick man has not been previously to confession he should receive the sacrament of Penance or at least make an act of contrition. The priest, if time will allow, is to instruct him about the blessing and he must see[172] that the patient *(a)* invokes the name *Jesus* (at least mentally), *(b)* and willingly accepts the sufferings of his illness in expiation for his past life and offers himself to God ready to accept whatever is pleasing to Him, and patiently undergo *even death itself* in satisfaction of the punishments which he has merited by his sins. The priest is also to console the patient by reminding him of the divine generosity, etc.[173]

The *Confiteor, Misereatur (tui)*, etc., need not be repeated for the blessing if they had been said shortly before for Viaticum or Extreme Unction.[174]

The ritual gives two shorter forms of imparting the blessing in case of imminent danger of death. Should the blessing be given to several together all the prayers, etc., are said once only, changing the singular into the plural wherever necessary.[175]

---

[172] The invocation of the Holy Name and resignation to death are conditions necessary for the future gaining of the indulgence, if the patient be of sound mind and conscious when he receives the blessing. The best time to secure the necessary resignation (which should be expressed) is during his confession, when the priest can speak to him about it.

[173] R.R., VI, vi, 4; *Excerpta,* p. 60.

[174] S.R.C., 30 October 1953.

[175] R.R., VI, vi, 8; *Excerpta,* p. 61.

Chapter XXXI

Funerals

§ 1. The Complete Rite

A
S in the case of marriage, so in that of funerals, there are really several rites which follow one another. The complete function, as supposed normally by the Roman Ritual[1] and missal, consists of these five offices: 1. The bringing of the body to the church; 2. Matins and Lauds for the Dead; 3. Requiem Mass; 4. The Absolution; 5. The burying. In general these complete funeral rites are of obligation.[2] While the Office of the dead may be omitted for a reasonable cause, the prayers which follow the Absolution may never be omitted. The exequial Mass may be omitted (on the day of the funeral) only if it be liturgically impeded or the omission be *necessary*. The Absolution, too, is of obligation after the funeral Mass.

The bringing of the body to the church, the Office for the dead, requiem Mass, burying, are different functions, which may be performed by different priests. But if the Absolution follows Mass immediately it must always be carried out by the priest who has celebrated the Mass. Only the Bishop of the place is allowed to give the Absolution without having celebrated the Mass before it.[3]

The right and duty of officiating at a funeral belong, ordinarily, to the parish priest of the church in whose district the man lived, even when he died somewhere else. The rector may delegate another priest to perform the function.

As far as possible, funerals should not be held on days of the first class, and especially not on Sundays or holy days of obligation. They should be put off to the next day. But if this cannot be done the funeral may be held on such days, as long as it does not interfere with the solemnity of the day.

General Rules for the Exequial Mass. The exequial Mass is the one requiem Mass—solemn or low—directly connected with the obsequies of a dead person, and normally celebrated in the presence of the corpse.[4] It is excluded (*a*) during Exposition of the Blessed Sacrament, (*b*) in a church having only one Mass when a conventual Mass, or the Mass on 2

---

[1] R.R., VII (cf. C.I.C. 1203-1242); *Excerpta*, p. 71. For U.S.A., see Appendix.

[2] R.R., VII, i, 4; C.I.C. 1215.

[3] Cf. S.R.C. 3029 § 10, 3798 § 2.

[4] It is a Mass of the dead of the first class.

February or Ash Wednesday, or for Rogations, occurs and this cannot be said by another priest, *(c)* on greater Sundays and feasts.[5] When the exequial Mass is thus excluded, or for a reasonable cause could not be celebrated at the obsequies, it may be said on the nearest day not similarly impeded.

If the funeral must take place when the exequial Mass is impeded, it must be held without Mass, and the church bells should not be tolled.

Preparations. For the complete ceremony the following preparations are made: In the sacristy plain surplices are laid out, a black stole, a black cope, the lustral water and sprinkler, processional cross, acolytes' candles, which if possible should be of unbleached wax. The altar is prepared for requiem Mass. The frontal is black, unless the Blessed Sacrament is there reserved, in which case the frontal and tabernacle veil (conopæum) are violet. The altar candles should be of unbleached wax; the carpet covers only the footpace; the missal-stand and sedilia are bare or covered in black or violet.

In the middle of the church, outside the chancel in every case, a bier or trestles are set up on which the coffin will be laid, so that it is possible to move freely all round it. Candles, usually six, of unbleached wax, stand around on the ground. They are lit just before the coffin is placed on the trestles. Candles of bleached wax are prepared to be distributed to the clergy during the Mass and Absolution, if this be the custom.

Conducting the Corpse to the Church. The priest, with servers and clergy , goes first to the house where the coffin waits.[6] It may await them in some house other than that of the death.[7] The officiating priest wears surplice, black stole, and (for greater solemnity) may wear a black cope; he wears his biretta when walking. The processional cross is carried in front and may be accompanied by two acolytes with lighted candles,[8] then the singers or clergy in order. At the end of the procession comes the celebrant, immediately preceded by a server carrying the aspersory. If he wears the cope he should be assisted by two servers in surplice who hold its ends. The officiating priest (even within the church) and clergy (outside the church) wear the biretta on the way. At the house where the coffin waits it will be more convenient if, at once, the procession is formed in the order in which it will return to the church (as below). The

---

[5] For the list of these see R.G., 11, 406, or the current *Ordo.* This latter also gives the rubrics for Masses celebrated *pro die obitus.* If the *external solemnity* of any of these feasts is transferred to a Sunday, the exequial Mass is then prohibited on the Sunday and not on the feast.

[6] The body of a tonsured cleric or cleric in minor orders is vested in cassock, surplice and biretta; that of a subdeacon, deacon or priest in violet Mass vestments of his order (R.R., VII, i, 12-16).

[7] Or even, in case of necessity, at the entrance to the church (S.R.C. 3481 § 1).

[8] The acolytes, if available, may on occasions of greater solemnity accompany the cross. The Roman Ritual makes no mention of them here.

coffin should be already brought to the door of the house, with the feet foremost. Candles are handed to the clergy and lighted; all uncover. Standing before the coffin (at the foot of the corpse) the priest sprinkles it with lustral water three times, first in front of him, then at his left, lastly at his right. He hands back the sprinkler and recites *Si iniquitates* and the psalm *De profundis* with those around. Instead of the verses *Gloria Patri* and *Sicut erat,* at this and all psalms at funerals, the verses *Requiem æternam* dona ei,*[9] *Domine, Et lux perpetua* luceat ei*[10] are substituted. Then the whole antiphon *Si iniquitates* is said.

The procession now goes to the church. The cross is borne before the clergy wearing cassock and surplice. Regular clergy go before the secular clergy, all walking two and two, holding lighted candles (in the outside hand). The officiating priest goes immediately in front of the coffin. He does not hold a candle. Behind the priest the coffin is carried by bearers, or it may be drawn on a hearse. Men should walk on either side of it holding lighted candles. If there are wreaths of flowers (which are only tolerated by usage) they should be carried behind the coffin; then come the lay mourners. The church bells are tolled as soon as the procession leaves the house. As soon as it starts the priest recites the antiphon *Exsultabunt,* the cantors begin the psalm *Miserere,* and the clergy continue it. This and all other psalms on the way to the church are to be recited "devote, distincte, gravique voce." If the way is long, so that the *Miserere* is finished before they arrive at the church, they recite the gradual psalms or others from the Office for the dead. The lay mourners behind the coffin pray for the dead man silently. The procession should go to the church by the shortest way. As soon as it arrives at the church the psalm is interrupted, the verse *Requiem æternam dona ei* is said at once, then the antiphon *Exsultabunt.*

Arrival at the Church. As they walk up the church the cantor begins the responsory *Subvenite, Sancti Dei.* The choir continues it. This is sung. If the Office or Mass is to follow, all go to their places in choir.[11]

The coffin is set on the bier or trestles prepared, the candles around are lighted. The body of a layman, clerk in minor orders, subdeacon or deacon, is set with the feet towards the altar; that of a priest with the head towards the altar.[12] A black pall is usually laid over the coffin and

---

[9] The prayers special to the funeral rite are said in the singular; those of the Mass and Office, are, generally speaking, in the plural.

[10] If the rite is carried out for more than one person, in this verse *Requiem* and in all the other verses and prayers (except *Non intres*), the singular is changed into the plural.

[11] In the shorter form, when the Absolution follows at once, the clergy and choir will go to stand around the coffin.

[12] This is the rule when the body is present physically or morally (that is, at the funeral ceremony when, for some exceptional reason, the body cannot be brought to the church). When the body is not present, either physically or morally, the foot of the catafalque is always nearer the altar.

wreaths of flowers may be placed around.[13] In the case of a priest or deacon a violet stole and biretta may be placed on the coffin, a biretta alone for subdeacons and clerics in minor orders. Any suitable symbol of the dead person's rank or office may be placed here if it is not grotesque or irreverent.

As soon as the clergy are in their places in choir they put out their candles; the cross-bearer sets the cross near the credence. It may not be stood at the head of the coffin. The acolytes take their candles to the sacristy.[14]

Office of the Dead. The Office for the dead should follow. The priest who will officiate at this takes his place in the first stall. He wears a surplice and black stole.[15] The Office for the dead consists of (Vespers), Matins (with three nocturns) and Lauds. All antiphons are doubled. But the ritual contemplates that not all this Office be said always. For a reasonable cause Lauds may be omitted, or only one nocturn of Matins said.[16] The ritual supposes that the body is brought to the church in the morning, that requiem Mass follows after the Office. The Mass should always be said, if possible.[17] If another priest presides at the Office the celebrant of Mass, with deacon and subdeacon, goes to the sacristy and vests during Lauds or the last part of the Office. At the end of the Office *Pater noster* and the following prayers are sung or said kneeling (the priest who presides standing while he sings or says *Dominus vobiscum* and the prayer *Absolve*). The prayer will be *Absolve* or any other suitable one from those given at the end of Vespers for the dead. At N. the baptismal name of the deceased (the religious name for religious of either sex) is said and *Sacerdotis* is added in the case of a priest.[18] It is not followed by the versicles *Requiem*, etc., if Mass or Absolution immediately follows.[19]

The Exequial Mass. Mass is then celebrated according to the rules for a requiem (cf. Chapters VII & XII). If the same priest celebrates the Office and Mass he may not go to vest till the Office is finished. There is no last Gospel if the Absolution follows at once, as it should.

A funeral oration may (but only with permission of the Ordinary) be preached after Mass. The preacher wears neither surplice nor stole.

---

[13] At the funerals of baptised children who die before the use of reason the rubric (R.R., VII, vii, I) prescribes the use of flowers "in signum integritatis carnis et virginitatis." The use of flowers at other funerals is alien to the mind of the Church and should be strongly discouraged. The national flag may be used instead of a pall for soldiers, sailors or airmen.
[14] Namely, in the complete rite, when the Office or Mass will follow. If the Office does not follow at once, see § 2 below.
[15] He may wear a black cope also.
[16] The first nocturn when the body is present (R.R., VII. iii, 16).
[17] R.R., VII, i, 4, 7. But a festal Mass may not be said before a dead body.
[18] *Mutatis mutandis* for a deacon or a bishop.
[19] R.R., VII, iii, 5.

The Absolution. After Mass follows the ABSOLUTION.[20]

The celebrant of Mass with the ministers goes to the seat. Here the celebrant takes off his chasuble and maniple and puts on a black cope. The ministers take off their maniples. If Mass is said without ministers there are none at the Absolution, a server carries the cross, and the MC or a server replaces the deacon.

The subdeacon takes the cross and stands between the acolytes; the thurifer, with a server carrying the aspersory on his right; the celebrant, deacon and MC (with the book) first stand before the altar in the order shown in fig. 46.

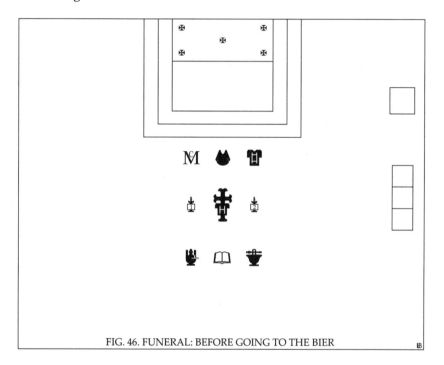

FIG. 46. FUNERAL: BEFORE GOING TO THE BIER

All make the usual reverence to the altar, turn and go to the coffin. The clergy, holding lighted candles, go after the cross, two and two. The celebrant and deacon (now on the celebrant's left) do not hold candles. The subdeacon, with the cross, and the acolytes stand at the head of the coffin, some way from it.[21] If the dead man is not a priest, this means that they stand at the end farther from the altar, facing the celebrant at the other end. In the case of a priest's funeral they stand at the end nearer the altar; the celebrant is then at the other end. The clergy with their candles stand in a line on either side, leaving room for the celebrant and ministers

---

[20] When the Absolution is given immediately after Mass it must be given by the celebrant. Only the Bishop of the diocese may give it if he has not celebrated the Mass.
[21] To allow space for the celebrant to pass between them and the coffin.

to go round the coffin. Those of higher rank are nearer to the celebrant. The celebrant stands at the foot of the coffin facing the cross at the other end;[22] when he moves the deacon holds the end of his cope at his left. The MC is at his right. The thurifer and bearer of holy water are at the deacon's left. When all are in their places the celebrant says or sings in the ferial tone *Non intres*,[23] the deacon holding the book before him. At the end all answer *Amen*.

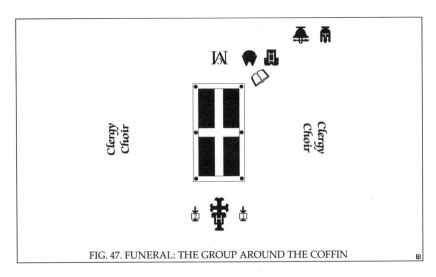

FIG. 47. FUNERAL: THE GROUP AROUND THE COFFIN

"Libera." Then the cantors begin the responsory *Libera me, Domine;*[24] the choir continues. During the repetition of *Libera* the celebrant puts incense in the thurible, the deacon assisting as usual (having passed to the celebrant's right), omitting the *solita oscula*. The incense is blessed with the usual form, the deacon having said *Benedicite, Pater reverende*. The MC holds the cope. When the responsory is finished, the cantor and clergy on the gospel side sing *Kyrie, eleison;* the cantor and the clergy on the other side answer *Christe, eleison;* all together sing *Kyrie, eleison*. The celebrant intones *Pater noster*, which all continue silently.

Sprinkling and Incensation of Coffin. The deacon takes the sprinkler, dips it in the lustral water, and hands it to the celebrant, not kissing it or his hand. The celebrant and deacon at his right, who holds the cope, reverence to the altar and go round the coffin, beginning at the right hand side as one faces it (i.e., on the left of the corpse). The celebrant sprinkles it with lustral water first towards the feet, next in the middle, then towards the head—not bowing, not pausing. As he passes the cross

---

[22] The rubric of the ritual for Absolution *absente corpore* says: "aliquantulum versus cornu Epistolæ, ita ut Crucem Subdiaconi respiciat." (R.R., VII, v, I).

[23] No change is made in this prayer whatever the sex of the dead person.

[24] The chant for this and all the funeral rite is in the Vatican Gradual and *Liber Usualis* in the Roman Ritual and in the *Missæ Defunctorum* issued by the Vatican Press.

he bows low to it; the deacon genuflects.[25] Coming back the other side, he sprinkles in the same way beginning towards the head of the coffin. Then the celebrant hands the sprinkler to the deacon, who gives it back to the server. The deacon takes the thurible and hands it to the celebrant, without kissing it or his hand. They again reverence to the altar, go round the corpse as before, incensing it with single swings of the thurible (three on each side). The celebrant gives the thurible back to the deacon, who hands it to the thurifer and takes the book, which he holds before the celebrant. The celebrant with joined hands chants *Et ne nos inducas in tentationem,* and the other versicles, the choir answering, then the prayer *(Deus cui proprium est)* in the ferial tone *(recto tono).* At N. he inserts the baptismal name of the deceased (except in the case of religious of both sexes, when the religious name is used) and adds *Sacerdotis* if the body is that of a priest.[26]

At the Graveside. If the coffin is taken at once to the place of burial, the procession is now formed, as when going from the choir to the coffin for the Absolution. The thurifer leads if the grave is to be blessed; otherwise the aspersory-bearer leads. As the coffin is carried to the cemetery the choir sings the antiphon *In paradisum deducant te angeli,* followed by *Ego sum* (in full) and *Benedictus.* If the distance is great, the psalm *De profundis* and other psalms from the Office of the dead are said. At the entrance to the cemetery the antiphon *Ego sum* is repeated in full. At the grave the coffin is laid by its side and all stand around, in the same order as during the Absolution, the celebrant at the foot of the grave. If the grave is not already blessed, the celebrant blesses it, using the prayer *Deus cuius miseratione.*[27] He then puts on incense, blessing it as usual, and standing where he is sprinkles the coffin and the grave (together) thrice with holy water, and incenses both. If the cemetery or grave is already blessed, neither is sprinkled or incensed. The celebrant then sings *Kyrie, eleison* to the simple tone, on one note, falling a half tone on the last syllable. The choir, in the same tone, answers *Christe, eleison* and *Kyrie, eleison;* the priest then intones *Pater noster.* While this is said silently, he sprinkles the coffin (cross-wise), not going around it. The other versicles and prayer follow, as in the ritual. The celebrant makes the sign of the cross over the coffin while saying *Requiem æternam,* etc.

Return to the Church. Then the procession leaves the grave, and the coffin is lowered into it.[28] The burial rite ends with *Anima eius...Amen.*

---

[25] If the deacon is a canon in his own capitular church, he bows low.

[26] It is permissible, if customary, to say prayers in the vernacular for the dead person after (not during) the Absolution (cf. S.R.C. 3790).

[27] If no other body is already buried in this grave the clause of the prayer that is in brackets must be changed into the singular, as is indicated in the ritual.

[28] The ritual does not suppose that the clergy remain while the body is lowered into the grave. It is, however, usual to do so. It is also permissible for the priest at the grave, when

§ 2. Modifications of the Funeral Rite

Various changes may be made in this ceremony, according to the necessity of time and place.[29]

(i) The first change is that, if the body is brought to the church in the evening, Vespers of the dead (as given in *Rituale Romanum*, VII, iv) may be recited. The psalm *Lauda* is not recited at the end of Vespers. The Office is terminated by *Pater noster*, etc., and the prayer suitable to the occasion (with a long conclusion) chosen from those assigned in the ritual (or breviary). Vespers are followed by Matins and Lauds or at least Matins (or one nocturn of it). (ii) If Lauds are not said, *Pater noster* and the other prayers which come at their end are said, kneeling, after Matins or the one nocturn which may be said. (iii) If the Office is not said at all on the arrival of the body, then after the singing of *Subvenite*, when the body is in its place, the prayers as at the end of Lauds (i.e., *Pater noster*, etc.) are said. These prayers are preceded by *Kyrie, eleison, Christe, eleison, Kyrie, eleison* and the conclusion to the prayer *Absolve* will be short[30] *(Per Christum Dominum nostrum).* At the end are added *Requiem* (in the singular) and *Requiescat.*

(iv) After Mass and the Absolution, if the body is not taken at once to be buried, the antiphons *In paradisum* and *Ego sum,* with the *Benedictus* and all that follows, are sung or said in the church. If the body is buried another day, or later, it is not necessary to repeat these prayers; but this may be done. The whole funeral service may be repeated another day, or at another church, if the burying is delayed.

(v) If it is not possible to bring the body in procession from the house to the church, the priest meets it at the entrance of the churchyard, or at the door of the church, there sprinkles it with lustral water, and says the *De profundis* and (if the procession lasts for some time) the *Miserere* with their antiphons, as above.[31] If the distance to the altar is short, the antiphon *Exsultabunt* and the *Miserere* may be omitted and *Subvenite* begun at once on entering the church.

---

the liturgical prayers have been said and the coffin lowered, to say *De profundis* and other prayers in the vernacular for the dead determined by the Ordinary.
[29] When because of special local conditions changes have to be made in the funeral Liturgy the general principle is that as far as possible the rite, as set forth in R.R., VII. iii, and the prescription of C.I.C. 1215, are to be followed (S.R.C. 4357).
[30] Being outside the Office (cf. R.R., VII, iii, 5).
[31] S.R.C. 3481 § 1.

§ 3. Private Funerals

Under this title *(exequiæ privatæ)* the *Ordo Administrandi Sacramenta* provides the shortest possible ceremony.[32] This may take place at any time of the day. The priest, in surplice and black stole, and uncovered, receives the body at the door of the church or churchyard. He sprinkles it thrice with lustral water and says *De profundis* with the antiphon *Si iniquitates,* and as he goes before it to the place in front of the altar he says *Subvenite sancti Dei, Pater noster,* etc. Immediately after the prayer *Absolve, quæsumus Domine*[33] he adds *Non intres in iudicium* and the full Absolution. As the coffin is carried to the cemetery he says *In paradisum deducant te angeli.*[34] He may say this as it is borne from the church. He will accompany the coffin to the cemetery (in England generally in a carriage). With him is a server who holds the lustral water and sprinkler and, if the grave is not yet blessed, another with incense. At the cemetery he blesses the grave, if it is not yet blessed, says the *Benedictus* with its antiphon *Ego sum,* and the rest of the prayers in the ritual.

It may even be that the body cannot be brought to the church at all. The priest accompanies it from the house to the grave, saying first *De profundis* and *Miserere* (if there is time), with their antiphons, *Subvenite,* the Absolution, then *In paradisum* and all that follows.]

§ 4. Office for the Dead when the Body is not Present

It is allowed under privileged conditions to say the Office and requiem Mass for a deceased person on the third, seventh and thirtieth days after either his death or burial, and on the anniversary of death or burial.[35]

The Mass for these occasions is a requiem Mass of III class and is permitted on liturgical days that are not of I or II class. One requiem Mass only — high or low — is permitted (unless the day be one on which requiem Masses of IV class are allowed) in any one church or oratory. If this Mass be rubrically impeded it may be celebrated on the nearest free date. One Mass on the receipt of the news of a death is a requiem Mass of II class. It is prohibited on any liturgical day of I class and on any Sunday.

If the Absolution[36] is to follow, a catafalque is set up in the place where the coffin would be placed, or the funeral pall or a black cloth is spread

---

[32] *Ordo Adm.,* VII, iii, n. 6, p. 171. There is nothing about this in *Excerpta.*

[33] It would seem (and it is the view of Martinucci and Vavasseur) that when the Absolution *immediately* follows the arrival of the body (the Office and Mass being omitted), after *Subvenite Non intres* should be said at once. But *Ordo Adm.* (p. 171) apparently prescribes *Pater noster,* etc., and the prayer *Absolve* before the Absolution is begun.

[34] And *Ego sum* (in full) and *Benedictus,* instead of at the graveside.

[35] For a detailed exposition of the rubrics which regulate these privileged Masses, see O'Connell, *The Celebration of Mass,* 1964, pp. 94-97.

on the floor to represent the coffin.[37] The Office of the dead is said or sung, either Matins and Lauds, or Matins only, or one nocturn and Lauds, or one nocturn.[38] The antiphons are doubled. At Matins the Invitatory is said. Then the requiem Mass is said or sung. The Mass is that appointed in the missal.[39]

The Absolution. The Absolution follows at the catafalque or pall spread on the ground, as when the body is present, except that the prayer *Non intres in iudicium* is omitted.[40] The clergy stand around with lighted candles, the subdeacon or a server holds the processional cross at the head of the coffin; the celebrant at the foot says the same prayers, sprinkles the catafalque with lustral water and incenses it, all as above in the case of funerals. The only other difference is in the final prayer.[41] Then the celebrant makes the sign of the cross over the catafalque, saying *Requiem æternam,* etc. The cantors sing *Requiescat in pace.* ℟. *Amen.* The celebrant chants *Anima eius,* etc., all as in the ritual.

If the Office is for a woman the gender is changed in the prayers. If it is for several people the plural is used; if for a bishop, priest or deacon, this rank is expressed in the prayers, after the man's name.

---

[36] R.R., VII, v. The Absolution is of obligation only at a funeral.

[37] This cloth should not be spread till just before the Absolution. In this simpler form of the Absolution (i) the cross-bearer and acolytes do not take part, (ii) the celebrant stands all the time on the footpace; cf. O'Connell, *The Celebration of Mass,* 1964, p. 542.

[38] The first nocturn is said on Monday and Thursday; the second on Tuesday and Friday; the third on Wednesday and Saturday.

[39] The Mass for anniversaries; or, the Mass on the third, seventh, or thirteenth day (i.e., the Mass *in die obitus,* with a special prayer according to the rubric in the missal after the burial Mass). For a deceased bishop or priest the Mass on an anniversary will be the first one given for All Souls' Day but with the prayer proper to the person for whom the Mass is offered; cf. O'Connell, *The Celebration of Mass,* 1964, p. 86.

[40] Nor in the case of a catafalque (unless the body be "morally" present) is the position changed for a priest. The head is supposed to be away from the altar, so the cross-bearer stands at that end, the celebrant between the catafalque and the altar.

[41] It is *Absolve, quæsumus Domine,* or the collect of the appropriate Mass (with the short conclusion), or other suitable prayer.

§ 5. Pontifical Absolution at the Throne[42]

According to the normal rule, after pontifical solemn Mass for the dead (Chapter XVIII) the Bishop proceeds to give the Absolution, either over the coffin or (if the body is not present) over a hearse *(castrum doloris)* or a catafalque, or over a black cloth spread on the ground.

Supposing, first, that the Bishop uses the throne and that the coffin or hearse or catafalque is in the usual place, namely in the centre of the church, outside the chancel, the following ceremonies are observed:

A faldstool covered with black is placed at the foot of the coffin (fig. 48),[43] on either side of it are stools for the assistant deacons, if they attend, on the right is a third stool for the A.P .

Vesting of Bishop. As soon as Mass is finished the Bishop goes to the throne and sits there. The two assistant deacons are at his side. Candles are distributed to the clergy and lighted; the Bishop's candle is held for him by a server at the right of the first assistant deacon. The deacon and subdeacon of the Mass take off their maniples and assist at unvesting the Bishop. Four servers[44] attend to take the Mass vestments, and another server brings the black cope. The three chaplains of the mitre, book and candle will assist at the Absolution. The crosier is not used. The mitre bearer comes and stands by the deacon of Mass. The subdeacon takes off the Bishop's maniple and gives it to a server; the deacon of Mass takes the Bishop's mitre and gives it to the mitre-bearer; the Bishop rises, the deacon, assisted by the subdeacon, takes his chasuble, dalmatic and tunicle. They give these to the servers who lay them on the altar, where they are arranged by the second MC. The ministers of Mass then vest the Bishop in a black cope and simple morse. The Bishop sits and the deacon puts on him the simple mitre.

If there is to be a funeral oration,[45] it is preached now, while the Bishop sits at the throne. The preacher does not ask his blessing, but genuflects first to the altar, then to the Bishop.

---

[42] C.E., II, xi, 10-12; *Pontificale Romanum* (Part 3). If the Bishop only *assists* at the requiem Mass and afterwards gives the Absolution he is assisted by the AP and assistant deacons in choir dress. It is a moot point, in this case, whether the subdeacon (vested) or a server (in surplice) carries the cross. If the Bishop merely assists at the Absolution he blesses the incense for the celebrant's use.

[43] That is to say, between the hearse and the altar for a layman, and always in the case of Absolution at a catafalque when the body is present neither physically nor morally. Only in the case of a priest or bishop whose body is present physically or morally is the faldstool at the end nearer the door of the church.

[44] Four would be the number if one takes each vestment, chasuble, dalmatic, tunicle, maniple. If there are not four they may take each vestment to the altar, leave it there (where the second MC will arrange it) and return for another; or take two vestments at a time.

[45] Cf. Chapter XII § 1; Chapter XVIII § 2.

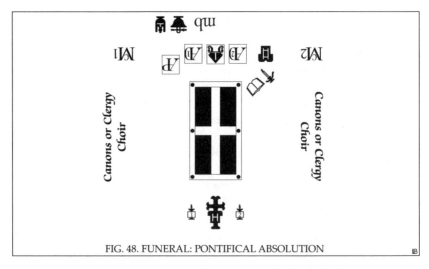

FIG. 48. FUNERAL: PONTIFICAL ABSOLUTION

Fig. 48 shows the place of those taking part at the Absolution for a layman
(the body being present), or for a priest or layman if the body be absent.

Procession to the Coffin. After the homily, if there is one, the subdeacon takes the processional cross, the acolytes take their candles. The
thurifer takes the thurible and incense boat; another server takes the
lustral and water sprinkler. The assistant priest now comes to the
Bishop's right. The procession goes to the altar, first the thurifer with the
holy-water bearer at his right; then the subdeacon with the cross[46]
between the acolytes; then the two masters of ceremonies; the AP and
deacon of Mass, side by side, the AP on the right; then the Bishop
between the two assistant deacons.[47] Then come the three chaplains of
mitre, book and candle. All stand before the altar and make the usual
reverences; then they go to the coffin. The canons or clergy join the
procession behind the cross and acolytes. The subdeacon with the cross
and the acolytes stand at the head of the coffin, some way from it;[48] the
Bishop goes to the faldstool at the foot,[49] between the assistant deacons;
the thurifer and bearer of lustral water go to the right of the Bishop, a
little distance back. The AP is at the right of the first assistant deacon, and
a little in advance of him; the deacon of Mass at the left of the second. The
bearers of book and candle stand on the same side as the deacon of Mass,

---

[46] If the Archbishop officiates it is his cross that is carried, the figure facing him; and if his
Chapter attends, the canons (alone) walk between the cross and the Archbishop.

[47] If there are no assistant deacons, the deacon accompanies the Bishop on his left, and the
AP takes no special part in the Absolution.

[48] To allow space for the Bishop and his assistants to pass between them and the hearse.

[49] In figure 48 it is supposed that the Blessed Sacrament is not present or that the coffin is a
long way down the church. If, however, the Blessed Sacrament is present and the coffin is
not a long distance away, the Bishop and his assistants will take their places somewhat to
the epistle side, in order to avoid directly turning their backs to the Blessed Sacrament.

the mitre-bearer at the Bishop's right, behind him. The first MC may stand at the right of the whole group, the second MC at the left. The Bishop sits on the faldstool. The canons or clergy stand in two lines on either side of the coffin (those of highest rank nearest the Bishop), leaving a space round it. The bearers of book and candle come before the Bishop. The second assistant deacon takes off the mitre; the Bishop rises, the AP holds the book, with the candle-bearer at his right.

"Non Intres" and "Libera." The Bishop sings, *in tono lectionis*,[50] the prayer *Non intres*. He sits again and the first assistant deacon puts on his mitre. The choir begins the antiphon *Libera me*. Towards the end of this the Bishop, sitting, puts on and blesses incense, the AP assisting and omitting the *solita oscula*. The thurifer kneels, as usual. Then the second assistant deacon takes off the mitre and hands it to the mitre-bearer. When the responsory is finished the Bishop rises, the cantors sing *Kyrie, eleison,* etc; the Bishop intones *Pater noster*. The AP hands him the sprinkler and he goes round the coffin sprinkling it with lustral water between the assistant deacons,[51] who hold back the cope.[52] Then, having come back to the faldstool, he takes the thurible from the AP and incenses the corpse. The Bishop sprinkles and incenses in the same way as a priest, and bows to the processional cross as he passes it. When this is finished, the bearers of book and candle come before him. The Bishop sings the verses *Et ne nos inducas in tentationem,* etc., as usual, the book-bearer holding the book; lastly, he makes the sign of the cross over the corpse as he sings *Requiem æternam dona ei, Domine*. The first assistant deacon holds the cope while he does so. The cantors sing *Requiescat in pace. R. Amen.* Nothing more is added. The Bishop sits, the first assistant deacon puts on his mitre. The procession goes to the throne as it came and the Bishop is there unvested.

Absolution if Body Absent. If there is no catafalque, a black cloth is spread in front of the throne. In this case the cross is not carried. The ministers of Mass go to the seat, take off their maniples, go to the throne and vest the Bishop, then return to the sedilia and stand there during the Absolution. But if there are no assistant deacons, then the ministers of Mass take their place at the throne. standing one on either side of the Bishop. The Bishop stays at the throne; the procession to the altar is not made. The clergy do not stand around the cloth. The AP ministers the incense and lustral water. *Non intres* is not said.[53] The Bishop puts on

---

[50] On one note, the last words of each sentence a little slower and softer .
[51] If the Blessed Sacrament be present and the coffin be not a long way from the altar the Bishop and his assistants genuflect to the Blessed Sacrament before the sprinkling and before the incensation.
[52] If there are no assistant deacons the deacon of the Mass accompanies the Bishop, on his right, and holds back the cope.
[53] At the Absolution *when the body is not present* (physically or morally) it is a moot point as to whether the Bishop should say the *Non intres* or not. The pontifical (part iii) prescribes it;

incense and blesses it at the throne. He sprinkles and incenses the cloth from the throne (not going round it), doing so thrice each time, once in the middle, once at his left, lastly at his right. The acolytes hold their candles one on either side of the throne before the Bishop for the prayers. For these the book-bearer holds the book. At the end of the Absolution the deacon and subdeacon go to the throne and aid the Bishop to unvest.

Only the Bishop may perform the Absolution, without having first sung the Mass.[54]

§ 6. Pontifical Absolution at the Faldstool

The ceremony in this case is almost the same as when the Bishop uses the throne. A faldstool is placed at the foot of the coffin or catafalque, outside the choir. There is no AP. There are no assistant deacons; so the deacon of Mass is at the bishop's left. He assists when incense is put on and blessed at the faldstool; he hands the holy-water sprinkler, puts on and takes off the mitre. The first MC is at the bishop's right. Meanwhile the subdeacon holds the cross at the head of the bier. *Non intres* is not said *absente corpore.* The deacon walks at the bishop's right when he goes round the bier. The book-bearer holds the book with the candle-bearer at his right.

If there is no coffin or catafalque, a black cloth is spread before the last step of the altar. The bishop does all the first part at the faldstool as at the throne when the Absolution is given over a cloth (as above) but he goes to the epistle corner of the altar (after the blessing of the incense) to chant the prayers; and from the footpace sprinkles and incenses the cloth.[55] The ministers of Mass are at his sides.

§ 7. The Five Absolutions

In certain cases of special solemnity the Absolution at the hearse is performed by five prelates.[56] These cases are the funerals of a greater prelate,[57] of a (Catholic) sovereign (or his wife) or the lord of the place.[58]

General Rules. The five Absolutions follow pontifical solemn Mass for the dead. There are, then, besides the bishop who sings the Mass, four

---

the Ceremonial (II, xi, 12), says nothing about it for the simpler form of the Absolution, and when a priest officiates it is not said. It would seem that when the Absolution is more solemn (given at a "castrum doloris" on an important occasion) and given by the Bishop, the *Non intres* is said; not otherwise.

[54] Cf. S.R.C. 3029 § 10, 3798 § 2, 4154 § 30. He may do so whether he presides at the throne or — in mozzetta — in the first stall in choir (S.R.C. 4355, ii, 3); and even if he were not present at the Mass.

[55] C.E., II, xi, 10-12; cf. O'Connell, *The Celebration of Mass,* 1964, pp. 542ff.

[56] This ceremony is in the pontifical, at the end of part iii: "De Officio quod post Missam Solemnem pro Defunctis Agitur," and in C.E., II, xi, 13-24.

[57] C.E., II, xi, 13 mentions the Pope, Cardinals, Metropolitans, Ordinaries.

[58] "Dux magnus aut Dominus loci" (ibid.).

other bishops. The ceremony may be performed only once for one person. It should take place at the occasion of the funeral if possible, or (failing that) soon afterwards, on the third, seventh or thirtieth day, not later. It is not done at anniversaries. It is generally performed at the cathedral church; but the Ordinary may appoint another for the purpose if the cathedral is not available. The five who perform the Absolutions should be bishops or prelates having the right to use pontificals. If so many cannot be procured, the other four may be dignitaries or canons.[59]

According to the Ceremonial of Bishops the five Absolutions are performed at the funeral of the Ordinary, which funeral is supposed to be celebrated by the highest dignitary of the Chapter, who is normally not a bishop. It is then clear that the ceremony may be carried out when no bishop is present. It is, however, usual, in this case, for the Chapter to invite a bishop to sing the Mass and preside at the Absolutions.

Besides the faldstool at the foot of the coffin, i.e., between it and the main door of the church (if the body be present and be that of a bishop or prelate; otherwise between the hearse and the altar), prepared for the celebrating bishop, four plain bare stools are set up at its corners (each on a black or violet carpet, if the prelates are bishops) and behind them a bench covered with black or violet, on both sides for the canons (who remain vested, if they were vested at Mass).

Vesting of Prelates. Supposing, in the first case, that five bishops will perform the ceremony, the four who assist, besides the celebrant of the Mass, go to the sacristy to vest at the end of Mass or of the funeral oration. Meanwhile the bishop-celebrant goes to the throne or faldstool.

The four other bishops vest in amice over their rochet, black stole and black cope, simple mitre. They come from the sacristy, each attended by a mitre-bearer and a servant or server, who carries a lighted candle.[60] The second MC comes first, then the bishops, two and two, those of higher rank behind. On the outer side of each are his mitre-bearer and server with a lighted candle, each in surplice. The prelates form in a straight line before the altar (the first and third at the epistle side, the second and fourth at the gospel side, leaving a space in the middle for the bishop-celebrant); the servers stand behind them. They take off their mitres and hand them to the bearers. (In this ceremony the assisting bishops take off the mitre themselves.) They bow to the bishop-celebrant at the throne or faldstool. The subdeacon goes to take the processional cross, the acolytes take their candles; other servers bring the thurible, lustral water and a pontifical. These stand behind the line of bishops. The first MC now invites the bishop-celebrant to join the others. He comes, with his assistant deacons, and takes his place in the middle of the four prelates. The deacons stand behind him. Meanwhile the deacon of Mass and AP

[59] S.R.C. 4119 § 1.
[60] If the assistants be not bishops they themselves carry their candles.

stand near the altar. The four bishops bow, with the celebrant, to the altar, then put on their mitres.

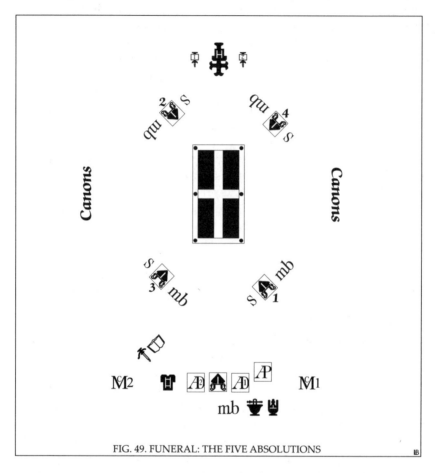

FIG. 49. FUNERAL: THE FIVE ABSOLUTIONS

If the body be not present, the celebrating bishop will be between the catafalque and the altar, with the assistant prelates placed in the same position in relation to him (beginning with the first prelate, who will be on the celebrating bishop's right) as when the body is present.

Procession to Hearse. The procession goes to the hearse in this order: first the thurifer with the server carrying the lustral water at his right; then the subdeacon of the Mass *(paratus)* holding the cross (processional or archiepiscopal) between the acolytes; the clergy and canons carrying lighted candles in the outer hand; the four bishops, two and two, those of higher rank behind, with their servers at their sides, as when they came in; the AP with the deacon of Mass at his left;[61] the bishop-celebrant between his assistant deacons. The server who holds his candle is at the

---

[61] If there are no assistant deacons, the deacon walks on the left of the bishop-celebrant; the AP on his right.

right of the first assistant deacon. Lastly come the three chaplains of mitre, book and hand-candle.

Pontifical Absolution for the Dead (C.E., II, xi ; Pontificale Romanum)

Cases	Who assist celebrant?	Non intres	Who ministers incense and lustral water?	Concluding prayers[62]
Five absolutions (body present or absent).	AP and assistant deacons (vested). Deacon (if Mass was at faldstool).[63]	Said always.[64]	Deacon. [65]	At foot of body or *castrum doloris*.
One pontifical Absolution after Mass *at the throne:* (i) at coffin or *castrum doloris*.	AP and ADs (vested)	Said always.[66]	AP	At foot of body or *castrum doloris*.
(ii) over cloth before the throne.	AP and ADs (vested)	Omitted.	AP	At throne.
One pontifical Absolution after Mass *at faldstool:* (i) at coffin or catafalque.	Deacon.	Omitted *absente corpore*.	Deacon.	At foot of coffin or catafalque.
(ii) at cloth before high altar.	Deacon.	Omitted.	Deacon.	On footpace.
Pontifical Absolution after Mass which Bishop *assists:*[67] (i) at coffin or catafalque.	AP and ADs in choir dress.	Probably omitted *absente corpore*.	AP	At foot of coffin or catafalque.
(ii) at cloth before throne.	AP and ADs in choir dress.	Omitted.	AP	At throne.

All stand around the hearse in the usual way, the subdeacon with the cross and acolytes at the head, the bishop-celebrant with his attendants at the foot before his faldstool, the clergy or canons around. The four other bishops are at the four stools prepared, in order of rank, the first (or senior) at the right of the celebrant, the second at the right of the cross at

---

[62] In every case (except for *Non intres*) the book-bearer (not the AP) holds the book (though some rubricians say the AP holds it for prayers sung by the bishop-celebrant, only, at the quintuple Absolution).

[63] In this case there are no ADs and AP takes no special part in the Absolution.

[64] Because of the *solemnity* of the Absolution in these two cases.

[65] For bishop-celebrant *Pontificale* says expressly the deacon, and C.E. makes no exception from the other four prelates, yet some rubricians say that AP ministers to the bishop-celebrant.

[66] Because of the *solemnity* of the Absolution in these two cases.

[67] It is a moot point whether, in this case, the cross is borne by the subdeacon (vested) or by a server (in surplice).

the other end, the third at the celebrant's left, the fourth at the left of the cross. The bishops and canons sit. At the right of each assisting bishop is his mitre-bearer, at his left the server with his candle. Then the second assistant deacon takes the mitre from the celebrant, the other bishops take off theirs, handing them to the bearers. All stand.

"Non Intres." The celebrant chants the prayer *Non intres*[68] in the ferial tone, the AP holding the pontifical, the candle-bearer by him. All sit again and put on their mitres. The first assistant deacon puts on the celebrant's mitre. The choir sings the responsory *Subvenite, Sancti Dei.*[69] Meanwhile the deacon of Mass — led by one of the MC's — goes to the first (or senior) of the assisting bishops with the thurifer, book-bearer, and bearer of lustral water, and stands at his right.

First Absolution. Towards the end of the responsory (when the verse *Requiem æternam* is begun) this bishop, seated, puts on and blesses incense, as usual, the deacon assisting.[70] The cantors sing *Kyrie, eleison,* etc. As soon as they begin the deacon takes off the first assistant bishop's mitre; all stand (uncovered). The first assistant bishop chants *Pater noster,* and then, continuing it silently, accompanied by the deacon on his right, he goes round the hearse twice (beginning on his right), first sprinkling it, then incensing — three times on each side, as usual. He bows as he passes each of the other bishops and to the cross. Then, having given back the thurible to the deacon, with hands joined the bishop sings the verses *Et ne nos inducas,* etc., and the prayer *Deus, cui omnia vivunt,* as in the pontifical (the book-bearer holding the book).[71] All sit again and the prelates put on the mitre, (the deacon presents that of the absolving prelate). The choir sings the second responsory, *Qui Lazarum resuscitasti.*

Second, Third and Fourth Absolutions. Meanwhile the deacon goes to the second bishop; all is done by him as before. He blesses incense, sprinkles and incenses (beginning to his right) and sings the verses and prayer *Fac, quæsumus Domine.* The choir sings the responsory *Domine, quando veneris;* and the third bishop performs the Absolution. His prayer is *Inclina, Domine, aurem tuam.* The choir sings *Ne recorderis peccata mea;* and the fourth (or junior) bishop gives his Absolution, singing at the end the prayer *Absolve, quæsumus Domine.*

---

[68] Even, in the case of the five Absolutions, if the body be not present (cf. C.E., II, xi, 15, 17; cf. also p. 399, n. 3). At the Absolution *when the body is not present* (physically or morally) it is a moot point as to whether the Bishop should say the *Non intres* or not. The pontifical (part iii) prescribes it; the Ceremonial (II, xi, 12), says nothing about it for the simpler form of the Absolution, and when a priest officiates it is not said. It would seem that when the Absolution is more solemn (given at a "castrum doloris" on an important occasion) and given by the Bishop, the *Non intres* is said; not otherwise.

[69] The five responsories, each with its versicles and prayer, are printed in order in the pontifical. The *Liber Usualis* gives the chants.

[70] The deacon asks the blessing, saying *Benedicite, reverendissime Pater.*

[71] The hand-candle-bearer holds the candle at the fifth Absolution only.

The Final Absolution. Then follows the last responsory *Libera me, Domine;* and the bishop-celebrant performs the last Absolution as usual, except that he, too, bows to the other bishops as he passes them. The deacon[72] assists with incense and holy water, and the book-bearer[73] (or AP) holds the book while he sings. The candle-bearer attends. At *Requiem æternam* the bishop-celebrant makes the sign of the cross over the coffin or catafalque.[74] No versicle or prayer follows after *Requiescat in pace.* All go to the altar as they came, the assisting bishops to the sacristy, the bishop-celebrant to the throne (or sacristy) where he is unvested (by the deacon and subdeacon).

If Assistants are not Bishops. If the assistants who make the Absolutions are not bishops and have no use of pontificals, the following exceptions occur.[75] They carry their own candles and have no mitre-bearers. They come in wearing the biretta, uncover and bow to the choir as usual; then make the proper reverence to the Bishop at the throne or faldstool. They wear the biretta while going to the hearse and coming from it, and while they sit on the stools there. While each gives the Absolution he hands his biretta and candle to the second MC or to a server to hold. If the presiding bishop is the Ordinary the priests do not bless the incense; but he does so for each of them. They bless incense if he is not the Ordinary.[76]

§ 8. The Funeral of Infants

The traditional Liturgy contains no liturgical ceremony for the burial of infants who die without baptism. When baptised infants die under the age of reason (seven years), there is a special rite for their funeral.[77] There are no signs of mourning; no prayers for the dead child are said. The colour is white. If the bells are rung at all they are rung joyfully. A crown of sweet-smelling flowers is put on the child's head as a sign of his bodily integrity and virginity.[78]

The priest goes to the house, to bring the coffin to the church, with a cross-bearer and a server who carries lustral water. He may be accompanied by clergy; there may be acolytes who go on either side of

---

[72] *Pontificale Romanum.* Nearly all rubricians say that AP does this for bishop-celebrant, but C.E. makes no exception for him, and *Pontificale* expressly directs deacon to minister to the bishop-celebrant as he had done to the other prelates.

[73] Cf. S.R.C. 2097 § 7, C.E., II, xi, 17 directs AP to hold book for bishop-celebrant at *Non intres.* It and *Pontificale* are silent about the other prayers, but some rubricians say the AP holds the book for the bishop-celebrant for these also.

[74] *Pontificale.*

[75] Cf. C.E., II, xi, 24.

[76] S.R.C. 2089 § 6.

[77] R.R., VII, vii. For the funeral of an unbaptised baby, see Mahoney, *Questions and Answers* II (1949), Q. 623.

[78] R.R., VII, vii, I.

the cross. The cross is borne without its shaft.[79] The celebrant wears surplice, white stole, and he may wear a white cope.

At the House. At the house he sprinkles the coffin, then intones the antiphon *Sit nomen Domini,* the choir chants or recites the psalm *Laudate, servi, Dominum.* When the antiphon after this psalm has been said the procession goes to the church in the same order as for a grown-up person. On the way they recite the psalm *Beati quorum immaculati* and (if there is time) *Laudate Dominum de cælis.* The verses *Gloria Patri* and *Sicut erat* are said at the end of these psalms.

If the priest cannot go to the house to bring the coffin to the church, he may meet it and carry out this rite at the gate of the churchyard or door of the church.

At the Church. When the procession arrives at the church, the psalm is interrupted; at once they say or sing *Gloria Patri* and *Sicut erat.*

Candles may be lighted around the coffin, placed in the usual place before the altar, outside the choir.[80] But they are not distributed to the clergy. If it is morning either the Mass of the day, or, if the rubrics permit, a private votive Mass, a suitable votive Mass—not for the child, but for some other intention (e.g., in thanksgiving for the blessing conferred on him; to beg consolation for his parents)—may be celebrated.

Then, instead of the Absolution, all stand around the coffin, the celebrant in white stole, and a white cope if he wishes. The cross (without shaft) is held at the head of the coffin, the celebrant stands at the feet. The psalm *Domini est terra* is said or sung, with the antiphon *Hic accipiet.*[81] The prayers *Kyrie, eleison,* etc., follow, as in the ritual. While *Pater noster* is said silently the priest sprinkles the coffin three times, crosswise before him. He does not go round it; nor is it incensed.

At the Graveside. After the prayer *Omnipotens et mitissime Deus* the coffin is carried to the grave. Meanwhile the choir in procession sings the psalm *Laudate Dominum de cælis,* with the antiphon *Iuvenes.* Incense and lustral water are taken in this procession. At the grave the celebrant says *Kyrie, eleison,* and the following prayers. After the collect *Omnipotens sempiterne Deus, sanctæ puritatis amator,* he puts incense into the thurible and blesses it. Then he sprinkles the coffin and grave together with lustral water and incenses them, not moving from his place. The procession returns to the church, and the body is buried.[82] On the way to the church they sing or recite the psalm *Benedicite,* with the antiphon

[79] The liturgical books make a special point of this. Not the whole processional cross with the long shaft, but a smaller hand-cross is carried. The processional cross should be so made that its upper part can be detached from the shaft for the funeral of infants.
[80] Or, preferably, in the mortuary chapel.
[81] R.R. supposes these prayers to follow immediately after the arrival of the body in the church. It makes no reference to the celebration of Mass.
[82] As in the case of adults, it is supposed that the celebrant and clergy have left the grave before the actual burial.

Benedicite Dominum. Before the altar the celebrant says *Dominus vobiscum,* and the prayer *Deus qui miro ordine.* All go to the sacristy.

If the body is not to be taken to the grave at once, all these prayers are said in the church.

If the priest does not accompany it to the grave, they may be said or sung at the door of the church, before it is taken farther .

If all the prayers have been said in church, it is not necessary to repeat them at the grave; but they may be repeated.

§ 9. Service on the Occasion
of the Death of a Non-Catholic Personage

On the occasion of the death of a non-Catholic personage, such as a king, queen or president, it is usual to hold a service in Catholic churches. The form of this service will be fixed by the Ordinary. Mass is not allowed, nor any form of exequial service (intercession for the dead) or one that resembles a non-Catholic "memorial service." Prayer may be offered for consolation for those who mourn the dead person, and — in the case of the head of a State — for the welfare of the State and for the successor of the dead potentate. The form of service usually prescribed by the Ordinary is: Exposition of the Blessed Sacrament, during which are recited or sung the psalm *Miserere* (with *Gloria Patri* at its conclusion), the prayer *Pro quacumque tribulatione,*[83] or *Deus qui culpa offenderis*[84] (with short conclusion), perhaps the Litanies of the Saints, then the prayer for the new King or Queen *(Salvum fac).*[85] The service ends with Benediction and the playing of the National Anthem on the organ.

---

[83] No. 13, *Orationes Diversæ* of the missal.

[84] Collect of Thursday after Ash Wednesday; it is also one of the prayers after the Litanies of the Saints.

[85] Before *Tantum ergo.*

Chapter XXXII

The Installation of a New Parish Priest

A newly appointed parish priest cannot *per se* validly perform certain functions, such as assisting at marriage (C.I.C. Canon 1095, § 1, 1°), until he has been installed in (or inducted into) his new parish. This installation, being a juridical rather than a liturgical function, is not provided for in the liturgical books, but is regulated by particular law[1] (e.g., synodal law) or by legitimate custom. The Ordinary, for a just cause, may dispense from the law requiring induction. If he does, the dispensation must be expressly given in writing, and then takes the place of the installation (C.I.C. Canon 1444, § 1).[2]

The rite followed for the induction of a parish priest varies in detail from diocese to diocese, but the general outline of the ceremony is normally as follows:

Ordinarily the function takes place in the parish church, either before the principal Mass, or in the afternoon before Vespers or Benediction. If the Bishop himself does not officiate he will appoint a delegate (his Vicar General, or a Vicar Forane, or some other priest) to represent him.

The officiant, vested in surplice (rochet), stole and cope of the colour of the Office, may go in procession with the attendant clergy and servers to the main door of the church. There he meets the parish priest wearing a surplice and carrying a stole of the colour of the day on his arm. The officiant presents a crucifix to the parish priest, who, kneeling, kisses it; and the officiant may then put the stole on the parish priest.[3] All kneel and *Veni Creator* is intoned by the officiant.[4] When the first strophe has been sung all rise and the procession is reformed—the parish priest walking before, or on the left of the officiant—and goes to the altar, while the hymn is continued. When it is over the officiant sings the versicle *Emitte* and the prayer *Deus qui corda.*

Then (or later) may be sung the antiphon, versicle and response (from Second Vespers) of the Titular of the church, and the prayer of the Titular chanted by the new parish priest.

---

[1] The Westminster Synod of 1925 permits a form once prescribed by Cardinal Vaughan to be used. It is set forth in Canon Mahoney's *Questions and Answers* II, Q. 524.

[2] Cf. also canon 527 of the 1983 C.I.C.

[3] In some places the officiant here puts on the parish priest his surplice, and later—at the altar, after *Veni* Creator—presents him with the stole.

[4] In the Vaughan form the hymn, with its versicle and prayer, are recited in English at the altar, and Psalm 66 follows.

A seat is placed for the officiant at the gospel corner of the footpace, and a prie-dieu may be placed at the foot of the altar for the parish priest. The officiant may now address the congregation and explain the rite that is taking place. He then sits and the episcopal document appointing the parish priest is read by one of the assisting clergy.

The parish priest kneeling at the prie-dieu, or on the lowest step of the altar, reads the profession of faith and the oath,[5] and at the closing declaration of each places his hand on the book of the Gospels, laid on the top of the prie-dieu or on the lap of the officiant.[6] The parish priest then signs the form of the profession of faith and the oath.

Next the officiant, still sitting, pronounces the form of canonical institution, as prescribed by local law or custom.

The officiant then presents the parish priest, kneeling before him, with the keys of the church, the missal and other symbols of his office, with the form of words prescribed for each.[7] In some places, the officiant leads the parish priest to the altar (which he kisses), to the credence (to touch the sacred vessels and Holy Oils), to the main door (which the parish priest opens and closes), to the confessional, to the baptismal font, to the belfry (where the parish priest rings the bell), and finally to the pulpit.[8] The parish priest may then address his flock, giving thanks for his appointment, and — if appropriate — outline his plans for his new parish.

After this he goes to the altar, kisses it in the middle, and — having raised his hands and his eyes heavenwards as he recites the opening words of the formula *(Benedicat* vos) — turns and blesses the people.

The function ends by the celebration of Mass by the parish priest; or by Vespers, or Benediction, at which the *Te Deum,* with its versicles and prayer, may be sung.

Afterwards the *procès-verbal* of the installation is drawn up for the diocesan archives. It may take some such form as this :

> Ego, infrascriptus (N.N.) Vicarius Foraneus (vel alius delegatus) a Revmo. Dno. (N.) Episcopo (N.) ad hoc delegatus, testor R.D.

---

[5] Canon 833 of the 1983 C.I.C. states the requirements.

[6] This part of the rite sometimes takes place beforehand, in private, in the presence of the Bishop or his delegate.

[7] In Ireland, the formula for presenting the keys and the stole is given in the Appendix of the Statutes of the Maynooth Synod of 1927.

[8] In the Vaughan form, after the presentation of the symbols Psalm 133, some versicles, and two concluding prayers are said.

(N.N.) emissa coram me professione fidei et iuramento anti-modernistico, per me missum fuisse in canonicam possessionem parœciæ ecclesiæ S. (N.) apud Diœcesis (N.) hac die... mensis...20....

Testes: ...

In quorum fidem, etc.

Appendix

Ceremonies of the Ritual in the U.S.A.[1]

§ 1. Use of the Roman Ritual

IN the United States the Roman Ritual of Pope Paul V is of obligation.[2] This has been true at least since the First Provincial Council of Baltimore (1829).[3] As noted in Chapter XXX, the differences between the Roman Ritual and the *Ordo Administrandi* used in England are largely theoretical. This means, in effect, that the descriptions of ceremonies in Chapters XXX and XXXI may generally be applied to the United States of America, although in the latter case the source of the text and rubrics is the Roman Ritual itself.

In addition to the prescriptions of the Roman Ritual, certain other rites, either required or approved by the Apostolic See for the United States, must be described. In the edition of the Roman Ritual published in the United States, these matters are included in a brief supplement.[4] They are also to be found in the various excerpts from the Roman Ritual published in the United States.

§ 2. The *Collectio Rituum*

In view of the approval given by the Apostolic See to the use of bi-lingual rituals in many parts of the world, the archbishops and bishops of the United States requested a similar concession and submitted a *Collectio Rituum* to S.R.C. After study of the proposed ritual, the S. Congregation, by decree of June 3, 1954, permitted its use, but placed the usual limitations upon the extent to which the vernacular might be employed in the administration of sacraments, and so forth.[5] Shortly thereafter, the

---

[1] The original text of this appendix is by Frederick R. McManus.

[2] The most recent *editio typica* of the ritual was approved on January 25, 1952.

[3] N. 10. This law was repeated in later Councils, including the Second Plenary Council of Baltimore (1866), n. 210. Cf. nn. 221, 275, of the Third Plenary Council of Baltimore (1884).

[4] "Supplementum Ritualis Romani ad usum cleri Americæ Septentrionalis Fœderatæ" in *Rituale Romanum,* New York: Benziger, 1953. A three-volume translation of the Roman Ritual, somewhat re-arranged in order, is also published in the United States: P. T. Weller, trans., *The Roman Ritual in Latin and English,* Milwaukee: Bruce, 1946-1950. Among other supplementary materials, this set contains a suggested rite of betrothal (I, 588-593).

[5] The dispositive part of the decree resembles very closely the indults allowing the use of the bi-lingual rituals in other places, e.g., France, Lugano. S.R.C. permitted the partial use of

volume was published "cum licentia Sacræ Congregationis Rituum."[6] S.R.C. next approved its use in certain other English-speaking countries.[7]

In 1961 a second version of the *Collectio Rituum* was issued in a limited edition, to serve as an exemplar for future rituals and manuals to be published in the United States; this volume had been authorised by a rescript of S.R.C. dated October 11, 1959.

The *Collectio Rituum* (1st ed.) has three parts: (1) *Sacramentale,* including Baptism, Confirmation, the sacraments for the sick and dying, and Matrimony; (2) *Benedictionale,* with twenty-six blessings; and (3) *Exsequiale,* with the funeral rites. In general its contents are similar to those of the European bi-lingual rituals, although it has more blessings.[8]

The second *Collectio Rituum* (1961) omits the *Benedictionale* and *Exsequiale,* and the *Sacramentale* contains only the sacraments of Baptism, Extreme Unction, and Matrimony, all with new translations of the permitted bi-lingual texts to replace the corresponding texts of the first *Collectio.*[9]

For the most part the rubrics of the *Collectio Rituum,* like those of the Roman Ritual, require no commentary. Two general principles may be set down very simply, as given in the first *Collectio Rituum:*

(1) Wherever the English translation is printed next to the Latin text, it is enough to recite the prayer in the English language only.[10]

(2) If the English text is *not* printed next to the Latin, only the Latin may be used; this applies to the forms of the sacraments and some other formulas. Even in these cases, however, the English translation may be read before or after the Latin.[11]

There is a great difference between these two uses of the vernacular language in the rites. In the first case, the English version is a substitute for the Latin and is in fact an authentic liturgical text. It follows that no version other than that given in the *Collectio Rituum* may be used.[12] In the

---

the vernacular in some rites which were unfortunately omitted from the first edition of the U.S. *Collectio Rituum,* especially the Baptism of adults.

[6] Milwaukee: Bruce, 1954.

[7] For English-speaking sections of Canada (February 12, 1955) ; for Australia and New Zealand (May 14, 1955).

[8] The *Collectio Rituum* approved by S.R.C. for the diocese of Lugano has 11 blessings, the German *Collectio Rituum I* only 4.

[9] The 1961 *Collectio* contains the following rites, omitted from the earlier edition: (1) Baptism of adults; (2) Nuptial Blessing outside Mass; and (3) prayers recited, by apostolic indult, in place of the Nuptial Blessing. Of the rites mentioned in the October 11, 1959 indult of S.R.C., only the English prayers after the Absolution of the dead are not provided.

[10] Although not expressly stated, it is clear that the English prayer-texts of the new *Collectio* are intended as emendations of and substitutes for the corresponding texts found in the 1954 edition. Cf. C.I.C. 22.

[11] *Prænotanda,* p. xi. Unlike the original *Collectio,* the 1961 edition does not give English translations to be used in addition to the prescribed Latin texts, but provides only those translations which are authentic substitutes for the Latin.

[12] Cf. C.I.C. 733, § 1; 1148; 1257.

second case, the supplementary recitation of an English translation is by way of explanation, commentary, or instruction; the Latin alone is the authentic liturgical text.

§ 3. Baptism

The rite for the administration of this sacrament has already been described in detail in Chapter XXX. In the original *Collectio* provision is also made for an instruction on the occasion of Baptism. This may be given at the church door, before the rite begins; or at the entrance to the baptistery, after the priest has put on the white stole; or, finally, at the end of the ceremony.[13] It is recommended, moreover, that Baptism be administered according to a "more solemn" form occasionally, in order to emphasise the social and public nature of the sacrament and to renew in the faithful the fervour of their Baptism. For "more solemn" Baptism the faithful in general are invited to assist; they recite all the responses provided in the text, the Creed and Lord's Prayer, and sing suitable hymns. On such an occasion the priest should vest in violet (later, white) stole and cope.[14] Although these recommendations are not renewed in the 1961 edition of the *Collectio Rituum*,[15] they may suitably be put into effect no matter what ritual is used.

If it is necessary to bless baptismal water in the course of the year, other than at the Easter Vigil, the usual rite given in the Roman Ritual may be followed.[16] In the United States a shorter formula for blessing baptismal water is also allowed, by apostolic indult.[17] This is the same as the shorter rite, also found in the Roman Ritual,[18] with the following addition (after the infusion of the holy oils): "Then the priest says, blessing the water itself: *Sanctificetur et fœcundetur Fons iste, et ex eo renascentes. In nomine Pa✠tris, et Fi✠lii, et Spiritus✠Sancti. ℟. Amen.*"

§ 4. Reception of Converts

The rites for the reception of converts into the Church are based upon the Roman Ritual, with some variations peculiar to the United States.[19] Three

---

[13] I, i, 2. Cf. R.R., I, 10.

[14] *Collectio Rituum,* I, i, 1, 3. At "more solemn" Baptism a hymn is sung during the procession from the church door to the baptistery (I, i; 14).

[15] The rubrical directions follow R.R. literally. Cf. *Collectio Rituum* (1961), p. ix.

[16] II, viii; *supra,* p. 363.

[17] S.C. de Prop. Fide, October 16, 1830.

[18] II, ix

[19] Instruction of the Holy Office, July 20, 1859; decrees of the Plenary Councils or Baltimore: II, n. 242; III, n. 122. The rites, not given in either edition of the *Collectio Rituum,* are found in various excerpts from R.R. in use in the United States and in the *Supplementum* to the Benziger edition of R.R., already mentioned.

cases may be envisioned: conversion of a person previously not baptised (whose reception into the Church is by Baptism itself), conversion of a baptised person (whose return from apostasy, heresy, or schism is chiefly a matter of absolution), or conversion of a doubtfully baptised person. In every case, a careful investigation of baptismal status must be made, preferably during the period of instruction.

Convert not already baptised. If the convert is certainly not baptised or if it is certain that his previous Baptism was invalid, he should be solemnly baptised according to the rite for the Baptism of adults.[20] It is very fitting that this Baptism should be administered at the Easter Vigil.

The candidate should be suitably instructed, have the proper intention, and be sorry for his sins. No abjuration of heresy, absolution from sin or censure, or special profession of faith (other than the Apostles' Creed itself) is required. After the Baptism, if a bishop should be present, the neophyte should be confirmed. In any event Mass should be celebrated if possible and the newly baptised should receive Holy Communion.[21]

For a grave and reasonable cause the local Ordinary may permit the use of the ceremonies for the Baptism of infants in the Baptism of adults.[22] If convenient, the Baptism of adults should be referred to the local Ordinary so that he may administer the sacrament more solemnly, if he wishes, either personally or through a delegate.[23]

In the case of a dying non-Catholic who is unbaptised, the prescriptions of canon 752 concerning instruction and intention should be followed, and private Baptism conferred, without preliminary ceremonies. If possible, the rites which follow the actual administration of the sacrament (anointing with Chrism, etc.) are added at once, as in the case of the private Baptism of an infant in danger of death.[24] The neophyte should be confirmed[25] and then receive Holy Communion, if circumstances permit. The baptismal ceremonies which were omitted are to be supplied in church *quamprimum* if the person recovers.[26]

Convert already baptised. If the convert has certainly been baptised, it would be a grave sacrilege to attempt to baptise him again. Instead he must abjure his error (by making the profession of faith) and be absolved from excommunication; thus he is readmitted into communion with the Church and may then be absolved from his sins and receive the other sacraments.

---

[20] R.R., II, iv. Detailed rubrics are given in the ritual.

[21] C.I.C. 753, § 2; R.R., II, iv, 52.

[22] C.I.C. 755, § 2; R.R., II, i, 26. In almost all dioceses of the United States this permission is given as one of the diocesan faculties.

[23] C.I.C. 744; R.R., II, iii, 2.

[24] C.I.C. 759, § 1; R.R., II, i, 28.

[25] If the priest has the faculty to administer Confirmation and may lawfully use it.

[26] C.I.C. 759, § 3: R.R., II, i, 28. The rite for adults is in R.R., II, vi; for infants, II, v; the latter is in the 1961 *Collectio*. Cf. *supra*, Chapter XXX.

In this case the absolution from the censure is granted according to canon 2314, § 2, in the external forum. The local Ordinary (but not the Vicar General without special mandate) may absolve, or the faculty may be delegated to any priest by the local Ordinary.[27] The abjuration or profession of faith[28] must be made before the local Ordinary or his delegate and before at least two witnesses.

The rite is as follows:[29] The priest vests in surplice and violet stole and sits before the altar (in the centre or, if the Blessed Sacrament is reserved at the altar, on the epistle side) facing the convert kneeling before him. The convert then recites the profession of faith, while touching with his right hand a book of the Gospels which the priest holds open on his knees.[30] If the convert cannot read the profession of faith, the priest reads it to him slowly so that he may understand and repeat the words.

Next the priest, still seated, recites the psalm *Miserere* or the *De profundis,* adding *Gloria Patri* at the end. He then stands and says *Kyrie, eleison* and the versicles and prayer which follow. The convert, witnesses, or people present should answer; if no one can, the priest himself answers. After the prayer the priest sits again and absolves the convert from heresy, according to the formula *Auctoritate Apostolica, qua fungor in hac parte...*[31] If there is any doubt as to whether the convert has incurred the excommunication, the priest inserts the word *forsan* before *incurristi.* Lastly he imposes a penance such as prayers or a visit to a church.

Converts who are under fourteen years of age do not make the formal abjuration and are not absolved from censure.[32] If they have reached the age of reason, they make a simple profession of faith, for example, by reciting the Apostles' Creed.

The ceremonies which were omitted at the time of the convert's Baptism should now be supplied.[33] For a reasonable cause, however, the local Ordinary may allow the supplying of ceremonies to be dispensed with in the case of heretics who are received into the Church.[34] Since he has been absolved in the external forum from the censure of

---

[27] In very many dioceses of the United States such a faculty is included among the ordinary diocesan faculties.

[28] The *abiuratio* of C.I.C. 2314, § 2, and the *professio fidei* are the same thing.

[29] Cf. R.R., IV, iii, which resembles this ceremony closely. The rite described in the text is intended for new converts, "born outside the Catholic Church." In the case of Catholics who are guilty of apostasy, heresy, or schism, absolution is given according to R.R. (IV, ii, for the internal forum only, or IV, iii, for the external forum); it must be preceded by the abjuration.

[30] The text approved by the Holy Office in 1942 is in Bouscaren, *Canon Law Digest,* II (Milwaukee: Bruce, 1943), 182-184, and in various U.S. rituals. On June 13, 1956, the Holy Office approved a shorter version for the reception of uneducated converts in the United States. Cf. Canon Law Digest Supplement, at canon 752.

[31] This differs somewhat from the usual absolution from excommunication (R.R., IV, iii, 6-7).

[32] S.C.S. Off., March 8, 1882. Cf. C.I.C. 2230.

[33] C.I.C. 759, § 3.

[34] R.R., II, iii, 12. Or there may be a custom of not supplying the baptismal ceremonies in the case of adult converts who have been baptised previously.

excommunication, the new convert may be absolved from his sins by any confessor.[35] He should be counselled to receive the sacrament of Confirmation and Holy Communion as soon as possible.

In the case of a dying non-Catholic who is already baptised, a brief abjuration or profession of faith is sufficient.[36] The last sacraments and last blessing are administered as usual.[37]

Convert doubtfully baptised. If, after careful investigation, the validity of the convert's Baptism remains doubtful, he must be baptised conditionally. The order to be followed is: (1) abjuration or profession of faith; (2) conditional Baptism; and (3) sacramental confession with conditional absolution.

The profession of faith is made as described above.[38] In the administration of Baptism the words *Si non es baptizatus* (or *baptizata*) are prefixed to the sacramental form.[39] Otherwise the usual rite for the solemn Baptism of adults is followed.[40] In the case of conditional Baptism of adult heretics, however, the local Ordinary may permit the use of private Baptism, that is, without the ceremonies preliminary to the actual Baptism.[41] When Baptism is repeated conditionally, the ceremonies performed in the earlier Baptism may be repeated or omitted; the ceremonies previously omitted must be supplied except in the case just mentioned, when the local Ordinary permits the private Baptism, *sub conditione,* of adult heretics.[42]

After the conditional Baptism, the new convert should go to confession and receive conditional absolution.[43] He should receive Confirmation and Holy Communion as soon as possible.

---

[35] C.I.C., 2314, § 2. There is no obligation for him to go to confession immediately, but he is bound to confess all grave sins committed after Baptism on the occasion of his first confession.

[36] Cf. *supra,* Chapter XXX § 13, and the *Supplementum* to the Benziger edition of R.R., p. (19).

[37] Including Confirmation, if the priest has the faculty and may lawfully use it.

[38] It is disputed whether the profession of faith must be followed by absolution from excommunication (as in England); it appears to be unnecessary and is not required by the Instruction of the Holy Office (July 20, 1859) which simply lists: *abiuratio seu fidei professio, baptismus conditionatus, confessio sacramentalis cum absolutione conditionata.* Cf. Goodwine, *The Reception of Converts* (Washington: Catholic University, 1944), p. 109.

[39] R.R., II, iv, 40; II, ii, 22.

[40] Or, for grave and reasonable cause, the local Ordinary may permit the use of the rite of infant Baptism (C.I.C. 755, § 2; R.R., II, i, 26).

[41] C.I.C. 759, § 2; R.R., II, i. 28. This permission is included in the usual faculties of many dioceses of the United States. In some places, moreover, a "short form" for the conditional Baptism of adults is permitted; this begins with the question *Quid petis ab Ecclesia Dei?* followed immediately by the interrogatory on faith. Cf. *Supplementum* to the Benziger edition of R.R., pp. (19)-(20).

[42] C.I.C. 760; R.R., II, i, 28. Because of the discretion allowed to local Ordinaries in this entire matter, particular legislation or diocesan faculties must be consulted.

[43] He need not, of course, confess to the priest who has baptised him conditionally. Although the order given in the text (abjuration, conditional Baptism, conditional absolution) is listed in the Instruction of 1859, the practice described in Chapter XXX § 11

As already noted, the convert under fourteen years of age does not make a formal abjuration, but only a simple profession of faith. In the case of the dying non-Catholic who is doubtfully baptised, the brief abjuration or profession of faith suffices (cf. Chapter XXX § 13), followed by conditional Baptism, conditional absolution, and the last sacraments.

In the United States, it is not permitted to use lustral water for the conditional Baptism of adult heretics; baptismal water must be used.[44]

§ 5. Matrimony

What has been said above in Chapter XXX, § 15 concerning Matrimony needs to be modified somewhat to conform to usage in the United States of America. Moreover, certain additional prayers are found in the *Collectio Rituum* of 1954 and are in use in some places.[45]

Nuptial Blessing. The ideal for Catholics is that the celebration of marriage should be followed by the Nuptial Mass (or other Mass which takes its place), at which they receive the Nuptial Blessing and then Holy Communion.[46] Failing this, there is a form of Nuptial Blessing which may be given outside of Mass, by apostolic indult.[47] As a final alternative, there are special prayers to be recited, again by apostolic indult, after a marriage celebrated without Mass.[48] In the United States local Ordinaries possess the faculty to permit the second form of the Nuptial Blessing outside Mass or these special prayers at a marriage outside Mass.[49] Thus there are several possibilities when Catholics marry: (1) Nuptial Mass and Blessing; (2) Nuptial Blessing at the Mass of the day;[50] (3) by indult, the second form of the Blessing;[51] (4) by indult, special prayers recited

---

may be followed. Cf. S.C.S. Off., December 2, 1874.

[44] S.C. de Prop. Fide, January 24, 1868. In emergency of course even ordinary water may be used.

[45] These prayers, not given in the 1961 *Collectio,* precede and follow the strictly liturgical rite for the celebration of Matrimony. For their use cf. R.R., VIII, ii, 6; S.R.C., instruction, September 3, 1958, § 12.

[46] For the times when the Nuptial Blessing may not be given without dispensation from the local Ordinary, see *supra* Chapter XXX § 15. If the Blessing may be given but the votive Mass is prohibited, the Mass of the day is celebrated (with the prayers of the Nuptial Mass added under one conclusion) and the prayers of the Blessing are said at the usual places. The regulations concerning the banns of marriage (*supra,* Chapter XXX § 15) need not be repeated here.

[47] R.R., VIII, iii.

[48] R.R., VIII, iv. These prayers are intended for marriages outside Mass (1) if the woman is a widow who has already received the Nuptial Blessing; or (2) *tempore clauso* when the local Ordinary does not permit the Nuptial Blessing (cf. C.I.C. 1108, § 3; R.R., VIII, i, 19).

[49] Quinquennial faculties (n. 5 from S.R.C.) in Bouscaren-O'Connor, *Canon Law Digest Annual Supplement* (Milwaukee: Bruce, 1953-), under canon 66. In some U.S. dioceses this faculty is sub-delegated in the ordinary diocesan faculties.

[50] *Supra,* Chapter XXX § 15.

[51] This differs completely from *the* Nuptial Blessing given only at Mass, but it may not be given if the woman is a widow who received the Blessing at her first marriage.

instead of the Blessing; (5) the marriage rite without Mass or added prayers.[52]

Civil Requirements. In the United States neither a civil declaration nor a separate exchange of consent for civil purposes is necessary.[53] The priest who assists at the marriage in accordance with the sacred canons acts in a civil capacity as well. Beforehand he must satisfy any civil requirements for recognition of his clerical status, and afterwards he must sign the license or certificate and return it to the proper civil official, all according to the laws of the several States.

Rite of Marriage. The priest wears the vestments for Mass, except for the maniple which is placed on the credence beforehand. If Mass is not to follow, he vests in surplice and white stole, and may wear a white cope. There should be at least one server who vests in surplice and who carries the book and the vessel of lustral water.[54]

While the man and woman to be married and all others kneel, the priest stands at the lowest step, facing the altar, and recites the introductory versicles and prayer. All who can, answer.[55] Then the priest gives a brief homily or instruction concerning marriage.[56] After it all stand for the matrimonial consent. The man and woman stand before the priest, with the man at the woman's right; the witnesses are at their sides or behind them.[57] The priest first asks the question of the man: N., *do you take* N., *here present,* etc.[58] The man answers *I do.* The priest then asks the question of the woman, and she answers. The priest directs the spouses to join their right hands, which they do. If convenient, the priest circles their joined hands with the ends of his stole.[59] Then, at the direction of the priest, the man first says the form, *I, N.N., take you, N.N., for my lawful wife,* etc., repeating it in short phrases after the priest. The woman in the same way says the form appointed for her. After this they keep the hands joined while the priest makes the sign of the cross over the persons, saying *Ego ·conjungo vos in matrimonium. In nomine Patris, et Fi✠lii, et*

---

[52] Mixed marriages will be described below.

[53] And any civil ceremony is prohibited for Catholics.

[54] These may be placed on the credence, together with the salver or plate to hold the ring (or rings).

[55] The versicles and prayer, recited prior to the rite of Matrimony, are found in the original *Collectio Rituum,* not in the edition of 1961.

[56] During this all sit. The priest may use one of the suggested "exhortations before marriage" which are found in various U.S. editions of the ritual.

[57] The place for the spouses, whether at the sanctuary entrance or within the sanctuary, varies in the United States according to local usage or particular legislation. The custom of the spouses' standing during the giving of consent is confirmed by the *Collectio Rituum* (1954), IV, i, 2.

[58] If the *Collectio Rituum* is not used, the text is: *Wilt thou,* etc., and (later): *With this ring I thee wed, and I plight unto thee my troth.*

[59] This practice, customary in some places, is found only in the 1954 *Collectio Rituum.*

Spiritus Sancti. ℞. Amen. He then sprinkles them thrice with lustral water (in front, to his left and to his right).[60]

The husband or best man places the ring or rings on the salver or plate held by the server. The priest recites the blessing, using the plural form if there are two rings, and sprinkles the ring or rings once with lustral water. Next[61] the husband takes the ring from the priest's hand and places it on the woman's left ring finger, saying after the priest, *Take and wear this ring as a sign of our marriage vows.*[62] If a second ring is used, the bride then takes it from the priest and places it on her husband's ring finger, saying the same words.

After the giving or exchange of rings, the priest makes the sign of the cross over the spouses, saying *In nomine Patris,* etc., and then concludes the rite of marriage.[63]

Conclusion of the Marriage Rite. According to the Roman Ritual and the 1961 edition of the U.S. *Collectio Rituum,* the liturgical rite is completed with the versicles and responses (beginning *Confirma hoc*) and the prayer *Respice, quæsumus.* After this the priest may give an instruction or exhortation[64] (especially if Mass is not to follow), recite one of the English prayers provided in ritual excerpts, or, according to local usage, recite the final prayers of blessing found in the 1954 *Collectio Rituum* and described below.

The Mass and the Nuptial Blessing follow.

In many places it is customary for the priest to recite the series of prayers in English (from the 1954 *Collectio*) after the *actio liturgica* of Holy Matrimony and before the beginning of Mass. These include psalm 127, versicles and prayer, and several invocatory prayers over the spouses.[65]

---

[60] The 1954 *Collectio Rituum* directs the priest to say, before sprinkling the spouses: *I call upon all of you here present to be witnesses of this holy union which I have now blessed. "What God has joined together, let not man put asunder."*

[61] The original *Collectio Rituum* gives a formal introduction to the "donatio anuli," said by the priest: *Now that you have sealed a truly Christian marriage, give this wedding ring (these wedding rings) to your bride (to each other), saying after me:... "* Even where such words are not used, it is customary for the priest to give this and similar directions to the spouses throughout the rite, to the extent necessary and in his own words.

[62] If the *Collectio Rituum* is used; otherwise, *With this ring I thee wed, and I plight unto thee my troth.* The 1954 *Collectio* has a longer formula: *In the name of the Father, and of the Son, and of the Holy Spirit. Take and wear this ring as a pledge of my fidelity.* In the United States, as witnessed by both editions of the *Collectio,* the rubric of R.R. directing the celebrant to say *In nomine Patris,* etc., during the giving of the ring is not observed.

[63] The 1954 *Collectio Rituum* omitted the concluding versicles and prayer of R.R. (VIII, ii, 3), but these have been restored in the 1961 edition.

[64] Suggested forms for this are found in various U.S. editions of the ritual. If Mass is celebrated, the proper time for the concluding instruction is after the prayer *Deus Abraham* and before the *Placeat.*

[65] In the 1954 *Collectio Rituum* these prayers are to be used "if the marriage is to be blessed," although they clearly do not constitute the Nuptial Blessing which is given at Mass and they differ from the "Benedictio Nuptialis extra Missam." A variant is given in the same *Collectio* "if the marriage is not to be blessed;" in this case only the psalm with versicles and

During the latter the server holds the book and the priest elevates and extends his hands over the spouses. All make the answers and the priest joins his hands for the conclusion *Through our Lord,* etc.[66] Then, as indicated above, the Mass and Nuptial Blessing are celebrated; otherwise the priest may conclude the rite with an instruction or exhortation and then dismiss the spouses.[67]

If more than one pair are married at the same time, having first received the consent of each pair and having said to each pair *Ego conjungo vos,* etc., the priest blesses the rings and carries out the other blessings once for all in the plural.

Nuptial Mass. The rules for the celebration of the Nuptial Mass (or of the Mass of the day with Nuptial Blessing), as well as the rite of the Blessing, are given in Chapter XXX.[68] The Nuptial Blessing within Mass, after the Lord's Prayer and before the *Placeat* must be given in Latin.[69]

Mixed Marriages. A simple rite is provided both in the original *Collectio* and in U.S. excerpts from the Roman Ritual for the case of a mixed marriage. It consists of the exchange of consent, to which is added the usual formula, *I, N.N., take you, NN., for my lawful wife,* etc., and the giving of the ring or rings. There may be instructions before and after the rite given by the priest in his own words or according to one of the texts suggested in various rituals.[70]

It is forbidden to celebrate such a mixed marriage in church or to add any sacred rites. In the United States, however, it is not uncommon for local Ordinaries to permit (1) the celebration of a mixed marriage in church, in order to avoid more serious evils,[71] and/or (2) the addition, for the same reason, of some ecclesiastical rites, always with the exception of

---

the prayer *Prætende, quæsumus* are said before the dismissal.

[66] The prayer *May you be blessed in your children,* etc., is omitted, "si Sponsi sunt nimis superadulti."

[67] Since the 1961 edition of the *Collectio Rituum* follows the Roman Ritual with very few exceptions, it does not provide additional prayers in English either before or after the liturgical rite itself, nor does it give suggested forms of instruction or exhortation. Cf. *præfatio* of 1961 *Collectio,* p. xi.

[68] In the United States local Ordinaries may allow either the second form of blessing or the special *Preces* mentioned in Chapter XXX. For the text see 1961 *Collectio Rituum,* based on R.R., VIII, iii-iv. In both cases psalm 127 is said in Latin, but the versicles and concluding prayer may be in Latin or in English.

[69] Although the original *Collectio* permitted the use of English for the Blessing, an instruction from S.R.C. later directed that "it is not permitted for priests to use the English translation for that part of the Nuptial Blessing that is read during the Holy Sacrifice of the Mass" (Letter from the Apostolic Delegate, June, 1956). This prohibition was incorporated in the rescript authorising the 1961 *Collectio Rituum,* n. 2d (October 11, 1959).

[70] Care must be taken not to use an instruction, in the case of a non-sacramental marriage, which makes reference to the sacrament.

[71] C.I.C. 1109, § 3; R.R., VIII, i, 20.

Mass.[72] For these permissions and for the extent of such rites particular legislation must be consulted.

§ 6. Sick Calls

The rites for the sick and the dying, as performed in the United States, do not differ from those of the Roman Ritual, described in Chapter XXX,[73] nor do the U.S. excerpts from the Roman Ritual list any local usages. The *Collectio Rituum* contains, in Title III, the order for administering Viaticum and Holy Communion to the sick, the order for administering Extreme Unction, the rite of the Apostolic Blessing with plenary indulgence, and part of the *Ordo Commendationis animæ* and *De Expiratione*.[74] It also gives the rite to be observed by a priest who confers the sacrament of Confirmation on a person in danger of death.[75] This entire title is omitted in the 1961 edition of the *Collectio*, with the exception of the rite for administering Extreme Unction.[76]

In the order of Extreme Unction, the following texts may be said either in Latin or in English: (1) introductory versicles and responses; (2) the three prayers *Intrœat, Oremus, et deprecemur* and *Exaudi nos*; (3) *Confiteor*, etc; (4) versicles and responses following the anointing. The Latin must be used for the prayer at the imposition of the priest's hand, for the words accompanying the anointings, and for the prayers which follow them.

Ritus continuus. In addition there is a very important rite in the *Collectio* of 1954 for the administration of all the last sacraments together.[77] This not only unifies the last sacraments (and the Apostolic Blessing) in a single rite but changes the order customarily followed.[78] After the introductory sprinkling with lustral water and prayers,[79] the succession is: Penance, Extreme Unction, Viaticum, Apostolic Blessing.[80]

---

[72] C.I.C. 1102, § 2.

[73] In the United States, as in England, it is not ordinarily possible to take the Blessed Sacrament to the sick in public procession, except in Catholic institutions.

[74] In some of these rites (for example, that of Extreme Unction) brief English texts are added to the existing rite. These are clear from the context in which they appear.

[75] Title II: vi *apostolici indulti diei* 14 *septembris* 1946. For a description of the Confirmation rite, cf. *supra*, Chapter XXIX.

[76] Sick call rituals in use in the United States ordinarily provide English translations of all or part of the sections *De Visitatione et Cura Infirmorum, Ordo Commendationis Animæ,* and *De Expiratione,* and these are generally used in pastoral care.

[77] III, iv.

[78] The "ritus continuus" is not given in the 1961 *Collectio Rituum,* although the changed (and restored) order of the last sacraments is generally observed in the United States, with Extreme Unction preceding Viaticum.

[79] These are in fact the introductory prayers of the rite of Extreme Unction.

[80] If Confirmation is conferred, this is done after the sacramental absolution.

§ 7. Funerals

Little need be said concerning any funeral rites peculiar to the United States.[81] The original *Collectio* gives the rite for the burial of adults and the order of burying infants,[82] the ceremonies for which do not differ substantially from those of the Roman Ritual. The use of the vernacular is restricted in the following fashion: "In funeral rites for the deceased faithful, the prayers and absolutions must be performed in Latin only. Yet it is permitted, once this rite has been completed, to add other prayers in the vernacular language, to be determined by Ordinaries according to circumstances of time and place and to be recited by the priest himself."[83] It is the almost universal practice in the United States to add such prayers,[84] versions of which are given in the 1954 *Collectio Rituum* and in other rituals. In many places, according to longstanding custom, these additional prayers take the form of English translations of such texts as *Non intres,* the collect of the rite of absolution, the antiphon *In paradisum,* etc.

Since it is not generally possible to conduct the corpse ceremonially from the house to the church, the rite properly performed at the house may take place at the entrance to the church.[85] Similarly, the ceremonial procession from church to cemetery does not take place (unless the cemetery adjoins the church): instead the procession of celebrant, ministers, clergy, and servers goes to the church door only, while the antiphon *In paradisum* is chanted.[86] The rite at the graveside begins with the *Benedictus* (or with the blessing of the grave if this is necessary).

---

[81] For the description of the funeral ceremonies, cf. *supra,* Chapter XXXI.

[82] Pars III, *Exsequiale.* Since English may not be substituted for the Latin texts in these instances, the rites are not found in the 1961 *Collectio Rituum.*

[83] S.R.C., June 3, 1954, repeated in rescript of October 11, 1959.

[84] In many places this is done in the church at the end of the absolution rite performed here, i.e., between the collect and the chanting of the antiphon *In paradisum,* as well as at the graveside.

[85] Cf. *supra,* pp. Chapter XXXI; S.R.C. 3481 § 1.

[86] Psalm 114 may be added if there is time.

Bibliography

Aertnys, Jos. & Dankelman, A., *Compendium Liturgiæ Sacræ* (Marietti, 1936).

Ahearne P. & Lane, M., *Pontifical Ceremonies,* Burns and Oates, 1942.

Alphonsus M. de Liguori (St), *Liber de Cæremoniis Missæ* (edition of G. Schober, Pustet, 1882).

Amicis, De, P., *Cæremoniale Parochorum, Ephemerides Liturgicæ,* 1948.

_____, *Il Cerimoniale Completo,* Pustet, 1921.

(Ab) Appeltern (P. Victorius), *Sacræ Liturgiæ Promptuarium,* Beyaert, 1913.

Attwater, D., *The Catholic Encyclopaedic Dictionary,* Cassell, 1931.

Augustine, C.A., *Liturgical Law,* Herder, 1931.

Baldeschi, G., *Esposizione delle Sacre Cerimonie,* Desclée, 1959.

Barin, L. R., *Catechismo Liturgico,* 1932, 1934, 1935.

Bauldry, M., *Manuale Sacrarum Cæremoniarum,* Venice, 1778.

Bootsma, G., *Tractatus de Officio Divino et Missa,* Herder, 1928.

Braun, J., *I Paramenti Sacri,* Marietti, 1914.

Brehm, F., *Synopsis Additionum et Variationum in Editione Typica Missalis Romani Factarum,* Pustet, 1920.

Britt, M., *How to Serve in Simple, Solemn and Pontifical Functions* (Bruce, 1934).

Bugnini, A. & Braga, C., *Ceremoniale della Settimana Santa, Ephemerides Liturgicæ,* 1957.

Cæremoniale Romano-Seraphicum (1927).

Callewaert, C., *Cæremoniale in Missa Privata et Solemni,* Beyaert, 1934.

_____, *De Missalis Romani Liturgia,* Beyaert, 1937.

_____, *De Exsequiis,* 1935.

Cappello, F., M., *Tractatus Canonico-Moralis de Sacramentis,* Marietti, 1948.

Carpo, De, A.M., & Moretti A, *Cæremoniale juxta Ritum Romanum,* Marietti, 1932.

Catalani, G., *Rituale Romanum...Commentariis Exornatum,* Rome, 1757.

_____, *Cæremoniale Episcoporum...Commentariis Illustratum,* Jouby, 1860.

Ceremonial for the Use of the Catholic Churches in the United States of America, Ninth Edition (revised by Rev. W. Carroll Milholland, S.S.), Kilner, 1935.

Clergy Review (1930-1962).

Coelho, A., *Corso di Liturgia Romana,* Marietti, 1936-1940.

Collins, H.E., *The Church Edifice and its Appointments,* Newman Press, 1953.

Croegaert, A., [See *Stappen*]

_____, *Tractatus de Rubricis Missalis Romani,* Dessain, 1935.

Deodati, G., & Toscano, A., *Manuale Pratico di S. Cerimonie,* Scuola Tipografica Salesiana, Catania, 1926, 1928.

Dictionnaire d'Archéologie Chrétienne et de Liturgie, Letouzey et Ané, 1907-1953.

Dictionnaire de Droit Canonique, Letouzey et Ané, 1924 -.

Dictionnaire Pratique de Liturgie Romaine, R. Lesage *et al.,* Bonne Presse, 1952.

Dictionnaire de Théologie Catholique, Letouzey et Ané, 1909-1950.

Directions for Altar Societies and Architects, (J. O'Connell), Burns and Oates, 1936.

Dubosq, R., *Le Guide de l'Autel,* Desclée, 1938.

Dunne, W., *The Ritual Explained,* A. Hickling, 1940.

Duret, D., *Mobilier, Vases, Objets et Vêtements Liturgiques,* Letouzey et Ané, 1932.

Enciclopedia Cattolica, Città del Vaticano, 1948-1954.

Ephemerides Liturgicæ [1] (1887-1962).

Eucharistia, Encyclopédie Populaire, Bloud et Gay, 1934.

Favrin, B., *Praxis Sollemnium Functionum Episcoporum,* Pustet, 1926.

Finnegan, S., & Paver, A., eds., *Ad Completorium,* Saint Austin Press, 2000.

Francis, J., *The Laws of Holy Mass,* Burns and Oates, 1949.

Gatterer, M., *Annus Liturgicus,* Rauch, 1935.

_____, *Praxis Celebrandi Functiones Ordinarias Sacerdotales,* Rauch, 1939.

Gavanti, B., & Merati, C.M., *Thesaurus Sacrorum Rituum,* Venice, 1744 & 1762.

Gemert, P.A., *Rubricarum ac Cæremoniarum Promptuarium,* 1935.

A Grammar of Plainsong, Stanbrook Abbey, 1926.

Gromier, L., *Commentaire du Cæremoniale Episcoporum,* La Colombe, 1959.

Hanin, A., *La Législation Ecclésiastique en matière de Musique Religieuse,* Desclée, 1933.

Hébert, L., *Leçons de Liturgie, III, Le Ceremonial,* Berche et Pagis, 1952.

Herdt, De, J.B., *Praxis Pontificalis,* Van Linthout, 1873.

_____, *Sacræ Liturgiæ Praxis,* Van Linthout, 1902.

Hove, Van, A., *Tractatus de Sanctissima Eucharistia,* Dessain, 1933.

Irish Ecclesiastical Record (1865-1962).

Johnson, Cuthbert, OSB, & Ward, Anthony, S.M., eds., *Missale Romanum Anno 1962 Promulgatum,* Centro Liturgico Vincenziano, Rome 1994.

Kieffer, G., & Guillaume, R., *Precis de Liturgie Sacrée,* Salvator & Casterman, 1937.

King, A.A., *Liturgies of the Primatial Sees,* Longmans 1957.

_____, *Liturgies of the Religious Orders,* Longmans 1955.

_____, *Liturgy of the Roman Church,* Longmans 1957.

Kuenzel, L., *A Manual of the Ceremonies of Low Mass,* Pustet, 1923.

[1] The issue of January-February, 1939, contains the text of decisions of S.R.C. from 1927 to 1938 (many of which did not appear in *Acta Apostolicæ Sedis*).

La Messe Commentée, Association Petrus a Stella, Abbaye Notre-Dame, Fontgombault, 1992.

Lane, J., *Notes on Some Ceremonies of the Roman Rite*, Burns and Oates, 1937, 1938.

Lechner & Eisenhofer, *The Liturgy of the Roman Rite*, Herder, 1961.

Liturgia, Encyclopédie Populaire, Bloud et Gay, 1930.

MacMahon, M., *Liturgical Catechism*, Gill, 1927.

McManus, F.R., *Handbook for the New Rubrics*, Geoffrey Chapman, 1961.

_____, *The Rites of Holy Week*, S. Anthony Guild Press, Paterson, New Jersey, 1957.

Mahoney, E.J., *Questions and Answers – The Sacraments*, Burns, Oates & Washbourne, 1947.

_____, *Questions and Answers Volume II – Precepts*, Burns, Oates & Washbourne, 1949.

Martimort, A.G., *L'Eglise en Prière*, Desclée, 1961.

Martinucci, P. & Menghini, J.B., *Manuale Sacrarum Cæremoniarum*, Pustet, 1911-1915.

Menghini, J.B.M., *Liturgia Eucharistica*, Desclée & Lefebvre, 1906.

_____, *Manuale Novissimo di S. Ceremonie*, Pustet, 1927.

Miller, J.H., *Fundamentals of the Liturgy*, Fides, 1959.

Moretti, A., *Cæremoniale Juxta Ritum Romanum*, Marietti, 1936-1937.

Miller, J.B., *Handbook of Ceremonies*, Herder, 1927.

Nabuco, J., *Pontificalis Romani Expositio Juridico-Practica*, Vozes, 1945.

_____, *Jus Pontificalium*, Desclée, 1956.

Noonan, James-Charles, Jr., *The Church Visible: The Ceremonial Life and Protocol of the Roman Catholic Church*, Viking, 1996.

O'Connell, J.B., *How to Serve Mass*, Brepols, 1928.

_____, *The Clementine Instruction* (Translation and Commentary), Burns and Oates, 1949.

_____, *The Celebration of Mass*, Burns and Oates, 1940-1942, 1956 and 1959; Bruce, 1964.[2]

_____, *Church Building and Furnishing*, Burns and Oates, 1955.

_____, *Simplifying the Rubrics*, Burns and Oates, 1955.

_____, *The Ceremonies of Holy Week*, Burns and Oates, 1957.

_____, *The Restored Order of Holy Week – The Simple Rite*, Burns and Oates, 1957.

_____, *Instruction on Sacred Music and Liturgy* (Translation and Commentary), Burns and Oates, 1959.

_____, *The Rubrics of the Roman Breviary and Missal* (Latin text with English translation), Burns and Oates, 1960.

---

[2] The 1964 edition of O'Connell's classic work, all too often passed over because of its publication date, is in fact the *only* book to have appeared in print in English which took full account of the stipulations of the 1962 *editio typica* of the *Missale Romanum* for the ceremonies of the celebration of Mass.

O'Connell, L., & Schmidtz, W.J., *The Book of Ceremonies*, Bruce, 1956.

O'Kane, J., & Fallon, M.J., *Notes on the Rubrics of the Roman Ritual*, Duffy, 1932.

O'Leary, J.C., *Fundamental Rubrics*, Newman, 1946.

O'Leary, P., *Pontificalia*, Browne and Nolan, 1895.

O'Shea, W., *The Worship of the Church*, Newman Press, 1957.

Oppenheim, P., *Institutiones Systematico-Historicæ in Sacram Liturgiam*, Marietti, 1938-1940.

Perardi, G., *La Dottrina Cattolica-Culto*, Torino, 1938.

Periodica de Re Morali, Canonica, Liturgica, 1922-1957.

Questions Liturgiques et Paroissiales, Les, Louvain, 1910-1957.

Radó, P., *Enchiridion Liturgicum*, Herder, 1961.

Romita, F., *Jus Musicæ Liturgicæ*, Marietti, 1936.

Schmidt, H.A.P., *Introductio in Liturgiam Occidentalem*, Herder, 1960.

Schmitz, W.I., *Holy Week Manual for Priests*, Bruce, 1956.

Schober, G., *Cæremoniæ Missarum Solemnium et Pontificalium*, Pustet 1909.

Schulte, A.J., & O'Connell, J.B., *Benedicenda*, Benziger, 1955.

——————————————————, *Consecranda*, Benziger, 1956.

Sessolo, G., *Appunti di Sacre Cerimonie*, 1938.

Stappen, J. Van Der, & Croegaert, A., *Cæremoniale*, Dessain, 1933, 1935.

Stehle, A., & Rettger, E.A., *Manual of Episcopal Ceremonies*, 5th edition, 2 vols, St Vincent Archabbey, 1961.

Sunol, G., *Text Book of Gregorian Chant*, Desclée, 1930.

Tamagnone, G, *Il Decoro della Casa di Dio, II – Le Sacre Funzioni*, Berruti, 1951.

Trimeloni, L., *Compendio di Liturgia Pratica*, Marietti, 1959.

Le Vavasseur, L., & Haegy, J., & Stercky, L., *Manuel de Liturgie et Cérémonial*, Gabalda, 1935.

——————————————————, *Les Fonctions Pontificales* 1932.

Veneroni, P., *Manuale di Liturgia*, Artigianelli, 1933 and 1936.

Vismara, E.M., *Le Funzioni della Chiesa*, Torino, 1934 and 1935.

Wapelhorst, I., *Compendium Sacræ Liturgiæ*, Benziger, 1931.

Webb, G., *The Liturgical Altar*, Burns and Oates, 1939.

Wuest, J., & Mullaney, T.W., & Barry W.T., *Matters Liturgical*, Pustet, 1956.

Zualdi, F., & Capoferri, S., *Cæremoniale Missæ Privatæ*, Marietti, 1922.

Zualdi, F., & Murphy, J., *The Sacred Ceremonies of Low Mass*, 1961.

Index

The Benedictine Abbey
of Saint Michael at Farnborough
was founded from the French
Abbey of Solesmes in 1895. The monks live
a traditional life of prayer, work and study
in accordance with the ancient
Rule of Saint Benedict.
At the heart of their life is the praise of God
expressed through the solemn
celebration of the Sacred Liturgy,
and supported through their work,
of which this publication is an example.